D1187597

SILVER BURDETT & GINN
UNITED STATES HISTORY

One Flag, One Land

RICHARD C. BROWN
Former University Professor of History,
State University of New York College at Buffalo

HERBERT J. BASS
Professor of History,
Temple University, Philadelphia, Pennsylvania

CONSULTANTS

Edgar A. Toppin   Professor of History and Dean of the Graduate School,
Virginia State University, Petersburg, Virginia
Barbara S. Bass   Reading Specialist,
Cheltenham School District, Cheltenham, Pennsylvania

SILVER BURDETT & GINN
MORRISTOWN, NJ   •   NEEDHAM, MA
Atlanta, GA   •   Cincinnati, OH   •   Dallas, TX   •   Deerfield, IL   •   Menlo Park, CA

ACKNOWLEDGMENTS

Page 40: By permission of the Smithsonian Institution Press from *Smithsonian Miscellaneous Collection, Vol. 80, No. 7.* "Aboriginal Indian Population North of Mexico," by James Mooney, Smithsonian Institution, Washington, D.C., 1928. Page 172: Excerpt adapted from THE AMERICAN HERITAGE BOOK OF THE REVOLUTION by Bruce Lancaster, 1958, © American Heritage, a division of Forbes, Inc. Reprinted with permission. Page 238: Excerpt from THE BOOK OF ABIGAIL AND JOHN, ed. by L. H. Butterfield, Cambridge, Mass.: The Belknap Press of Harvard University, Copyright © 1975 by the Massachusetts Historical Society. Reprinted by permission of the publishers. Page 638: Entry "platform" excerpted from THE WORLD BOOK DICTIONARY. © Copyright 1987 Doubleday & Company, Inc. By permission of World Book, Inc.

CONTENTS

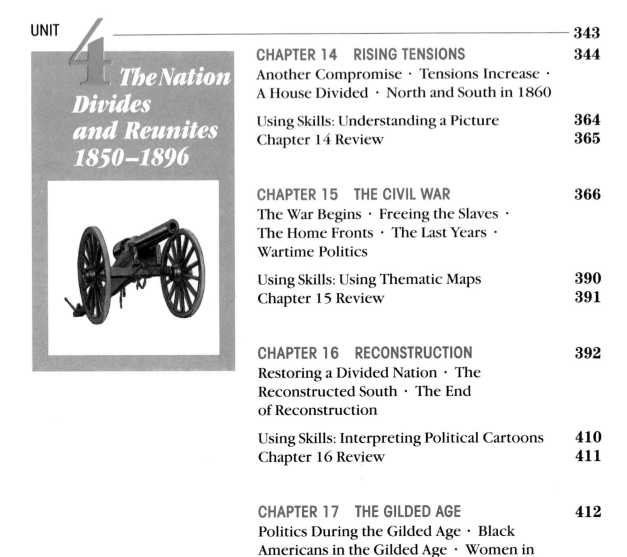

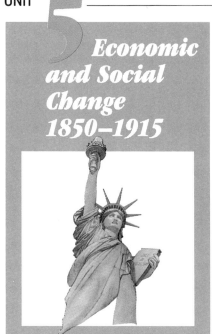

UNIT

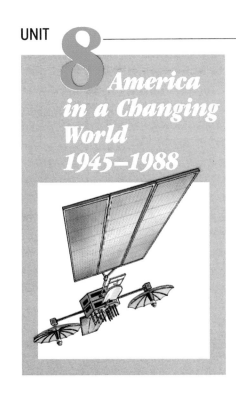

8
*America
in a Changing
World
1945–1988*

THE PRESIDENTS
OF THE UNITED STATES

PRIMARY SOURCE READINGS

UNIT *1*
Settling the Americas

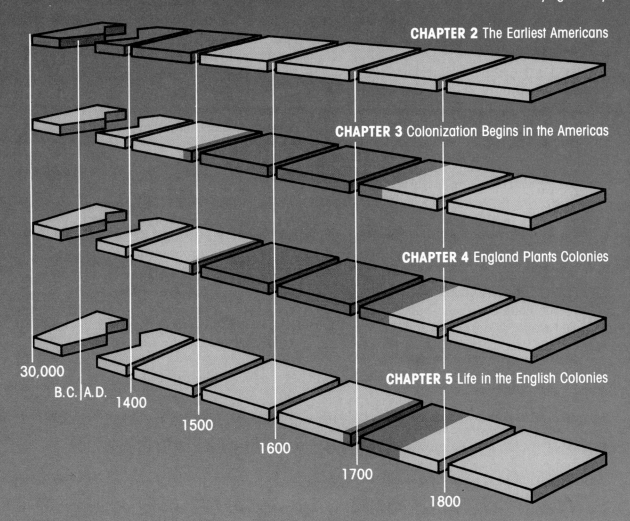

CHAPTER 1 Tools for Studying History

CHAPTER 2 The Earliest Americans

CHAPTER 3 Colonization Begins in the Americas

CHAPTER 4 England Plants Colonies

CHAPTER 5 Life in the English Colonies

30,000

B.C. A.D.

1400

1500

1600

1700

1800

1 *Tools for Studying History*

Using Maps

What are some things that a map can show?

VOCABULARY

astronaut	longitude
orbit	tributary
relief map	mass transit
elevation	precipitation
contour line	cartographer
political map	atlas
latitude	

The Bird Lifts Off On May 5, 1961, Commander Alan B. Shepard became the first American to enter outer space. Lucian C. Warren, a reporter, described the launching in this manner:

> There was deafening handclapping and cheering as the bird gracefully lifted itself into the sky, its rocket belching from the lower end, soared through a few thin clouds, began a vapor trail, then disappeared into space history. . . .

This was a historic day. Yet it was only a new chapter in the continuing history of our country. This book is dedicated to helping you understand history.

The Astronauts The first people chosen as **astronauts**, or people who travel in space, became as close as the members of a large family. (Words in heavy type appear in the Glossary, which begins on page 782.) They trained together and ate, slept, and lived under the same roof. Three of them died together in an accident at Cape Canaveral (kə nav′ə rəl) on the east coast of Florida in January 1967. (See the Key to Pronunciation, page 782.) The seven-member crew of the space shuttle *Challenger* died in an explosion shortly after takeoff in January 1986. The brave crew members had risked their lives to explore the unknown.

John H. Glenn, later a senator from Ohio, was the first to **orbit**, or circle, the earth. His successful three-orbit flight took place on February 20, 1962. Other astronauts have reached heights equal to or greater than Glenn's. A dozen have had the thrill of walking on the moon. The first astronaut to set foot on the moon was Neil Armstrong in 1969. From the moon, astronauts have an unusual experience. In one glance they can see the *whole* United States.

Only a few of us will ever see the whole United States as space travelers can now see it. (See the photograph on page 3.) However, we can see our whole country in other ways. Maps can show the entire

Astronaut Edward H. White II floats into space secured to the Gemini 4 spacecraft. White became the first United States astronaut to walk in space.
■ What planet can you see in the background?

THE METRIC SYSTEM OF MEASUREMENT

Kilometers and miles are both units of measure used to express distance or length. A kilometer is a unit of measure in the metric system. The system is called metric because it uses the meter in measuring length. A meter is 39.37 inches, or a little more than 1 yard.

The metric system is used to measure such things as distance, weight, area, and temperature. This system is in use or is being introduced in all the major countries of the world except the United States. Someday the United States will probably "go metric" also, adopting the measurement system that is used so widely.

To get you ready for this change, both American and metric measurements are used in this book. When an American measurement appears, it is followed in parentheses ( ) by the metric measurement that is about equal to it. Inches are changed to centimeters (cm), feet and yards to meters (m), miles to kilometers (km), and acres to hectares (ha). Pounds are changed to kilograms (kg), and quarts to liters (L). Pecks and bushels are also changed to liters. Degrees Fahrenheit (°F) are changed to degrees Celsius (°C).

United States. Indeed, maps can show aspects of the United States that are invisible from space.

Relief Maps   As space travelers speed through space above the United States, they can perhaps make out certain landforms, such as mountain ranges. Whether they can or cannot, *you* can see them by looking at the **relief map** on page 5. A relief map shows the **elevation**, or height, of the earth's surface. The elevation of land is expressed in feet or meters above or below sea level. Elevation is often shown by **contour lines**. All points along a contour line are exactly the same distance above or below the level of the sea. Sometimes color is added between contour lines as on the relief map on page 5 to show different elevations more clearly.

Among the mountain ranges shown on the relief map on page 5 are the Appalachians and the Rockies. Can you find them? Which ocean is the Appalachian range closer to? The Rocky Mountains make up the largest range in the United States. Between the Appalachians and the Rockies, there are plains and plateaus. West of the Rockies are three other mountain ranges. What are their names?

Mountain ranges have been important in United States history. They were barriers, or walls, that slowed for a time the movement of the American people. Nevertheless, as you will learn, these barriers were overcome as the United States spread across the continent.

Political Maps   No space traveler can see the boundaries dividing our country into 50 states. But you can, by looking at the map on pages 774 – 775. It is a **political map**. A political map shows such things as national and state boundaries and the names and locations of towns and cities. Find your state on the map. Does it share a common boundary with other states? If so, which ones?

Can you find states on the political map that do not touch any of the other

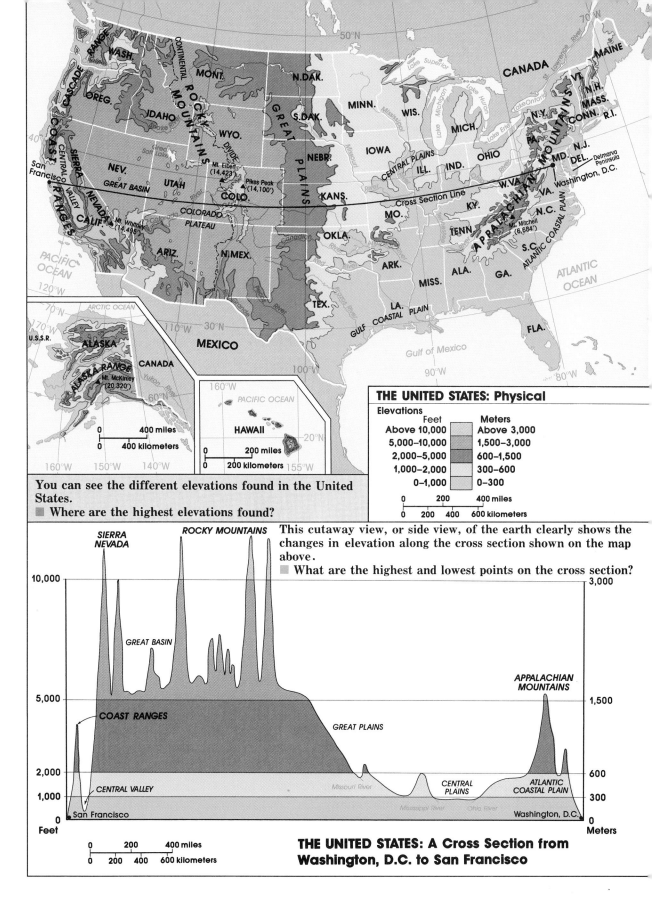

THE UNITED STATES: Physical

Elevations

Feet	Meters
Above 10,000	Above 3,000
5,000–10,000	1,500–3,000
2,000–5,000	600–1,500
1,000–2,000	300–600
0–1,000	0–300

You can see the different elevations found in the United States.

■ Where are the highest elevations found?

This cutaway view, or side view, of the earth clearly shows the changes in elevation along the cross section shown on the map above.

■ What are the highest and lowest points on the cross section?

THE UNITED STATES: A Cross Section from Washington, D.C. to San Francisco

5

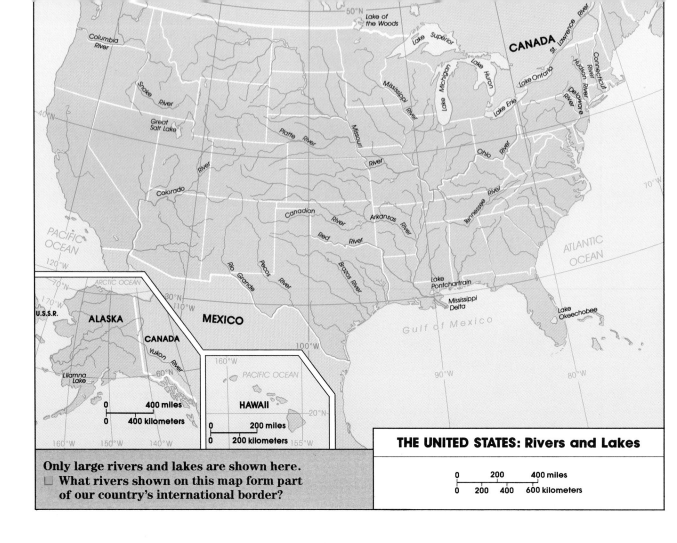

THE UNITED STATES: Rivers and Lakes

Only large rivers and lakes are shown here.
☐ What rivers shown on this map form part of our country's international border?

states? That touch only one other state? How many foreign countries share a common boundary with the United States? Some states have no water boundaries, only land boundaries. Find three states having only land boundaries with their neighbors. Then find a water boundary between two states.

The political map on pages 774–775 shows the capital city of each state. Could space travelers pick out your state's capital city as they orbit the earth? Probably not. But *you* can tell the name of the capital city of each state by looking at the map on pages 774–775 again. How many states have capital cities named for United States Presidents? (See page 781 for a list of our Presidents.)

You can also find the location of each capital city on the political map on pages 774–775. You can do this by using lines of **latitude** and **longitude**. Lines of latitude circle the earth in an east-west direction. They are numbered north and south of the Equator. Lines of longitude run north-south between the two poles. The lines are numbered east and west of the Prime Meridian. What are the latitude and longitude coordinates for Memphis, Tennessee? What city is located near 33°N, 97°W? What are the coordinates for your state capital?

Rivers and Lakes　　The map on this page shows the largest rivers and lakes in the United States. As you can see, the

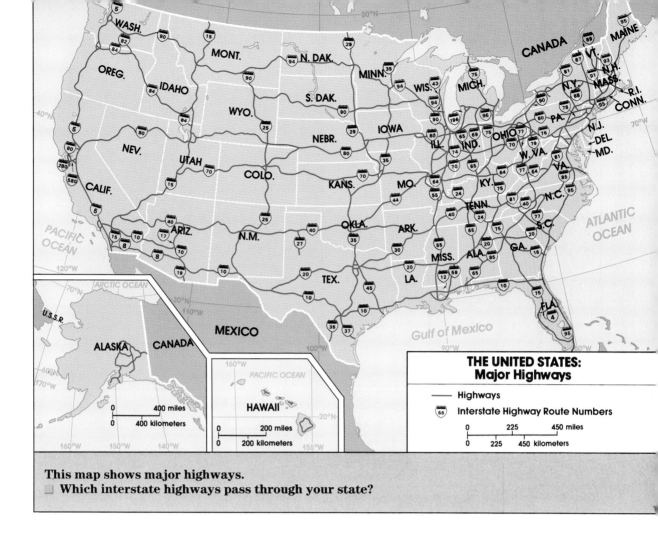

This map shows major highways.
☐ Which interstate highways pass through your state?

Mississippi River and its **tributaries** — rivers that run into the Mississippi — stand out as features of the land. During the entire span of human life in North America, the Mississippi River system has provided food and transportation for the people of the region.

In the northeastern section of the United States are the Great Lakes. Can you find the names of these five lakes on the map on page 6? Which is the only one entirely within the United States?

Our Highway System Rivers and lakes provided a natural system of transportation in our land for thousands of years. But nineteenth-century Americans added to this natural system by building canals and railroads. In the twentieth century, Americans added an extensive highway system.

The map on this page shows our Interstate Highway System. Interstate highways are identified by route markers that look like red, white, and blue shields. The even-numbered interstates, such as 40, 70, and 80, run east and west. Those with odd numbers, such as 5, 25, and 95, are north-south routes. Find these routes on the map above.

The first interstates were begun in 1956. Today the system is 95 percent complete. At times of gasoline shortages some Americans have criticized the Interstate Highway System. These critics say it is not wise to spend large sums of money on a

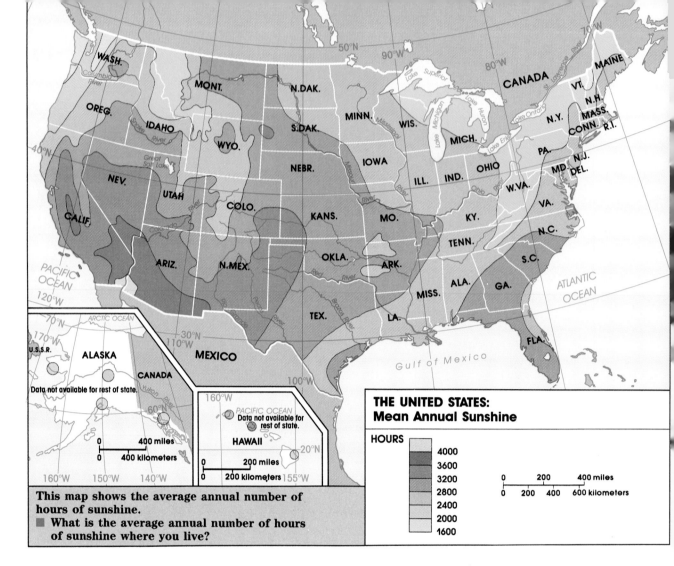

THE UNITED STATES:
Mean Annual Sunshine

HOURS
4000
3600
3200
2800
2400
2000
1600

This map shows the average annual number of hours of sunshine.
■ What is the average annual number of hours of sunshine where you live?

system that encourages travel by private automobile. It would be better, they say, to spend the money on **mass transit**. Mass transit is the carrying of people by buses, trains, and subways. How do you think the money should be spent — for interstate highways or for mass transit?

No doubt you have been on interstate highways. Which ones have you traveled on? Which interstate is nearest to your community? Though you may have ridden on the interstates, have you ever had a train ride? Or a ride on a canal boat?

Climate Any nation as large as the United States has a great variety of climates. Maps can demonstrate this vari-

ety. For example, the map above shows the average annual number of hours of sunshine in the United States. You can see how the amount of sunshine differs from one part of the country to another. The amount of sunshine a region receives affects its climate. Which regions of the United States have the most sunshine? Which have the least?

On the map on page 9, note the area of very low annual **precipitation** (pri sip ə tā′ shən), that is, moisture falling to earth as rain, snow, hail, sleet, or mist. For many years in the nineteenth century, this area in the West was labeled on maps *The Great American Desert*. It was thought to be almost unfit for human settlement. And

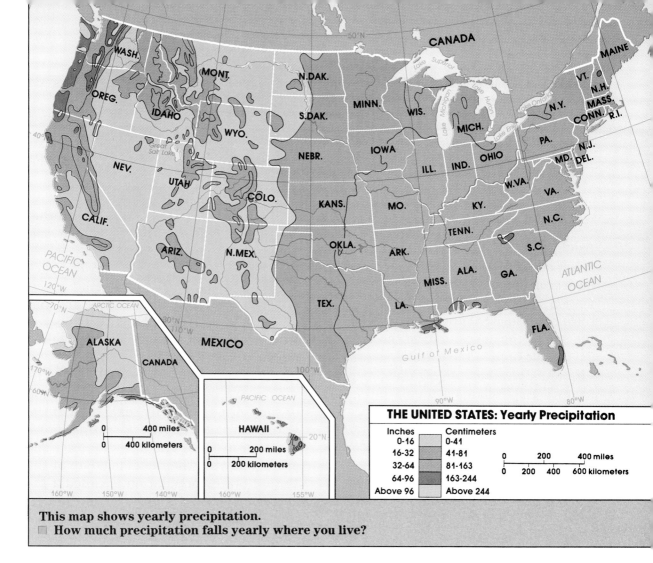

THE UNITED STATES: Yearly Precipitation

Inches	Centimeters
0-16	0-41
16-32	41-81
32-64	81-163
64-96	163-244
Above 96	Above 244

This map shows yearly precipitation.
How much precipitation falls yearly where you live?

yet today this area supports millions of people. What changes, do you think, took place so that people could live there?

The Many Uses of Maps   People who make maps are known as **cartographers** (kär tog′ rə fėrz). They make a useful product. The maps in this history book will help to teach you how the United States began, how it grew, and how it got to be the nation it is today.

Maps are a part of our lives. There are many other uses of maps. Drivers taking long-distance trips depend on road maps. There are state maps, city maps, maps of fairgrounds, maps of the world, and even maps of our universe. The seating plan of a theater, a baseball park, or a football stadium is a kind of map. A collection of maps is called an **atlas**.

CHECKUP

1. What is shown on a political map of the United States?
2. How have mountain ranges influenced American history?
3. What waterways have provided a natural system of transportation in the United States?
4. How have Americans added to this natural system of transportation?
5. **Thinking Critically**   Choose one kind of map and give at least three ways people can use it.

Using Tables and Graphs

How does the information shown on tables and graphs differ from that shown on maps?

VOCABULARY

demographer

Learning from Tables Information about our states can be presented, as you have seen, on a map. But for some information, a table is handier than a map. A table can be used to present many facts, as the one on the opposite page shows.

A map of the United States shows you Virginia's location. The Atlas map on pages 774–775 shows you that the capital of Virginia is Richmond. Still, the map does not show you the area of the state or the state's population. Can you learn this information from the table?

By looking at the map you can guess that Virginia and Kentucky are about the same size. The table, on the other hand, shows you *exactly* which is larger. Which *is* larger, Virginia or Kentucky? What is the nation's largest state? The smallest?

How does your state rank in area as compared with other states? How large is your state? How many states have a larger population than your state? What state has the largest population? Use the table on page 11 as a reference.

Learning from Graphs Still another way to show information about the United States is by using a graph. Graphs are useful because they can pack a lot of information into a small space. On this page and page 12 there are four different kinds of graphs. Each tells you something about the people of the United States.

Each kind of graph is named. The *pictograph* below shows the population of the United States by sex. Look at the graphs on page 12. The *bar graph* shows the size of different age groups. The graph showing the racial makeup of the United States population is called a *pie graph*. The *line graph* shows the percentage of women in the labor force between 1890 and 1980.

The statistics, or numbers, shown in these graphs were gathered by **demographers** (di mog' rə fėrz). A demographer is a person who studies the characteristics

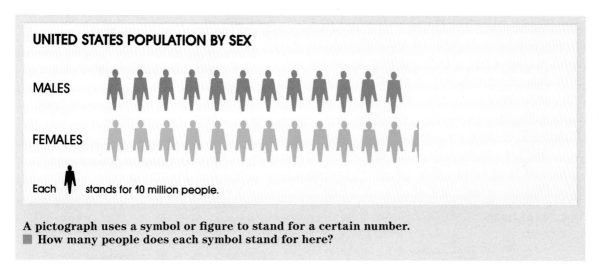

UNITED STATES POPULATION BY SEX

MALES

FEMALES

Each 🧍 stands for 10 million people.

A pictograph uses a symbol or figure to stand for a certain number.
■ How many people does each symbol stand for here?

FACTS ABOUT THE UNITED STATES

State	Area (sq mi) and Rank		Area (sq km)	Population and Rank		Capital City
Alabama	50,767	(28)	131,487	4,083,000	(22)	Montgomery
Alaska	570,767	(1)	1,478,458	525,000	(49)	Juneau
Arizona	113,508	(6)	293,986	3,386,000	(25)	Phoenix
Arkansas	52,078	(27)	134,883	2,388,000	(33)	Little Rock
California	156,299	(3)	404,814	27,663,000	(1)	Sacramento
Colorado	103,595	(8)	268,311	3,296,000	(26)	Denver
Connecticut	4,872	(48)	12,618	3,211,000	(28)	Hartford
Delaware	1,932	(49)	5,005	644,000	(47)	Dover
Florida	54,153	(26)	140,256	12,023,000	(4)	Tallahassee
Georgia	58,056	(21)	150,365	6,222,000	(11)	Atlanta
Hawaii	6,425	(47)	16,641	1,083,000	(39)	Honolulu
Idaho	82,412	(12)	216,432	998,000	(42)	Boise
Illinois	55,645	(24)	144,120	11,582,000	(6)	Springfield
Indiana	35,932	(38)	93,064	5,531,000	(14)	Indianapolis
Iowa	55,965	(23)	144,950	2,834,000	(29)	Des Moines
Kansas	81,778	(14)	211,805	2,476,000	(32)	Topeka
Kentucky	39,669	(37)	102,743	3,727,000	(23)	Frankfort
Louisiana	44,521	(33)	115,310	4,461,000	(20)	Baton Rouge
Maine	30,995	(39)	80,277	1,187,000	(38)	Augusta
Maryland	9,837	(42)	25,477	4,535,000	(19)	Annapolis
Massachusetts	7,824	(45)	20,265	5,855,000	(13)	Boston
Michigan	56,954	(22)	147,511	9,200,000	(8)	Lansing
Minnesota	79,548	(15)	206,030	4,246,000	(21)	St. Paul
Mississippi	47,233	(31)	122,333	2,625,000	(31)	Jackson
Missouri	68,945	(18)	178,568	5,103,000	(15)	Jefferson City
Montana	145,388	(4)	376,555	809,000	(44)	Helena
Nebraska	76,644	(10)	198,508	1,594,000	(36)	Lincoln
Nevada	109,894	(7)	284,624	1,007,000	(41)	Carson City
New Hampshire	8,993	(44)	23,292	1,057,000	(40)	Concord
New Jersey	7,468	(46)	19,342	7,672,000	(9)	Trenton
New Mexico	121,335	(5)	314,258	1,500,000	(37)	Santa Fe
New York	47,377	(30)	122,707	17,825,000	(2)	Albany
North Carolina	48,843	(29)	126,504	6,413,000	(10)	Raleigh
North Dakota	69,300	(17)	179,486	672,000	(46)	Bismarck
Ohio	41,004	(35)	106,201	10,784,000	(7)	Columbus
Oklahoma	68,655	(19)	177,817	3,272,000	(27)	Oklahoma City
Oregon	96,184	(11)	249,117	2,724,000	(30)	Salem
Pennsylvania	44,888	(32)	116,260	11,936,000	(5)	Harrisburg
Rhode Island	1,055	(50)	2,732	986,000	(43)	Providence
South Carolina	30,203	(40)	78,227	3,425,000	(24)	Columbia
South Dakota	75,952	(16)	196,715	709,000	(45)	Pierre
Tennessee	41,155	(34)	106,591	4,855,000	(16)	Nashville
Texas	262,017	(2)	678,623	16,789,000	(3)	Austin
Utah	82,073	(13)	212,569	1,680,000	(35)	Salt Lake City
Vermont	9,273	(43)	24,017	548,000	(48)	Montpelier
Virginia	39,704	(36)	102,832	5,904,000	(12)	Richmond
Washington	66,511	(20)	172,264	4,538,000	(18)	Olympia
West Virginia	24,119	(41)	62,468	1,897,000	(34)	Charleston
Wisconsin	54,426	(25)	140,964	4,807,000	(17)	Madison
Wyoming	96,989	(9)	251,202	490,000	(50)	Cheyenne
District of Columbia	69		178	622,000		
United States	3,539,295		9,169,762	243,399,000		Washington

UNITED STATES POPULATION BY AGE

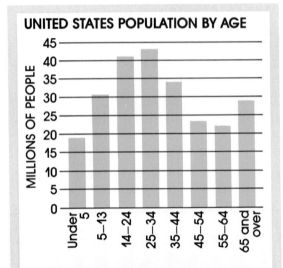

UNITED STATES POPULATION BY RACE

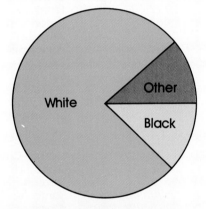

WOMEN IN THE LABOR FORCE OF THE UNITED STATES
(as a percentage of total employed)

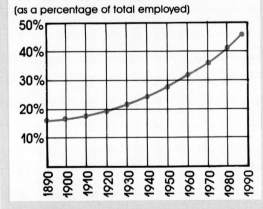

Each kind of graph presents information in a different way, so each has special uses.
■ **Which kind of graph best shows changes over time?**

of human populations. According to the demographers, which sex is more numerous today? About how many millions of people are in your age group?

The pie graph divides the United States population according to race. About how many white people are there for every black person in the United States? What races are included in the group labeled *Other*?

Explaining Facts   The line graph shows that the percentage of women in the work force has grown over the years. About what year did the percentage go above 40?

When you try to answer this question, you are going a step beyond the facts shown on the graph. You are getting into an *explanation* of the facts. Knowing the facts of history is not enough—the facts need to be explained.

Usually there is more than one explanation for a historical fact. Certainly there is more than one explanation for the increasing number of working women in the United States. This textbook, your teacher, outside sources, your classmates, even you yourself will help to provide explanations for the facts you learn this year. We can make a formula that applies to this learning. It looks like this:

facts + explanation = understanding

CHECKUP

1. Explain the differences between tables and graphs.
2. What kinds of graphs are there?
3. What facts about the United States population are revealed by the graphs in this chapter?

4. **Thinking Critically** Why are facts and explanations both important for understanding history?

Learning About History

What features of this book will help you learn United States history?

VOCABULARY

unit	annotation
caption	

Why Study History?   Perhaps most of you have at least studied parts of United States history in school before. You might well ask, "Why study it again?" There are good reasons. One excellent reason is that you are older than you were when, in a lower grade, you last learned about the history of our country.

We can compare your life to climbing a mountain. As you grow older, you reach a higher place than you occupied 3 or 4 years ago. Having now reached a higher level, you can see more than you could before. Things you were unable to understand several years ago will now seem clearer to you.

Furthermore, good citizenship in our complex world requires almost constant study and thought. The great American patriot Patrick Henry once said: "I know of no way of judging the future but by the past." Learning about United States history will make you a more alert and effective citizen.

No one studying United States history can learn all there is to know about it. Men and women who devote a lifetime to studying United States history still confess they have an incomplete knowledge of our past. Since no one can learn everything, teachers in the earlier grades had to choose those things they thought you could learn best at that time.

You will find some familiar names and events in this year's work. But you are not about to study them *once more*. You are continuing your study at a higher level. As you continue your study, you will be practicing and improving learning skills that are immensely important to your future success.

A Guide to Learning   Maps, tables, and graphs are *guides* to learning. This section is a guide, too. It describes the parts of this book so that you can find your way through it in the months ahead. It will help you make the best use of the book's features.

Look in the front part of this book at the Table of Contents pages. These pages show that the book is divided into eight **units,** or major parts. Each unit deals with a period of time. The first unit contains five chapters. Most other units contain four chapters. Two units have three chapters. Each chapter is listed along with its title and page number. There are 31 chapters in this book.

Already you have learned about maps, tables, and graphs. They will help you learn about the history of your country during the coming year. You will also find pictures and cartoons in this book. Each map, graph, picture, and cartoon has a **caption.** A caption is a description or explanation of the meaning of an illustration. There is a question with each caption. As you study, be sure to read the captions and answer the questions.

Time Lines   Another visual that can help you learn is a *time line*. Time lines can help you understand the order in which historical events occurred. The time line that appears on the page that begins each new unit of this book compares the periods covered by the different

UNIT **1**

Settling
the
Americas

CHAPTER 1 Tools for Studying History

CHAPTER 2 The Earliest Americans

CHAPTER 3 Colonization Begins in the Americas

CHAPTER 4 England Plants Colonies

CHAPTER 5 Life in the English Colonies

30,000
B.C. A.D.   1400
1500
1600
1700
1800

**EVENTS
IN OUR
COUNTRY**

1492 Columbus sails to the Americas
1500 Cabral lands in Brazil
1513 Ponce de León explores Florida/Balboa discovers the Pacific Ocean
1519 Cortés conquers the Aztecs
1531 Pizarro conquers the Incas
1534 Cartier explores the St. Lawrence River
1540 Coronado and Alarcon explore the Southwest
1608 Champlain founds Quebec
1609 Dutch settle on Manhattan Island
1673 Marquette and Joliet explore the Mississippi River
1682 La Salle claims the Mississippi River valley
1728 Bering explores Alaskan waters

1500
1550
1600
1650
1700

1669 First French trading post in India
1642 Dutch take the Gold Coast in Africa from the Portuguese
1615 Dutch seize the Moluccas from the Portuguese
1574 Portuguese colonize Angola (Africa)
1551 Portuguese establish a colony at Macao
1543 Portuguese arrive in Japan
1526 Portuguese land in New Guinea (East Indies)
1519 Magellan begins voyage around the world
1498 Da Gama sails around Africa to discover India

**EVENTS
ELSEWHERE**

**Time tiers (left) and time lines (right) appear throughout this book.
What can these visual tools tell us about events in United States history
and events elsewhere?**

chapters in that unit. The time lines at the beginning of each chapter show important events that you will learn in that chapter. They also describe events that were happening elsewhere in the world at that time.

Look at the time line for Unit 1 (left). How many chapters are in Unit 1? What color is used to designate the time period you will study in Chapter 3? Now look at the time line for Chapter 3 (right). What color is used here to designate the time period covered in the chapter? How is the chapter time line like the unit time line?

Historical Documents   You will find the Declaration of Independence and the Constitution printed in full in Unit 2. Along with the text of these historical documents are comments in the margins. These comments are called **annotations.** Annotations point out and explain important parts of these two great historical documents.

Other historical documents are placed in appropriate sections in the text. They are called Primary Source Readings. Sometimes excerpts from documents are included within the text itself. Often these passages are accounts of historical events written by persons who saw the event or took part in it. They add color and realism to your study of history.

Vocabulary and Checkup   You will note that each chapter is divided into sections. At the beginning of each section is a question that should focus your thinking as you read the section. After that is a list of words or phrases. You may already know the meaning of some of these terms. Each word or phrase will appear in the section that follows and its meaning will be explained. The word or phrase is also defined in the Glossary, beginning on page 782. Thus, as the year goes on, you will find your own vocabulary increasing.

14

At the end of each section are questions labeled Checkup. They are designed to review your understanding of what you studied in that section.

Using Skills and Chapter Review At the end of each chapter you will find a page called Using Skills. The exercises on these pages will help you learn about United States history. In addition, the Using Skills pages will help you develop skills that are important for living in the twentieth century.

Knowing how to read a map, a table, or a graph is a skill. It is a skill you will make use of at different times during your life. Will you use a library only this next year? Of course not — or at least we hope not. So developing skills in using the library will benefit you now and later.

On the last Contents page, look over the list of skills you will get a chance to practice as you learn from this book. Which skills do you consider most important? Try to think of a way in which you might use each of these skills in the coming years.

Also, at the end of each chapter you will find a list of main ideas from the chapter, a review of the chapter vocabulary, a series of questions, and a number of activities. The purpose of the review page is to help you check up on what you have studied, learn more about the material in the chapter, and apply what you have learned.

How Americans Lived At the end of each of several units is a section entitled How Americans Lived. These sections describe the way people lived at specific times, at 50-year intervals. They also give a good picture of the United States and its people at a particular time in history. Since most people live as members of families, family life is emphasized here.

In fact, families are an important emphasis throughout this book. Perhaps there is no such thing as the "typical" American family. Nevertheless, families have been and will remain an important part in our society. Mainly through families, values are passed from generation to generation. In this book you will learn about important individuals in United States history. You will also learn about the families of some of these individuals.

This family is at the site of the Civil War battlefield at Gettysburg, Pennsylvania.
■ What purpose do you think the tower at the left might serve?

15

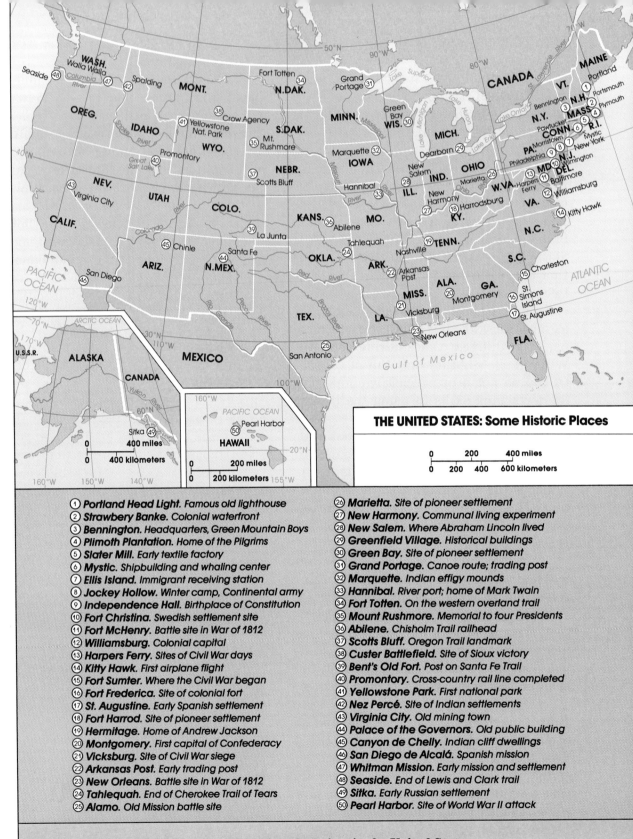

THE UNITED STATES: Some Historic Places

0   200   400 miles
0   200   400   600 kilometers

1. **Portland Head Light.** Famous old lighthouse
2. **Strawbery Banke.** Colonial waterfront
3. **Bennington.** Headquarters, Green Mountain Boys
4. **Plimoth Plantation.** Home of the Pilgrims
5. **Slater Mill.** Early textile factory
6. **Mystic.** Shipbuilding and whaling center
7. **Ellis Island.** Immigrant receiving station
8. **Jockey Hollow.** Winter camp, Continental army
9. **Independence Hall.** Birthplace of Constitution
10. **Fort Christina.** Swedish settlement site
11. **Fort McHenry.** Battle site in War of 1812
12. **Williamsburg.** Colonial capital
13. **Harpers Ferry.** Sites of Civil War days
14. **Kitty Hawk.** First airplane flight
15. **Fort Sumter.** Where the Civil War began
16. **Fort Frederica.** Site of colonial fort
17. **St. Augustine.** Early Spanish settlement
18. **Fort Harrod.** Site of pioneer settlement
19. **Hermitage.** Home of Andrew Jackson
20. **Montgomery.** First capital of Confederacy
21. **Vicksburg.** Site of Civil War siege
22. **Arkansas Post.** Early trading post
23. **New Orleans.** Battle site in War of 1812
24. **Tahlequah.** End of Cherokee Trail of Tears
25. **Alamo.** Old Mission battle site
26. **Marietta.** Site of pioneer settlement
27. **New Harmony.** Communal living experiment
28. **New Salem.** Where Abraham Lincoln lived
29. **Greenfield Village.** Historical buildings
30. **Green Bay.** Site of pioneer settlement
31. **Grand Portage.** Canoe route; trading post
32. **Marquette.** Indian effigy mounds
33. **Hannibal.** River port; home of Mark Twain
34. **Fort Totten.** On the western overland trail
35. **Mount Rushmore.** Memorial to four Presidents
36. **Abilene.** Chisholm Trail railhead
37. **Scotts Bluff.** Oregon Trail landmark
38. **Custer Battlefield.** Site of Sioux victory
39. **Bent's Old Fort.** Post on Santa Fe Trail
40. **Promontory.** Cross-country rail line completed
41. **Yellowstone Park.** First national park
42. **Nez Percé.** Site of Indian settlements
43. **Virginia City.** Old mining town
44. **Palace of the Governors.** Old public building
45. **Canyon de Chelly.** Indian cliff dwellings
46. **San Diego de Alcalá.** Spanish mission
47. **Whitman Mission.** Early mission and settlement
48. **Seaside.** End of Lewis and Clark trail
49. **Sitka.** Early Russian settlement
50. **Pearl Harbor.** Site of World War II attack

This map shows only a few of the many historical sites in the United States.
■ **Which of these sites would you like to visit? Why?**

Other Features   Interesting places, events, and other subjects are topics of special features in this book.   Throughout the text are boxes about the Presidents.   They include a picture of each President and facts about his life.   Still another feature is called What's in a Name?   There is a lot of history wrapped up in the names of our states, our cities, and even our streets. Curiosity about names can be a fascinating hobby, one that you can follow throughout your life.

Learning Aids   A number of valuable learning aids come near the end of the book.   You will find the Biographical Dictionary interesting and useful.   It lists alphabetically more than 225 people who have played significant roles in United States history.   Each person is described briefly.   A page reference tells you where you can find more information about his or her activities.

Still another valuable aid is the Atlas. It contains a map of the world, maps of the major continents, and a map of the United States.   You will want to refer to the Atlas often as you study our nation's history.

Finally, there is the Index.   In the Index you can quickly find page references for persons, places, and things that are mentioned in this book.   You can use the page numbers to look up more information.

The Fun Factor   Many Americans find a hobby in some aspect of the past.   For them there is a fun factor in the study of history.   Perhaps they restore antique automobiles or collect old stamps and coins. Perhaps they like to read good historical novels or biographies of famous people. They may concern themselves with the history of the state or community in which they live, or do research into the history of their own families.

Perhaps they travel to historic places. The map on page 16 shows 50 historic places in the United States.   Each place is numbered and is identified and briefly described in the key below the map.   The places listed are only a small fraction of the historic places in the United States. Practically every community has places of historic interest.   What historic places are there in your community?

As you study United States history this year, you will read about what happened at many of the places shown on the map.   Have you visited any of these historic places?   Have you visited other historic places?   Doesn't a visit to a historic place mean more if you know what took place there?

There is history all around you.   History is in the streets where you walk.   It is in the place where you live.   It is in your family, and in your place of worship, and in your school.   In fact, there is a history to everything you see or read or touch.   Keep this in mind in your study of United States history.   Perhaps this book will encourage you to develop a continuing interest in the past, present, and future of your country, the United States of America.   If so, *One Flag, One Land* will have done what it was meant to do.

CHECKUP

1. How is this book divided?
2. Which two historical documents appear in full and are annotated?
3. Why is there a Using Skills page at the end of each chapter?
4. What are the purposes of the boxes about the Presidents and What's in a Name?
5. **Thinking Critically**   Why do we study United States history?

Using Your Textbook

FINDING YOUR WAY

You have read that this book is organized to help you learn about your country's history. But knowing the book's organization cannot help you unless you know how to use its various learning aids.

The following exercise is meant to give you practice in using the parts of this book. By finding the answers to the questions you will be sharpening skills that you will use many times in your study of United States history. Moreover, you will often use these same skills in future years as you read magazines, newspapers, and books.

SKILLS PRACTICE

On a separate sheet of paper, write the answer to each of the following questions.

1. What is the title of the page in this book on which a listing of all the units and chapters starts?
2. What is the number of the unit in which you can find an account of World War II?
3. What time period does Unit 7 cover?
4. What chapter deals with each of the following topics? (a) Andrew Jackson's presidency (b) the Civil War (c) the 1920s
5. What page has a map showing all of the English colonies?
6. What page has a graph showing the estimated Native American population in 1492?
7. Which is longer, the Declaration of Independence or the Constitution?
8. Which of these documents begins with the words "When, in the course of human events . . ."?
9. How many amendments are there to the Constitution?
10. How many vocabulary terms are there in the box at the beginning of Chapter 14?

11. How many other vocabulary lists are there in Chapter 14?
12. According to the time line on page 295, what took place in 1848?
13. What is the title of the primary source reading in Unit 6?
14. How many sections entitled How Americans Lived are there in the book?
15. What skill is practiced on page 410?
16. How many presidential boxes are there in the book?
17. On what page would you look to find a map of the world?
18. In the feature entitled Biographical Dictionary, find the home state of each of the following persons. (a) John C. Calhoun (b) Henry Cabot Lodge (c) Belva Lockwood
19. On what page would you find a definition for the word *mercantilism?*
20. In the Index, find the page number on which each of the following topics is described. (a) the siege of Vicksburg (b) the impeachment of President Andrew Johnson (c) the children's writings of Louisa May Alcott

MAIN IDEAS

1. Maps help us to learn because they can show large areas in a small space.
2. Maps can show many kinds of facts, such as information about landforms, boundaries, cities and towns, rivers, highways, precipitation, and climate.
3. Maps can show us not only how things are now but also how they were in the past.
4. Tables and graphs are effective tools for presenting information in a small space.
5. Learning about United States history will make you a more alert and effective citizen.
6. Some features in this book that will help you are tables, graphs, maps, table of contents, captions, time lines, historical documents, annotations, vocabulary, checkup, skills, chapter reviews, special interest features, Biographical Dictionary, Glossary, Atlas, and Index.

VOCABULARY REVIEW

On a separate sheet of paper, write the letter of the vocabulary word next to the number of its definition.

a. precipitation
b. atlas
c. demographer
d. caption
e. elevation
f. cartographer
g. unit
h. index
i. contour lines
j. mass transit

1. The height of the earth's surface
2. Any form of moisture that falls to the earth
3. A collection of maps
4. A person studying the characteristics of human populations
5. A description or explanation of a picture, map, or graph
6. The transporting of people by buses, trains, or subways
7. A person who makes maps
8. An alphabetical listing of names, places, and subjects that are in a book
9. A way of showing elevation on a map
10. A division of a book

CHAPTER CHECKUP

1. What can maps show that cannot be seen by space travelers?
2. Name three famous American astronauts, and describe their accomplishments.
3. What differences are there between political maps and relief maps?
4. Explain the kinds of information that can be shown on tables and graphs.
5. Why is there often more than one explanation for a historical fact?
6. **Thinking Critically** If you wanted to make a graph that would show average monthly precipitation in your community, what type of graph mentioned in this chapter would you use? Why?
7. **Thinking Critically** What did Patriot leader Patrick Henry mean when he said: "I know of no way of judging the future but by the past"?

APPLYING KNOWLEDGE

1. Bring to class a table or graph from a newspaper or magazine. Explain to the class what the table or graph shows.
2. In your school library or in a classroom reference book, look up the population of the five largest cities in your state. Round off the population of each to the nearest thousand. Using those figures, make a bar graph to show how the cities compare in population.
3. Draw a map showing the route you take from your home to your school. Include directions and distances.
4. Using a road atlas, show the route you would take for traveling by automobile from your community to one of the places shown on the map on page 16.
5. On page 17 you were told that many Americans find a hobby in some aspect of the past. Name three hobbies not mentioned in the text and explain how they are related to history.

2 The Earliest Americans

30,000 B.C.–A.D. 1492

Origins of the Native Americans

Where did the first Americans come from?

VOCABULARY

prehistoric	tribe
archaeologist	Folsom man
Ice Age	geologist
glacier	radioactivity
Mongoloid	carbon 14
extinct	

A Flight Toward the Rising Sun Fear of enemies behind them drove Omuk the Leader and his small band along. Out of the fog these enemies had come 2 days earlier. They were men and women dressed in furs, looking much like the people Omuk led. There were at least 100 of these enemies. But Omuk's band had no more than 20 fit fighters.

Omuk and his people had fled. The enemies had not followed for long. But they had taken over the good hunting grounds that Omuk and his followers had enjoyed. Now Omuk must find food for his people, or else they all would die.

The flight had led the band away from familiar landmarks. Now Omuk the Leader was lost. He kept the open water to the side of him as he moved on. Always he moved in the direction of the rising sun. Omuk and his band may have been the first people to enter America.

We do not know that there was really a man named Omuk. But we do know there were people like Omuk in **prehistoric** times — that is, in those early years before there were written records. **Archaeologists** (är kē ol' ə jists) say that the flight of this prehistoric band of people might well have taken place. Archaeologists study objects, ruins, and other evidence of human life in the past.

A Land Bridge from Asia Omuk the Leader and others like him lived at a time known as the **Ice Age**. Huge sheets of ice called **glaciers** had pushed down from the north to cover much of North America. Beneath the ice a narrow strip of land connected Siberia, in Asia, and Alaska, in North America.

As the Ice Age ended, the glaciers melted. In time, the water from the melting ice covered the land bridge. Today the land that Omuk and his band walked on is covered by the waters of the Bering Strait, which separates Siberia and Alaska.

Most scholars today accept the idea that the first people in America came across the land bridge from Asia. But there are other ideas advanced by some.

The Native Americans of the Pacific Northwest had many natural resources available to them. The Native Americans were the first people to come to the Americas.
■ What kinds of natural resources can you find in the painting?
■ When did people come to the Americas?

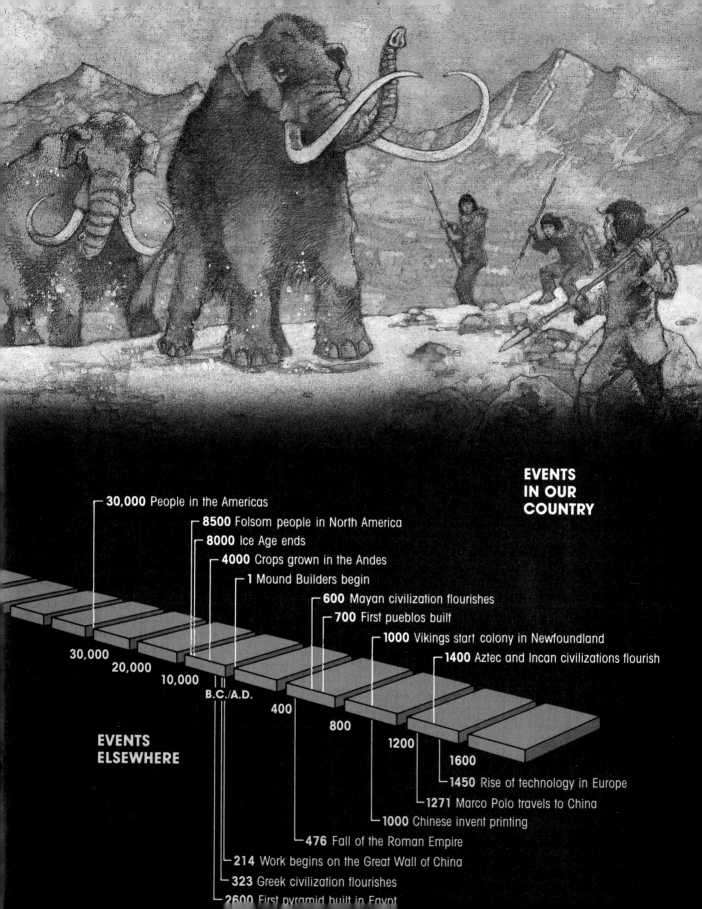

EVENTS
IN OUR
COUNTRY

30,000 People in the Americas
8500 Folsom people in North America
8000 Ice Age ends
4000 Crops grown in the Andes
1 Mound Builders begin
600 Mayan civilization flourishes
700 First pueblos built
1000 Vikings start colony in Newfoundland
1400 Aztec and Incan civilizations flourish

30,000
20,000
10,000
B.C./A.D.
400
800
1200
1600

EVENTS
ELSEWHERE

1450 Rise of technology in Europe
1271 Marco Polo travels to China
1000 Chinese invent printing
476 Fall of the Roman Empire
214 Work begins on the Great Wall of China
323 Greek civilization flourishes
2600 First pyramid built in Egypt

Some Other Explanations Some people believe that these first people in America were descendants of the ten lost tribes of Israel. Others believe that America's earliest inhabitants were related to ancient Egyptians or Greeks or perhaps to the Phoenicians or Romans. Some think that the first Americans crossed the Atlantic by way of a lost continent called Atlantis. It may be, some have said, that the ancestors of the American Indians were from Wales or Ireland and were blown in their boats to North America by an Atlantic storm.

Still others think that the first Americans crossed the Pacific Ocean by boat or raft from China, Japan, or the islands of Polynesia (pol ə nē′ zhə). There is indeed some physical evidence that they did come

from an Asian land, whether by boat, by raft, or by the land bridge.

Physical Evidence The American Indians are of the **Mongoloid** race. So are the people of China. The American Indians and the people of China differ in many ways. Yet in some ways they are much alike.

Most Indians have a fold of skin along the inner edge of their eyes. So do Asiatic people of the Mongoloid race. This fold probably developed over thousands of years, passed along from generation to generation. Such a physical characteristic would help the people having it to survive the harsh climate. Certainly it would have helped Omuk as he narrowed his eyes to peer into the fog and snow along the Ice Age bridge.

Babies of the first Americans probably had a bluish-black spot on the lower back. Many American Indian babies are born with this spot. The spot tends to disappear when they grow older. The same thing happens to the spot that marks most of the children of eastern Asia. The mark is called the Mongoloid spot.

American Indians vary in appearance. However, many have straight black hair on their heads but little hair on the rest of their bodies. Many have dark brown eyes and reddish or brownish-red skin. These are physical characteristics of the Mongoloid race. Indian and Chinese babies often resemble each other. This may be one more indication that the ancestors of the American Indians came from Asia.

ROUTES OF EARLY NATIVE AMERICANS

| 0 | 2000 miles |
| 0 | 2000 kilometers |

You can see some of the routes the first Americans might have followed as they spread throughout the Americas.
■ How far is it from Asia to the southern tip of South America?

Life in the Ice Age Omuk and his Ice Age descendants lived by hunting. They hunted animals that are now **extinct**— that is, they hunted kinds of animals that have died out. Among them were ancient

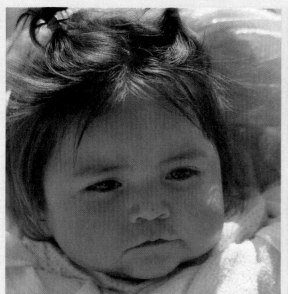 

The photograph at the left is an Indian baby, and the photograph at the right is a Chinese baby.
▢ Do these photographs give any support to the idea that the ancestors of Native Americans might have come from Asia?

bison and huge elephantlike animals called mammoths. No doubt the lives of these first Americans were harsh and short. (See the picture on page 21.)

Still the number of people increased. The first group to come across the land bridge was followed by others. However, the main increase in population came from the children born in the new land. Though many died young, enough lived to populate hundreds of places.

Moving Southward   Omuk's people and their descendants roamed from place to place, depending on the climate and food supply. Slowly they spread eastward and southward into the Yukon River valley, away from the coast. They moved southward from Alaska into western Canada. Finally they reached lands the glaciers had left uncovered. As time passed, some small bands joined together and formed larger groups called **tribes.**

By the time the Ice Age ended, these early Americans had reached at least as far as present-day New Mexico. How do we know this? We know it partly through a find made by a black cowhand on a ranch in northeastern New Mexico. His name was George McJunkin.

The Mysterious Buried Bones   One day in the spring of 1926, George McJunkin was following the trail of some missing cows. The trail led him along the edge of Dead Horse Gulch. McJunkin saw some bones sticking out of the mud on the side of the gulch. Being a curious person, he got off his horse to take a closer look at the bones.

The bones were about the size of cow bones and buried 20 feet (6 m) below the surface. This seemed strange to McJunkin. Even stranger was the flint spearhead he pried from a bone with his cattle knife. It had a groove, or channel, on each

An Ice Age spearhead was found next to some bison bones in New Mexico.
■ **What might an archaeologist learn from this evidence?**

side and was different from any other spearhead that George McJunkin had ever seen. Why, he asked himself, were the animal bones and the flint spearhead buried so deep?

This also seemed strange to the people whom McJunkin told of his discovery. As the news spread, an expert on animal bones came to have a look. He found that the bones belonged to a kind of bison that had lived in North America during the last years of the Ice Age. The spearhead proved that human beings were living in New Mexico thousands of years ago.

Bones of other ancient bison were dug up at the site of McJunkin's discovery. Several more flint spearheads were found. These discoveries were all made near the town of Folsom, so whoever made the spearhead and killed the bison came to be known as the **Folsom man.**

No human bones were found at the site of McJunkin's discovery. Scholars guessed that the bison bones might have come from a single hunt. Perhaps a herd of the ancient bison drank from a pool or lake that no longer exists. The Folsom people might have surprised the bison, killing them on the spot. They might then have cut up the dead animals and carried the meat back to their campsite. This would explain the absence of human bones near the bison bones.

How Long in America? How long have people been in America? **Geologists** (jē ol′ ə jists) are scientists who learn about the earth and its history mostly through the study of rocks. They are able to tell much about the Ice Age but nothing that helps a great deal in dating the time that Omuk and his people crossed the land bridge from Asia. Nor are they able to give more than a very rough estimate of the time when the Folsom people lived.

Counting tree rings on the ends of logs or the stumps of trees is one way of time dating. Each tree ring shows a year's growth. Another method is counting the layers of soil or gravel laid down at the bottom of what was once a glacial lake. The most accurate method of time dating, however, makes use of what scientists have discovered about living matter and **radioactivity.** Radioactivity is caused when atoms change and give off energy.

Carbon Dating Scientists have discovered that all living things have a radioactive substance called **carbon 14.** In living matter the amount of carbon 14 is always the same. But when a living thing dies, the carbon 14 in it decreases at a fixed rate. Think of a kettle of water boiling dry as the water evaporates. This is much like the way once-living matter gives off radiation.

It is known that a pound of carbon 14 will be reduced by radioactivity to half a pound in 5,568 years. In another 5,568 years it will weigh only a quarter of a

Gary Smith ©1980 National Geographic Society

These ancient Indian petroglyphs, or rock paintings, are in Nine Mile Canyon in Utah.
▪ Why do you think the Indians made these rock paintings?

pound. Even then it will continue to throw off radiation. Delicate instruments can measure the amount of carbon 14 in anything that has been alive. By carbon dating we know that the bison at Dead Horse Gulch died about 10,000 years ago.

In Sandia Cave, near Albuquerque, New Mexico, hunters left the bones of ancient camels, mastodons, and small horses. All these animals have long been extinct. But by using carbon 14 dating, we find that hunters killed the camels, mastodons, and small horses about 25,000 years ago.

No one has ever found conclusive evidence of the date when the first people crossed the Ice Age land bridge from Asia. Probably no one ever will. Nevertheless, that crossing must have been made more than 25,000 years ago according to the evidence found in Sandia Cave. Other finds have pushed the date back even further. For example, mammoth bones found on Santa Rosa Island, off the coast of California, date back about 30,000 years.

The southward journey of the Ice Age people did not stop in New Mexico or California. They pushed on into Mexico and South America. In fact, there is proof that humans lived in Fell's Cave, near the southern tip of South America, from 8,000 to 10,000 years ago. If prehistoric people had spread so far across the American continents by that time, their date of entry must have been very early indeed.

CHECKUP

1. Name at least three points that are used as evidence that the first people in America came from Asia.
2. How did these early people meet their daily needs?
3. What did the discovery of Folsom man help to prove?
4. Explain how prehistoric bones are dated.
5. **Thinking Critically** Why do you think the early Americans migrated from Alaska southward?

Agriculture in the Americas

Why was agriculture important to the development of early American civilizations?

A Great Discovery   Leel the Clever One was the first to notice. First, you put seeds from plants into holes in the ground. Then, when spring came, plants like the ones the seeds came from grew from the earth. It was a great discovery because it allowed people to settle in one place. On this discovery was based the rise of civilization in the Americas.

The Ice Age had ended. Animals of the late Ice Age had become extinct. Early Americans had lived by killing these animals and eating their flesh. Human beings in the Americas might have become extinct, too, had it not been for an important fact. Human beings are **omnivorous** —that is, they can eat plants as well as meat. They do not have to depend on meat alone. In the centuries following the end of the Ice Age, prehistoric Americans turned more and more to plants for food.

Agriculture Develops   Even during the Ice Age, hunters had probably learned that many roots, berries, and nuts were good to eat. As the large animals vanished, tribes continued to move about.

The use of terraces made it possible to raise crops on the steep slopes of the Andes Mountains.
■ How would you describe the terrain of the Andes?
■ What kind of tools do you think these farmers used?

The pyramid El Castillo and a statue of Chac Mool, the Mayan rain god, can be seen at Chichèn Itzá in Yucatán.
■ Why do you think a rain god would be important to the Mayas?

Their members lived by gathering these wild foods and by eating the flesh of such small animals as they were able to trap and kill. This was probably the time that Leel — or someone like her — began the practice of **agriculture.**

Agriculture is the planting of seeds and the care of growing plants. It also involves saving the very best of the plant seeds to improve the next year's crop. It is believed that agriculture was first practiced in Asia and Africa. Leel and her tribe may have brought this practice to the Americas and then taught it to others. Or clever people may have started practicing agriculture in the Americas on their own.

Where and when agriculture began in the Americas have been matters for debate. Most scholars now believe, however, that agriculture was first practiced in the Andes Mountains of South America. Crops were grown there at least 4,000 years ago. Some of the crops that these people grew were potatoes, peanuts, kidney beans, and tomatoes.

Although the earliest movement of people in the Americas was almost certainly from north to south, evidence shows that the practice of agriculture advanced from south to north. In the places where agriculture had been practiced the longest, the greatest civilizations arose.

The Mayas The Mayas (mī′ əz) developed the first advanced civilization in the Americas. They lived in the jungles of Central America and southern Mexico. Their civilization flourished from 1,200 to 700 years before Europeans arrived in America. The Mayas built large cities, supported by croplands carved from the jungle. One of their main crops was maize (māz), or Indian corn. From this area, the cultivation of maize spread throughout North America and South America.

About the year 900 the Mayan civilization declined for unknown reasons. But reminders of its greatness can still be seen in the jungles. There are ruins of temples, pyramids, and other stone buildings.

The Aztecs   By the 1400s the Aztecs (az′ teks) ruled what is now central Mexico. Like the Mayas, the Aztecs built beautiful cities. Their capital, Tenochtitlán (tä nôch tē tlän′), was built on islands in the middle of Lake Texcoco. It stood on the site of today's Mexico City. Tenochtitlán had a population of about 300,000. The surrounding farmlands produced abundant food supplies.

The Aztecs developed an accurate calendar with 365 days. They wrote their history in a series of pictographs on long strips of paper. They learned to fashion jewelry with jade, gold, and silver.

The Aztecs were a warlike people. They practiced human sacrifice because they believed that their gods needed blood in order to live. As a result, other tribes lived in dread of the Aztecs.

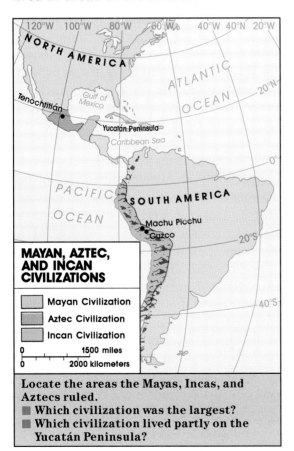

MAYAN, AZTEC, AND INCAN CIVILIZATIONS

- Mayan Civilization
- Aztec Civilization
- Incan Civilization

0   1500 miles
0   2000 kilometers

Locate the areas the Mayas, Incas, and Aztecs ruled.
■ **Which civilization was the largest?**
■ **Which civilization lived partly on the Yucatán Peninsula?**

The Incas   The Incas (ing′ kəz) were the descendants of those first Andean tribes who learned to farm long ago. By conquering their neighbors, they greatly expanded the region they controlled. In the 1400s, they ruled over all the tribes in the areas of present-day Peru and Ecuador and parts of Chile, Bolivia, and Argentina. Cuzco in Peru was their capital.

The Incas developed a complex system of farming. On the steep sides of the Andes, the Incas cut **terraces,** or ledges, into the land for planting. Water from mountain streams **irrigated,** or supplied water to, the dry soil. By using these methods, the Incas were able to raise more crops to feed the many people they ruled. To transport these crops and other goods, the Incas built an extensive highway and bridge network. There were more than 7,000 miles (11,200 km) of roads. Messages or communications were carried across their lands by relay runners.

The Pueblo Indians   About 700 years ago, Indian civilization in the Southwest United States reached its height. Agriculture had probably come to this region 2,000 years earlier. Still, it took centuries for farming to develop enough to support a large population.

Much of this population lived in **pueblos** (pwe′ blōz) — the Spanish word for "towns." Indian pueblos were, however, more like apartment houses than towns. At one time there were thousands of pueblos. They were scattered over the region between the Mexican state of Chihuahua (chē wä′ wä) in the south to Kansas and Colorado in the north. One of the most famous is Pueblo Bonito (bō nē′ tō) in Chaco (chäk′ ō) Canyon, New Mexico.

About 1,000 years ago Pueblo Bonito housed at least 1,500 people. Until a bigger apartment house was built in New York

The Cliff Palace Pueblo at Mesa Verde, Colorado, was inhabited from about
A.D. 1100 to 1275.
■ How did the cliffs protect the pueblos?

in 1882, Pueblo Bonito and some of the other pueblos were the largest dwellings ever built in the Americas.

To support so many people, Pueblo agriculture had to be well developed. Farmers raised corn, squash, and beans. They looked upon these vegetables as gifts from the gods they worshiped. Like farmers to the south, the Pueblo Indians irrigated their crops with water brought from distant streams. They raised cotton, too. From its fibers, cloth was woven and decorated with a variety of fancy designs.

At Mesa Verde (mā' sə vər' dā), in southwestern Colorado, pueblos were built along the sides of steep cliffs. Some of these dwellings were several stories high. They were probably built along the sides of cliffs as a means of protection from the tribe's enemies.

Most pueblos in the Southwest were abandoned long before Europeans came to America. Invaders from the north may have driven the peaceful Pueblo Indians from their towns. Or changes in climate may have caused a **drought,** that is, a long period of dry weather. A lengthy drought would have been a disaster for farming. People would have had to leave the pueblos to find other sources of food. As people scattered in search of food, the Pueblo civilization would have declined.

CHECKUP

1. After the Ice Age ended, how did the source of food supplies change?
2. Where did agriculture in the Americas most likely originate?
3. Describe three early American civilizations south of the present-day United States.
4. What were the main features of the Pueblo Indian civilization?
5. **Thinking Critically** Compare the crops grown by the American Indians with those grown now in your state.

29

The Mound Builders

What is the mystery surrounding the Mound Builders?

VOCABULARY

Mound Builders	temple mound
artifact	geometric mound
burial mound	effigy mound

A Pile of Earth   Aru the Strong carried the heavy earth-filled basket to the top of the ramp. After emptying the basket, he trod on the soil with his bare feet, making it solid. Aru did the same thing many times each day. He did it day after day, year after year. Was he a slave captured from a neighboring tribe? Was he a paid worker? Or did he carry the baskets as part of his religious duties?

No one knows exactly why Aru did this work. And yet we know what he was doing. He was helping to build a large earthen mound.

A Unique Civilization   The civilizations of the Mayas, the Incas, and the Aztecs flourished in areas south of what is now the United States. Still, within the area of the present-day United States, there were thriving native civilizations. You have already learned about the Pueblo Indians. Hundreds of miles to the east lived the **Mound Builders.** This civilization developed in stages. Each stage was more advanced than the one before it.

Some Europeans saw at first hand the glories of the Aztec civilization. The high level of Incan civilization is also a matter of historical record. However, no European ever saw the Mound Builders at the high point of their civilization. And they left no written records. They left only mounds such as Aru the Strong helped to build.

Mysterious Mounds   When settlers moved into the river valleys of the United States in the eighteenth and nineteenth centuries, they saw in many of the valleys strange mounds of earth. Farmers and others who were puzzled by these piles of earth dug into them. One person who wondered about the mounds and the people who built them was Thomas Jefferson, later our third President. He excavated, or dug into, a mound on his Virginia farm.

Unlike Jefferson, most diggers were interested only in collecting **artifacts** from the mounds. Artifacts are objects that people have made. Among these objects are necklaces, tools, and pottery. Only a few of the diggers wondered why the mounds were built. But as time went on, the mysterious mounds attracted the attention of scholars.

In 1890 a group of scholars working for the Smithsonian Institution published a report on the mounds. The Smithsonian Institution, in Washington, D.C., is widely known for the scientific research it carries on. Its report on mounds was based on 10 years of study. The report described vast numbers of mounds in an area extending from Ontario, Canada, southward to the Gulf Coast of Florida, Mississippi, and Louisiana. The mounds are especially numerous in the Ohio and Mississippi river valleys. (See the map on page 36.) In the states of Illinois and Ohio, thousands of mounds have been counted.

Types of Mounds   These mounds, built by several groups over hundreds of years, are of different types. The type found most often is the small round **burial mound.** These mounds nearly always contain skeletons and objects buried with them. Another common type is called the

temple mound. It is flat on top but sometimes has terraced sides. This kind of mound was used as a foundation for a wooden building or temple.

There are several other types of mounds besides the two main ones. **Geometric mounds** were built in the form of circles, squares, or parallel lines. Sometimes these geometric mounds enclose an area of 100 acres (40 ha) or more.

The **effigy mounds** are especially interesting. An effigy mound is built in the shape of a bird, snake, animal, or human being. The state of Wisconsin has many effigy mounds, and some can be seen in Indiana, Ohio, and other states. The Great Serpent Mound in southern Ohio and the Opossum Mound in Tennessee are famous effigy mounds. Effigy Mounds National Monument is located in eastern Iowa.

The Mound Builders worked with a purpose. They had a reason for building each mound. Some experts believe that the custom of mound building came from the south, as did agriculture. There is some resemblance between the earthen temple mounds and the pyramids of the Mayas and Aztecs.

Tribes were building mounds at different times in different places. The years A.D. 1 to A.D. 1000 were a time of great building activity. Artifacts found in some of the mounds of those years showed that a lively trade took place among well-to-do tribes of Mound Builders. Among the materials and objects found in the mounds are copper from the Lake Superior region, shells from both the Atlantic and Gulf of Mexico coasts, and grizzly bear teeth from the area of the Rocky Mountains.

This aerial view shows the Great Serpent Mound in Ohio.
■ Why do you think it is called the Great Serpent Mound?

Cahokia City   Perhaps the most remarkable work of the Mound Builders stands today near Collinsville, Illinois, about 15 miles (24 km) east of St. Louis. Its name is Cahokia (kə hō′ kē ə) Mounds State Historic Site. It could just as well be called Cahokia City. The site includes a great number of different mounds. They were built by a skilled Indian civilization that disappeared about 500 years ago.

Cahokia Mounds is known as the only prehistoric Indian city north of Mexico. At its height it had a population of up to 40,000 people. Probably 30,000 more Mound Builders lived in villages nearby.

At Cahokia Mounds the main mound is a flat-topped pyramid 1,080 feet (330 m) long, 710 feet (216 m) wide, and 100 feet (30 m) high. It covers 14 acres (6 ha). It is believed to have held a massive wooden building, used for religious purposes. It is known today as Monks Mound.

Nearly 100 burial mounds surround Monks Mound. At the center of this old cemetery is the grave of a prominent ruler. Buried with him were attendants meant to serve him in the next world. Around the site of the Cahokia Mounds are the traces of a stockade that required 50,000 logs.

Cahokia Mounds, the only prehistoric Indian city that has been found north of Mexico, probably looked something like this.
- Would this city have been easy to defend from attackers?
- How might such a defense have been organized?

Richard Schlecht © National Geographic Society

The Banjo-Playing Collector

In the nineteenth century, Cyrus Moore made a fortune in the cotton business. Having plenty of money, he was able to pursue his hobby of collecting Mound Builder treasures. Each winter Cyrus Moore had a houseboat built to order in either St. Louis or Cincinnati. Each spring he moved aboard his new boat with a crew of strong-armed diggers. In summer, Moore's houseboat was towed or floated along the banks of the Mississippi and its many tributaries.

There were thousands of mounds near these rivers. Moore's diggers had plenty of sites for their busy shovels. The pottery, tools, ornaments, and other objects they found —like the mica hand shown here—were cleaned and brought aboard the houseboat. While the diggers worked, Cyrus Moore sat on deck in a special chair, playing his banjo. He always played a lively tune when his men found something special.

Each fall the summer's collection was unloaded at New Orleans. Then the houseboat was sold. The next spring Moore and his crew went north to take over another new houseboat. Then they repeated the process of the previous summer. In this way Cyrus Moore built up a great collection. It was the envy of other collectors. Oddly enough, Moore displayed little curiosity about the Mound Builders or what had happened to them. He was mostly interested in collecting objects buried in their mounds. He was also interested in sitting on the deck of his houseboat and playing his banjo.

Imagine the length of time and the many baskets of earth it took to build the Cahokia Mounds! Mound Builders knew nothing about wheels, so they worked without wagons or wheelbarrows. They had no animals to haul earth from many miles away. All they had was the labor of thousands of persons like Aru the Strong.

Why did the custom of mound building die out? What happened to the highly organized tribes of Mound Builders? No one knows for certain. Perhaps they suffered the fate of other great civilizations of the past. Savage, warlike people have time and again invaded the lands of more civilized people and have overthrown them. This may have been what happened to the Mound Builders.

CHECKUP

1. Why do we know so little about the Mound Builders' civilization?
2. Describe four types of mounds.
3. Why are the Cahokia Mounds so remarkable?
4. What knowledge would have made the Mound Builders' work easier?
5. **Thinking Critically** What are some possible explanations for the disappearance of the Mound Builders?

33

Life-styles of the American Indians

How did environment shape the culture of the American Indians?

culture	Western
environment	civilization
tepee	technology
llama	

A Tribal Rite   Salma the Priest Woman buried the salmon bones carefully. It was her religious duty to do so. Salma was a member of the Makah (mä′ kä) tribe. The Makahs lived along the coast of what is now the state of Washington. The Pacific Ocean and the rivers that run into it made this good country for fishing.

Fishing for salmon and halibut was important to the Makahs. It touched upon every aspect of their **culture.** Culture is the way of life of a people. Salmon became almost sacred to the Indians of the Pacific Northwest. That is why Salma treated the bones of the fish in such a respectful manner.

Many Cultures   When Europeans first came to America, there were at least 200 different Indian tribes in the territory that would become the United States. Each tribe had its own distinctive culture. Such a culture set each tribe apart from other tribal groups.

Some tribes, however, shared certain ways of doing things with other tribes in the same area. This occurred because nearby tribes shared the same **environment.** Environment means everything in an area—land, water, plants, animals, and climate. These physical surroundings are important to any group. This is especially true of the Indians because they had few means of changing their physical surroundings.

Fishing was an important part of the daily life of the Indians in the Pacific Northwest.
- What clues tell you about the way these people lived?
- Do you think these Indians were skilled craftworkers?

The environment of the Makahs favored fishing, so salmon became an important part of their lives. In fact, *salmon* was the word for "fish" among several of the Indian tribes of the Northwest. In the dry Southwest, of course, fishing played little or no part in the lives of the tribes living there.

Farming in North America At the time that Europeans came, most North American Indians knew how to grow a few crops. Maize, squash, and beans were the most common. Nevertheless, crops varied, depending on the climate where a tribe lived. Indians of the Southwest could grow cotton. In the Southeast, tobacco was grown.

Indians worked out ways to grow better crops. Eastern Woodland Indians used dead fish as fertilizer when planting maize or beans. The Pueblo Indians and other tribes in the dry Southwest knew how to irrigate their fields.

Most Indian tribes stayed in the same place for only a few years. A tribe suffering from unusual weather conditions would move to escape from drought, or too much rain or cold. Also, tribes would have to move if their ways of farming wore out the soil. Occasionally a tribe would lose its crops because of raids by stronger, more aggressive Indians. This might force them to move to a safer place.

Indian Dwellings Since certain Indian tribes often moved, they seldom built permanent homes. An exception is the pueblos, which you read about earlier. Pueblos were built of stone or adobe, which is a brick made of sun-dried earth and straw. Even though most pueblos were abandoned by the time the first Europeans came to America, a few are still used. People have lived in Oraibi (ō rī′ bē), a pueblo in

This tribal house is located in Ketchikan, Alaska.
■ What figures form these totems?

Arizona, for more than 800 years. About 600 people still live there. Oraibi is thought to be the oldest continuously inhabited community in the United States.

In the Pacific Northwest, cedar trees were plentiful. So Indians there built their shelters of cedar boards or logs. The cedar was fitted or tied together because the Indians had no metal nails.

In the wooded lands of the Northeast and the Great Lakes region, lodges were made from logs, branches, and the bark of trees. Deer hides might have been stretched over cracks to keep out the winter cold.

The area bordering the Gulf of Mexico had a hot, humid climate. Therefore, Indians in this region usually built their houses without walls so cooling breezes could enter. Poles supported roofs made of wood, bark, thatch, or reeds.

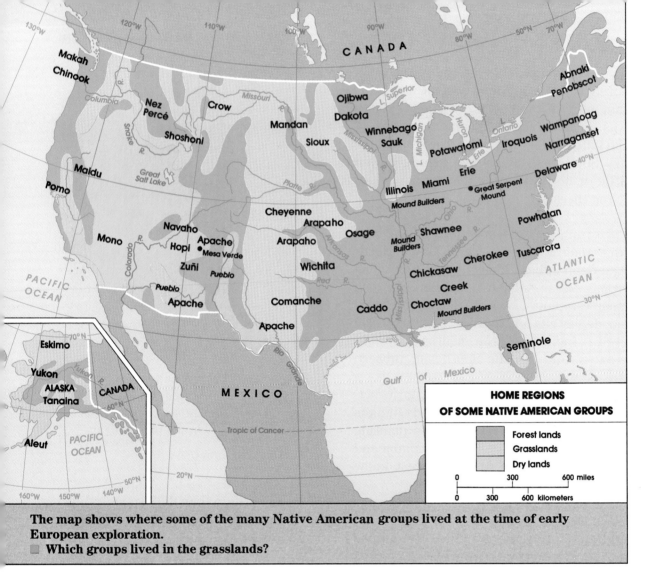

The map shows where some of the many Native American groups lived at the time of early European exploration.

■ Which groups lived in the grasslands?

Culture of the Plains Indians At first, Indians living on the western plains hunted and farmed in much the same way as Indians to the east and south. But their culture changed as buffalo herds increased in numbers. The Indians trailed the herds and cleverly invented ways to bring down the big animals. Sometimes the Indians surrounded a herd and drove it over a cliff. At other times, a hunter wrapped himself in a buffalo skin and crept close enough to the herd to kill one or more animals with a bow and arrows.

Following the herds made it necessary to have shelters that were light and easy to carry. To make such shelters the women stitched buffalo hides together. Then they stretched the hides over a framework of poles. This form of dwelling was called a **tepee.**

The women not only provided the basic dwelling but also did the cooking. They prepared rich buffalo meat, using buffalo stomachs as cooking pots. To serve the food, they used ladles and spoons made from buffalo horns.

With the arrival of Europeans in America, the buffalo became even more important in the lives of the Plains Indians. The use of horses and guns brought to America by the Europeans made buffalo hunting much easier. In later years the Plains Indians became almost totally dependent on the buffalo for their livelihood.

Culture of the Eastern Woodland Indians   In the eastern region the Indians also practiced farming. They cleared trees to make fields where they raised beans, corn, pumpkins, and squash. They fished in the streams, and those who lived near the ocean gathered shellfish.

The Eastern Woodland Indians hunted deer. They ate venison, the meat of the deer. They made the deer hides into clothing and the antlers into arrowpoints. But they never became as dependent on deer as the Plains Indians became on buffalo. Yet, like the Plains Indians, the Eastern Woodland Indians made the best use of the animals and natural resources.

The Five Nations   The Iroquois (ir′ ə kwoi) lived in what is today the state of New York. The Iroquois were not a single tribe but rather a confederacy. In a con-federacy, several groups join in a loose union to act together for certain purposes. The Cayuga (kä yü′ gə), Mohawk, Oneida (ō nē′ də), Onondaga (on ən dä′ gə), and Seneca tribes were members of the confederacy. At the beginning the main purpose of the Iroquois Confederacy was to stop warfare among the five tribes, or the Five Nations as they called themselves.

In the tribes of the Iroquois Confederacy, women occupied a unique position. Like women in other tribes, they cultivated the crops, prepared food, made clothing, and took care of the children. In addition, Iroquois women chose the 50 sachems, or chiefs, who met as a council each year to discuss matters of common concern. The Senecas sent 8 representatives; the Cayugas, 10; the Onondagas, 14; and the Mohawks and Oneidas, 9 each to this council. Each tribe voted as a unit, and each

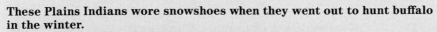
These Plains Indians wore snowshoes when they went out to hunt buffalo in the winter.
■ **How were snowshoes helpful to the Plains Indians?**

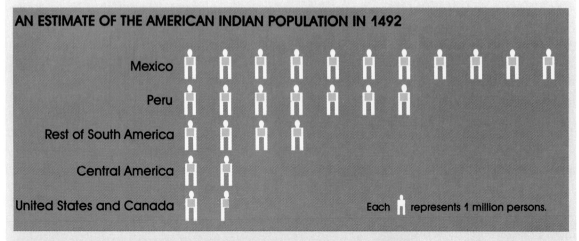

AN ESTIMATE OF THE AMERICAN INDIAN POPULATION IN 1492

Mexico
Peru
Rest of South America
Central America
United States and Canada

Each represents 1 million persons.

This pictograph shows scientists' best guess of the Indian population when the Europeans arrived in the Americas.
▪ In what area was the largest Indian population located?

had its own special tasks within the confederacy. The two war chiefs were always Senecas. The meeting place for the council was in the territory of the Onondagas. They had charge of the central council fires and always kept them burning.

Each tribe was made up of several families, or groups of families. Each village had a governing council. The women chose the members of this council, just as they chose the 50 sachems of the confederacy council. The members of all the councils were men, though. Iroquois families lived in villages of from 10 to 50 families, numbering 50 to 250 people. A palisade, or fence of sharpened logs, enclosed the village. Outside the palisade lay the fields where the women cultivated and tended rows of corn, squash, and pumpkins.

Indian Civilizations   Indians in the Americas had made different kinds of adjustments before the arrival of the Europeans. Some tribes had risen to more advanced levels of civilization. Others had remained at lower levels.

Except for the Mayas and the Aztecs, the tribes in early America did not develop a written language. What they knew was passed on by word of mouth. The wheel was not known to the Native Americans. Nor was the secret of exploding gunpowder. Thus, Indians had no guns.

Except for the Incas, Indians lacked large animals for transportation or use as beasts of burden. In the Andes, the Incas had trained wild **llamas** (yä′ mäs). These animals were probably descendants of prehistoric camels. Like the small horses that once roamed the plains of North America, the camels had become extinct. But llamas were much less useful than the horses, oxen, and mules brought to America by the Europeans.

Adapting to the Environment   Still, the Indians had the knowledge and skills that enabled them to survive in the Americas. Outsiders coming to these continents at first had to learn from the Indians.

American Indians had great respect for nature. Their religions differed from tribe to tribe, from culture to culture. But all the religions showed in many ways the Indians' respect for the natural wonders they saw about them.

American Indians had a long history in what came to be called the New World. Of course, to the Indians it was really a very old world. They had developed complex civilizations that had adapted to various environments in the Americas. Some of these civilizations, to be sure, had declined or vanished entirely. But so had other civilizations elsewhere.

A Clash of Civilizations   In Europe a new kind of civilization had developed by the fifteenth century. It was a rising civilization, ready to expand its influence. This **Western civilization,** as it has been called, put a high value on **technology** (tek nol' ə jē). Technology is the amount of scientific knowledge and the kinds of tools a people have. Some of this technology had been borrowed from cultures in Africa and Asia. Some had been invented or improved upon by the Europeans.

Whatever the sources, Western technology was more advanced than that of the Indian cultures of the Americas. In any conflict between the Indians and the European settlers, the Europeans' technology would give them a big advantage. In basic values, however, American Indian civilizations were at least an even match for Western civilization.

Indian Influences   Indeed, today there are many parts of the Americas showing a blend of Western and Indian civilizations. Thousands of names for cities, states, lakes, mountains, and rivers throughout the Americas are taken from Indian languages. Half the states in our nation have Indian names. Americans daily use such Indian words as *squash, tobacco, chipmunk, skunk, moose, pecan, woodchuck,* and *toboggan.* Phrases such as "walking Indian file" and "enjoying Indian summer" are frequently heard.

In spite of Western civilization's superior technology, the first European explorers and colonists had to learn from the Indians. Indians taught them how to plant, fish, and hunt in the Americas. Indian medicine men and women often were called on to doctor pioneer colonists when no other physicians were available. The Indians' knowledge of herbs and plants as medicines proved enormously useful to grateful pioneers.

Today we are still making use of Indian knowledge and skills. Indian jewelry designs are popular. Boy Scouts and Girl Scouts learn Indian woodcraft. Today's conservation movements owe much to Indian ideas of the relationship between human beings and nature. Books, movies, and television make use of Indian themes. Unfortunately, the way Indian history, culture, and characters are portrayed is often inaccurate. Sometimes it seems as if Western civilization overwhelmed the Indians. Actually, there is evidence all around us to show that the civilization of the Native Americans has had a lasting influence.

CHECKUP

1. In what ways did their environment influence the culture of the North American Indians?
2. What development changed the way of life of the Indians on the western plains?
3. What did Native American civilizations lack in their clash with Western civilizations that came to the Americas?
4. What were the strengths of the American Indian cultures?
5. What contributions were made by Indians to modern American life?

6. **Thinking Critically**   How did not living in permanent homes affect Indians' ways of life?

Reading a Table

NATIVE AMERICAN POPULATION

A table can be used to present many facts in a small space. Usually these facts are arranged in columns and rows to show some relationship between them. The table below shows the estimated Native American, or Indian, populations north of Mexico in the years when the various regions were explored.

SKILLS PRACTICE

Using the table, answer the following questions on a separate sheet of paper.

1. Which region had the largest Native American population?
2. Which region had the smallest Native American population?

3. What was the estimated population of the Gulf States area in 1650?
4. What states are included, wholly or in part, in the Columbia River basin?
5. In what year were estimates of population made for New Mexico and Arizona?
6. What area now in the United States had the smallest population?
7. Was the population larger on the Northern Plains or the Southern Plains?
8. In what area is Utah?
9. When were estimates made in Alaska?
10. If you were to add another column to this chart, showing the Native American populations in these regions today, would you expect the numbers to be larger or smaller? Why?

NATIVE AMERICAN POPULATION NORTH OF MEXICO		
Area	Date	Estimated population
North Atlantic New England, New York, New Jersey, Pennsylvania	1600	55,600
South Atlantic Delaware, Maryland, Virginia, West Virginia, the Carolinas except Cherokee country	1600	52,200
Gulf States Georgia, Florida, Alabama, Mississippi, Louisiana, Arkansas, Tennessee, Cherokee country	1650	114,400
Central States Ohio Valley from Alleghenies to Mississippi; Chippewa in Canada	1650	75,300
The Plains Canada to Gulf of Mexico		
Northern	1780	100,800
Southern	1690	41,000
Columbia River Basin Washington, most of Oregon, northern half of Idaho	1780	89,300
California	1769	260,000
Central Mountain Nevada, Utah, parts of surrounding states	1845	19,300
New Mexico and Arizona	1680	72,000
British America Eastern Canada, central Canada, British Columbia	1600–1780	190,950
Alaska	1740	72,600
Greenland	1721	10,000

MAIN IDEAS

1. Physical evidence indicates that the first Americans probably came from Asia by crossing a land bridge thousands of years ago.
2. Carbon dating has proved to be the best method of finding out when ancient peoples were living in the Americas.
3. Agriculture enabled the Indians to develop civilizations because they no longer had to search for food.
4. The Mayas, the Aztecs, the Incas, the Pueblo Indians, and the Mound Builders were among the more advanced Indian civilizations to develop in the Americas.
5. Very little is known about the Mound Builders' civilization and disappearance because they left no written records.
6. A tribe's environment affected its life-style, type of dwelling, and diet. It also affected its cultural development.

VOCABULARY REVIEW

On a separate sheet of paper, write **T** if the statement is true and **F** if it is false. If the statement is false, replace the underlined word or words to make the statement true.

1. The Ice Age bridge between Siberia and Alaska is now covered by water known as the Bering Strait.
2. A geologist is an expert in studying rocks.
3. Every living thing has a radioactive substance called earth beams.
4. Human beings are omnivorous.
5. The Aztecs lived in Peru.
6. In 1890 the Smithsonian Institution made a report on agriculture.
7. The Cahokia Mounds are an ancient Indian site in New Mexico.
8. An Indian tribe's culture can best be described as its ability to enjoy music.

9. The wheel was unknown to America's prehistoric Indians.
10. Planting seeds and taking care of growing plants is known as technology.

CHAPTER CHECKUP

1. What significant fact, event, or achievement is associated with each of the following imaginary characters in this chapter?

   a. Omuk the Leader
   b. Leel the Clever One
   c. Aru the Stong

2. How have scientists contributed to the study of ancient human life in America?
3. Why do we know so little about the American Indian cultures?
4. Why do you think small bands of Indians formed tribes?
5. What skills or knowledge would the Mound Builders have needed to build their mounds?
6. **Thinking Critically** Compare the culture of the Pueblo Indians with that of the Eastern Woodland Indians.
7. **Thinking Critically** In your opinion, which is more important to civilization — its level of technology or its basic values?

APPLYING KNOWLEDGE

1. Most Native Americans had no written language. However, they communicated through pictures and symbols and in some cases through sign language. Write a sentence. Then try to communicate the same thought with pictures.
2. Research and write a report about the Indian tribe(s) that lived in your state. For information, you might visit your local library, museum, or historical society.
3. Write an account of the way in which carbon dating might be used to learn how long ago a group of people occupied a cave.

3 Colonization Begins in the Americas 1492–1755

Columbus Leads the Way

Who is considered the discoverer of America?

VOCABULARY

Far East	Vinland
Indies	colony
Vikings	New World

A Man from Genoa Christopher Columbus was born in the old seaside city of Genoa (jen′ ō ə), Italy, in 1451. His father and his grandfather were weavers. His mother was a weaver's daughter. But Columbus chose to go to sea.

Christopher Columbus had two brothers. Bartholomew (bär thol′ ə myü), the older, was tough, skillful, and loyal. He became a partner in the project that resulted in Columbus's voyages to America. The other brother was named Diego (dē ā′ gō). Though willing enough, Diego failed as a sailor and colonist in the New World. Later he became a priest.

Columbus had a sister named Bianchinetta (byäng′ kē net′ ə). She married a wine merchant in Genoa. Little more is known of Bianchinetta.

A Plan for Reaching the Indies When Christopher Columbus was 25, he sailed with a fleet of merchant ships from the port of Genoa. Off the coast of Portugal, Columbus's ship was attacked and sunk. He saved himself by grabbing a large oar. Hanging onto it, he floated to the coast of Portugal, 6 miles (10 km) away.

Columbus stayed in Portugal for several years. There he sailed with and talked to many experienced sailors. At that time Europeans were talking of finding a water route to the **Far East,** or East Asia. There was a great demand in Europe for the silks, spices, and other products of eastern Asia. Trade with the Far East by way of land routes had proved to be slow, costly, and dangerous. A water route would be much better.

Some sailors talked of reaching Asia by sailing south from Portugal and then east around Africa. In this way they hoped to reach the rich islands off the southeastern coast of Asia called the **Indies.**

Gradually, Columbus formed another plan. Like other people of the time, he believed the world was round. If so, Columbus could reach the Indies by sailing west from Europe.

Christopher Columbus presented his plan to the king of Portugal. Much to his disappointment, the king's advisers turned down Columbus's plan. For this

Columbus and his crew landed in the West Indies. They thought they had landed on an island off the coast of Asia.
■ When did Columbus land in the West Indies?

EVENTS IN OUR COUNTRY

1492 Columbus sails to the Americas
1500 Cabral lands in Brazil
1513 Ponce de León explores Florida/Balboa discovers the Pacific Ocean
1519 Cortés conquers the Aztecs
1531 Pizarro conquers the Incas
1534 Cartier explores the St. Lawrence River
1540 Coronado and Alarcón explore the Southwest
1608 Champlain founds Quebec
1609 Dutch settle on Manhattan Island
1673 Marquette and Joliet explore the Mississippi River
1682 La Salle claims the Mississippi River valley
1728 Bering explores Alaskan waters

1500
1550
1600
1650
1700

EVENTS ELSEWHERE

1669 First French trading post in India
1642 Dutch take the Gold Coast in Africa from the Portuguese
1615 Dutch seize the Moluccas from the Portuguese
1574 Portuguese colonize Angola (Africa)
1551 Portuguese establish a colony at Macao
1543 Portuguese land in Japan
1526 Portuguese land in New Guinea (East Indies)
1519 Magellan begins voyage around the world
1498 Da Gama sails around Africa to Calicut, India

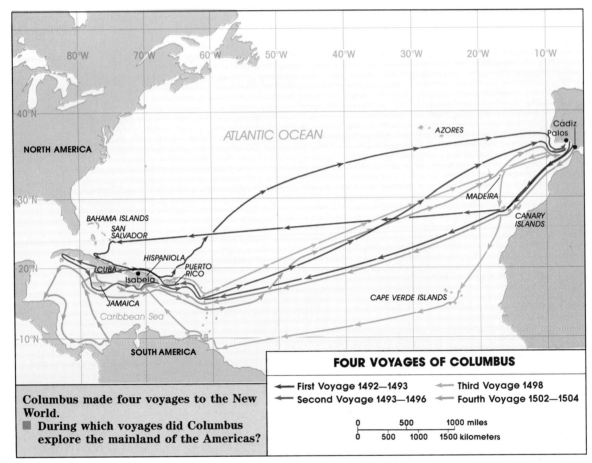

FOUR VOYAGES OF COLUMBUS

← First Voyage 1492—1493 ← Third Voyage 1498
← Second Voyage 1493—1496 ← Fourth Voyage 1502—1504

| 0 | 500 | 1000 miles |
| 0 | 500 1000 | 1500 kilometers |

Columbus made four voyages to the New World.
■ **During which voyages did Columbus explore the mainland of the Americas?**

reason the Columbus brothers traveled to the court of King Ferdinand and Queen Isabella of Spain. They succeeded in getting approval there, though it took 6 years.

The king and queen of Spain furnished the Columbus brothers with three ships — the *Niña*, the *Pinta*, and the *Santa María*. Each ship was less than 100 feet (30 m) in length. The little fleet sailed from the harbor of Palos (päl′ ōs), Spain, on August 3, 1492. At the Canary Islands, off the west coast of Africa, the ships made their first stop. The crews rested there and made needed repairs on their ships. They took on supplies for a long voyage before lifting anchor once more. This time they sailed directly westward. On September 9 the three ships passed the last island then known to European sailors.

Land! After sailing for more than a month, Rodrigo de Triana (rôd rē′ gō dä trë ä′ nə), a lookout on the *Pinta*, doubted the ships would ever reach land. But as a good sailor, he still kept watch carefully. Several hours before sunrise on October 12, he thought he saw something like a white cliff shining in the moonlight. "Land! Land!" he shouted.

Within a few minutes the captain of the *Pinta* also saw the land. He ordered a cannon fired as a signal that land had been sighted. As the three ships sailed closer together, Columbus called from the *Santa María* that the *Pinta* had sighted land first.

The rising sun revealed an island in the distance. When Columbus went ashore he knelt to kiss the soil. With tears of joy in his eyes, he named the island San

Salvador, Spanish for "Holy Savior." It was one of the many small islands in the Bahamas. (See the picture on page 43.)

The West Indies   Columbus and his crew stayed for a few months in the islands they had discovered. They believed these were the rich Indies near the coast of Asia. For this reason, Columbus called the people there Indians. To this day the islands he explored are known as the West Indies.

After his first voyage, Columbus sailed to the New World three more times. On these voyages his ships carried colonists, seeds for planting, pigs, cattle, chickens, sheep, and goats. On his third voyage, Columbus reached the coast of South America. However, he never saw any part of the mainland of what is now the United States.

Family Fortunes   Columbus had an agreement with the Spanish rulers and businesspeople who backed his first voyage. He was to be made admiral and also governor of the islands and continents he might discover. Moreover, these titles were to pass to his elder son and the son's heirs. In addition Christopher Columbus was to receive 10 percent of the profits from "pearls, precious stones, gold, silver, spices, and all other things" obtained as the result of his discoveries.

Had things worked out differently, Christopher Columbus might have been the richest man in the world. Instead he never received anything close to the 10 percent promised him. Disappointment, poverty, and ill health clouded his last years. He died in 1506, a bitter man.

The Vikings   As you read in the last chapter, the first people to reach America were probably those who came from Asia by way of the Bering Strait land bridge. Nor was Columbus even the first European to reach America. Centuries before Columbus's first voyage, the **Vikings** had visited the North Atlantic islands of Iceland and Greenland. The Vikings were a bold, seagoing people who came from what are today the countries of Norway, Sweden, and Denmark. According to legend a Viking named Bjarni Herjulfson (byär′ nə hėr′ yŭlf sən) set out for a small Viking settlement in Greenland but was blown off course. The storm drove his ship to a coast west of Greenland. In time he returned to Greenland with the exciting news of a land to the west.

A few years later another Viking, Leif Ericson (lāv er′ ik sən), accidentally reached this new land. He and his crew spent a winter there. They called it **Vinland,** which means "land of vines," because of the wild grapes they found there.

The Vikings were a great seagoing people. Their ships were powered by oar as well as by sail.
■ What purpose do you think was served by the shields on the side of this boat?

America

Christopher Columbus not only lost the chance to become the richest man in the world—the lands to which he led the way were named for someone else.

Amerigo Vespucci (ä mə rē′ gō   ves pü′ chē) was a skillful navigator born in Florence, Italy. He took part in several Spanish and Portuguese voyages to the New World. He claimed to have been a member of an expedition that in 1499 discovered the mainland of a continent.

Martin Waldseemüller (vält zā mül′ ėr), a German geographer and mapmaker, published some of Amerigo Vespucci's accounts in 1507. Along with the accounts Waldseemüller printed 12 pages of maps with the name "America" spread across each page. The maps showed all the discoveries made in the New World up to that time. Waldseemüller called the New World "the fourth continent," suggesting it be named for Amerigo Vespucci because he had discovered it.

Not many people agreed with Waldseemuller about the discovery. But the book and Waldseemüller's maps became so popular that people got into the habit of calling the New World that was being explored "America."

Still the name of Columbus is remembered in a number of ways in the lands he discovered. The republic of Colombia in South America is named for him. Twenty-seven of the United States have counties, towns, or cities named Columbus or Columbia.

The District of Columbia is the site of our nation's capital. The mighty Columbia River drains a good part of the Pacific Northwest.

No one in the United States celebrates Amerigo Vespucci Day, but 40 states make Columbus Day a legal holiday. So Christopher Columbus is far from being forgotten as the foremost European discoverer of America.

Other Vikings founded a **colony** in Vinland. A colony is a settlement that is ruled by another country.

Although no one actually knows the location of the Vinland colony, archaeologists have discovered the remains of a Viking colony on Newfoundland. The buildings and artifacts prove that the Vikings lived there around the year 1000. The Viking colonies, however, were short-lived. The discovery of a land across the sea was soon forgotten.

In contrast, news of Columbus's discovery spread through Western Europe. His first voyage led directly to the exploration and colonization of the **New World.** That is why Columbus, even though others came before him, is called the discoverer of America.

Other Early Explorers Soon after Columbus's third voyage, Pedro Cabral (kä bräl′), a Portuguese sea captain, set out on a voyage down the coast of Africa. Storms blew his ship far off course, and he landed on the coast of South America. Cabral claimed for Portugal the land that we now call Brazil. You can follow Cabral's route on the map on page 50.

It was, however, the Spaniards who led the way in exploring the mainland of the American continents. In 1513, Vasco Núñez de Balboa (vas′ kō nü′ nyäs də bal bō′ ə) crossed the Isthmus of Panama. He became the first European to see the Pacific Ocean from the shores of the New World. In the same year, Juan Ponce de León (wän pon′ sə də le on′) discovered the peninsula he named Florida, while searching for a fountain of youth.

These and other explorers soon suspected there was more land in the New World than anyone had first realized. Still they hoped there was a way around or through this land. Such a passage would

Juan Ponce de León searched for the fountain of youth in Florida.
■ Were these men dressed for the climate?

make it possible to reach Asia by sailing west, as Columbus had believed.

The First Voyage Around the World In 1519 the Spanish king, Philip II, sent Ferdinand Magellan (mə jel′ ən) to look for a passage through the newly discovered lands. Magellan was Portuguese but had enlisted in the service of Spain. After crossing the Atlantic in five ships, Magellan's expedition spent the winter on the coast of South America. One ship was lost in a storm, but the other four sailed south in the spring. At the southern end of South America, they entered the strait, or narrow passage of water, that today bears Magellan's name.

In the stormy strait the crew of one ship seized control of the vessel and headed back to Spain. The other three ships sailed into the ocean that Magellan named the *Pacific*, which means peaceful, because it seemed so calm. For months they sailed across this huge ocean. Food

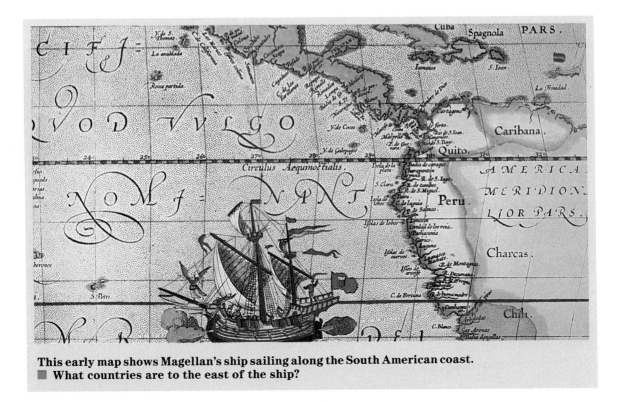

This early map shows Magellan's ship sailing along the South American coast.
■ **What countries are to the east of the ship?**

supplies ran out, forcing the men to eat rats and to chew pieces of leather. At last they reached Guam, an island in the Pacific. After finding food, they sailed west until they reached a group of islands, later named the Philippines for King Philip of Spain. On one of these islands Magellan was killed when he took part in a battle between rival Filipino groups.

With the death of its commander, this voyage might have ended in the Philippines. But it did not. Juan Sebastián del Cano took charge of the one remaining ship, the *Victoria*. He and his crew sailed south, picked up a cargo of spices in the Indies, and then sailed westward across the Indian Ocean. After passing the Cape of Good Hope, at the southern tip of Africa, the ship turned north into the Atlantic. In 1522 it reached Spain, 3 years after it had first set sail. The *Victoria* was the first ship to sail around the world. Follow Magellan's route on the map on page 50.

The voyage proved it was possible to reach Asia by sailing west from Europe. Even so, very few explorers wanted to suffer the hardships of such a lengthy voyage. In the years that followed, they devoted their attention to exploring and colonizing the American continents.

CHECKUP

1. What was Columbus's goal on his first voyage across the Atlantic?
2. How did the Native Americans come to be called Indians?
3. Since Columbus was not, in fact, the first person to reach America, who else might also be called the discoverer of the Americas?
4. Tell briefly what each of the following did in the age of exploration: Cabral, Balboa, Ponce de León, Magellan.

5. **Thinking Critically** What role did chance play in the discovery of the Americas? Explain.

Spain Builds an Empire in the New World

What areas of the Americas did Spain colonize?

VOCABULARY

empire	viceroy
conquistador	peninsular
encomienda	creole
hacienda	mestizo
mission	mulatto
presidio	vaquero
viceroyalty	

Spaniards Conquer the Aztecs and the Incas Columbus started Spain's first colony on the West Indian island of Hispaniola, which today is Haiti and the Dominican Republic. Using this and other island bases, Spanish explorers and colonizers sailed to the mainland of North and South America. Within 100 years after Columbus's first voyage, Spaniards had explored, conquered, and colonized a great **empire** in the Americas. An empire is made up of the territories and peoples under the control of a powerful country or ruler. The richest parts of Spain's New World empire were in the West Indies, Mexico, and Peru.

Hernando Cortés (kôr tez′) had learned to command troops in the Spanish conquest of the West Indies. In 1519 this Spanish explorer led an expedition to Mexico. It consisted of 600 men with 17 horses and 10 cannons. The Spaniards landed near present-day Vera Cruz and marched inland into the great empire of the Aztecs. The Spaniards' goals were to claim land for Spain, to seek gold and other treasure, and to convert the Indians to Christianity. The men who led the Spanish expeditions were called **conquistadores** (kon kē stä dôr′ ās). This word means "conquerors" in Spanish.

The Aztecs built this Temple of the Sun at Teotihuacán, in Mexico.
■ What are some of the skills that the Aztecs would have used to build this temple?

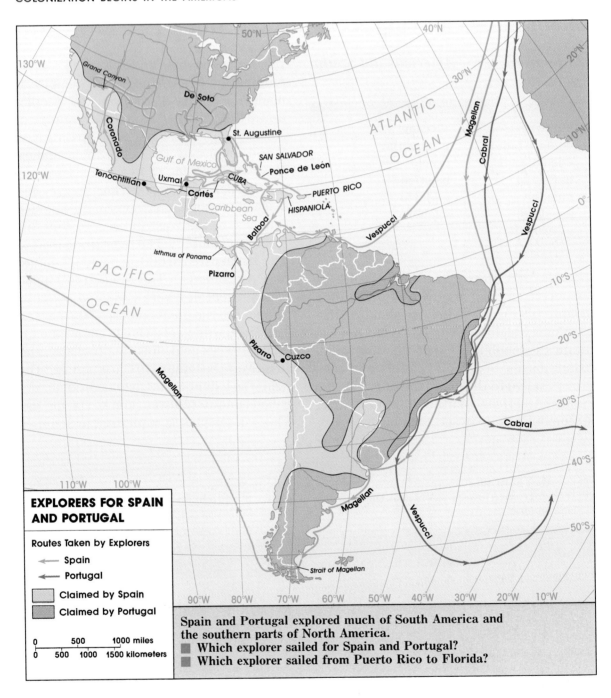

EXPLORERS FOR SPAIN AND PORTUGAL

Routes Taken by Explorers

← Spain

← Portugal

Claimed by Spain

Claimed by Portugal

0   500   1000 miles
0   500   1000   1500 kilometers

Spain and Portugal explored much of South America and the southern parts of North America.
■ Which explorer sailed for Spain and Portugal?
■ Which explorer sailed from Puerto Rico to Florida?

The Spanish horses amazed the Aztecs. At first the Aztecs treated Cortés and his men like gods. But Cortés ordered the seizure of Montezuma (mon tə zü′ mə), the Aztec ruler. Then Cortés forced the Indians to hand over their gold and silver ornaments to him. He made them dig new supplies of precious metals from deep mines.

Finally the Aztecs rebelled and drove the Spaniards from their capital city. But the Aztecs' victory was only temporary. More troops from the West Indies came to Cortés's aid, as did thousands of Indians who had been conquered by the Aztecs and who hated them. In the fighting that followed, Montezuma was killed, and the Spaniards again took the Aztec capital.

With the Aztec empire under his control, Cortés directed further conquests in Mexico. Mexico was used as the base from which other Spanish explorers moved north into what is now the southwestern United States.

In South America, another Spaniard, Francisco Pizarro (pə zär′ ō), conquered the Incan empire of Peru. Pizarro commanded fewer than 200 men. Yet the Spaniards, mounted on horses and armed with swords and guns, attacked and killed thousands of Incas. Pizarro then seized the Incas' gold and silver. Most of these precious metals went into the royal treasury of Spain.

The conquering of the Aztec and Incan empires destroyed two powerful Native American civilizations. With the flow of wealth from the Americas, Spain became the richest and most powerful country in Europe for more than a century.

De Soto's March to the Mississippi In 1539, Hernando de Soto led an expedition that landed in Florida. For 4 years the expedition marched through the wilderness. From Florida it moved north into present-day Georgia and the Carolinas. In 1541 the Spaniards reached the Mississippi River at a point south of the present location of Memphis, Tennessee.

De Soto died of fever while his expedition was camped on the banks of the Mississippi. One of his lieutenants led the surviving men west to the Brazos River in what is now Texas and then back to the Mississippi. After building boats and rafts, the Spaniards floated down the Mississippi to the Gulf of Mexico.

De Soto's expedition failed to find gold or any other wealth. Nearly half of the 600 Spanish soldiers died in the wilderness. However, the expedition made it possible for Spain to add the southeastern part of what is now the United States to the Spanish empire.

The "Golden Cities" Tales of "golden cities" led the Spaniards to explore the mountains, plains, and deserts of the American Southwest. Francisco Coronado entered this region in 1540 with an army of 300 Spaniards and 1,300 Indians.

Francisco Coronado and his men discovered Indians living in pueblos. But these were not the golden cities they sought. To cover more territory in the search, the expedition split up. One group became the first Europeans to see the Grand Canyon of the Colorado River. Coronado himself led another group as far north as present-day Kansas and Nebraska. All he found were grass-covered plains and large herds of buffalo.

Disappointed, Coronado led his expedition back to Mexico. He reported to the governor, "There is not any gold nor any other metal in all that country."

While Coronado explored by land, Hernando de Alarcón (ä lär kōn′) tried to link up with Coronado's expedition by sailing up the Colorado River from the Gulf of California. The plan failed because neither Coronado nor Alarcón knew the vast extent of the American Southwest.

Pacific Coast Exploration About the same time, Juan Rodríguez Cabrillo (wän ro drē′ gāz kä brē′ yō) was ordered to explore the Pacific coast by sea. Cabrillo died along the way, but the two ships he had commanded sailed as far north as present-day Oregon. When exploring parties from the ships went ashore, they saw and spoke to many Indian tribes.

Spaniards gave the name *California* to the land they explored along the Pacific coast. The name came from an imaginary land described in a popular book of the time. But reports on the actual land were discouraging. There were no Aztec or Inca empires along the western coast of North America.

Spanish Settlements   The Spaniards used three different methods of settlement in the New World. Sometimes a large land grant was given to a Spanish noble or other person as a reward for that person's service to Spain. The Spanish king also awarded **encomiendas** to certain colonists. An encomienda (en kō myen′ dä) was a large estate where a group of Indians lived under the colonist's care and supervision. The colonist was to teach and protect the Indians, and convert them to Christianity. In return the Indians were to spend most of their working time in the colonist's fields or mines. The encomienda system was misused, however, and the Indians became little more than slaves.

The large estates on which these colonists lived were called **haciendas** (hä syen′ däs). A hacienda could be a plantation or ranch. Sometimes the word *hacienda* also referred to the owner's house.

Another type of settlement was the **mission.** A mission usually consisted of a church, living quarters for the priests and Indians, and workshops. At the mission the Indians were converted to Christianity, taught Spanish, and introduced to European customs. They were also taught to raise livestock and to grow crops in the fields surrounding the mission. Many learned crafts such as weaving, carpentry, and blacksmithing. Missions were the most common form of Spanish settlement in the present-day United States.

The Mission Nuestra Señora de la Purísima Concepción was established in 1731 in San Antonio, Texas. (29°N/99°W; map p. 326)
■ Could this mission also serve as a fortress? Why or why not?

Spanish soldiers also helped to settle the New World. They built **presidios,** or small forts, to protect the colonists from invasion by the Indians, the English, and the French. Some of these presidios grew into towns or cities. St. Augustine, Florida, is the oldest permanent European settlement in the continental United States. It began as a presidio in 1565.

Spanish Colonial Government To rule their vast territories in the New World, the Spaniards divided their empire into two great **viceroyalties,** or regions, called New Spain and Peru. New Spain included all of Spanish America north of Panama. Florida, New Mexico, Arizona, California, and part of Texas formed the northern boundary of New Spain. The viceroyalty of Peru included the present countries of Panama, Venezuela, Colombia, Peru, and Chile. Each viceroyalty was governed by a **viceroy,** or vice-king. He stood in the place of the Spanish king in America.

The Spanish system of government gave rise to four social classes in the Americas. At the top were the major officeholders of the empire. These were the viceroys, judges, high church officials, and governors. Most of these officials were born in Spain. Usually they returned to their homeland after their term of service in the New World. They were called **peninsulares** (pe nēn sü lär′ ās) because they came from the Iberian Peninsula.

Below this group were the **creoles,** people born of Spanish parents in the Americas. They were priests, army officers, merchants, and small landowners. The **mestizos** were of mixed European and Indian ancestry. **Mulattoes** were of mixed European and black ancestry. They formed a lower middle class of small farmers and shopkeepers. The Indians

and the blacks, who were imported as slaves, belonged to the lowest class.

Spanish Influence in America Signs of Spanish influence are readily seen in the United States today. Churches, public buildings, and ranch-style houses in the Southwest show the influence of Spanish colonial architecture. Some laws regulating the use of water in this dry region are of Spanish origin.

We think of the cowhand as being typically American. But the **vaquero** (vä kär′ ō), or Spanish cowhand, invented most of the equipment used on the range. The cowhand's hat is called a *sombrero*, and his rope, the lariat, comes from the Spanish term *la reata*. Longhorn cattle were brought to the West by Spanish colonists, as were the ancestors of the cowhand's horse. Riding and roping contests called *rodeos* date from an old Spanish custom.

Spain's worldwide empire lasted for more than four centuries. Today immigrants from former colonies of that empire are numerous in several regions of the United States. In the areas where these immigrants and descendants of immigrants live, the Spanish language is still widely spoken.

CHECKUP

1. Why did the empires of the Aztecs and the Incas come to an end?
2. How did Francisco Coronado contribute to Spain's New World empire?
3. Describe the three types of Spanish settlements in the New World.
4. In what ways does Spanish influence show itself in the United States today?
5. **Thinking Critically** What obstacles did the Spanish explorers face in the Americas?

The French Empire in North America

What were the explorers from France searching for in the New World?

VOCABULARY

Northwest Passage	aristocrat
portage	bilingual

The Northwest Passage   The desire to find a water route to the riches of the Far East first sent French explorers to North America. Magellan's voyage had shown there was no short route through the southern continent. But French explorers thought that there might be such a route through the northern landmass. Several expeditions sailed from France in search of this northern route, which was called the **Northwest Passage.**

Giovanni da Verrazano (jō vän′ nē dä vär rä tsä′ nō), an Italian sea captain living in France, commanded the first of these expeditions. In 1524 he sailed from what is now North Carolina northward to New-foundland. Verrazano did not find the Northwest Passage, but he taught map-makers something about the eastern coast of North America.

The French in North America   Ten years after Verrazano's explorations, Jacques Cartier (kär tyā′) made the first of three voyages to North America. During these voyages he discovered the Gulf of St. Lawrence. He sailed up the broad St. Lawrence River as far as present-day Mon-treal. France based its claims to the St. Lawrence region on Cartier's discoveries.

Samuel de Champlain (sham plān′) started the first permanent French colony along the St. Lawrence River at Quebec in 1608. He explored as far west as Lake Huron and as far south as New York State.

Jacques Cartier brought some settlers to French North America on one of his voyages, but most chose to return to France a year later.
■ Does this picture—from a French map made in 1547—tell you anything about why the French wanted to leave?

La Salle's expedition leaves a French fort on Lake Ontario to explore the Midwest.
Why do you think La Salle took Indians along with him?

In his honor the body of water along the boundary between present-day New York and Vermont is called Lake Champlain. Samuel de Champlain made 20 exploring trips to the region, gaining the title Father of New France. Champlain became the governor of France's first colony in the New World.

It was Champlain who sent Jean Nicolet (nik ō lā′) west to visit the Winnebago Indians of Wisconsin. Nicolet claimed the lands he saw for the king of France. Years later the French returned to explore this land. Father Jacques Marquette (mär ket′), a missionary, and Louis Joliet (zhô lyä′), a trader, reached the northern part of the Mississippi River in 1673. By canoe, they traveled as far as the Arkansas River before turning back.

It remained for another French explorer, Robert Cavalier, Sieur (sër) de La Salle (lä sal), to travel all the way down the Mississippi to the Gulf of Mexico. Before this, La Salle had explored the Ohio River

country and claimed it for France. He traveled down the Mississippi in 1682, claiming all the land drained by that mighty river for France. La Salle named the land Louisiana in honor of King Louis XIV of France.

"Water Highways"   At its greatest extent the French empire in North America stretched from the St. Lawrence River in the north to the Gulf of Mexico in the south. In addition, France claimed vast unsettled lands between the Appalachians and the Rocky Mountains. Water routes held together this far-reaching empire.

Travelers could go by canoe from Quebec, on the St. Lawrence, to New Orleans, on the Mississippi. Canoes had to be carried around rapids or for short distances from waterway to waterway. Such a task on land was called a **portage,** from the French word *porter* (pôr tä′), which means "to carry." But even with the portages, water travel was much easier and faster than overland travel. The St. Lawrence, the Great Lakes, the Ohio, and the Mississippi and its tributaries were "water highways" for the French in North America.

The Fur Trade None of these water highways was the Northwest Passage through the North American continent. Still they permitted the French to carry on a rich business in furs. Sailors on fishing boats visiting the St. Lawrence region brought iron weapons, tools, and trinkets, which they bartered for furs.

Fur-bearing animals had become scarce in France. But it was the custom for French nobility and wealthy business leaders to wear clothing made of fur or decorated with fur. For these reasons the price of furs was high. Thousands of people living in the region called New France made their living from the fur trade.

French fur traders traveled long distances into the interior of the North American continent. Often they lived for years with Indians, learning their languages and their ways. The French government tried

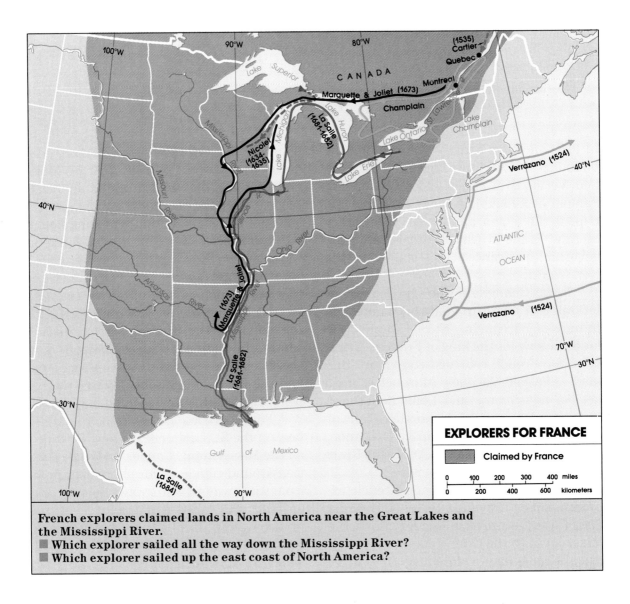

French explorers claimed lands in North America near the Great Lakes and the Mississippi River.
■ Which explorer sailed all the way down the Mississippi River?
■ Which explorer sailed up the east coast of North America?

to control traders by requiring each to have a license to trade furs. However, many traders broke the law. They kept on the move, and few settled anywhere for long.

French Settlements Most of France's New World empire remained unsettled. Probably no more than 100,000 people moved there from France. In an effort to attract permanent colonists, the French king granted land to **aristocrats,** or people of high social standing. The aristocrats had to find settlers and pay for their passage to New France. But this failed.

Some of the people who settled New France were missionaries. Thousands of French soldiers came from Europe to North America. Although most of the soldiers returned to France, some remained in the new lands. While stationed in New France, the soldiers built many forts. Most were located on "water highways."

French settlers did little to profit from the rich lands of the Mississippi River valley. Instead, settlements in that region were chiefly trading posts or forts designed to protect people from the Indians, the English, or the Spanish. The same was true of French settlements west of the Mississippi. Fort St. Jean Baptiste de Natchitoches (now called Natchitoches) on the Red River in Louisiana was an early center of the western fur trade. So, too, was St. Louis, which later became known as the Gateway to the West.

French Influence in America The most heavily settled parts of the French empire in North America were along the St. Lawrence River. Today this area is in Quebec, one of the provinces of Canada. The Canadian cities of Quebec and Montreal contain large numbers of French-speaking people. Indeed, Canada is now a **bilingual** nation; that is, two languages —

Montreal is Canada's largest city. It is the second largest French-speaking city in the world. (47°N/90°W; map, p. 56)
■ Do you think this photograph shows old Montreal or new Montreal?

English and French — are officially used there. The widespread use of French in the province of Quebec stems from the time when eastern Canada was part of France's North American empire.

Two of the 50 United States have French names. They are Vermont, which means "green mountain," and Louisiana. Not long after La Salle claimed Louisiana, the French took steps to found permanent settlements along the lower Mississippi River. In this region you can clearly see French influence in the United States today.

French Louisiana The land the French called Louisiana included not only the present-day state, but also parts of Alabama, Mississippi, Tennessee, and Texas. In 1689, the Sieur de Bienville and the Sieur d'Iberville, sons of a prominent Quebec family named Le Moyne, received permission from Louis XIV to colonize the mouth of the Mississippi. Mobile in Alabama, New Orleans in Louisiana, and Biloxi and Natchez in Mississippi were the results of their efforts.

This is the French Quarter in New Orleans. The style of the buildings and the streetlamps shows French influence.
■ **What is unusual about the style of the buildings?**

In 1718, the Sieur de Bienville laid out the city of New Orleans on a site he had chosen about twenty years earlier. Almost overnight, New Orleans began to rival Montreal and Quebec as the largest city in New France. It became the capital of French Louisiana in 1722. To promote the city's growth, Bienville had a shipload of young, single women sent from France. They were accompanied by nuns until suitable husbands could be found. Fur traders and other men traveled down the Mississippi from as far away as Illinois to claim a bride. Bienville also welcomed immigrants from all nations. Today the French Quarter reminds us that New Orleans was originally a French city.

Other parts of the lower Mississippi region also show French influence. Louisiana's present capital, Baton Rouge, has a French name. French influence in Louisiana was increased when thousands of Acadians settled there. The Acadians were exiled from Nova Scotia by the English in 1755. At first the French-speaking Acadians were scattered throughout the English colonies, but eventually most of them settled in Louisiana.

CHECKUP

1. Why was the Northwest Passage important?
2. Where did the following explore?
   (a) Samuel de Champlain
   (b) Jacques Cartier
   (c) Marquette and Joliet
   (d) Robert Cavalier, Sieur de La Salle
3. How did "water highways" contribute to the French empire?
4. What regions of the French North American empire were most heavily populated?
5. **Thinking Critically** The French empire was connected by waterways. How are different regions of the United States connected today?

The Netherlands, Sweden, and Russia Claim Land

Where did the Dutch, the Swedes, and the Russians settle in North America?

VOCABULARY

Spice Islands	**patroon system**
patroon	**tsar**

Trade with the Spice Islands   The Netherlands, sometimes known as Holland, was a great trading country in the seventeenth century. Dutch merchants had a thriving business with islands off the coast of Southeast Asia. There they obtained spices such as cloves, pepper, and nutmeg. As a result these islands were known as the **Spice Islands.** Today they are called the Moluccas. To reach the Spice Islands, Dutch ships used the long route around Africa and across the Indian Ocean. The voyage to the Spice Islands and the return to the Netherlands took at least two years and was very costly.

After a time the merchants became dissatisfied with this long, expensive route. They knew that Spanish, Portuguese, and French explorers were trying to find a shorter route by sailing west. So the Dutch merchants hired an English sea captain named Henry Hudson to look for a shorter route.

Hudson's Explorations   Hudson first tried sailing northeast around northern Europe. After two unsuccessful attempts he decided this was impossible. Next he sailed west across the Atlantic in 1609. In his ship, the *Half Moon,* he explored the Atlantic coast of what is now the United States.

Henry Hudson's *Half Moon* entered three bays along the coast. Today they are known as New York Bay, Delaware Bay, and Chesapeake Bay. He also sailed up the river that flows into New York Bay. His ship got as far as present-day Albany before turning back. Today this waterway is known as the Hudson River because of Henry Hudson's explorations.

Dutch Colonies in North America   Although Henry Hudson did not find the Northwest Passage, his explorations gave the Netherlands a claim to the land along

In the *Half Moon,* **Henry Hudson sailed along America's eastern coast, searching for the Northwest Passage.**
■ **How does this ship compare to the Viking ship on page 45?**

the eastern coast of North America. Taking advantage of this claim, a Dutch trading company started a colony near the mouth of the Hudson River, on Manhattan Island. The company bought the island from Indians. Dutch settlers built a fort there, calling it Fort Amsterdam. Later it became known as New Amsterdam, after the city of Amsterdam in the Netherlands.

The Dutch also built forts along the Connecticut and the Delaware rivers. At the spot on the Hudson River that the *Half Moon* had reached in 1609, they built Fort Orange. It became a center for trade with the Iroquois Indians. The Dutch, however, were interested in more than trade. New Amsterdam was made into a strong naval base. Dutch warships sailed from New Amsterdam in search of Spanish vessels carrying gold and silver from America to Spain.

Settling farm families on the land was a lesser interest of the Dutch trading companies. Like the French, the Dutch tried to promote settlement by giving away large grants of land. The **patroons** (pǝ trüns′), or owners of these large grants, were supposed to rent the land to settlers whose

Peter Minuit, the first governor of New Amsterdam, displays the goods he will trade to the Indians in exchange for Manhattan Island. The goods were worth about $24.
■ What kinds of goods did Minuit offer the Indians?
■ Why do you think he did not offer them money?

passage they paid to New Netherland. This idea, known as the **patroon system,** failed because land was easy to obtain in North America. Most people wanted to own land rather than to rent it.

Dutch Influence Nevertheless the independent Dutch families that did settle on the land became some of the best farmers in America. Their style of barns and farmhouses can still be seen in the Hudson River valley. On Manhattan Island, Dutch merchants formed thriving business establishments. Three American Presidents—Martin Van Buren, Theodore Roosevelt, and Franklin D. Roosevelt—had ancestors who came to the Dutch colony in America.

Some Dutch names still survive in the New York City area. For example, the Bowery section was originally *bouwerie,* meaning "a Dutch farm." The names *Harlem* and *Brooklyn* came from the Dutch towns Haarlem and Breucklen. At Christmastime, Santa Claus, or Saint Nicholas, owes his appearance and name to Dutch customs brought to America. Sauerkraut is a Dutch dish, and the Dutch were the first bowlers in America.

Sweden's Little Colony On the Delaware River, near present-day Wilmington, a company chartered by the Swedish government started a colony in 1638. It was a small colony with only a few hundred settlers. However, they made—according to some historians—an important contribution to American frontier life.

The Swedish colonists came from a heavily forested region of northern Europe. They were skilled in cutting down trees and using logs for various purposes. Therefore, it is believed that Swedish colonists may have built the first log cabins in America. Such wooden dwellings became

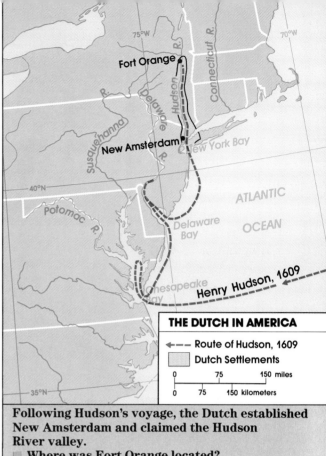

THE DUTCH IN AMERICA

←--- Route of Hudson, 1609
☐ Dutch Settlements

0   75   150 miles
0   75   150 kilometers

Following Hudson's voyage, the Dutch established New Amsterdam and claimed the Hudson River valley.
☐ **Where was Fort Orange located?**

so popular, especially on the frontier, that the log cabin is considered the typical dwelling of American pioneers.

The land settled by the Swedish colonists was part of the Dutch claims. Still the Dutch in New Netherland left the little colony undisturbed until 1655. But in that year a Dutch force commanded by Governor Stuyvesant came from New Amsterdam and easily overcame the feeble resistance of the Swedish colonists.

Russia in North America At one time, Russia, too, had claims to land in North America. Russia's claims came through the explorations of Vitus Bering in the waters between Siberia and Alaska. Bering was from Denmark but served Russia's **tsar** (zär), or ruler, as a sea captain. In 1728 and again in 1741, Bering explored the land and the waters east of Siberia. He discovered the passage between Alaska

61

This wooden church in Alaska is a reminder of the time when the Russian empire extended into North America.
■ How does this Russian church differ from the Spanish mission on page 52?

and Siberia that is today called the Bering Strait. This is the region, you will recall, where a land bridge once existed and by which people came to America.

Bering's explorations revealed that Alaska was rich in furs, timber, and fish. Wealthy Russians, like the French, wore furs for warmth and to be stylish. Individuals and small companies traded in Alaskan furs until 1799. In that year the tsar of Russia granted the Russian American Company the right to take charge of all Russian interests in North America.

The tsar required the company not only to trade in furs but also to promote settlement and to teach Christianity to the Indians. Priests of the Russian Orthodox faith converted Indians to the Russian form of Christianity. Today older Alaskan towns, such as Kodiak and Sitka, still contain Russian Orthodox churches.

Conflicting Claims Not many Russians came to settle in Alaska. But the Russian army and navy built outposts along the west coast of North America. At one time Russians occupied a fort only 40 miles (64 km) north of San Francisco, California. This expansion of Russian claims alarmed Spanish officials. It caused them to add more settlements and military bases in California. Through these methods they hoped to halt the Russian advance down the west coast.

The west coast of North America was but one of the places where European powers had conflicting claims. Spain and France clashed over rival settlements in Florida and the Carolinas. New Orleans, at the mouth of the Mississippi, changed hands a number of times during the colonial period.

In fact nearly every part of what is now the United States was claimed by one or more European powers. The exception is our fiftieth state, Hawaii.

CHECKUP

1. Why did Dutch merchants hire Henry Hudson?
2. How did the Dutch promote settlement of their colony?
3. What contribution to American frontier life may have been made by the Swedish colonists?
4. Whose explorations gave Russia claims to Alaska?
5. **Thinking Critically** Why were colonies established along waterways?

Africans in America

How did Africans contribute to the development of colonies in the New World?

People from Africa   Africans were among the early explorers of the Americas. Some of the Africans were servants. Some were slaves. Some were free.

Columbus had black sailors in his crews. Blacks marched with Balboa across the Isthmus of Panama in 1513. They helped build the first ships on the Pacific coast. Six years later, blacks dragged the heavy Spanish artillery that helped Cortés conquer the Aztecs. Blacks accompanied Pizarro in his conquest of Peru. In 1565, blacks assisted in building St. Augustine. Blacks sailed up the St. Lawrence River with the French and helped to explore the Mississippi Valley.

"Little Steven"   One black explorer who wrote his name on the pages of history was Estevanico (ās tā vä nē′ kō), which means "Little Steven" in Spanish. In English he probably would have been called Stevie. Estevanico served as an adviser to Hernando Cortés. As a guide he traveled

These are the ruins of a pueblo in the Southwest.
■ Why might a person seeing this or a similar sight believe in the legend of the Seven Cities of Gold?

through Florida, Mexico, and parts of Arizona, New Mexico, and Texas.

While exploring Florida in 1528, Estevanico and three companions were captured by Indians. They escaped but spent 8 years wandering before they reached the Spanish headquarters in Mexico. From Indians that Estevanico met during these wanderings, he first heard of **Cíbola** (si′ bō lə), the **Seven Cities of Gold.** These fabulous cities were said to be located somewhere north of Mexico.

In 1539 the Spanish explorer Father Marcos de Niza (mar′ kōs dā nē′ sä) led an expedition to search for the Seven Cities of Gold. Estevanico acted as a scout for the expedition. He also served as interpreter, for he could speak the Indians' language. One member of the expedition later wrote: "He inquired about the roads we should follow, and the villages; in short, about everything we wished to know."

Unfortunately Estevanico's skills led to his death. Father Marcos sent him ahead of the main group to scout out the best way to the golden cities. Weeks later, a wounded Indian staggered into the Spanish camp with the news that Estevanico had been killed near the Seven Cities of Gold. Father Marcos's expedition fled back to Mexico.

No one ever knew if Estevanico had reached the golden cities. Nevertheless the story of Estevanico spurred De Soto, Coronado, and other Spanish explorers to search for these cities. Hundreds of years later the Zuñi (zü′ nyē) Indians still told stories of a black man who had met his death as he approached their pueblos.

Blacks in New France Black Africans also joined in French explorations of the New World. Blacks paddled down the Mississippi with Marquette and Joliet. At least 70 blacks served as farmers, carpenters, blacksmiths, and stonemasons in the French colony at Kaskaskia, Illinois. In 1720 a Paris banker named Phillipe Renault (rė nō′) brought white and black laborers to the mines of New France.

Probably the best-known black in New France was Jean Baptiste Pointe du Sable (dü säh′ bəl). A tall handsome man, he had been educated in Paris before coming to New France. Like many other French traders and trappers, du Sable married an Indian woman. The couple set up a trading post at the mouth of the Chicago River. The trading post expanded to include a house, a bakery, a dairy, a stable, a workshop, and a barn. The site is now within the modern city of Chicago.

Blacks in New Amsterdam There were 11 male African slaves at the found-

Jean Baptiste Pointe du Sable, a French trader, was the first European to live at what is now the site of Chicago, Illinois.
■ Why do you think Du Sable, an educated man, became a fur trader?

Chicago Historical Society

These African slaves worked on a tobacco plantation in the West Indies.
■ What jobs did these slaves do on the plantation?

ing of the Dutch colony of New Amsterdam in 1626. A few years later, women slaves were brought to the colony. Dutch merchants were prominent in the slave trade, but the Dutch often freed their slaves.

In 1644 the Dutch freed a dozen slaves in New Amsterdam. In 1661 the first American slave **petition** (pə tish′ ən), or request, for freedom was sent to the governor of the colony. It was granted, giving the 12 slaves "their freedom on the same footing as other free peoples."

Ten Million Slaves   In the New World there was a great shortage of laborers. As colonies grew, more people were needed to tend the fields and work the mines. At first, settlers tried to force the Indians to work for them. But many Indians died or ran away, so the colonists began to import African slaves as a source of cheap labor.

The first African slaves were brought to the Spanish colony of Hispaniola in the West Indies in 1501. From then until slavery finally was ended in the Americas, about 10 million people were brought to the New World as slaves. About three quarters of them were sent to the Portu-

guese colony of Brazil and to the Caribbean islands. In Brazil, slaves worked in the gold mines and in the fields where sugarcane, coffee, and cotton were raised. In the West Indies, slaves worked to produce sugar and other crops. The slaves' lives were usually harsh and often short.

The English colonies in North America received about 400,000 slaves directly from Africa. Other slaves, however, came to the English colonies after working for a time in the West Indies. Some slaves worked at skilled trades. But the great majority were unskilled laborers.

CHECKUP

1. How did Africans help build New World empires?
2. How did Estevanico and Jean Baptiste Pointe du Sable contribute to American history?
3. Why were Africans brought to the New World as slaves?
4. Describe what happened to some slaves in New Amsterdam in 1661.
5. **Thinking Critically**   How did slavery affect the growth of the colonies?

Making a Time Line

PUTTING EVENTS IN SEQUENCE

Chronology (kro nol′ ə jē) deals with time and putting historical events in sequence, or in the order in which they happened. It is especially important to understand chronology in history. A time line is a good way to put events in sequence. At the bottom of this page is a time line with dates marked below it, running from 1400 to 1800. Note that the time line is drawn to scale—1½ inches stands for 100 years.

Several explorations and settlements are described in Chapter 3. Some of these events are listed below with the date when each event took place. Each event is identified by a letter at the left.

SKILLS PRACTICE

On a separate sheet of paper, draw a time line like the one below. Find the proper place on the time line for each event. Make a dot on the line for each event. Above the dot write the letter that identifies the event.

a. Vitus Bering explores in Alaskan waters. (1728 and 1741)
b. The Dutch conquer the Swedish colony. (1655)

c. Columbus sails from Palos, Spain, on his first voyage to America. (1492)
d. Marquette and Joliet reach the Mississippi. (1673)
e. Balboa sees the Pacific Ocean. (1513)
f. Coronado explores the American Southwest. (1540)
g. Samuel de Champlain starts a French colony at Quebec. (1608)
h. St. Augustine, the oldest permanent European settlement in the continental United States, is founded. (1565)
i. La Salle claims Louisiana for France. (1682)
j. Magellan begins his historic voyage. (1519)
k. Swedish settlers start a colony on the Delaware River. (1638)

By doing this exercise with the time line, you not only put events in sequence, but you also show the time span between events. You can see that the Spanish were the first to explore and colonize the Americas. The other powers established colonies here a century later. Finally, you can see that the whole process of exploring and colonizing in the New World and the Pacific occurred over a period of more than 3 centuries.

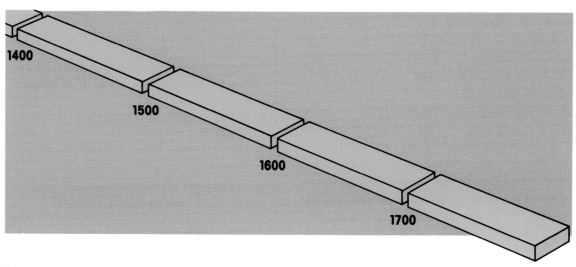

MAIN IDEAS

1. The Vikings visited North America around A.D. 1000, but their discovery was not common knowledge.
2. Columbus is considered the discoverer of America because his voyage in 1492 led to the exploration and colonization of the Americas.
3. Within 100 years after Columbus's first voyage, Spain had become the richest nation in Europe by establishing an empire that extended from what is now the southwestern United States to Chile in South America.
4. The French began to explore North America as a result of their search for the Northwest Passage to the Far East.
5. The Dutch settled along the northeastern coast of North America, especially around the Hudson River Valley; the Swedes settled along the Delaware River; and the Russians settled Alaska.
6. Some Africans were among the early explorers and settlers of the Americas.
7. Many Africans were brought to the New World to work as slaves in the fields and mines.

VOCABULARY REVIEW

On a separate sheet of paper, write the letter of the vocabulary word next to the number of its definition.

a. aristocrats   **f.** Vikings
b. presidio   **g.** empire
c. bilingual   **h.** portage
d. creoles   **i.** Indies
e. patroon system   **j.** tsar

1. An attempt to settle tenant farmers in New Amsterdam
2. Having two languages
3. People of high social standing
4. Russia's ruler
5. People born in the Americas of Spanish parents
6. Rich islands off the coast of Asia
7. A Spanish fort
8. Carrying boats from one waterway to another waterway
9. A bold, seagoing people
10. Territories and peoples under the control of a powerful country or ruler

CHAPTER CHECKUP

1. Why did Columbus, an Italian, lead an expedition for Spain?
2. What were the goals of the early Spanish explorers?
3. Why were the Spaniards able to build such a large empire in the New World?
4. Describe the class system in Spanish colonial America and explain why it developed.
5. What parts of America were claimed by the French?
6. Why did France have little success in attracting settlers to North America?
7. Where in the New World were there conflicting claims among the European empires? Why?
8. **Thinking Critically** Why was the Northwest Passage never discovered?
9. **Thinking Critically** How did slavery change life in the New World?
10. **Thinking Critically** If astronauts from the United States found people living on another planet, do you think the astronauts would treat the people like the Spanish or the French explorers treated the Native Americans? Explain.

APPLYING KNOWLEDGE

1. Besides those described in this chapter, what other signs of European colonial influence can you find in the United States? Look for these signs on maps, in the names of foods, in customs, and in words we commonly use.
2. Each of the explorers in this chapter has biographies or encyclopedia articles written about him. Find an unusual fact about each explorer and present it to the class.

4 England Plants Colonies

1497–1733

The First English Settlements

Why was Virginia a successful colony?

VOCABULARY

legend	charter
sea dog	oronoco
Invincible Armada	plantation
Lost Colony	cash crop
joint-stock company	House of Burgesses
stock	self-government
	royal colony

A Lively Indian Girl   Her Indian name was Matoaka (mä tō ä′ kə). English colonists at Jamestown, however, knew her best as Pocahontas (pō kə hon′ təs), which meant "lively." Her father was the chief of the Powhatans (pou ə tan′), Indians living along the coast of what is now the state of Virginia.

Pocahontas was about 13 years old when the English colonists founded Jamestown in 1607. She is the subject of many **legends** — stories from the past that may or may not be true. One legend tells how she saved the life of Captain John Smith, the colonists' leader at Jamestown. He had roamed onto Powhatan land and was captured. Chief Powhatan ordered Smith's head cut off. As Smith later told it, Pocahontas covered his body with

her own. She pleaded for his life. Her father gave in. Chief Powhatan let the English leader go.

In 1613 the English colonists took advantage of Chief Powhatan's great love for his daughter. They lured Pocahontas onto an English ship and carried her off to Jamestown. To get his daughter back, Chief Powhatan had to return some English colonists his warriors had captured.

Pocahontas and John Rolfe   While Pocahontas was living at Jamestown, she met John Rolfe. Pocahontas and John Rolfe fell in love. She became a Christian, baptized under the name of "the lady Rebecca." In April 1614, "the lady Rebecca" and John Rolfe were married.

About 2 years after their marriage, Mr. and Mrs. John Rolfe went to England. She was received as a princess there. King James I and Queen Anne welcomed her at their royal court. John Rolfe soon got word to return to Virginia on business.

Before the Rolfes could leave, however, Pocahontas became sick and died. Pocahontas and John Rolfe had one son, Thomas Rolfe. Eventually he returned to Virginia. Among his long line of descendants were the Randolphs, one of Virginia's most famous families.

Reconstructed Jamestown pictured to the right looks much like the early village did. (37°N/77°W; map, p. 72)
■ When was Jamestown founded?

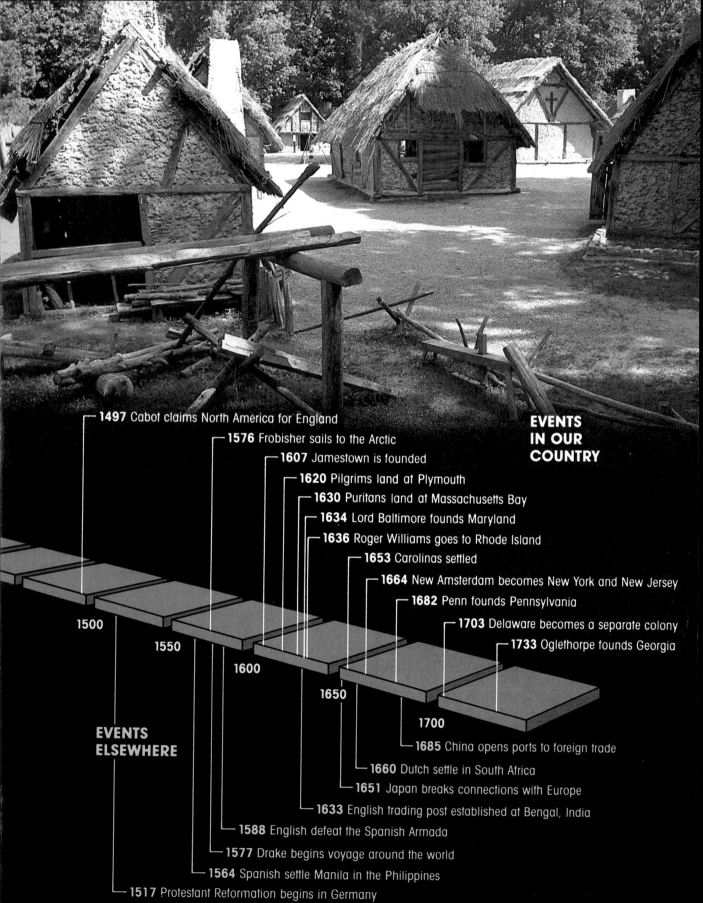

EVENTS IN OUR COUNTRY

1497 Cabot claims North America for England
1576 Frobisher sails to the Arctic
1607 Jamestown is founded
1620 Pilgrims land at Plymouth
1630 Puritans land at Massachusetts Bay
1634 Lord Baltimore founds Maryland
1636 Roger Williams goes to Rhode Island
1653 Carolinas settled
1664 New Amsterdam becomes New York and New Jersey
1682 Penn founds Pennsylvania
1703 Delaware becomes a separate colony
1733 Oglethorpe founds Georgia

1500
1550
1600
1650
1700

EVENTS ELSEWHERE

1685 China opens ports to foreign trade
1660 Dutch settle in South Africa
1651 Japan breaks connections with Europe
1633 English trading post established at Bengal, India
1588 English defeat the Spanish Armada
1577 Drake begins voyage around the world
1564 Spanish settle Manila in the Philippines
1517 Protestant Reformation begins in Germany

Pocahontas, Chief Powhatan, John Rolfe, and Captain John Smith lived at the time England was struggling to start colonies in the New World. Unlike Spain, England entered late in the race for a colonial empire. Let us look back and see how England, in spite of its late start, was finally able to plant its first successful colony on the mainland of North America.

John Cabot's Voyages   After the news of Columbus's discovery reached England, King Henry VII wanted to know more about the land that lay across the North Atlantic. So the king and some English merchants backed Giovanni Caboto (jō vän′ nē kä bō′ tō), an Italian sea captain who had taken the English form of his name — John Cabot.

Cabot made two voyages across the stormy North Atlantic. In 1497 he claimed "New Found Land" (now Newfoundland) for the English king. The next year Cabot sailed south along the North American coast, also claiming it for England.

However, England did not begin settlement of this land for almost a century. It was first believed that colonies in the New World would not be profitable. By the time this idea was proven false, England became involved in wars and had neither the time nor money to spend on settlement.

England Challenges Spain   In 1558, Elizabeth I became queen of England. She ruled England until 1603. During her reign, England prospered and developed a strong navy, which challenged Spain's military power.

To undermine Spain's power, Queen Elizabeth secretly encouraged English sea captains, called **sea dogs**, to raid Spanish settlements and ships carrying gold and silver from the Americas. Two of the most famous sea dogs were Sir John Hawkins and Sir Francis Drake.

Queen Elizabeth I of England honored the sea dog Francis Drake by making him a knight.
■ Why would the queen want to honor someone that some people called a pirate?

In 1577, Drake sailed through the Straits of Magellan and made a series of surprise attacks on the Spanish settlements along the Pacific coast. He may have sailed as far north as present-day Oregon. Fearing that his ships, which were filled with riches, would be captured, Drake set sail across the Pacific. He sailed around the world and arrived back in England in 1580. Drake was the first person since Magellan's expedition to accomplish this feat of sailing around the world.

The Spanish Armada   Angered by the raids on Spanish treasure ships and alarmed by England's growing power, King Philip II decided to invade England. In 1588 he ordered a large fleet to sail to the island. He called this fleet the **Invincible Armada** because he thought it could not be defeated. It consisted of 130 armed ships, carrying 8,000 sailors and 22,000 soldiers.

As the Spanish Armada sailed toward England, Queen Elizabeth rallied her subjects. "I have resolved to live or die amongst you," she told them. "I know I have but the body of a weak and feeble woman, but I have the heart of a king."

Inspired by their queen, English sea captains, led by Sir Francis Drake, prepared to meet the Armada. Making use of their accurate cannons and superior sailing skill, they fought the larger Spanish ships from long range. In a running battle that lasted more than 4 days, 200 English ships drove the Spanish Armada away from England and into the North Sea. Fierce storms there finished the work that the English cannons had begun. More than half of the ships and more than two thirds of the crew were lost. The invasion attempt by Spain had been beaten back.

This crushing defeat was a blow to Spain. It opened a door, however, for England, where there was mounting inter-est in colonization. No longer could Spain prevent other European countries from colonizing the east coast of North America. Soon England, France, the Netherlands, and Sweden began to plant colonies along the Atlantic coast.

Martin Frobisher's Voyages   Queen Elizabeth I also encouraged exploration. In 1576, Martin Frobisher set sail in search of the Northwest Passage. He reached the bay in the Arctic that is named after him. When he returned to England, he brought some lumps of ore believed to be gold. Frobisher made two more voyages in 1577 and 1578 to the bay for the purposes of mining gold. After he had brought back tons of ore to England, it was discovered to be "fool's gold" and totally worthless.

The Lost Colony   Sir Walter Raleigh (rôl' ē) was another one of Queen Elizabeth's favorite sea captains. He had hoped to plant English colonies in northern Ireland. But in 1587 he shifted his attention to North America. The spot he chose was on Roanoke (rō' ə nōk) Island, a short distance off the coast of what is now North Carolina.

Sir Walter Raleigh's colonists included men, women, and children. John White, in charge of the expedition, stayed only long enough to get the colonists settled. A week before White returned to England for more supplies, his daughter, Elizabeth White Dare, gave birth to his grandchild. Sir Walter Raleigh called his colony Virginia, and this was the name given to the little girl. Virginia Dare was the first English child born in what is now the United States.

England's war with Spain kept John White from returning to Virginia until 1590. When he did return to Roanoke, however, he found none of the colonists he

71

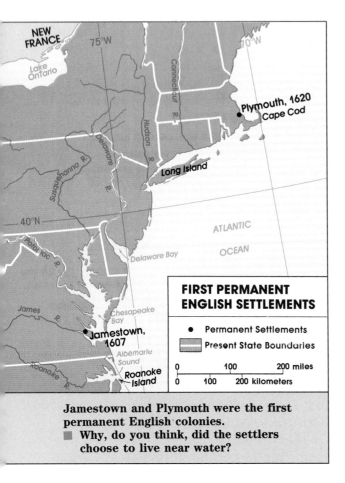

FIRST PERMANENT ENGLISH SETTLEMENTS

- ● Permanent Settlements
- Present State Boundaries

0   100   200 miles
0   100   200 kilometers

Jamestown and Plymouth were the first permanent English colonies.
■ Why, do you think, did the settlers choose to live near water?

A joint-stock company was like a modern corporation. Many people could buy **stock**, shares of ownership in a company. If the company succeeded and made a profit, the stockholders would share in the profit. If the company failed, the stockholders lost only the amount that each person had invested.

Hundreds of joint-stock companies were formed in England for the purpose of establishing colonies. These companies started colonies in the West Indies, in Canada, and in what is now the United States. In 1606, rich English merchants organized the Virginia Company of London. Its goal was to start a colony on the coast of North America.

Jamestown Survives   King James I of England gave a **charter** to the Virginia Company of London. A charter is a written agreement giving permission to settle or trade in a certain area. In December 1606 the *Susan Constant*, the *Godspeed*, and the *Discovery* sailed for North America. These three company ships carried 104 men and supplies. On May 24, 1607, the ships anchored near a sandy peninsula on the north shore of the James River. There the settlers built a village and a fort. They called it Jamestown in honor of their king.

From the very beginning, everything seemed to go wrong at Jamestown. The settlement was in a low, swampy area, and the first flimsy shelters let rain leak in. So there was much sickness. In 1607 the settlers failed to get a crop planted, and food became scarce. Only 53 colonists lived through the first winter.

The story you read about earlier of Pocahontas saving John Smith's life may or may not be true. What is true is that John Smith saved Jamestown at this time. In the winter the desperate colonists elected

had left there 3 years before. John White and other men kept looking for the missing people. There was no trace of what had happened except the word *Croatoan* (krō ə tō an′) carved on a post in the crude fort the colonists had built. This was the name of another island, held by Indians friendly to the colonists. To this day no one knows for sure what happened to Raleigh's **Lost Colony** and to little Virginia Dare.

Joint-stock Companies   In the failure of the Roanoke colony, Sir Walter Raleigh lost his entire fortune. His loss served as a lesson to others. Colonization was too risky and costly for one person to undertake. So the English formed **joint-stock companies** to obtain the large sums of money needed for starting colonies.

him as their leader. He saved the colony by forcing the colonists to do the necessary work and by getting food from the Indians.

The next year a gunpowder explosion injured Captain John Smith. He returned to England for medical attention. Without his leadership, Jamestown went through a winter so hard it was called the "starving time." At the end of this terrible time, the survivors were digging roots and catching snakes for food.

In the spring the Virginia Company once more sent colonists and supplies. The stockholders still hoped to make a profit from their colony. Their profit soon came from an unexpected source—tobacco.

Profit from Tobacco   The Spaniards had brought tobacco from the New World to Europe. Its use had spread to England. The English liked the mild tobacco from South America best. They called this mild tobacco **oronoco** (ō rə nō′ kō) because it came from near the Orinoco River in present-day Venezuela.

Two years before John Rolfe married Pocahontas, he managed to get some seeds of mild oronoco. He planted them in Virginia. John Rolfe's first crop sold for a good price in London. More and more Virginians started raising tobacco. People with small tobacco farms were called oronocos because that was the kind of tobacco they raised.

Plantations and Slave Labor   As time went on, some colonists expanded their farms for growing tobacco. Such large farms, usually devoted to growing a single crop, were called **plantations**. In Virginia plantations raised tobacco as a **cash crop**, that is, a crop grown for sale rather than for private use by the farmer. With tobacco as a cash crop, settlers were able to greatly improve the outlook for the success of the Virginia colony.

Tobacco growing also fastened the system of slavery on the colony. The first Africans to arrive in English North America landed at Jamestown in 1619. The Dutch ship that brought them had been headed for a Caribbean island but was blown off course. The ship's captain exchanged the Africans for food and supplies. Records are unclear, but it appears

Tobacco farming made some settlers wealthy and gave rise to slavery.
■ **How can you tell which people in the picture are the owners?**

73

The Virginia House of Burgesses, an elected assembly, met for the first time in 1619.
■ How was this meeting recorded?

King James I of England, however, was suspicious of the elected House of Burgesses. King James mistrusted this small amount of self-government in Virginia. Likewise, he mistrusted the leaders of the Virginia Company of London. Perhaps this was reason enough to be suspicious of the colony from which so much English tobacco came. King James hated tobacco. He called smoking it "a custom loathsome to the eye, hateful to the nose, harmful to the brain and dangerous to the lungs."

In 1624, King James took back the charter he had granted to the Virginia Company. Virginia was then made a **royal colony**, that is, a colony directly under the king's control. King James also planned to do away with the House of Burgesses, but he died in 1625. His successor, Charles I, permitted the House of Burgesses to meet.

Virginia remained a royal colony for the next 150 years. The English king appointed Virginia's governor and a council to advise the governor. In time the appointed governor and council were certain to clash with the House of Burgesses.

that these first 20 Africans worked as servants rather than as slaves and eventually earned their freedom. In 1624, five years after the Africans arrived in Jamestown, William Tucker was born. He was the first black child born in the English colonies. As more plantations were established along the rivers of Virginia, there was increased demand for laborers. By the latter part of the 1600s, slavery was firmly established in Virginia and had spread to all the English colonies in North America.

Two Kinds of Government   In 1619 the Virginia Company allowed the colonists to elect members to a **House of Burgesses**. Burgess meant "free citizen" in England. So the House of Burgesses represented the free citizens of Virginia. It gave white male landowners the chance to help make the laws under which they were to live. The Virginia House of Burgesses was a first step in the English colonies toward **self-government** — the belief that people can and should rule themselves.

CHECKUP

1. Explain the roles played by John Smith and John Rolfe in helping to make Virginia a success.
2. Why was the defeat of the Armada important to English colonization?
3. What are the known facts about the colony set up by Sir Walter Raleigh?
4. How were joint-stock companies helpful in planting English colonies?
5. Why was the creation of the Virginia House of Burgesses important?
6. **Thinking Critically** Which of the following do you think was most important to the success of the Virginia colony — tobacco, the Virginia Company of London, or the Virginia House of Burgesses? Explain.

The New England Colonies

Why were the New England colonies founded?

VOCABULARY

Separatist	Puritan
Pilgrim	constitution
Mayflower Compact	Fundamental Orders

Settlements in New England   After Jamestown the next successful English settlements were started far to the north. Massachusetts became the first of the New England colonies. Religion was of great importance in the early days of these colonies. In fact, religion was the major reason most of the first colonists came to New England.

In Virginia most of the colonists were members of the Church of England, which, by law, was England's official church. In New England, on the other hand, the first two groups to arrive had had disagreements with the official church.

The Travels of the Pilgrims   The first group to settle successfully in New England wanted to separate from the Church of England. Some of these **Separatists**, as they are sometimes called, left Scrooby, England, in 1608. They moved to Leiden, a town in the Netherlands, where they felt they could worship as they pleased. But during the next few years, the Separatists began to worry as they saw their children learning the Dutch language and Dutch ways in the Netherlands.

These deeply religious people wanted to live where they could worship in their own way. And yet they wanted their children to grow up as English boys and girls.

So they decided to move once more, this time to land that England claimed in North America. Thus they earned the name of **Pilgrims**, meaning persons traveling on a religious journey. It is the name by which they are known in United States history.

The Pilgrims were poor. They needed money for supplies and transportation. London merchants gave them money and supplied a ship called the *Mayflower*. In return the Pilgrims agreed to give the merchants a share of all the profits earned by the colony after 7 years in America.

The Pilgrims Find a Home   In September 1620 the *Mayflower* picked up Pilgrims from Leiden. Then the ship sailed to Plymouth, England, where more people boarded for the journey to America. In November the *Mayflower*, carrying about 100 passengers, reached the New England coast. It anchored in a bay at the end of Cape Cod, near the site of present-day Provincetown, Massachusetts. From this point, exploring parties searched for a suitable spot to settle.

The Pilgrims had permission to settle on land owned by the Virginia Company of London, but Massachusetts was far north of Virginia. If they settled in Massachusetts, the Pilgrims would be living on land they had no right to occupy. For this reason the leaders of the group decided they needed some form of government for the colony, even before landing. While still on board ship, they wrote a document known as the **Mayflower Compact**.

The 41 men who signed it agreed to obey several simple rules and regulations. Like the Virginia House of Burgesses, the Mayflower Compact was a step toward self-government in the English colonies. Because of the Mayflower Compact, adult males in the Pilgrim colony soon began meeting to make laws for their new colony.

The Pilgrims Live Quietly   Most of the Pilgrims had left England from the port of Plymouth. So they decided to call the colony in New England by the same name. They built their first houses along what they called Leiden Street, after their temporary haven in the Netherlands. As at Jamestown, the first years at Plymouth were hard. By March 1621, 44 members of the original Mayflower company had died. Those who survived were mainly the young and fit. In fact, more than half the survivors were under 16 years of age.

It was then that an Indian named Samoset appeared. His greeting—"Much welcome, Englishmen"—startled the Pilgrims. They found that Samoset had learned English from sailors fishing near islands off the New England coast. His offer of friendship must have been one of the few pleasant moments for the Pilgrims during that first winter.

In the spring the Indian chief Massasoit (mas′ ə soit) and 60 of his men came to Plymouth. The Indians offered help and hospitality to the Pilgrims. Squanto, another Indian, showed them where to hunt and fish and how to raise corn. The Pilgrims harvested the corn and other crops in the fall. These became part of the first Thanksgiving Day dinner.

By living quietly, working hard, and worshiping God in their own way, members of the Pilgrim colony survived in the wilderness. Thirty times in annual elections they chose William Bradford as their governor. He wrote *Of Plimoth Plantation*, a history of the Pilgrims in New England and how they got there.

The Pilgrim town of Plymouth was the first permanent colony in New England. Like Jamestown, Plymouth Plantation has been reconstructed.
■ **How would a New England town today be different from this town?**

Pilgrim Society, Plymouth, MA

The Mayflower Compact

The Mayflower Compact was signed on November 11, 1620. In this document the signers agreed to set up a government and make laws for the colony. All promised to abide by the colony's laws. The responsibility for establishing the new government would be shared by the signers. This compact remained in effect until the Plymouth colony merged with the Massachusetts Bay Colony in 1691.

This day, before we came to harbor, observing some not well affected to unity and concord, but gave some appearance of faction, it was thought good there should be an association and agreement that we should combine together in one body, and to submit to such government and governors as we should by common consent agree to make and choose, and set our hands to this that follows word for word.

. . . We whose names are underwritten. . . . Having undertaken, for the glory of God, and advancement of the Christian faith and honor of our king and country, a voyage to plant the first colony in the northern parts of Virginia, do by these present solemnly and mutually in the presence of God, and one of another, covenant and combine ourselves together into a civil body politic, for our better ordering and preservation and furtherance of the ends aforesaid; and by virtue hereof to enact, constitute, and frame such just and equal laws, ordinances, acts, constitutions, and offices from time to time, as shall be thought most meet and convenient for the general good of the colony; unto which we promise all due submission and obedience. . . .

USING SOURCE MATERIAL

1. What were the Pilgrims' motives in writing the Mayflower Compact?
2. What major points were covered in this document?
3. Why do you think the new government would be decided upon by common consent?

TO HELP YOU READ

There are certain rules to keep in mind when reading a quotation such as the one from the Mayflower Compact. Words shown within brackets, [ ], are put in by the editor to make the meaning of the passage clearer. The words within the brackets are not part of the original quotation. If any words are left out of the quotation, the place where they originally appeared is marked by three periods (. . .) known as an ellipsis. If the ellipsis comes at the end of a sentence, a fourth period is added.

The Puritans   Within a few years, other settlements were founded on the shores of Massachusetts Bay, north of Plymouth. Among these were several started by a group known as the **Puritans**. Unlike the Pilgrims, the Puritans wanted to stay within the Church of England. But they wanted a more simple church organization, with the church governed by its worshipers rather than by bishops. Their desire to "purify," or reform, the church is why they were called Puritans.

There were other differences between Pilgrims and Puritans. While many Pilgrims were poor, most Puritans were prosperous. They were also generally better educated than the Pilgrims. Moreover the Puritans came to America in much greater numbers than the Pilgrims. More than 1,000 came in 1630, the Puritans' first year in Massachusetts. In the next 13 years, more than 20,000 English people joined the Puritan settlements.

Before they left England, Puritan leaders organized the Massachusetts Bay Company with a charter from King Charles I. The charter, which the Puritans brought with them, served for many years as a **constitution** for the colony. A constitution is a set of basic laws by which people are governed. The Puritan settlements prospered through fishing, fur trading, and shipbuilding. Still the Puritans never forgot that religious reasons had first brought them to Massachusetts.

Religion's Role   Although founded as a trading company, the Massachusetts Bay Colony quickly changed into a self-governing colony. Laws were based on the Bible and Puritan belief. During the early years of the colony, Puritan ministers had a great deal of influence. They watched over their congregations to protect them from sin. The ministers' fiery sermons sometimes lasted for hours. In the Massachusetts Bay Colony, there was a close relationship between the Puritan church and the colonial government.

The ministers held no government offices, but only members of the Puritan church could vote and hold office. Only about one fifth of the adult white males had political rights as more and more non-Puritans came to Massachusetts.

A Belief in Education   The Puritans are remembered for their belief in education. Because many Puritans had been well-educated in England, they put great emphasis on education in Massachusetts. In 1636 at Cambridge, near the prominent Puritan town of Boston, they started the first college in the English colonies. It soon became known as Harvard College. Today it is one of the most famous universities in the United States. The main purpose of Harvard College in its early years was to train Puritan ministers.

In 1647 the government of the Massachusetts Bay Colony passed an education

In early colonial days, children often learned to read and write in a class in the teacher's home.
■ How is this classroom different from a classroom today?

law. It required every town of more than 50 families to start a school in which children could learn to read and write. Puritans believed that all persons should know how to read so they could study the Bible. That was the main reason for the School Law of 1647. Because of it, Massachusetts set up the first public schools in the English colonies.

An Expanding Colony   It has been said of Massachusetts that "all earlier settlements [in New England] grew into it — all later colonies grew out of it." The first part of that statement refers to the Puritan takeover of three other settled areas in New England.

In 1641, Massachusetts took control of settlements in New Hampshire. They remained part of Massachusetts until the king of England made New Hampshire a royal colony in 1679. Massachusetts in 1677 bought the land that is today the state of Maine. This land was a part of Massachusetts until 1820, when Maine became the twenty-third state of the United States. In 1691 the older Pilgrim colony at Plymouth merged with Massachusetts, its larger neighbor to the north.

The Founding of Rhode Island   The second part of the statement about Massachusetts is also true — that all later New England colonies grew out of it. Most Puritan leaders were capable men. Indeed, they were often brilliant. Sometimes, however, they were narrow-minded and unwilling to admit that others might also have good ideas.

In 1631 Roger Williams, a well-educated Puritan minister, came to Massachusetts. He soon began to disagree with other Puritan ministers. Williams believed that the Puritan church leaders had

WHAT'S IN A NAME?

New England

John Smith had a spectacular career in early Virginia. Yet his contributions to the settlement of New England were possibly more important. In fact, he gave the name *New England* to what is now the northeastern part of the United States.

In 1614 a group of London merchants hired John Smith to explore the rocky coast that John Cabot had explored more than a century before. Smith brought back a valuable cargo of fish and furs. He talked of the value of the fishing places among the islands and along the coast.

After he got back to England, John Smith wrote a book about his voyage. He

called his book *A Description of New England*, saying a part of that coast looked like Devonshire, in "old" England. He used the name *New England* many times in his book, so it became familiar. So, 6 years later, when King James I gave a charter to that land, the king wrote, "The same shall be called by the name New England in America."

Smith's maps fastened another name on part of New England, placing the location of an Indian town. He called the Indians who lived there, Massachusetts. By the time the Pilgrims and Puritans arrived, New England and Massachusetts were already named.

---

too much control over the Massachusetts government. He wanted to separate the church and the state, or religion and government. He argued that all people should be free to worship in their own way. Also, he felt that the Indians should be paid for the land on which the Puritans had settled.

Roger Williams expressed his views openly in sermons preached at Plymouth and Salem. Because of this, the General Court of Massachusetts ordered him to leave the colony. With the aid of Indians, he made his way southward. On the shores of Narragansett (nar ə gan' sət) Bay, Williams built a settlement he called Providence. Out of this settlement grew the colony of Rhode Island.

Other settlements on Narragansett Bay also offered refuge to persons disagreeing with the church leaders in Massachusetts. Among those who came was Anne Hutchinson, a highly intelligent and spirited woman. She was married to William Hutchinson. Twelve of their 15 children were born in England. The other three were born after the family moved to Massachusetts in 1636.

Anne Hutchinson had a deep interest in religion. It was this interest that eventually led her to move to Rhode Island. In her own home she had begun to hold religious meetings that were popular and well attended. But what she discussed there was different from what the Puritan church leaders taught. So they ordered her to leave Massachusetts.

Others followed Anne Hutchinson to Rhode Island, and by 1643 there were four settlements on Narragansett Bay. Rhode Island offered more religious freedom than any of the other English colonies. Its government provided for a firm separation of church and state. Rhode Island also became a thriving center of trade. Its merchants made Newport one of the busiest ports in the American colonies.

Connecticut's Constitution In 1636 the Reverend Thomas Hooker led a group of people out of Massachusetts. The minister and his followers left for at least two reasons. First they felt that their voice in the government of Massachusetts was not as strong as it should have been. But a second reason was to find better farmland than there was in Massachusetts.

Hooker and his followers found good land for crops in the broad Connecticut River valley. As time passed, this rich soil proved to be the most fertile in New England. Other people moved into the valley, settling in communities they named Windsor, Wethersfield, and Hartford.

Representatives from these towns organized the Connecticut Colony. In 1639 these organizers drew up a document called **Fundamental Orders.** People living in the colony agreed to be governed by this constitution. Connecticut's Fundamental Orders have been called the world's first written constitution. It provided the settlers in Connecticut with one of the most democratic of all the governments in the American colonies.

Thus Rhode Island, Connecticut, and New Hampshire all grew out of Massachusetts in one way or another. These were the four New England colonies. Of the four, Rhode Island was the smallest and

For her beliefs, Anne Hutchinson was put on trial and ordered to leave Massachusetts. ■ What did the artist who made this engraving think of Anne Hutchinson?

Massachusetts the largest in area and population. Second oldest of the colonies, Massachusetts was a leader from the start.

CHECKUP

1. How did the Indians help the Plymouth colonists to survive?
2. Explain the differences between the Pilgrims and the Puritans.
3. Why were the New England colonies founded?
4. How did other New England colonies grow out of Massachusetts?
5. **Thinking Critically** Anne Hutchinson was ordered to leave Massachusetts because her beliefs differed from those of the church leaders. Do you think this was a fair decision? Explain.

The Middle Colonies

How did England gain the middle colonies?

VOCABULARY

legislature	pamphlet
Quaker	

A Soldier and a Governor Peter Stuyvesant (stī′ və sənt) served in the Dutch army. Fighting for the Dutch, he lost his right leg in a campaign against the French on the West Indian island of St. Martin. As a reward for his loyal service, he was made governor-general of the Dutch colony of New Netherland. He arrived in the port city of New Amsterdam, the capital of that colony, in 1647.

Peter Stuyvesant was a stern, energetic governor. He kept peace with neighboring Indian tribes. He settled a boundary dispute with the English colony of Connecticut. He drove the Swedes out of their colony in Delaware and he kept tight control of his own colony.

In spite of these successes, Peter Stuyvesant could not prevent an English fleet from sailing into the harbor of New Amsterdam in September 1664. By this time the English and the Dutch were not as friendly as they had been earlier in the seventeenth century. England had claimed *all* of the Atlantic coast north of Florida because of John Cabot's voyages. Also, English rulers were unwilling to have

Governor Peter Stuyvesant eventually decided not to resist the British fleet when it came to take over his Dutch colony of New Amsterdam.
▇ Why might Stuyvesant have made this decision?

Dutch New Amsterdam was renamed New York when the British took it over. It had a natural harbor.

■ What business activities would such a harbor make possible?

a Dutch colony between the New England colonies and England's southern colonies.

The English Take New York King Charles II of England ordered the capture of the Dutch colony. An English fleet dropped anchor in New Amsterdam's harbor. The guns of the fleet's four warships were trained on the city. Peter Stuyvesant had the desire and courage to fight the English. But he had few weapons, and the colonists refused to fight. He was forced to surrender. The colony was then renamed for the Duke of York, the king's brother. In this way, New Netherland and New Amsterdam both became *New York.*

Even so, Dutch influence remained strong in New York. Dutch ships sailed in and out of New York Harbor, as they had when the settlement was called New Amsterdam. Most Dutch farmers and traders stayed in the colony after the English took control. In fact, Peter Stuyvesant returned to live there after a brief visit to his homeland.

New Jersey and Delaware Besides New York, two other former Dutch possessions along the Atlantic coast became English colonies. The two colonies were New Jersey and Delaware. Among the Duke of York's friends were two English noblemen, Sir George Carteret and Lord John Berkeley. In gratitude for their friendship, the Duke of York gave them land across the Hudson River from New York. They called the land New Jersey because Carteret had been governor of an island named Jersey.

The two English noblemen cared little for their land in far-off America. They soon sold part of it. The remaining land changed owners a number of times. Nevertheless, small towns and farms eventually dotted the New Jersey landscape. After several changes in government, New Jersey became a prosperous royal colony.

The land Peter Stuyvesant took from the Swedes became the English colony of Delaware. The name came from Lord De La Warr, an early governor of Virginia.

For many years Delaware was considered to be part of nearby Pennsylvania. Then in 1703 the people of Delaware won the right to elect their own **legislature**, or law-making body. After that, Delaware was counted as a separate colony.

Peaceful Pennsylvania   William Penn was born into a wealthy English family. He was named for his father, an admiral in the English navy. Young William grew up as a member of the Church of England. For a time he served in the English navy. Then he took charge of several estates his father owned in Ireland.

A great change came in Penn's life when he joined the Society of Friends, or **Quakers**. At that time Quakers were persecuted in England because of their religious beliefs. Quakers refused to serve in the army or navy. They would not swear oaths of loyalty to the king. Penn went to jail for these Quaker beliefs.

But Penn's father was wealthy and had influence, and King Charles II owed him a debt. When Penn's father died, the king offered to pay the debt by giving young William some land in America. Penn agreed and in 1681 he received a large land grant. The king named the land Pennsylvania, meaning "Penn's woods," in memory of Penn's father.

Pennsylvania, like Massachusetts, was a success almost from the beginning. William Penn thought of Pennsylvania as a *"holy experiment"* for furthering the Quaker way of life. He worked hard to make the experiment succeed. He insisted on paying the Indians for the land on which his colonists settled.

Penn named the chief settlement in his colony Philadelphia. The name meant "city of brotherly love." He encouraged Quakers to come to Pennsylvania, but everyone who believed in God was welcome there. Only Rhode Island had as much religious freedom as Pennsylvania did.

The principles of toleration and peace on which William Penn founded Pennsylvania attracted thousands of settlers.
■ What can you tell about Penn's background from this portrait?

Advertising for Settlers   Penn attracted settlers by advertising. His agents wrote and distributed **pamphlets** describing attractive features of the colony. These paper-covered booklets told of Pennsylvania's fertile soil, good government, peaceful Indians, and healthy climate.

Because the pamphlets were sent to different countries, people came from many places. Whether rich or poor, whether Quaker or not, they helped Pennsylvania grow. Some who came were wealthy merchants or landowners. Experienced farmers came from lands along the Rhine River in Europe. Families from northern Ireland and Scotland settled in the western parts of Pennsylvania.

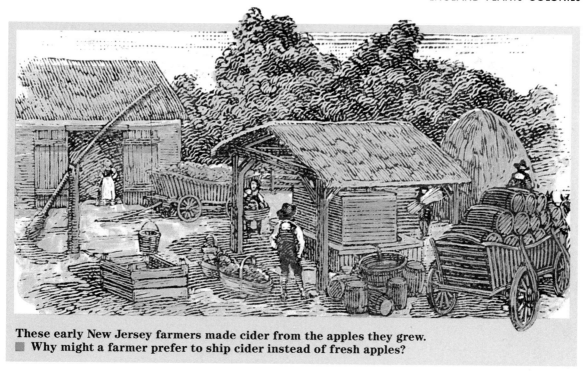

These early New Jersey farmers made cider from the apples they grew.
■ Why might a farmer prefer to ship cider instead of fresh apples?

Why "Middle Colonies"?   New York, New Jersey, Delaware, and Pennsylvania were in the middle of the English colonies. To the north were the New England colonies; to the south, the southern ones. Thus their location is one reason they were called the middle colonies.

But they were in the middle of the English colonies in other ways, too. New York and Pennsylvania were neither the largest nor the smallest colonies. Virginia and Massachusetts exceeded them in population, yet there were colonies in New England and the South that had fewer people. As for religious freedom, these colonies were in the middle on this issue, too. None was as free in religious matters as Rhode Island. Nor was any as strict as Massachusetts.

The people of the middle colonies were a varied group. There were not as many English people as there were in New England. Though slavery was legal in all four of the middle colonies, there were far fewer blacks in these colonies than there were in the southern colonies.

The middle colonies were not as heavily dependent on agriculture as the southern colonies, though most of the residents were farmers. Only along the Hudson River in New York could any farms be found as big as Virginia plantations. Yet life in the middle colonies depended more on agriculture than life in New England.

CHECKUP

1. How did New Amsterdam become New York?
2. What other English colonies originally belonged to the Dutch?
3. Why were settlers attracted to the Pennsylvania colony?
4. How were the middle colonies different from the New England colonies?
5. **Thinking Critically**   If you had been William Penn, how would you have attracted settlers to Pennsylvania?

The Southern Colonies

What groups of people found refuge in Maryland and Georgia?

The Founding of Maryland   Three of England's southern colonies were founded by **proprietors**. A proprietor was a person to whom the king gave a large grant of land. You have already learned about William Penn who was a proprietor. Pennsylvania was a **proprietary colony**. Penn made money by selling his land to colonists. The proprietors who founded southern colonies hoped to do the same thing that had been done for the middle colony of Pennsylvania.

A few prominent families in England were members of the Roman Catholic Church. Since the Church of England was the official church, Roman Catholics had many restrictions placed on them. King Charles I of England had Roman Catholic friends, such as Lord Baltimore.

Because of the Toleration Act, the Maryland colony was settled by many English Roman Catholics.
■ Why are so many settlers and Indians in this painting carrying weapons?

Because of their friendship, King Charles I gave Lord Baltimore a large grant of land to the north and east of Virginia. Through this, Lord Baltimore became proprietor of the colony he called Maryland. He gave his colony this name in honor of Henrietta Maria (or Mary), the king's wife. In 1634, St. Marys became the first settlement in Maryland.

Like other southern colonies, Maryland became a tobacco-growing plantation colony. Its land was fertile and its location made it easy to trade with England. So Maryland soon prospered.

A Refuge for Roman Catholics Lord Baltimore wanted to make money by selling his land. He also had the idea of making his colony a refuge for Roman Catholics from England. Many of Maryland's first settlers were Catholics, but the majority were English Protestants. It seemed possible that the Protestant majority might impose the same restrictions in Maryland that Roman Catholics had experienced in England.

Lord Baltimore had appointed a governor to represent him in Maryland. In 1649 he ordered the governor to try to pass the **Toleration Act**. The act would guarantee freedom of worship to all Christians in Maryland, whether Protestant or Catholic. The governor introduced the act into Maryland's local **assembly**, or legislature. The assembly passed the Toleration Act.

The Carolina Colony Until the 1660s there were several hundred miles of uncolonized land between Spanish settlements in Florida and the growing colony of Virginia. Both Spain and England claimed this land.

Earlier, Spanish missionaries had tried to establish missions along the coast of present-day South Carolina. However,

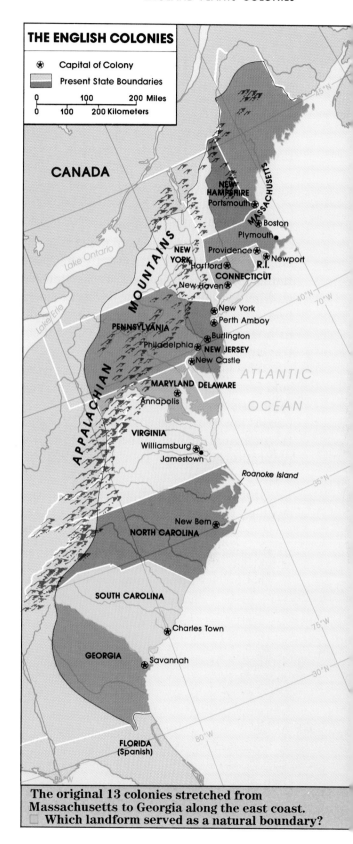

THE ENGLISH COLONIES

⊛ Capital of Colony

Present State Boundaries

0   100   200 Miles

0   100   200 Kilometers

CANADA

Lake Ontario

Lake Erie

NEW HAMPSHIRE

Portsmouth

MASSACHUSETTS

Boston

Plymouth

NEW YORK

Providence ⊛

Hartford ⊛

R.I.

⊛ Newport

CONNECTICUT

New Haven ⊛

MOUNTAINS

New York ⊛

Perth Amboy ⊛

PENNSYLVANIA

Burlington

Philadelphia ⊛ NEW JERSEY

New Castle ⊛

ATLANTIC

APPALACHIAN

MARYLAND DELAWARE

Annapolis ⊛

OCEAN

VIRGINIA

Williamsburg ⊛

Jamestown

Roanoke Island

New Bern ⊛

NORTH CAROLINA

SOUTH CAROLINA

⊛ Charles Town

GEORGIA

⊛ Savannah

FLORIDA
(Spanish)

The original 13 colonies stretched from Massachusetts to Georgia along the east coast.
☐ Which landform served as a natural boundary?

Indians had driven them out. In 1653, English colonists from Virginia settled in the disputed land. Ten years later it was the Spanish colonists' turn to be angry. At that time the Spaniards learned that King Charles II of England had granted ownership of the land south of Virginia to eight English noblemen.

The eight noblemen became known as lords proprietors of Carolina. The name *Carolina* came from the Latin word for Charles. The lords proprietors were chiefly interested in the land nearest to the islands the English claimed in the West Indies. So they made their first settlement at what is today Charleston, South Carolina. They named it Charles Town, again in honor of the king who had given them the land.

The lords proprietors either gave or sold large plantations near Charleston to their aristocratic friends. Instead of tobacco, however, rice and **indigo** became the principal cash crops on these Carolina plantations. Indigo is a plant used to make a blue dye.

Both rice and indigo need sun and swampy land to grow successfully. There was a great demand for slave labor to cultivate these crops. Most slaves brought to the Carolina mainland came from the West Indies. A century after Charleston, South Carolina, was founded, there were twice as many black slaves as white people living in South Carolina.

Carolina Is Divided In 1729 the English government bought back all the land owned by descendants of the original lords proprietors of Carolina. At that time the colony was divided into North Carolina and South Carolina. There were several reasons for this.

Poor people from Virginia had drifted southward into the unsettled northern part of Carolina. In most cases they were **squatters**. This means that they settled on land to which they had no legal claim. There they raised families on the small farms they cleared from the wilderness.

These small farmers had left Virginia because the colony was controlled by plantation aristocrats. Now the farmers feared control by aristocrats from the southern part of Carolina. People in the northern and southern parts had little in

By 1740, Charles Town, South Carolina, had become a busy seaport.
■ **Why are so many houses built so close to the shore?**
■ **What problems might come about because of that?**

James Oglethorpe and his partners got British debtors out of prison and brought them to settle Georgia.
■ **What do the British bystanders think of Oglethorpe and his crew?**

common, so they often quarreled. Recognizing this difference, the English government split the huge colony in two. Both North Carolina and South Carolina became royal colonies.

Georgia Is Last Georgia, the last of the southern colonies, was founded in 1733. It was the last of the 13 English colonies on the mainland of North America. There were two reasons for its existence. First, it was set up to protect prosperous South Carolina from raids by Spaniards and Indians in Florida. Second, it was thought of as a home for English **debtors**—people unable to pay the money they owed to others.

In England at that time, persons unable to pay their debts had to go to jail. A group of wealthy men thought this system was unfair. They asked King George II to release some of the male debtors so they could go to America and start new lives. The king agreed to this plan but asked that

the debtors become part-time soldiers. They could then be used to prevent Spanish raids on South Carolina.

After the king gave the wealthy men a charter, one of them—James Oglethorpe—became the governor of the new colony. It was named Georgia to honor King George II. By the time Georgia was founded in 1733, Virginia, the first colony, was 126 years old. It had taken England a long time to plant its 13 colonies along the Atlantic coast of North America.

CHECKUP

1. How did the proprietors of colonies hope to profit from their holdings?
2. For what two purposes was Maryland founded?
3. How did the colonists in North and South Carolina differ?
4. Why was Georgia founded in 1733?
5. **Thinking Critically** Why did it take England more than 100 years to establish colonies in North America?

Using the Library

FINDING INFORMATION

A library can be used to find more information on a subject that interests you. Perhaps you would like to know more about one of the English colonies or about a person connected with the colonies. Or later in the year you may want to know more about another aspect of United States history. Even after your school days are over, you may want or need to know something about a subject that concerns you.

Your school library or the public library in your community can be very helpful. To obtain the greatest benefit from a library, you must know how to use it. Most libraries are arranged the same way, with certain aids to finding what you want to know.

LIBRARY AIDS

Card catalogs in libraries contain cards for every book in the library. There probably is a card listing the book by *title*, another card filed under the name of the *author* or *authors*, and often a third card under the *subject* of the book.

Libraries have a reference section. It includes encyclopedias, almanacs, dictionaries, atlases, and other books of general interest. One helpful reference book is called the *Dictionary of American Biography*. It contains biographical information on more than 15,000 famous Americans. *Notable American Women* has biographical details for hundreds of famous American women.

Librarians are persons with special skills in finding the right source for information. Librarians also have many other duties, so they are usually quite busy. Although they are willing to help, you should first try to find what you need on your own.

SKILLS PRACTICE

Study the following card from a library catalog. Then answer the questions below.

1. What type of card is this?
2. What is the title of this book?
3. Who is the author?
4. What does the number in the left-hand corner tell you?
5. What other information is included on this card?

```
                    ◯
        UNITED STATES--SOCIAL LIFE AND CUSTOMS--
           COLONIAL PERIOD, CA. 1600-1775

  E      Tunis, Edwin, 1897-1973.
  162       Colonial living / written and
  .T8     illustrated by Edwin Tunis. -- New York
  1976    : Crowell, [1976] c 1957.
            155 p. : ill. ; 31 cm.
            SUMMARY: Describes the industries,
         schools, society, culture, and growth
         of the coastal settlements during the
         colonial period.
            ISBN 0-690-01063-X

            1.  United States--Social life and
         customs--Colonial period, ca. 1600-1775
```

MAIN IDEAS

1. Between 1607 and 1733, England founded 13 colonies on the mainland of North America.
2. Virginia, the first successful English colony, was the creation of a joint-stock company.
3. The Pilgrims and the Puritans left their homes in England to found colonies in Massachusetts for religious reasons.
4. New Hampshire and Maine were originally part of the Massachusetts Bay Colony.
5. England seized Dutch possessions in North America and created the three middle colonies — New York, New Jersey, and Delaware.
6. William Penn started Pennsylvania with land granted to him by the King of England, making the fourth middle colony.
7. Maryland, and the two Carolinas were proprietary colonies.
8. Maryland was a refuge for Catholics. Georgia was a buffer colony and a refuge for debtors.

VOCABULARY REVIEW

On a separate sheet of paper, write the letter of the vocabulary word next to the number of its definition.

a. joint-stock company
b. House of Burgesses
c. Pilgrims
d. Fundamental Orders
e. Puritans
f. Quakers
g. legislature
h. indigo
i. proprietor
j. debtor

1. Said to be the first written constitution in the world
2. A person to whom the king of England gave a large grant of land
3. An organization in which people buy shares and receive part of the profits
4. A person who owes money
5. A crop that was grown extensively in South Carolina
6. The first representative government in the English colonies
7. The largest group of settlers in the Massachusetts Bay Colony
8. A lawmaking body
9. The group that went on a religious journey to Massachusetts in 1620
10. A group that refused to serve in the English military

CHAPTER CHECKUP

1. Who were the first English explorers and what areas did they claim?
2. Why was England slow in starting colonies in North America?
3. Why were the Puritans important in the New England colonies?
4. Describe the different types of colonies established by the English in North America. Give examples.
5. Which colonies granted a certain amount of religious freedom? How did some colonies limit that freedom?
6. **Thinking Critically** Which English colonies were the most successful? Explain.
7. **Thinking Critically** Where did self-government begin to appear in the colonies? Why?

APPLYING KNOWLEDGE

1. Make a chart showing: (a) the name of each of the 13 colonies, (b) the date of establishment, (c) whether it was a New England colony, a middle colony, or a southern colony, and (d) a person or group closely associated with each colony.
2. In which of the English colonies would you have chosen to live? Write an essay describing your choice and explaining the reasons for that choice.
3. Write a pamphlet to attract people to live in your town or city. Be sure to list as many favorable points as you can think of.

CHAPTER 5

Life in the English Colonies 1650–1760

A Land of Promise

Why did people come to settle in the English colonies?

VOCABULARY

apprentice	indenture
promotional literature	

A New Arrival in Philadelphia   It was October 1723. A young man, 17 years old, had just arrived in Philadelphia. He had left his home in Boston. He walked to a bakery where he bought three big, puffy bread rolls, too large to fit in his pockets. Carrying a roll under each arm and eating the third, he walked to Market Street. On the way he passed the Reads' home.

The Reads' young daughter, Deborah, stood in the doorway of the home. She laughed at the awkward appearance of the young man. His name was Benjamin Franklin. During the next year, the two young people got to know each other better.

In 1730 Benjamin Franklin and Deborah Read were married. In the same year he became sole owner of a prosperous printing business. He also became owner of a newspaper. Franklin made *The Pennsylvania Gazette* one of the leading newspapers in the English colonies. He did so well in the printing business that he could

retire at the age of 48 and devote the rest of his life to the service of his country.

Growing Up in Boston   Josiah Franklin was Benjamin Franklin's father. He was one of thousands who left England in search of a better life in the colonies. His wife and three children came with him from England. The family settled in Boston where four more children were born. After Josiah's first wife died, he married Abiah Folger, by whom he had ten more children. Benjamin, born in January 1706, was their youngest son.

Josiah Franklin had been a silk dyer in England, but there was little demand for his trade in colonial Boston. So he worked as a soap-boiler and candlemaker. Benjamin went to the Boston Grammar School until he was 10 years old. For the next 2 years Benjamin helped his father at work.

Twelve-year-old Benjamin Franklin hated boiling soap and making candles. He wanted to go to sea on one of the merchant ships sailing from Boston's busy harbor. To prevent him from running away, his father made young Benjamin an **apprentice** to his older half brother James Franklin, a printer. An apprentice is one who learns a craft, or trade, by working with one who is skilled at it.

This painting of the Pennsylvania countryside in 1750 shows that the wilderness in many colonies had given way to orderly fields and farms.
■ What occupation do you think most of the colonists had in 1750?

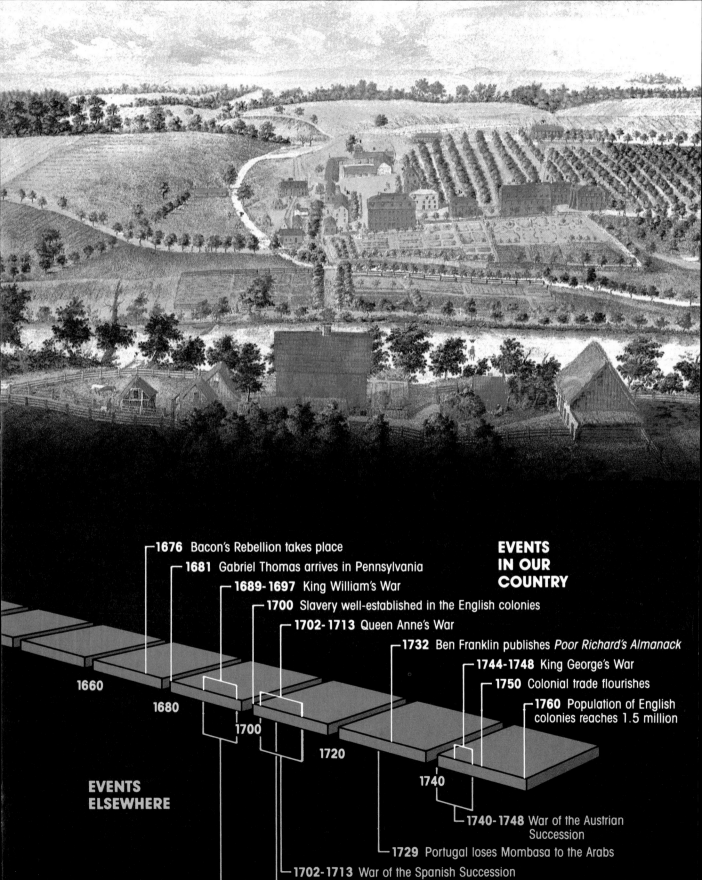

1676 Bacon's Rebellion takes place

1681 Gabriel Thomas arrives in Pennsylvania

1689-1697 King William's War

1700 Slavery well-established in the English colonies

1702-1713 Queen Anne's War

1732 Ben Franklin publishes *Poor Richard's Almanack*

1744-1748 King George's War

1750 Colonial trade flourishes

1760 Population of English colonies reaches 1.5 million

**EVENTS
IN OUR
COUNTRY**

1660

1680

1700

1720

1740

**EVENTS
ELSEWHERE**

1740-1748 War of the Austrian Succession

1729 Portugal loses Mombasa to the Arabs

1702-1713 War of the Spanish Succession

Two Brothers Quarrel Along with his printing business, James Franklin published a newspaper called the *New England Courant*. Some things he printed in his paper angered the Massachusetts General Court. The court ordered him to give up the paper. Instead, he merely transferred ownership to Benjamin Franklin. Benjamin had written some pieces for the paper, so it was not strange that his brother gave the paper to him.

But the arrangement worked poorly. Before long, the half brothers quarreled. So at the age of 17, Benjamin Franklin decided to strike out on his own.

Franklin's Success Benjamin Franklin's life was one of the great success stories in eighteenth-century America. He became the publisher of four newspapers, but he is best known for his publication of *Poor Richard's Almanack*. This

Benjamin Franklin learned the printer's trade as an apprentice in a shop owned by his brother James.
■ What skills would he need for this job?

book included a calendar, weather predictions, jokes, useful bits of information, and—most important—the sayings of "Poor Richard." Many of these sayings, such as "A penny saved is a penny earned," are still popular today. Franklin also gained fame with his inventions and his scientific experiments with electricity.

Benjamin Franklin was not alone in climbing from poor beginnings to fame and fortune. The English colonies were booming. There were opportunities everywhere. Even those who did not climb as high as Franklin were generally better off in America than in Europe.

Advertising America People across the Atlantic learned about the opportunities in America through **promotional literature.** This literature was in the form of pamphlets, advertisements, books, and letters from people already in the English colonies. Much of the promotional literature was exaggerated and unreliable in terms of fact. But it dealt with the topics that most interested the people who were thinking of going to America. The promotional literature reflected the people's hopes and dreams of what they might find in the English colonies.

A young Welshman named Gabriel Thomas wrote a well-known piece of promotional literature. Thomas was a Quaker from a small town in Wales. He was among the first colonists in Pennsylvania, coming there by himself on a ship named the *John and Sarah* in 1681. Many other young unmarried persons came to the English colonies. But many families came, too. In fact, Gabriel Thomas's parents and sisters followed him to William Penn's colony.

Gabriel Thomas stayed 15 years in Pennsylvania. Then he returned to Wales and England for a visit. While there he

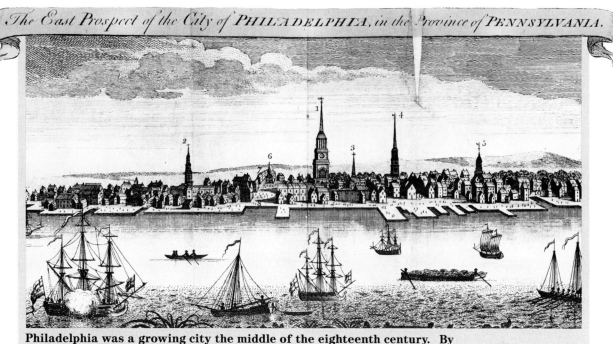

The East Prospect of the City of PHILADELPHIA, in the Province of PENNSYLVANIA.

Philadelphia was a growing city the middle of the eighteenth century. By 1750, Philadelphia had 13,000 people. (40°N/75°W; map p. 87)
■ **What evidence can you find in the picture that shows many people lived in Philadelphia?**

published a little book with a big title, *An Historical and Geographical Account of the Province and Country of Pennsylvania. . . .* He wrote the book to inform and to encourage people thinking of coming to Pennsylvania.

The Good Life There was plenty of food in Pennsylvania, Gabriel Thomas wrote. Wild turkeys weighed 40 or 50 pounds (about 20 kg). There were red deer in the woods as well as pheasants, partridges, and pigeons. Likewise, there were "prodigious quantities" of fish waiting to be caught.

Gabriel Thomas's list of wild fruits must have made mouths water. If his readers needed further encouragement, they could have read: "Their sorts of grain are wheat, rye, pease, oates, barley, buckwheat, rice, Indian corn, Indian pease, and beans." In addition, there were turnips,

potatoes, carrots, and parsnips. All these fruits, grains, and vegetables were produced yearly in greater quantities than in England, according to Gabriel Thomas.

Gabriel Thomas described many other attractive features of Pennsylvania. Land was inexpensive. Government was just. Good schools were available. The Indians were peaceful. The climate was healthful. And "poor people, both men and women, will get near three times more wages for their labor in this country than they can earn either in England or Wales."

After Gabriel Thomas wrote his book, he returned to Pennsylvania to live the rest of his life. Certainly some of what he wrote, though exaggerated, was close to the truth about other English colonies as well as about Pennsylvania. Pennsylvania's population grew rapidly in the eighteenth century, but so did that of the other colonies. (See the picture on page 93.)

Indentured servants had no idea when they would see home and loved ones again.
■ **Why did so many choose to leave home?**

The Atlantic Voyage   Hundreds of thousands of people felt they would be better off in the English colonies than in their homelands. They had to be willing to undergo great hardships, for the voyage to America was not an easy one.

Usually the voyage across the Atlantic from England or a port on the European continent took from 7 to 12 weeks. It was not a pleasant journey. One man wrote:

> There is on board these ships terrible misery, stench, fumes, horror, vomiting, many kinds of sea-sickness, fever, dysentery, headache, heat, constipation, boils, scurvy, cancer, mouth-rot, and the like, all of which come from old and sharply salted food and meat, also from very bad and foul water, so that many die miserably.

It seems a miracle that anyone survived conditions like these, but hundreds of thousands did.

Most people coming to the colonies were too poor to pay their way across the Atlantic. To come to the colonies, a person

would sign an **indenture**, or contract. The indenture pledged the person to work for a certain number of years after arriving in America. Usually the term of service was from 4 to 7 years.

Indentured Servants   The contract was held by the ship's captain. Upon arrival at a port in the English colonies, the ship's captain would sell the contract to someone wanting to buy the service of the person who had signed the indenture. Sometimes whole families would sign indentures to get to America. Occasionally husband, wife, and children would be separated when their contracts were sold to different purchasers.

The advantages of coming to America as an indentured servant usually outweighed the disadvantages of this arrangement. Upon becoming free at the end of the term of service, an indentured servant might receive new clothes, tools, money, or some land. Courts in America made masters treat their indentured servants well. Masters were forced to live up to the terms of the contract. It was not unknown for a woman servant to marry her master or one of his sons. There was no disgrace attached to being an indentured servant. In fact, at least half of the white people coming to the English colonies came as indentured servants.

CHECKUP

1. Why did Benjamin Franklin move to Philadelphia?
2. Explain the purpose of promotional literature and give examples.
3. What hardships were involved for those coming by ship to America?
4. Describe the indenture system.
5. **Thinking Critically** How did indenture differ from slavery?

A Variety of People

What large groups of non-English people came to the English colonies?

VOCABULARY

Huguenot	Middle Passage
Bacon's Rebellion	population explosion

Many Nationalities Until about 1700 most of the colonists came from England. The Pilgrims and the Puritans came for religious reasons, at least in part. But the great majority of people came because the English colonies offered better opportunities for getting ahead in life. Younger sons with no chance to inherit the family farm came to find land in the colonies. After the frequent wars in Europe of the 1600s and 1700s, thousands of discharged soldiers and sailors came to the colonies to find work. Anyone unemployed in England could always try for a better life by coming to the colonies.

Yet even in the 1600s some non-English people came to the colonies. French Protestants, known as **Huguenots** (hyü′ gə notz), who were persecuted in their home country, came in small numbers. They settled near the area of what is now Charleston, South Carolina, as well as in other colonial communities. People of the Jewish faith, forced out of Spain and Portugal by religious persecution, found new homes at Newport, Rhode Island. In 1658, the first Jewish congregation in America was founded in Rhode Island. Thousands of Dutch people were added to the English population when New Amsterdam became New York in 1664. Slaves from Africa or the West Indies and some free blacks could be found in all the colonies. Still, in 1700 the great majority of people in the English colonies were of English descent.

German Colonists The first non-English people to migrate from Europe to the English colonies in large numbers were of German background. Many of them came from the Upper Rhine Valley, where they had suffered from invading armies in time of war. They came to America searching for a land where they could live in peace. At first these German-speaking people settled in Pennsylvania because of the advertising distributed by agents of William Penn. In time, some of them and their descendants migrated north into New York or south into Virginia, Maryland, and the Carolinas.

Wherever they settled, most German immigrants worked hard, obeyed the laws, and kept to themselves. Most were farmers, though a few turned to industry, making cloth, paper, or glass. Some of them were the ancestors of the people who are today called the Pennsylvania Dutch. The term "Dutch" here comes from a common mispronunciation of the German word *Deutsch* (doich), which means "German."

Scots and Scots-Irish During the 1700s about 300,000 people from Scotland and northern Ireland migrated to the English colonies in America. Those from northern Ireland were descendants of Scots who had settled there 100 years before. They were known as the Scots-Irish.

At first these people prospered by raising sheep and turning wool into heavy, warm cloth. Late in the 1600s, the English government denied them the right to sell their cloth in England. This destroyed the market that many of these colonists depended on.

Whether Scots or Scots-Irish, these people were usually poor. By the time they arrived in the colonies, good land near the coast was expensive. So the new-comers went to the edge of settlement, where few people lived. The new settlers settled on land along the western edge of all the colonies, particularly in Pennsylvania, Virginia, North Carolina, South Carolina, and Georgia.

On the edge of the settlements these Scots and Scots-Irish cleared land, built homes, and put up churches. Often these people quarreled with government officials who represented the more settled eastern part of the colonies. The settlers in the west wanted more protection from the Indians. Also they quarreled about taxes. Some of the tax money collected from all residents of the southern colonies was used to support the official Church of England. The Scots and Scots-Irish in Virginia especially resented this. They were Presbyterians, unwilling to be taxed to support the Church of England.

Bacon's Rebellion   One of the most famous clashes to occur between Virginia's western settlers and the royal government was called **Bacon's Rebellion**. In 1676 there was an outbreak of Indian raids on western settlements. The farmers appealed to Governor Berkeley for help. The governor preferred to do nothing because he wanted to avoid a war.

So a group of farmers led by Nathaniel Bacon took matters into their own hands. They fought and defeated the Indians. Encouraged by their success, they decided to settle other complaints against the governor. For years settlers in western Virginia had objected to what they considered unfair taxes and laws favoring wealthy people who lived near the coast. They also did not think that they were fairly represented in the House of Burgesses.

To make their point, Bacon and his followers marched on Jamestown, the capi-

Bacon and his enraged followers burned Jamestown in 1676 after the governor fled. What conclusion had these rebellious farmers reached about the governor?

tal, and forced Governor Berkeley to flee to Maryland. However, Nathaniel Bacon died shortly thereafter. The rebellion collapsed, and Governor Berkeley regained control of Virginia's government.

Still, "Bacon's Rebellion" achieved results. When news of the trouble reached England, Governor Berkeley was removed from office and a new governor appointed. The new governor made a treaty with the Indians and tried to resolve the farmers' complaints.

Black People in the Colonies   You read in the last chapter how the first blacks came to Jamestown in 1619. It seems likely that they were sold as indentured servants rather than slaves and in time earned their freedom. By 1700, however, slavery had fastened itself on the colonies. After that date, the number of black people brought to the colonies as slaves increased rapidly.

There were several reasons for this rapid increase. The rapid growth of the plantation system in the 1700s created a need for laborers. And large profits could be made from the slave trade. Most plantation owners purchased slaves rather than indentured servants because slaves did not have to be released after a certain time. Children of slave mothers were born into slavery; thus there was a natural increase in the number of slaves.

Portuguese, Dutch, and English sea captains, as well as some from New England, took part in the slave trade. The sea captains bought the slaves at trading posts in the present-day countries of Angola, Ghana, Senegal, Gambia, Sierra Leone, and southern Nigeria along the west African coast. African chiefs whose tribes had taken captives from rival tribes sold these captives to the slave traders for cotton cloth, beads, weapons, utensils, rum, and other goods.

The **Middle Passage**, or the long voyage from Africa to the Americas, was a terrible ordeal for the Africans. The ships were crowded and dirty. Often the slaves were chained and packed so tightly together in the hold of the ship that they barely had enough room to lie down. They were given little food to eat. It is no wonder that a great many slaves died before reaching the Americas. Find the Middle Passage on the map on page 104.

Distribution of Slaves Usually Africans were brought first to the West Indies. Many of them worked on the sugar plantations. Others were sold in the English colonies on the mainland. Slavery was legal in all the colonies, but by 1750 it was most closely linked with the South.

Of the colonies north of Maryland, New York had the most slaves. By the middle 1700s, 1 New Yorker out of every 8 was black. No more than 1 in every 50 New Englanders was black. Only in South Carolina were there more blacks than

European slave traders visited African slave markets like this one in Zanzibar to buy slaves they could sell in America.
■ **Why, do you think, are so few of the captives standing?**

whites, although in colonial Virginia blacks and whites were nearly equal in number.

Not all blacks in colonial times were slaves. Whether slave or free, some blacks practiced a skilled trade such as that of a carpenter or blacksmith. Most slaves worked in the fields on plantations and farms, but some were house servants and cooks. The labor of blacks contributed greatly to the prosperity of the colonies in the 1700s.

What Colonists Brought Even the poorest indentured servant from Europe was better off than the slaves in America. Most indentured servants brought a few possessions with them. Slaves arrived with no more than the clothes on their backs. However, both Europeans and Africans brought the language, religious beliefs, and ideas of government they had known in their homeland.

Since the English controlled the colonies along the Atlantic Coast between Florida and Canada, the colonies based their governments on English models. The early settlers from England brought English ideas of liberty and law to America. They introduced into most of the colonies the customs of the Church of England — or, as with the Puritans and Quakers, the customs of the offshoots of the official English church.

Because these were English colonies, English became the common language. But other languages were spoken in some colonial homes. One third of the population of Pennsylvania spoke German. In neighboring New York, the Dutch language held on long after the English government had taken over. Huguenots spoke French, and many educated English colonists spoke that language. Still, the language of business and government was English.

A Leap in Population In the 1700s the 13 English colonies experienced a **population explosion**, or a rapid increase in the number of people. By 1760 the population had climbed to more than 1.5 million. Immigration explained only part of this rapid increase. Families were quite large, so there were many native-born Americans. Josiah Franklin's family of 17 children by two wives was above average in number, but families with 10 or 12 children were not at all uncommon. A large family meant more hands to do the hard work that was necessary for the family to survive.

This population explosion had a number of effects. First, it meant the colonies expanded, especially along the western settlements. Second, the population explosion created scores of new towns, while at the same time it increased the population of the older ones. Third, farming, trade, and industry grew because there were more workers and more customers. Finally, the population explosion indicated the rising strength of the English colonies.

By 1760 the 13 colonies not only had survived but had grown and prospered. Many kinds of people had started new lives there. The colonists had begun to develop their own characteristics. They were becoming different from the English.

CHECKUP

1. Where did the groups of non-English people settle in the colonies during the 1700s?
2. Why did newcomers to the colonies generally go to the western settlements?
3. Why did the number of slaves increase rapidly during the 1700s?
4. How did the population explosion benefit the colonies?
5. **Thinking Critically** What steps could Governor Berkeley have taken to avoid Bacon's Rebellion?

Colonial Economy

VOCABULARY

bread colonies	commission
triangular trade route	mercantilism
factor	

A Variety of Occupations   The 1.5 million residents of the English colonies in 1760 had many occupations. Most people lived in rural surroundings. Yet by no means did all colonists make their living by farming.

Gabriel Thomas listed occupations in Pennsylvania in which the pay was better than it was in England. His list describes the many ways of making a living in the English colonies. Among the occupations he named were blacksmith, carpenter (for houses and ships), bricklayer, mason, shoemaker, tailor, sawyer (one who saws boards), weaver, wool comber, potter, tanner (one who makes animal hides into leather), currier (one who makes leather goods), brickmaker, hatmaker, glazier (one who puts glass into place), cooper (one who makes wooden barrels, tubs, and pails), baker, butcher, brewer, silversmith, plasterer, wheelwright (one who makes wheels), millwright (one who builds mills), brazier (one who works with brass), gunsmith, locksmith, watchmaker and clockmaker, saddler, barber, printer, bookbinder, and rope maker.

Most colonial communities had cooper shops like this one, where pails, tubs, barrels, and butter churns were made.
■ What else would a community need if it wanted these products?

These modern craftworkers demonstrate early bootmaking at Colonial Williamsburg. ■ Why would a modern museum want to recreate this activity?

There also were lawyers and physicians in the colonies. Thomas omitted them from his list, explaining, "Of lawyers and physicians I shall say nothing, because this country is very peaceable and healthy." He also omitted surveyors, whose services were greatly in demand where so much land was bought and sold.

There were no real factories in the colonies. People working at crafts and trades generally had small shops. During the 1700s American cabinetmakers fashioned furniture as good as any made in England or France. They used such native woods as cherry, maple, or oak. Sometimes they made furniture from mahogany, a heavy hardwood shipped from the West Indies. Usually they worked from pattern books, following models of the master furniture makers of England. Often, however, the American craftworkers added distinctive touches of their own.

Farming in the Colonies   In the early days of each colony, almost all settlers were farmers. Families raised the food they needed and some of the materials from which their clothing was made. But as life became a little easier, groups of colonies developed products for trade.

In Virginia, Maryland, and North Carolina, tobacco proved to be the most profitable crop. In South Carolina and Georgia the leading products were rice and indigo. These crops were grown mainly by slave labor on large plantations. Nevertheless, small farms contributed a share of southern agricultural production.

By the 1700s the middle colonies were known as the **bread colonies**. Much grain, which was mainly used to make bread, was raised there. Farmers in New York and Pennsylvania also sent large amounts of beer, beef, and pork to England and the West Indies. At the same time, Albany, New York, was a fur-trading center. Furs obtained through trade with Indians were collected in Albany. Then they were shipped to England or to one of the colonial cities to be made into hats, blankets, rugs, or clothing.

New England's rocky soil made farming difficult. However, forests and the sea offered opportunities for making a living. As a result, New Englanders turned to shipbuilding, fishing, and trading as their major occupations.

Oak Trees, Codfish, and Whales   An English ship's carpenter was among the early settlers at Plymouth. Soon afterward, six shipwrights (carpenters skilled in shipbuilding) settled at Salem, in the Massachusetts Bay Colony. They brought pitch, tar, ships' ropes, and sailcloth with them from England. Oak trees in New England forests provided fine lumber for building ships. Before long, ships built in

Massachusetts were sailing along the coast, from Maine to Virginia.

Because of the abundant supply of lumber, it cost only half as much to build ships in the colonies as it did in England. For this reason, English merchants bought many of the ships built in colonial shipyards. By 1665, some 300 ships built in New England sailed the seas. By 1720 Boston shipyards alone produced 200 ships a year, and Philadelphia shipyards launched nearly as many.

Hundreds of New Englanders made their living fishing for cod. Salted or dried codfish were packed in barrels and shipped out in great quantities. Many Massachusetts merchants made their fortunes from this business. A model of a codfish still hangs in the State House in Boston as a reminder of how much the fish meant to the colony.

The most adventurous of all who made their living from the sea were those going after the great whales. Sometimes the whales were caught close to the New England coast. The whales' fat was boiled down to make oil for lamps.

In the early 1700s, whalers from Nantucket captured a kind of whale they had not heard of before. It was the sperm whale. Spermaceti (spər mə sēt′ ē), a waxy substance from the oil in its head, made excellent candles. This oil burned with a clear, bright flame. Before long, whaling ships from New England ports sailed forth in every ocean of the world in search of the valuable sperm whale.

A whaling ship would not return until it had its hold full of oil. A man signing on for a voyage on a whaler knew that he might not see his home port for 3, 4, or even 5 years.

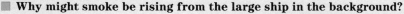

Among those who made their living from the sea, the whalers faced the most startling dangers.
■ Why might smoke be rising from the large ship in the background?

Colonial Trade   By the middle of the 1700s, the colonies were active members of an Atlantic trading community. Generally this trade was carried on by merchants whose offices were in Boston, Philadelphia, or New York. But every section of the colonies took part in trade. The southern colonies sold tobacco and rice. The middle colonies traded grain, livestock, and furs. New England sold lumber and fish, and, in addition, built many of the ships that carried colonial products to England, the West Indies, and countries bordering on the Mediterranean.

Some New England merchants made fortunes through what became known as a **triangular trade route**. The triangular trade route was so named because the ships traded at two other ports before returning home. For example, rum made in New England was carried to Africa. There it was traded for African slaves. The slaves were carried to the West Indies where they were traded for molasses. This molasses was then brought back to New England and used in the making of more rum. Merchants and sea captains counted on making a good profit from each

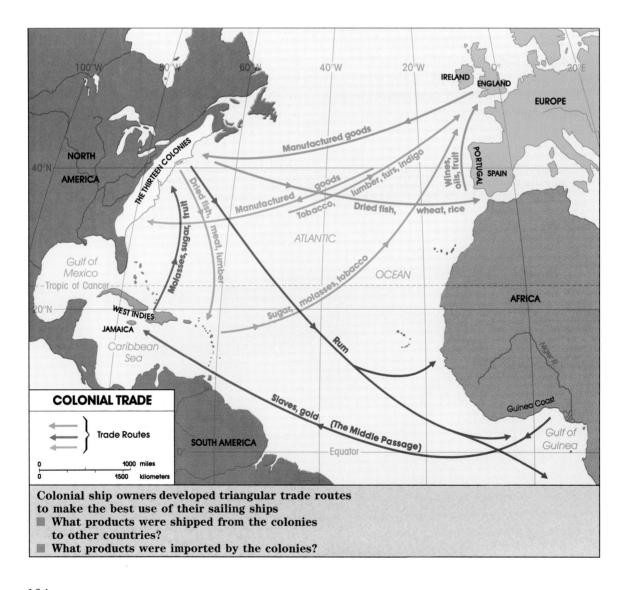

COLONIAL TRADE

Colonial ship owners developed triangular trade routes to make the best use of their sailing ships
■ What products were shipped from the colonies to other countries?
■ What products were imported by the colonies?

of the three sides or stages in this triangular trade route. Find the triangular trade routes on the map on page 104.

In Virginia, ships sailed up a river to a plantation wharf. Slaves then rolled large barrels packed with tobacco along the wharf and into the hold of the ship. Before the ship sailed, the owner of the plantation would give the ship captain an order for English goods. He might order a fine set of dishes. Or perhaps he would order cloth from which clothes could be made.

When the ship anchored in an English harbor, its cargo of tobacco would be turned over to a **factor**, or trading agent, for sale. The factor kept part of the sale price as his **commission**, or payment for his services. He used some of the remainder to buy the items the plantation owner had ordered. Perhaps the same ship carried these items back to Virginia. Then it took on a cargo of tobacco, and the process would be repeated.

Trade with England   The English believed that colonies should exist for the benefit of the country that held them. This belief was part of a system called **mercantilism**. Under this system the colonies were to produce raw materials and send them to England. There they would be made into manufactured goods and sold back to the colonies. English leaders thus encouraged commerce and the development of colonial resources. But they had no intention of encouraging manufacturing in the colonies. Trying to protect their own industries, English leaders passed laws that were aimed at forcing the colonies to buy all their manufactured goods from England.

Increasingly, colonial leaders felt strong enough to try to get around these laws. Some manufacturing developed in Massachusetts and Pennsylvania. More-

Baltimore Harbor was a busy trading center in colonial times.
■ What kinds of goods do you think were loaded on ships at Baltimore?

over, smuggling manufactured goods from France or from other countries apart from England began to be a feature of colonial trade. Sooner or later, England and its American colonies were bound to disagree over trade.

Women's Roles   Most women in colonial times worked in, or close to, their homes. Still, women were by no means confined to the traditional tasks of cooking, cleaning, and child care. Numbers of women owned and ran their own farms and businesses.

Usually skilled craftworkers had their homes above or behind their shops. This made it possible for wives and children to help in the work. Wives waited on customers, perhaps leaving older children to care for the younger ones. Likewise, in the numerous taverns of the time, wives often served customers during busy hours.

Some colonial women of the 1700s owned and ran their own businesses.
■ What does this shopkeeper sell?

On southern plantations, black men, women, and children held in slavery did nearly all the housework. The plantation owner's wife supervised them in the household tasks. She also supervised the spinning, weaving, and food preserving, while her husband directed the field work. In her husband's absence, she was responsible for managing the activities of the entire plantation.

On the small farms where most colonial families lived, there was no specific division of labor. Every member of the family did what had to be done. The farm family functioned as a unit. Women and children worked in the fields, especially at harvesttime. In the West, where life was more difficult, women had to know how to handle a musket as well as a plow and a spinning wheel. In the West, women did many jobs usually performed by men.

There were so many tasks to be done that it was almost impossible for a single man or woman to survive alone. Widows or widowers did not stay single very long. Stories have been told of women who received proposals of marriage on the way back from the cemetery after the burying of their husbands.

Colonial marriages took place at about the same average age as marriages today. The colonial town of Dedham, Massachusetts, has been closely studied. In Dedham, over a span of time, the average age of the first marriage for men was 25; for women, it was 22.

Before marriage, girls got years of instruction and practice in the duties of being a wife and mother. Older girls were expected to take over much of the care of younger brothers and sisters.

An extremely important role for colonial women was that of doctor-nurse. Physicians were few and far between. In the home it was the role of the woman to care for the sick. Therefore, a woman had to learn the use of the few available medicines. She learned what herbs and roots were useful for treating certain illnesses. She splinted the broken bones and bound up the wounds of the adults and children in her home.

CHECKUP

1. What products were most typical of the southern colonies?
2. How did most New Englanders make their living?
3. Why was mercantilism profitable for England?
4. What roles did women have in colonial America?
5. **Thinking Critically** How have occupations changed from colonial times to today?

New World Rivalries

What was the relationship between the English colonies and the French colonies?

VOCABULARY

allies

Conflicting Claims   To the north of the 13 English colonies lay New France. The population of New France had grown slowly. By 1700 New France had only 15,000 colonists in its vast territory. The population of the English colonies at that time was nearly 20 times larger.

As you read in Chapter 3, the French built a string of forts along the Mississippi River and its tributaries to protect New France from invasion. In the late 1600s and the early 1700s, England and France were rivals. They both wanted to build worldwide colonial empires. In North America the English government and the colonists saw the empty land west of the Appalachian Mountains as a desirable place to settle. Both the French and English governments claimed some of the same land. For years there were minor clashes between French and English colonists in this region.

The West Indies was another area of conflict. Planting settlements on the West Indian islands followed much the same

The French and Indians attack English settlers at Deerfield, Massachusetts.
■ Why would the Europeans want to involve Indians in their conflict?

pattern as the colonization of the mainland of North America. For 100 years after Columbus's voyages, the Spaniards were the major power in the Caribbean Sea. Beginning in the 1600s, however, England, France, and the Netherlands began to colonize some of the islands in this region.

In time, each of these European empires claimed one or more of the West Indian islands. Because of the sugar plantations located in the West Indies, some islands were at first considered more valuable than any of the mainland colonies. Providing slaves to owners of sugar plantations was a profitable business as well. Much of the salted cod shipped from New England went to the West Indies to feed the slaves on the sugar plantations.

During the colonial wars some of these islands changed hands. Great naval battles took place in the West Indies as fleets from France and England fought each other.

Colonial Wars   Between 1689 and 1750, New France and the English colonies were drawn into three wars. Usually these wars started in Europe between France and England, or Great Britain. (The term *Great Britain* came into use in 1707 after the union of England and Scotland.) In North America these three wars were known as King William's War (1689–1697), Queen Anne's War (1702–1713), and King George's War (1744–1748). In each of these wars the American colonists fought alongside British troops against the French. Both sides had Indian **allies**, or groups that fought with them against the enemy.

Western settlements in the colonies suffered in these wars. From their base in Canada, French soldiers and Indians attacked and wiped out the village of Schenectady, New York, in 1690. In 1704 Indian allies of the French attacked the frontier town of Deerfield, Massachusetts, killing or capturing more than half the residents.

The British and the colonists fought back. In 1710, Port Royal, a French settlement in Nova Scotia, fell to the British and their allies. But an attempt to take Quebec and Montreal the next year was abandoned after ten British troopships were wrecked in the Gulf of St. Lawrence.

In the last of these three wars, New Englanders invaded Canada. With the help of a British fleet, the New England farmers and fishers captured Louisburg. Louisburg was a French fort built on Cape Breton Island, at the entrance to the Gulf of St. Lawrence. A few months later a French and Indian force raided towns in Maine. Other groups of French-led Indians burned Saratoga and Albany in New York. Find Louisburg on the map.

THE BRITISH COLONIES AND NEW FRANCE: 1740

- British
- French
- ▲ French Forts

0   250   500 miles
0   250   500 kilometers

The boundaries between British and French areas are approximate. They were generally disputed.
▢ Which nation claimed the largest territory in North America in 1740?

British ships unload an attack force from New England at Cape Breton Island in 1745. The British captured the French fort at Louisburg.
■ **Do you think this picture might have been done by an eyewitness?**

detail, Yale University Art Gallery

The treaty of peace that ended King George's War gave Louisburg back to France. This angered people in New England, especially those who had taken part in the capture of the French fort.

In two of these colonial wars France and Spain were allies against Great Britain. In the south, Carolinians and Indians seized and burned the town of St. Augustine in Spanish Florida, but they were unable to capture the fort there.

Another expedition from Carolina marched across northern Florida toward French Louisiana. It destroyed 13 of the 14 Catholic missions that formed a link between Florida and Louisiana. But Choctaw Indians, allied with the French, turned back this invasion before it could reach any actual French settlements.

The struggle between Britain and France for control of North America did not end with these wars. There was an uneasy truce between settlers in disputed areas. In 1755, warfare soon broke out.

CHECKUP

1. How did the French government attempt to protect New France from invasion?
2. Why were some West Indian islands considered so valuable?
3. What part did American colonists play in the three colonial wars fought between 1689 and 1750?
4. **Thinking Critically** Would the French and English colonists have fought each other even if their governments had been at peace? Explain.

Using Context Clues

THE WAY THAT WORDS ARE USED

The following paragraphs are taken from *Colonials and Patriots*, a 1964 publication of the United States National Park Service. As you read them, you will see that some words are underlined. You may not know these words, but you should be able to understand what they mean by the *context*—that is, the way the words are used in relation to words around them.

Cities and towns reflected the population boom. In 1700, Boston was the colonial <u>metropolis</u> with 7,000 people, and only Philadelphia came close, with 5,000. By 1775, however, Philadelphia's population had risen to 34,000, making her the largest city, and 11 other cities had passed the 5,000 mark. During the same period, colonial towns increased in number by 3½. But the <u>urban</u> centers could <u>accommodate</u> only a <u>fraction</u> of the <u>mushrooming</u> population.

In 1700, settlements dotted the <u>seaboard</u> from Penobscot Bay, in present Maine, southward to the Edisto River in South Carolina. They were not <u>continuous</u>, and only in the valley of the Hudson River had they penetrated inland more than 100 miles. Seventy years later, however, settlement had spread down the coast another 150 miles, to the St. Marys River, and inland 200 miles and more to the <u>crest</u> of the Appalachians. . . .

The westward movement flowed continuously but not evenly. Before 1754 it was slowed by the <u>hostility</u> of Indian tribes angered by the English invasion and <u>incited</u> by French and Spanish agents. . . .

SKILLS PRACTICE

Show that you understand the underlined words in the text by matching each word with its correct meaning. Write your answers on a separate sheet of paper.

1. metropolis (**a**) major city (**b**) a large center of government
2. urban (**a**) farm (**b**) city
3. accommodate (**a**) occupy (**b**) take care of
4. fraction (**a**) part (**b**) broken bone
5. mushrooming (**a**) agricultural (**b**) increasing rapidly
6. seaboard (**a**) coastal area (**b**) islands
7. continuous (**a**) touching each other (**b**) separated from each other
8. crest (**a**) highest ridge (**b**) farthest point
9. hostility (**a**) hospitality (**b**) warlike action
10. incited (**a**) stirred up (**b**) stopped

SKILLS PRACTICE

Show how well you understand what you have read by answering the following questions.

11. Which colonial city was the second largest in 1700?
12. How many cities had more than 5,000 people in 1775?
13. Where were the southernmost colonial settlements in 1700?
14. How far west had settlements reached by 1770?
15. What slowed the westward movement of colonial people in some places before 1754?
16. Who had incited Indian tribes against the English?

MAIN IDEAS

1. People were attracted to the English colonies by promises of plentiful food, inexpensive land, and a healthy climate.
2. A great many settlers came to America through the indenture system.
3. Huguenots, Germans, Scots, Scots-Irish, and Africans were the largest non-English groups to come to the colonies.
4. Though most settlers in the English colonies were farmers, there was an increasing variety of occupations in the crafts and trades.
5. Great Britain's and France's desire for empire resulted in three wars being fought in North America between 1689 and 1750.

VOCABULARY REVIEW

On a separate sheet of paper, write the letter of the vocabulary word next to the number of its definition.

a. apprentice
b. indenture
c. Huguenots
d. Middle Passage
e. promotional literature
f. factor
g. commission
h. triangular trade route
i. mercantilism
j. allies

1. One who arranged for the sale of Virginia tobacco in England
2. Usually a young person learning a trade from a master craftworker
3. French Protestants
4. A system in which England got raw materials from the colonies, made the raw materials into manufactured goods, and sold the goods back to the colonies.
5. The long voyage from Africa to the Americas of slaves on board slave ships.
6. Groups that work together against a common enemy
7. A contract pledging a person to serve for a specified number of years
8. Written matter intended to persuade people to come to America

9. Trade between New England, Africa, and the West Indies
10. A payment for making a sale

CHAPTER CHECKUP

1. How did Benjamin Franklin's early life prepare him for the occupation he followed in Philadelphia?
2. In what ways was life in the English colonies more attractive than it was in Europe?
3. Why was there a population explosion in the English colonies during the 1700s?
4. What caused the system of slavery to become fastened on the colonies?
5. What actions did the French take to strengthen their control over the lands they claimed in North America?
6. Name the colonial wars that took place between 1689 and 1750.
7. **Thinking Critically** How did trade influence the growth of the English colonies?
8. **Thinking Critically** Why do you think both Britain and France wanted to expand their empires?

APPLYING KNOWLEDGE

1. Benjamin Franklin started to write his *Autobiography* but never got much beyond his early years. Obtain a copy of his *Autobiography* and write a summary of an interesting incident described in it.
2. Make a chart comparing jobs held by colonial women with jobs held by women today. Show similarities as well as differences.
3. Write an essay that explains why colonial America was considered a highly mobile society. Answer the following questions in your essay. What opportunities awaited a newly arrived immigrant in colonial days? What opportunities are available today? What degree of social mobility is there in the United States today? Describe examples of social mobility in your family's history. Use specific examples.

How Americans Lived: 1750

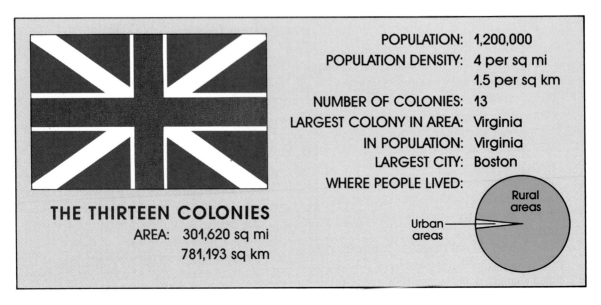

THE THIRTEEN COLONIES

AREA: 301,620 sq mi

781,193 sq km

POPULATION: 1,200,000

POPULATION DENSITY: 4 per sq mi

1.5 per sq km

NUMBER OF COLONIES: 13

LARGEST COLONY IN AREA: Virginia

IN POPULATION: Virginia

LARGEST CITY: Boston

WHERE PEOPLE LIVED:

Rural areas

Urban areas

What was life like in 1750 for Americans?

In 1750 about 1.2 million people lived in the 13 British colonies on the mainland of North America. These people were of different races, religions, and social classes, and they lived in different geographical locations. So it is impossible to describe how *all* the colonial people lived in 1750. What we can do, however, is select people who were living at that time and see how they carried on their everyday lives to get an idea of how some people lived in 1750.

Going to School In the South and in the middle colonies, education was left for a long time to parents and to private schools. Only in New England was there anything like a school system. John Adams, later to be the second President of the United States, was 15 years old in 1750. What was school like for young John Adams?

John Adams was born in a plain frame house, which still stands in Quincy, Massachusetts. His father was a farmer and the village shoemaker. John Adams learned to read at home, like many New England boys of the time. Those not learning to read at home attended a **dame school**. These were small private schools taught by women in their homes.

The dame schools were somewhat like kindergarten today. Children were taught the alphabet and the simplest addition and subtraction. While mostly boys went to the dame schools, a few girls attended. It was probably the only formal education girls ever had. They were expected to become wives and mothers, and it was felt that they did not need much book learning to fill those roles. Instead, girls worked at home with their mothers, learning to cook, sew, and run the household.

John Adams started in **grammar school** at the age of 7. Grammar schools then were quite different from our schools today. Their sole purpose was to prepare boys to attend college. Girls did not go to grammar school in colonial times, and some boys who attended were judged unable to do college work. Preparing for college in grammar school, John Adams learned Latin and Greek. These were the main subjects taught there, but grammar school students also learned advanced mathematics.

Most schoolhouses were freezing cold in winter. Benches were narrow and backless, yet students were expected to sit on them for 8 hours. Schoolmasters enforced rigid discipline. If a boy failed to recite correctly, the schoolmaster might whip him with a birch rod. The slightest disorder could bring the same punishment. And yet parents approved this discipline. They felt that a student who had never been whipped could not be learning much.

Having survived grammar school, John Adams left home to study at Harvard College. Life there was more of the same hard study. His living quarters were cold, heated poorly by an open fireplace. Meals were usually meager—hardly enough for growing boys. Hours of study were long, with only an hour after the evening meal for relaxation. How could John Adams be anything other than happy when he graduated from Harvard in 1755!

Young John Adams studied here, at Harvard College in Cambridge, Massachusetts.
■ How do these buildings compare to other school buildings you have seen?

Abigail Smith, the young woman John Adams married in 1764, had no formal education at all. She was 6 years old in 1750. What she learned after that, as she later wrote, she "picked up as an 'eager gatherer' rather than from systematic instruction." She picked up a good deal, for she was the daughter of a minister, himself a Harvard graduate. Conversation in the Smith home was lively, and books were plentiful.

Abigail Smith taught herself French. She also learned to write in a witty style, becoming one of the greatest of American letter writers. Anyone who reads the love letters she exchanged with her future husband might think she was the Harvard graduate.

Building a House Daniel Boone, the pioneer and trailblazer, was a year older than John Adams, having been born near Reading, Pennsylvania, in 1734. While John Adams was preparing to enter Harvard in 1750, 16-year-old Daniel Boone and his family were moving from Pennsylvania to North Carolina.

Daniel Boone had become a hunter and trapper at the age of 12. This was not unusual—the largest wolf ever killed in western Pennsylvania was shot by a 10-year-old boy. Boone and his family spent about a year in the Shenandoah Valley before settling at Buffalo Lick, on the north fork of the Yadkin River, in North Carolina. There in the wilderness they built their house of logs.

As was customary, the whole community helped the Boones build their house. With sharp axes enough timber could be cut to finish the job in 3 days. This included the **clapboard** roof and the **puncheon** (pun' chən) floor. A clapboard is a narrow board that is thicker at one edge

Families like the Boones who settled in the western parts of the colonies lived in log houses and grew or hunted all their own food.
■ What kinds of different uses of wood logs can you see in this illustration?

than the other. A puncheon is a log split in half lengthwise. For floors, puncheons were laid flat side up. Puncheons were also used to make tabletops and benches. Puncheon floors, tables, and benches were as smooth and splinterless as hand tools could make them.

The Boone family was only one of thousands of colonial families living in log houses. Most western cabins had only one room. Often they had a dirt floor rather than a puncheon floor. Windows had no glass but were merely holes in the wall. At night wooden shutters closed them from the inside. Greased paper that let light in might later be stretched across the windows to keep out rain and snow.

A fireplace with a log chimney lined with mud or clay provided heat and was used for cooking. The family ate meals from wooden dishes called **table furniture**. There were plenty of trees in the forests. With wood, an ax, and a few other hand tools, a western family could fashion many of the articles it needed.

Getting Married   On Wednesday, April 4, 1750, the Reverend John Moncure, an Anglican (Church of England) clergyman, performed the marriage of George Mason and Ann Eilbeck. At that time, only Anglican clergymen were licensed to perform legal marriages in Virginia, where the Church of England was recognized by law as the established, or official, church.

George Mason was a Virginia aristocrat. The Mason and Eilbeck families had been neighbors when George and Ann were children. After they were married, George ordered the building of a new home for his wife and the children they expected. Eventually there were nine Mason children living in this home, which George Mason called Gunston Hall.

George Mason and Ann Eilbeck had portraits painted about the time they married in 1750. Later they had Gunston Hall built to be their home.
■ Why do you suppose Gunston Hall took 3 years to build, while a log cabin (page 114) might take only 3 days?

Gunston Hall was no log cabin built in 3 days. Started in 1755, it was finally completed in 1758. William Buckland directed the construction and personally designed the elaborate woodwork inside the house. Buckland was a skilled craftworker, brought from England as an indentured servant.

From Gunston Hall, George Mason went on to become a leader in colonial politics and government. Today visitors to Gunston Hall, near Lorton, Virginia, can see the colonial home and gardens of George Mason. It is remarkable that the heroes of colonial America came from homes as different as John Adams's plain frame house in Massachusetts, Daniel Boone's cabin on the North Carolina frontier, and George Mason's Gunston Hall in Virginia.

Managing a Plantation   Six years before 1750, Eliza Lucas had married Charles Pinckney, a prominent South Carolinian. Eliza was born in 1722 in the West Indies, the daughter of a British army officer. He owned a plantation called Wappoo, near Charleston, South Carolina. In 1738 he took Eliza there. Then he returned to England, leaving his daughter to manage Wappoo, though she was only 16 years old.

Eliza Lucas set out to learn all she could. Wappoo was a large plantation, with 20 slaves. But Eliza had to plan carefully to pay off its debts, for Wappoo was heavily mortgaged. She ordered the planting of oak trees, hoping they would grow into sturdy timber for ships of the British navy. She experimented with growing indigo from seeds her father sent from the West Indies, although indigo had never been grown successfully before in South Carolina.

Managing Wappoo kept Eliza Lucas busy. Still, along with her business duties,

she found time for music and reading. In nearby Charleston she became popular because she was a witty young woman with the ability to carry her part of the conversation in any gathering.

At the time of their marriage in 1744, Eliza gave Charles Pinckney some of the indigo plants grown successfully at Wappoo. Her husband later gave some of the seeds to neighbors. From this wedding gift came most of the indigo grown in South Carolina.

In 1750 Eliza Pinckney was living at Belmont, a plantation owned by her husband. She no longer had the responsibility of managing a plantation by herself. Nevertheless, she continued her agricultural experiments. She found better ways to raise hemp and flax. She became interested in using silkworms to produce threads to be woven into silk cloth. Dresses made from this silk are still on exhibit in South Carolina.

Eliza Pinckney was the first to grow indigo plants successfully in South Carolina.
■ **How was the indigo plant used in 1750?**

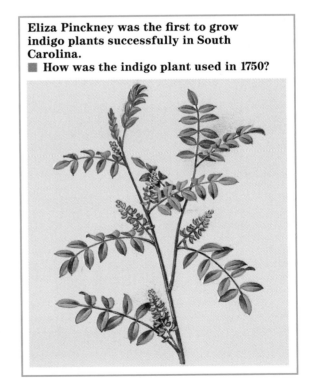

Workers bring indigo plants from the fields to be made into blue dye.
■ What group of people do you think did this kind of work on the indigo plantations of South Carolina?

Two sons, Charles and Thomas, were born to Eliza Pinckney and her husband before he died in 1758. As a widow with small children, she again had the responsibility of managing large properties. Few mothers in America in 1750 were able to give their sons the advantages Eliza Pinckney gave to hers, for she was a skillful manager in a prosperous land.

Both sons were educated in England. Later they helped make the Pinckney name famous in the history of South Carolina and the United States. Eliza Pinckney lived to see South Carolina become one of the 13 original United States. By that time she was as well known as her famous sons. George Washington, who knew Eliza Pinckney, asked for the honor of helping to carry her casket to the grave when she died in 1793.

In 1750 there were hundreds of thousands of women living in America. Not many managed plantations as Eliza Pinckney did. Still, they were good wives and mothers, as she was. And, like Eliza Pinckney, a great many talented women found time for other activities.

CHECKUP

1. Describe schools in 1750.
2. Why did girls receive so little formal education in colonial times?
3. What was Boone's house like?
4. How did Eliza Lucas improve her husband's plantation?

5. **Thinking Critically** Which of the people mentioned in this section do you think would most likely have owned slaves? Explain your answer.

REVIEWING VOCABULARY

1. prehistoric   The first people came to the Americas in prehistoric times — that is, before there were written records. Where did these early Americans come from? How did they get here? How do we know anything about these people?

2. environment   A people's way of life is affected by its geographical environment, or the land, water, plants, animals, and climate of the area in which the people live. Give four examples of the way in which the geographical environment affected American Indians' lives.

3. empire   Six countries at one time or another gained control of land in what is now the United States. In this way, each established an empire. Name the six countries. How did each first gain control of its empire? How did it maintain control? Which of the six empires had the most lasting influence in North America?

4. constitution   A constitution is a set of basic laws by which a nation, state, or group is governed. What, do you think, would life be like in the United States if we did not have the Constitution?

5. archaeologist   Archaeologists are scientists who study objects, ruins, and other evidence of human life in the past. Suppose you were an archaeologist digging at the site of an abandoned Indian village in New York. According to the rings of trees found at the site, the trees died in the 1500s. Digging reveals stone axes, clay pots, and iron knives. What conclusions might you draw about contact between the Indians and Europeans? Explain.

EXPRESSING YOURSELF

1. Through their eyes.   Hernando Cortés landed in Mexico with 600 men, 17 horses, and 10 cannons. The Aztecs had never seen such people or things before. How would these men, horses, and cannons have looked to Aztec warriors? How do you think the Aztecs reacted to their sudden appearance?

2. What if . . . ?   Suppose Verrazano, Cartier, and Henry Hudson had each found a water route through North America to the Far East. How would the history of the New World have been changed?

3. In what ways?   Imagine you were born in colonial Boston but moved with your family to the Virginia frontier when you were fourteen. In what ways would your life be different?

4. You make the decision.   Suppose you lived in England in 1700 and read a copy of Gabriel Thomas's *Account of the Province and Country of Pennsylvania.* Which of Pennsylvania's features would be of most interest to you? What factors would you take into consideration in deciding whether to migrate to Pennsylvania or stay in England? Would you go or stay?

5. Who would you rather be?   Would you rather be the fourteen-year-old child of Christopher Columbus, Anne Hutchinson, Josiah Franklin, Daniel Boone, or George and Ann Mason? Why?

UNIT 2
Founding a New Nation

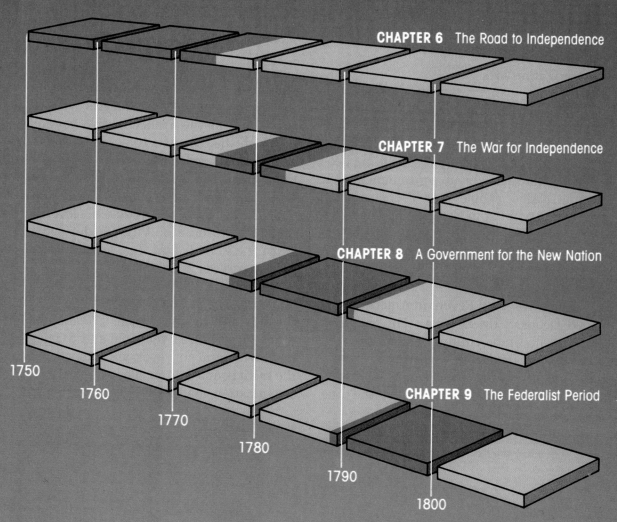

CHAPTER 6 The Road to Independence

CHAPTER 7 The War for Independence

CHAPTER 8 A Government for the New Nation

CHAPTER 9 The Federalist Period

1750

1760

1770

1780

1790

1800

6 The Road to Independence 1750–1775

British Policy Changes

Why did the attitude of the British government toward the American colonists change after the French and Indian War?

VOCABULARY

militia	enumerated articles
Albany Plan of Union	warrant
prime minister	Sugar Act
Treaty of Paris (1763)	Parliament
Proclamation of 1763	Quartering Act
Navigation Acts	Stamp Act

The Reveres of Boston Apollos Rivoire (ə pol′ əs rē vwär) had come to America from France in 1716 as a 13-year-old boy. He soon found that English-speaking people in Boston had trouble pronouncing his name. Also, people with French names were not popular in New England because of the wars between France and Great Britain. So Apollos Rivoire called himself Paul Revere when he became a silversmith in America.

The first Paul Revere in America married Deborah Hitchbourn. Mr. and Mrs. Revere had nine children and named the eldest boy Paul after his father. Young Paul learned the secrets of the silversmith's trade from his father. By the time he was 13, he could turn out a silver bowl, a tray, or a cup as well as any other silversmith in Boston.

After his father's death in 1754, Paul Revere took over added duties in the family business. His mother managed the silversmith's shop on Fish Street in Boston. So Paul taught the trade to his younger brother, Thomas, so he could help the family. Then in 1756, 21-year-old Paul Revere marched off to war.

George Washington's First Mission War had begun in the wilderness far to the south of Massachusetts. It was the fourth of the French-British conflicts in which the colonists took part. During the peaceful years following the third of these wars, the French had pushed south from the Great Lakes into the Ohio River valley. Alarmed by this action, Governor Robert Dinwiddie of Virginia decided to warn the French that they were invading British territory.

Young George Washington was the man Governor Dinwiddie chose to carry the warning to the French. Washington was a Virginian, 21 years old at the time, a landowner and surveyor, and a member of the **militia** (mə lish′ ə). The militia was an organization made up of the able-bodied

George Washington, on horseback, directs his troops against the French in the Pennsylvania wilderness as the French and Indian War gets under way.
■ When did the French and Indian War begin?

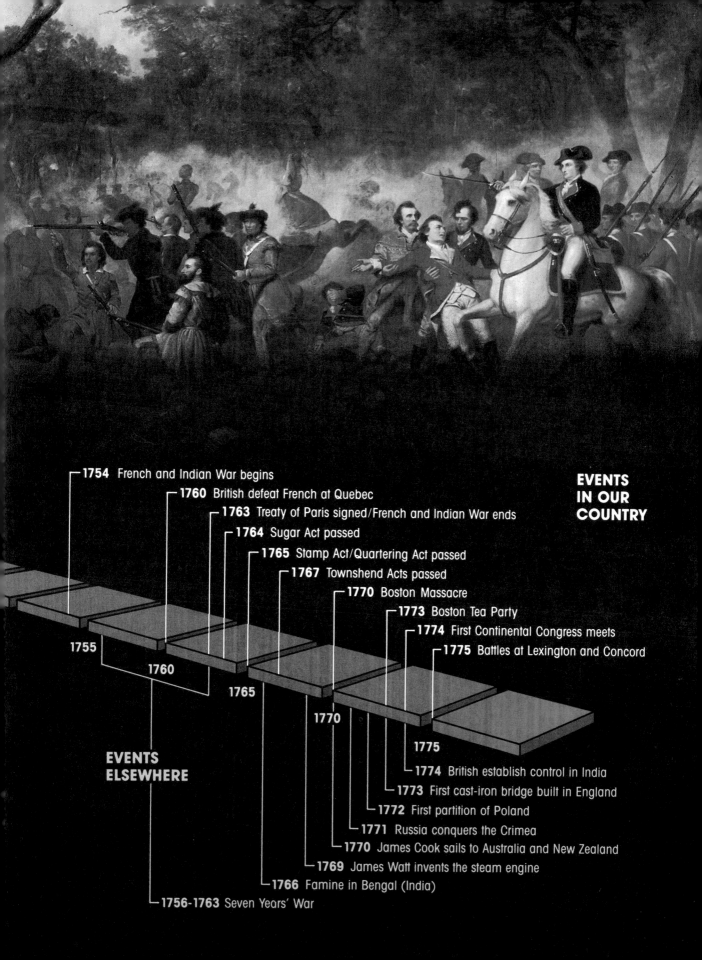

**EVENTS
IN OUR
COUNTRY**

1754 French and Indian War begins

1760 British defeat French at Quebec

1763 Treaty of Paris signed/French and Indian War ends

1764 Sugar Act passed

1765 Stamp Act/Quartering Act passed

1767 Townshend Acts passed

1770 Boston Massacre

1773 Boston Tea Party

1774 First Continental Congress meets

1775 Battles at Lexington and Concord

1755

1760

1765

1770

1775

**EVENTS
ELSEWHERE**

1774 British establish control in India

1773 First cast-iron bridge built in England

1772 First partition of Poland

1771 Russia conquers the Crimea

1770 James Cook sails to Australia and New Zealand

1769 James Watt invents the steam engine

1766 Famine in Bengal (India)

1756-1763 Seven Years' War

men in the colony. They could be called into military service in an emergency. George Washington returned from his wilderness journey with grim news. He reported that the French were determined to stay in the Ohio River valley and could not be removed except by force.

A Setback at Fort Necessity   In 1754, Governor Dinwiddie made Washington a lieutenant-colonel, in command of the Virginia militia. His orders were to seize a fort occupied by the French.

Fort Duquesne (dü kān′), as it was called, was located at the point where the Allegheny and Monongahela rivers meet to form the Ohio River. As the soldiers proceeded through the wilderness, they met a small band of French soldiers. Washington ordered an attack. The first shots of what became known to the colonists as the French and Indian War were fired. On one side were the government of France, the French colonists in America, and their Indian allies. On the other side were the government of Great Britain, the British colonists in America, and their Indian allies. (See the picture on page 121.)

After the Virginians had driven off the French soldiers, Washington ordered his troops to build a fort about 40 miles (64 km) south of Fort Duquesne, in western Pennsylvania. He named this outpost Fort Necessity. More French soldiers from Fort Duquesne soon arrived and surrounded Fort Necessity. Though Washington and his troops fought bravely, the French finally forced them to surrender. Washington and his troops were, however, allowed to march away without giving up their weapons.

The Albany Plan of Union   Even before Washington's defeat at Fort Necessity, the British colonists had felt threatened by the French in the Ohio River valley. They also feared that the powerful Iroquois might join forces with the French to push them out of the valley.

In June 1754, delegates from the New England colonies and from New York, Pennsylvania, and Maryland met with leaders of the Iroquois in Albany, New York. The purpose of the meeting was to discuss Indian relations and defense problems. As a result of this meeting, the Iroquois did not join the French.

At the meeting Benjamin Franklin proposed the **Albany Plan of Union**. This plan called for a Grand Council with representatives from each colony and a president general to be appointed by the British king. The president, with the advice of the Grand Council, would raise taxes to pay for an army to defend the colonies and would settle boundary disputes and negotiate treaties with the Indians. The delegates at the meeting approved the plan. However, all the colonial assemblies rejected it. They did not want to give up any of their own powers. Nevertheless, the Albany Plan was the first step toward uniting the colonies.

Braddock's Defeat   In 1755, General Edward Braddock was sent to America from England with a strong force of soldiers. His mission was to drive the French from the Ohio River valley. As Braddock set off toward Fort Duquesne, he ordered his men to cut a road through the dense woods and march along it as if they were on parade.

George Washington went with Braddock's army. Now a colonel, Washington commanded 450 colonial soldiers. Washington and others warned Braddock that his troops should be cautious in their advance. However, the British general refused to listen to the advice. He thought that Washington and the colonial soldiers knew nothing about the proper way to fight a war.

General Braddock's stubbornness brought on a disaster. A few miles from Fort Duquesne, French soldiers and Indian warriors ambushed the advancing columns of the British army. The bright red coats of the British soldiers made them easy targets. General Braddock himself was mortally wounded. Colonel George Washington had two horses shot from under him. But in spite of these close calls, Washington was able to lead what was left of the defeated British army back to safety.

William Pitt's Leadership By 1756 the British leaders knew they were in for a long, hard fight. In 1757, William Pitt became Britain's **prime minister**. As prime minister, Pitt was the leader of the British legislature. The brilliant Pitt realized the value of Britain's North American colonies. He poured men and money into destroying France's New World empire. He replaced unsuccessful generals and admirals with more able men. His leadership soon paid off with victories in battle. British and American troops once more captured the great French fort at Louisburg in Canada. Fort Duquesne was captured and renamed Fort Pitt. From that

British General Edward Braddock, mortally wounded in a French ambush, is taken from the scene of battle in a Pennsylvania forest.
◼ How can you tell the British troops from the colonial militia in this picture?

Chicago Historical Society

The British captured Fort Duquesne in 1758 and renamed it Fort Pitt.
■ Why was the location of this fort very important to both the French and the British?

fort the present-day city of Pittsburgh got its name.

Some of the greatest British victories were won in Canada. A combined British land and naval force advanced up the St. Lawrence River to Quebec. There in 1759, General James Wolfe's army defeated a French army led by General Louis Montcalm. Both Wolfe and Montcalm lost their lives in the battle fought on the Plains of Abraham, outside the fortress of Quebec. The next year the British captured Montreal, winning control over the settled parts of Canada. France was defeated by Great Britain in America and in Europe.

Results of the French and Indian War

The peace treaty signed in Paris in 1763 changed the map of North America. Under the **Treaty of Paris**, France gave all of Canada (except two small islands off the southern coast of Newfoundland) and the part of Louisiana east of the Mississippi River to Great Britain.

Spain had helped France during the war. As a reward, France gave Spain New Orleans at the mouth of the Mississippi and all of Louisiana west of the Mississippi. But since Spain was on the losing side, Spain was forced to give up its Florida lands to the victorious British.

Thus Great Britain added more territory to its empire. But it was a costly victory. When the war ended, Great Britain had a large army and a large navy to support. It also had a large war debt. Somehow the expenses of the army and the navy and the war debt would have to be paid.

The French and Indian War had important effects on the American colonists. During the war 25,000 of them had fought at one time or another alongside the British. Many of their leaders, like George Washington, had gained valuable military experience. Most of the 13 colonies had prospered during the war, as their farmers, shipbuilders, and merchants sold supplies to the British and sometimes to the French. Probably most importantly, the outcome of the war meant that France could no longer discourage the movement of Americans into the lands west of the Appalachians. French and Indian raiders could no longer swoop down on settlements along the colonial frontier.

The outcome of the war greatly benefited the American colonists. In view of this fact, the British decided that the colonists should help pay the cost of the war. Acting on this idea, the British government made a series of moves that had far-reaching effects in the American colonies.

The Proclamation of 1763 The first problem the British faced after the war was an Indian uprising in the Ohio River valley. Fearful of losing tribal lands, Pontiac, chief of the Ottawa, organized some of the tribes in the area. In the spring and summer of 1763, Pontiac's forces attacked and captured many British forts along the western settlements. Pontiac's Rebellion, as it was called, ended when British troops recaptured the forts. To keep the settlers and Indians apart, King George III issued the **Proclamation of 1763**.

This proclamation prohibited settlers from entering the land west of the Appalachians. Thousands of colonists had planned to move into this region. Indeed, thousands were already there. Now they were ordered to move back east of the mountains. To the colonists it seemed that the western lands won from the French were to be reserved for the Indians. In addition, the Proclamation of 1763 said that only merchants licensed by a

Pontiac and other Indian leaders kept their people fighting against the British and the settlers even after the French had surrendered.
■ What do you think this war council might have been discussing?

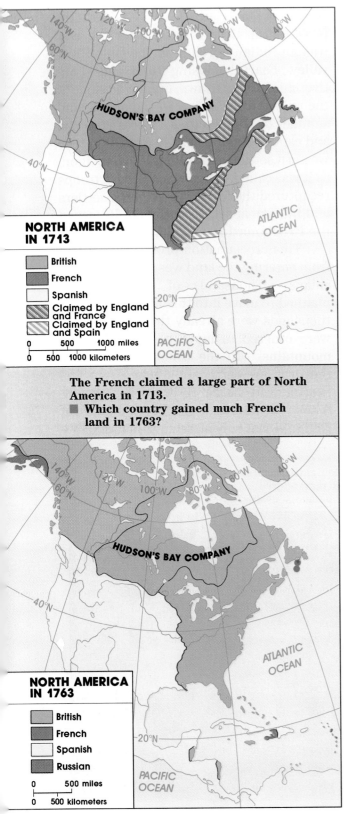

NORTH AMERICA IN 1713

- British
- French
- Spanish
- Claimed by England and France
- Claimed by England and Spain

0   500   1000 miles
0   500   1000 kilometers

The French claimed a large part of North America in 1713.
- Which country gained much French land in 1763?

NORTH AMERICA IN 1763

- British
- French
- Spanish
- Russian

0   500 miles
0   500 kilometers

representative of King George III could trade with the Indians.

The Proclamation of 1763 aroused great resentment in the colonies. To many Americans the Proclamation of 1763 looked like an example of British greed. It seemed that only the British would profit from the lands won from France.

The Grenville Program In the year 1763, George Grenville became the prime minister of Great Britain. He was also chief adviser to King George III. In 1764, Grenville announced some new policies for Britain's American colonies.

Grenville shaped his new policies with two goals in mind. First he wanted his government to have tighter control over the American colonies. Second he wanted to make the colonies pay a share of the large British war debt. To tighten control, he ordered stricter enforcement of the **Navigation Acts**. These acts had been passed in the 1600s for the purpose of regulating colonial trade.

Some of these laws said that certain colonial products could be shipped only to Britain or to other British colonies. The products listed were known as **enumerated articles**. By the 1760s the list of enumerated articles included raw materials such as tobacco, indigo, cotton, furs, lumber, and sugar. Other laws regulated the sale of products manufactured in the colonies. For example, colonists could not make fur hats, ironware, or woolen goods to be sold outside the colony in which they were made.

Still other laws provided that only British or colonial ships could carry products to or from the colonies. Furthermore, products from other countries had to go through British ports before proceeding to the colonies. In the British ports these foreign products were taxed. This meant

British troops camped on the Boston Common during the mid-1760s.
■ Why might this situation shock local citizens?

that they cost more in the colonies than if they had been shipped directly.

Before Grenville's time, British officials had seldom enforced the Navigation Acts. Colonial merchants and manufacturers had conducted their business as if the laws did not exist. In 1764, Grenville took steps to enforce these laws and sent more British officials to America. These officials sometimes made searches for illegal goods without a **warrant** to do so. A warrant is a paper signed by a judge that gives officials the right to make a search or carry out other acts.

The Sugar Act Besides enforcing the Navigation Acts, Grenville persuaded Parliament to pass the **Sugar Act** in 1764. This act raised the duties on sugar, wine, cloth, and coffee imported from areas not belonging to Great Britain.

The extra duties on sugar and the strict enforcement hurt New England merchants because they relied on sugar produced in the West Indies to make rum. As

you read in Chapter 5, rum was shipped to Africa, where it was exchanged for slaves who were taken to the West Indies and exchanged for sugar and molasses. The extra duties meant a lower profit for the New England merchants.

The Quartering Act In March 1765, under Grenville's urging, **Parliament**, Great Britain's lawmaking body, passed another unwanted act. After the French and Indian War, about 7,000 British troops remained in the colonies. The **Quartering Act** ordered colonial governments to furnish quarters — that is, a place to live — and food for these troops.

However, since the war was over, most Americans thought they no longer needed British soldiers to protect them. The colonists were shocked to learn that they were expected to pay for housing and feeding these soldiers. Soon some colonists began to suspect that the British troops remained not to protect American colonists but to enforce British laws.

Much violence broke out in Boston in reaction to the Stamp Act.
What one effect would the Stamp Act have had on all of these people?

The Stamp Act   None of Grenville's policies aroused so much anger as the **Stamp Act**, which became effective in 1765. The act listed about 50 items that had to be printed on stamped paper or have official stamps glued to them. The list included newspapers, almanacs, pamphlets, marriage licenses, wills, deeds, and other legal documents. Special officials sold the stamps and stamped paper, turning the money over to the British government and keeping a small fee as their pay. Money raised by the Stamp Act helped pay for the British troops stationed in America.

American colonists resisted the stamp tax with a fury that amazed the British government. For many years people in Great Britain had paid a stamp tax nearly three times as high. But Grenville and other British leaders failed to realize two important things.

First of all, the Stamp Act was a direct tax imposed on the colonists by the British government. Before the Stamp Act, only the colonial legislatures had passed laws providing for taxes within the colonies. Second, the Stamp Act affected nearly everyone in the colonies. No newspaper could be printed, no land could be legally sold, no couple could be married unless the stamp tax was paid. For these reasons, Americans resisted the Stamp Act.

CHECKUP

1. Why did the French and Indian War begin?
2. What were the results of the war?
3. What were the goals of Grenville's policies for the American colonies?
4. Explain why the colonists objected to (**a**) the Proclamation of 1763 (**b**) the Sugar Act (**c**) the Quartering Act (**d**) the Stamp Act.
5. **Thinking Critically**   Was the Proclamation of 1763 a fair order or not? Explain your answer.

American Colonists Resist

How did the American colonists oppose British policies?

VOCABULARY

tyranny	Declaratory Act
"taxation without representation"	Townshend Acts
	veto
Stamp Act Congress	governor's council
repeal	
nonimportation agreements	writ of assistance

A Fiery Speech   Patrick Henry of Virginia was 29 years old when he was elected to the House of Burgesses in 1765. He represented the northern and western counties of Virginia. And he defended the rights of all Virginians against what he believed to be the illegal acts of the British.

Consequently, though he was a very new member of the House of Burgesses in 1765, Patrick Henry spoke out against the Stamp Act. He called it an example of British **tyranny**, or harsh and unfair government. In one fiery speech he came close to calling King George III a tyrant, or dictator. In the same speech he declared that the Virginia Assembly had "the sole exclusive right and power to levy taxes" upon the colony.

Violent Actions   Some angry people in the American colonies threatened violence to the tax collectors. In many towns men organized secret societies. In Boston a man named Samuel Adams organized the Sons of Liberty. The Sons paraded openly and held picnics and other social events, but they sometimes met secretly. Women joined the Daughters of Liberty. On occasions members of the secret societies tarred and feathered stamp-tax collectors as well as colonists suspected of being too friendly to the new British policies.

One night in August 1765, a mob invaded the home of Thomas Hutchinson in Boston. Thomas Hutchinson was lieutenant governor and chief justice of the colony of Massachusetts. He could understand the anger that Massachusetts people felt because of the stamp tax. But he was part of the official British colonial government, and he felt that Parliament had a right to pass the Stamp Act. Because Hutchinson held this last belief, his home was invaded.

Other Ways of Resistance   Some leaders argued that only their colonial legislatures could levy taxes within the colonies. American colonists were not represented in Parliament. Therefore,

In protest of the Stamp Act, groups of colonists met and burned the hated stamps. ■ Who participated in the stamp burning?

these colonial leaders pointed out, the Stamp Act was **"taxation without representation."**

Some colonial leaders thought the time had come to unite in opposition to the new British policies. In October 1765, delegates from nine colonies assembled in New York for what became known as the **Stamp Act Congress**. Leaders of the nine colonies talked about colonial problems and got to know each other better. Some of the resolutions passed by the Stamp Act Congress stated what the delegates believed were the rights of the American colonists. Others listed objections to the new British policies. A final resolution asked the British government to **repeal**, or do away with, the Stamp Act.

In London, customs officials collected import duties from colonial ships.
■ What, do you think, did the import duties do to the price of colonial goods?

Stopping Imports Before they went home, delegates to the Stamp Act Congress urged colonial merchants to stop buying imports from Great Britain until Parliament repealed the Stamp Act. This turned out to be the most effective way of resisting the hated tax. Merchants in the colonial ports signed **nonimportation agreements**. They pledged not to import any British goods.

It took only a short time for the sale of British goods to drop far below what it had been. In Great Britain, merchants and manufacturers became worried. Ship captains complained about losses in trade. Those British merchants hurt most asked Parliament for an end to the Stamp Act so that trade with the colonies could begin again.

Good News and Bad News In 1766 good news came to the American colonists. Parliament had given in to pressure from the British merchants. British leaders had also come to see that enforcing the Stamp Act would cost more than the money gained from it. Because of this, the act was repealed.

Americans celebrated when they heard the good news. They lit bonfires, they sang, and they cheered. They had come close to rebellion in their resistance to the Stamp Act. Now it seemed their troubles were over. Few colonists were aware of the bad news that came along with the good news.

The bad news was the **Declaratory Act**, passed the same day Parliament repealed the Stamp Act. The Declaratory Act said that Parliament had the right to tax and to pass laws for the colonies "in all cases whatsoever." In other words, Parliament refused to accept the complaint of the colonists that "taxation without representation" was illegal.

Punishing the Legislatures   The legislatures of New York and Massachusetts had refused to pay the expense of the Quartering Act. The next year Charles Townshend (toun′ zənd) became the most powerful man in the British government. He resolved to punish these rebellious legislatures. First he turned to New York, because the British army had its headquarters there. He ordered New York's legislature suspended, meaning it was forbidden to meet.

Later the British government suspended the colonial legislatures of Massachusetts and Virginia. The British government did this because of the legislatures' opposition to the Quartering Act and to some new taxes put on the colonies by Parliament.

The Townshend Acts   The new taxes were called the **Townshend Acts**. They placed taxes on glass, lead, paint, and tea imported from Great Britain by the colonial merchants. British leaders thought the colonists would willingly pay these duties because they were indirect taxes, collected *before* the goods were sold in colonial ports. They were not direct taxes as the stamp tax had been.

However, the colonists did not accept this line of reasoning. In fact, Townshend's actions brought even more opposition than the Stamp Act. Some colonial leaders believed that keeping the legislatures from meeting might end all self-government in the colonies. The colonists were upset, too, to learn that tax money raised by the Townshend Acts would be used to pay the salaries of the royal governors and other British officials in America. If this was done, colonial legislatures could no longer put pressure on government officials by threatening to hold back their pay.

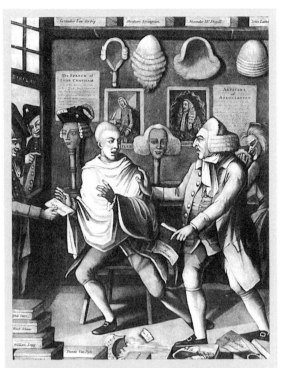

This political drawing shows a patriotic barber in New York.
■ How can you tell that the man getting a shave represents the government?

In making a stand against the Townshend Acts, colonial leaders used the same methods that had worked in fighting the Stamp Act. They declared the new taxes were "taxation without representation." They urged merchants to once again support the nonimportation agreements. The Sons of Liberty in Boston and in other colonial ports threatened violence to merchants who imported British goods.

Many merchants had been alarmed by the violence at the time of the Stamp Act. For this reason, they were less willing to oppose the Townshend Acts. Some merchants paid the Townshend taxes and passed the cost along to those who bought goods from them. These merchants thought this was better than running the risk of arousing more violence. Other merchants managed to avoid the new taxes

Colonial Government

Each of the 13 colonies had a governor. Most of the colonial governors were appointed by the British king. Only the governors of Connecticut and Rhode Island were elected by voters. The governor of Pennsylvania was still chosen by that colony's proprietor.

A colonial governor could appoint people to certain jobs in his colony. He commanded the armed forces of the colony. He was responsible for seeing that the laws were enforced. He could **veto** — that is, refuse to approve — acts that had been voted on and passed by the legislature of his colony.

By the 1760s each colony had a legislature, usually divided into two parts. One part — often referred to as the upper house — was made up of members appointed by the governor. For this reason the upper house in most colonies was known as the **governor's council**. Generally the other part of the legislature — or lower house — was called the assembly.

Voters elected the members of the assemblies. Only white men over 21 years of age could vote. To vote, a man also had to own a certain amount of property. These elected assemblies had been in existence for a long time. Over the years, the power of such elected assemblies had grown.

One source of power came from the assembly's control over taxes imposed within each colony. In several colonies the governor was paid his salary from these taxes. If a governor did something to displease the assembly, its members could vote to withhold his pay. Even though the assembly was the lower house, it was the most important part of self-government in a colony.

by smuggling in the taxed goods. Smuggling means bringing in the goods secretly, without paying taxes on them.

Years of Turmoil If those who led the opposition to the Townshend Acts expected the British to give in, they were mistaken. More customs officials were sent to colonial ports to collect the Townshend taxes. The British army and navy received orders to help the tax collectors enforce the law. **Writs of assistance** were made legal in the colonies. These documents gave an official who was looking for smuggled goods the right to enter and search a ship or building.

Between 1767 and 1770, Americans started to disagree among themselves, thus adding to the turmoil. Some colonists favored giving in to the British. Others wished to continue the resistance. None, however, spoke out openly for breaking the ties between the colonies and Great Britain. Most colonists still considered themselves to be loyal subjects of the king. In fact, they argued that Parliament was trying to take away a right that they held as British citizens — to be taxed only by legislatures they had helped to elect.

A Change in British Policy Charles Townshend died in 1767, but the British government continued to follow his policies until 1770. However, in that year new British leaders decided to end the turmoil in the colonies. They repealed the Townshend Acts except the tax on tea. At the same time, the new British leaders allowed the suspended legislatures in New York, Massachusetts, and Virginia to meet again.

To Americans, this seemed like another victory. Most were tired of the uproar of the preceding 3 years. Therefore, when the British leaders gave in, a great wave of relief swept over the colonies.

WILLIAM JACKSON,

an *IMPORTER*; at the

BRAZEN HEAD,

North Side of the TOWN-HOUSE,

and *Opposite the* Town-Pump, *i*

Corn-hill, BOSTON.

It is defired that the Sons and DAUGHTERS of *LIBERTY*, would not buy any one thing of him, for in fo doing they will bring Difgrace upon *themfelves*, and their *Pofterity*, for *ever* and *ever*, AMEN.

This leaflet urges freedom-loving colonists not to do business with a merchant who is still trading with the British.
■ **What kind of an appeal is being made here?**

Yet even after the repeal of the Townshend Acts, the Sons of Liberty and other groups continued to meet. The groups mainly talked about the ways in which British policies were harming the colonies and not about independence from Great Britain.

CHECKUP

1. How did the colonists resist the Stamp Act?
2. Why did the British repeal the stamp tax?
3. Why did the colonists object to the Townshend Acts?
4. **Thinking Critically** If the British had refused to repeal the Townshend Acts, would the colonists have given in and eventually paid the taxes? Explain.

Armed Conflict Begins

What events increased the tension between the colonists and the British government?

VOCABULARY

Boston Massacre	Intolerable Acts
acquit	Quebec Act
propaganda	First Continental Congress
Committee of Correspondence	Continental Association
Tea Act	Minuteman
monopoly	
Boston Tea Party	

Bloodshed in Boston On the snowy evening of March 5, 1770, five men in Boston were shot down by British soldiers. Among the five was Crispus Attucks, a tall black man who had once been a slave in Framingham, Massachusetts. After gaining his freedom, Attucks worked for 20 years as a sailor. How did he happen to die in Boston?

The British government had sent two regiments of troops to Boston in 1768 to preserve law and order. To most colonists, these soldiers were unwelcome. Residents of Boston hooted and jeered at them and sometimes threw stones.

On the evening of March 5, a crowd gathered in front of the Boston Customs House, where a British soldier was standing guard. Some men and boys started throwing snowballs and chunks of ice at the soldier. As the crowd became more threatening, the soldier called for help. A British officer named Captain Preston and seven soldiers hastened to the aid of the guard.

The crowd, jeering and hooting, kept increasing in size. Some men waved clubs at the soldiers. As the crowd surged forward, British soldiers and colonists were separated by no more than an arm's length. Suddenly a musket shot rang out. Whether the British soldier who fired did so out of panic or because he thought he had been ordered to fire, no one knows. But other soldiers then fired into the crowd. When the smoke from the British muskets cleared, four men lay dead and one was seriously wounded.

Later it was said that Crispus Attucks had led an advance on the British troops. Killed along with him were Jonas Baldwell, also a sailor; Samuel Maverick, a lad of 17; and Samuel Gray. Patrick Carr died 4 days later from his wounds. The skirmish in which these men died became known in the colonies as the **Boston Massacre**. Accounts of the affair, often exaggerated, quickly spread throughout Massachusetts and the other colonies.

Captain Preston and the British soldiers were put on trial for murder. Two young Massachusetts lawyers, John Adams and Josiah Quincy, thought the soldiers deserved a fair trial and agreed to defend them. Adams and Quincy defended the accused men so skillfully that Captain Preston and all but two of the soldiers were **acquitted**, or freed without punishment. The remaining two were convicted of manslaughter, a lesser charge than murder. They were branded on their hands and dishonorably discharged from the British army.

Whether Paul Revere saw the shooting or not is uncertain. However, he made a diagram that was used at the trial. The diagram showed the positions of the soldiers and the persons killed. Revere also made a copper engraving from which prints were produced and sold. The prints were first-class pieces of **propaganda**. Propaganda is the spreading of ideas or facts for the purpose of helping a cause.

The details of Paul Revere's engraving of the Boston Massacre are not accurate. The colonial crowd was larger, many carried clubs or chunks of ice, and they had virtually surrounded the soldiers.
■ Why might Revere have wanted to show the Massacre this way?

Revere's print showed a line of British soldiers firing into a crowd of innocent-looking people. Thousands of people learned to hate the British because of Paul Revere's version of what happened on the night of March 5, 1770.

A Communications Network Samuel Adams, a cousin of the lawyer John Adams, acted quickly to spread the word of the Boston Massacre. Samuel Adams was now convinced that Americans could only keep their liberties by breaking away from the British Empire. He set about trying to convince others in the American colonies that such a break was necessary.

In Boston, Adams set up a **Committee of Correspondence**. Its members wrote letters to people in other colonies. In time, there were committees in most towns from Massachusetts to Georgia. Letters from one group to another told of British actions

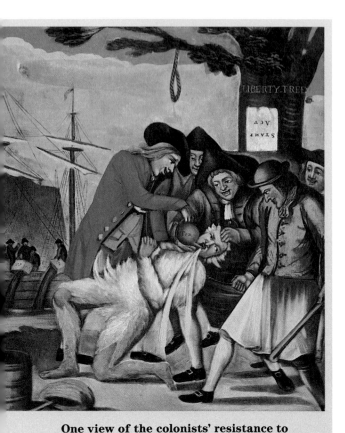

One view of the colonists' resistance to the tea tax is reflected in this drawing of a tarred and feathered tax collector.
■ What are the clues in the drawing that this is a British view?

that threatened colonial liberties. The letters also suggested ways of dealing with these actions.

The Committees of Correspondence kept alive the sparks of colonial resistance to British policies. Moreover, the committees built unity among the leaders of this resistance.

The Tea Act   When the British government repealed the Townshend taxes on various articles in 1770, it kept the tax on tea sold in the colonies. At that time more than 1 million Americans drank tea. The colonists continued to protest this tax. Many of them avoided it by buying tea that had been smuggled past tax collectors by

colonial merchants and ship captains. But despite resentment over the tea tax, the period of relative calm beginning in 1770 continued until 1773. In that year the British government made a decision that marked another step along the road to war.

In 1773 the powerful British East India Company had 17 million pounds of unsold tea. Though it was a private company, it had a great deal of influence with Parliament. To help the company, Parliament passed the **Tea Act**. This act granted the British East India Company a **monopoly** on the sale of tea to the American colonies. A monopoly is the complete control of an industry or product by a single company. In other words, only the British East India Company could sell tea to the colonies. The company arranged to sell the tea through its own agents rather than through colonial merchants. But the company did not raise the price on tea, as it could have done. Instead it lowered the price of British tea.

With tea now at lower prices, Parliament hoped the colonists would no longer object to the tea tax. The British leaders thought, too, that now it would not pay the colonists to risk smuggling tea. But Parliament was wrong. The colonists were angered that only one company could sell tea. Colonial merchants were upset over their loss of business. Smugglers feared there would no longer be a profit in breaking the law. Other people thought Parliament might make similar grants to other British companies and put all colonial merchants out of business. For many in America, it seemed as if cheap tea was being offered as a bribe to get them to pay the tea tax.

By this time the well-organized Committees of Correspondence had plans for united action. They warned that tea shipped by the British East India Company must not be unloaded. At Philadelphia and New York, determined colonists forced the tea ships to carry their cargoes back to British ports. At Annapolis, Maryland, both the tea and the vessel that had brought it from Great Britain were burned in the harbor.

The Boston Tea Party   The most famous "tea party" of all took place in Boston. In December 1773 three tea ships — the *Beaver,* the *Eleanor,* and the *Dartmouth* — were tied to Griffin's Wharf in Boston Harbor. One dark night more than a hundred men disguised themselves as Mohawk Indians. They slipped on board the three ships and dumped about $90,000 worth of tea into the harbor.

Thousands of people watched this event, which came to be known as the **Boston Tea Party**. But no one seemed to know who the "Indians" were. Some of them certainly were Sons of Liberty.

The British Response   In response to the Boston Tea Party, Parliament passed four laws to punish the people of Massachusetts. The outraged Massachusetts colonists called these laws the **Intolerable Acts** because they felt they could not tolerate or endure them.

One law ordered the closing of the port of Boston until the colonists paid for the destroyed tea. A second law restricted town meetings to once a year. It also gave the king the right to appoint the members

Bostonians disguised as Indians dump cases of tea into Boston Harbor. The Boston Tea Party actually occurred on a dark December night.
■ Why do you suppose this artist shows the event in daylight?

of the governor's council rather than their being elected by the people.

A third law changed the Quartering Act, first passed in 1764. The new Quartering Act said that British soldiers could be housed in privately owned buildings, even in the homes of Massachusetts citizens. Thus it seemed to colonists that British soldiers could spy on and control the activities of private citizens. A fourth law allowed British officials to be tried in Great Britain for crimes they might have committed in the colonies. In this way, they might avoid facing hostile colonial juries and judges.

The Quebec Act   At the same time as the Intolerable Acts were passed, Parliament also passed the **Quebec Act**. This law extended the boundaries of the Canadian province of Quebec to include all territory north of the Ohio River and east of the Mississippi River. It permitted the people of Quebec to keep their French laws and their language. It guaranteed religious freedom for the Roman Catholics of Quebec, and it set up a council to pass laws for the people.

The Quebec Act angered American colonists. It threatened the claims of Massachusetts, Connecticut, Virginia, and New York to land north of the Ohio River. Moreover, most British colonists were Protestants. They did not want a strong Roman Catholic province to the west. The colonists considered the Quebec Act to be yet another of the Intolerable Acts.

The Committees of Correspondence spread the news of the Intolerable Acts and the hardships being faced by the people of Boston. Nearly all the colonies responded. South Carolina sent shipments of rice. North Carolina offered money. Connecticut farmers herded sheep to Boston to feed the hungry people there.

The First Continental Congress   In Virginia the House of Burgesses sent out a call for another meeting of delegates from each of the colonies. This meeting was meant to discuss colonial grievances against Great Britain. Committees of Correspondence spread the word. Fifty-five colonial leaders assembled in Philadelphia in September 1774. This time only Georgia failed to send delegates. This meeting in Philadelphia became known as the **First Continental Congress**.

Samuel Adams and Patrick Henry from Virginia met for the first time at the First Continental Congress in Philadelphia. No two men had done more to arouse resistance to British policies. George Washington was also there as one of the delegates from Virginia. He listened as the other delegates debated for 7 weeks.

From these debates came several resolutions. One was a declaration of the rights of the colonists. Another demanded the repeal of the Intolerable Acts. Before the delegates went home, they organized the **Continental Association**. One of its purposes was to unite the colonies in a refusal to buy or sell British goods. The Continental Association was the first written agreement pledging the colonies to act together.

Another Fiery Speech   In some of their declarations, delegates to the First Continental Congress had called themselves "His Majesty's most loyal subjects." Perhaps so, but already some of them wanted independence from Great Britain. And back in their home colonies, people were preparing to fight to defend their liberty if that became necessary. In Massachusetts the Committee of Public Safety was authorized to call out the militia to protect American lives, American property, and American rights.

The militia drilled openly in Massachusetts and the other colonies. However, many members of the militia lived on farms that were far apart. Often it took several hours for all the militia to come together when called to action.

As a result, special groups were formed within various militia units. They were made up of men who could be counted on to answer at once, ready to fight if need be. These special groups were called **Minutemen**, implying that they could be ready for action in a minute. Colonial leaders gathered powder, shot, and other military necessities. The leaders stored these in secret places.

At a meeting in Richmond, Virginia, on March 3, 1775, Patrick Henry made another fiery speech (page 140). At its conclusion came the inspiring words: "I know not what course others may take, but as for me, give me liberty, or give me death!"

The War Begins General Thomas Gage was the British military governor of Massachusetts. His headquarters were in Boston. In 1775 he received orders to put down all signs of rebellion against King George III. Gage knew colonial leaders had stored military supplies at Concord, a small town about 20 miles (32 km) northwest of Boston. The British general was determined to seize the supplies. On the night of April 18, 1775, a force of about 700 British soldiers marched out of Boston, bound for Concord.

They were being watched. As they marched, Paul Revere, William Dawes, and Dr. Samuel Prescott rode ahead of them. These riders warned, "The British are

Colonial Minutemen and British soldiers exchange fire on Lexington Green. This encounter marked the beginning of the War for Independence.
■ **How might each of these armies react to the sight of the other?**

Liberty or Death

Patrick Henry became a member of the Virginia House of Burgesses in 1765. He also served on a Committee of Correspondence and attended the First and Second Continental Congresses as a delegate. He was one of the most eloquent speakers of his time and a strong advocate for freedom. On March 23, 1775, Patrick Henry rose from his seat to address the members of the Virginia convention.

Sir, we have done everything that could be done to avert the storm which is now coming on. We have petitioned; we have remonstrated; we have supplicated; we have prostrated ourselves before the throne and have implored its interposition to arrest the tyrannical hands of the Ministry and Parliament. Our petitions have been slighted; our remonstrances have produced additional violence and insult; our supplications have been disregarded; and we have been spurned, with contempt, from the foot of the throne. In vain, after these things, may we indulge the fond hope of peace and reconciliation.

There is no longer any room for hope. If we wish to be free; if we mean to preserve inviolate those inestimable privileges for which we have been so long contending; if we mean, not basely to abandon the noble struggle in which we have been so long engaged, and which we have pledged ourselves never to abandon, until the glorious object of our contest shall be obtained; we must fight! I repeat it, sir, we must fight!! An appeal to arms and to the God of hosts is all that is left to us! . . . It is vain, sir, to extenuate the matter. Gentlemen may cry, peace, peace; but there is no peace. The war is actually begun! The next gale that sweeps from the north will bring to our ears the clash of resounding arms! Our brethren are already in the field! Why stand we here idle? What is it that gentlemen wish? What would they have? Is life so dear or peace so sweet as to be purchased at the price of chains and slavery?

Forbid it, Almighty God—I know not what course others may take, but as for me, give me liberty, or give me death!

USING SOURCE MATERIAL

1. Why does Henry say that there is no hope for peace?
2. What does Henry mean when he says "give me liberty, or give me death"?
3. How would you have reacted to this speech if you had been a member of the convention?

coming!" Early the next morning, part of the British forces reached Lexington on their way to Concord.

On the village green at Lexington, about 70 soldiers in the Massachusetts militia had assembled. The British commander ordered them to disperse. Captain John Parker, commander of the militia, told his men: "Stand your ground. Don't fire unless fired upon, but if they mean to have a war, let it begin here."

Suddenly the sound and smoke of musket fire filled the morning air. Eight soldiers were killed and several were wounded. After the brief skirmish, the militiamen withdrew and the red-coated British soldiers continued on their march toward Concord. Who fired the first shot is a mystery even today.

The Massachusetts Militia in large numbers had gathered at Concord. However, they were unable to keep the British from searching the town and destroying all the military supplies they could find. A small battle took place at the North Bridge in Concord, and both sides suffered casualties. News of the fighting at Lexington and Concord spread rapidly. Thousands of Massachusetts fighters picked up their muskets and hurried across the fields toward the sounds of battle. No one who heard the call to arms was too young or too old to go.

Around noon the outnumbered British force began the long march from Concord back to Boston. No one now opposed the British openly. Instead, colonists fired from farmhouse windows, and from behind stone walls, trees, and barns. Every Massachusetts citizen fought a personal battle, but the damage they did together was immense.

The exhausted British soldiers reached their camp near Boston after dark. For 24 hours they had been on the

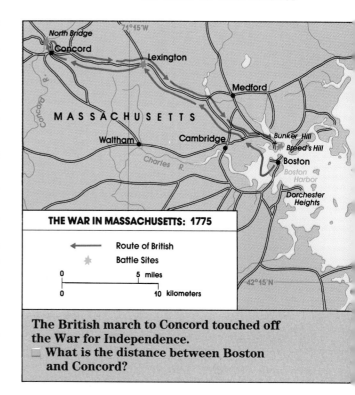

THE WAR IN MASSACHUSETTS: 1775

← Route of British
✶ Battle Sites

0   5 miles
0   10 kilometers

The British march to Concord touched off the War for Independence.
☐ What is the distance between Boston and Concord?

march and, during much of that time, under fire. Seventy-three British soldiers had been killed. More than 200 were wounded or missing. American casualties numbered 49 killed and 41 wounded. Though Americans did not know it at the time, they had started on the road to independence. The events of April 19, 1775, are still recalled each year in Massachusetts and in Maine on Patriots' Day.

CHECKUP

1. What was the Boston Massacre?
2. Why did the colonists protest the Tea Act?
3. List the Intolerable Acts.
4. Where did the first fight between British soldiers and Massachusetts militiamen take place?
5. **Thinking Critically** Why do you think most of the protest against British policies was centered in Massachusetts?

Stating a Point of View

PAUL REVERE'S ACCOUNT

On page 139 you read that Paul Revere, William Dawes, and Dr. Samuel Prescott rode to warn the militia and the minutemen on the night of April 18, 1775, that the British were coming. Here is Paul Revere's account of that night, written 23 years later.

> In the fall of 1774 and winter of 1775, I was one of upwards of thirty, chiefly mechanics, who formed ourselves into a committee for the purpose of watching the movements of the British soldiers. . . . On Tuesday evening, the 18th, it was observed that a number of soldiers were marching toward the bottom of the Common. . . . About 10 o'clock Dr. Warren sent in great haste for me and begged that I would immediately set off for Lexington. . . .
>
> I went home, [got] my boots and coat [and] set off upon a very good horse. It was then about 11 o'clock and very pleasant. After I had passed Charlestown Neck . . . I saw two men on horseback under a tree. When I got near them, I discovered they were British officers. . . . I turned my horse very quick and galloped . . . for the Medford Road. The [British officer] who chased me . . . got into a clay pond. . . . I got clear of him, and went through Medford [where] I awaked the captain of the minutemen; . . . I alarmed almost every house, till I got to Lexington. . . .
>
> After I had been there about half an hour, Mr. Dawes came. We refreshed ourselves and set off for Concord. We were overtaken by a young Dr. Prescott, whom we found to be a high Son of Liberty. . . .

On their way to Concord the three men ran into six British officers on horseback. Dawes and Prescott got away, but this time Revere was caught. The letter resumes.

> One of [the British officers] whom I afterwards found to be a Major Mitchell, of the 5th Regiment, clapped his pistol to my head, called me by name and told me he was going to ask me some questions, and if I did not give him true answers, he would blow my brains out.

After questioning Revere, Major Mitchell turned him over to a sergeant, and the whole party rode back toward Lexington.

SKILLS PRACTICE

On a separate sheet of paper, write an account of the night of April 18, 1775, from the point of view of Major Mitchell or of a colonist who was being warned.

MAIN IDEAS

1. In the Treaty of Paris (1763), France gave Britain all of Canada and the part of Louisiana east of the Mississippi.
2. After the French and Indian War, the British began new policies in an attempt to exert more control over its American colonies and to make those colonies help pay for the war.
3. The American colonists opposed British policies by refusing to buy British goods, by writing formal protests to the king and Parliament, and by threatening violence to British officials.
4. Each new British policy led to a stronger colonial response until warfare erupted at Lexington and Concord in April 1775.

VOCABULARY REVIEW

On a separate sheet of paper, write **True** if the statement is true and **False** if it is false. If the statement is false, replace the underlined word or words to make the statement true.

1. The Proclamation of 1763 <u>opened</u> the lands west of the Appalachian Mountains to settlement by the American colonists.
2. In military terms, "<u>quarters</u>" refers to a place where soldiers stay.
3. The stamp tax was an example of a <u>direct</u> tax.
4. As a result of the French and Indian War, <u>France</u> won control over the settled parts of Canada.
5. The British legislature is <u>Parliament</u>.
6. The repeal of the Townshend Acts saw all indirect taxes on the colonies lifted except the tax on <u>glass</u>.
7. The militia was a <u>larger</u> group than the minutemen at the beginning of the War for Independence.
8. The first shots of the War for Independence were fired on the village green in <u>Boston</u>.
9. Smuggling means to <u>import</u> goods illegally.
10. During the <u>Boston Massacre</u>, colonists dumped tea into Boston Harbor.

CHAPTER CHECKUP

1. Why did the American colonists object to the Quebec Act?
2. How did the British respond to the Boston Tea Party?
3. What was the purpose of the First Continental Congress?
4. What evidence is there that the colonies were becoming more united between 1753 and 1775?
5. Choose one event between 1763 and 1775 and explain how it was a step toward the War for Independence.
6. **Thinking Critically** Why did the phrase "no taxation without representation" become the cry of many American colonists?
7. **Thinking Critically** Name three ways in which American colonists opposed acts passed by Parliament. Which do you think was the most effective? Why?

APPLYING KNOWLEDGE

1. Using a biographical collection such as the *Dictionary of American Biography*, prepare a written report on the activities of one of the following people in the 1700s.

   Paul Revere   John Adams
   Patrick Henry   Thomas Jefferson
   Samuel Adams   George Mason

2. Make a chart listing the advantages and disadvantages of being a British colony.
3. Look at the maps on page 126. Describe how the geography of the United States might have been different if the French had won the French and Indian War. How might the history of the United States have been different?
4. Following the Boston Massacre, there was a trial of the British soldiers involved in the incident. Their defense lawyer was John Adams, who although a Patriot, felt bound to defend the soldiers in the name of justice. Investigate this trial and present the information in essay form.

7 The War for Independence

1775–1783

The Break with Britain

*What events led to the colonists'
declaration of independence?*

VOCABULARY

Second Continental Congress	Tory
	Patriot
Continental army	*Common Sense*
Loyalist	Declaration of Independence

George Washington George Washington was the eldest son of Augustine Washington and his second wife, Mary Ball Washington. When George was 11 years old, his father died. Young George then went to live with his elder half brother, Lawrence, who was 25 at the time.

Lawrence Washington was the owner of Mount Vernon, a large plantation on the Potomac River. After Lawrence's death in 1752, George Washington inherited the estate. Following his service in the French and Indian War, George Washington returned to Mount Vernon to live. Thereafter, he only left the plantation to serve Virginia or the United States. In 1759 he married a widow, Martha Dandridge Custis.

George worked hard at managing his plantation. In fact, some Virginians recognized him as the best farmer in their colony. But Washington was more than a good farmer and major landowner. He was to play an important role in the War for Independence. Before independence was declared, the British and the colonists had engaged in several conflicts.

Fort Ticonderoga Fort Ticonderoga (tī kon də rō′ gə) was the site of a bloodless conflict. The fort was located about 150 miles (240 km) northwest of Boston. It stood at the southern end of Lake Champlain. That lake was an important link in the land-and-water route between Canada and the middle colonies.

At daybreak on May 10, 1775, Ethan Allen, Benedict Arnold, and a band of Vermont militia called the Green Mountain Boys won an almost bloodless victory there. The attack was such a surprise that the British commander of the fort surrendered while still dressed in his nightclothes. By capturing Ticonderoga, the militia gained a key fort. They also captured valuable cannons and supplies.

Under the direction of General Henry Knox, these cannons were dragged over snowy trails through forests by teams of oxen. The 43 cannons and 16 mortars from Ticonderoga finally reached the Boston area on January 24, 1776.

George Washington (on horseback) takes command of the Continental army in July 1775.
■ **When did the Americans invade Canada?**

144

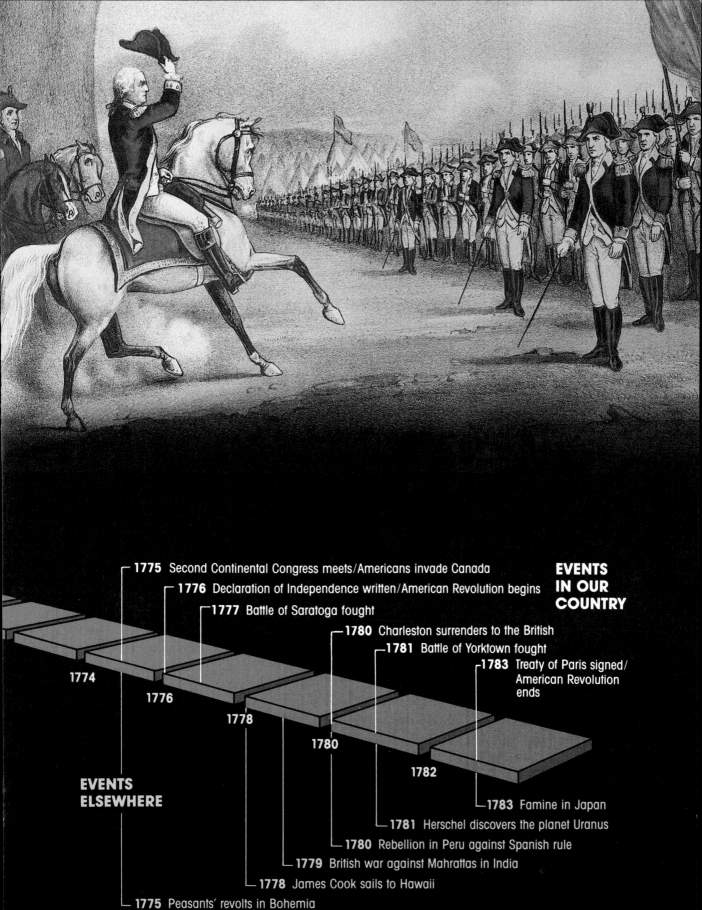

EVENTS IN OUR COUNTRY

1775 Second Continental Congress meets/Americans invade Canada

1776 Declaration of Independence written/American Revolution begins

1777 Battle of Saratoga fought

1780 Charleston surrenders to the British

1781 Battle of Yorktown fought

1783 Treaty of Paris signed/ American Revolution ends

1774

1776

1778

1780

1782

EVENTS ELSEWHERE

1783 Famine in Japan

1781 Herschel discovers the planet Uranus

1780 Rebellion in Peru against Spanish rule

1779 British war against Mahrattas in India

1778 James Cook sails to Hawaii

1775 Peasants' revolts in Bohemia

Ethan Allen, waving his sword, calls on the British to surrender Fort Ticonderoga. The Green Mountain Boys captured the fort without losing one soldier.
■ Why, do you think, are so few of the British defenders shown in this picture?

The Second Continental Congress On the same day that Ethan Allen and the Green Mountain Boys captured Fort Ticonderoga, delegates from all 13 colonies came together in Philadelphia. The meeting became known as the **Second Continental Congress**. Until 1781 that group acted as a central government in the American fight for independence.

George Washington was a delegate from Virginia to the Second Continental Congress and commander of the Virginia militia. On June 15, 1775, members of the Second Continental Congress chose him to take charge of the troops around Boston. They had gathered in Cambridge and other nearby towns after the fighting at Lexington and Concord.

The Continental Army Washington's troops were little more than a loosely organized group of poorly trained militia. The enlistments of most of its members would run out in a few months. And yet the Congress had named the militia the **Continental army**. Thousands served in its ranks for various periods of time, but George Washington remained its commander in chief throughout the long years of the war.

The militia that made up the Continental army around Boston fought one major battle before Washington took command. Two months after Lexington and Concord, a large force of American troops under the command of Colonel William Prescott took up positions across the Charles River from Boston on Bunker Hill and Breed's Hill.

The Battle of Bunker Hill   A little after noon on June 17, 1775, British troops led by General Thomas Gage crossed the Charles River. They marched in orderly ranks toward the trenches on Breed's Hill. As they drew close, a blast of musket fire shattered the silence. The British fell back, but then charged again. Once more, the determined colonial militia drove them back. After reforming their ranks, the British infantry charged up the hill a third time.

This time the British were successful. The militia, with ammunition running low after 2 hours of fighting, had to retreat. Though most of the fighting took place on Breed's Hill, the struggle became known in United States history as the battle of Bunker Hill.

The battle was a victory for the British, but they suffered more than 1,000 casualties, compared to less than 400 for the Continental troops. Moreover, the militia gained the confidence they badly needed. Until their ammunition was nearly gone, the Continental troops had stood up to the British regulars.

Invasion of Canada   Soon after the battle of Bunker Hill, Congress received news that Sir Guy Carleton was gathering a force to invade New York. Carleton was the British commander in Canada. Congress sent Philip Schuyler (skī′ lėr) of New York to seize any forts vital to the security of the northern colonies. Schuyler assembled a force of about 1,000 men at Ticonderoga. From there he began an invasion of Canada. First, Schuyler tried to capture St. John's. The city surrendered on November 2, 1775. When Schuyler became ill, General Richard Montgomery took command. On November 13, 1775, General Montgomery and his army captured Montreal, Canada.

Back at Cambridge, Massachusetts, General Washington had authorized Benedict Arnold to recruit volunteers for another invasion of Canada. After a long and difficult march, Arnold reached the St. Lawrence River opposite Quebec early in November of 1775 with about 650 men. General Montgomery joined him with 300 men from Montreal on December 3. Together Arnold and Montgomery planned an attack on Quebec.

The attack on Quebec began on December 31, 1775. It ended in disaster. General Montgomery was killed, and Arnold was wounded. Nearly 100 other Americans were killed or wounded, and over 300 were taken prisoner. However, Arnold and the survivors did not give up. They laid siege to the city for the remainder of the winter. In the spring, when British reinforcements arrived, the Americans retreated to Ticonderoga.

American leaders were disappointed in the failure of the Canadian invasion. They had expected the Canadians to join them in the fight against Great Britain. But they did not. Benedict Arnold was disappointed, too. He felt his efforts during the invasion of Canada were unappreciated and unrewarded.

Boston Is Free   Early in March 1776, units of the Continental army captured Dorchester Heights. From there, Boston and most of the harbor were in range of General Knox's cannons. These were the same cannons that had been brought from Fort Ticonderoga.

Because of this threat, General Howe, who had taken over command from General Gage, decided to evacuate, or withdraw from, Boston. On March 17 the British troops left on ships, sailing to Halifax, Nova Scotia. They never returned to Boston. At last the city was free.

Loyalists and Patriots   About 1,000 civilians left Boston with the British troops. They were colonists who remained loyal to King George III, so they were called **Loyalists**. Sometimes they were called **Tories** because that was the name of the political party that supported the king.

The colonists who actively supported independence from Great Britain were called the **Patriots**. Most of them did not yet think of themselves as Americans. They thought of themselves as Virginians or New Yorkers or members of one of the other 11 English colonies.

The well-informed John Adams believed that only one third of the colonists were Patriots. Adams said that one third remained Loyalists. In fact, during the Revolution about 40,000 Loyalists signed up to fight against the Patriots. Adams felt that the other third of the people remained neutral. This group did not care which side won.

Action in the Carolinas   There were large numbers of Loyalists in North Carolina and South Carolina. For this reason, British leaders thought it would be easy to put down any revolt there. In February 1776 a British fleet sailed toward Wilmington, North Carolina. At the same time, about 1,500 Loyalists marched to aid in the capture of Wilmington. They never got

South Carolinians built their fort at Charleston from the logs of the palmetto. British cannons were unable to shoot it down.
■ Why, do you think, did the South Carolinians choose to use the palmetto?

there, because a force of Patriots defeated the Loyalists in battle at Moore's Creek Bridge.

Without the help of land forces, the British fleet had little chance to capture Wilmington. So the fleet sailed farther south, to Charleston, South Carolina. The British ships shelled the city's defenses. These defenses had been built quickly with logs cut from the palmetto tree. British cannonballs were unable to penetrate these thick, tough logs. After failing in several attempts to capture Charleston, the British fleet sailed north to New York.

Patriots in South Carolina wanted people to remember how they had resisted the British fleet. So they put a palmetto tree as a symbol on their new state flag. To this day, South Carolina is known as the Palmetto State.

Paine's Pamphlet The Patriot leaders waited for more than a year before breaking their ties with Great Britain. Some favored a form of self-government that would keep them within the British Empire. Gradually, however, those favoring independence gained the upper hand.

Thomas Paine helped swing public opinion in favor of independence. He was a poor young writer from England who came to Philadelphia less than a year before the fighting broke out at Lexington and Concord. In January 1776, Paine published a pamphlet called *Common Sense*. It was a best seller for its time, with sales of more than 120,000 copies.

Paine's pamphlet stated that it was only common sense for the colonies to declare their independence from Great Britain. "How is it that a continent should be ruled by an island?" he asked. *Common Sense* convinced thousands of doubtful readers that independence from Great Britain was proper and logical. Abigail

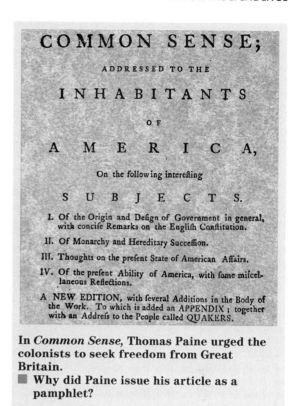

COMMON SENSE;

ADDRESSED TO THE

INHABITANTS

OF

AMERICA,

On the following interesting

SUBJECTS.

I. Of the Origin and Design of Government in general, with concise Remarks on the English Constitution.

II. Of Monarchy and Hereditary Succession.

III. Thoughts on the present State of American Affairs.

IV. Of the present Ability of America, with some miscellaneous Reflections.

A NEW EDITION, with several Additions in the Body of the Work. To which is added an APPENDIX; together with an Address to the People called QUAKERS.

In *Common Sense,* Thomas Paine urged the colonists to seek freedom from Great Britain.
▪ Why did Paine issue his article as a pamphlet?

Adams wrote to her husband, John, at the Second Continental Congress in Philadelphia, "*Common Sense* . . . has come to clear our doubts and fix our course." George Washington wrote to a friend, "By private letters, which I have lately received from Virginia, I find Paine's *Common Sense* is working a wonderful change there in the minds of many men."

The Declaration of Independence On June 7, 1776, Richard Henry Lee of Virginia introduced a resolution into the Second Continental Congress. Its main part stated that "these United Colonies ought to be free and independent states." For nearly a month the members of Congress debated Lee's resolution. They approved it on July 2, 1776. This was all that was needed to declare independence. But the Congress had also chosen a committee to prepare a suitable statement to accompany Lee's resolution. This statement

KEY 1. *Richard Stockton, N.J.;* 2. *Josiah Bartlett, N.H.;* 3. *Thomas Nelson, Jr., Va.;* 4. *George Clymer, Pa.;* 5. *Francis Lightfoot Lee, Va.;* 6. *John Penn, N.C.;* 7. *Abraham Clark, N.J.;* 8. *John Morton, Pa.;* 9. *George Ross, Pa.;* 10. *James Smith, Pa.;* 11. *Samuel Adams, Mass.;* 12. *Robert Treat Paine.* *Mass.;* 13. *Button Gwinnett, Ga.;* 14. *Robert Morris, Pa.;* 15. *Benjamin Harrison, Va.;* 16. *Carter Braxton, Va.;* 17. *John Hart, N.J.;* 18. *John Adams, Mass.;* 19. *Roger Sherman, Conn.;* 20. *James Wilson, Pa.;* 21. *Thomas Jefferson, Va.;* 22. *Charles Thompson, (Secretary);* 23. *John* *Hancock, Mass.;* 24. *Francis Hopkinson, N.J.;* 25. *William Ellery, R.I.;* 26. *Edward Rutledge, S.C.;* 27. *Benjamin Franklin, Pa.;* 28. *Charles Carroll, Md.;* 29. *Richard Henry Lee, Va.;* 30. *George Read, Del.;* 31. *George Taylor, Pa.;* 32. *Stephen Hopkins, R.I.*

Members of the Continental Congress prepare to approve the Declaration of Independence.
■ **How would you describe the general appearance of this group?**

explaining Congress's action has become known to history as the **Declaration of Independence**.

A committee of five prepared the statement. Its members were Benjamin Franklin of Pennsylvania, John Adams of Massachusetts, Robert Livingston of New York, Roger Sherman of Connecticut, and Thomas Jefferson of Virginia. Jefferson was chosen to chair the committee.

Thomas Jefferson came to Philadelphia to attend the Second Continental Congress. After sessions of Congress each day, Jefferson spent the nights working on the Declaration of Independence. Sometimes other members of the committee brought suggestions. It was Thomas Jefferson, though, who was most responsible for the words, phrases, and ideas in this historic document. Congress received the committee's report on June 28. All the delegates except those from New York approved the Declaration of Independence on July 4. That is why we celebrate Independence Day on this date.

The News Spreads Congress ordered the Declaration of Independence printed and sent to Patriot officials, military units, and the press. On July 8, outside the Pennsylvania State House, the declaration was first read to the public. During the celebration that followed, people cheered, bells rang, and soldiers paraded.

Within a month, more than 25 newspapers had spread the words of the Declaration of Independence from New Hampshire to South Carolina. Ships carried copies of the declaration to Europe. It was read with interest by the British government and other governments in Europe.

The Importance of the Declaration The text of the Declaration of Independence is on the following pages. Although it is a short document, the effects of the declaration have been widespread. In 1776 it had an immediate effect on the undecided colonists. They had to choose between independence and loyalty to Great Britain. Probably most important, the declaration gave foreign nations that were enemies of Great Britain the opportunity to harm it by helping the new United States of America gain independence.

The Declaration of Independence is the best-known American document thoughout the world. People in colonies everywhere have used its ideas in support

Copies of the Declaration of Independence were hung up in public places for the colonists to read.
■ What were the colonists' reactions?

of their own movements toward independence. Here in the United States it has been a source of inspiration for people fighting for equal rights for all Americans. In 1776, it put into words the reasons for peoples' willingness to fight for independence. Yet, declaring independence left the task of winning independence.

CHECKUP

1. Why were battles fought at Ticonderoga and Bunker Hill?
2. Name two accomplishments of the Second Continental Congress.
3. Why did the Americans invade Canada?
4. How did Thomas Paine contribute to the drive for independence?

5. **Thinking Critically** If you had been a colonist, would you have been a Loyalist, a Patriot, or a neutral? Explain.

The Declaration of Independence

☆ ☆ ☆ ☆ ☆ ☆ ☆ ☆ ☆ ☆ ☆ ☆ ☆

Why the Declaration of Independence Was Issued
This paragraph states that it has become necessary for the American colonists to break their political ties with Great Britain, and that it is only proper to explain why they are taking this step. (One reason was that the colonists hoped to get help from other nations.)

The Purposes of Government
This paragraph is the very heart of the Declaration of Independence. It states that all men are born with equal claims to "life, liberty, and the pursuit of happiness." These rights, given by the Creator, are "unalienable," that is, they cannot be given away, nor can a government take them away.

In Congress, July 4, 1776

When, in the course of human events, it becomes necessary for one people to dissolve the political bands which have connected them with another, and to assume, among the powers of the earth, the separate and equal station to which the laws of nature and nature's God entitle them, a decent respect to the opinions of mankind requires that they should declare the causes which impel them to the separation.

We hold these truths to be self-evident; that all men are created equal, that they are endowed by their Creator with certain unalienable rights, that among these are life, liberty, and the pursuit of happiness. That to secure these rights, governments are instituted among men, deriving their just powers from the consent of the governed; that whenever any form of government becomes destructive of these ends, it is the right of the people to alter or to abolish it, and to institute new govern-

ment, laying its foundation on such principles, and organizing its powers in such form, as to them shall seem most likely to effect their safety and happiness. Prudence, indeed, will dictate that governments long established should not be changed for light and transient causes; and accordingly all experience hath shown that mankind are more disposed to suffer, while evils are sufferable, than to right themselves by abolishing the forms to which they are accustomed. But when a long train of abuses and usurpations, pursuing invariably the same object, evinces a design to reduce them under absolute despotism, it is their right, it is their duty, to throw off such government, and to provide new guards for their future security.

*S*uch has been the patient sufferance of these colonies; and such is now the necessity which constrains them to alter their former systems of government. The history of the present king of Great Britain is a history of repeated injuries and usurpations, all having in direct object the establishment of an absolute tyranny over these states. To prove this, let facts be submitted to a candid world.

He has refused his assent to laws the most wholesome and necessary for the public good.

He has forbidden his governors to pass laws of immediate and pressing importance, unless suspended in their operation till his assent should be obtained; and when so suspended, he has utterly neglected to attend to them.

He has refused to pass other laws for the accommodation of large districts of people, unless those people would relinquish the right of representation in the legislature, a right inestimable to them, and formidable to tyrants only.

He has called together legislative bodies at places unusual, uncomfortable, and distant from the depository of their public records, for the sole purpose of fatiguing them into compliance with his measures.

He has dissolved representative houses repeatedly, for opposing, with manly firmness, his invasions on the rights of the people.

He has refused, for a long time after such dissolutions, to cause others to be elected; whereby the legislative powers, incapable of annihilation, have returned to the people at large for their exercise; the state remaining, in the meantime, exposed to all the dangers of invasion from without and convulsions within.

The paragraph goes on to state that governments were created to protect these human rights. Whenever a government interferes with them, its citizens have the right as well as the duty to change or do away with the government. A government must be based on the consent of the governed. Changing or doing away with a government will be carried out, however, only after events have proved that the government has abused its powers.

The Charges Against the British King

Here the Declaration of Independence reviews the years between 1763 and 1776, stating that the colonists believed the king's government had many times denied their basic human rights. King George III and his government are charged with committing a long list of misdeeds. Because of these acts, the declaration states that the king is no longer entitled to rule the American colonies. He no longer has the consent of the governed.

He has endeavored to prevent the population of these states; for that purpose obstructing the laws for the naturalization of foreigners, refusing to pass others to encourage their migrations hither, and raising the conditions of new appropriations of lands.

He has obstructed the administration of justice, by refusing his assent to laws for establishing judiciary powers.

He has made judges dependent on his will alone for the tenure of their offices, and the amount and payment of their salaries.

He has erected a multitude of new offices, and sent hither swarms of officers to harass our people and eat out their substance.

He has kept among us, in times of peace, standing armies, without the consent of our legislatures.

He has affected to render the military independent of, and superior to, the civil power.

He has combined with others to subject us to a jurisdiction foreign to our constitution and unacknowledged by our laws, giving his assent to their acts of pretended legislation:

For quartering large bodies of armed troops among us;

For protecting them, by a mock trial, from punishment for any murders which they should commit on the inhabitants of these states;

For cutting off our trade with all parts of the world;

For imposing taxes on us without our consent;

For depriving us, in many cases, of the benefits of trial by jury;

For transporting us beyond seas, to be tried for pretended offenses;

For abolishing the free system of English laws in a neighboring province, establishing therein an arbitrary government, and enlarging its boundaries, so as to render it at once an example and fit instrument for introducing the same absolute rule into these colonies;

For taking away our charters, abolishing our most valuable laws, and altering fundamentally the forms of our governments;

For suspending our own legislatures, and declaring themselves invested with power to legislate for us in all cases whatsoever.

He has abdicated government here, by declaring us out of his protection and waging war against us.

He has plundered our seas, ravaged our coasts, burned our towns, and destroyed the lives of our people.

He is at this time transporting large armies of foreign mercenaries to complete the works of death, desolation, and tyranny already begun with circumstances of cruelty and perfidy scarcely paralleled in the most barbarous ages, and totally unworthy the head of a civilized nation.

He has constrained our fellow-citizens, taken captive on the high seas, to bear arms against their country, to become the executioners of their friends and brethren, or to fall themselves by their hands.

He has excited domestic insurrection among us, and has endeavored to bring on the inhabitants of our frontiers, the merciless Indian savages, whose known rule of warfare is an undistinguished destruction of all ages, sexes, and conditions.

*I*n every stage of these oppressions we have petitioned for redress in the most humble terms; our repeated petitions have been answered only by repeated injury. A prince whose character is thus marked by every act which may define a tyrant is unfit to be the ruler of a free people.

Nor have we been wanting in attentions to our British brethren. We have warned them, from time to time, of attempts by their legislature to extend an unwarrantable jurisdiction over us. We have reminded them of the circumstances of our emigration and settlement here. We have appealed to their native justice and magnanimity; and we have conjured them, by the ties of our common kindred, to disavow these usurpations, which would inevitably interrupt our connections and correspondence. They, too, have been deaf to the voice of justice and consanguinity. We must, therefore, acquiesce in the necessity which denounces our separation, and hold them, as we hold the rest of mankind, enemies in war; in peace, friends.

The Attempts to Obtain Justice
These two paragraphs state that the American colonists have asked the British king for justice. They have also appealed to the British people. Yet neither the king nor the British people have responded to the colonists' pleas.

*W*e, therefore, the representatives of the United States of America, in General Congress assembled, appealing to the Supreme Judge of the world for the rectitude of our intentions, do, in the name and by the authority of the good people of these colonies, solemnly publish and declare that these United Colonies are, and of right ought to be, free and independent states; that they are absolved from all allegiance to the British crown, and that all

The Colonies Declare Their Independence
This final paragraph actually proclaims independence. It also lists those things that the new United States of America may do as an independent country.

155

In the last sentence the signers pledge their lives and all they own to support the cause of independence. This was a serious matter, for as Benjamin Franklin said, "Now we must all hang together, or we will all hang separately." Still, they took the risk and signed the document that proclaimed to the world the independence of the United States of America.

political connection between them and the state of Great Britain is, and ought to be, totally dissolved; and that, as free and independent states, they have full power to levy war, conclude peace, contract alliances, establish commerce, and do all other acts and things which independent states may of right do. And, for the support of this declaration, with a firm reliance on the protection of Divine Providence, we mutually pledge to each other our lives, our fortunes, and our sacred honor.

John Hancock, President
(MASSACHUSETTS)

NEW HAMPSHIRE
Josiah Bartlett
William Whipple
Matthew Thornton

MASSACHUSETTS
John Adams
Samuel Adams
Robert Treat Paine
Elbridge Gerry

NEW YORK
William Floyd
Philip Livingston
Francis Lewis
Lewis Morris

RHODE ISLAND
Stephen Hopkins
William Ellery

NEW JERSEY
Richard Stockton
John Witherspoon
Francis Hopkinson
John Hart
Abraham Clark

PENNSYLVANIA
Robert Morris
Benjamin Rush
Benjamin Franklin
John Morton
George Clymer
James Smith
George Taylor
James Wilson
George Ross

DELAWARE
Caesar Rodney
George Read
Thomas McKean

MARYLAND
Samuel Chase
William Paca
Thomas Stone
*Charles Carroll of
  Carrollton*

VIRGINIA
George Wythe
Richard Henry Lee
Thomas Jefferson
Benjamin Harrison
Thomas Nelson, Jr.
Francis Lightfoot Lee
Carter Braxton

NORTH CAROLINA
William Hooper
Joseph Hewes
John Penn

SOUTH CAROLINA
Edward Rutledge
Thomas Heyward, Jr.
Thomas Lynch, Jr.
Arthur Middleton

CONNECTICUT
Roger Sherman
Samuel Huntington
William Williams
Oliver Wolcott

GEORGIA
Button Gwinnett
Lyman Hall
George Walton

Victories and Defeats

What major battles were fought between 1776 and 1778?

VOCABULARY

mercenary	**treaty of alliance**
Hessian	

The British Attack   In the spring of 1776, word came that an overwhelming British force was moving to attack New York City. The British had assembled 32,000 soldiers and 500 ships for this attack. Washington's Continental army had only 19,000 men. Nevertheless, he ordered the army south from Boston to meet the expected British attack.

British troops landed first on Staten Island in July. Later, 20,000 more came ashore on Long Island. They easily defeated the poorly trained American soldiers. Under cover of darkness and fog, the retreating Americans escaped to New York City.

It was at this time that Nathan Hale, a young Connecticut schoolmaster who had become a captain in the Continental army, volunteered to spy on British positions. Posing as a Dutch schoolmaster, he worked his way through the front lines. On his return with valuable information, Hale was captured, and a day later he was hanged as a spy. His last words are said to have been, "I only regret that I have but one life to lose for my country."

A Long Retreat   In September the advancing British drove the Continental army from New York City. After an indecisive battle at White Plains, General Washington ordered a retreat.

The Americans retreated all the way across New Jersey into Pennsylvania. This put the Delaware River between them and their enemies. If General Howe's troops had followed more closely, they might have won the war at this time. Expiring enlistments, desertions, and sickness had shrunk the Continental army to no more than 5,000 soldiers.

Instead of crushing this remnant, however, Howe ordered his army into winter quarters. Most of the British troops were housed in New York and New Jersey. In Trenton and several other communities, Howe stationed German soldiers who had been hired to fight for the British. People who serve for pay as soldiers in the army of a foreign country are known as **mercenaries**. These mercenaries were called **Hessians** because many of them came from the German state of Hesse.

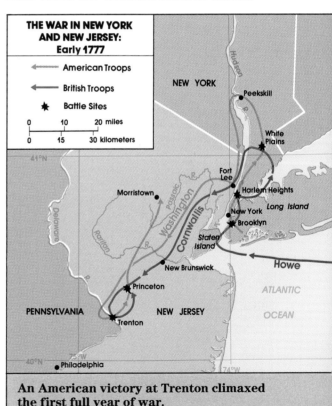

THE WAR IN NEW YORK AND NEW JERSEY: Early 1777

American Troops
British Troops
★ Battle Sites

0   10   20 miles
0   15   30 kilometers

NEW YORK

Peekskill

White Plains

Fort Lee

Morristown

Harlem Heights

New York   Long Island

Brooklyn

Staten Island

New Brunswick

Howe

Princeton

PENNSYLVANIA   NEW JERSEY

ATLANTIC OCEAN

Trenton

Philadelphia

An American victory at Trenton climaxed the first full year of war.
☐ Why, do you suppose, Washington took his troops into Pennsylvania?

A Christmas Victory   On December 25, 1776, the Delaware River was in full flood. Heavy sheets of ice spun and whirled on its wild surface. Yet on Christmas night, boatloads of shivering American soldiers crossed the river. The Continental army was about to make a surprise attack on Trenton, New Jersey.

By four o'clock in the morning, the army had crossed the river. It then began marching the 9 miles (14 km) to Trenton. The soldiers' wet muskets were useless, so Washington ordered, "Use the bayonet —I am resolved to take Trenton." The Continentals took Trenton, capturing about 900 Hessians and seizing valuable supplies.

News of the Christmas victory spread through the country. It was good news, because it came after a series of near disasters for the fighting Americans. Even more encouraging news came 8 days later when Washington won another surprise victory at Princeton, New Jersey.

After that battle, the Continental army marched to Morristown, New Jersey.

A Plan to Split the Colonies   In spite of Washington's successes in New Jersey, British generals thought they could deliver a knockout blow in 1777. They planned a campaign to invade New York State and seize the rich Hudson River valley. If successful, this campaign would cut off New England from the rest of the United States. It would put New York under British control and crush American spirits.

The campaign got under way as British General John Burgoyne (bėr goin') advanced south from Canada along the Lake Champlain route. Burgoyne had 7,000 men under his command. British Colonel Barry St. Leger (lej'ər) led a somewhat smaller force east from Lake Ontario toward Albany. The British plan also called for General Howe to send troops up the Hudson from New York City. All three forces were to meet near Albany.

General Washington directs his troops at the battle of Princeton.
■ **Based on the evidence in the picture, which army do you think had occupied the town at the beginning of the battle?**

The Night Ride of Sybil Ludington

Two years after Paul Revere made his ride, a 16-year-old girl named Sybil Ludington also made a night ride for the cause of independence.

She lived in New York State, just across the line from Connecticut. One rainy night in April 1777, an exhausted man rode up to the Ludington home. He brought word to Colonel Henry Ludington, Sybil's father, that the British had captured Danbury, Connecticut. Now the British soldiers were looting and burning homes.

Colonel Ludington, the militia commander, could see the red glow in the sky. Danbury was burning, but part of it could be saved if his men were assembled. But who could tell them to meet at his house? He would have to stay and organize them. The exhausted messenger could go no farther. Besides, the messenger knew nothing of the country roads where the militiamen lived.

Then Sybil spoke up. "I'll go, Father," she said.

"It will be a hard ride," her father warned. "There will be dangers." But Sybil was already out the door, running toward the stable. It took no more than a minute to get Star, her big bay horse, saddled and bridled.

Sybil Ludington rode hard through the night. She pounded on doors, shouting for the militiamen to assemble at her father's house. By the time she got home the next morning, she had ridden 40 miles (74 km). Nearly every militiaman had responded. Colonel Ludington led them to join other forces who drove the redcoats out of Danbury.

Highway signs today mark the road that Sybil Ludington traveled more than 200 years ago. A statue of Sybil and Star stands on the shore of Lake Gleneida, New York, not far from where they set out.

But General Howe, instead of ordering an advance up the Hudson, took most of his troops by sea to a point near Philadelphia. By this time Philadelphia had become America's largest city and was the meeting place of the Continental Congress. Apparently Howe thought he could capture Philadelphia and still have time to take part in the Hudson Valley campaign.

Howe's troops did capture Philadelphia after defeating Washington's army in the battle of Brandywine. The Continental Congress had to flee, first to Lancaster, Pennsylvania, and then farther west to

159

York. When the Americans tried to retake Philadelphia, the British beat them back at Germantown. But Howe's army was never able to go back and take part in the Hudson Valley campaign.

Saratoga   Meanwhile, General Burgoyne, advancing through the forests of New York State, was in trouble. His was an unusual army. It was made up of British soldiers, Canadians, Hessians, and Indian allies. Though Fort Ticonderoga surrendered to Burgoyne, he met stronger resistance as he moved farther south.

General Philip Schuyler and General Horatio Gates had organized their militiamen into an able fighting force. General Washington sent a company of sharpshooters under Daniel Morgan to help the American northern army. In August, Americans turned back an expedition sent by Burgoyne to seize supplies stored at Bennington, Vermont. Nearly 1,000 of his men were killed, wounded, captured, or missing at the end of the battle of Bennington. To make matters worse, Burgoyne learned that American resistance had driven Colonel St. Leger's small army back to its base at Oswego.

In September the American militiamen turned back an attack by Burgoyne's desperate army at Saratoga, New York. Three weeks later the militiamen defeated the British once more. Now Burgoyne's army was nearly surrounded. His Indian allies had deserted him. Supplies were almost gone. Faced with these conditions, Burgoyne had no choice but to give up. He surrendered the remainder of his army on October 17, 1777.

General Burgoyne surrenders to General Gates at Saratoga in 1777.
■ How can you tell, without knowing any of the story, which side is the winner here and which is the loser?

detail, Yale University Art Gallery

The Turning Point   Burgoyne's surrender was the turning point in the War for Independence. Although there were hard years ahead, American spirits rose with this victory and the capture of a major British army. It seemed that the Americans now had a very good chance to win. With this in mind, the French government decided to help openly in the American struggle against the British.

In 1776 the Second Continental Congress had sent a commission to France. Among its members was Benjamin Franklin. Franklin was a key figure in persuading the French finance minister to secretly help the Americans with money and supplies. Then came news of Burgoyne's surrender at Saratoga. Four months later, France and the United States signed a **treaty of alliance**. The next year Spain pledged its support to the American struggle for Independence. In 1780 Holland joined the growing list of Great Britain's enemies.

Foreign Aid   Wars cost money, and the Americans had trouble financing their struggle for independence. Congress was powerless to tax the states or individuals. Though the states voluntarily furnished a small amount of money, it was never enough. To pay for the war, Congress had to issue paper money and to borrow. Robert Morris, who served as American superintendent of finance, lent part of his own fortune when money was needed. Haym Salomon, an immigrant from Poland, lent so much money to Congress that he ruined himself financially.

Loans and gifts from other countries were part of the aid the Americans received during the war. France gave the most financial help. In some ways America's fight for independence was another war between France and Great Britain.

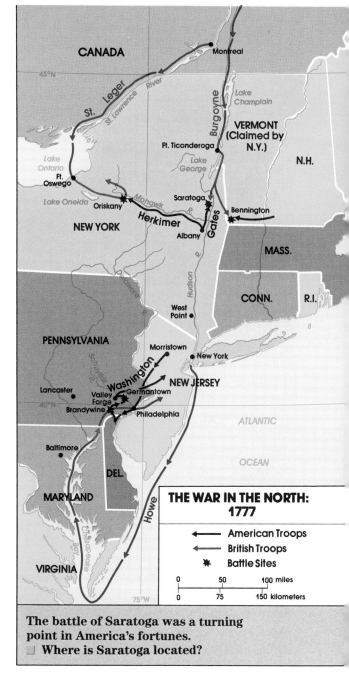

The battle of Saratoga was a turning point in America's fortunes.
■ Where is Saratoga located?

The two nations fought each other in several parts of the world. This kept Great Britain from giving its entire attention to putting down the American colonial rebellion. France furnished the United States with tons of equipment, thousands of soldiers, and the help of its large naval fleet because it hoped to profit from trade with the new nation.

Still, foreign aid did not end the War for Independence immediately. For 6

161

years after Burgoyne's surrender in 1777, the war continued. During these years Americans experienced many hardships and bitter disappointments.

Valley Forge   One of the hardest times for the Continental army came during the winter following Burgoyne's surrender. General Howe's British soldiers were warm, well-fed, and comfortable in Philadelphia. Conditions were different at Valley Forge, only a little more than 20 miles (32 km) from Philadelphia. The Continental army camped there for the winter of 1777–1778.

The Continental camp was on a low plateau, already cold and windswept when the troops arrived in December. Washington later said, "You might have tracked the army to Valley Forge by the blood of their feet." Ice and frozen ground had cut through the soldiers' worn shoes and boots. The men lived in tents until small huts were built at Valley Forge. But the huts were drafty, sunless, and damp inside, bringing on sickness and infection among the soldiers on the snow-covered plateau.

Food was always in short supply during that terrible winter. Soap was also scarce. Men could not wash their clothes or their bodies. This resulted in a tormenting itch. Thousands of men deserted, and more might have done so had they been strong enough to leave the camp. By spring the ranks of the Continental army had shrunk to fewer than 4,000 soldiers.

Without Washington's courage and strength of character, the Continental army might have disappeared completely. In the spring, news of the French alliance raised the spirits of the discouraged men. Fresh clothing, more plentiful food, and money to pay the soldiers brought an upsurge in morale. As the army prepared for

The winter at Valley Forge was bitter.
■ What, do you think, were the single most valuable items of clothing to a Continental soldier at Valley Forge?

its summer campaigns, new recruits entered the camp. The ranks of the Continental army increased, and the fight for independence continued.

CHECKUP

1. Why were the victories at Trenton and Princeton important?
2. Describe the British plan to divide the colonies.
3. Why might Burgoyne's surrender at Saratoga be considered a turning point of the war?
4. Why was the winter at Valley Forge a difficult time for the Continental army?
5. **Thinking Critically** Why do you think other countries gave aid to the American colonies?

Independence!

When did the United States gain its independence?

Warfare at Sea   In 1775, Congress authorized the formation of an American navy. Though it had too few ships to fight as a fleet, single ships and their crews fought hard against the British. John Paul Jones was one of the outstanding naval officers. He specialized in sinking or seizing British merchant ships in their home waters.

In 1779, Jones fought a now famous naval battle off the English coast with the British warship *Serapis*. Jones commanded the *Bonhomme Richard*. The first part of the fight went against him and his ship. But when the British commander asked if he wanted to surrender, Jones replied, "I have not yet begun to fight." With renewed determination, he ordered his crew to continue to fire and finally forced the captain of the *Serapis* to surrender.

In addition to the regular navy, Congress and some of the states authorized **privateers** to make war on British commercial shipping. Privateers were privately owned vessels especially built to attack and capture enemy merchant ships. About 2,000 American privateers sailed the high seas during the War for Independence. They captured nearly 600 British merchant ships. Because of the

In 1779, John Paul Jones and his crew on the *Bonhomme Richard*, along with two French ships, fought a vicious four-hour sea battle with the *Serapis* and another British ship off the east coast of England.
■ Why was America's navy more active in English waters than at home?

damage done by privateers and the regular American navy, British merchants brought increasing pressure on Parliament to bring the war to an end.

War in the West   In the fall of 1777 George Rogers Clark was a militia leader living at Fort Harrod in Kentucky. At that time Kentucky was still part of Virginia. Clark asked Governor Patrick Henry of Virginia to let him lead an expedition against the British in the west. The British were holding many of the forts once owned by France, near the Great Lakes. From these forts the British, aided by Loyalists and Indian allies, were making attacks on western settlements. Their goal was to take over the entire region that lay to the west of the Appalachian Mountains.

Patrick Henry liked the idea and made Clark a colonel. In May 1778, Clark took command of 175 militiamen from Virginia and Kentucky. They traveled down the Ohio River almost to the Mississippi, then marched northwestward. On July 4 the daring expedition captured Kaskaskia, originally a French settlement in the Illinois country. With the help of the French settlers, Colonel Clark's men took control of Cahokia, Vincennes, and other settlements in the region.

But the British had no intention of withdrawing from the Illinois country. Colonel Henry Hamilton, the British lieutenant governor at Detroit, led an attack on Vincennes, and recaptured it. But British occupation of the former French fort lasted only a short time. In February 1779, Clark gathered 150 men at Kaskaskia. He led them toward Vincennes, often through swamps and icy streams. His surprise attack left Colonel Hamilton with no choice but to surrender.

Clark's brilliant campaign left Americans in control of the vast territory north of the Ohio River from the Appalachian Mountains to the Mississippi River. When peace came at the end of the War for Independence, American diplomats would argue that this region, which became known as the **Northwest Territory**, should be part of the new United States.

Action in New Jersey   While George Rogers Clark was winning in the west, New York and New Jersey became the scene of action in the east. General Henry Clinton replaced General Howe as commander of the British army in Philadelphia. Clinton learned that a French fleet was sailing for America and was probably headed for New York. Therefore, he decided to move his army to New York.

As the British marched across New Jersey, Washington ordered an attack at Monmouth. It was during this battle, fought under a blazing summer sun, that Mary Ludwig Hays, the wife of a soldier, won her place in American history. During the fighting, she carried water in a pitcher to the soldiers, who gratefully nicknamed her Molly Pitcher. Later, when her husband suffered a heatstroke, she took his place in a gun crew.

The Continental army fought well at Monmouth, but there was no decisive victory. Clinton's army left the battlefield and marched to New York. Washington led his army northward and took up a position along the Hudson River at White Plains, north of New York City. The presence of the Continental troops threatened the British and held them in this area for most of the remainder of the war.

War in the South   Late in 1778, British officials decided that their main military effort should be in the southern colonies. The British believed that there were more Loyalists in the south than in the north.

British leaders also felt they could use their naval strength to better advantage along the southern coast. British ships sailed from the north and, with the aid of Loyalists, captured the port of Savannah, Georgia. Within a year all of Georgia was under British control.

In 1780 Clinton's army and a British fleet forced the surrender of Charleston, South Carolina. The surrender of Charleston was the biggest American disaster of the entire War for Independence. More than 5,000 American soldiers and huge amounts of supplies were captured by the British. Many of the Patriot leaders in the area were seized.

General Clinton turned over command of the British southern campaign to General Charles Cornwallis in June 1780. Clinton sailed back to New York with 4,500 of his troops. But before sailing, he sent a long report to the British war office in London. In the report Clinton said, "I venture to assert that there are few men in South Carolina who are not our prisoners or in arms with us."

Guerrilla Warfare As it turned out, Clinton's report was an exaggeration. There were plenty of fighting Patriots left in South Carolina. Among them was Francis Marion, a genius at **guerrilla**, or hit-and-run, warfare. Marion's exploits earned him the name *Swamp Fox* because he conducted surprise attacks from secret bases in the Carolina swamps. Andrew Pickens and Thomas Sumter carried out attacks similar to Marion's. The three guerrilla leaders struck British outposts, cut supply lines, and attacked small detachments of British troops and Loyalists. These tactics weakened the British southern campaigns by pinning down regular troops.

In October 1780 a hastily gathered force of 900 American fighters won a deci-

Francis Marion leads a band of guerrillas across the Pee Dee River to harass the British in South Carolina.
◼ Why would Marion want his soldiers to bring their hunting dogs along?

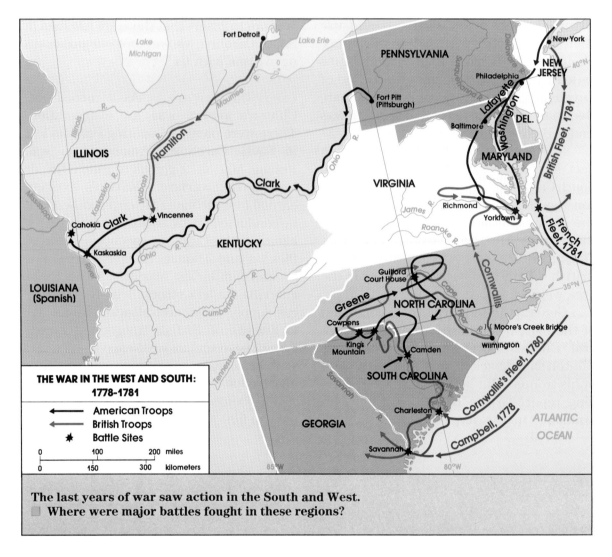

THE WAR IN THE WEST AND SOUTH: 1778-1781

← American Troops
← British Troops
★ Battle Sites

| 0 | 100 | 200 miles |
| 0 | 150 | 300 kilometers |

The last years of war saw action in the South and West.
Where were major battles fought in these regions?

sive battle at Kings Mountain, on the western border between North Carolina and South Carolina. These western fighters trapped 1,100 Loyalists led by British Major Patrick Ferguson, on top of the mountain. Their accurate shooting turned back bayonet charges by the Loyalists. Ferguson was killed, and his entire force was either killed or captured.

The main Continental army in the Carolinas met with less success than did the guerrilla and western fighters. After the army suffered a bloody defeat at Camden, South Carolina, Washington sent General Nathanael Greene of Rhode Island to take command. Greene promised no miracles. "We fight, get beat, rise, and fight again," he said. For a time, that is what happened. When Cornwallis pursued him, Greene took his army across the Dan River into Virginia.

In the spring of 1781, Greene moved into the Carolinas again and captured a number of smaller British outposts. This convinced General Cornwallis that British control could not be restored in the Carolinas while Virginia remained a supply and training base for the Americans. Cornwallis decided to remedy this situation by leading his army into Virginia.

166

Treason and Mutiny   In the fall of 1780, the news that General Benedict Arnold had committed **treason** shocked all Americans. The crime of treason is that of making war against one's country or aiding its enemies. A person who commits treason is called a **traitor**.

In 1780 Washington placed Arnold in command of West Point on the Hudson River. This fort guarded against a British advance up the river from New York City. Arnold had shown great courage and ability as an officer. Yet Arnold, who was deep in debt, thought Congress had not rewarded him sufficiently. Arnold offered to turn this key fort over to the British in exchange for a large sum of money and a commission as a brigadier general. The plot was stopped and Arnold himself escaped into British lines.

In 1781 at their camp at Morristown, New Jersey, the Pennsylvania soldiers **mutinied**, that is, rebelled against their officers. The soldiers had not been paid for a year. Many claimed they had enlisted only for 3 years, not for as long as the war lasted. The problem was settled by promising part of the back pay and releasing from service many of the men who claimed they had enlisted for only 3 years.

Surrender at Yorktown   During the summer of 1781, Washington and the French General Rochambeau (rô sham bō′) were planning an attack on New York City. Then came word that Cornwallis had taken his army to Yorktown, Virginia. Yorktown was located on a small peninsula in the Chesapeake (ches′ ə pēk) Bay. Cornwallis felt safe there as long as the

General Cornwallis's army surrenders to the Americans at Yorktown in October 1781.
▪ **Do you think this picture was painted by an eyewitness to the British surrender? Why or why not?**

Yale University Art Gallery

Heroes of the Revolution

One of the ways in which Americans have honored military and civilian heroes of the Revolution is to name counties after them. George Washington's name is found in more counties than is the name of any other individual. Thirty-one states have counties named Washington in honor of the commander in chief of the Continental army. Thomas Jefferson ranks second to Washington, with 26 counties named Jefferson. Benjamin Franklin ranks third. Twenty-three states have counties named Franklin.

Virginia has a Patrick County and a Henry County, both named for Patrick Henry. Eight other states have Henry counties named for the great Virginia patriot. Seventeen states have Marion counties to commemorate the Swamp Fox. Nine states have Knox counties, named for Henry Knox, who supervised the removal of Ticonderoga's cannons to the heights outside Boston. Nine states also have honored Daniel Morgan, the commander of sharpshooters, by naming counties after him.

Americans have remembered that foreign heroes came to fight in the War for Independence. Eleven states have Fayette counties and 6 have Lafayette counties, making a total of 17 named in honor of the gallant young French officer. Seven states have Pulaski counties, named for the Polish hero and cavalry commander who perished in the fight for Savannah. Six counties are named for Johann Kalb, also known as Baron de Kalb. Born in Germany, he came to America and gave his life charging the enemy at the battle of Camden, South Carolina.

This is only a partial account of counties named for heroes of the Revolution. What is the origin of the name of your county?

British navy could reach him with more soldiers and supplies. But a French fleet under Admiral François de Grasse (gräs), sailed from the West Indies to drive British ships from the Chesapeake.

Washington and Rochambeau hurried their armies southward to join troops already in Virginia. Under Washington's command they surrounded Yorktown on land. With the French fleet blocking the mouth of the Chesapeake, Cornwallis was trapped. On October 19, 1781, he surrendered his force of about 8,000 soldiers and sailors. The war, however, continued for more than a year after the surrender.

The Peace Treaty Formal negotiations for a peace treaty began at Paris in September 1782. It took more than a year before agreement was reached. The peace treaty was signed at Paris on September 3, 1783, and formally approved by the American Congress the following March.

Great Britain recognized the independence of the United States in the Treaty of Paris. The new country's boundaries were the Mississippi River on the west, Florida on the south, and the Great Lakes on the north. In the treaty, Congress agreed to recommend to the states that property that had been taken from Loyalists be returned, but most states did not return their lands. Britain agreed to let fishing fleets from the United States fish off the Grand Banks of Newfoundland.

Women in the Revolution It would be wrong to think that it was only the fighting men of the Continental and French armies and navies who won independence for the new United States. Other groups made important contributions to victory. Women played a major role. Some managed farms and shops while husbands, brothers, and fathers went off to war.

Molly Pitcher brought pitchers of water to American soldiers.
■ What is Molly Pitcher shown doing?

Other women helped more directly by following the armies in the field or in camp. They washed, cooked, and sewed for the soldiers. They nursed the sick and cared for the wounded in makeshift hospitals. In fact, women were considered an essential part of eighteenth-century armies.

It was not unusual for women to work as part of a gun crew, as Molly Pitcher did. (See page 164.) Margaret Corbin, the 25-year-old wife of John Corbin, took over his position at a small cannon during the American retreat across New Jersey in November 1776. She was badly wounded. Congress, recognizing that her wounds would leave her crippled, awarded her a pension of half a soldier's pay each year for the rest of her life.

A few women distinguished themselves in unusual ways during revolutionary times. Phillis Wheatley was bought directly off a slave ship from Africa. She became noted for her poetry. One of her poems was about General George Washington, and she was invited to visit his headquarters at Cambridge in 1776. Deborah Sampson dressed in men's clothes, served as an American soldier, and won a pension from Congress. "Number 355" was an American spy in New York. No one knew her name, but she was one of the most valuable agents the Americans had.

The Help of Other Groups   Blacks also did essential work on the home front and with the fighting armies. Crispus Attucks, a black sailor, has been called "the first casualty of the American Revolution."

Once fighting began, blacks and whites together served in the militia and the Continental army. Peter Salem, Prince Hall, and Salem Poor were black militiamen at the battle of Bunker Hill. One historian has written that two thirds of a Rhode Island regiment at Yorktown were blacks.

Slaves were encouraged to join the Continental army because some Patriot commanders promised them their freedom. British commanders in Virginia made the same kind of promises. Though these promises were sometimes broken, many slaves won their freedom.

In New York most tribes in the Iroquois confederacy supported the British. But the Oneidas and some of the Tuscaroras aided the American cause. In the west nearly all the Indians fought alongside the British. George Rogers Clark had Indian guides and some Indian support.

Many blacks fought in a Rhode Island regiment during the War for Independence.
■ **Do you think the fighters were fighting for their freedom as well?**

detail, Rhode Island Historical Society

George Washington spent much of his life at Mount Vernon, Virginia.
■ **Why, do you think, would tourists visit Mount Vernon?**

Washington Returns Home The Treaty of Paris allowed British troops to remain in New York until November 1784. In that month the last British soldiers left.

A few days later, General George Washington rode into the city with the governor of New York at his side. On December 4, Washington bade goodbye to his officers at Fraunces Tavern. His journey back to Mount Vernon was a triumphal procession, as cheering Americans honored the man who had done so much to win independence for their country. On the way, Washington passed through Annapolis, where Congress was meeting.

Two days before Christmas, 1784, Washington appeared before Congress to resign his commission as commander in chief. In doing so, he said, "I now take leave of all the employments of public life." But this was not to be. After a few years of peace and quiet at Mount Vernon, Washington would answer his country's call for service in another role.

CHECKUP

1. Why was George Rogers Clark's campaign in the west important?
2. What kind of military tactics proved successful in South Carolina? Why?
3. What events brought about the surrender of Cornwallis at Yorktown?
4. List the provisions of the Treaty of Paris.

5. **Thinking Critically** Do you think the Americans would have continued with the war if they had lost at Yorktown? Explain.

Using Source Material

PRIMARY AND SECONDARY SOURCES

Documents, letters, artifacts, and books written by historians are some of the material available for the study of history. Historians must be able to determine whether a source is primary or secondary material. Knowledge of the type of source and its origin is very helpful in evaluating the source and understanding its contribution to history.

Primary source material is composed of original documents, speeches, eyewitness accounts such as those recorded in letters or diaries, and artifacts including photographs and some paintings. Primary source materials are firsthand accounts, recorded at the time an event occurred.

Secondary source material is made up of generalizations by historians who have studied primary source materials. Secondary sources are not firsthand observations but are descriptions of events based on what others have written. This textbook is an example of secondary source material. However, it includes some primary source materials.

Below are two selections of historical material. Read the selections and see if you can distinguish the primary source material from the secondary source material.

1. . . . My situation is inexpressibly distressing, to see the winter fast approaching upon a naked army, the time of their services within a few weeks of expiring, and not provision yet made for such important events. Added to this, the military chest is totally exhausted; the paymaster has not a single dollar in hand: the commissary-general assures me he has strained his credit to the utmost for the subsistence of the army. The quartermaster general is precisely in the same situation; and the greater part of the army are in a state not far from mutiny . . . if the evil is not immediately remedied . . . the army must absolutely break up.

2. From his headquarters on the edge of Morristown Common, the commander in chief watched his army settle itself in long huts on the south slope of Thimble Mountain, ready to face still another winter in the field. Despite the lingering glow of Trenton and Princeton, the future must have appeared ominous to him, for all his never-failing outward calm. Smallpox broke out, and Washington had to set up isolation areas and struggle with the then almost impossible problem of camp sanitation.

The first selection is part of a letter George Washington wrote to the Congress. It is a primary source. The second is part of a historian's description of the winter the Continental army spent in Morristown, New Jersey. It is a secondary source.

SKILLS PRACTICE

On a separate sheet of paper, write **P** if the source is primary and **S** if it is secondary.

1. Thomas Paine's pamphlet *Common Sense*
2. The authors' description of Valley Forge on page 162
3. The Declaration of Independence
4. A composition you might write about the signers of the Declaration of Independence
5. The diary of a soldier during the American Revolution
6. A letter written by Martha Washington to George Washington
7. A picture painted last year of Benjamin Franklin
8. A musket used in the American Revolution

MAIN IDEAS

1. Before war was officially declared, conflicts took place at Ticonderoga, Bunker Hill, Montreal, Quebec, and Charleston.
2. Only about one third of the American people actively supported the Revolution.
3. The battles of Trenton and Princeton were great victories for the Americans.
4. Burgoyne's surrender after the battle of Saratoga marked the turning point of the war.
5. Foreign nations, particularly France, helped the United States in its struggle for independence.
6. The War for Independence officially ended with the signing of the Treaty of Paris in 1783.
7. The United States boundaries were the Mississippi River, Florida, and the Great Lakes.

VOCABULARY REVIEW

On a separate sheet of paper, write the letter of the term next to the number of its definition.

a. treaty of alliance   **f.** mutiny
b. Tory   **g.** treason
c. privateer   **h.** mercenary
d. guerrilla   **i.** *Common Sense*
e. Northwest Territory   **j.** Patriot

1. A rebellion against military leaders
2. A member of a political party that supported King George III of England
3. A hired soldier in the army of a foreign country
4. A region lying west of the Appalachian Mountains
5. A pamphlet
6. An agreement by two or more countries to fight a common enemy
7. A hit-and-run fighter
8. A civilian ship fitted for war
9. A colonist who sought American independence from England
10. Aiding the enemies of one's country

CHAPTER CHECKUP

1. What was George Washington's role in the American Revolution?
2. How did the seizure of Fort Ticonderoga help the Continental cause?
3. Why is the Declaration of Independence an important document?
4. What role did women play in the War for Independence?
5. How did the Revolution help the slaves?
6. **Thinking Critically** Which battle of the war do you think was most important to the American cause?
7. **Thinking Critically** Why do you think the poorly trained and outfitted Continental army was able to defeat the British army?

APPLYING KNOWLEDGE

1. Make a chart listing the advantages and disadvantages that the Americans and the British faced during the War for Independence.
2. Make a drawing to illustrate Thomas Paine's *Common Sense*.
3. Imagine that the colonists had not won the Revolution. Write an essay explaining what life would be like in the United States today.
4. Write an essay explaining your viewpoint on the following: Suppose that Country A ruled and dominated Country B, and that Country B wished to be free and independent. Suppose the United States was in a position to give Country B the necessary help to achieve independence. Answer the following questions: Should the United States help Country B? What information might you want to have before answering that question? When should a nation mind its own business and refrain from becoming involved? What situations have arisen in America's history where the question of becoming involved or remaining neutral has been an issue?

8 A Government for the New Nation 1777–1791

The First Union of States

What problems did the central government face under the Articles of Confederation?

VOCABULARY

confederation	Shays's Rebellion
Articles of Confederation	Northwest Ordinance

Alexander Hamilton   A hurricane seldom brings anyone good fortune. And yet a hurricane proved to be lucky for Alexander Hamilton, who was born in the British West Indies.

When young Alexander was 11, his mother died. His father's business had been ruined, and Alexander soon had to give up school. He was working as a clerk in a store in 1772 when, in the late summer, a hurricane swept across the West Indian island of St. Croix (kroi). In a letter, the 15-year-old youth wrote of the damage that had been done to the island by the hurricane. The letter was so impressively written that a local newspaper published it.

Several plantation owners on the island read Hamilton's letter. They decided that the boy should be sent to the mainland to college. With their help, Alexander Hamilton went to New York. He enrolled in what is now Columbia University.

From Aide to Legislator   The War for Independence interrupted Alexander Hamilton's education. His skill at writing won him a position as secretary and aide to General George Washington. Later, at Yorktown, Hamilton commanded troops and led a daring charge against the British.

After the War for Independence ended, Hamilton practiced law in New York. Beginning in 1782 he served a term in Congress. However, he did not seek another term because he did not think the central government was strong enough.

The Articles of Confederation   Plans for a new government had begun at the time of the Declaration of Independence. When Richard Henry Lee had introduced his resolution for independence in 1776, he had urged the Second Continental Congress to form a government for the 13 states. Lee wanted a **confederation**, that is, a loose union of independent states organized to take action on a few — but only a few — matters.

After months of discussion, the delegates agreed in November 1777 on the **Articles of Confederation**. This document listed the powers of the central government and the powers of the states in the new United States of America.

Delegates to the Constitutional Convention bring their session to a successful ending.
■ When did the Constitutional Convention take place?

EVENTS IN OUR COUNTRY

1781 Articles of Confederation go into effect

1786 Shays's Rebellion

1787 Northwest Ordinance passed/Constitutional Convention meets

1788 Constitution goes into effect

1791 Bill of Rights passed

1782

1784

1786

1788

1790

EVENTS ELSEWHERE

1789 Martin Klaproth discovers uranium

1788 Bread riots in France

1787 English settlement for freed slaves founded in Sierra Leone

1786 Lord Cornwallis becomes Governor-General of India

1785 Russians settle the Aleutian Isles

1784 Serfdom abolished in Denmark

The 13 states were slow to approve the Articles of Confederation. Some leaders felt the states should run their own affairs independently. They feared that any kind of central government would limit the power of the states.

There was one other major reason for delay. Several states claimed land west of the Appalachian Mountains. The Articles of Confederation provided that the new central government should control these lands. But some states were reluctant to give up their western land claims.

Western Land Claims When the new government was formed, some states had no claims or very weak claims to western territories. These states felt that if the

This postage stamp was issued on the 200th anniversary of the drafting of the Articles of Confederation.
■ When was the stamp issued?

stronger claims of other states were recognized, those other states would become too large and powerful.

Leaders in Maryland in particular feared this development. Therefore, they refused to approve the Articles of Confederation until all states agreed to yield their western land claims to the central government. Since all 13 states had to approve the Articles of Confederation before they became effective, Maryland's refusal delayed the first union of the states.

One by one, the states agreed to give up their western land claims. New York was first, partly because its claims to western lands were weak. Virginia probably had the strongest claims of any state. But Virginia, too, promised to turn over its western lands to the central government. Maryland then was satisfied. In 1781 it became the last of the 13 states to approve the Articles of Confederation.

The Confederation Government The United States operated under the Articles of Confederation for 8 years. Congress was the major part of the Confederation government.

The government during that time differed greatly from our government today.

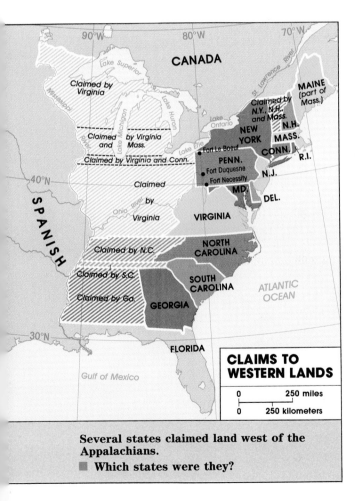

CLAIMS TO WESTERN LANDS

0   250 miles
0   250 kilometers

Several states claimed land west of the Appalachians.
■ Which states were they?

Depending on its population, each state had from two to seven representatives in Congress. However, each state had only one vote, so small states had as much power as larger ones in the Confederation Congress. Furthermore, it took a two-thirds majority, or 9 states, to pass important legislation. Thus any 5 states could block action by Congress.

Congress under the Articles of Confederation had several important powers. It could wage war and make peace. Under its guidance the United States finally won independence in the peace treaty signed in Paris. In addition, the Confederation Congress could conduct negotiations between the United States and foreign countries. It could control trade with Indian tribes. It could, and did, organize a mail service. And it could borrow money in the name of the United States. Under this power, Congress borrowed heavily from foreign countries, not only during the War for Independence but also in later years.

Weaknesses   Because of its limited powers, the Confederation government had a difficult time. It lacked power to regulate trade and commerce between states or between states and foreign countries. Each state could, therefore, arrange its own trade regulations. The Confederation Congress had no power to tax the states or the people. It could only *ask* the states for money. Neither did it have power to draft people for an army. It could only *ask* the states for people to help protect the nation. Furthermore, the Confederation government lacked a system of courts in which those who broke national laws could be tried.

Confusion spread through the money system because each state issued its own coins. Some states issued paper money, which was unstable in value. In 1786,

storekeepers in New Jersey closed their shops and would not accept paper money as payment for their goods.

In the same year a serious uprising took place in Massachusetts. Times were hard, and many farmers could not pay their taxes and other debts. When their lands were seized for overdue taxes, the farmers rebelled. Led by Daniel Shays, a Revolutionary War veteran, the farmers armed themselves. They refused to let the courts, which were going to take away their lands, convene. They even attacked an arsenal. The Massachusetts militia had to be called out to put down what is known as **Shays's Rebellion**. Congress, lacking the power to keep order, stood by helplessly.

The American negotiators of the Treaty of Paris in 1783 posed for this group portrait. The part that was supposed to show the British negotiators was never completed.
■ Why might the British have refused to pose?

The Stars and Stripes

The Stars and Stripes, or Old Glory, as our flag is often called, is a symbol of our nation. It represents the land, the people, the government, and the ideals of the United States. The flag was the inspiration for our national anthem, "The Star-Spangled Banner," written by Francis Scott Key in 1814.

Our flag has a long history. It has grown as our nation has grown. In colonial times many different flags were carried on ceremonial occasions. During the War for Independence, Americans fought under various banners. For example, one New England flag had a pine tree and the words *An Appeal to Heaven*. Another flag pictured a rattlesnake with 13 rattles and the slogan *Don't Tread Upon Me*.

PINE TREE FLAG (1775)

FIRST NAVY JACK (1775)

George Washington's army carried the Continental Colours, which had 13 alternating red and white stripes and the British flag in the corner. The Bennington

CONTINENTAL COLOURS (1775)

BENNINGTON FLAG (1777)

flag also had 13 alternating red and white stripes, but the 13 stars were arranged around the number 76. This number stood for 1776, the year in which the colonists declared their independence. None of these flags, however, was a national flag.

On June 14, 1777, the Second Continental Congress enacted a flag resolution. It said that the flag of the United States would have 13 alternating red and white stripes and 13 white stars on a field of blue, but it did not describe how the stars should be arranged.

Who designed the first national flag? One story tells of a group of women in Portsmouth, New Hampshire, making the first flag from ballroom dresses. This flag was supposedly flown on John Paul Jones's ship, the *Ranger*, when it went into battle. Another story says that Francis Hopkinson, a member of the naval committee and a signer of the Declaration of

Independence, designed the first flag. The best-known story is of George Washington's visit to Betsy Ross, a Philadelphia seamstress, and his request that she make the first national flag. However, there is no real proof that any one of these stories is true. The origin of our national flag is still a mystery.

Although the designs varied, the number of stars and stripes on the flag remained the same until 1795. In that year, Congress passed a new flag resolution. It stated that there should be 15 stars and 15 stripes because two new states (Vermont and Kentucky) had joined the Union. The plan was to add a new star and a new stripe for each new state. This soon became impossible as the nation grew larger.

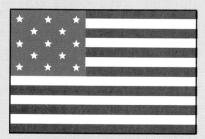

FIRST NATIONAL FLAG (1777)

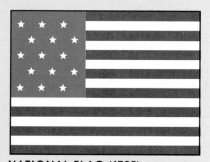

NATIONAL FLAG (1795)

By 1817 five more states had joined the Union. Realizing that the flag would keep increasing in size because of the number of stripes, Congress passed the

Act to Establish the Flag in 1818. The new flag was to have 13 stripes, 7 red and 6 white, and as many stars as there were states. The 13 stripes represented the 13 original colonies. A star was to be added for each new state on July 4 following the state's admission to the Union. But the act still did not describe how the stars were to be arranged. The Great Star Flag of 1818 displayed 20 stars in the shape of a large star.

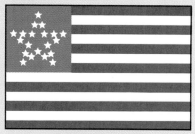

GREAT STAR FLAG (1818)

Since then, orders by Congress or the President have set the arrangement of the stars. At times the stars have been in even rows or in staggered rows, depending on how many states were in the Union at a given time. Our flag has been changed 24 times since 1818.

The present flag has 50 five-pointed stars in staggered rows. It has been in use since 1960. To honor our flag, Congress declared June 14 as Flag Day in 1949. June 14 was chosen because the first flag resolution was passed on this date.

NATIONAL FLAG (1960)

Angry farmers, under the informal command of Daniel Shays, closed the courts in western Massachusetts in 1786. How did this upheaval reveal a weakness of the Confederation?

Congress was equally weak in its dealings with other countries. After the war, Great Britain refused to enact trade treaties with the United States. Moreover, it kept its soldiers on American territory at western forts and trading posts such as Detroit and Fort Niagara. This action was contrary to the Treaty of Paris. Still, the Confederation Congress could do little except protest.

Spain had been an ally of the United States for a time during the War for Independence. Nevertheless, after the war it denied western Americans the right to ship their products through the port of New Orleans. From France, Thomas Jefferson reported that the government there paid little attention to any action of the Confederation Congress. Thus, even though the Confederation Congress was authorized to deal with foreign countries, it had trouble gaining respect abroad for the new United States.

The Confederation's Accomplishments

The Confederation government was not entirely unsuccessful. It directed the War for Independence to a successful conclusion, and it held the country together for 6 years following that war. Its most lasting accomplishment was the passage of the **Northwest Ordinance** in 1787. An ordinance is a law.

The Northwest Ordinance set up a system for governing the Northwest Territory. It also provided a series of steps through which this territory could be divided into three, four, or even five states and admitted to the Union. For residents of this territory and the later states, the ordinance guaranteed public support of education, trial by jury, and freedom of worship.

Significantly, the ordinance declared that any states formed from the territory would be equal to any of the existing states in all respects. Finally, the law prohibited slavery in the territory.

Washington Fears a Coming Crisis

In the summer of 1786, George Washington received a letter from John Jay. Jay, a New Yorker, had once been president of the Continental Congress. Now he was the secretary of foreign affairs for the Confederation government. "I am uneasy and apprehensive [nervous]," wrote Jay, "more so than during the war." He feared

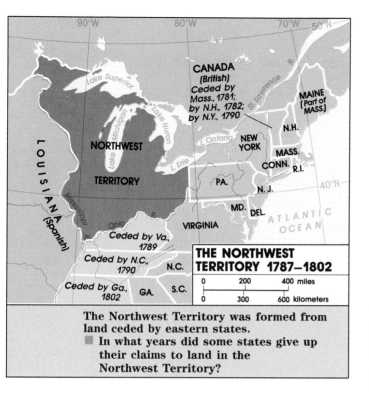

THE NORTHWEST TERRITORY 1787–1802

0   200   400 miles
0   300   600 kilometers

The Northwest Territory was formed from land ceded by eastern states.
■ In what years did some states give up their claims to land in the Northwest Territory?

that greed and "personal rather than national interests" were driving Americans apart, keeping the states from becoming a true nation.

Washington agreed. He knew a crisis would come soon unless changes were made:

> I do not conceive we can exist long as a nation without having lodged somewhere a power, which will pervade the whole Union in as energetic a manner as the authority of the State government extends over the several states.

A Call for a Stronger Government By 1787 many people in the United States believed the country needed a stronger central government. Among these were Alexander Hamilton and James Madison, a Virginian and a friend and follower of Thomas Jefferson.

Hamilton and Madison had already taken the lead in calling for a strong central government. They met with others holding the same views at a conference in Annapolis, Maryland, in 1786. Not all the states sent delegates to this meeting. The delegates were supposed to discuss matters of trade. Most agreed that trade problems arose from the weaknesses of the Confederation government.

Alexander Hamilton had a plan. He urged those attending the Annapolis meeting to ask Congress to hold a convention of all the states in Philadelphia. Its purpose, Hamilton said, would be to suggest changes in the Articles of Confederation. It seems likely, however, that Hamilton wanted the people attending the meeting to decide on an entirely new government. Changes to the Articles of Confederation required the consent of all 13 states, and Hamilton undoubtedly knew that this was impossible.

At first, Congress was reluctant to call the convention. But despite Congress's attitude, some states started to name delegates to the convention. James Madison wisely persuaded the Virginia legislature to name George Washington as a delegate from that state. Washington's prestige was so great that Congress could hardly refuse any longer. Its members gave in and issued a formal call for a convention to meet in Philadelphia in May 1787.

CHECKUP

1. Why did it take so long for the states to adopt the Articles of Confederation?
2. What were the main powers of the government under the terms of the Articles of Confederation?
3. What was the Northwest Ordinance?
4. Who led the movement for a stronger central government?
5. **Thinking Critically** What other solutions to the problem of western land claims might have been proposed?

The Constitutional Convention

What problems did the delegates have to resolve while writing the Constitution?

VOCABULARY

amendment	executive branch
Virginia Plan	judicial branch
New Jersey Plan	Three-Fifths
Great Compromise	Compromise
legislative branch	

Independence Hall   Few places in the United States had more to do with our nation's beginnings than the red brick building that stands on Chestnut Street, between Fifth and Sixth Streets, in Philadelphia. Completed in 1748, it was designed to be the meeting place for the Pennsylvania legislature. In 1753 a tower was added, and hung in it was a "bell of about two thousand pounds weight," as the records show. Today we know it as the Liberty Bell.

The First and Second Continental Congresses and Congress under the Articles of Confederation met in this red brick building. Thomas Jefferson first read the Declaration of Independence there, so it is now called Independence Hall. You will remember that the British held Philadelphia for a time during the War for Independence. For a while British soldiers were housed in the red brick building. Later, after the battle of Germantown, they used it as a hospital.

The Declaration of Independence and the Constitution of the United States were both drafted at Philadelphia's Independence Hall.
■ Why, do you think, was this building named Independence Hall?

The Convention Meets Less than 10 years later, the red brick building became the meeting place for the convention called by Congress. In May of 1787, delegates began to drift into Philadelphia. They had differing instructions from their states. Some delegates were there only to suggest **amendments**, or additions, to the Articles of Confederation. Others believed they should write an entirely new constitution for the government of the United States. The view of the latter group won out as the convention began 4 months of debate in the sweltering heat of summer. Because its members wrote a new constitution, the meeting in Philadelphia in 1787 is known as the Constitutional Convention.

Fifty-five delegates from 12 states were at the opening meetings of the Constitutional Convention. (See the picture on page 175.) Rhode Island refused to send any delegates. The convention unanimously chose George Washington of Virginia to preside over the meetings. James Madison of Virginia took notes of the proceedings. Delegates decided to bar the public from the meetings so that they could speak more freely. For this reason, much of what went on was known only to the delegates until Madison's notes were published 50 years later.

Distinguished and experienced people served as delegates to the Constitutional Convention. Most were prosperous, earning a good living as lawyers, merchants, bankers, or plantation owners. At 81, Benjamin Franklin was the oldest. James Madison and Alexander Hamilton, who represented New York, were among the youngest. Madison was 36 and Hamilton was 4 years younger.

Four great American leaders were absent from the Constitutional Convention. Thomas Jefferson was in France, and John Adams was in England. These two men were serving the United States as representatives to foreign governments. Samuel Adams had not been chosen as a delegate. Patrick Henry stayed in Virginia, even though he had been chosen as a delegate. He suspected the convention would draw up a plan for a stronger central government, which he opposed.

The Great Compromise One problem faced by the delegates was the question of how states should be represented in the lawmaking body of the new central government. Virginia delegates got to the convention early. Before the convention opened, they drew up a plan. It was called the **Virginia Plan**. This plan was favored by the large states because it proposed that states should be represented in the Congress according to population.

William Paterson of New Jersey took the opposite view. "New Jersey," he declared, "will never submit to a plan in which she could always be outvoted by a large state." His plan, in which the states would be represented equally in Congress, was called the **New Jersey Plan**. This plan was favored by the small states.

Two months passed before the convention accepted the **Great Compromise**, which solved this problem. This arrangement is also sometimes called the Connecticut Compromise because Roger Sherman, a Connecticut delegate, played a major role in working it out.

At this point in the convention, there was already general agreement among the delegates that Congress should consist of two houses. The Great Compromise suggested that the states be represented according to population in one body, the House of Representatives. In the other body, the Senate, each state would be represented equally. In both the House of Representatives and the Senate, each

The Liberty Bell

One of the most famous patriotic symbols of the United States is the Liberty Bell. But it has not always been known by that name. For many years it was called the State House Bell. The superintendents of the State House of the Province of Pennsylvania ordered it made in England in 1751. The bell was cast with a biblical quotation on its crown: "Proclaim liberty throughout all the land, unto all the inhabitants thereof."

The bell was hung in the steeple of the State House in Philadelphia. The bell cracked the first time it was rung, but it was repaired and its tone restored. When the British occupied Philadelphia in 1777, the State House Bell and other bells were hastily moved for fear that the British would melt them down for making cannons. The State House Bell was hidden for more than a year under the floor of a church in nearby Allentown, Pennsylvania.

After the British left Philadelphia, the bell was returned to the State House. Until 1835 it was rung every year on July 4, the anniversary of the adoption of the Declaration of Independence. It was sometimes called Old Independence or the Bell of the Revolution. In 1837 someone recalled the quotation on the old bell. Supporters of the movement to free slaves quickly realized the significance of the quotation, "Proclaim liberty throughout the land. . . ." It was they who first called the old State House Bell the Liberty Bell.

The bell cracked again in 1835 while being rung during the funeral of John Marshall, who had been Chief Justice of the United States. The Liberty Bell is now kept on display in Philadelphia's historic area, where independence was declared and the Constitution written. It is a treasured symbol of our country's independence.

member would have one vote. This solution satisfied both the small and the large states, and the compromise was written into the new constitution.

The Branches of Government   The delegates did not want a central government that was all-powerful. It solved this problem by dividing power among three equal branches. One would be the **legislative branch**, a Congress that would pass laws. A second branch, headed by a President, would execute, or carry out, the laws passed by Congress. This would be known as the **executive branch**. Third would be the **judicial branch**, which would set up courts to try people who disobeyed national laws. This branch would also interpret the laws. Each branch of government would be able to limit the power of the other two branches in some specific ways. The workings of this system of checks and balances are explained by the flowchart on page 192.

Having established the form of the new government, the convention debated over the details. How long should the terms be for the various offices? Should the President or a member of Congress have to meet a minimum-age requirement? Could a foreign-born person serve as an elected official in the new government? Settling these questions took time, but the answers were finally written into the new constitution.

The Slavery Issue   After resolving the problem of representation in Congress, slaves and slavery entered into the debates. The delegates had agreed that direct taxation should be divided among the states, according to population. Southern delegates did not want slaves counted for taxation purposes. If slaves were counted, southern states would be more heavily taxed. And yet southern delegates wanted slaves counted when the number of members in the House of Representatives for each state was decided.

Another compromise was arranged to settle this problem. For every five slaves in a state, the new constitution allowed three to be counted for the purpose of taxation and for representation in Congress. This solution was known as the **Three-Fifths Compromise**.

The opposition of southern delegates made it impossible for the new constitution to end slavery in the United States. But ending the importation of slaves was another matter. Virginia and Maryland, as well as most of the northern states, had

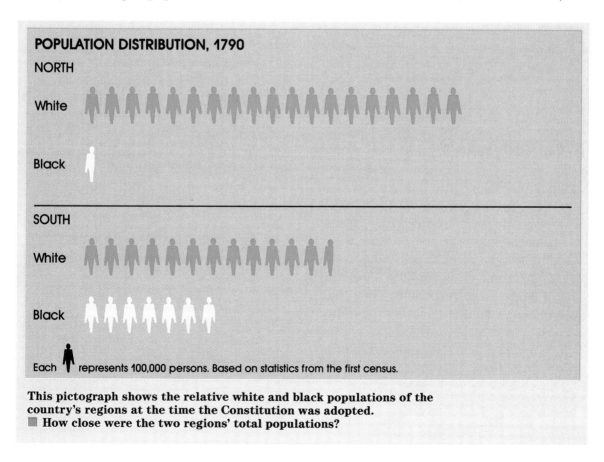

This pictograph shows the relative white and black populations of the country's regions at the time the Constitution was adopted.
■ How close were the two regions' total populations?

Gouverneur Morris, a delegate to the Constitutional Convention from Pennsylvania, headed the committee that prepared the final draft of the Constitution.
■ What important skills would have been required to do this job?

forbidden the importation of slaves by the time of the Constitutional Convention. However, delegates from South Carolina and Georgia said that their states would never approve a constitution that barred the importation of slaves into the entire United States. Nevertheless, they were willing to let Congress prohibit the importation of slaves after 20 years had passed. This agreement was still another compromise that helped the delegates to continue their work.

Writing the Constitution   The delegates worked in the red brick building on Chestnut Street from May 1787 through the whole summer. By September they had agreed on the most important matters. They turned over to the Committee on Style the task of writing down what they wanted. The organization and the wording of the Constitution came from the work of this group. It was headed by Gouverneur Morris of Pennsylvania. He wrote the Preamble, or introduction, beginning "We the people of the United States" and ending "do ordain and establish this Constitution for the United States of America." The new government was not to be a loose union of the states. It was to be a union of *the people*.

On September 17, 1787, the Committee on Style presented the Constitution to the Congress. Thirty-nine delegates, including George Washington, the presiding officer, signed the document. The other sixteen delegates had gone home for one reason or another. Some had left because they disapproved of one part or another of the Constitution and refused to sign it.

Drawing up and signing a new constitution was only one part of forming a stronger central government. There remained the task of having the Constitution approved by the necessary number of states. (See pages 194–219 for the text of the Constitution.)

CHECKUP

1. Why was the Constitutional Convention called?
2. What three important compromises were written into the Constitution?
3. What was the function of each of the three branches of government under the Constitution?
4. How was the issue of slavery resolved?
5. **Thinking Critically** Why were compromises so important in writing the new Constitution?

"A More Perfect Union"

Why did some people oppose the ratification of the Constitution?

Winning State Approval   Alexander Hamilton played only a small part in the Constitutional Convention. His legal work in New York kept him busy during much of the time the convention met. Even when he was present, he was always outvoted by the other two delegates from New York, Robert Yates and John Lansing. They opposed a stronger central government, fearing it would take away the power of their state. In fact, they refused to sign the Constitution.

So Hamilton knew that the task of those who favored the new Constitution would be difficult. In his own state the opposition was strong. Still, Hamilton knew the convention had done two things to make it easier to get the states to **ratify**, or approve, the Constitution.

First, the convention had provided that when 9 states accepted the Constitution, it would go into effect for those states. This would certainly be easier than trying for approval by all 13 states. This meant, too, that once the new government was formed, it would be hard for the other 4 states to stay out of the Union. Second, the delegates had directed that the Constitution be considered for approval by special conventions in each state, not by the state legislatures. Knowing this, Alexander Hamilton decided to work hard.

Opposing Views   The group favoring the Constitution wanted a **federal government**. In such a government the powers are either shared or divided between the states and the central government. This group took the name **Federalists**.

Their opponents had little choice but to take the name **Anti-Federalists**. They had three main reasons for opposing the Constitution. First, they said the Constitution provided no guarantees of certain

POWERS OF CONGRESS UNDER THE CONSTITUTION

- Make laws for the federal government
- Make foreign policy
- Regulate foreign and interstate trade
- Levy taxes
- Borrow money
- Coin money
- Declare war
- Raise and maintain armed forces
- Establish federal courts
- Set up post offices
- Admit new states
- Fix standard weights and measures

Many of the powers of the new Congress had previously belonged to the states.
■ **Which power do you think is the most useful?**

rights or freedoms for the people of the United States. Second, they believed the new government would take too much power away from the states. Third, they argued the new government would favor the rich, setting up a wealthy ruling class.

The last argument in particular appealed to people living on western settlements, poorer people living in towns and cities, and to people with small businesses. But not all who opposed the Constitution were poor. Some wealthy plantation owners opposed it because they were powerful within their states. Several state officials, who feared that the central government would overshadow state governments, also opposed the Constitution. Patrick Henry in Virginia and Governor George Clinton in New York led the fight against ratification in their states.

The Federalist Papers   As New Yorkers prepared to elect delegates to their state convention, a series of articles began to appear in four New York newspapers. Eighty-five articles in all appeared, signed with the name *Publius*. Alexander Hamilton wrote at least 45 of them and James Madison about 30. These articles became known as the **Federalist papers**. They received this name because each article supported the Federalist arguments in favor of the Constitution. Later they were published in a book called *The Federalist*.

The Federalist papers answered every question raised about the new Constitution. They explained each part of the document, showed how the new government would work, and praised the benefits that would come if the Constitution were approved. The articles were written to influence the vote in New York State, but they were read in the other states, too. They helped convince people that the new government would be good for the nation.

Alexander Hamilton argued in favor of approval of the new Constitution. He and James Madison cooperated to write the essays known as the Federalist papers.
■ Why was ratification by Hamilton's home state of New York so important?

The State Conventions   Federalist leaders were well organized. They worked hard to get their supporters chosen to attend the state conventions. Small states favored the Constitution because it gave them equal representation in the Senate. Delaware was the first state to ratify the Constitution. It did so by unanimous vote. In Pennsylvania the vote was closer but still in favor of ratification. New Jersey, Georgia, and Connecticut soon gave their approval. Thus five states had ratified the Constitution by the time the Massachusetts convention met.

Samuel Adams was still a respected leader in Massachusetts. At first he was against the Constitution. He said it did not give enough liberty to the people. The Federalists promised to add a **bill of rights**, guaranteeing basic rights and freedoms to the citizens of the United States. This promise satisfied Adams, and Massachusetts ratified the Constitution. Maryland and South Carolina followed. In June 1788, New Hampshire became the ninth state to approve the Constitution. The new national government could now be put into effect.

Virginia and New York   Still, the future of the new government was in doubt if Virginia and New York did not ratify the Constitution. In Virginia James Madison led the fight for ratification. He was supported by George Washington. Hoping to gain the support of Thomas Jefferson, Madison wrote to him in France. Jefferson replied that, like Samuel Adams, he believed a bill of rights should be added to the Constitution. Madison took Jefferson's advice, promising to see that citizens' rights would be protected. Virginia's convention then voted approval.

In New York, Alexander Hamilton had persuaded the convention to delay voting until after Massachusetts and Virginia had voted. When those two states ratified the Constitution, Hamilton argued that New York could hardly afford to stay out of the new government. The final vote in the New York convention showed 30 in favor of the Constitution and 27 opposed. Without Alexander Hamilton, the vote would surely have been different.

A Stronger Government   The word **revolution** means "a sudden and complete change." Sometimes the change is brought about by arms and war, as in the American Revolution. But revolution can happen in other ways, as the Federalists proved. In 14 months they had brought

On July 23, 1788, New York State celebrated the ratification of the Constitution. The "federal ship" was pulled along the streets of lower Manhattan.
■ Who was the ship named after?

about a revolution. They had written the new Constitution and 11 states had accepted it. This was a peaceful revolution but, all the same, a revolution.

During the summer of 1788, the machinery for choosing a President and members of Congress under the Constitution was set in motion. Voters elected members of the House of Representatives directly, while state legislatures elected two senators each, as the Constitution provided. State legislatures also followed the Constitution by choosing people called **electors**, who in turn would choose the President. Most people assumed George Washington would become the first President under the new Constitution. And so he did, being named by a unanimous vote of the electors.

Partly through Alexander Hamilton's influence, New York City was named the temporary capital of the United States. In April 1789, George Washington left Mount Vernon once more to serve his country. Every village and city he passed through wanted to honor him—a great man on his way to becoming the first President of the United States. So numerous were the celebrations that it took Washington a week to reach New York.

The people of the United States had created a new kind of government, called a **federal republic**. It was *federal* because the central government shared its powers with the states. It was a *republic* because it was based on the consent of the people, acting through their representatives.

Amending the Constitution The writers of the Constitution knew that this new government was not perfect. In time it might be necessary to make changes. Under the Articles of Confederation, all the states had to approve a change in the

George Washington passes through Trenton, New Jersey, on his way to New York to be inaugurated as the first President.
Why did crowds gather to see Washington all along his journey?

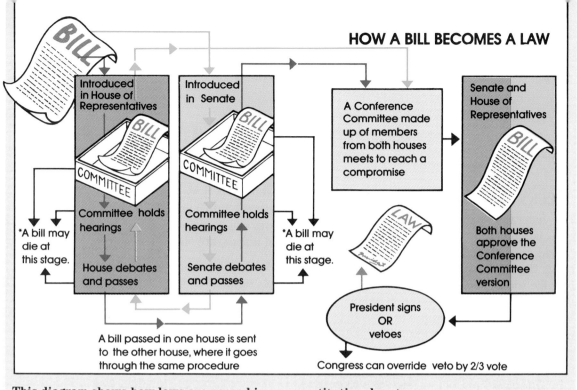

HOW A BILL BECOMES A LAW

Introduced in House of Representatives

Introduced in Senate

A Conference Committee made up of members from both houses meets to reach a compromise

Senate and House of Representatives

COMMITTEE

COMMITTEE

*A bill may die at this stage.

Committee holds hearings

Committee holds hearings

*A bill may die at this stage.

Both houses approve the Conference Committee version

House debates and passes

Senate debates and passes

President signs OR vetoes

A bill passed in one house is sent to the other house, where it goes through the same procedure

Congress can override veto by 2/3 vote

This diagram shows how laws are passed in our constitutional system.
■ Why do you think the President got the power to veto new laws?

government. The writers of the Constitution, realizing that it would be difficult for all the states to agree, had made the amending process less difficult.

The Constitution provided that an amendment had to be approved by a two-thirds majority vote of both houses of Congress. Then it had to be ratified by three fourths of the states before it became part of the Constitution. In the 200 years since the Constitution was put into effect, only 26 amendments have been added.

The Bill of Rights   When the new Congress met in 1789, one of its first acts was to propose the first ten amendments to the Constitution. James Madison introduced nine of these ten amendments. The ten amendments were ratified by the states, and the Bill of Rights became an official part of the Constitution in 1791.

The First Amendment guarantees the freedom of religion, the freedom of speech, the freedom of press, and the freedom of

assembly. Other amendments protect people from unreasonable searches and seizures of their property, and from cruel and unusual punishment. There is an amendment that protects people who are accused of crimes and guarantees them speedy trials. The Tenth Amendment states that all powers not granted to the federal government remain with the states or the people, unless the Constitution prohibits it.

CHECKUP

1. What were the Federalist papers?
2. What arguments were used by those who opposed the new Constitution?
3. Why did smaller states generally give approval to the Constitution?
4. What is the purpose of the Bill of Rights?
5. **Thinking Critically**   Which of the rights or freedoms mentioned in the first ten amendments to the Constitution is the most important to you? Why?

Reading a Flowchart

CHECKS AND BALANCES

The federal government under our Constitution is sometimes called a government of checks and balances. That is, each branch may check the other two so that no one of them can become too powerful.

You can see how the system of checks and balances works by studying the flowchart below. A flowchart is a graphic drawing that can be used to show how organizations or activities are related.

This flowchart shows how the executive branch (President) checks the legislative branch (Congress) and the judicial branch (Supreme Court). It also shows how the legislative branch checks the executive and judicial branches, and, too, how the judicial branch checks the executive and legislative branches.

SKILLS PRACTICE

Use the information from the flowchart to answer the questions below. Write your answers on a separate sheet of paper.

1. Which branch passes laws?
2. How can the federal courts check the power of Congress?
3. Which branch appoints justices to the federal courts?
4. How can Congress control the power of the President's veto?
5. How can the President check the power of Congress?
6. Which branch has the power to impeach federal officials?
7. What check does the Congress have on the decisions of the Supreme Court?
8. Which branch grants pardons?

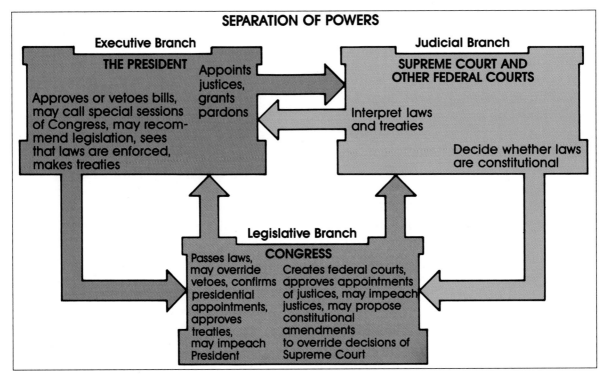

SEPARATION OF POWERS

Executive Branch

THE PRESIDENT

Approves or vetoes bills, may call special sessions of Congress, may recommend legislation, sees that laws are enforced, makes treaties

Appoints justices, grants pardons

Judicial Branch

SUPREME COURT AND OTHER FEDERAL COURTS

Interpret laws and treaties

Decide whether laws are constitutional

Legislative Branch

CONGRESS

Passes laws, may override vetoes, confirms presidential appointments, approves treaties, may impeach President

Creates federal courts, approves appointments of justices, may impeach justices, may propose constitutional amendments to override decisions of Supreme Court

MAIN IDEAS

1. The Articles of Confederation set up the first union of the United States, which lasted from 1781 to 1789.
2. The Northwest Ordinance provided a system of government for the Northwest Territory and a series of steps by which this territory could be divided into states.
3. The Confederation government was unsuccessful because it had no power to tax or to regulate trade.
4. The major issues facing the writers of the Constitution were the powers of the central government, the states' representation in Congress, and the counting of slaves for taxation purposes.
5. The Anti-Federalists opposed the Constitution because they believed that the new government would take too much power away from the states and because the Constitution did not contain a bill of rights.

VOCABULARY REVIEW

On a separate sheet of paper, write the best ending for each sentence.

1. A loose union of states able to act only on certain matters is a _____ .
2. An uprising that showed the weakness of the central government in 1786 was called _____ .
3. A law forbidding slavery west of the Appalachian Mountains and north of the Ohio River was the _____ .
4. A proposal at the Constitutional Convention that states be represented in Congress according to population was called the _____ .
5. Under the Constitution, the President is chosen by people called _____ .
6. The three equal branches of government are the executive, the legislative, and the _____ .
7. The Three-Fifths Compromise in the Constitution had to do with the counting of _____ .

8. Persons favoring the ratification of the Constitution were known as _____ .
9. An addition to the Constitution that was favored by Samuel Adams and Thomas Jefferson was the _____ _____ _____ .
10. In a federal republic like ours, powers are shared by the central government and the _____ .

CHAPTER CHECKUP

1. What evidence shows that the Confederation government lacked respect at home and abroad?
2. Name the accomplishments of the Confederation government, and explain which one you believe to have been the most important accomplishment.
3. What were the major differences between the central government under the Articles of Confederation and the central government under the Constitution?
4. Explain what is meant by a system of checks and balances.
5. **Thinking Critically** In 1787, which would you have favored, a strong or a weak central government? Why?
6. **Thinking Critically** Why do you think the framers of our Constitution considered it necessary to have a provision for making amendments to the Constitution? Explain your answer.

APPLYING KNOWLEDGE

1. Make a list of the qualities a person would need to be a good President of the United States. Then explain why you think these qualities are desirable, and under what circumstances a President would need them.
2. Write a bill to be considered by Congress. Present your bill to the class and explain why you are proposing this legislation. Then ask the class to conduct a debate and to vote on your bill.

The Constitution of the United States of America

Preamble
The Preamble is a beautifully written introduction stating the purposes for which the government under the Constitution is established.

LEGISLATIVE BRANCH

Congress
The lawmaking branch of the federal government is Congress. It is made up of two bodies — a Senate and a House of Representatives.

House of Representatives
The writers of the Constitution intended this body to be closer than the Senate to the people. Its members are elected every 2 years.

Qualifications
To be a member of the House of Representatives, one must be at least 25 years old, a United States citizen for 7 years, and a resident of the state from which elected.

Apportionment
Each state, no matter how small its population, has at least one representative, but each member of the House no longer represents 30,000 people. If this were true today, the House of Representatives would have nearly 8,000 members! For some years, laws passed by Congress have limited the House of Representatives to 435 voting members.

We the people of the United States, in order to form a more perfect union, establish justice, insure domestic tranquility, provide for the common defense, promote the general welfare, and secure the blessings of liberty to ourselves and our posterity, do ordain and establish this Constitution for the United States of America.

ARTICLE I

SECTION 1.
All legislative powers herein granted shall be vested in a Congress of the United States, which shall consist of a Senate and House of Representatives.

SECTION 2.
The House of Representatives shall be composed of members chosen every second year by the people of the several States, and the electors in each State shall have the qualifications requisite for electors of the most numerous branch of the State legislature.

No person shall be a representative who shall not have attained to the age of twenty-five years, and been seven years a citizen of the United States, and who shall not, when elected, be an inhabitant of that State in which he shall be chosen.

Representatives and direct taxes shall be apportioned among the several States which may be included within this Union, according to their respective numbers, which shall be determined by adding to the whole number of free persons, including those bound to service for a term of years, and excluding Indians not taxed, three fifths of all other persons:* The actual enumeration shall be made within three years after the first meeting of the Congress of the United States, and within every subsequent term of ten years, in such manner as they shall by law direct. The number of representatives shall not exceed one for every thirty thousand, but each State shall have at least one representative; and until such enumeration shall be made, the State of New Hampshire shall be entitled to choose three, Massa-

NOTE: Items that have been changed or replaced are underlined.
* Changed by the Fourteenth Amendment

chusetts eight, Rhode Island and Providence Plantations one, Connecticut five, New York six, New Jersey four, Pennsylvania eight, Delaware one, Maryland six, Virginia ten, North Carolina five, South Carolina five, and Georgia three.

When vacancies happen in the representation from any State, the executive authority thereof shall issue writs of election to fill such vacancies.

The House of Representatives shall choose their speaker and other officers, and shall have the sole power of impeachment.

SECTION 3.

The Senate of the United States shall be composed of two senators from each State, _chosen by the legislature thereof,_* for six years; and each senator shall have one vote.

Immediately after they shall be assembled in consequence of the first election, they shall be divided as equally as may be into three classes. The seats of the senators of the first class shall be vacated at the expiration of the second year, of the second class at the expiration of the fourth year, and of the third class at the expiration of the sixth year, so that one third may be chosen every second year; _and if vacancies happen by resignation, or otherwise, during the recess of the legislature of any State, the executive thereof may make temporary appointments until the next meeting of the legislature, which shall then fill such vacancies._*

No person shall be a senator who shall not have attained to the age of thirty years, and been nine years a citizen of the United States, and who shall not, when elected, be an inhabitant of that State for which he shall be chosen.

The Senate

The states are equally represented in the Senate, with two senators from each state. A senator must be at least 30 years old, a United States citizen for 9 years, and a resident of the state from which elected. Senators serve a 6-year term, although only one third of them are elected every 2 years. The writers of the Constitution wanted the Senate to consist of experienced lawmakers; therefore, they arranged this rotating plan so that two thirds of the Senate will always consist of experienced lawmakers.

* Changed by the Seventeenth Amendment

195

The Vice President

This is the only part of the Constitution that assigns duties or powers to the Vice President. However, recent Presidents have given their Vice Presidents important duties as aides.

Impeachment

Both the House of Representatives and the Senate have roles in the process known as impeachment. The House of Representatives states the misconduct of which the federal official is accused. The Senate then acts as a court to determine if the official is guilty. If two thirds of the senators judge the official to be guilty, he is removed from office.

Elections and Meetings

Congress has decided that federal elections will take place in even-numbered years on the Tuesday after the first Monday in November. A new Congress now meets on January 3 after its election the preceding November.

The Vice President of the United States shall be president of the Senate, but shall have no vote, unless they be equally divided.

The Senate shall choose their other officers, and also a president pro tempore, in the absence of the Vice President, or when he shall exercise the office of President of the United States.

The Senate shall have the sole power to try all impeachments. When sitting for that purpose, they shall be on oath or affirmation. When the President of the United States is tried, the Chief Justice shall preside: and no person shall be convicted without the concurrence of two thirds of the members present.

Judgment in cases of impeachment shall not extend further than to removal from office, and disqualification to hold any office of honor, trust or profit under the United States: but the party convicted shall nevertheless be liable and subject to indictment, trial, judgment and punishment, according to law.

SECTION 4.

The times, places, and manner of holding elections for senators and representatives shall be prescribed in each State by the legislature thereof; but the Congress may at any time by law make or alter such regulations, except as to the places of choosing senators.

The Congress shall assemble at least once in every year, and such meeting shall be on the first Monday in December,* unless they shall by law appoint a different day.

* Changed by the Twentieth Amendment

SECTION 5.

Each house shall be the judge of the elections, returns and qualifications of its own members, and a majority of each shall constitute a quorum to do business; but a smaller number may adjourn from day to day, and may be authorized to compel the attendance of absent members, in such manner, and under such penalties as each house may provide.

Each house may determine the rules of its proceedings, punish its members for disorderly behavior, and, with the concurrence of two thirds, expel a member.

Each house shall keep a journal of its proceedings, and from time to time publish the same, excepting such parts as may in their judgment require secrecy; and the yeas and nays of the members of either house on any question shall, at the desire of one fifth of those present, be entered on the journal.

Neither house, during the session of Congress, shall, without the consent of the other, adjourn for more than three days, nor to any other place than that in which the two houses shall be sitting.

SECTION 6.

The senators and representatives shall receive a compensation for their services, to be ascertained by law, and paid out of the Treasury of the United States. They shall in all cases, except treason, felony and breach of the peace, be privileged from arrest during their attendance at the session of their respective houses, and in going to and returning from the same; and for any speech or debate in either house, they shall not be questioned in any other place.

No senator or representative shall, during the time for which he was elected, be appointed to any civil office under the authority of the United States, which shall have been created, or the emoluments thereof shall have been increased during such time; and no person holding any office under the United States shall be a member of either house during his continuance in office.

SECTION 7.

All bills for raising revenue shall originate in the House of Representatives; but the Senate may propose or concur with amendments as on other bills.

Every bill which shall have passed the House of Representatives and the Senate, shall, before it become a law, be presented to the President of the United States; if he approve he shall sign it, but if not he shall return it, with his objections to that house in which it shall have originated, who shall enter the objections at

Rules of Procedure
Congress makes nearly all its own rules of operation and controls its own membership. Both the Senate and the House of Representatives keep journals, which are published daily. In these journals, people can find out how their representatives voted on bills.

Pay and Privileges
Under the Articles of Confederation, each state paid its members in Congress. This caused trouble because state legislatures could withhold salaries if Congress did something that displeased them. The Constitution resolves this problem by stating that the members of Congress will be paid from the national treasury. Several privileges are spelled out. They are intended to make members of Congress as free as possible from undue influence.

Lawmaking
The main business of Congress is passing laws, but no bill can become a law unless the President signs it or unless Congress passes it over his veto.

large on their journal, and proceed to reconsider it. If after such reconsideration two thirds of that house shall agree to pass the bill, it shall be sent, together with the objections, to the other house, by which it shall likewise be reconsidered, and if approved by two thirds of that house, it shall become a law. But in all such cases the votes of both houses shall be determined by yeas and nays, and the names of the persons voting for and against the bill shall be entered on the journal of each house respectively. If any bill shall not be returned by the President within ten days (Sundays excepted) after it shall have been presented to him, the same shall be a law, in like manner as if he had signed it, unless the Congress by their adjournment prevent its return, in which case it shall not be a law.

Every order, resolution, or vote to which the concurrence of the Senate and House of Representatives may be necessary (except on a question of adjournment) shall be presented to the President of the United States; and before the same shall take effect, shall be approved by him, or being disapproved by him, shall be repassed by two thirds of the Senate and House of Representatives, according to the rules and limitations prescribed in the case of a bill.

SECTION 8.

The Congress shall have power to lay and collect taxes, duties, imposts and excises, to pay the debts and provide for the common defense and general welfare of the United States; but all duties, imposts and excises shall be uniform throughout the United States;

To borrow money on the credit of the United States;

To regulate commerce with foreign nations, and among the several States, and with the Indian tribes;

To establish a uniform rule of naturalization, and uniform laws on the subject of bankruptcies through the United States;

To coin money, regulate the value thereof, and of foreign coin, and fix the standard of weights and measures;

To provide for the punishment of conterfeiting the securities and current coin of the United States;

To establish post offices and post roads;

To promote the progress of science and useful arts by securing for limited times to authors and inventors the exclusive right to their respective writings and discoveries;

To constitute tribunals inferior to the Supreme Court;

To define and punish piracies and felonies committed on the high seas, and offenses against the law of nations;

To declare war, grant letters of marque and reprisal, and make rules concerning captures on land and water;

Checks and Balances
The relationship between Congress and the President in making laws is a clear example of the checks-and-balances system in the Constitution.

Powers of Congress
This is one of the most important parts of the Constitution. The powers of the national government as exercised by Congress are listed here. This section shows that the makers of the Constitution wanted a national government strong enough to do the things they thought needed to be done. Among the most important powers given to the national government are the powers to tax and spend for the general welfare, to regulate interstate and foreign commerce, and to wage war and to provide for the common defense.

To raise and support armies, but no appropriation of money to that use shall be for a longer term than two years;

To provide and maintain a navy;

To make rules for the government and regulations of the land and naval forces;

To provide for calling forth the militia to execute the laws of the Union, suppress insurrections and repel invasions;

To provide for organizing, arming, and disciplining the militia, and for governing such part of them as may be employed in the service of the United States, reserving to the States respectively the appointment of the officers, and the authority of training the militia according to the discipline prescribed by Congress;

To exercise exclusive legislation in all cases whatsoever, over such district (not exceeding ten miles square) as may, by cession of particular States and the acceptance of Congress, become the seat of the government of the United States, and to exercise like authority over all places purchased by the consent of the legislature of the State in which the same shall be, for the erection of forts, magazines, arsenals, dockyards, and other needful buildings; and

To make all laws which shall be necessary and proper for carrying into execution the foregoing powers, and all other powers vested by this Constitution in the government of the United States, or in any department or officer thereof.

Elastic Clause
The last paragraph in this section contains the famous "elastic clause." It permits Congress to make whatever other laws it thinks necessary to carry out its "enumerated powers" as listed in the previous paragraphs of Section 8.

CONSTITUTION OF THE UNITED STATES

Forbidden Powers

This section contains several provisions to protect the people of the United States against injustice. A writ of *habeas corpus* requires that an arrested person be brought promptly before a court to determine if he or she is being held legally. A bill of attainder is a legislative act by which a person can be declared guilty of treason and executed without a trial. An *ex post facto* law is one that makes an act a crime after it has been committed. Therefore, it could turn an innocent person into a criminal.

Powers Denied to the States

One purpose of our Constitution is to limit the powers of the states and strengthen those of the national government. This section forbids the states to exercise any of those powers given to Congress. The states are also forbidden to do certain things that the national government is forbidden to do.

SECTION 9.

The migration or importation of such persons as any of the States now existing shall think proper to admit, shall not be prohibited by the Congress prior to the year one thousand eight hundred and eight, but a tax or duty may be imposed on such importation, not exceeding ten dollars for each person.

The privilege of the writ of habeas corpus shall not be suspended, unless when in cases of rebellion or invasion the public safety may require it.

No bill of attainder or ex post facto law shall be passed.

No capitation, or other direct,* tax shall be laid, unless in proportion to the census or enumeration herein before directed to be taken.

No tax or duty shall be laid on articles exported from any State.

No preference shall be given by any regulation of commerce or revenue to the ports of one State over those of another; nor shall vessels bound to, or from, one State be obliged to enter, clear, or pay duties in another.

No money shall be drawn from the Treasury, but in consequence of appropriations made by law; and a regular statement and account of the receipts and expenditures of all public money shall be published from time to time.

No title of nobility shall be granted by the United States: and no person holding any office of profit or trust under them, shall, without the consent of the Congress, accept of any present, emolument, office, or title of any kind whatever, from any king, prince, or foreign State.

SECTION 10.

No State shall enter into any treaty, alliance, or confederation; grant letters of marque and reprisal; coin money; emit bills of credit; make anything but gold and silver coin a tender in payment of debts, pass any bill of attainder, ex post facto law, or law impairing the obligation of contracts, or grant any title of nobility.

No State shall, without the consent of the Congress, lay any imposts or duties on imports or exports, except what may be absolutely necessary for executing its inspection laws: and the net produce of all duties and imposts laid by any State on imports or exports, shall be for the use of the Treasury of the United States; and all such laws shall be subject to the revision and control of the Congress.

No State shall, without the consent of Congress, lay any duty of tonnage, keep troops, or ships of war in time of peace, enter into any agreement or compact with another State, or with a

* Changed by the Sixteenth Amendment

foreign power, or engage in war, unless actually invaded, or in such imminent danger as will not admit of delay.

ARTICLE II

SECTION 1.

The executive power shall be vested in a President of the United States of America. He shall hold his office during the term of four years, and, together with the Vice President chosen for the same term, be elected as follows:

Each State shall appoint, in such manner as the legislature thereof may direct, a number of electors, equal to the whole number of senators and representatives to which the State may be entitled in the Congress: but no senator or representative, or person holding an office of trust or profit under the United States, shall be appointed an elector.

The electors shall meet in their respective States, and vote by ballot for two persons, of whom one at least shall not be an inhabitant of the same State with themselves. And they shall make a list of all the persons voted for, and of the number of votes for each; which they shall sign and certify, and transmit sealed to the seat of the government of the United States, directed to the president of the Senate. The president of the Senate shall, in the presence of the Senate and House of Representatives, open all the certificates, and the votes shall then be counted. The person having the greatest number of votes shall be the President, if such number be a majority of the whole number of electors appointed;

EXECUTIVE BRANCH

President, Vice President

The writers of the Constitution felt that the President's and Vice President's terms of office (4 years) should be different from the terms of members of Congress, and that the executive officers should be chosen in a different way. Therefore they set up a system of electors who were to choose the President and Vice President. However, hardly anything about the electoral system works today as the writers of the Constitution intended. For one thing, the Twelfth Amendment changed the method somewhat by requiring each elector to indicate separately his choice for President and Vice President. Furthermore, the rise of political parties changed the system markedly.

CONSTITUTION OF THE UNITED STATES

The Electors

Today each political party in a state selects people to be candidates for the position of electors. These people pledge that if they become electors, they will vote for the presidential and vice presidential candidates of their party.

When people vote in a presidential election today, they seem to be voting only for electors. Actually, however, they are voting for the President and Vice President since the voters know which candidates the electors are pledged to vote for.

Election Day

Congress has determined that presidential elections shall take place every 4 years on the Tuesday after the first Monday in November.

Salary

The President's salary is now $200,000 a year, and he receives $50,000 for expenses. He pays income taxes on both sums. He also receives a sum not to exceed $100,000 a year for travel expenses. This fund is not taxed.

and if there be more than one who have such majority, and have an equal number of votes, then the House of Representatives shall immediately choose by ballot one of them for President; and if no person have a majority, then from the five highest on the list the said house shall in like manner choose the President. But in choosing the President, the votes shall be taken by States, the representation from each State having one vote; a quorum for this purpose shall consist of a member or members from two thirds of the States, and a majority of all the States shall be necessary to a choice. In every case, after the choice of the President, the person having the greatest number of votes of the electors shall be the Vice President. But if there should remain two or more who have equal votes, the Senate shall choose from them by ballot the Vice President.*

The Congress may determine the time of choosing the electors, and the day on which they shall give their votes; which day shall be the same throughout the United States.

No person except a natural-born citizen, or a citizen of the United States, at the time of the adoption of this Constitution, shall be eligible to the office of President; neither shall any person be eligible to that office who shall not have attained to the age of thirty-five years, and been fourteen years a resident within the United States.

In case of the removal of the President from office, or of his death, resignation, or inability to discharge the powers and duties of the said office, the same shall devolve on the Vice President, and the Congress may by law provide for the case of removal, death, resignation, or inability, both of the President and Vice President, declaring what officer shall then act as President, and such officer shall act accordingly, until the disability be removed, or a President shall be elected.

The President shall, at stated times, receive for his services a compensation, which shall neither be increased nor diminished during the period for which he shall have been elected, and he shall not receive within that period any other emolument from the United States, or any of them.

Before he enter on the execution of his office, he shall take the following oath or affirmation: —"I do solemnly swear (or affirm) that I will faithfully execute the office of President of the United States, and will to the best of my ability, preserve, protect and defend the Constitution of the United States."

SECTION 2.

The President shall be commander in chief of the army and navy of the United States, and of the militia of the several States,

* Changed by the Twelfth Amendment

when called into the actual service of the United States; he may require the opinion, in writing, of the principal officer in each of the executive departments, upon any subject relating to the duties of their respective offices, and he shall have power to grant reprieves and pardons for offenses against the United States, except in cases of impeachment.

He shall have power, by and with the advice and consent of the Senate, to make treaties, provided two thirds of the senators present concur; and he shall nominate, and by and with the advice and consent of the Senate, shall appoint ambassadors, other public ministers and consuls, judges of the Supreme Court, and all other officers of the United States, whose appointments are not herein otherwise provided for, and which shall be established by law: but the Congress may by law vest the appointment of such inferior officers, as they think proper, in the President alone, in the courts of law, or in the heads of departments.

The President shall have power to fill up all vacancies that may happen during the recess of the Senate, by granting commissions which shall expire at the end of their next session.

SECTION 3.

He shall from time to time give to the Congress information of the state of the Union, and recommend to their consideration such measures as he shall judge necessary and expedient; he may, on extraordinary occasions, convene both houses, or either of them, and in case of disagreement between them with respect to the time of adjournment, he may adjourn them to such time as he shall think proper; he shall receive ambassadors and other public ministers; he shall take care that the laws be faithfully executed, and shall commission all the officers of the United States.

Military Powers

By making the President, a civilian, the Commander in Chief of the armed forces, the writers of the Constitution made sure that an elected representative of the people would control the military power of the nation. This is a basic principle of a free society. In the missile age, when Congress may not have time to declare war, the President has an awesome responsibility as head of the defense forces of the nation.

The President and Congress

Congress makes the laws, but the President signs most of them before they go into effect. In addition, the President suggests needed legislation each year when he gives his State of the Union message to Congress.

SECTION 4.

The President, Vice President, and all civil officers of the United States, shall be removed from office on impeachment for, and conviction of, treason, bribery, or other high crimes and misdemeanors.

ARTICLE III

SECTION 1.

The judicial power of the United States shall be vested in one Supreme Court, and in such inferior courts as the Congress may from time to time ordain and establish. The judges, both of the Supreme and inferior courts, shall hold their offices during good behavior, and shall, at stated times, receive for their services, a compensation which shall not be diminished during their continuance in office.

SECTION 2.

The judicial power shall extend to all cases, in law and equity, arising under this Constitution, the laws of the United States, and treaties made, or which shall be made, under their authority;—to all cases affecting ambassadors, other public ministers and consuls;—to all cases of admiralty and maritime jurisdiction;—to controversies to which the United States shall be a party;—to controversies between two or more States;—between a State and citizens of another State;—between citizens of different States;—between citizens of the same State claiming

JUDICIAL BRANCH

Federal Courts

The President, with the consent of the Senate, appoints the judges for the federal courts. They are the only officials of the national government to hold office for life.

Cases in Federal Courts

The Constitution names the kinds of cases to be handled in federal courts. Only a few are handled directly by the Supreme Court. Most of these kinds of cases start in a lower federal court. If the verdict is questioned, the case may go to a court of appeals, and it may in time be appealed again and

lands under grants of different States, and between a State, or the citizens thereof, and foreign States, citizens or subjects.

In all cases affecting ambassadors, other public ministers and consuls, and those in which a State shall be party, the Supreme Court shall have original jurisdiction. In all the other cases before mentioned, the Supreme Court shall have appellate jurisdiction, both as to law and fact, with such exceptions, and under such regulations as the Congress shall make.

The trial of all crimes, except in cases of impeachment, shall be by jury; and such trial shall be held in the State where the said crimes shall have been committed; but when not committed within any State, the trial shall be at such place or places as the Congress may by law have directed.

SECTION 3.

Treason against the United States shall consist only in levying war against them, or in adhering to their enemies, giving them aid and comfort. No person shall be convicted of treason unless on the testimony of two witnesses to the same overt act, or on confession in open court.

The Congress shall have power to declare the punishment of treason, but no attainder of treason shall work corruption of blood, or forfeiture except during the life of the person attainted.

ARTICLE IV

SECTION 1.

Full faith and credit shall be given in each State to the public acts, records, and judicial proceedings of every other State. And the Congress may by general laws prescribe the manner in which such acts, records, and proceedings shall be proved, and the effect thereof.

SECTION 2.

The citizens of each State shall be entitled to all privileges and immunities of citizens in the several States.

A person charged in any State with treason, felony, or other crime, who shall flee from justice, and be found in another State, shall on demand of the executive authority of the State from which he fled, be delivered up to be removed to the State having jurisdiction of the crime.

No person held to service or labor in the State, under the laws thereof, escaping into another, shall, in consequence of any law or regulation therein, be discharged from such service or labor, but shall be delivered up on claim of the party to whom such service or labor may be due.*

reach the Supreme Court. The judgment of the Supreme Court is final.

One of the great powers of our federal courts is their right to declare an act of Congress or a state legislature unconstitutional, though this right is not specifically mentioned in any part of the Constitution.

Treason
This crime is carefully defined. The last sentence in Section 3 says that if a person is convicted of treason, the taint of the crime cannot legally be passed on to his or her children or later descendants.

THE STATES

Relations among the States
The Constitution insures that persons cannot escape a legal obligation by moving from one state to another. Also, citizens moving from one state to another shall be treated the same as are citizens of the state they have moved to.

* Changed by the Thirteenth Amendment

New States

Without this section we might still be a nation of only 13 states. This permits Congress to admit new states to the Union. No state may be divided into two or more states without the consent of its people. This explains why the people of Massachusetts had to consent before Maine could become a state at the time of the Missouri Compromise. (See page 269.)

SECTION 3.

New States may be admitted by the Congress into this Union; but no new State shall be formed or erected within the jurisdiction of any other State; nor any State be formed by the junction of two or more States, or parts of States, without the consent of the legislatures of the States concerned as well as of the Congress.

The Congress shall have power to dispose of and make all needful rules and regulations respecting the territory or other property belonging to the United States; and nothing in this Constitution shall be so construed as to prejudice any claims of the United States, or of any particular State.

SECTION 4.

The United States shall guarantee to every State in this Union a republican form of government, and shall protect each of them against invasion; and on application of the legislature, or of the executive (when the legislature cannot be convened) against domestic violence.

AMENDMENTS

Changing the Constitution

Two methods are provided for proposing amendments, but the second—that is, on the application of the legislatures of two thirds of the states—has never been used.

ARTICLE V

The Congress, whenever two thirds of both houses shall deem it necessary, shall propose amendments to this Constitution, or, on the application of the legislatures of two thirds of the several States, shall call a convention for proposing amendments, which, in either case, shall be valid to all intents and purposes, as part of this Constitution, when ratified by the legislatures of three fourths of the several States, or by conventions in three fourths thereof, as the one or the other mode of ratification may be proposed by the Congress; provided [that no amendment which may be made prior to the year one thousand eight hundred and eight shall in any manner affect the first and fourth clauses in the ninth section of the first article, and] that no State, without its consent, shall be deprived of its equal suffrage in the Senate.

GENERAL PROVISIONS

The Supremacy Clause

The second paragraph of Article VI is often called the supremacy clause. It makes clear that when national and state authority collide, state authority must give way, for the Constitution is the supreme law of the nation.

ARTICLE VI

All debts contracted and engagements entered into, before the adoption of this Constitution, shall be as valid against the United States under this Constitution, as under the Confederation.

This Constitution, and the laws of the United States which shall be made in pursuance thereof; and all treaties made, or which shall be made, under the authority of the United States, shall be the supreme law of the land; and the judges in every State shall be bound thereby, anything in the Constitution or laws of any State to the contrary notwithstanding.

The senators and representatives before mentioned, and the members of the several State legislatures, and all executive and judicial officers, both of the United States, and of the several States, shall be bound by oath or affirmation to support this Constitution; but no religious test shall ever be required as a qualification to any office or public trust under the United States.

No Religious Test
A person's religion shall never be used officially to keep him or her from holding office under the government of the United States.

ARTICLE VII

The ratification of the conventions of nine States shall be sufficient for the establishment of this Constitution between the States so ratifying the same.

Done in Convention by the unanimous consent of the States present the seventeenth day of September in the year of our Lord one thousand seven hundred and eighty-seven, and of the independence of the United States of America the twelfth. In witness whereof we have hereunto subscribed our names.

George Washington, President
(VIRGINIA)

RATIFICATION

Conventions
All states had ratifying conventions in which they gave approval to the Constitution. The table below gives the date and the vote in each of the state conventions.

1787

Del.	Dec. 7	Unanimous
Pa.	Dec. 12	46–23
N.J.	Dec. 18	Unanimous

1788

Ga.	Jan. 2	Unanimous
Conn.	Jan. 9	128–40
Mass.	Feb. 6	187–168*
Md.	Apr. 28	63–11
S.C.	May 27	149–73
N.H.	June 21	57–46*
Va.	June 25	87–76*
N.Y.	July 26	30–27*

1789

N.C.	Nov. 21	187–77

1790

R.I.	May 29	34–22

*Strongly urged Bill of Rights

MASSACHUSETTS
Nathaniel Gorham
Rufus King

NEW YORK
Alexander Hamilton

GEORGIA
William Few
Abraham Baldwin

DELAWARE
George Read
Gunning Bedford
John Dickinson
Richard Bassett
Jacob Broom

VIRGINIA
John Blair
James Madison

PENNSYLVANIA
Benjamin Franklin
Thomas Mifflin
Robert Morris
George Clymer
Thomas FitzSimons
Jared Ingersoll
James Wilson
Gouvernor Morris

NEW HAMPSHIRE
John Langdon
Nicholas Gilman

NEW JERSEY
William Livingston
David Brearley
William Paterson
Jonathan Dayton

CONNECTICUT
William Samuel Johnson
Roger Sherman

NORTH CAROLINA
William Blount
Richard Dobbs Spaight
Hugh Williamson

SOUTH CAROLINA
John Rutledge
Charles Cotesworth
  Pinckney
Charles Pinckney
Pierce Butler

MARYLAND
James McHenry
Daniel of St. Thomas
  Jenifer
Daniel Carroll

BILL OF RIGHTS

The first ten amendments are known as the Bill of Rights. The First Amendment sets forth several basic rights and freedoms. Congress cannot interfere with freedom of religion or a person's right to speak freely. It cannot curb the right to print the truth. It cannot prevent citizens from meeting peaceably to discuss their problems and to ask the government to do something about them.

FIRST AMENDMENT—1791

Congress shall make no law respecting an establishment of religion, or prohibiting the free exercise thereof; or abridging the freedom of speech, or of the press; or the right of the people peaceably to assemble, and to petition the government for a redress of grievances.

SECOND AMENDMENT—1791

The Second and Third Amendments are not so pertinent today as they were in 1791. Today, for example, it is not likely that the national government would quarter soldiers in a private home.

A well-regulated militia, being necessary to the security of a free State, the right of the people to keep and bear arms, shall not be infringed.

THIRD AMENDMENT—1791

No soldier shall, in time of peace, be quartered in any house, without the consent of the owner, nor in time of war, but in a manner to be prescribed by law.

FOURTH AMENDMENT—1791

The Fourth Amendment is still very important. It protects people against illegal invasions of their homes and against seizure of their property by government officials without a proper search-and-seizure warrant.

The right of the people to be secure in their persons, houses, papers, and effects, against unreasonable searches and seizures, shall not be violated, and no warrants shall issue, but upon probable cause, supported by oath or affirmation, and particularly describing the place to be searched, and the persons or things to be seized.

FIFTH AMENDMENT—1791

No person shall be held to answer for a capital or otherwise infamous crime, unless on a presentment or indictment of a grand jury, except in cases arising in the land or naval forces, or in the militia, when in actual service in time of war or public danger; nor shall any person be subject for the same offense to be twice put in jeopardy of life or limb; nor shall be compelled in any criminal case to be a witness against himself, nor be deprived of life, liberty, or property, without due process of law; nor shall private property be taken for public use without just compensation.

SIXTH AMENDMENT—1791

In all criminal prosecutions, the accused shall enjoy the right to a speedy and public trial, by an impartial jury of the State and district wherein the crime shall have been committed, which district shall have been previously ascertained by law, and to be informed of the nature and cause of the accusation; to be confronted with the witnesses against him; to have compulsory process for obtaining witnesses in his favor, and to have the assistance of counsel for his defense.

SEVENTH AMENDMENT—1791

In suits at common law, where the value in controversy shall exceed twenty dollars, the right of trial by jury shall be preserved, and no fact tried by a jury shall be otherwise reexamined in any court of the United States, than according to the rules of the common law.

Rights of Persons Accused of Crimes

The Fifth, Sixth, Seventh, and Eighth Amendments set forth the procedures that courts must follow regarding persons involved in criminal or civil court actions. Among the rights are trial by jury within a reasonable time, the services of a lawyer, and the right to call witnesses. If the accused person is found not guilty, he or she cannot be tried again for the same crime.

Bail, Penalties

An accused person cannot be required to put up an unreasonable sum of money as bail if he or she is released from jail while awaiting trial. If found guilty, the accused person cannot be tried again for the same crime.

People's Rights and Reserved Powers

The people may retain rights that were not stated earlier. Moreover, any power that the Constitution does not forbid to the states is retained by them or by their people.

Election of President and Vice President

This amendment was made necessary because of the rise of political parties during the 1790s. The amendment changed the details for electing a President through the electoral system.

In 1800 the most famous tie vote in American political history occurred. At that time, electors voted for two candidates without distinguishing between President and Vice President. The electors of the victorious party—the Democratic-Republicans—were pledged to vote for Thomas Jefferson and Aaron Burr. They cast their votes in this way, meaning that they wanted Jefferson to be the President and Burr to be the Vice President. It had been expected

EIGHTH AMENDMENT—1791

Excessive bail shall not be required, nor excessive fines imposed, nor cruel and unusual punishments inflicted.

NINTH AMENDMENT—1791

The enumeration in the Constitution of certain rights shall not be construed to deny or disparage others retained by the people.

TENTH AMENDMENT—1791

The powers not delegated to the United States by the Constitution, nor prohibited by it to the States are reserved to the States respectively, or to the people.

ELEVENTH AMENDMENT—1795

The judicial power of the United States shall not be construed to extend to any suit in law or equity, commenced or prosecuted against one of the United States, by citizens of another State, or by citizens or subjects of any foreign State.

TWELFTH AMENDMENT—1804

The electors shall meet in their respective States, and vote by ballot for President and Vice President, one of whom, at least, shall not be an inhabitant of the same State with themselves; they shall name in their ballots the person voted for as Vice President, and they shall make distinct lists of all persons voted for as President and of all persons voted for as Vice President, and of the number of votes for each, which lists they shall sign and certify, and transmit sealed to the seat of government of the United States, directed to the president of the Senate;—The president of the Senate shall, in the presence of the Senate and House of Representatives, open all the certificates and the votes shall then be counted;—The person having the greatest number of votes for President shall be the President, if such number be a majority of the whole number of electors appointed; and if no person have such majority, then from the persons having the highest numbers not exceeding three on the list of those voted for as President, the House of Representatives shall choose immediately, by ballot, the President. But in choosing the President, the votes shall be taken by States, the representation from each State having one vote; a quorum for this purpose shall consist of a member or members from two thirds of the States, and a majority of all the States shall be necessary to a choice. And if the House of Representatives shall not choose a President whenever the right of choice shall devolve upon them, <u>before the fourth day of March next following,</u>* then the Vice President shall act as President, as in the case of the death or other constitutional disability of the President. The person having the greatest number of votes as Vice President shall be the Vice President, if such number be a majority of the whole number of electors appointed, and if no person have a majority, then from the two highest numbers on the list, the Senate shall choose the Vice President; a quorum for the purpose shall consist of two thirds of the whole number of senators and a majority of the whole number shall be necessary to a choice. But no person constitutionally ineligible to the office of President shall be eligible to that of Vice President of the United States.

THIRTEENTH AMENDMENT—1865

SECTION 1.

Neither slavery nor involuntary servitude, except as a punishment for crime whereof the party shall have been duly convicted, shall exist within the United States, or any place subject to their jurisdiction.

SECTION 2.

Congress shall have power to enforce this article by appropriate legislation.

*Changed by the Twentieth Amendment

that at least one elector would vote for Jefferson and not for Burr, avoiding a tie. But none did, and each got 73 electoral votes.

Under the Constitution the election then had to be decided in the House of Representatives. At such times, each state had one vote. The Federalists still controlled the House of Representatives, and they saw the opportunity to keep Jefferson, whom they disliked, from becoming President. Only the personal influence of Alexander Hamilton kept the Federalists from making Burr President. To prevent such a mixup from happening again, the Twelfth Amendment was adopted. It instructs electors to cast separate votes for the candidates for President and Vice President.

Slavery Abolished
The Thirteenth Amendment, added soon after the Civil War, prohibited slavery.

FOURTEENTH AMENDMENT—1868

Rights of Citizens

The Fourteenth Amendment defines citizenship and forbids the states to interfere with the rights of citizens of the United States. Also added soon after the Civil War, this amendment protects citizens' rights against state action. Section 2 says that if a state denies the right to vote to any group, that state's delegation in Congress will be reduced.

Apportionment

If a state denies voting rights to any group for any reason except for taking part in a rebellion or other crime, that state's delegation in Congress will be reduced.

Dealing with Rebels

This section denies the privilege of serving in any public office to any former officeholder who took part in the rebellion of the 1860s. In 1898, Congress removed this limitation so that former Confederate officers could serve in the Spanish-American War.

Civil War Debt

No part of the national government's debts can ever be canceled. No part of the debt of the Confederate states or any claim for loss of slaves will be paid.

SECTION 1.

All persons born or naturalized in the United States, and subject to the jurisdiction thereof, are citizens of the United States and of the State wherein they reside. No State shall make or enforce any law which shall abridge the privileges or immunities of citizens of the United States; nor shall any State deprive any person of life, liberty, or property, without due process of law; nor deny to any person within its jurisdiction the equal protection of the laws.

SECTION 2.

Representatives shall be apportioned among the several States according to their respective numbers, counting the whole number of persons in each State, excluding Indians not taxed. But when the right to vote at any election for the choice of electors for President and Vice President of the United States, representatives in Congress, the executive and judicial officers of a State, or the members of the legislature thereof, is denied to any of the male inhabitants of such State, being twenty-one years of age, and citizens of the United States, or in any way abridged, except for participation in rebellion, or other crime, the basis of representation therein shall be reduced in the proportion which the number of such male citizens shall bear to the whole number of male citizens twenty-one years of age in such State.

SECTION 3.

No person shall be a senator or representative in Congress, or elector of President and Vice President, or hold any office, civil or military, under the United States, or under any State, who, having previously taken an oath, as a member of Congress, or as an officer of the United States, or as a member of any State legislature, or as an executive or judicial officer of any State, to support the Constitution of the United States, shall have engaged in insurrection or rebellion against the same, or given aid or comfort to the enemies thereof. But Congress may by a vote of two thirds of each house, remove such disability.

SECTION 4.

The validity of the public debt of the United States, authorized by law, including debts incurred for payment of pensions and bounties for services in suppressing insurrection or rebellion, shall not be questioned. But neither the United States nor any State shall assume or pay any debt or obligation incurred in aid of insurrection or rebellion against the United States, or any claim for the loss or emancipation of any slave; but all such debts, obligations and claims shall be held illegal and void.

SECTION 5.

The Congress shall have power to enforce, by appropriate legislation, the provisions of this article.

FIFTEENTH AMENDMENT—1870

SECTION 1.

The right of citizens of the United States to vote shall not be denied or abridged by the United States or by any State on account of race, color, or previous condition of servitude.

Right to Vote
This third and last Reconstruction amendment was meant to guard the people against the misuse of state power.

SECTION 2.

The Congress shall have power to enforce this article by appropriate legislation.

SIXTEENTH AMENDMENT—1913

The Congress shall have power to lay and collect taxes on incomes, from whatever source derived, without apportionment among the several States, and without regard to any census or enumeration.

Income Taxes
Article I said that "direct taxes shall be apportioned among the several states . . . according to their respective numbers (population)." This amendment was necessary in order to make the income tax constitutional.

SEVENTEENTH AMENDMENT—1913

The Senate of the United States shall be composed of two senators from each State, elected by the people thereof, for six years; and each senator shall have one vote. The electors in each State shall have the qualifications requisite for electors of the most numerous branch of the State legislatures.

Direct Election of Senators

By the time of the twentieth century, many people had come to feel that it would be more democratic to have senators chosen by direct vote of the people instead of by state legislatures as the Constitution provided. In accordance with this idea, the Seventeenth Amendment was added.

Prohibition

In 1919 the American people decided to prohibit the manufacture, sale, or transportation of intoxicating liquors. Many people felt that such a prohibition would be good for the health and welfare of all the people in the United States. Nevertheless, 14 years after it became a part of the Constitution, the Eighteenth Amendment was repealed by the Twenty-first Amendment.

When vacancies happen in the representation of any State in the Senate, the executive authority of such State shall issue writs of election to fill such vacancies: Provided, that the legislature of any State may empower the executive thereof to make temporary appointments until the people fill the vacancies by election as the legislature may direct.

EIGHTEENTH AMENDMENT*—1919

SECTION 1.

After one year from the ratification of this article the manufacture, sale, or transportation of intoxicating liquors within, the importation thereof into, or the exportation thereof from the United States and all territory subject to the jurisdiction thereof for beverage purposes is hereby prohibited.

SECTION 2.

The Congress and the several States shall have concurrent power to enforce this article by appropriate legislation.

SECTION 3.

This article shall be inoperative unless it shall have been ratified as an amendment to the Constitution by the legislatures of the several States, as provided in the Constitution, within seven years from the date of the submission hereof to the States by the Congress.

* Repealed by the Twenty-first Amendment

NINETEENTH AMENDMENT—1920

SECTION 1.

The right of citizens of the United States to vote shall not be denied or abridged by the United States or by any State on Account of sex.

SECTION 2.

Congress shall have power, by appropriate legislation, to enforce the provisions of this article.

Women's Suffrage

By 1920 it was plain that denying women the right to vote was a denial of the principles of democracy. Any woman who met the qualifications required of men could henceforth vote.

TWENTIETH AMENDMENT—1933

SECTION 1.

The terms of the President and Vice President shall end at noon on the 20th day of January, and the terms of senators and representatives at noon on the 3d day of January, of the years in which such terms would have ended if this article had not been ratified; and the terms of their successors shall then begin.

SECTION 2.

The Congress shall assemble at least once in every year, and such meeting shall begin at noon on the 3d day in January, unless they shall by law appoint a different day.

SECTION 3.

If, at the time fixed for the beginning of the term of the President, the President-elect shall have died, the Vice President-elect shall become President. If a President shall not have been chosen before the time fixed for the beginning of his term, or if the

Terms of President, Members of Congress

This amendment shortens the time that passes between the election of a President or member of Congress and the beginning of his or her term of office. Now the newly elected Congress meets on January 3 and the President is inaugurated on January 20 following his election. This change reflects the swifter means of communication and travel that are available today. This amendment also clarifies the procedure to be followed in case a President-elect or Vice President-elect dies or is not qualified for some reason before the time of inauguration. It also specifies the procedure in case of the death of a candidate in an election that has been thrown into the House of Representatives because no candidate has received a majority of electoral votes.

President-elect shall have failed to qualify, then the Vice President-elect shall act as President until a President shall have qualified; and the Congress may by law provide for the case wherein neither a President-elect nor a Vice President-elect shall have qualified, declaring who shall then act as President, or the manner in which one who is to act shall be selected, and such persons shall act accordingly until a President or Vice President shall have qualified.

SECTION 4.

The Congress may by law provide for the case of the death of any of the persons from whom the House of Representatives may choose a President whenever the right of choice shall have devolved upon them, and for the case of the death of any of the persons from whom the Senate may choose a Vice President whenever the right of choice shall have devolved upon them.

SECTION 5.

Sections 1 and 2 shall take effect on the 15th day of October following the ratification of this article.

SECTION 6.

This article shall be inoperative unless it shall have been ratified as an amendment to the Constitution by the legislatures of three fourths of the several States within seven years from the date of its submission.

TWENTY-FIRST AMENDMENT—1933

SECTION 1.

The eighteenth article of amendment to the Constitution of the United States is hereby repealed.

National Prohibition Repealed
The Twenty-first Amendment repealed the Eighteenth Amendment, which provided for prohibition by the national government of the sale, manufacture, or transportation of intoxicating liquors. However, it is still possible for states, counties, or local communities to forbid the manufacture, sale, or use of intoxicating liquors within their borders.

SECTION 2.

The transportation or importation into any State, territory, or possession of the United States for delivery or use therein of intoxicating liquors, in violation of the laws thereof, is hereby prohibited.

SECTION 3.

This article shall be inoperative unless it shall have been ratified as an amendment to the Constitution by conventions in the several States, as provided in the Constitution, within seven years from the date of submission hereof to the States by the Congress.

TWENTY-SECOND AMENDMENT—1951

No person shall be elected to the office of the President more than twice, and no person who has held the office of President, or acted as President, for more than two years of a term to which some other person was elected President shall be elected to the office of the President more than once.

But this Article shall not apply to any person holding the office of President when this Article was proposed by the Congress, and shall not prevent any person who may be holding the office of President, or acting as President, during the term within which this Article becomes operative from holding the office of President or acting as President during the remainder of such term.

Two-term Limit

Throughout most of our history, the tradition that a President should serve only two terms was a part of our unwritten Constitution. In 1940, Franklin D. Roosevelt broke the tradition by running successfully for a third term. In 1944 he was elected once more but died a few months after his inauguration. When the Republicans gained control of Congress a few years later, they introduced this amendment. It makes the two-term tradition a part of our written Constitution.

TWENTY-THIRD AMENDMENT—1961

SECTION 1.

The District constituting the seat of government of the United States shall appoint in such manner as the Congress may direct:

A number of electors of President and Vice President equal to the whole number of senators and representatives in Congress to which the District would be entitled if it were a State, but in no event more than the least populous State; they shall be in addition to those appointed by the States, but they shall be considered, for the purposes of the election of President and Vice President, to be electors appointed by a State; and they shall meet in the District and perform such duties as provided by the twelfth article of amendment.

Presidential Vote for D.C.

When the Constitution was drawn up, there was no District of Columbia. The right to choose electors for President and Vice President was granted only to the states. This amendment states that the District of Columbia shall have electors who may vote for President. However, they are limited in number to the number of electors for the least populous state. At the present time, it is three.

SECTION 2.

The Congress shall have power to enforce this article by appropriate legislation.

TWENTY-FOURTH AMENDMENT—1964

SECTION 1.

The right of citizens of the United States to vote in any primary or other election for President or Vice President, for electors for President or Vice President, or for senator or representative in Congress, shall not be denied or abridged by the United States or any state by reason of failure to pay any poll tax or other tax.

SECTION 2.

The Congress shall have power to enforce this article by appropriate legislation.

TWENTY-FIFTH AMENDMENT—1967

SECTION 1.

In case of the removal of the President from office or his death or resignation, the Vice President shall become President.

SECTION 2.

Whenever there is a vacancy in the office of the Vice President, the President shall nominate a Vice President who shall take the office upon confirmation by a majority vote of both houses of Congress.

SECTION 3.

Whenever the President transmits to the president pro tempore of the Senate and the speaker of the House of Representatives his written declaration that he is unable to discharge the powers and duties of his office, and until he transmits to them a written declaration to the contrary, such powers and duties shall be discharged by the Vice President as Acting President.

SECTION 4.

Whenever the Vice President and a majority of either the principal officers of the executive departments or of such other body as Congress may by law provide, transmit to the president pro tempore of the Senate and the speaker of the House of Representatives their written declaration that the President is unable to discharge the powers and duties of his office, the Vice President shall immediately assume the powers and duties of the office as Acting President.

Thereafter, when the President transmits to the president pro tempore of the Senate and the speaker of the House of Repre-

Poll Tax Outlawed

The poll tax is a levy that some states impose on all adult citizens. It is usually not more than three dollars a year. A main purpose of the poll tax is to provide revenue, but in a few states a citizen could not vote if he or she had not paid the poll tax. This requirement sometimes kept poor people from voting. This amendment says that payment of the poll tax, or any other tax, can no longer be required for voting in a federal election.

Presidential Succession

At what time the Vice President should take over the President's duties in case of disability had never been defined. The illnesses of Dwight Eisenhower in the 1950s and the tragic death of John F. Kennedy in 1963 were behind the movement that resulted in this amendment. It sets forth the procedure to be followed in case a President is disabled. It also provides for the selection of a Vice President in case the office becomes vacant.

This procedure for selecting a Vice President has been used just twice—in 1973, when Richard Nixon selected Gerald R. Ford, and a year later, when Ford selected Nelson A. Rockefeller.

sentatives his written declaration that no inability exists, he shall resume the powers and duties of his office unless the Vice President and a majority of either the principal officers of the executive department or of such other body as Congress may by law provide, transmit within four days to the president pro tempore of the Senate and the speaker of the House of Representatives their written declaration that the President is unable to discharge the powers and duties of his office. Thereupon Congress shall decide the issue, assembling within 48 hours for that purpose if not in session. If the Congress, within 21 days after receipt of the latter written declaration, or, if Congress is not in session, within 21 days after Congress is required to assemble, determines by two-thirds vote of both houses that the President is unable to discharge the powers and duties of his office, the Vice President shall continue to discharge the same as Acting President; otherwise, the President shall resume the powers and duties of his office.

TWENTY-SIXTH AMENDMENT—1971

SECTION 1.

The right of citizens of the United States, who are eighteen years of age or older, to vote shall not be denied or abridged by the United States or by any State on account of age.

SECTION 2.

The Congress shall have power to enforce this article by appropriate legislation.

Voting Age of 18
This amendment lowers the voting age from 21 to 18. It recognized that people from 18 to 21 are as well qualified as their elders to cast ballots in elections.

9 The Federalist Period

1789–1800

The New Government Begins

What patterns of government were established by George Washington and the first Congress?

VOCABULARY

inauguration	loose interpretation
tariff	strict interpretation
Cabinet	
Judiciary Act of 1789	Bank of the United States

Our First President   April 30, 1789, was a sunny day in New York City. A happy and curious crowd had gathered in front of the new Federal Hall. The crowd had come to see the first **inauguration** of a President of the United States. An inauguration is a ceremony that is held when a person begins a term of service in an elected office.

A little after noon a group of people stepped onto the balcony of Federal Hall. Everyone recognized the tall white-wigged figure of George Washington. Few recognized Robert Livingston, the chief judge of New York's highest state court. Livingston was there to read the oath of office, which the new President would take.

Not many on the street below the balcony heard the words. Still, they knew that George Washington was taking the Presi-dent's oath of office. As soon as the oath was administered, Livingston turned to the crowd and cried, "Long live George Washington, President of the United States!" The people responded with a cheer. Washington bowed and they cheered again. Then the group on the balcony moved inside Federal Hall. There Washington gave his first inaugural address.

Congress Acts   Most of the members of the first Congress had supported the Constitution. Nearly half of the 26 senators had taken part in the Constitutional Convention. Most of the others had worked for ratification. James Madison led a powerful group in the House of Representatives. Like their leader, members of this group supported the new central government.

The new government badly needed money to meet its expenses. Some money would come from the sale of western lands, but it was not enough. So Congress passed a **tariff** bill. A tariff is a tax on goods imported into or exported from a country. The tariff of 1789 put a tax of from 5 to 15 percent on about 80 manufactured articles imported into the United States. For more than a century, tariffs on imported goods supplied most of the money the government needed.

George Washington took the oath of office as first President of the United States in New York in 1789.
■ What was happening in Europe that same year?

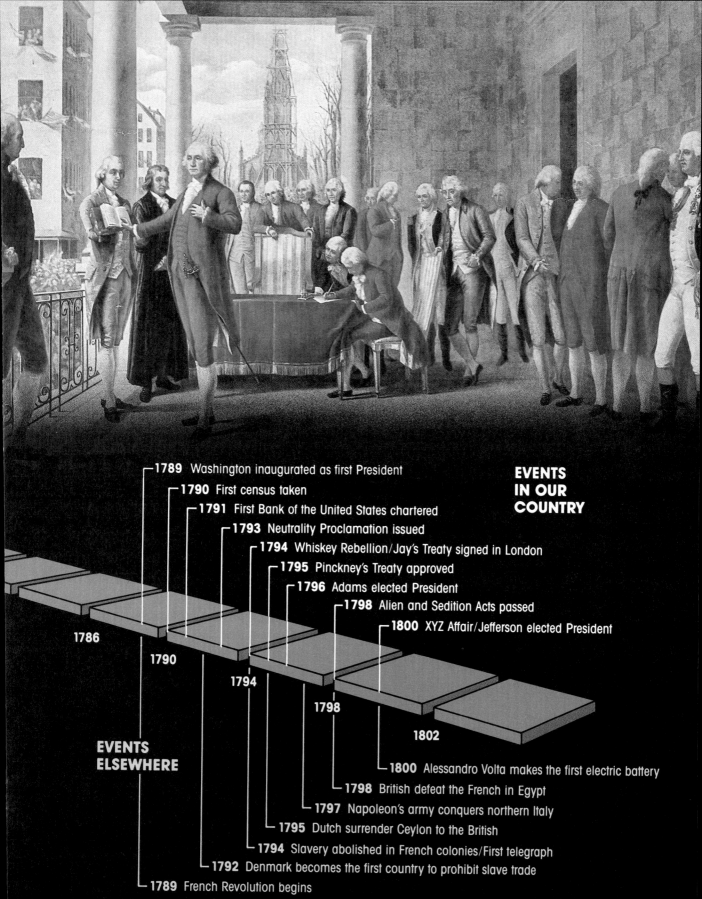

**EVENTS
IN OUR
COUNTRY**

—1789 Washington inaugurated as first President
—1790 First census taken
—1791 First Bank of the United States chartered
—1793 Neutrality Proclamation issued
—1794 Whiskey Rebellion/Jay's Treaty signed in London
—1795 Pinckney's Treaty approved
—1796 Adams elected President
—1798 Alien and Sedition Acts passed
—1800 XYZ Affair/Jefferson elected President

1786
1790
1794
1798
1802

**EVENTS
ELSEWHERE**

—1800 Alessandro Volta makes the first electric battery
—1798 British defeat the French in Egypt
—1797 Napoleon's army conquers northern Italy
—1795 Dutch surrender Ceylon to the British
—1794 Slavery abolished in French colonies/First telegraph
—1792 Denmark becomes the first country to prohibit slave trade
—1789 French Revolution begins

The President's Cabinet Congress knew that President Washington would need help to run the executive branch of government. So within the executive branch, Congress created the Departments of State, Treasury, and War. Each was headed by an official called a secretary. Congress also authorized the office of attorney general to handle legal affairs. The postmaster general was to run the mail service. The chart on page 223 shows the duties of these officials and the names of the five men first appointed to these offices in the new government.

President Washington is pictured with his first Cabinet. Today the Cabinet has 13 departments.
■ **Why, do you think, has the Cabinet grown?**

It was Washington who began the practice of consulting with the heads of the major departments in the executive branch of the government. These advisers soon became known as the President's **Cabinet**, which means "a group of advisers." The Constitution says nothing about advisers to the President, but every President since Washington has had a Cabinet. The number of Cabinet members has increased over the years as Congress has added new departments to the executive branch.

In making appointments to his Cabinet, the President tried to gain support from different parts of the country. Thomas Jefferson and Edmund Randolph were from Virginia, Henry Knox was from Massachusetts, and Alexander Hamilton was from New York. Since Washington's time, Presidents have sought geographical balance in their Cabinets.

Washington — and the Presidents following him also — tried to have Cabinet members with different points of view. For example, Edmund Randolph and Samuel Osgood had opposed ratification of the Constitution. And Thomas Jefferson was not so firmly in favor of a strong central government as Hamilton and Knox were.

The Federal Courts Article III of the Constitution states that the judicial branch of the federal government will consist of a Supreme Court and any lower courts Congress wishes to establish. Acting under this authority, Congress passed the **Judiciary Act of 1789**. This act provided for a Supreme Court with a chief justice and five associate justices. The Judiciary Act of 1789 also set up lower courts on two levels. At the lower level were 13 district courts, one for each state. There were three circuit courts at a higher level, between the district courts and the United States Supreme Court.

WASHINGTON'S FIRST CABINET		
Office	Official	Duties
Secretary of State	Thomas Jefferson	To conduct the relations of the United States with other nations
Secretary of the Treasury	Alexander Hamilton	To handle the government's finances
Secretary of War	Henry Knox	To take charge of all military matters
Attorney General	Edmund Randolph	To act as chief legal adviser to the executive branch
Postmaster General	Samuel Osgood	To run the post office and mail service

Postmaster General did not become a Cabinet department until 1829.
Which Cabinet position do you think is the most important one?

Since 1789, Congress has changed the number of associate justices on the Supreme Court as well as the number of district and circuit courts. Still, our federal court system today has the same framework as the one set up by the Judiciary Act of 1789. Through this court system, justice is served.

Hamilton's Debt Plan   Article VI of the Constitution required the new government to pay all debts contracted by the old government under the Articles of Confederation. Most of the states were still in debt from the War for Independence. The new federal government had no responsibility for the state debts. However, it arranged to pay these debts, too.

Payment came about through a plan proposed by Alexander Hamilton. In 1789, Congress asked him, as secretary of the treasury, to prepare a report on government finances. In his report, Hamilton suggested that the new government pay both the federal and the state debts. Hamilton argued that the federal government would be strengthened by taking responsibility for the state debts. People who had lent money to the states would look to the federal government for payment. Therefore, they would support the federal government and would work for its success.

The Federal District   Virginia and other southern states had paid nearly all their state debts. They had no quarrel with the plan to pay the federal debt. But their leaders were unwilling to have the federal government take over the task of paying the state debts. Southern leaders thought their citizens would be taxed to help pay the debts of northern states.

At that time Congress was trying to decide the location of a new capital and at the same time Hamilton's debt plan was being considered. Thomas Jefferson knew that people in the South wanted the permanent capital of the United States to be in or near their part of the country. So he persuaded some Virginia members of Congress to vote for Hamilton's plan. In return, Hamilton used his influence to place the new capital in a federal district between Maryland and Virginia. Philadelphia was to be the capital for 10 years. Then the United States government would move to Washington in the newly formed District of Columbia.

A National Bank   Alexander Hamilton and Thomas Jefferson were successful in working out a compromise on the debt question. On another matter, however, the two leaders disagreed. Hamilton proposed that the United States Congress charter a national bank, modeled on the Bank of England. A national bank, Hamilton said, should be owned partly by the government and partly by private individuals. Such a bank would be a safe place for the federal government to keep its money. Moreover, it could help the government borrow money.

Hamilton and Jefferson disagreed on the question of whether Congress had the power to charter a national bank. Hamilton said that the Constitution (Article I, Section 8) gave Congress the power to pass any laws necessary to carry out its listed powers. He argued that Congress clearly had the power to tax and spend for the general welfare. A bank, he said, would help Congress carry out this power. Therefore, Hamilton declared, Congress did have the power under the Constitution to charter a bank.

Hamilton's argument is known as the **loose interpretation** (or broad interpretation) of the Constitution. The makers of the Constitution could not possibly write in all the details of government. Therefore, they included a clause permitting Congress to create whatever agencies were "necessary and proper" to carry out the functions of government. This clause made a loose interpretation of the Constitution possible. It is sometimes referred to as the *elastic* clause.

Jefferson, on the other hand, believed the federal government could do only what the Constitution specifically gave it the power to do. In his opinion, the Constitution should be interpreted exactly as it was

The site that would become the District of Columbia was a little river port in 1790. What were some of the advantages of such a location?

The newly chartered Bank of the United States set up its headquarters in Philadelphia.
■ According to the picture, in what year was the bank founded?

written. Jefferson's view is known as the **strict interpretation** (or narrow interpretation) of the Constitution. According to this interpretation, the government could not charter a bank because the Constitution did not give the legislative branch the specific power to do so.

Actually, Congress had already passed a bill chartering the first **Bank of the United States**. President Washington, however, had cautiously held off signing the bill into law. He wanted to hear his Cabinet's views on whether the Constitution gave Congress the power to establish a bank. After listening carefully, Washington decided to accept Hamilton's arguments. He signed the bank bill in 1791. It provided a charter for the Bank of the United States. Under its charter, which

would last 20 years, the headquarters of the bank would be in Philadelphia. It could, however, set up branches in other parts of the country.

CHECKUP

1. How did the tariff of 1789 raise money for the new government?
2. What was the purpose of the President's Cabinet?
3. How did the Judiciary Act of 1789 establish a federal court system?
4. Why was Hamilton's debt plan adopted?
5. Explain the difference between Hamilton and Jefferson's interpretations of the Constitution.

6. **Thinking Critically** Why do you think Washington wanted people with different points of view in his Cabinet?

The Rise of Political Parties

Why did political parties form in the United States?

VOCABULARY

political party	Whiskey Rebellion
Federalist party	nominate
Democratic-Republican party	caucus

A "Fishing" Trip   In the summer of 1791, Thomas Jefferson and his friend James Madison took a trip through the northern states. The two men said they were going on a "fishing and botanizing" journey. But it was neither fish nor rare plants that sent them north. They were looking for northern leaders opposed to the policies of Alexander Hamilton.

Jefferson and Madison found what they were looking for in New York. There they talked with Aaron Burr, an opponent of Alexander Hamilton. They also spoke with George Clinton, who had long been governor of New York. Out of these talks in New York grew an organization called a **political party**.

Political Parties   A political party is an organization of people holding similar views on the policies a government should follow. The party members work to elect people of their choice to office and to shape government policies. The writers of the Constitution had not foreseen the development of political parties, and the Constitution makes no mention of them. Nevertheless, political parties have become important to all levels of government in the United States. Our first two political parties grew from the opposing views of Thomas Jefferson and Alexander Hamilton. As you have read, the two men had different opinions on the Bank of the United States. In time they differed on other questions, too.

Both Jefferson and Hamilton had many followers. Those with views similar to Hamilton's joined in what became known as the **Federalist party**. The leaders of this party had helped to write the Constitution. They believed in a strong central government. For more than 10 years, they had held most of the important offices in the government.

The people who had been against ratification of the Constitution were called Anti-Federalists. In the 1790s many of them became followers of Thomas Jefferson. His party was called the **Democratic-Republican party**. Later the name was shortened to the Democratic party.

Political parties were not written about in the Constitution. Some functions of political parties are listed above.
■ Which function do you think is most important?

WHAT POLITICAL PARTIES DO

- Political parties select candidates for office by means of caucuses or conventions.

- Political parties draw up *platforms*, which are statements of the stands the parties take on important issues.

- Political parties collect money to finance their candidates' campaigns.

- Candidates and other party leaders provide information to voters through speeches, written position statements, and advertisements.

- When members of political parties are elected to office, they direct the activities of the government.

- When leaders of a political party are out of office, they act as watchdogs, checking to see that the party in power conducts the activities of the government properly.

Angry farmers batter a whiskey-tax collector they have tarred and feathered.

■ **How do you think the tax collector responded to this treatment?**

Washington's Second Term   In 1792 President Washington wanted to retire to Mount Vernon. However, he consented to accept a second 4-year term. Once more he was chosen President by the unanimous vote of the electors.

During Washington's second term a crisis arose. In order to help pay back the government's debt, Hamilton had persuaded Congress to put a tax on whiskey. The whiskey tax angered western farmers. Since they had difficulty getting their grain to eastern markets, the farmers distilled some of their corn and rye into whiskey. Jugs, kegs, and barrels of whiskey could be more easily transported to the East and were less likely to rot than could wagonloads of bulky grain.

Many western farmers refused to pay the whiskey tax because they felt it was unfair. When the federal government sent tax collectors, the angry farmers threatened them with violence. Washington was alarmed by this threat, and in 1794 he called the militia of three states into federal service. With Alexander Hamilton in command, 15,000 men marched into west-

ern Pennsylvania. This display of force brought about the collapse of the **Whiskey Rebellion**, the name given to the farmers' brief resistance to the federal government.

The Whiskey Rebellion had two results. First, it showed that the federal government could enforce the laws that Congress had passed. The Whiskey Rebellion had the opposite effect on the people than Shays's Rebellion. Second, it convinced many western farmers that violence was a very poor way of opposing Federalist policies. Joining Jefferson's Democratic-Republican party began to look like a better way.

The Election of 1796   No doubt George Washington could have been elected to a third term as President. However, he believed two terms were enough. He also believed that political parties would weaken the national government. In a farewell message to the country, Washington warned against the harmful effects of the "spirit of party." His advice came too late. Political parties had already begun.

227

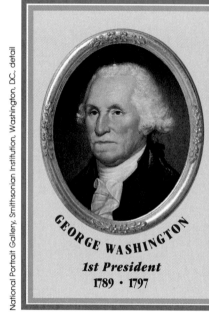

National Portrait Gallery, Smithsonian Institution, Washington, DC, detail

GEORGE WASHINGTON
1st President
1789 · 1797

Born: 1732, Westmoreland County, Virginia.
Education: Private tutors and relatives.
Training: Surveyor, militia officer, plantation owner.
To presidency from: Virginia.
Position when elected: Plantation owner.
Political party: Belonged to no party.
Married: Martha Dandridge Custis.
Children: None, though his wife had two children by a former marriage.
Died: 1799, from a cold and sore throat that doctors of the time could not cope with.
Other facts: Tall, broad-shouldered, and muscular. Large land holdings made him one of the richest persons of his time. Yet he was so short of cash that he had to borrow money to travel to his inauguration.
During his presidency: Saw the first successful balloon flight in America in Philadelphia in 1793.

As the end of Washington's second term neared, the two political parties **nominated,** or chose, candidates for election to the presidency. Federalist leaders wanted to nominate Alexander Hamilton, but they feared he had too many enemies to be elected. Instead they chose John Adams of Massachusetts as the Federalist presidential candidate. For Vice President they nominated Thomas Pinckney of South Carolina, the youngest son of Eliza Lucas Pinckney, whom you have already read about on pages 116–117.

Democratic-Republican leaders held a meeting to choose candidates for their party. Such a meeting of party leaders is called a **caucus.** From 1796 to 1832, parties used this method to choose those who ran for office. In 1796 the Democratic-Republican caucus named Thomas Jefferson as the party's presidential candidate. For Vice President, they chose Aaron Burr of New York.

The election showed how the power of the Democratic-Republican party was growing. Although John Adams won the presidency, he received only three more electoral votes than Thomas Jefferson. The Constitution at that time stated that the person with the second highest number of electoral votes would be Vice President. Therefore, Jefferson became Vice President even though he and John Adams were members of different political parties. The Twelfth Amendment to the Constitution, ratified in 1804, called for separate balloting for Vice President in the electoral college.

CHECKUP

1. Name the first two political parties and explain the differences between them.
2. What are the main functions of political parties in the United States?
3. How did the presidential election of 1796 show the growing strength of the Democratic-Republican party?
4. What did the Whiskey Rebellion prove?

5. **Thinking Critically** Would you have agreed with George Washington's view that political parties weaken the national government? Why or why not?

Treaties and Troubles

What problems in foreign relations did Presidents Washington and Adams have to solve?

VOCABULARY

Neutrality Proclamation	Pinckney's Treaty
impress	XYZ affair
Jay's Treaty	

The Last Federalist President John Adams was one of the leaders of the American Revolution. His writings had put forth many of the arguments in favor of revolution. Adams had helped draft the Declaration of Independence, had signed it, and had helped persuade the Second Continental Congress to approve it. He had served as his country's diplomatic representative abroad. He had been Vice President during Washington's two terms as President. Very few Americans in 1796 had as much experience in politics and government as John Adams.

Nevertheless, John Adams won only a narrow victory over Thomas Jefferson. This was one reason why he did not have greater success as President. Another reason was his stubborn personality. John Adams refused to change his ways to make himself popular. Even though Federalists were in control of the Senate and the House of Representatives, President Adams had trouble with Congress.

President Adams's main troubles, however, were in dealing with other countries. In 1789, the year that George Washington was inaugurated for his first term, a revolution broke out in France. John Marshall, who later became Chief Justice of the United States, wrote in 1789, "In no part of the globe was this revolution hailed with more joy than in America."

At first, most Americans looked on the French Revolution with favor. But as time passed, the French Revolution took a violent turn, with much bloodshed. Events in France as well as in other countries became matters of great concern in the United States. The way the Federalists dealt with these problems turned out to be unpopular. The foreign relations of the United States during the years that the Federalists were in power helped make John Adams the last Federalist President.

The Old Treaty with France You have read that the United States and France signed a treaty of alliance in 1778. At the time the United States was struggling for independence. France helped greatly in that struggle. In fact, without France's aid, the United States might not have won its War for Independence.

Fifteen years later, war broke out again between France and Great Britain. Because of the treaty of alliance, some Democratic-Republicans thought the United States should join France in this war against Great Britain. But Federalists argued that the treaty was no longer in force. They said that the revolution in France had changed the government that had signed the treaty. In addition, the Federalists feared that the French Revolution would go too far.

President Washington knew that the United States was too weak to get involved in another war so soon after its War for Independence. Therefore, he issued the **Neutrality Proclamation**. This meant the United States would not take sides in the war between France and Great Britain. It also made plain that the treaty of alliance between France and the United States was no longer in effect.

Jay's Treaty   Though President Washington declared American neutrality, the French-British conflict still caused trouble for the United States. British war vessels seized or sank American merchant ships suspected of trading with France. The British **impressed** American sailors — that is, they took sailors off American ships and forced them to serve on British warships.

Moreover, as late as the 1790s, the British still held western forts and trading posts in United States territory. They justified this action by saying that Americans had not paid the debts owed to British merchants from before the war. In 1794, Washington sent John Jay, the first Chief Justice of the United States, to Great Britain to try to arrange solutions to these problems.

John Jay's treaty with Great Britain was so unpopular that it sparked many demonstrations.
■ **What are the demonstrators in this picture doing?**

Jay succeeded in coming to an agreement with the British. In what became known as **Jay's Treaty**, Great Britain agreed to move out of the forts and trading posts on America's western lands. In exchange, a commission would be formed to work out the payment of American debts.

However, Jay was not able to solve all the problems that had caused trouble between the United States and Great Britain. There was nothing in Jay's Treaty about Great Britain's interference with American shipping. And the trade terms that were agreed on seemed to favor Great Britain. Also, impressment was not stopped, although it lessened somewhat.

The Democratic-Republicans and even some Federalists were unhappy with Jay's Treaty. President Washington was not pleased with it either. Still, he thought it might keep the United States out of war. So he presented it to the Senate for approval, as the Constitution required. Ratification in the Senate turned into a fight between the two political parties. Finally, in 1795, the Senate ratified Jay's Treaty and President Washington signed it. Nevertheless, the split between Democratic-Republicans and Federalists had widened.

Pinckney's Treaty   The year after Jay's Treaty, Thomas Pinckney, also a Federalist, was sent to Spain to try to work out problems between Spain and the United States. France had turned over its holdings west of the Mississippi River to Spain as part of the Treaty of Paris in 1763. As long as the colonists were confined to the region east of the Appalachians, it made little difference who laid claim to the wilderness region beyond the Mississippi. But as Americans moved into the lands beyond the mountains after the Revolution, trouble developed between the settlers and the Spanish officials.

Americans along the Mississippi River recognized the importance of New Orleans, near the river's mouth, as a port for shipping their crops. In 1795 Thomas Pinckney secured for these farmers the right to use the port. Not until 8 years later would the United States buy the city—and with it all of Louisiana—outright. (See page 253.)

◼ What is the meaning of the banner held by the eagle here?

A major issue was the use of the Mississippi River as a water highway. Spain did not want the river opened to free navigation. It saw such an act as a threat to its landholdings in North America. To western farmers, however, use of the Mississippi was essential to getting their crops to market. The crops could be sent down the river on flatboats. Near the mouth of the Mississippi river they could then be transferred to oceangoing vessels for shipment to ports on the Atlantic coast or foreign ports in Europe.

Pinckney had more success than John Jay. The treaty he negotiated with Spain was popular. In **Pinckney's Treaty**, Spain granted Americans the right to travel on the Mississippi River. Even more important, the treaty allowed Americans to ship goods through the port of New Orleans, at the mouth of the Mississippi. For many a western farmer, the right to use the

port was the difference between failure and success.

In addition, Pinckney's Treaty cleared up the disputed boundary between American and Spanish territory in the southeastern United States. Spain and the United States agreed to accept the 31st parallel as the northern boundary of Spanish Florida. Thomas Pinckney won such popularity through this treaty that Federalist leaders nominated him as their party's candidate for Vice President of the United States in 1796. Pinckney lost the race for Vice President to Jefferson.

Trouble with France Washington's proclamation of neutrality had angered French leaders. They had expected the United States to aid them in their war against Great Britain because of the old treaty of alliance. In fact, the French ambassador had made plans to have armed

231

ships use United States' harbors as naval bases for French ships.

America's relations with France reached their lowest point during John Adams's term as President. French warships seized American merchant ships in the West Indies, and the French government refused to receive the American ambassador. Some Federalists thought Adams should ask Congress to declare war on France because of these actions. Adams refused. Instead, he sent three special ambassadors to France with instructions to try for a peaceful solution to the difficulties.

The XYZ Affair When the three American ambassadors got to Paris, three French officials met them. The French officials suggested that the Americans pay them a bribe of $240,000 before negotiations could begin. They also wanted the United States to grant France a loan. The Americans refused and sent a report to President Adams about what had happened. Adams then reported the whole affair to Congress.

In his report to Congress, President Adams refused to name the French officials who had asked for the bribe. He identified them as X, Y, and Z. For this reason, the negotiations with France became known as the **XYZ affair**. When news of it reached the American public, demands for a declaration of war against France increased. The Federalists' slogan was "Millions for defense, but not one cent for tribute."

Adams Stands Firm President Adams continued to withstand pressure to declare war. Still, he realized his duty to protect the United States against a possible invasion by French forces. He called George Washington out of retirement and asked him to take command of an army of volunteers. Alexander Hamilton was named Washington's second-in-command.

Congress established a Department of the Navy headed by Benjamin Stoddert of Maryland. Stoddert served with great ability as America's first secretary of the navy. He established several navy yards in which American warships were built. Some French and American naval vessels actually fought battles between 1798 and 1800, though no declaration of war was ever made.

During these years, President Adams stood firm. His patience was rewarded in 1800 when Napoleon Bonaparte came to power in France. Napoleon was willing to end the undeclared naval warfare. When new American diplomatic representatives were sent to France, they were treated with courtesy.

In 1800, France and the United States canceled the troublesome treaty of alliance of 1778. To take its place, the two countries signed a trade treaty. By showing firmness and patience, John Adams had kept the United States out of war with France. Later, John Adams spoke of this as the greatest achievement of his term as President. However, some Federalist leaders never forgave him for his refusal to go to war with France.

CHECKUP

1. Why did President Washington issue the Neutrality Proclamation?
2. What problems did Jay's Treaty and Pinckney's Treaty resolve?
3. Why were relations between France and the United States poor in the 1790s?
4. What was the XYZ affair?
5. **Thinking Critically** Do you think John Adams was right in refusing to help France in the war against Britain? Explain.

The Federalist Record

Why did the Federalists lose control of the national government?

VOCABULARY

White House	census
mint	Alien and
patent	Sedition Acts

The President's House During the winter of 1801, Abigail and John Adams were getting ready to move out of the President's house. They had lived there only a few months. It was the first public building in Washington, the new capital city. The cornerstone for the President's house had been laid on October 13, 1792, by George Washington. President and Mrs. Adams moved in 8 years later. More than 20 years would pass before the President's house would be called the **White House**.

Some people complained about the size and the cost — $400,000 — of the President's house. Abigail Adams had other complaints. "We had no fence, yard, or other conveniences," she wrote. The house stood on the edge of a swamp. It lacked bathrooms. Water had to be carried by hand from a distance of five city blocks. Several of the rooms were unfinished. Mrs. Adams dried clothes in one of the largest unfinished rooms.

Abigail Adams may have been happy to leave the President's house. It is doubtful that her husband was. John Adams thought he had done well in his 4 years as President. Nevertheless, the electors in 1800 preferred Thomas Jefferson and Aaron Burr, the candidates of the Democratic-Republican party, for President and Vice President. A new party with new

William Birch made this picture of the Capitol in 1800, while it was under construction. The President's house can be seen in the distance.
■ What would a picture of the Capitol today show to be different?

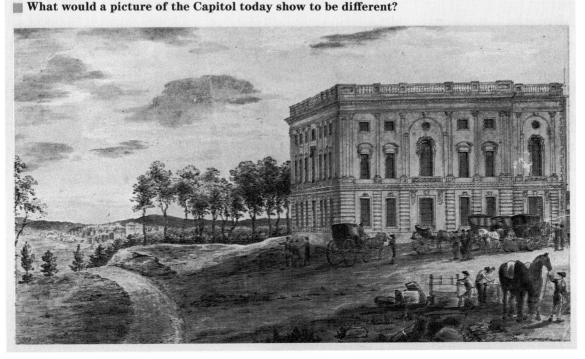

policies was about to take over the federal government.

Perhaps the Federalists deserved better treatment from the voters. Their party had done a great deal for the young United States. Their leaders had established the powers of the federal government, making the Constitution a working document. Much of what they did for the first time has lasted to the present day.

Coins and Patents For 16 years following the Declaration of Independence, people in the United States used British and other foreign coins. Also, some states had issued their own coins. It was the Federalists, in 1792, who first set up a system of American coins. Philadelphia was chosen as the home for the government's first **mint**, or place where coins are made. Some of the first United States coins were made from silverware given by George Washington.

The Federalists also started the issuing of **patents** to inventors. A patent is a document that gives an inventor the sole right to his or her invention for a certain number of years. No one else can make, use, or sell the invention without the inventor's permission. The first patent issued by the new patent office went to Samuel Hopkins. In 1790, Mr. Hopkins perfected a process for using potash in the manufacture of soap. Since 1790 about 4.5 million patents have been issued through the United States Patent Office.

Federalist Achievements In spite of criticisms, Presidents Washington and Adams had kept the country out of war. Moreover, they had arranged treaties that solved problems existing between the United States and foreign countries. At the same time, Alexander Hamilton's financial policies had worked wonders for the credit of the United States government. During the 1790s, the federal government was able to borrow money from foreign countries at very favorable rates of interest.

In 1790 the government undertook the first **census**, or count of people, in the United States. Between the first census and the second census, in 1800, the United States had increased its population by 35 percent. Foreign trade had tripled during the same 10-year period. With this kind of record during the first 12 years under the Constitution, why were the Federalists turned out of office? Why was Thomas Jefferson moving into the President's house in 1801?

One answer to these questions lay with the public image of the Federalist party. Somewhat unfairly it had the reputation of being a party for the wealthy. There were wealthy people in the Federalist party, but there were also many other people. At the same time, many of the rich favored the Democratic-Republican party, the party of Thomas Jefferson. Jefferson was himself a large landowner in the state of Virginia.

The Alien and Sedition Acts No political party can remain in power for 12 years without losing some backing. The unpopular treaty that John Jay worked out with Great Britain, the whiskey tax, and the way the government crushed the Whiskey Rebellion created opposition to the Federalists. By 1798 the Federalist leaders knew their power was slipping. Some of them were willing to chance a war with France if, by doing so, they could retain their control over the federal government. When it became clear that Adams wanted peace, not war, desperate Federalists pushed the **Alien and Sedition Acts** through Congress.

From Thalers to Dollars

Several questions had to be settled in the early 1790s before the Philadelphia Mint could start producing United States coins. Should the new coins be based on the British system of coinage—pounds, shillings, and pence? Or should the United States use an entirely new system? If a new system were used, what should be the worth of the various coins?

At this time Holland was a friend of the United States. Dutch bankers had lent the federal government a great deal of money. When it was decided to use an entirely new system for United States coins, it was also decided to name the basic unit after a Dutch coin, the thaler. Americans knew about this Dutch coin, but they pronounced its name in a way that sounded something like "dollar." In this way the Dutch coin known as the thaler became the American dollar.

The Mint Act of 1792 provided for coins valued at $10, $5, $2.50, $1, 50¢, 25¢, 10¢, 5¢, 1¢, and ½¢. Coins worth more than $1 were made of gold. The $1 coin and others down through 5¢ were made of silver. The 1¢ and ½¢ coins were made of copper. It may seem odd to have need of a ½¢ coin, but in those days even the penny had considerable purchasing power. And fractional pricing of goods was common. For example, apples might sell for 5½¢ a half dozen.

Today our coins are still based on their relationship to the dollar. The penny, or cent, is 1/100 of a dollar. The dime is 1/10 of a dollar. The quarter is ¼ (one quarter) of a dollar. The 50¢ piece is ½ of a dollar. And it all goes back to the days when Treasury officials chose the Dutch thaler as the basis for the money system of the United States.

THE FIRST POLITICAL PARTIES IN THE UNITED STATES

	Federalist	Democratic-Republican
Political beliefs	• The "best people" should control the government. • Strong national government • Favored loose interpretation of the Constitution • Restrictions on free speech and press	• The average citizen is capable of choosing representatives who will govern. • Limited national government to preserve states' rights • Favored strict interpretation of the Constitution • Relatively free speech and press
Economic beliefs	• Favored active government aid to business, finance, commerce, and industry • Favored United States Bank to ensure stable finances • Whiskey tax necessary to finance governmental expenditures • Favored high tariffs	• No special favors for business; farming preferred • Against Bank; thought it united the national government and the wealthy people against the poor • Rigid economy in government, to reduce taxes • Favored low tariffs
Foreign affairs	• Favored Great Britain because of commercial ties and fear of the French Revolution • Favored Jay's Treaty	• Sympathized with the French Revolution and its leaders • Opposed Jay's Treaty
Sources of strength	• Strong in New England and sea-coast areas • Supported by manufacturers, bankers, and merchants • Brilliant leadership under Alexander Hamilton	• Strong in South, Southwest, and frontier areas • Supported by small farmers, tradesmen, and mechanics • Brilliant leadership under Thomas Jefferson

The chart above shows the differences in the first political parties.
■ Which political party would you have supported?

The Federalist leaders thought these acts would weaken the Democratic-Republican party. Three of the acts applied to aliens, people not yet citizens of the country in which they live. One of these three acts increased the waiting period before aliens could become citizens of the United States. Aliens now had to wait 14 years instead of 5 years before becoming citizens with the right to vote. Most new citizens had been voting for Jefferson's party. This law, the Federalists thought, would hurt the Democratic-Republican party.

Naturalized citizens thought the Federalists were questioning their loyalty by passing the Alien Acts. Therefore, they supported the Democratic-Republican party more strongly than ever. Thus these acts did not have the effect that the Federalists had hoped they would have.

The Sedition Act was meant to silence criticism of Federalist officials. It called for the arrest and trial of anyone who spoke or published anything "false, scandalous, and malicious" about Congress or the President. Soon, 25 persons were ar-

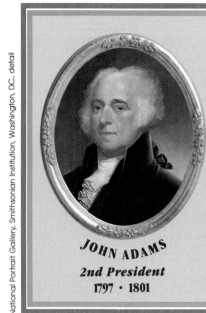

JOHN ADAMS
2nd President
1797 · 1801

Born: 1735, Braintree (now Quincy), Massachusetts.
Education: Harvard College.
Training: Lawyer.
To presidency from: Massachusetts.
Position when elected: Vice President.
Political party: Federalist.
Married: Abigail Smith.
Children: Three sons, two daughters. A son, John Quincy Adams, served as President, 1825–1829.
Died: July 4, 1826, on the fiftieth anniversary of the Declaration of Independence, which John Adams had signed. His age was 90 years, 8 months—the longest life span of any President.
Other facts: A short, stout man with a ruddy complexion. Never popular but highly respected.
During his presidency: The religious fervor known as the Great Revival swept over Kentucky and Tennessee.

rested and tried for violations of the Sedition Act. Most of the people who were arrested were editors or publishers of papers opposing the Federalists.

Thomas Jefferson and other Democratic-Republican leaders were quick to protest the Sedition Act. They pointed out that it clearly violated the First Amendment, which guarantees freedom of speech and freedom of the press. After Jefferson became President, he pardoned the men convicted under the Sedition Act, and Congress returned their fines.

The Election of 1800 The Federalists again nominated John Adams. However, many members of his own party refused to support him. The Democratic-Republicans once more nominated Thomas Jefferson. This time Jefferson won 73 electoral votes to 65 for Adams. The Democratic-Republican party also gained control of both the House of Representatives and the Senate.

Jefferson called the election of 1800 the *Revolution of 1800*. The government was now in the hands of the Democratic-Republicans. Jefferson and his party had attracted enough popular support to take control of the government. Moreover, the Federalists had accepted their defeat and had peacefully given up their control. Federalists continued to be elected to state offices, particularly in New England. But never again would a Federalist be chosen to serve as the nation's chief executive. Never again, either, would the Federalists have a majority in either the Senate or the House of Representatives.

CHECKUP

1. Name at least three contributions of the Federalist party during the 12 years it controlled the federal government.
2. What were the Alien and Sedition Acts?
3. How did the Alien and Sedition Acts contribute to the defeat of the Federalists in 1800?
4. Why might the election of 1800 be called a peaceful revolution?
5. **Thinking Critically** In the election of 1800, who would you have voted for — John Adams or Thomas Jefferson? Why?

Reading Eyewitness Accounts

LETTER OF ABIGAIL ADAMS

Eyewitness accounts are written by people who saw or who took part in the events they are writing about. Historical eyewitness accounts tell us a lot about events that happened long ago. These written accounts, in the form of diaries and letters, are also known as primary sources.

Some eyewitness accounts written during the eighteenth and nineteenth centuries show grammar and spellings that are different from those in use today. As you read the letter below, notice how some words are misspelled. In some cases they are errors. In others they reflect the style during that time.

In 1784, Abigail Adams sailed from the United States to join her husband, John Adams, in Europe. While on board the ship *Active*, Abigail wrote a letter to her sister Elizabeth. The following portion of that letter is an eyewitness account of Abigail's voyage.

This day 3 weeks I came on Board this Ship; and Heaven be praised, have hietherto had a favourable passage. Upon the Banks of Newfoundland we had an easterly Storm, I thought, but the Sailors say it was only a Brieze. We could not however sit without being held into our chairs, and every thing that was moveable was in motion, plates Mugs bottles all crashing to peices: the Sea roaring and lashing the Ship, and when worn down with the fatigue of the voilent, and incessant motion, we were assisted into our Cabbins; we were obliged to hold ourselves in, with our utmost Strength, without once thinking of closeing our Eyes, every thing wet, dirty and cold, ourselves Sick; you will not envy our Situation: yet the returning sone, a smooth sea and a mild Sky dispelld our fears, and raised our languid heads.

SKILLS PRACTICE

The words below are misspelled in the passage you just read. On a separate sheet of paper, write the correct spelling for each word. If you do not know the correct spelling, use a dictionary to find it.

1. hietherto
2. brieze
3. peices
4. voilent
5. closeing
6. sone
7. dispelld

Now answer the following questions about the eyewitness account.

8. What changes other than spelling would you make in Mrs. Adams's letter if you were to write it today?
9. How did Abigail Adams's description of the weather differ from the sailors' description of the same conditions?
10. What was the weather like after the storm?

MAIN IDEAS

1. The first Congress established a series of departments in the executive branch of the government and set up the federal court system.
2. Alexander Hamilton's financial plans put the credit of the United States on a firm and stable basis.
3. The disagreements between Alexander Hamilton and Thomas Jefferson on whether Congress could charter a national bank and on other matters resulted in the formation of the first political parties.
4. Federalists controlled the national government from 1789 to 1801.
5. In foreign affairs, Presidents Washington and Adams steered a careful course, avoiding war and attempting to solve disagreements by negotiations.
6. In 1800 the Federalists lost control of the federal government because of unpopular acts, such as the whiskey tax, Jay's Treaty, and the Alien and Sedition Acts.

VOCABULARY REVIEW

On a separate sheet of paper, write the best ending for each sentence.

1. Department heads who advised the President came to be referred to as members of the _____.
2. The interpretation of the United States Constitution favored by Alexander Hamilton was _____.
3. Western farmers protested a tax on alcoholic beverages by staging the _____.
4. The Democratic-Republican party was the forerunner of the party we know today as the _____.
5. In the 1790s, each party chose its candidates for President and Vice President in a meeting called a _____.
6. In the 1790s, the Presidents and the Vice Presidents were chosen by people called _____.

7. At the time of a new war between France and Great Britain, President Washington issued the _____.
8. The XYZ affair made relations worse between the United States and the European country of _____.
9. An inventor has the sole right to his or her invention for a certain number of years by means of a _____.
10. In 1795, Pinckney's Treaty settled the boundary between the United States and the Spanish territory of _____.

CHAPTER CHECKUP

1. List the first acts of Congress under the Constitution.
2. Which five offices made up the first President's Cabinet?
3. What are some practices that Washington began and other Presidents have followed?
4. How did the Federalists and Democratic-Republicans differ in their economic views?
5. Why was Pinckney's Treaty more popular than Jay's Treaty?
6. **Thinking Critically** What do you consider to be the greatest achievement of the Federalists? Explain.
7. **Thinking Critically** What does the slogan "Millions for defense, but not one cent for tribute" mean? Does it still apply today? Why or why not?

APPLYING KNOWLEDGE

1. Make a chart that contrasts the achievements of the Federalists when they were in power with the mistakes they made during the time of their rule.
2. Appoint two people in your class to act as Democratic-Republicans and two to act as Federalists. Have the four hold a panel discussion so each pair can recruit other members of the class for their party and discourage them from joining the others' party.

239

How Americans Lived: 1800

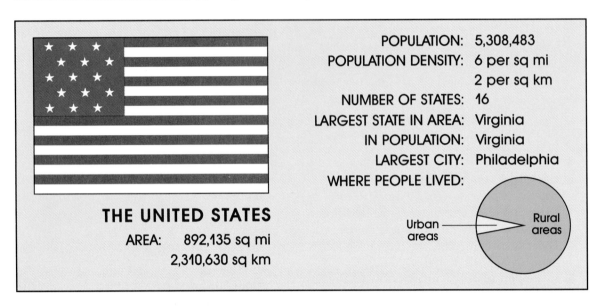

THE UNITED STATES

AREA: 892,135 sq mi

2,310,630 sq km

POPULATION: 5,308,483

POPULATION DENSITY: 6 per sq mi

2 per sq km

NUMBER OF STATES: 16

LARGEST STATE IN AREA: Virginia

IN POPULATION: Virginia

LARGEST CITY: Philadelphia

WHERE PEOPLE LIVED:

Urban areas — Rural areas

How had the production of goods in America changed by 1800?

According to the census of 1800, there were 5,308,483 people in the United States of America. These Americans were spread unevenly across the land. Two thirds of them lived within 50 miles (80 km) of the Atlantic coast. In this narrow band were all the American cities. In these cities were a few painting schools, music halls, and theaters. Much of what went on in these places imitated European art, music, and drama. Nor was there much typically American literature.

Acting on the Stage   Many of the actors appearing in American theaters in 1800 had trained in England. This was true of Mrs. Arnold, who brought her 8-year-old daughter Elizabeth to Boston in 1796.

When Elizabeth Arnold made her first stage appearance at the old Boston Theater, she was 9 years old. From then until her death at the age of 24, she sang, danced, and played numerous roles in American theaters. At first, Elizabeth Arnold played young boys in Shakespeare's plays. Then she learned light comedy roles, at which she was very successful. In Philadelphia in the spring of 1800, she met Charles Hopkins. They were married in 1802, although Elizabeth was barely 15.

Charles and Elizabeth Hopkins joined a company of actors known as the Virginia Players. Not long afterward, Charles Hopkins died. Some time later the young actress married another member of the Virginia Players, David Poe.

After their marriage, Elizabeth and David Poe acted together in Richmond, Philadelphia, and New York. Then they settled down for 3 years of appearances at the Federal Street Theater in Boston. Their two sons were born in Boston. The younger, Edgar, was born in January

1809. A few months later the Poes moved to New York. At the Park Theater, Elizabeth played the Shakespearean roles of Ophelia in *Hamlet* and Desdemona in *Othello.*

Tragedy struck in New York. David Poe disappeared from the American stage. Perhaps he deserted his wife. Perhaps he became ill. At any rate, Elizabeth had to support two small children and possibly her husband. In the fall of 1811, she joined a theatrical company in Richmond,

Elizabeth Poe appeared in stage productions at the Park Theater in New York.
■ How is this theater different from a theater in which plays appear today?

Virginia. Elizabeth Arnold Hopkins Poe died there the following December, possibly of pneumonia, and was buried in St. John's churchyard.

Elizabeth Poe was a pleasing, versatile actress. During her short life, she enacted 201 varied roles besides numerous singing and dancing parts. Often she portrayed two or three characters in the same evening. Such rigorous schedules were common for actors and actresses of the time, and very few people earned good wages in the acting profession.

John Allan, a Richmond merchant, and his wife took over the care of little Edgar Poe. As a young man, Edgar Poe took Allan as his middle name. Not even 3 years old when his mother died, he probably had no memory of her. Nor does the world remember much about Elizabeth Poe. However, the world does remember her brilliant son. Though his life was as tragic as hers, Edgar Allan Poe is remembered as one of America's greatest writers. Along with Washington Irving, James Fenimore Cooper, Nathaniel Hawthorne, and Herman Melville, Edgar Allan Poe created a distinctively American literature during the first half of the nineteenth century.

Studying Law Three members of the United States Senate came to dominate the political life of the nation in the early 1800s. They were John C. Calhoun, of South Carolina; Daniel Webster, of Massachusetts; and Henry Clay, of Kentucky. All were lawyers.

In those days people preparing to be lawyers studied law differently from people today. Generally, they "read law" in the office of an experienced lawyer. That is, they studied the collections of laws and other books kept in every lawyer's office. John C. Calhoun was 18 in 1800. The death of his father in 1796 had forced the 14-year-old boy to take on some family responsibilities. Nevertheless, he was able to go to Yale University, beginning in 1800. After graduation he returned to South Carolina to read law in the office of a Charleston lawyer, Henry W. DeSaussure.

Daniel Webster was a sickly, highly emotional boy. He had a good mind, however, and did well in his studies. In his early teens he was shy and sensitive about his unfashionable clothes and clumsy manners. Like Calhoun, Webster was also 18 in 1800. But he was ahead of Calhoun in formal education, having only one more year to go before graduation from Dartmouth College, in his home state of New

Hampshire. Eventually Daniel Webster moved to Massachusetts to become a clerk in the law office of Christopher Gore.

Henry Clay was born in Hanover County, Virginia. He was 5 years older than Calhoun and Webster. As a boy, he was poorer than either of them. His formal education was limited to 3 years in a backwoods school. When he was 14, his family moved to Richmond, Virginia. Young Henry worked in a store and then as a clerk in one of Virginia's highest courts. He studied law in the office of the attorney general of Virginia, Robert Brooke. Within a year, Clay had learned enough law to earn his license to practice before the bar of Virginia.

Calhoun, Webster, and Clay dominated public life in their time. No President of the era except Andrew Jackson had a more lasting impact.
▉ Do you think you would be able to find portraits like this of most of the young men of this time? Why or why not?

John C. Calhoun

Daniel Webster

Henry Clay

Corcoran Gallery of Art (left): National Portrait Gallery, Smithsonian Institution (center): New-York Historical Society (right)

Samuel Slater's mill stood beside the Blackstone River in Pawtucket, Rhode Island.
■ What are some of the reasons Slater would have wanted to locate his mill on a river?

In 1797, Henry Clay moved to Lexington, Kentucky. At that time 220,000 people, including 40,000 slaves, lived in Kentucky. Five years earlier, Kentucky had become the first state west of the Appalachian Mountains to be admitted to the Union. By 1800, Clay had gained a fine reputation as an up-and-coming lawyer, though he was only 23 years old. Already he was in **politics**—the business of getting elected to public office and governing. Calhoun and Webster became involved in politics just a few years later. Then, as today, the study of law was one avenue to a career in politics.

Setting Up Factories Machines to spin and weave cotton fibers were developed in Britain before America's War for Independence. These developments were the beginning of what is known as the **Industrial Revolution**. The Industrial Revolution was the period of change brought about through the development of power-driven machines—the change from muscle power to machine power. The British government passed laws against taking these machines out of their country. If other countries got the machines, they could build factories and compete with those in Britain.

However, the British government could not keep people from leaving the country. A young man named Samuel Slater left Great Britain for the United States in 1789. He had studied and memorized all the details of the valuable spinning and weaving machines. In the United States, Slater settled in Rhode Island. At first he built machines for Almy and Brown, partners in a factory in Pawtucket. This was the first successful spinning mill in America. In 1798, Samuel Slater started his own company. By 1800, he had several factories making cloth.

Samuel Slater's factories employed many children who were no more than 10 years old. In Rhode Island's early factories, supervisors saw to it that the children were decently clothed and fed. Working children were read to and drilled in their ABCs as they tended the machines. In 1800 the infant textile industries depended on hundreds of young workers who were hardly more than infants themselves.

A Yankee Inventor   In 1800 a man whose name was already well known was working in a Connecticut factory. He was Eli Whitney. After graduating from Yale in 1792, Whitney set out for Savannah, Georgia. The job Eli Whitney expected in Savannah fell through. He gratefully accepted an invitation from Catherine Greene to live at Mulberry Grove, one of the plantations she owned.

Eli Whitney built and repaired all kinds of things for Mrs. Greene. Impressed by his skill, Mrs. Greene asked him to make a machine that could strip seeds from the short-fibered cotton that was grown in Georgia and other parts of the South. The time it took to remove the seeds by hand kept the crop from being profitable.

In 10 days Whitney invented a machine that would do what Mrs. Greene wanted though it worked poorly at first. He called it a gin, short for *engine*. Whitney spent 6 months perfecting his machine. On March 14, 1794, Whitney received a patent for an improved **cotton gin**. With the improved machine, one worker could clean 50 pounds (23 kg) of cotton in a day. By this time, however, it was too late for Whitney to profit because so many others were making cotton gins.

The invention of the cotton gin had a great effect on slavery. The production of cotton in the United States increased from 140,000 pounds (63,560 kg) in 1791 to 35,000,000 pounds (15,890,000 kg) in 1800. In the latter year, slaves made up almost 20 percent of the population of the United States. Yet only 10 years before, the slave-labor system had seemed to be on its way out. But the invention of the cotton gin changed that. As cotton plantations became more and more profitable, many more slaves were needed in the cotton fields, and the possibility of freedom for slaves became more and more remote.

Interchangeable Parts   The invention of the cotton gin was not the only accomplishment of Eli Whitney. In 1798 he obtained a government contract to make 10,000 guns for the army in a Connecticut factory. Gunsmiths had been accustomed to making one gun at a time—lock, stock,

The cotton gin easily and quickly separated the seeds from the clean cotton. Cotton plantations became more profitable with this invention.
■ What kind of power was used to run this engine?

Yale University Art Gallery

Eli Whitney pioneered the use of interchangeable parts at his gun factory in New Haven, Connecticut.
■ **For what reasons do you think Whitney built his plant here?**

and barrel—but Whitney proposed to mass-produce guns. Factory machines would make the same part of each gun exactly alike. For example, every one of 10,000 gun locks would be interchangeable with the other 9,999 gun locks. The method Whitney used is known as the system of **interchangeable parts**.

When Whitney's guns were assembled, some parts may have had to be finished by hand to make them fit. But Whitney's idea was sound and caught on. Improvements in the system were made by others.

Today we take it for granted that parts of machines are interchangeable. If a part wears out in an automobile or a washing machine, we can replace the worn-out part with a new one just like it. But before Eli

Whitney set to work in his Connecticut factory, that was not the case. Whitney's idea of interchangeable parts has played an important role in the development of modern industry.

CHECKUP

1. Where were many American actors and actresses trained in 1800?
2. How did John C. Calhoun, Daniel Webster, and Henry Clay prepare themselves for a career in politics?
3. Who built the first spinning and weaving machines in America?
4. What were the effects of each of Eli Whitney's inventions?
5. **Thinking Critically** If you could invent a new machine, what would it be? Explain its purpose.

REVIEWING VOCABULARY

1. treaty   A treaty is a formal agreement between two or more independent countries. Article II, Section 2 of the Constitution gives the President the power to make treaties "with the advice and consent of the Senate." Name the treaties described in this unit. What problem did each solve? Why do you think the writers of the Constitution required a two-thirds vote of the Senate to ratify a treaty?

2. compromise   Compromise is an important process in every aspect of life. Individuals and groups, as well as nations, sometimes have to settle differences by giving up some demands in order to reach a peaceful solution. Our Constitution has been described as a "great bundle of compromises." How is this true?

3. tariff   Tariffs have been a subject of controversy since the beginning of our nation. Tariffs, or taxes on goods imported into or exported from a country, may be low or high. A tariff may be passed to produce revenue for a government or to keep out foreign competition. Were the first tariffs passed by the United States Congress low or high? What was their purpose?

4. census   A census is a count of the people in a country. When was the first census taken in the United States? According to our Constitution (Article I, Section 2), when is a census required? What is the stated purpose of the census?

5. propaganda   Propaganda refers to a plan or method of spreading ideas. The ideas may be good or bad, true or false. A number of illustrations in this unit were originally used as propaganda. Identify three of these pictures and tell what ideas each is trying to spread.

EXPRESSING YOURSELF

1. Thinking like a President. Ideally the President of the United States represents all the people and must therefore do what is best for the country as a whole. If you had been President, how would you have responded to the Whiskey Rebellion? How would you have responded to the XYZ Affair?

2. What if . . . ?   Suppose General Washington and his army had crossed the Delaware River on December 25, 1776, and had been defeated by the British at the battle of Trenton. Would the War for Independence have ended any differently? Explain.

3. Could you do it better?   The Mint Act of 1792 established a coinage system for the new United States. Why was the Mint Act passed? What could you have done to make the monetary system better than the one ordered by the Mint Act? Why would you have made these changes?

4. Through other eyes.   Many Americans agreed with President Washington's Neutrality Proclamation. However, French leaders and some American leaders believed the United States should honor the treaty of alliance of 1778. Explain how Washington's Neutrality Proclamation might have looked to France's leaders.

5. In what ways . . . ?   In 1798, Federalist leaders sought to maintain control of the federal government by passing the Alien and Sedition Acts. Why did these acts make the party unpopular? How did they lead to the defeat of the Federalists in the election of 1800? In what ways could the Federalists have stayed in power?

UNIT 3
Building a Nation

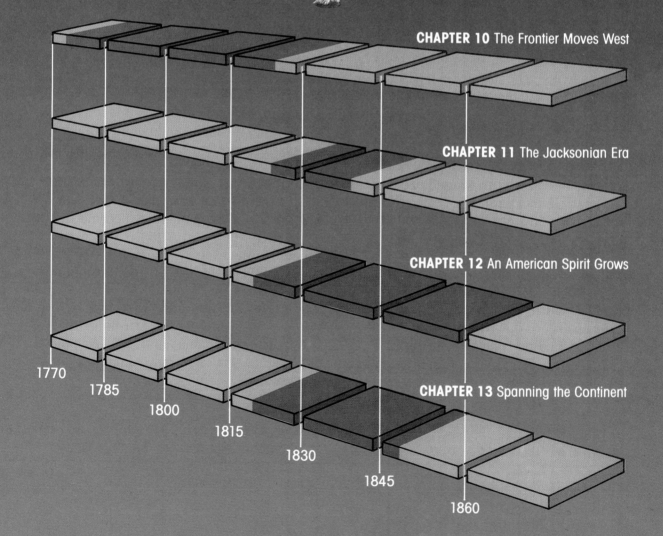

1770

1785

1800

1815

1830

1845

1860

10 The Frontier Moves West

1774–1825

Across the Appalachians

How were the lands between the Appalachian Mountains and the Mississippi River opened to settlement?

VOCABULARY

Wilderness Trail	Treaty of Greenville
township	frontier
battle of Fallen Timbers	

Shooting Star   Warfare with white settlers from the east was a family tradition with Tecumseh (tə kum′ sə), chief of the Shawnee (shô nē′) tribe. His father, also a chief, had died fighting the pioneers in 1774, when Tecumseh was a boy of 6. Two of his older brothers later fell in battles with American soldiers.

Tecumseh, whose name may be translated as Shooting Star, wanted to organize a great Indian alliance. He traveled through the western lands, urging Indians to unite in resisting the advance of the settlers. He and his one surviving brother helped a group of more than 1,000 Indians settle on the Wabash (wô′ bash) River in what is today the state of Indiana. Tecumseh argued that the white people's government had no right to buy land from a single tribe. The western lands belonged to all the tribes together, Tecumseh said.

Indians and non-Indians alike felt the force of his personality. One white observer who heard him speak to an Indian gathering reported that Tecumseh "hurled out his words like thunderbolts."

The Tide of Settlement   Tecumseh and his brother had reason to fear the advancing tide of white settlement. In 1774 the first permanent settlement west of the Appalachians was made at Harrodsburg in the region called Kentucky. The next year Daniel Boone blazed the **Wilderness Trail** through the Cumberland Gap. A gap is a natural pass through the mountains. Thousands of people followed Boone's trail into Kentucky. Thousands more came by way of the Ohio River, which was a great natural water highway to the West.

In 1792, Virginia gave up its claim to Kentucky, and Kentucky became the fifteenth state. (Vermont had become the fourteenth state in 1791.) Tennessee gained statehood in 1796. By 1800 more than 225,000 people lived in Kentucky and Tennessee, the first states west of the Appalachians. Other settlers, especially from Georgia and South Carolina, had moved into Alabama and Mississippi. This rush of settlers overwhelmed the region's Indians.

Daniel Boone leads a party of pioneers through the Cumberland Gap into Kentucky, land south of the Northwest Territory.
■ When was the Northwest Ordinance passed?

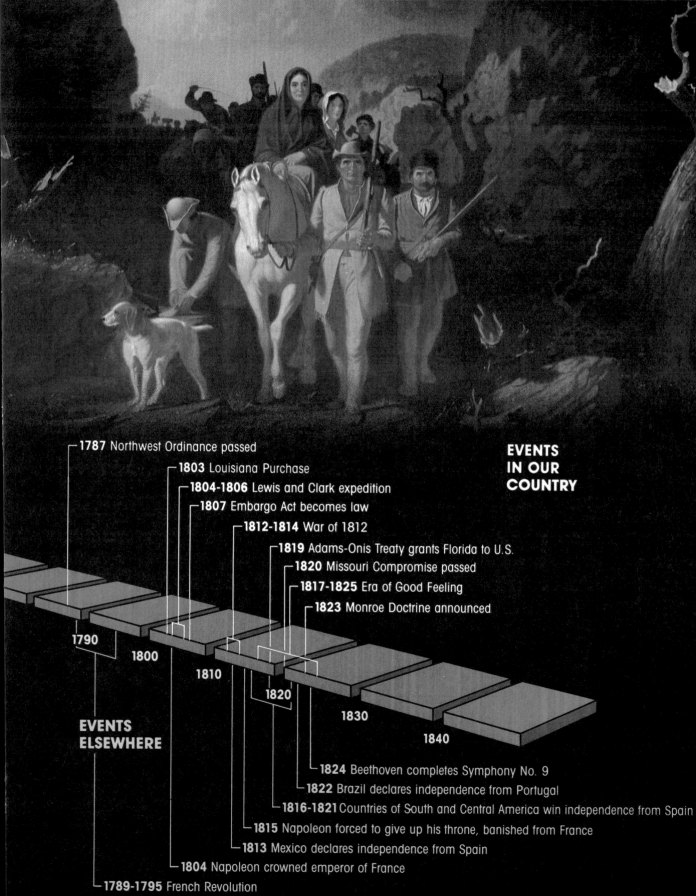

1787 Northwest Ordinance passed

EVENTS IN OUR COUNTRY

1803 Louisiana Purchase

1804-1806 Lewis and Clark expedition

1807 Embargo Act becomes law

1812-1814 War of 1812

1819 Adams-Onis Treaty grants Florida to U.S.

1820 Missouri Compromise passed

1817-1825 Era of Good Feeling

1823 Monroe Doctrine announced

1790

1800

1810

1820

1830

1840

EVENTS ELSEWHERE

1824 Beethoven completes Symphony No. 9

1822 Brazil declares independence from Portugal

1816-1821 Countries of South and Central America win independence from Spain

1815 Napoleon forced to give up his throne, banished from France

1813 Mexico declares independence from Spain

1804 Napoleon crowned emperor of France

1789-1795 French Revolution

The Northwest Territory There were important historical differences between the lands south of the Ohio River and the Northwest Territory. Land in the Northwest Territory was surveyed and sold according to the terms of a law passed by the Confederation Congress in 1785. Surveyors divided the land into square **townships**. Each township measured 6 miles (10 km) along each side. Within each township, surveyors marked off 36 sections. Each section was a square, measuring 1 mile (1.6 km) on each side. This 1 square mile contained 640 acres (259 ha) of land. Surveyors could later divide the sections into halves, quarters, or even smaller areas if necessary. One whole section in each township was set aside to support public schools for the township. Land marked off in this orderly way could be sold without disputes over boundaries.

South of the Ohio there was no such orderly land policy. Boundaries were irregular. A boundary might run from a large rock to a tall tree to a bend in a river to other visible points. These landmarks, however, tended to disappear or change as time passed. This caused many boundary disputes among southern neighbors.

The status of slavery marked another important difference between the Northwest Territory and the lands south of the Ohio. The Northwest Ordinance of 1787 barred slavery from that territory. Thus slavery was illegal in Ohio, Indiana, Illinois, Michigan, and Wisconsin. No such ordinance applied to Kentucky, Tennessee, Mississippi, and Alabama.

The Treaty of Greenville Settlement of the Northwest Territory lagged behind that of the regions south of the Ohio River. For one thing, white settlers in the Northwest were always threatened by attacks from the strong Indian tribes of the region. Some 12 of these tribes had banded together to keep white settlers out. In 1791 they badly defeated an untrained army led by General Arthur St. Clair, the first governor of the Northwest Territory. More than 600 of St. Clair's men were killed.

President Washington sent General Anthony Wayne to drive the Indians out of the Northwest Territory. Wayne's reck-

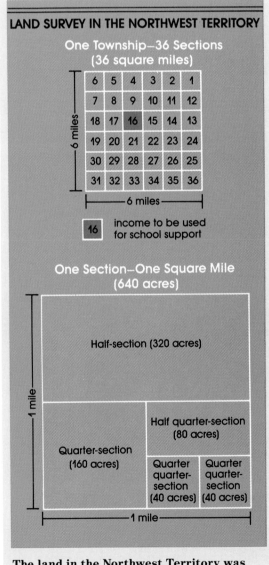

LAND SURVEY IN THE NORTHWEST TERRITORY

One Township—36 Sections
(36 square miles)

6	5	4	3	2	1
7	8	9	10	11	12
18	17	16	15	14	13
19	20	21	22	23	24
30	29	28	27	26	25
31	32	33	34	35	36

6 miles

6 miles

16 income to be used for school support

One Section—One Square Mile
(640 acres)

Half-section (320 acres)

1 mile

Quarter-section (160 acres)

Half quarter-section (80 acres)

Quarter quarter-section (40 acres) | Quarter quarter-section (40 acres)

1 mile

The land in the Northwest Territory was to be divided according to a grid of squares. ■ How many acres made up a township?

Anthony Wayne led his troops to victory in the battle of Fallen Timbers. Wayne's own men nicknamed him Mad Anthony.
■ **Why did this artist show Wayne looking away from the battle?**

lessness and daring in the Revolutionary War had earned him the nickname Mad Anthony. Still, he was a competent commander and trained his troops well. In August 1794 his army defeated the 12 tribes at the **battle of Fallen Timbers**. This battle took place near present-day Toledo, Ohio.

A year later, unable to resist their better-armed foe any more, the chiefs of the 12 tribes signed the **Treaty of Greenville**. This treaty set up a boundary line between Indian lands and the lands on which newcomers could settle.

The existence of such a boundary encouraged settlement in the Northwest Territory. Soon 50,000 people had moved there. Most of them settled in Ohio, which became a state in 1803.

For years the treaty kept Indians and settlers apart and at peace. In time, the settlers broke the Treaty of Greenville by invading Indian lands as settlers pushed the **frontier** westward. The frontier is the newly settled area that separates the older, more populated settlements from the wilderness.

Frontier Life A pioneer family's first task was to clear the land. Food for the winter depended on getting a crop raised before the first frost. With axes and scythes, husband, wife, and children cut trees and brush. Then, in ground slashed with a shovel, an axe, or a crude plow, they planted corn and a few vegetables.

A family's first shelter was probably a rough cabin, good enough to get them through the winter. During the next year, friends and neighbors might help in putting up a sturdier building. As time passed, more rooms would be added. Glass would take the place of greased paper in the windows. Iron hinges would replace leather straps on the doors.

Only the more prosperous pioneer families owned pigs, cows, or sheep. Squirrels, turkeys, deer, and other wildlife furnished most of the meat. Berries, honey, and maple syrup sweetened an otherwise dull diet. Salt was needed for flavoring and as a preservative. Pioneers got their salt from natural springs or from salt licks. Salt licks are natural deposits of salt found on the ground.

Flatboats, like this one on the Ohio River, carried settlers west with their belongings.
■ Why would this boat's crew want to keep a canoe lashed to the side?

Rivers and Streams   Many pioneers in the lands west of the Appalachians had traveled at least part of the way by water to reach their new homes. Generally river travel was easier than travel by land since there were few roads west of the mountains. The western pioneers also used the rivers to get their surplus farm crops to market. They built flatboats, large boats with flat bottoms that are especially useful in shallow water. They loaded these flatboats with grain and livestock. Then they set out on the long voyage down the Ohio and Mississippi rivers to New Orleans. This city near the mouth of the Mississippi remained in European hands —first Spanish, then French — until 1803.

In New Orleans, merchants bought the farm products and the flatboats. The boats were broken up for lumber. Farm products and lumber might be shipped to the West Indies or Europe. Meanwhile, those who had ridden downriver on the flatboats started on the long walk back to their homes. After the following year's harvest, many of them would again be making the long voyage by flatboat.

Rivers and streams were also sources of waterpower. The current of a stream could run a sawmill or a mill to grind grain. A store and blacksmith shop might be started nearby. Soon, as newcomers continued to arrive, there would be a sizable settlement. Thus, towns often grew up along the rivers and streams.

CHECKUP

1. Why did Tecumseh want the Indian tribes to organize?
2. What were some of the differences between the Northwest Territory and the region south of the Ohio River?
3. How was the Treaty of Greenville typical of the agreements signed by the American government and Indian tribes?
4. Why were rivers and streams important in the settlement of the western lands?

5. **Thinking Critically** Why do you think it was so hard for Indians to keep settlers from moving onto Indian lands?

Jefferson Buys Louisiana

What aroused the interest of the Americans in the lands of the West?

VOCABULARY

cede	Old Northwest
Louisiana Purchase	Old Southwest
Lewis and Clark expedition	

A Great Bargain   Thomas Jefferson was disturbed by rumors that reached the United States soon after he became President. It seemed that Napoleon Bonaparte, the French dictator, was interested in building a colonial empire in America to replace the one that France had lost in 1763. At that time, you will recall, France lost Canada to Great Britain and **ceded**, or gave up, Louisiana to Spain.

In 1801 it became known that Spain had secretly agreed to return Louisiana to France. The area then known as Louisiana stretched from the Mississippi River to the Rocky Mountains. It included the port of New Orleans, near the Gulf of Mexico and the mouth of the Mississippi River. Pinckney's Treaty with Spain had given Americans the right to ship goods through New Orleans. But would Napoleon honor that treaty? Or would he "put a cork in the bottle" and close the outlet to world trade that was so important to the western settlements?

To keep New Orleans open to American goods, Jefferson offered to buy the port. He instructed our representatives in France to offer Napoleon up to $10 million in payment for New Orleans. Much to Jefferson's amazement, the American representatives reported that Napoleon was willing to sell *all* of Louisiana for $15 million. Napoleon needed money for new wars in Europe and had given up plans to regain France's empire in North America.

The Constitution did not specifically give the President the power to buy land, but after much thought, Jefferson decided to accept Napoleon's offer. The Senate approved. Thus, in 1803 the United States was doubled in size by the **Louisiana Purchase** at a cost of about three cents an acre.

The Lewis and Clark Expedition   Thomas Jefferson wanted to know more about the land acquired in the Louisiana Purchase. He was curious, too, about the land west of the Rocky Mountains, even though the United States had little claim to it. He decided to send an expedition to explore the entire region.

As commander of the expedition, Jefferson named Captain Meriwether Lewis of the United States Army. Lewis was an

Lewis, Clark, Sacajawea, and York explored the Louisiana Territory.
■ What area of the country does this painting show?

The Thomas Gilcrease Institute of American History and Art, Tulsa, Oklahoma.

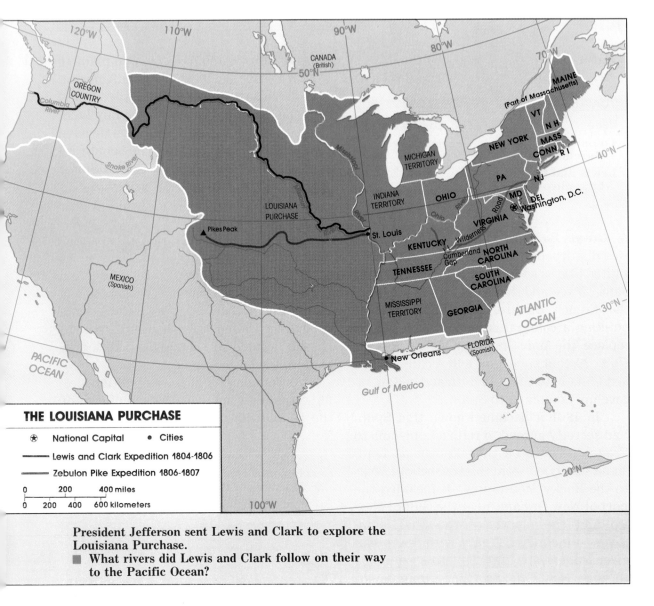

THE LOUISIANA PURCHASE

⊛ National Capital • Cities

—— Lewis and Clark Expedition 1804-1806

—— Zebulon Pike Expedition 1806-1807

0   200   400 miles
0   200 400   600 kilometers

President Jefferson sent Lewis and Clark to explore the Louisiana Purchase.

■ What rivers did Lewis and Clark follow on their way to the Pacific Ocean?

experienced explorer, but at the time, he was serving in Washington as Jefferson's private secretary. Lewis asked William Clark, the younger brother of George Rogers Clark, to share the leadership.

The **Lewis and Clark expedition** consisted of 23 soldiers, 3 interpreters, and Clark's slave, whose name was York. In the spring of 1804, the group left from the small fur-trading town of St. Louis. The expedition traveled in boats up the Missouri River. By autumn they reached

Indian villages near the site of present-day Bismarck, North Dakota. After wintering with the friendly Mandan Indians, the expedition moved west toward the Rocky Mountains in the early spring of 1805.

The Role of Sacajawea   Living among the Mandans were a French-Canadian fur trader, Toussaint Charbonneau (tü san´ shär bô nō´), and his young Indian wife, Sacajawea (sak ə je wē´ ə). When the expedition left Mandan country, Charbonneau went along as an interpreter and was accompanied by Sacajawea, carrying their newborn baby on her back. One reason Sacajawea went along was probably her longing to see her own Shoshone (shō shō′ nē) people. Crow Indians had kidnapped Sacajawea from her Rocky Mountain home 5 years earlier, when she was about 12 years old. They had sold her to the Mandans, who in turn had sold her to Toussaint Charbonneau.

Sacajawea has inspired many legends. It seems, however, that she served the expedition mainly as a peacemaker. Clark wrote, "Sacajawea reconciles all the Indians as to our friendly intentions — a woman with a party of men is a token of peace." When the expedition met a band of Shoshones, Sacajawea danced with joy. Soon she was reunited with her brother, who had become chief of the tribe.

Once the explorers got through the Rocky Mountains, they built canoes and followed the Columbia River to the Pacific Ocean. The group spent the winter on the Pacific coast before heading back east.

Sacajawea, standing next to Captain Lewis, converses in sign language with a party of Indians.
■ **Why would Sacajawea have needed to use sign language?**

Courtesy Amon Carter Museum, Fort Worth

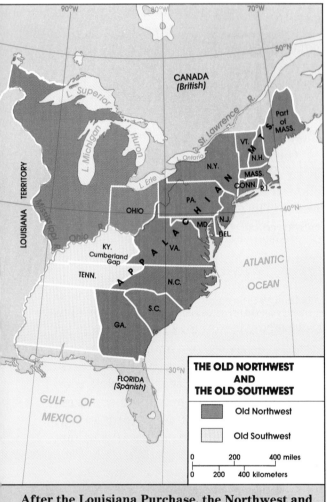

THE OLD NORTHWEST
AND
THE OLD SOUTHWEST

Old Northwest

Old Southwest

0   200   400 miles

0   200   400 kilometers

After the Louisiana Purchase, the Northwest and the Southwest came to be known as the Old Northwest and Old Southwest.
■ What river divided the two regions?

Americans Learn About the West
The journals of Lewis and Clark, published in 1814, created a growing fascination with the little-known lands along and beyond the Missouri River. Other adventurous Americans began to push into the Far West.

Major Zebulon Pike was an army officer who spent part of his career as an explorer. In a book published in 1810, he told of his journeys. On one expedition, he had explored the upper reaches of the Mississippi River. A second expedition had taken him into Colorado and New Mexico. A snowcapped mountain peak that he had observed in Colorado is today called Pikes Peak.

Americans added to their geographical knowledge by reading books or reports written by Pike and others. What they learned changed their way of speaking about different parts of their country. With the purchase of Louisiana from France, the Northwest Territory was no longer in the northwest corner of the United States. It was now called the **Old Northwest**. Similarly, after the Louisiana Purchase, the area south of the Ohio River and between the Appalachians and the Mississippi became the **Old Southwest**.

Charbonneau and Sacajawea returned to the Mandan village from which they had started. The rest of the expedition reached St. Louis on September 23, 1806. The country rejoiced. No one dreamed their journey would take 30 months. Later, Clark wrote to Charbonneau:

> The woman who accompanied you that long, dangerous, and fatiguing route to the Pacific Ocean and back deserved a greater reward for her attention and services than we had in our power to give her.

CHECKUP

1. How did Jefferson's offer to buy New Orleans result in the purchase by the United States of the entire Louisiana territory?
2. What parts of the Louisiana Purchase were explored by the Lewis and Clark expedition?
3. How did Sacajawea help the expedition?
4. **Thinking Critically** Why do you think President Jefferson decided to go ahead and buy Louisiana, even though the Constitution did not specifically give him the power to do so?

The War of 1812

What were some of the major results of the War of 1812?

VOCABULARY

Barbary States	national anthem
neutral rights	Treaty of Ghent
Embargo Act	Hartford
War Hawks	Convention

Mediterranean Pirates After the Revolution, American merchants sought new areas for trade. One of these areas was the region bordering on the Mediterranean Sea.

In the Mediterranean Sea, pirate ships became threats to merchant vessels from northern Europe and the United States. The pirate raiders came from the **Barbary States**, the countries along the northern shore of Africa. The Barbary States included Morocco (mə rok′ ō), Algeria (al jir′ ē ə), Tunis (tü′ nis), and Tripoli (trip′ ə lē). To keep their ships from being captured, European and American governments had been forced to make payments to the rulers of these countries.

In 1801 the ruler of Tripoli became

dissatisfied with the amount of tribute money the United States was paying. He declared war. Jefferson sent a naval squadron and some marines into the Mediterranean. Finally, in 1805, this show of force caused Tripoli to make peace with the United States. Tripoli's ruler promised that pirates would stop interfering with American merchant ships. Payments to the other Barbary States did not end, however, until 10 years later.

Thomas Jefferson disliked war and the use of force. Still, he knew how important it was for American ships to sail the world's oceans and seas freely. Any interference with shipping would be harmful to America's overseas trade. Poor transportation made it hard to trade by land within the boundaries of the United States. Moreover, the United States at that time had few factories to manufacture necessary items. For these two reasons, foreign trade was vital to the prosperity of our country.

The Rights of a Neutral In 1803, war broke out once more between France and

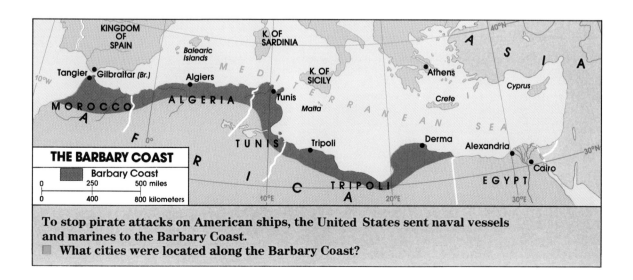

THE BARBARY COAST

■ Barbary Coast

0 — 250 — 500 miles

0 — 400 — 800 kilometers

To stop pirate attacks on American ships, the United States sent naval vessels and marines to the Barbary Coast.
▪ What cities were located along the Barbary Coast?

Great Britain. President Jefferson declared America's neutrality, as President Washington had done in 1793 when the same two countries had fought each other. Jefferson also asserted our **neutral rights**. He claimed that the United States, as a neutral country, had the right to trade with both France and Great Britain. Each of these countries disputed that claim, and each tried to keep American products from reaching the other.

French privateers seized or sank American merchant ships heading for England. British warships seized or sank American ships bound for France. In addition, the British increased the practice of impressment. This meant they would seize a few American sailors from ships they stopped or captured. The British claimed that these sailors were deserters from the British navy. They would then impress these men into service for the British navy.

In June 1807 the *Leopard,* a British warship, attacked the American naval vessel *Chesapeake* near the entrance to the Chesapeake Bay. After a bloody battle, British marines boarded the *Chesapeake* and impressed four sailors. News of this encounter shocked and angered the American people. Some of them demanded that the United States go to war against Great Britain.

Actually, both Great Britain and France were interfering with our neutral rights. Jefferson had no wish to fight either of them, and certainly not both. Instead, he decided to defend American rights by putting economic pressure on the two warring countries. This was done by a law that Jefferson got Congress to pass in December 1807.

Stephen Decatur and the crew of the *Intrepid* managed to destroy the *Philadelphia* after Barbary pirates had captured that American frigate.
■ **Why would the American navy want to destroy its own captured ship?**

Born: 1743, Albemarle County, Virginia.
Education: College of William and Mary.
Training: Lawyer, plantation owner, public official.
To presidency from: Virginia.
Position when elected: Vice President.
Political party: Democratic-Republican.
Married: Martha Wayles Skelton.
Children: Five daughters, one son.
Died: July 4, 1826, the same day that John Adams died.
Other facts: Called Long Tom by some because of his height. A man of many interests. Played the violin, experimented in raising crops and flowers, and designed his lovely home, Monticello. Wrote the Declaration of Independence.
During his presidency: In 1807, Robert Fulton's *Clermont*, the first commercially successful steamboat, went up the Hudson River from New York to Albany in 32 hours.

THOMAS JEFFERSON
3rd President
1801 · 1809

The Embargo Act   An embargo is the act of a government to limit or stop trade with other countries. The **Embargo Act** of 1807 said that American ships would not be allowed to sail to other countries. The law also said that foreign ships could not carry American goods to other countries. Jefferson thought that this law would make British and French leaders realize the importance of American trade and cause them to change their attitudes. But, for the most part, the embargo failed. British farmers raised ample supplies of food the next summer, making it unnecessary to rely on American corn or wheat. France proved able to get along well without American trade, too.

As a result of the Embargo Act, idle ships clogged American harbors. About 150,000 sailors, clerks, and dockworkers lost their jobs. Tons of cotton, tobacco, and grain piled up in seaport warehouses. Clearly, Jefferson's Embargo Act was hurting the United States more than it hurt Great Britain and France.

The embargo hit New England merchants and sea captains especially hard.

Opponents in that region turned the word *embargo* around, calling Jefferson's policy "The O-grab-me Act." Federalist leaders in New England threatened to take their states out of the Union unless the law was repealed.

Madison Becomes President   In 1809, Thomas Jefferson left the White House after serving two terms as President. He was succeeded by James Madison, who, like Jefferson, was a Virginian and a leader in the Democratic-Republican party. It seemed likely that Madison would carry out Jefferson's embargo policy and other peaceful means of protecting our neutral rights.

Three days before Jefferson left office, however, Congress repealed the Embargo Act. In its place, Congress passed a law permitting trade with any country except Great Britain and France. A year later Congress tried another plan. This plan allowed trade for one year with France and Great Britain. In addition, if one of those countries were to stop interfering with our merchant ships, the plan would call for us

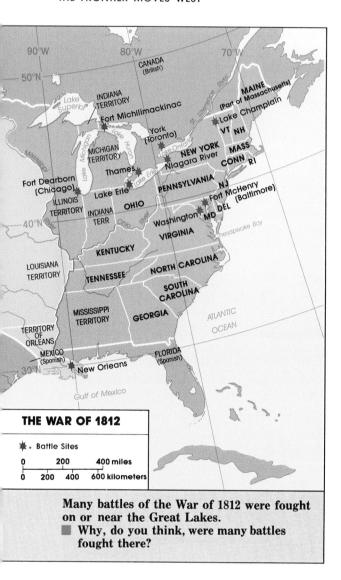

THE WAR OF 1812

✳ • Battle Sites

0   200   400 miles

0   200   400   600 kilometers

Many battles of the War of 1812 were fought on or near the Great Lakes.
■ Why, do you think, were many battles fought there?

Henry Clay of Kentucky as the Speaker of the House. John C. Calhoun of South Carolina was also one of the **War Hawks**, as these young men from the South and West came to be called. The War Hawks were members of Congress who favored war.

The War Hawks were more than ready for a war with Great Britain. Their battle cry became "On to Canada!" That British colony looked defenseless now that Great Britain was involved in a great war with France. The War Hawks believed that the United States could add more territory for its settlers by declaring war on Great Britain and then invading Canada. In addition, an invasion of Canada might destroy bases from which Indians had been raiding frontier settlements throughout the Northwest Territory.

Still, the War Hawks were more than land grabbers. Proud and patriotic, they resented the way Great Britain had violated the neutral rights of the United States and impressed American sailors. Urged on by the War Hawks' demands, President James Madison asked Congress in 1812 to declare war on Great Britain.

A Poor Beginning   Americans call this the War of 1812 because it began in that year. Canadians call it the War for Defense because it began with American invasions across the Canadian border. In 1812 there were 8 million Americans and only 500,000 Canadians. Conquering Canada appeared to be an easy matter, especially since there were but a small number of British troops stationed there.

However, Americans soon found that their own troops were hastily organized, improperly trained, poorly supplied, and badly commanded. Consequently, three American attempts to invade Canada failed. The map above shows the battle sites of the war.

to increase trade with that country and stop all trade with the other. But neither of these plans worked. Both Britain and France continued to harass American shipping.

"On to Canada!"   Some Americans were unhappy with economic weapons. The election of 1810 brought a number of eager young Democratic-Republicans from the southern and western states into the House of Representatives. They won control of that body of Congress and chose

Naval Victories   At the beginning of the War of 1812, the American navy had fewer than 20 ships. The British navy had more than 800. Even though many of these were busy against the French, Americans could not challenge Britain's mighty fleet in a sea battle. Still, in contests between single warships, Americans won several victories. The most famous of these took place early in the war. It involved the American war vessel *Constitution* against the British *Guerrière* (gə rē ãr′). Captain Isaac Hull commanded the *Constitution*. In a fierce sea battle, Captain Hull and his crew left the *Guerrière* a burning wreck. In this encounter the *Constitution* earned the nickname *Old Ironsides* because cannonballs seemed to bounce off its thick, oaken sides.

On Lake Erie energetic Oliver H. Perry directed the building of some American warships. With these he defeated and captured a small British fleet in 1813. Americans now controlled the lake. The British and Canadians with their Indian allies could no longer hold Detroit. They retreated into Canada, followed by an army led by William Henry Harrison.

The Death of Tecumseh   William Henry Harrison was the son of Benjamin Harrison, who was a signer of the Declaration of Independence and later the governor of Virginia. After joining the army, William Henry Harrison served in the Northwest Territory. By the Treaty of Fort Wayne in 1809, Harrison had obtained about 2.5 million acres (1 million ha) of Indian land along the Wabash River. There, in 1811, Harrison, who had become governor of the Indiana territory, had his first encounter with Tecumseh.

Tecumseh warned Harrison that he would oppose settlers occupying the Indian lands. The Indian chief directed about 1,000 Indians to place themselves in a camp near the point where the Tippecanoe Creek flowed into the Wabash. Harrison sent 900 American soldiers to Tippecanoe. They camped near the Indian settlement. In the spring of 1811, Tecumseh left for the south, attempting to persuade Creeks, Choctaws, and Chickasaws to join his alliance.

While Tecumseh was gone, his brother Tenskwatawa ordered the Indians to attack the Americans, thus touching off the battle of Tippecanoe. At its end the Indians were defeated and scattered. They had believed Tenskwatawa's claim that white men's bullets could not hurt them. Tecumseh returned to find his alliance shattered, his hopes all but destroyed. He went to Canada as the War of 1812 was beginning. The British greatly respected

Tecumseh, chief of the Shawnee, tried to turn back the rush of settlers moving west.
■ Why is Tecumseh wearing the coat shown?

Tecumseh. They made him a brigadier general. As a British officer, Tecumseh led white soldiers and Indians in four major battles against the Americans.

Meanwhile, William Henry Harrison had become a general in the American army. Perry's victory on Lake Erie made it possible for Harrison's army to reach Canada by water. On October 5, 1813, his force of about 4,500 soldiers met the British and Indians in battle. On the north bank of the Thames River, Americans won a great victory. Tecumseh was killed in the battle. Perhaps he had felt the approach of death. Before the battle he had taken off his army uniform and dressed himself in his traditional Indian buckskins.

British Invasions   By 1814 the British had defeated Napoleon and his armies in Europe. This made it possible to send thousands of veteran British soldiers and sailors to fight against the United States. As a result, Americans in 1814 had to face invasions of American soil.

One invading army moved south from Montreal into the state of New York. Instead of marching through the forests, it tried to use the Lake Champlain water route. Near Plattsburgh a hastily constructed American fleet commanded by Captain Thomas Macdonough met the British. After a desperate battle, the small American fleet turned the British back. New York was saved.

The Burning of Washington   A more successful British invasion took place in the Chesapeake Bay area. At Bladensburg, Maryland, British marines defeated American militia. On August 24, 1814, a British force of about 5,000 marched into Washington. President Madison and other government officials fled to the hills surrounding the city. The British set fire

The British burned much of Washington, D.C., during their successful invasion of August 1814.
■ How would Washingtonians of the time have reacted to this?

to the Capitol, where Congress met. They burned the President's House and nearly every other government building in Washington. Before leaving the President's House, Dolley Madison, the President's wife, hurriedly grabbed everything of worth she could, including a valuable portrait of George Washington. When the government eventually returned to Washington, the President's House had to be painted white to hide the scorch marks. From that time on it came to be known as the White House.

Our National Anthem   After leaving Washington, the British marines boarded their warships and sailed up Chesapeake Bay to Baltimore. There the guns of the British fleet bombarded Fort McHenry. Had the fort been captured or had it surrendered, Baltimore might have suffered the same fate as Washington. British guns thundered throughout the day and night of September 13, 1814. On the morning of September 14, a man watching anxiously saw that "our flag was still there." He was Francis Scott Key, a prisoner on board one of the attacking ships.

Inspired by the Americans' defense of Fort McHenry, Key wrote the words to "The Star-Spangled Banner." It was published as a poem, and later that year it was sung to the music of an old English tune. It took more than 100 years, however, before "The Star-Spangled Banner" was officially adopted as our **national anthem**.

The Battle of New Orleans   A third British invasion in 1814 threatened the American ports on the Gulf of Mexico and the entire Mississippi River Valley. General Andrew Jackson of Tennessee commanded the American forces in the South. He had gained a reputation as an Indian fighter. When Jackson learned of the British plan to attack New Orleans, he hurried to the city's defense.

The defenders of New Orleans were a mixed group. They included regular army troops, militiamen from Kentucky and Tennessee, free blacks, and Choctaw Indians. For a time, Jackson refused the help of Jean Lafitte (zhän la fēt′), the leader of pirates who had preyed on merchant ships sailing in the Gulf of Mexico. But Lafitte persuaded Jackson that the pirate cannons and cannoneers would be of great help against the British—and they were.

The decisive battle of New Orleans took place on January 8, 1815. Jackson's army won an overwhelming victory. Americans rejoiced when they heard of it. Only later did they learn that the peace treaty ending the War of 1812 had been signed in Europe 2 weeks before the battle. No one in the United States knew the

At dawn Francis Scott Key saw the American flag still waving over Fort McHenry.
■ What passages of the national anthem does this painting call to mind?

war was over at the time because of the slowness of communications.

Peace Without Victory   Negotiations to end the war had begun when American and British representatives met in Ghent (gent), Belgium, in August 1814. They signed the **Treaty of Ghent** in December of that year, although it was February 1815 before the news reached the United States. The treaty said nothing about American grievances, and no territory changed hands. The country forgot that the War Hawks had shouted "On to Canada!" at the beginning of the war. Even though the United States failed to gain territory, neither had it lost any. In spite of these inconclusive results, the Treaty of Ghent was so popular that the Senate approved it without a dissenting vote.

The truth was, the War of 1812 never had the support of the whole country at

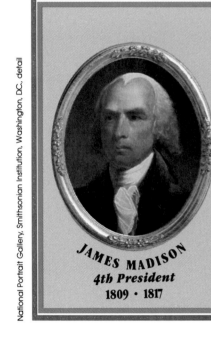

National Portrait Gallery, Smithsonian Institution, Washington, DC, detail

JAMES MADISON
4th President
1809 · 1817

Born: 1751, Port Conway, Virginia.
Education: College of New Jersey (now Princeton University).
Training: Lawyer, public official.
To presidency from: Virginia.
Position when elected: Secretary of State.
Political party: Democratic-Republican.
Married: Dolley Payne Todd.
Children: None, though his wife had one child from an earlier marriage.
Died: 1836, the last surviving signer of the Constitution.
Other facts: The smallest President, standing 5 feet 4 inches (1.6 m) tall and weighing about 100 pounds (45 kg). Often called "Father of the Constitution."
During his presidency: Work began, in 1811, on building the National Road, leading west from Cumberland, Maryland. It was the chief road into the region west of the Appalachians.

any one time. Blunders during the invasion attempts, failures in supplying the armies, and incompetent leadership had brought on storms of criticism. Opposition to the war was particularly strong in New England. Federalist leaders there declared that their section was suffering because of the war. They called it "Mr. Madison's War," indicating they wanted nothing to do with it.

Discontent in New England brought about a meeting of Federalist leaders at Hartford, Connecticut, in December 1814. At this **Hartford Convention** were 26 top leaders from five New England states. Some of the men at the meeting talked of having their states leave the Union. Calmer views won out, though. The protests were greeted with anger in other parts of the country, but they were soon forgotten with the joyful news that the war was over.

The War's Results   In spite of its indecisive ending, the War of 1812 had some important results. It convinced Great Britain and other European countries that the United States could defend itself from outside attack. Europeans had a greater respect for and interest in the United States after the war ended. The war also broke once and for all the power of the Indians in the Northwest Territory. More and more white settlers now moved into the region. Finally, as you shall see, the war caused a lasting change in the political life of the young republic.

CHECKUP

1. How did Presidents Jefferson and Madison try to defend the neutral rights of the United States?
2. Who were the War Hawks?
3. Why did the War Hawks want to go to war against Great Britain?
4. What were some of the results of the War of 1812?
5. **Thinking Critically** Was the Treaty of Ghent really a "peace without victory"?

An Era of Good Feeling

Why was the time of James Monroe's presidency called the Era of Good Feeling?

VOCABULARY

Virginia Dynasty	Adams-Onìs Treaty
revenue	Monroe Doctrine
protective tariff	Missouri Compromise
nationalism	slave state
Era of Good Feeling	free state

The Virginia Dynasty   The Federalists' opposition to the War of 1812 had made them seem unpatriotic to many Americans. This badly weakened their party. This loss of strength was seen in the voting for President in 1816. James Monroe, the candidate of the Democratic-Republicans, received 183 electoral votes. Rufus King, his Federalist opponent, got only 34.

James Monroe was the last of three Presidents who, as a group, have been called the **Virginia Dynasty**. A dynasty is a family or group that maintains power for a long period of time. Thomas Jefferson, James Madison, and James Monroe were not members of the same family. But they were members of a group of great Virginians who headed the United States government during the first quarter of the nineteenth century. And Jefferson, who protected and guided the careers of the two younger men, was seen as the father of this dynasty.

The Burr-Hamilton Duel   Alexander Hamilton had been the guiding light of the Federalist party in its early years. Had he lived, the Federalists might have challenged the Virginia Dynasty. Indeed, Hamilton himself might have been elected President. But Alexander Hamilton was killed in a duel with Aaron Burr at Weehawken, New Jersey, in July 1804.

The duel came as the result of a long series of private and public disputes between Hamilton and Burr. Finally Burr challenged Hamilton to a duel with pistols. Hamilton tried to avoid the duel, but Burr persisted. Each man fired one shot during the duel, with Burr's bullet plowing its way into Hamilton's stomach. Hamilton died the next day.

Burr's shot killed Hamilton, but it also wrecked Burr's political career. At the time, he was Vice President under President Thomas Jefferson. After the duel, Democratic-Republicans refused to nominate Aaron Burr for a second term as Vice President.

Hamiltonian Policies Are Adopted   Though Alexander Hamilton died in 1804, his influence lived on. This was

Alexander Hamilton was mortally wounded in a duel with Aaron Burr. Hamilton fired the first shot—straight up in the air.
■ Why might Hamilton have done that?

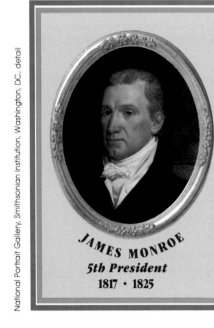

JAMES MONROE
5th President
1817 · 1825

Born: 1758, Westmoreland County, Virginia.
Education: College of William and Mary, from which he withdrew to join the Continental army.
Training: Lawyer, public official.
To presidency from: Virginia.
Position when elected: Secretary of State.
Political party: Democratic-Republican.
Married: Elizabeth Kortright.
Children: Two daughters, one son.
Died: 1831, New York City.
Other facts: A tall blue-eyed man of military bearing. Wounded in the battle of Trenton. In 1819, at Savannah, Georgia, the first President to ride on a steamboat.
During his presidency: The first public high school in the United States opened in 1821 in Boston. The English Classical School admitted only boys for instruction in reading, writing, English grammar, and mathematics.

so because the Democratic-Republicans adopted some of the policies Hamilton had favored. Hamilton favored a Bank of the United States, and, as you will recall, the bank was chartered in 1791 for a period of 20 years. When its charter ran out, the Democratic-Republicans chartered a second Bank of the United States with powers similar to the first one.

As Secretary of the Treasury in the 1790s, Hamilton had urged that the United States adopt a tariff on imported goods. This would allow the government to collect a fee on all imports. Congress had passed tariff laws from the 1790s onward. However, until 1816, these were chiefly for **revenue** — that is, for money to pay the expenses of government.

During the years of Jefferson's embargo and during the War of 1812, manufacturing increased in the northeastern United States. After the war a flood of low-priced British manufactured goods threatened to destroy these budding industries by taking over their markets. To prevent this, Congress in 1816 approved a **protective tariff**, a policy that Hamilton had urged years before. The protective tariff raised duties enough so that imported goods would be sold at higher prices than American-made products. The effect in many cases was to keep foreign manufacturers from trying to sell their goods in the United States.

The Years of National Unity   Among Americans, the War of 1812 created an increasing feeling of **nationalism**, or loyalty to the whole nation as opposed to a single state or region. The war also made popular heroes of Andrew Jackson and William Henry Harrison. The nation had not known such military heroes since George Washington in the Revolution. The two generals would eventually go on to become the seventh and ninth Presidents of the United States.

With the Federalists in decline, James Monroe, the fifth President, won a second term in 1820. Monroe received every electoral vote but one — and even that went to another Democratic-Republican. With the exception of Washington, who was twice elected unanimously, no President has ever received so large a share of the electoral college's vote.

The years of Monroe's presidency have been called the **Era of Good Feeling**. This was a period of calm in the nation's political life, prosperity for farms and businesses, and great unity in dealings with other nations. Five new states were added to the Union during these years. These included Illinois in the Old Northwest, and Mississippi and Alabama in the Old Southwest. The term *Era of Good Feeling* was coined by a newspaper in Boston, which had once been a Federalist stronghold. The paper used the term to welcome Monroe on a visit to the state of Massachusetts, the home territory of his former opponents.

The Purchase of Florida   In the early 1800s, Florida was owned by Spain. At that time, Florida was larger than it is today. It included parts of Alabama, Mississippi, and Louisiana. The exact boundary between the United States and Florida, however, remained in doubt.

The United States acquired Florida in three stages. In 1810, American colonists north of New Orleans revolted against Spanish rule. The United States took this opportunity to seize the territory between the Pearl and Mississippi rivers. During the War of 1812, American troops captured the Spanish fort at Mobile, Alabama. As a result, all the land between the Perdido and Pearl rivers came under United States control by 1813.

Concern over the Spanish presence in eastern Florida grew. Escaped slaves

This painting of an Independence Day Celebration in Philadelphia in 1819 captures some of the spirit of the Era of Good Feeling.
■ **Does this picture remind you of Fourth of July celebrations today?**

THE ACQUISITION OF FLORIDA

0   150   300 miles
0   150   300 kilometers

By acquiring Florida, the Untied States extended its southeastern boundary.
■ In which three years did the United States acquire parts of Florida?

from Georgia and other southern states fled to Florida. Smugglers and pirates used Florida as a base of operations. Seminole Indians living in Florida began raiding settlements in southern Georgia.

In 1818, American troops led by Andrew Jackson pursued a Seminole raiding party into Florida. Along the way they captured several Spanish forts. Thus pressured to negotiate, Spain reached an agreement with the United States in 1819.

This agreement, the **Adams-Onìs Treaty**, gave the United States the rest of Florida for $5 million. Another part of the treaty fixed the boundary between the United States and Spanish territory west of Louisiana, in what are today the states of Texas and New Mexico.

At about the same time, the northern boundary of the Louisiana Purchase was formally worked out between Great Britain (which owned Canada) and the United

States. The boundary ran along the 49th parallel, from Lake of the Woods in present-day Minnesota westward to the crest of the Rocky Mountains.

The Monroe Doctrine Early in the nineteenth century, revolutions against Spanish rule broke out in many of Spain's colonies in South America and Central America. One after another, these Spanish colonies fought for their independence as the United States had done.

By itself, Spain had little chance of regaining its lost colonies. It might do so, however, with help from Austria, France, Prussia, or Russia. At that time, Russia claimed territory along the Oregon coast that was also claimed by the United States. If Austria or France helped Spain, would they also help Russia in North America?

In 1823, President Monroe, following the advice of his secretary of state, John Quincy Adams, decided to issue a warning to these European countries. His statement, known as the **Monroe Doctrine**, has been called the American "declaration of independence from Europe."

The Monroe Doctrine promised European nations that they could keep whatever holdings they had in the Western Hemisphere as of 1823. However, they must not claim any additional territory in this hemisphere. Moreover, the United States would oppose any effort to extend the European system of rule by kings and queens to the Western Hemisphere. In return the United States promised not to interfere in events in any European country.

At the time, the Monroe Doctrine was more brave talk than anything else. The young United States could not hope to enforce it against any serious threat from one of Europe's great powers. Many years would pass before anyone even tried to invoke the Monroe Doctrine against a specific European action. Nevertheless, its principles remained a cornerstone of American foreign policy.

The Missouri Compromise The Monroe Doctrine was not the only important event during the Era of Good Feeling. The **Missouri Compromise** rivaled the Monroe Doctrine in importance. By 1819, 9 additional states had joined the original 13 in the Union, making a total of 22. These 22 states were evenly divided: 11 were **slave states**—states in which slavery was legal—and 11 were **free states**—states in which slavery was illegal. The 9 new states had been admitted with little or no controversy. It was different, however, in 1819, when Missouri asked to be admitted as a slave state.

Northerners opposed to slavery objected to the admission of Missouri as a slave state. The admission of Missouri would give the southern slave states two more votes in the Senate, and therefore a majority. An additional danger, some northerners claimed, was that the admission of Missouri as a slave state might set a pattern. It might mean that all the other states that would be made from the Louisiana Purchase territory would become slave states.

Some southerners, on the other hand, argued that Missouri had a right to be admitted as a slave state if that is what its people wanted. Furthermore, they said the North had a larger population than the South. That gave the North a majority in the House of Representatives. It would be only fair, they argued, to give the South a majority in the Senate—which had just two members from each state—by admitting Missouri as a slave state.

Feeling about the Missouri question ran high throughout the country as well as in Congress. Thomas Jefferson wrote from Monticello that the controversy alarmed him like "a fire bell in the night." Then in December 1819, Massachusetts agreed to give up its three northern counties. These counties then asked for admission to the Union as a free state, to be called Maine. This made possible what became known as the Missouri Compromise, which was guided through the Congress by the ambitious young Speaker of the House, Henry Clay.

By the terms of the compromise, Missouri was admitted to the Union as a slave state and Maine as a free state. This preserved the balance between slave and free states in the Senate. In the Louisiana territory, slavery would from now on be prohibited north of the $36°30'$ line, except in Missouri. It was agreed that Congress would make no laws that attempted to exclude slavery from the territory south of that line of latitude.

By means of the Missouri Compromise, Congress avoided a dangerous confrontation between North and South. But the dispute had only been postponed, not resolved. A deadly confrontation was yet to come.

CHECKUP

1. Name three leaders who were called members of the Virginia Dynasty.
2. What Hamiltonian policies were eventually adopted by the Democratic-Republicans?
3. In what three years did the United States gain control over the three parts of Florida?
4. What were the main points of the Monroe Doctrine?
5. **Thinking Critically** Why do you think the Missouri Compromise could only be a temporary solution to the conflict between North and South?

Understanding Cause and Effect

WHAT HAPPENED AND WHY

When an event occurs, it sometimes causes something else to happen. For example, during a thunderstorm, lightning struck a tree. The tree fell across a road. This is called a cause-and-effect relationship. The cause was the storm, and the effect was lightning striking the tree. The cause was lightning striking the tree, and the effect was the tree falling across the road. To understand cause and effect, you must ask what happened and why it happened. *What* happened tells you the effect. *Why* it happened tells you the cause.

Many events in history have a cause-and-effect relationship. In this chapter you have read how the Embargo Act of 1807 put a halt to American trade overseas. This resulted in the

loss of many jobs in the United States. The cause was the Embargo Act of 1807. The effect was the loss of jobs.

SKILLS PRACTICE

The following incomplete sentences are about events mentioned in this chapter. Each sentence is followed by three endings. On a separate sheet of paper, write the letter of the ending that gives the correct cause of each event.

1. The United States nearly doubled in size because
   a. of the purchase of Louisiana from France.
   b. Tennessee gained statehood in 1796.
   c. Ohio became a state.
2. European countries had a greater respect for the United States as a result of
   a. the Missouri Compromise of 1820.
   b. the Treaty of Greenville.
   c. the War of 1812.
3. General William Harrison was able to reach Canada by water because
   a. Daniel Boone blazed the Wilderness Trail.
   b. Wayne's army defeated the Indians at Fallen Timbers.
   c. Perry defeated the British at Lake Erie.
4. In 1816, Congress passed a protective tariff because
   a. the United States was flooded with British manufactured goods.
   b. salt was necessary to preserve food.
   c. pirate ships became a threat.
5. Canadians called the war that started in 1812 the War for Defense because
   a. slavery was illegal in the Old Northwest.
   b. the British began impressing seamen.
   c. American troops invaded Canada.

MAIN IDEAS

1. From 1774 on, white settlers moved westward toward the Mississippi, forcing many Indians off the lands they lived on.
2. President Thomas Jefferson's purchase of Louisiana from France more than doubled the size of the United States.
3. Lewis and Clark explored the Louisiana Purchase lands and brought back reports that inspired many Americans to want to settle that new territory.
4. The War of 1812 between the United States and Great Britain came to an inconclusive end, but it brought about a growth in national pride.
5. The years of prosperity and national unity during James Monroe's presidency came to be called the Era of Good Feeling.
6. The Monroe Doctrine said that European powers must stay out of the Americas and that the United States would not interfere in European affairs.

VOCABULARY REVIEW

On a separate sheet of paper, write **True** if the statement is true and **False** if it is false.

1. In the Northwest Territory, the land was divided into square townships.
2. General Anthony Greenville negotiated the Treaty of Greenville for the United States.
3. The Louisiana Purchase cost the United States $15 million.
4. The Wilderness Trail was the route Lewis and Clark followed to the Pacific.
5. Americans saw the Embargo Act as a way of defeating the Barbary pirates.
6. The War Hawks were young members of the House of Representatives from the South and West.
7. The Hartford Convention was called to support the War of 1812.
8. The members of the Virginia Dynasty were all close relatives.
9. The Era of Good Feeling is most closely tied to the presidency of James Monroe.

10. The Missouri Compromise was a decision made in the Missouri state legislature.

CHAPTER CHECKUP

1. In what ways were rivers and streams used by frontier settlers?
2. What were the contributions of (**a**) Sacajawea and (**b**) Zebulon Pike in exploring the western United States?
3. List two complaints against Great Britain that helped bring on the War of 1812.
4. How did the Missouri Compromise avoid a dangerous confrontation?
5. **Thinking Critically** With so many of their policies being adopted by the nation, why did the Federalist party die out?
6. **Thinking Critically** What do you think President Monroe and the nation would have done if Spain or Russia had challenged the Monroe Doctrine in 1823 or 1824?

APPLYING KNOWLEDGE

1. Make a list of the states admitted from territory west of the Appalachians in the order of their admission between 1792 and 1821. Put *S* next to any that were part of the Old Southwest; *N* next to any from the Old Northwest; and *L* next to any admitted from the Louisiana Purchase territory.
2. Much good historical fiction has been written about pioneers in the Old Southwest or the Old Northwest. Ask your teacher or your school librarian for suggestions, read an appropriate piece of historical fiction, and report on it orally to the class or in writing.
3. Use the table of contents of this book to find all the boxes that contain information about the Presidents of the United States. Make a list of all the Presidents in order and their home states at the time they were elected. Is there a "dynasty" from any other state or states like the Virginia dynasty of 1801–1825?

271

11 *The Jacksonian Era*

1824–1840

A New Kind of President

Why was Andrew Jackson considered a new kind of President?

VOCABULARY

favorite son	Democrat
sectionalism	

Inauguration Day   March 4, 1829, was Andrew Jackson's inauguration day. Crowds gathered in Washington to see the man from Tennessee take the oath of office as President. Jackson walked from his hotel down Pennsylvania Avenue to the Capitol. He walked, hat in hand, to indicate he was "a Servant, in the presence of his Sovereign, the People," as one observer put it.

After Jackson had taken the oath and given his acceptance speech, a crowd broke through the barriers. Everyone wanted to shake Jackson's hand. The new President made his way to his horse and rode to the White House. Behind him there followed a procession of carriages, wagons, and people on foot.

That afternoon the "presidential palace" witnessed a mob scene. Some 20,000 people came to the reception that honored President Andrew Jackson. Nothing like this had ever happened before. One person who attended had this to say:

Ladies fainted, men were seen with bloody noses, and such a scene of confusion took place as is impossible to describe — those who got in could not get out by the door again and had to scramble through the windows. . . .

In this way Andrew Jackson began his presidency. He was a new kind of President. Unlike Washington, Adams, and Jefferson, he was not a descendant of an old colonial family. Instead he was the son of an immigrant, raised on the frontier and grown to manhood in the newly opened lands west of the Appalachians.

Jackson's Early Years   Andrew Jackson's parents and their sons, Hugh and Robert, immigrated to the American colonies from northern Ireland in 1765. Mr. Jackson died shortly before Andrew's birth in 1767. During the War for Independence, Hugh was killed and Robert died of smallpox. Andrew's mother died in 1781, leaving him completely without family at the age of 14. For a time he studied law at Salisbury, North Carolina. In 1788 he crossed the mountains into Tennessee before that region became a state.

Jackson lived a busy and varied life in Tennessee. He was at different times a judge, a member of Congress, and a major

In 1829 over 20,000 people came to the reception honoring President Andrew Jackson.
■ When was Jackson elected President?

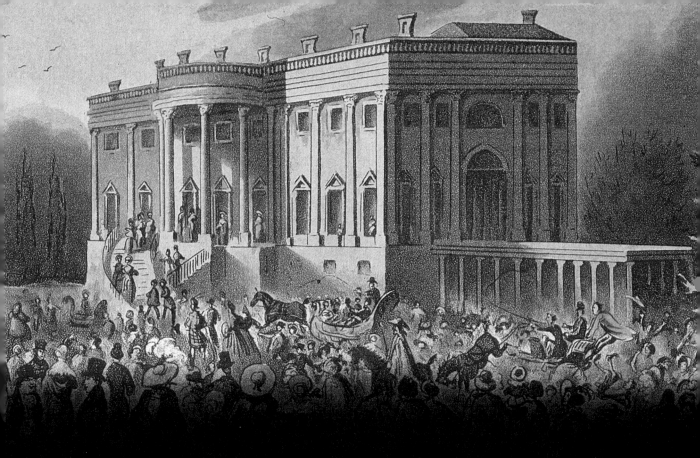

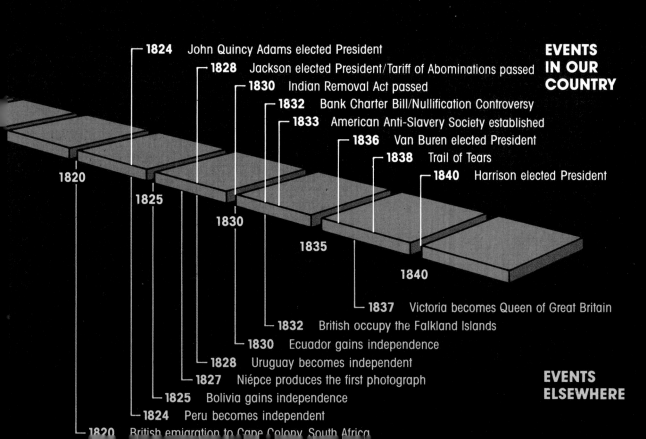

**EVENTS
IN OUR
COUNTRY**

1824 John Quincy Adams elected President
1828 Jackson elected President/Tariff of Abominations passed
1830 Indian Removal Act passed
1832 Bank Charter Bill/Nullification Controversy
1833 American Anti-Slavery Society established
1836 Van Buren elected President
1838 Trail of Tears
1840 Harrison elected President

1820
1825
1830
1835
1840

**EVENTS
ELSEWHERE**

1837 Victoria becomes Queen of Great Britain
1832 British occupy the Falkland Islands
1830 Ecuador gains independence
1828 Uruguay becomes independent
1827 Niépce produces the first photograph
1825 Bolivia gains independence
1824 Peru becomes independent
1820 British emigration to Cape Colony, South Africa

general of the Tennessee militia. He sold land to settlers, had slaves, raised cotton and tobacco, kept packs of hunting dogs, and owned some of the finest racehorses in the United States. The home Jackson built outside Nashville is called the Hermitage. Andrew Jackson and his wife, Rachel, had no children of their own, but the Hermitage was like a home for several of his wife's nephews and nieces.

In 1814, Jackson led the Tennessee militia's campaign against the Creek Indians, defeating them at the battle of Horseshoe Bend. A few months later, as you read in the last chapter, General Andrew Jackson defended New Orleans against the British invaders. After the United States acquired all of Florida, Jackson served as its first territorial governor for 6 months. With his rise to fame as the victor at New Orleans, Jackson began to be mentioned as a presidential candidate.

The Election of 1824 The campaign for President in 1824 was unusual because all four leading candidates claimed to be members of the Democratic-Republican party. When the party failed to agree on a single candidate, each section of the country nominated a **favorite son**. A favorite son is a candidate favored by the delegates from one state or section. The South backed William H. Crawford of Georgia, who was serving at the time as President Monroe's secretary of the treasury. John Quincy Adams, son of our second President, was New England's favorite. The West offered two candidates. One was Henry Clay of Kentucky. Clay was the Speaker of the House of Representatives. The other was Andrew Jackson, the war hero from Tennessee.

In the voting, Jackson received 99 electoral votes. He had nearly as many popular votes as those of the next two candidates together. (Popular votes are the votes of the people of the nation.) John Quincy Adams finished second with 84 electoral votes. Crawford had 41, and Clay had 37. Clearly, Andrew Jackson was the

Andrew Jackson became a popular hero after the battle of New Orleans pictured below.
■ How can you tell which two countries are fighting each other?

National Portrait Gallery, Smithsonian Institution, Washington, D.C., detail

JOHN QUINCY ADAMS

6th President
1825 • 1829

Born: 1767, Quincy, Massachusetts.
Education: In France and Holland and at Harvard College.
Training: Lawyer, diplomat.
To presidency from: Massachusetts.
Position when elected: Secretary of state.
Political party: National Republican.
Married: Louise Catherine Johnson.
Children: Three sons, one daughter.
Died: 1848. The only man to serve in the House of Representatives after being President, he suffered a stroke on the floor of the House and died in the Speaker's Room.
Other facts: Served at the age of 14 as private secretary to the first United States diplomat in Russia. As President, he liked to swim in the Potomac River.
During his presidency: Noah Webster published a dictionary of the English language, considered the finest of its time.

people's choice. However, no one of the four candidates had a majority of the electoral votes.

The Constitution stated that if no one had a majority, the House of Representatives should choose the President from the three leaders in electoral votes. Henry Clay had finished fourth, so he had to drop out. However, as Speaker of the House, Clay could influence the choice. Crawford had suffered a stroke during the campaign, so Clay knew that Crawford was too sick to be President. Clay and Jackson disagreed on a number of points, even though both represented the West at the time. This left John Quincy Adams, whose political views were close to those of Henry Clay.

Thus Henry Clay gave his support to John Quincy Adams. As a result the House of Representatives chose the man from Massachusetts as the successor to President James Monroe. After his inauguration, Adams named Henry Clay his secretary of state. Jackson's supporters quickly charged that Adams and Clay had made a "corrupt bargain." By this, they meant that Clay had supported Adams in a deal he made in return for his appointment as secretary of state.

The Second President Adams   John Quincy Adams entered office under the handicap of the "corrupt bargain" charges. He was a "minority President," having received fewer than one third of the popular votes in the election of 1824. His distinguished father, John Adams, had never been a popular President. The second President Adams was even less popular than his father had been.

John Quincy Adams had served brilliantly in diplomatic posts before he became President. Nevertheless he lacked political skill. He had none of the warmth that would attract the support of the common people. Part of his failure as a President stemmed from these personal characteristics. He also had to combat the increasing **sectionalism** that was dividing the country. Sectionalism is the attaching of great importance to a single region, or section, of the country.

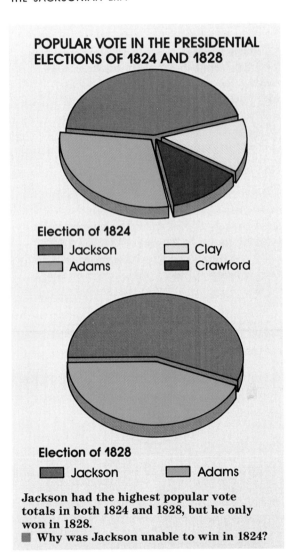

POPULAR VOTE IN THE PRESIDENTIAL ELECTIONS OF 1824 AND 1828

Election of 1824

■ Jackson   □ Clay
■ Adams   ■ Crawford

Election of 1828

■ Jackson   ■ Adams

Jackson had the highest popular vote totals in both 1824 and 1828, but he only won in 1828.
■ Why was Jackson unable to win in 1824?

Adams was not popular, and his policies had failed to win wide support. However, Jackson's campaign managers took no chances. They worked hard to win votes for Jackson. As the election drew closer, they made sure that newspapers carried articles praising Jackson. They held meetings in every city and town where they could gather a crowd of people. With this help and with his standing as a war hero, Jackson won easily. He received more than 56 percent of the popular votes and more than twice as many electoral votes as Adams.

During the years of Adams's presidency, people who favored the strong national program supported by Adams and Clay had begun to call themselves National Republicans. On the other hand, Jackson's supporters had kept the name of Democratic-Republicans. When Jackson became President, however, they shortened the name to **Democrats**. Thus Andrew Jackson joined Thomas Jefferson as a founder of what is today the Democratic party. In this way the election of Andrew Jackson marked another step in the development of one of the two major political parties of today.

President John Quincy Adams believed that the national government, rather than the states, should build roads and canals that would help the whole country to grow. He proposed to raise money for these internal improvements in two ways — by raising the tariff and by increasing the price of public land. These policies were popular in New England and in other parts of the East. However, they failed to win support from the West and the South.

Jackson Wins in 1828   It was almost certain that Andrew Jackson would win the presidency in 1828. John Quincy

CHECKUP

1. How did John Quincy Adams become President?
2. Why did Jackson's supporters charge that a "corrupt bargain" had been made in 1824?
3. Why was the administration of John Quincy Adams generally unsuccessful?
4. What were the reasons for Jackson's easy victory in the election of 1828?

5. **Thinking Critically** Do you think it was fair that Adams was made President when Jackson received more popular and electoral votes than Adams did? Explain.

Sectionalism

How did sectionalism cause problems during Jackson's presidency?

A Sectional Issue   During the presidential campaign, Jackson had been thought of as a sectional candidate from the West. During his two terms in office, however, he skillfully balanced sectional and national interests. Whenever sectional interests threatened national unity, Jackson struck hard.

The most serious sectional dispute during Jackson's presidency had to do with the tariff issue. In 1828, during John Quincy Adams's administration, Congress had raised the tariff again as a way of protecting eastern industries. Higher tariffs were unpopular in the South where, at that time, there was little industry. Higher tariffs meant that southerners had to pay more for manufactured products from Europe, or buy the more expensive products of the North. Southerners called the new tariff the Tariff of Abominations.

Consequently the legislature of South Carolina protested this action by Congress. As part of its protest, the legislature supported a statement issued by John C. Calhoun. Calhoun was a defender of state's rights. He said that a state could **nullify**—that is, cancel or veto—a national law within its own boundaries. The belief that a state could do this was called the **nullification** doctrine.

Huge textile mills were operating in New England by the 1830s.
■ **How would these workers' lives be different from farmers' lives?**

277

John C. Calhoun was Andrew Jackson's Vice President, but Jackson kept to himself his views on Calhoun's stand. Jackson did, however, use his influence to get Congress to pass a new tariff law in 1832. The new law brought the tariff rates down by a small amount. Yet the 1832 law continued to protect American industry.

The Nullification Controversy In 1832 a convention took place in Columbia, the capital of South Carolina. By a large vote, South Carolina leaders stated that the tariff acts of both 1828 and 1832 were "null, void, and no law." The people of South Carolina were authorized to refuse to pay the tariff duties after February 1, 1833. The convention went even further in its challenge to the national government. It added that any attempts by the national government to enforce the tariff acts in South Carolina "would be a just cause for the **secession** [withdrawal] of the state from the Union." The governor of South Carolina then asked for 10,000 volunteers to defend the state.

In 1830, Andrew Jackson had made a firm public statement that the Union *must* be preserved. Until 1832, however, he said nothing more about nullification. But when faced with South Carolina's challenge, he acted swiftly and decisively. First, he issued a statement strongly opposing the nullification doctrine. Then he let it be known that he would send 50,000 soldiers to South Carolina to enforce the tariff laws.

Bloodshed seemed certain to occur if neither side backed down. South Carolina appealed to the other states for help but got no promises of military assistance. John C. Calhoun realized his home state had gone too far. He turned to Henry Clay for help in arranging a compromise. Clay responded by supporting a law that would lower tariff rates annually over a period of 10 years.

Under Clay's plan, the tariff rates

Many Americans traveling westward stopped briefly at this inn near the beginning of the National Road in Maryland.
■ What kinds of transportation can you find in the picture?

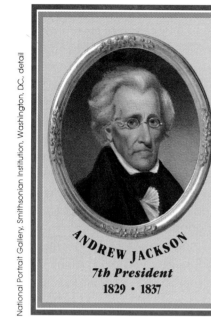

National Portrait Gallery, Smithsonian Institution, Washington, DC., detail

ANDREW JACKSON

7th President
1829 · 1837

Born: 1767, Waxhaw, South Carolina.
Educated: Very little formal schooling.
Training: Lawyer, soldier, landowner.
To presidency from: Tennessee.
Position when elected: Private citizen living on his estate, the Hermitage, near Nashville.
Political party: Democratic.
Married: Rachel Donelson Robards.
Children: One adopted son.
Died: 1845 at the Hermitage.
Other facts: The first President to have been born in a log cabin. As a 13-year-old, served in the South Carolina militia in the War for Independence. Had a quick temper and as a young man fought several duels. Owned racehorses. The first President to ride on a railroad train.
During his presidency: Cyrus McCormick invented a machine for reaping grain.

would by 1842 be nearly as low as they were in 1816. By a narrow margin, Congress passed the Compromise Tariff of 1833. At the same time, Congress passed the **Force Bill**. This authorized the President to use the army and navy, if necessary, to collect tariff duties.

The Crisis Ends   It was now up to South Carolina to compromise. Once more a convention met in Columbia. This convention repealed the nullification of the tariffs of 1828 and 1832. But to show that it still supported the principle of nullification, the convention nullified the Force Bill. However, the national government now had no need to use force because South Carolina had accepted the Compromise Tariff of 1833.

Both sides claimed victory in this crisis. The fact was, though, that neither the state nor the national government had won completely. South Carolina had won a reduction in the tariff. When its convention nullified the Force Bill, South Carolina held to the principle of nullification. On

the other hand, Jackson had kept the Union together without bloodshed. He had blocked the threat of secession.

Other Sectional Issues   Should the national government pay for highways and other improvements? On that question, Jackson took the middle road. He backed measures providing funds for improvements that helped more than one state. For example, he favored funds for building the National Road that ran from Cumberland, Maryland, westward through several states. He refused, however, to support national government expenditures for improvements within a single state.

Before Jackson became President, Congress had lowered the price of public land to $1.25 an acre and permitted it to be sold in amounts as small as 80 acres (32 ha). During the Jacksonian era, new land laws made it even easier for people to buy cheap land in the West. If land could not be sold at $1.25 an acre, it could now be sold at less than that. By 1840 these laws made it possible for poor people to settle

279

on government land and pay for it later. Some people thought government land should be given away free. Jackson never quite went that far, but he always favored a policy of cheap government land. By doing so, he favored the sectional interest of the West, along with the hopes of many eastern working people who dreamed of someday owning a little farm in the West.

The Second Bank The Democratic-Republicans had adopted a Hamiltonian policy in 1816 by setting up the Second Bank of the United States. The national government kept its funds in the Second Bank and in that bank's branches. This gave the Second Bank of the United States an advantage over other banks.

Thousands of people in the South and West disliked the Second Bank. They thought that the national government's funds should be spread out among other banks. Moreover, southerners and westerners blamed the Second Bank for the high interest rates they had to pay when they borrowed money. President Jackson also disliked the Second Bank. Still, he felt there was little he could do about it because the bank's 20-year charter would not run out until 1836.

However, Henry Clay hoped to defeat Jackson in the election of 1832, and he hit upon an idea that he thought would help him. Clay persuaded Nicholas Biddle, head of the Second Bank, to ask Congress for a new charter in 1832, 4 years before the old one ran out. Biddle did what Clay wished. Clay and his friends in Congress then passed the **Bank Charter Bill**. The bill was then sent to Jackson for his signature.

Clay thought that this would cause great trouble for Andrew Jackson. If Jackson signed the bill, he would surely lose votes in the South and the West. But if he vetoed it, the Second Bank would use its influence against Jackson in the coming election. Actually, Henry Clay thought Jackson would never dare to veto the Charter Bill.

Jackson not only vetoed the Charter Bill, he also sent Congress a stinging message along with his veto. In this message he said he thought that the Second Bank was unconstitutional because Congress had no power to charter a bank in the first place. Moreover, said Jackson, the Second Bank was a monopoly. It was also un-American, Jackson concluded, because many of its stockholders were British.

Critics of Andrew Jackson's presidency said that he acted like a king. One critic drew this cartoon to illustrate the point.
■ What is by "King" Andrew's feet?

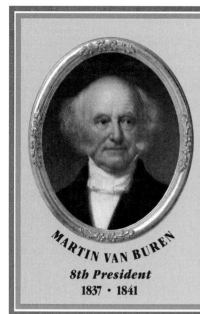

Born: 1782, Kinderhook, New York.
Education: Village school, read law.
Training: Lawyer, public official.
To presidency from: New York.
Position when elected: Vice President.
Political party: Democratic.
Married: Hannah Hoes.
Children: Four sons.
Died: 1862, Kinderhook, New York.
Other facts: Small, dapper, an elegant dresser. Served in the United States Senate and as governor of New York. The first President who was born a United States citizen — that is, after the Declaration of Independence. Considered to have been a master politician. Called "the Little Magician" by political enemies, who charged him with being sly.
During his presidency: Mount Holyoke, the first permanent women's college, was established.

MARTIN VAN BUREN
8th President
1837 · 1841

End of the Bank Henry Clay's supporters in Congress could not get the two-thirds vote needed to pass the Bank Charter Bill over Jackson's veto. Furthermore, Jackson's veto message proved to be so popular with voters that he easily defeated Henry Clay in the election of 1832. After the election, Jackson ordered his secretary of the treasury to remove the national government's funds from the Second Bank and put them into state banks throughout the country. Many business people who had borrowed money from the Second Bank had to repay it sooner than they had intended. Some of them went bankrupt and blamed Jackson for their troubles.

Like all strong Presidents, Andrew Jackson made enemies. The bankrupt business people were only a few of these enemies. Others opposed Jackson's belief that the President was as important as Congress because he represented all the people. Still others were angry when he said a President had as much right as the Supreme Court to declare an act of Congress unconstitutional.

The Whig Party Because Andrew Jackson took on such presidential power, his opponents started calling him King Andrew. They pointed out that Jackson had vetoed more acts of Congress during his first term than all previous Presidents together. So, in the early 1830s, Jackson's opponents started calling themselves **Whigs** after the party of that name that opposed the king in England.

A **depression** takes place when business slows down for many months and a large number of people lose their jobs. Near the end of Jackson's second term, a depression began. Because of this, the Whigs hoped they could beat Jackson's party, the Democrats, in 1836. However, the Whigs could not agree on one candidate, so they nominated four favorite-son candidates. They hoped that one would win a majority of the electoral votes. But if no one did, it would be up to the House of Representatives to make the choice from among the three leaders. If this happened, the Whigs believed that one of their candidates might be able to win the presidential election.

Van Buren Wins Perhaps Andrew Jackson could have been elected to a third term as President in 1836, for he was still very popular with the common people. But Jackson was old and tired. Moreover, by 1836 it was tradition that a President should serve only two terms. So Jackson retired to the Hermitage. While still in office, however, he was able to get the Democratic party to choose Martin Van Buren of New York as its presidential candidate in 1836. Van Buren had served as secretary of state during Jackson's first term, and then as Vice President during Jackson's second term.

The Whig candidates failed to get enough votes to throw the election into the House of Representatives, as they had hoped to do. Van Buren was elected quite handily. But as President, he received the chief blame for the severe depression that began even before he entered that office. As Vice President, Van Buren had helped Jackson defeat the bill to recharter the Second Bank of the United States. Now, as the depression deepened, many state banks failed. Depositors lost their money, factories closed down, and thousands of workers were unemployed. In the South the price of cotton fell by 50 percent. Many western farmers lost their farms because they were unable to pay their debts.

The Election of 1840 As the election of 1840 approached, the Whigs were sure they could win the presidency from Van Buren and the Democrats. All that was needed, the Whigs believed, was to agree on one candidate. Henry Clay was their real leader, and Clay was certain he would be chosen as the Whig candidate. However, he had made some enemies within his party, and the Whig nominating convention chose William Henry Harrison. Harrison's electoral vote total had been the highest of all four Whig candidates in 1836. Like Jackson, William Henry Harrison was a hero of the War of 1812. He had led Americans to victory in the battle of the Thames, in which Tecumseh was killed. And a year before that he had defeated the Indians at the battle of Tippe-

In the election of 1840 the Whig presidential candidate was William Henry Harrison. The cover of a song sheet favoring his election is shown below.
■ How would a campaign song be useful in an election?

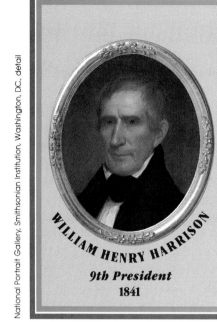

WILLIAM HENRY HARRISON

9th President
1841

Born: 1773, Berkeley, Charles City County, Virginia.
Education: Hampden-Sydney College.
Training: Army officer, public official.
To presidency from: Ohio.
Position when elected: County clerk of Hamilton County, Ohio.
Political party: Whig.
Married: Anna Symmes.
Children: Six sons, four daughters.
Died: 1841, a month after his inauguration. Made the longest inaugural speech on record (1 hour, 45 minutes) on a stormy winter day, catching a cold that caused pneumonia.
Other facts: A military hero of the War of 1812. Governor of the Indiana Territory for 12 years.
During his presidency: For the first time, copies of an inaugural address were carried by railroad. Philadelphians read Harrison's address the day it was delivered.

canoe. For Vice President the Whigs chose John Tyler of Virginia. Formerly a Democrat, Tyler had joined the Whigs because he disagreed with President Jackson over nullification.

In 1840, the Whig party showed it had learned from the Democrats. The Whigs borrowed the methods the Democrats had used to win votes for Jackson. This time, however, the methods were used to win votes for William Henry Harrison. The Whigs described their presidential and vice presidential candidates with the clever slogan **"Tippecanoe and Tyler too."** Whig orators attacked Martin Van Buren, calling him an aristocrat who wore corsets. They said that Van Buren ate fancy French foods with golden teaspoons from golden plates.

Slogans, parades, and shouting drowned out any serious discussion of the issues. The Whigs refused to adopt a party platform explaining what they stood for. Instead, they shouted "Tippecanoe and Tyler too" and "Van, Van is a used-up man." When the votes were counted, the Whigs had won. Democrats complained that they had been shouted down, sung down, and lied down. Basically, however, the Democrats lost because of the depression that lasted through most of Van Buren's single term in office.

Whig leaders had hoped to persuade the newly elected President to follow their policies. However, the plans of the Whigs fell apart when Harrison died of pneumonia a month after his inauguration at the age of 68.

CHECKUP

1. How did the tariff issue turn into a nullification controversy in 1832?
2. What was the result of the nullification controversy between South Carolina and the national government?
3. Why did Jackson veto the Bank Charter Bill?
4. How did the Whigs win the presidential election of 1840?
5. **Thinking Critically** Why do you think slogans such as "Tippecanoe and Tyler too" are effective in political campaigns?

Jacksonian Democracy

What changes led to a more political democracy during the Jacksonian era?

Nominating Conventions   The years between 1824 and 1840 are often called the Jacksonian era. During that period Jackson's beliefs about freedom, democracy, and equality influenced every aspect of American life.

One of the most significant new developments of the Jacksonian era was the expansion of **political democracy**. That is, more people than ever before took part in the process of choosing their leaders and influencing their government. One development of these years was the presidential **nominating convention**. Before this time, candidates for President, Vice President, governor, and lesser offices had been chosen by caucus. That is, a group of influential politicians would meet to choose their party's candidates in the next election. This was an undemocratic way of choosing candidates because it put the power of nomination in the hands of very few people.

In 1832 the two major political parties

In Jackson's time, more people were able to vote than ever before.
■ **What evidence can you find in this picture to illustrate high interest in this election?**

held their first presidential nominating conventions. All party members could vote for delegates from their state to attend the nominating convention. This gave even the humblest members the feeling that they had a voice in choosing their party's candidates for the highest office in the national government. Andrew Jackson was chosen to run for a second term by Democratic delegates, who came from every state except Missouri. Since 1832 each major party has held a nominating convention every 4 years.

More Voters   There were other developments that showed a growing democratic spirit. When Indiana became a state in 1816 and when Illinois followed in 1818, their constitutions permitted all white men over 21 years of age to vote. Other states at that time required voters and officeholders to own property or to pay a certain amount of tax. Gradually the reform pioneered by Indiana and Illinois spread to the older states. By 1840 only a few states kept their property requirements for voting and holding office.

Before Jackson's time, some states had religious requirements for voting. To be eligible to vote, a man had to be a member of an approved church. By the end of the Jacksonian era, all religious requirements were removed. Because of this change, three times as many men voted in the presidential election of 1828 as had in 1824.

The growth in political democracy never reached women, blacks, or Indians during the Jacksonian era. But for white male citizens there was a sizeable expansion of political rights in the years between 1824 and 1840.

Lively Campaigns   Before the Jacksonian era, presidential campaigns were quiet, dignified affairs. In fact, not much campaigning was done. Things were different from 1828 on. Many voters needed excitement to get them to the polls. Busy with their farms or their town jobs, the voters had little time to read lengthy arguments for one candidate or another.

Jacksonian Democrats were the first to use slogans to attract voters. Democratic newspapers featured cartoons that any voter could understand. Parades, songs, and band concerts brought men out to support the Democratic party and its candidates. As you have read, the Whigs adopted these tactics in 1840. Since then, political campaigns in America have been generally lively and usually noisy. They seem to have to be that way to attract the average voter's attention.

Political Organizations   Another development during Jackson's time was the strengthening of political-party organizations. After Jackson was defeated in 1824, those who had backed him started planning for victory in 1828.

At first these political organizations were small and simple. As time went by, however, they became large and lasting. Some of Jackson's supporters worked full time at the task. Only a few were wealthy enough to work without pay. Full-time workers were paid through dues or gifts of party members. Or they were given government jobs while still spending much of their time working for their political party. The practice of rewarding party members with government jobs came to be known as the **spoils system**.

The Spoils System   The spoils system received its colorful name from Senator William Marcy of New York. In a speech to the Senate in January 1832, Marcy said, "They [the Jacksonians] see nothing wrong in the rule that to the victor belong the spoils [possessions] of the enemy."

Jackson and his political supporters preferred to call the practice "rotation in office." When Jackson became President, many employees of the national government had held their jobs for 25 years or more. Some did their jobs well, but some were inefficient. Others regarded their jobs as lifetime appointments and thought they could serve the public in any way they wanted to.

Jackson favored short-term appointments to prevent the growth of a permanent office-holding group. In addition, he believed in equality and thought one person had as much right to a government job as any other. Therefore, he saw nothing

wrong with replacing some government employees with those who supported him politically. During his two terms in office, he "rotated" the employees in about one fifth of the positions available in the national government.

An old soldier himself, Jackson was reluctant to remove old soldiers from their government jobs. He refused to replace the aged postmaster in Albany, even though that postmaster was a supporter of Henry Clay. "I will not remove the old man," Jackson declared. "He carries a pound of British lead in his body." Neither would he rotate in office a veteran who had lost his leg on the battlefield, although the man had voted for Jackson's opponent. "If he lost a leg fighting for his country, that is vote enough for me," Jackson said.

To Jackson, rotation in office was a way of showing his faith in the intelligence and ability of the common man. Furthermore, his enemies greatly exaggerated the number of men he replaced with his own supporters. And, at least in the case of deserving war veterans, Jackson made exceptions to the spoils system. He started a practice that went on for many years. It often put people who were not qualified for their jobs into government posts.

Jackson's Cabinets Jackson well knew how strong sectional feelings were in the United States. When his first term began, he tried to please each part of the country. He chose a person from each section as a member of his Cabinet. Secretary of State Martin Van Buren of New York represented the East. John Eaton of Jackson's home state of Tennessee came from the West to serve as secretary of war. Jackson's first attorney general was John M. Barrien, from the southern state of Georgia. However, the keen-witted Van Buren was the only member of the official

This cartoon shows Jackson as a master of the spoils system.
■ To whom do the spoils belong?

Old Hickory

Do you have a nickname, or do you know someone who does? A nickname may be a shortened form of a given name. Examples are "Bob" for Robert; "Debbie" for Deborah; "Steve" for Steven; "Bill" for William. Or a nickname can be given because of a characteristic or physical feature a person possesses. "Red," "Skinny," "Slim," or "Curly" are nicknames of this type. Or a nickname may have some other origin.

Generally, nicknames are affectionate and are used for people we like and respect. Such was the case with Andrew Jackson, who had a number of nicknames. His friends and supporters affectionately called him "Old Andy" and "Old Hickory." Andrew Jackson seemed old to many Americans when he was inaugurated in 1829 at 61 years of age. And "Andy," of course, is a short name that is often used in place of Andrew.

Why did people call Andrew Jackson "Old Hickory"? The future President earned the nickname during the War of 1812 because of his toughness and endurance—characteristics associated with the wood of the hickory tree. He carried the nickname up to and through his presidency until his death. People gave these nicknames to Andrew Jackson because they liked and admired him. They felt he was one of them—a man of the people.

detail, Chicago Historical Society

Cabinet that President Jackson relied on for advice. So within a few months Jackson stopped holding regular meetings of his Cabinet.

The President had another group of advisers, however. The group included several politicians and newspapermen, some of whom held minor government jobs. Jackson's opponents called this informal group of advisers the **Kitchen Cabinet**, and pictured them sitting around Jackson's kitchen stove, chewing over political questions. The group probably did not actually meet in the kitchen. However, Jackson did rely on the group for advice because he knew its members were in close touch with ordinary people.

Equal Opportunities In Jackson's time, democracy in America came to mean more opportunity for many and special privileges for none. This was one of the ideas that led to the free public school system in the United States. There were schools in America as early as colonial times. Only a few of these were free, however, and they were free only to children of poor parents. The poor parents had to sign an oath saying they were unable to pay the fees that other parents had to pay.

Henry Clay is shown stitching Andrew Jackson's lips.
■ Why, do you think, was Clay stitching Jackson's lips?

During the Jacksonian era, several states experimented with free public elementary schools. In 1834 Thaddeus Stevens, a member of the Pennsylvania legislature, pointed out that there were 100,000 voters in his state who were unable to read. Surely, he argued, this was sufficient reason to establish free public schools. New York City and Philadelphia had free elementary school systems in the 1830s. By that time Massachusetts had a state law requiring towns with more than 500 families to provide opportunities for high school education at public expense. All these schools were started to create equal opportunities for students. As Thaddeus Stevens expressed it: "Let them all fare alike in the . . . schools and be animated by a feeling of perfect equality."

No Special Privileges   During the 1830s and 1840s, Jacksonian Democrats attacked what they called monopolies. To them, a monopoly was any business that had a special privilege. For example, Jackson called the Second Bank of the United States a monopoly because it had a charter giving it privileges no other bank possessed. Therefore, when Jackson destroyed the Second Bank, he took away a privilege it had and created equal opportunities for all banks.

Other businesses had special privileges in their charters. Many of these charters had been given to businesses by state legislatures during the early years of the United States. Often these special privileges prevented new companies from competing with those already chartered. However, during Jackson's second term, states began to change their charter laws. The changes made it much easier for companies to get charters to do business of one kind or another. All the new charters were alike. None contained a special privilege for the chartered company. Thus, the emphasis on equality of economic opportunity in Jackson's time opened the door to free competition among businesses.

CHECKUP

1. How did the presidential nominating conventions help to give more political rights to people?
2. What led to an increase in the number of voters during the Jacksonian era?
3. How did political organizations and the spoils system get started in the Jacksonian era?
4. Why did Jackson pay more attention to the Kitchen Cabinet than to the official Cabinet?
5. **Thinking Critically** Why do you think free public education became important as more people gained the right to vote?

Inequalities in the Jacksonian Era

What groups of people did not benefit from Jacksonian democracy?

Indian Removal   When Jacksonian Democrats spoke of equality of opportunity, they usually thought only of white men. They gave little thought to the unequal treatment of Indians, blacks, and women.

By Jackson's time, Indians east of the Mississippi were no longer a danger to white settlements. Most eastern Indians lived peacefully on land granted to them by treaties with the national government. But many white people wanted to take this land away from the Indians. These people believed the Indians should be forced to live west of the Mississippi.

Congress gave in to the demands of these people in 1830 by passing the Indian Removal Act. This act ordered Indians to give up their land east of the Mississippi River in exchange for lands west of the river. The Indian Removal Act had Jackson's backing. Even earlier, he had allowed people in Georgia to take land away from the Cherokee.

By treaties made earlier, Indians had to agree to their removal. Also, they were supposed to be paid for any lands they gave up. However, the government made the eastern Indians move without any regard for their wishes. Furthermore, Jackson ignored the protests of many white people who protested the government's treatment of the Indians.

Indian removal reached a tragic height in the 1830s. During that decade the Choctaw, Chickasaw, Seminole, Cherokee, and Creek peoples were forced to leave their lands in Georgia, Alabama, Florida, Mississippi, and Tennessee. These Indians were known as the Five Civilized Tribes. The Cherokee in particular had

The Cherokee are forced to Oklahoma on what came to be known as the Trail of Tears.
■ Why, do you think, did the artist show so little detail of the land and sky?

Philbrook Art Center, Tulsa, Oklahoma

accepted white people's culture by becoming Christians and inviting missionaries to live among them. One of their leaders, Sequoya, had created an alphabet for their language. The Cherokee also published a newspaper called *The Cherokee Gazette*.

Nevertheless, the Cherokee were required to move. Under guard by the United States Army, about 15,000 of them set forth on what became known as the **Trail of Tears**. Heartbroken at being forced from their homes, they were herded westward in the fall and early winter of 1838. Rain and cold brought on sickness, and about 4,000 died before they reached Oklahoma. Not a single family made the trip without losing at least one member along the trail.

Indian Resistance   Some southern Indians refused to move. Bands of Seminole, Cherokee, and Creek resisted as white families waited to settle on their land. A few Indians managed to hide out near their homes. Others died of starvation or were hunted down and killed. Sometimes those removed to the western lands were killed by other Indians, who resented new intruders on their hunting grounds.

Indians of the Old Northwest also were moved west of the Mississippi during Jackson's time. Some of them refused to stay there. Under the leadership of Chief Black Hawk, a group of Indians tried to return to their former homes near Rock Island, Illinois, in 1832. Fighting broke out and the governor of Illinois called out the state militia. A large number of Sac and Fox Indians were killed in what became known as **Black Hawk's War**. Black Hawk himself was captured. Several months later he was sent on a trip to the East, which included a visit with President Jackson. "We did not expect to conquer the whites," Black Hawk told Jackson. "I

took up the hatchet to revenge injuries which my people could no longer endure."

Black Inequality   Between 2 million and 3 million black people lived in the United States during the Jacksonian era. Most of these people were slaves, but even free black Americans were denied equality. Some Americans had protested against the evils of slavery in colonial times. During and soon after the American Revolution, most northern states had begun the process of ending slavery within their borders. By the time of the Jacksonian era, **abolitionists** — people who wanted slavery abolished, or legally prohibited everywhere — were active in all parts of the nation.

As early as 1800, free black Americans in Philadelphia sent an antislavery petition to Congress. Individual white southerners like Levi Coffin, James G. Birney, Angelina Grimké, and her sister, Sarah, were early supporters of the antislavery movement. They joined northerners in working for *gradual abolition*, that is,

Frederick Douglass, a former slave, helped other slaves escape to freedom.
■ How could a former slave help other slaves escape?

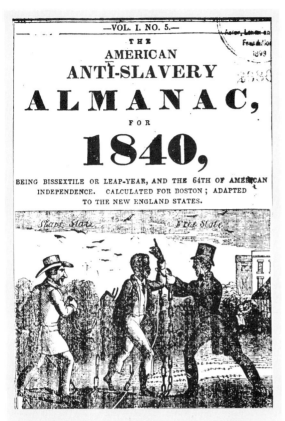

─VOL. I. NO. 5.─

THE
AMERICAN
ANTI-SLAVERY
ALMANAC,
FOR
1840,

BEING BISSEXTILE OR LEAP-YEAR, AND THE 64TH OF AMERICAN
INDEPENDENCE. CALCULATED FOR BOSTON; ADAPTED
TO THE NEW ENGLAND STATES.

In 1833 abolitionist leaders formed the American Anti-Slavery Society.
■ **When was this almanac published?**

emphasis on equality as well as by humane concerns. As the movement spread, the American Anti-Slavery Society gained 200,000 members. Nevertheless, in spite of these efforts, slavery continued. It would take a bloody war to eliminate slavery once and for all.

Women's Inequality Equality between men and women had little meaning during the Jacksonian era. No male leader of the 1830s seriously argued that women should have the right to vote or to hold office. In fact, throughout the country the laws treated women as children, no matter how old they were. Most states refused women the right to own property. Women were denied entry into the professions of law, medicine, and the ministry.

Yet, at the same time, expanding prosperity freed some women from work in their homes. Immigrant girls and black servants often took over household duties in middle- and upper-class homes. This allowed women from these homes to work for causes they believed in. They became active in antislavery societies and in missionary work. From these activities grew a **women's rights** movement. It would be years before changes were made in the laws that denied equality to women. Nevertheless, the seeds for these changes and for many other reforms were planted in the days when Andrew Jackson was President.

ending slavery over a period of years. However, beginning about 1830 a group of northerners became *extreme abolitionists.* Probably William Lloyd Garrison of Massachusetts was the most widely known of the extreme abolitionists, who wanted to end slavery immediately. Garrison published a paper in Boston that he called *The Liberator.*

Frederick Douglass, a self-educated former slave, also published an abolitionist newspaper. He called it *The North Star* and suggested that slaves escaping from the South could use the North Star in the sky as a guide to freedom.

In 1833 abolitionist leaders organized the American Anti-Slavery Society. These leaders were influenced by the Jacksonian

CHECKUP

1. Why were eastern Indians removed to lands west of the Mississippi?
2. What evidence indicates that an antislavery movement was growing?
3. In what ways were women denied equality during the Jacksonian era?
4. **Thinking Critically** Why do you think abolitionists began to gain support for their cause during the Jacksonian era?

Using Synonyms

WORDS THAT REPLACE OTHER WORDS

Usually there is more than one way to say the same thing. For example, one sentence in this chapter reads: A favorite son is a candidate favored by the delegates from one state or section. The underlined word could be replaced by a synonym without changing the meaning of the sentence. The new sentence would read: A favorite son is a candidate preferred by the delegates from one state or section. Synonyms are different words or terms that have the same or similar meanings.

SKILLS PRACTICE I

Listed below is a series of statements. Each statement is followed by three words. One of the words could be used in place of the underlined word without changing the meaning of the numbered statement.

On a separate sheet of paper, write the number of the statement and the word in parentheses that could replace the underlined word.

1. Immense crowds gathered in Washington to see the man from Tennessee take the oath of office as President of the United States. (Small, Large, Angry)
2. Jackson had to combat the increasing sectionalism that was dividing the country. (help, start, fight)
3. The Tariff of 1832 retained the principle of protecting American industry. (kept, changed, started)

4. As the depression deepened, many state banks failed. (collapsed, expanded, increased in size)
5. Jackson favored short-term appointments to prevent the growth of a permanent office-holding group in the federal government. (aid, stop, expand)

SKILLS PRACTICE II

For the following statements think of a word that could be used in place of the underlined word without changing the meaning of the statement. On a separate sheet of paper, write the number of each statement and the word you think of. Use your dictionary if you need to look up any of the underlined words.

1. Land laws passed during the Jacksonian era permitted some land to be sold at less than $1.25 an acre.
2. Most eastern Indians lived peacefully on land granted them by treaties with the national government.
3. In 1833, abolitionist leaders organized an American Anti-Slavery Society.
4. During the 1828 election, Jackson's campaign managers worked hard to attract the votes of the common man.
5. Immigrant girls and black servants often took over household duties in middle- and upper-class homes.

MAIN IDEAS

1. Andrew Jackson represented a new kind of President because he was the son of an immigrant and not from an old colonial family, and he had been raised on the frontier west of the Appalachians.
2. During Jackson's presidency, disputes arose because of sectional interests over the raising of the tariff and the use of government funds for building roads.
3. Jackson crushed the Second Bank of the United States because he regarded it as an un-American monopoly.
4. Jacksonian democracy expanded the role of the common person in politics through presidential nominating conventions, lively campaigns, and permanent political organizations.
5. During the Jacksonian era, Native Americans, black Americans, and women continued to be denied rights held by white males.

VOCABULARY REVIEW

On a separate sheet of paper, write the letter of the ending that best completes each sentence.

1. A favorite-son candidate is one who is (a) seeking office for the first time, (b) the son of an officeholder, (c) favored by one state or region, (d) the oldest son.
2. "Tippecanoe and Tyler too" was a slogan that helped to win the presidency for (a) Andrew Jackson, (b) Martin Van Buren, (c) William Henry Harrison, (d) John Tyler.
3. John C. Calhoun of South Carolina was chiefly responsible for (a) the Bank Charter Bill, (b) the Force Bill, (c) the doctrine of nullification, (d) the Indian Removal Bill of 1830.
4. The expansion of political democracy in Jackson's time resulted in (a) the election of a woman as governor of Indiana, (b) an increase in the number of voters, (c) a denial of voting rights to people who owned no land, (d) the Indian Removal Act.

5. The practice that Democrats called "rotation in office" (a) originated in Georgia and Kentucky, (b) became known as the spoils system, (c) caused 90 percent of the national government's employees to lose their jobs, (d) ended when Jackson left office.

CHAPTER CHECKUP

1. Why did many people admire Andrew Jackson?
2. Why were favorite-son candidates nominated by the Democratic-Republicans in 1824 and the Whigs in 1836?
3. What was Jackson's attitude toward each of the following?
   a. the Second Bank of the United States
   b. the doctrine of nullification
   c. the Indians
4. Why were permanent political organizations and the appearance of the spoils system linked together?
5. How did Jackson encourage free competition in business?
6. **Thinking Critically** Would you consider Jackson a sectionalist or a nationalist? Give reasons to support your answer.
7. **Thinking Critically** Who do you think had a more important role in the federal government during the Jacksonian era—Congress or the President? Explain.

APPLYING KNOWLEDGE

1. Plan an automobile trip to the Hermitage, near Nashville, Tennessee. Use road maps to locate the routes you would follow. List these routes and the states you would pass through.
2. Draw a cartoon on one or more of the following subjects:
   a. The Second Bank of the United States as seen by Jacksonian Democrats
   b. A Whig view of "King Andrew"
   c. John C. Calhoun's view of the protective tariff

12 An American Spirit Grows 1820–1860

The Spirit of Reform

What were the goals of reformers in the 1830s and 1840s?

reform	suffrage
Declaration of Sentiments	

A Determined Young Woman   On July 14, 1848, there appeared in the *Seneca Falls Country Courier* the following unusual announcement:

> Woman's Rights Convention—a Convention to discuss the social, civil, and religious conditions and rights of woman, will be held in the Wesleyan Chapel, at Seneca Falls, N.Y., on Wednesday and Thursday, the 19th and 20th of July . . . commencing at 10 o'clock A.M. . . .

With this announcement Elizabeth Cady Stanton and Lucretia Mott called upon women to organize and work for rights that had been denied them.

As a child, Elizabeth Cady sometimes hid in her father's law office. From her hiding place she heard pitiful stories of married women who had come to her father for help. Often they told of having their property and their children taken from them because of laws that favored men. When her only brother died, Elizabeth's father cried because he had no more sons. Elizabeth resolved to prove to her father that a daughter was as good and as valuable as a son.

The determined girl became a skillful horseback rider. She learned to play chess and other games that many men thought to be above the mental powers of girls and women. She studied Greek, Latin, and mathematics. She begged to go to Union College, a men's school in Schenectady, New York. Instead she was sent to Emma Willard's Troy Female Seminary.

Wider Interests   After graduating, Elizabeth Cady became interested in movements for **reform**. Reform is the improving of conditions by change. Elizabeth Cady heard about women's rights at the meetings she attended. Sometimes Henry Stanton, a journalist and reformer, spoke at these meetings. Stanton and Cady soon realized they shared many of the same views. In May 1840, they were married.

Elizabeth Cady Stanton and her husband spent their honeymoon in London, England, where he was a delegate to a World Anti-Slavery Convention. She found women delegates were barred from the convention. This seemed unfair and

Elizabeth Cady Stanton addresses the first women's rights convention in the United States in 1848 at Seneca Falls, New York.
■ Did men as well as women attend this convention?

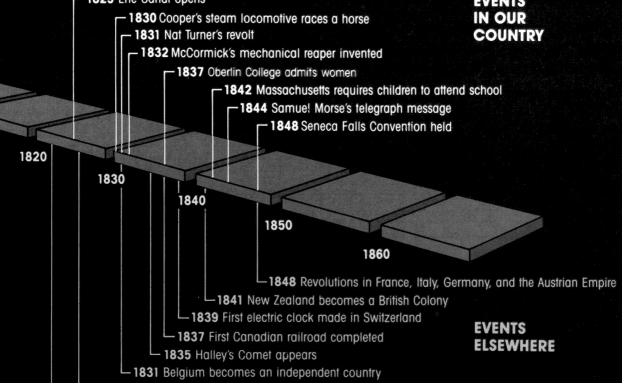

EVENTS IN OUR COUNTRY

- **1825** Erie Canal opens
- **1830** Cooper's steam locomotive races a horse
- **1831** Nat Turner's revolt
- **1832** McCormick's mechanical reaper invented
- **1837** Oberlin College admits women
- **1842** Massachusetts requires children to attend school
- **1844** Samuel Morse's telegraph message
- **1848** Seneca Falls Convention held

1820

1830

1840

1850

1860

- **1848** Revolutions in France, Italy, Germany, and the Austrian Empire
- **1841** New Zealand becomes a British Colony
- **1839** First electric clock made in Switzerland
- **1837** First Canadian railroad completed
- **1835** Halley's Comet appears
- **1831** Belgium becomes an independent country
- **1826** Pan-American Congress in Panama
- **1822** First iron railroad bridge built in England

EVENTS ELSEWHERE

turned Elizabeth Cady Stanton's thoughts to the many ways that society discriminated against women. At the convention she met Lucretia Mott, and the two resolved to work together for women's rights.

After returning to the United States, the Stantons lived for several years in Boston. Elizabeth Cady Stanton met other reformers there. She met the abolitionist Frederick Douglass; John Greenleaf Whittier, an abolitionist poet; and Lydia Maria Child, an author whose husband had protested against President Andrew Jackson's treatment of the Cherokee Indians. (See pages 289–290.)

"All Men and Women . . ." The damp climate around Boston was not good for Henry Stanton's health. The drier air of central New York seemed to be better for him. The Stantons moved to Seneca Falls in 1847 with their three small children. Later they had four more children.

The women's rights convention that met at Seneca Falls in July 1848 was attended by both men and women reformers. (See the picture on page 295.) The convention issued a **Declaration of Sentiments**, written by Cady Stanton. She used the Declaration of Independence as her model, beginning her Declaration of Sentiments with the words "All men and women are created equal." She followed this with a long list of ways in which society discriminated against women.

At the end of her declaration came the demand that women be given **suffrage**— that is, the right to vote. Not all reformers believed this was a good idea at that time. But Frederick Douglass, among others, spoke in favor of it. Later women's rights conventions also demanded woman suffrage. Still, many years passed before women were granted the right to vote throughout the United States.

Susan B. Anthony became a leading voice in the struggle for women's rights.
■ In what year was this coin minted?

Some influential women reformers were missing from the Seneca Falls Convention. Susan B. Anthony, for example, was teaching school at the time. However, she joined Elizabeth Cady Stanton in 1851 as a crusader for women's rights. They made a good team. While Stanton stayed home and wrote speeches, Anthony traveled around delivering them and organizing local groups. As Mrs. Stanton's husband is said to have remarked to his wife, "You stir up Susan and she stirs up the world."

Sojourner Truth Elizabeth Cady Stanton and Susan B. Anthony worked with another influential woman reformer of the time who went by the name of Sojourner (sō jėr′ nėr) Truth. Originally named Isabella Baumfree, she had been a slave in a New York family of Dutch descent. When New York did away with slavery in 1828, she became a member of the African Zion Church and worked in religious causes in New York City.

UNITED STATES POSTAGE

ELIZABETH STANTON CARRIE C. CATT LUCRETIA MOTT

3¢ 100 YEARS OF PROGRESS 1848 · OF WOMEN · 1948 3¢

The Declaration of Sentiments

On July 19, 1848, over 300 people gathered at a small church in Seneca Falls, New York, for the first women's rights convention. James Mott, Lucretia Mott's husband, was chosen to chair the convention. In the opening speech, Elizabeth Cady Stanton described the inequalities that existed between men and women.

The history of mankind is a history of repeated injuries and usurpations on the part of man toward woman, having in direct object the establishment of an absolute tyranny over her. To prove this, let facts be submitted to a candid world.

He has never permitted her to exercise her inalienable right to elective franchise.

He has compelled her to submit to laws, in the formation of which she had no voice.

He has withheld from her rights which are given to the most ignorant and degraded men—both natives and foreigners. . . .

He has made her, if married, in the eyes of the law, civilly dead.

He has taken from her all rights in property, even to the wages she earns. . . .

He has monopolized nearly all the profitable employments. . . .

He has denied her the facilities for obtaining a thorough education, all colleges being closed against her. . . .

He has endeavored, in every way that he could, to destroy her confidence in her powers, to lessen her self-respect and to make her willing to lead a dependent and abject life.

Now in view of . . . the unjust laws above mentioned, and because women do feel themselves aggrieved, oppressed, and fraudulently deprived of their most sacred rights, we insist that they have immediate admission to all the rights and privileges which belong to them as citizens of the United States. . . .

USING SOURCE MATERIAL

1. Name four inequalities between men and women in the 1840s.
2. What was the goal of these women?
3. Which of the objections mentioned in the declaration would have mattered most to you at the time?

Sojourner Truth, a former slave, worked to help other slaves gain their freedom.
■ Do you think this painting was made before or after she was freed? Explain.

which it should be ended. Moreover, the abolitionists were generally interested in other reforms besides the abolition of slavery. Whether black or white, male or female, they worked together to make the United States — and the entire world — a better place to live in.

Frederick Douglass was not only an abolitionist, but he also worked for women's rights. Susan B. Anthony spoke and wrote in favor of abolition, temperance in the use of alcoholic beverages, and the right of women to vote. William Lloyd Garrison borrowed some ideas from David Walker, a free black who urged slaves to revolt if their masters refused to free them. Garrison argued as strongly for women's rights and better treatment of Indians as he did for the abolition of slavery.

A dedicated woman named Dorothea Dix worked during the 1830s and 1840s for better treatment of the mentally ill. At the time, these unfortunate people were put in prisonlike cells. They were chained, whipped, and left with very little care. Dorothea Dix investigated this shameful treatment of the mentally ill in several parts of the country.

Baumfree's magnificent voice attracted large audiences. She spoke of her dreams and her visions as she traveled from town to town. In the 1840s she took the name Sojourner Truth and became one of the most sought-after speakers in the cause of abolition and other reforms.

The Goals of Reformers   Nearly all reformers of the time were abolitionists. However, they often disagreed about the best way to end slavery and the speed with

Methods of Reform   To help the mentally ill, Dorothea Dix appeared before committees of state legislatures. She described the hopeless conditions she had seen in jails and other places where these people were held. She called upon the committees to use the power of the state to improve the lives of the mentally disturbed. As a result of her investigations, state after state took mental patients out of jails and prisons. They were put into hospitals where they could be better cared for.

Many other reformers used methods like those of Dorothea Dix. Reformers who worked for women's rights set out to bring about changes in state laws that

You can see some of the conditions mentally ill people were kept in at the time of Dorothea Dix's reform efforts.
■ What can you tell about the living conditions of mental patients?

discriminated against women. Abolitionists hoped to convince southern states to pass laws against slavery, as had been done in all northern states by 1850. Temperance advocates petitioned for laws limiting the sale of liquor or prohibiting it completely. Sometimes reformers organized tiny political parties made up of people who believed that certain specific reforms were needed.

Most reformers of the time spoke long and loud in public. Going to a lecture was a favorite form of entertainment in those days. Sometimes a reformer's lecture might last two or three hours. Occasionally fights broke out between those who sympathized with the lecturer and those who opposed him or her. At first, women were denied the right to speak in public, but in time they won this right as well as other rights long denied them.

Convincing others of the need for reform by lecturing was slow and limited in the number of people it reached. A better way was to use the printed word. Consequently, many reformers wrote about the reforms they favored and had their arguments published in books, magazines, newspapers, or pamphlets.

CHECKUP

1. What reformers were in favor of women's rights?
2. Why could some men and women of the 1830s and 1840s be described as "all-purpose reformers"?
3. Who did Dorothea Dix try to help? Why?
4. What methods did reformers use?
5. **Thinking Critically** If you had lived in the 1840s, which reform(s) would you have supported? Why?

Educating the Public

VOCABULARY

egalitarian

Better Education   Until the 1840s most Americans opposed the idea of free public schools. However, when workers in the cities and other people without property got the right to vote, many who had opposed free public schools began to change their minds. Voters needed to be able to read and write. Factory owners realized that their workers might be more productive if they could read instructions and perhaps do a little simple arithmetic. Gradually, opposition lessened to the idea of free public schools.

In 1842, Horace Mann persuaded the Massachusetts legislature to pass a law that required every child to attend school for a certain length of time each year. To educate these children, Massachusetts provided free public schools. The Massachusetts idea spread, as Horace Mann lectured all over the country in support of free public schools. By the 1850s many states had free public education for children through the elementary school years. In the elementary schools of the

This picture is an idealized view of a public school classroom in the middle of the 1800s.
■ How is this classroom different from your classroom?

Yale University Art Gallery, The Mabel Brady Garven Collection

time, youngsters studied reading, spelling, writing, arithmetic, and perhaps a little geography and history.

The new interest in education for all brought about the growth of some high schools, colleges, and universities. However, the idea of free high schools spread very slowly. The colleges and universities of the time were usually supported by churches or other private groups. College and university students were required to pay tuition. But the idea of tax-supported state universities was spreading. Michigan, Mississippi, Iowa, Indiana, Missouri, and Wisconsin had them by 1850.

Educational opportunities for girls and women increased during this time. Emma Willard started a school for girls in Vermont in 1814 and another in Troy, New York in 1821. (The latter was the school in which Elizabeth Cady Stanton studied.) As the free public elementary schools spread, girls studied alongside boys in many states. Oberlin College in Ohio allowed four women to enroll in 1837, along with men students. Later, other western colleges and universities admitted women as well as men. Separate colleges for women were established at about the same time.

More Reading Material   As more people learned to read, more books, magazines, and newspapers were published. Reformers furnished some of this reading material. Frederick Douglass had his paper, *The North Star.* William Lloyd Garrison published *The Liberator,* an abolitionist paper. Elizabeth Cady Stanton wrote articles for a New York newspaper and for a women's rights magazine, called the *Una.*

One women's magazine of the time that had a large circulation was called *Godey's Lady's Book.* Sarah Hale became

This illustration is from the cover of the 1840–1860 *Godey's Lady's Book.*
■ How is women's clothing different today?

editor of the *Godey's Lady's Book* in 1837. She remained as the magazine's editor for 40 years and was largely responsible for its success. *Godey's Lady's Book* had beautiful drawings of women's fashions of the time. It also contained editorials, written by Sarah Hale, favoring women's rights and other reforms.

More Newspapers   Americans of the 1830s and 1840s liked to read newspapers. In 1790 there were 92 newspapers in the United States, but only eight were published every weekday. Sixty years later there were more than 3,000 newspapers, and 387 of them were dailies. One of these was *Freedom's Journal,* the first newspaper in the United States directed to black people. Samuel Cornish and John B. Russwurm began its publication in New York in 1827. Another successful New York paper was the *Sun*, published by Benjamin H. Day beginning in 1833. The *Sun* was a daily and sold for only one cent a copy.

Newspaper publication had spread widely throughout the United States by 1850. The Nashville *Union* and the Detroit *Free Press* both began publication in 1835. *The Telegraph and Texas Register* first appeared that same year in San Felipe, Texas. Later it became the Houston *Telegraph*. An influential southern paper, the New Orleans *Picayune* (pik ə yün'), started in 1836. The Monterey *Californian* began in 1846 as the first newspaper in California. Three years later it changed its name to the *Alta Californian* and became the first daily newspaper in California. *Spectator*, Oregon's first paper, also started in 1846.

The 1830s and 1840s were years of very heavy immigration to the United States. Between 1841 and 1850 nearly 1,750,000 Irish and German people crossed the Atlantic to settle in America. These immigrants wanted to read news about their homelands and about the new country to which they had come. By 1856 there were 56 German-language newspapers published in the United States.

In 1841 Horace Greeley started the *Tribune* as a daily newspaper in New York City. He was a brilliant editor and his paper rapidly gained national influence. Greeley fearlessly expressed his own views in *Tribune* editorials. He opposed slavery, believing it to be both immoral and uneconomical. He despised and feared monopoly of any kind. He supported labor unions, argued against capital punishment, and urged restrictions on the sale of liquor. In other words, Horace Greeley was an all-purpose reformer, and he made

the New York *Tribune* one of the great voices of reform in the land.

Religion and Reform   Many reforms of the time were based on the idea of dignity and equality of individuals. It was no accident that the women at the Seneca Falls Convention began their Declaration of Sentiments with the phrase "All men and women are created equal." Jacksonian democracy stressed special privilege for none. Horace Greeley was known as an **egalitarian** because he favored *equal* political, economic, and legal rights for all American citizens.

Religious beliefs were also a source of reform during the 1830s and 1840s. Many male reformers were ministers. Many women reformers, such as Sojourner Truth, were deeply religious. Some southern clergy argued that the Bible sanctioned slavery, but an equal number of reformers pointed out that slavery was immoral. For many black people, whether slave or free, religion was both a comfort and a guide.

Opposition to Reform   It would be wrong to think that many Americans in the 1830s and 1840s were reformers or even to think that most people favored reform. A few brave women argued for the rights of all. Most women, however, kept busy with their traditional tasks in the home. Most men were too busy earning a living for themselves and their families to think much about reforms. Organized workers did back the movement for free public schools. Some also campaigned for a shorter working day. In 1834 a national federation of workers was formed. However, when hard times hit the country in 1837, this group collapsed.

Outspoken opposition to slavery was dangerous in many parts of the country. Elijah Lovejoy, an abolitionist editor, had

Members of a mob, angered by Elijah Lovejoy's antislavery editorials, set fire to his newspaper's printing plant and then killed him.
■ Besides setting fire to the plant, what else is the mob doing to it?

his printing press destroyed by a mob in Alton, Illinois. The Ohio Anti-Slavery Society sent him another press. When the mob came once more, Lovejoy was shot dead while trying to defend the new press. James G. Birney left his native state of Kentucky because of opposition to his antislavery views. After moving to New York, Birney was the presidential candidate of an Anti-Slavery party in 1840 and of the Liberty party in 1844.

Slave revolts were punished with great severity. Nat Turner, a black preacher and leader, led a revolt in Southampton County, Virginia, in 1831. Fifty-one white persons were killed in a single day and night. Turner and his associates were hunted down or killed outright. Some slaves were tried and hanged.

In Boston a mob threatened to hang William Lloyd Garrison because of his abolitionist views. Women reformers were often hooted at and jeered as they attempted to speak out against injustice. In fact, reformers in general had a difficult time. What they asked for was change, and most people were against change.

Yet, even with the resistance that reformers met, the 1830s and 1840s are looked upon as one of the great reform periods in American history. By 1850 women enjoyed more rights than they had had 20 years earlier, more tax-supported schools were in existence, and more people were aware that slavery was a gigantic blot on the principles of dignity and equality.

CHECKUP

1. How were better educational opportunities made available in the 1830s and 1840s?
2. What kinds of newspapers were published at this time?
3. Who was Horace Greeley?
4. Why was there opposition to reform?
5. **Thinking Critically** In the 1830s and 1840s, lecturing and printing were the most effective methods of gaining reform. What would be the most effective methods today? Explain.

An American Spirit in the Arts

How did American literature, art, and music change in the first half of the 1800s?

VOCABULARY

Leatherstocking Tales	**Hudson River School**
Concord group	

Independence in the Arts The United States of America won political independence from Great Britain at the time of the American Revolution. Nearly 50 years passed, however, before Americans won independence in the arts. During those years American authors, painters, and sculptors generally followed European models. At that time, a Britisher might sneer as he or she asked, "Who reads an American book?"

The Britisher would have asked a good question. Some Americans had written books before that time. Other Americans had painted pictures and shaped statues. And yet there was no way to tell that these were *American* achievements. These works of art were only imitations of what European artists had done before.

Ralph Waldo Emerson, one of America's great thinkers, urged an end to this situation. In a speech at Harvard in 1837 he asked for an "intellectual Declaration of Independence." By this Emerson meant that Americans should stop relying on foreign models and should create stories, pictures, and statues based on American ideas and American scenes.

Irving and Cooper At least two American writers had already done what Emerson asked. Under the pen name Diedrich Knickerbocker, Washington Irving had published a history of New York in 1809.

Actually, it was more a history of the old Dutch colony of New Amsterdam. Washington Irving later wrote *The Sketch Book,* a collection of stories about the early Dutch settlers in colonial America. "Rip Van Winkle" and "The Legend of Sleepy Hollow" are two of his most famous tales.

James Fenimore Cooper wrote of other American scenes and other kinds of Americans. In a series of novels called the *Leatherstocking Tales*, he created a character named Natty Bumppo. This character appeared at different times and in different places but was always the honest, brave, and true American frontiersman. Cooper's Indian characters, too, were always noble and uncorrupted by civilization. *The Deerslayer* and *The Last of the Mohicans* were included in this series. Cooper's *Leatherstocking Tales* were immensely popular not only in the United States but also in Europe. In fact, some European authors began imitating *him.* They wrote stories about American Indians without ever having seen one.

The Concord Group By the 1840s a group of New England writers lived in and near the town of Concord, Massachusetts. Ralph Waldo Emerson was probably the most famous member of the **Concord group**. Henry David Thoreau, a close friend of Emerson's, would become well known when he published *Walden* in 1854. In the book, Thoreau wrote of his experience living alone for a year in a hut beside Walden Pond, near Concord, observing nature and the changes of seasons.

Nathaniel Hawthorne lived in Concord for several years, where he was a neighbor of Emerson and Thoreau. Hawthorne first made a reputation for himself by publishing collections of short stories. He gained even greater fame later with two novels, *The Scarlet Letter* and *The House of the Seven Gables.* Both were about Puritan ideas during the time Massachusetts was a colony of Great Britain.

The poet Henry Wadsworth Longfellow was also a member of the Concord group. Longfellow used historical themes in many of his poems. Many Americans could quote all or parts of "Paul Revere's Ride." Longfellow also wrote story-poems such as *The Song of Hiawatha, Evangeline,* and *The Courtship of Miles Standish.*

Like many American writers and poets, the Concord group borrowed some European ideas. But they mixed these borrowed ideas with their own thoughts and set their work in American locations.

It made for a product that was distinctly American.

American Painters Several American artists had begun to depict American scenes by the time Ralph Waldo Emerson advocated an intellectual Declaration of Independence. Thomas Cole, Thomas Doughty, and Asher Durand were among these. They were members of a group called the **Hudson River School**, since they painted scenes along the Hudson River. They were the first to concentrate on painting American scenes in a distinctive style of their own.

The Hudson River School of artists painted landscapes. Other American artists became well known by painting people. George Caleb Bingham, for example,

In one of Washington Irving's best-known tales, "The Legend of Sleepy Hollow," schoolteacher Ichabod Crane is chased by a headless horseman. ■ **How did the artist capture the mood of Crane's terror?**

National Gallery of Art. Washington

The Versatile Mr. Morse

Few people become famous in even one field. Samuel F. B. Morse became famous in two fields, painting and inventing. Like other young American artists, he studied abroad for a time. Morse studied at the Royal Academy of London, between 1811 and 1815. When he returned to the United States, Morse found that portraits were the only works of art Americans would buy. So he became a portrait painter — and a good one.

Then tragedy struck. First, Morse's young wife died, then his parents. Saddened by these deaths, he found it difficult to paint. He went to Europe, hoping to rekindle his artistic imagination. On the voyage home he talked with a scientist who mentioned that electric impulses could travel any distance in an instant. This set Morse to thinking about the use of electrical force to send messages over long distances.

It took Samuel F. B. Morse many years to perfect his telegraph. In 1838 he developed the Morse code, which is an alphabet of dots and dashes used in transmitting telegraph messages. Finally, Congress appropriated money to build a telegraph line between Washington and Baltimore. The first telegraph message in the United States was sent over that line in 1844. The telegraph proved to be a great aid to American enterprise, especially for railroads and newspapers. Telegraph lines ran along railroad lines around the country. By means of the telegraph, railroads could operate more efficiently and more safely. Newspapers could receive news from all parts of the country almost as the events happened.

painted scenes of American frontier life. His *Daniel Boone Coming Through Cumberland Gap* was painted from imagination because Bingham was born long after the event shown in his picture. Other scenes, however, Bingham saw and remembered from his early years in Missouri. Among these scenes of frontier life are *Jolly Flatboat Men, Raftsmen Playing Cards, Fur Traders Descending the Missouri,* and *Verdict of the People.*

American Indians of the early nineteenth century were painted from life by George Catlin. He traveled extensively west of the Mississippi in the 1830s and 1840s. There he recorded scenes of the West and the lives of western Indians. Catlin's *Bird's Eye View of the Mandan Village,* painted in 1832, shows the same scene the members of the Lewis and Clark expedition might have witnessed some 30 years before.

American birds and animals were the subjects of John James Audubon's paintings. Though Audubon was born on the island of Santo Domingo, he lived most of his adult life in the United States. He had prints of his pictures fastened together and sold as huge books.

During the 1840s inexpensive copies of famous paintings became available. Demand increased as more Americans developed a taste for art. Most of the copies they bought were of paintings by European artists. However, prints sold by Nathaniel Currier and James M. Ives became very popular. They flooded the country with reproductions of pleasant scenes of American life.

Folk Art   Artistic creations made by common people are known as folk art. An example might be the lovely quilts handmade by women of the 1800s. However, much of American folk art dating from

that time is made of wood, which, of course, was readily available. With their sharp knives, many early nineteenth century men developed great skill in carving wood into all kinds of shapes.

Nearly every large sailing vessel had a wooden figurehead at its bow. Some of these figureheads were fine examples of folk art. Well-designed weathervanes, sign boards for country taverns, and

This folk art carving of Andrew Jackson was once on the front of a sailing ship.
■ How does this image of Jackson compare to the cartoons you saw of Jackson in Chapter 11?

Painter Eastman Johnson called this 1859 painting "My Old Kentucky Home" after Stephen Foster's song of the same name.
■ What did Johnson want to show about plantation life?

kitchen utensils can also be considered folk art. The best of these objects are in American museums today. They remind us of the skills and artistic sense that were part of the character of many Americans in the 1830s and 1840s.

Popular Music   Stephen Foster is probably the best known of a small number of American composers whose songs are still sung a century and a half after they were written. He never earned much money from them, but Foster's compositions were very popular in his time. An Albany newspaper had this to say about Stephen Foster's song "Old Folks at Home," which appeared in 1851: "Sentimental young ladies sing it; sentimental young men warble it in midnight serenades . . . All the bands play it. . . ." Other Stephen Foster songs still sung by Americans today are "My Old Kentucky Home," "Camptown Races," and "O Susanna."

As folk art was created at this time, so was folk music. Examples of folk music are sea chanteys, songs sung by sailors as they worked together to raise a ship's anchors and sails. Negro spirituals, sung in the fields or at religious services, are other examples of Americans creating their own folk music.

CHECKUP

1. What did Ralph Waldo Emerson mean by an "intellectual Declaration of Independence"?
2. Who were the members of the Concord group?
3. What were the subjects of each of the following painters? (a) Asher Durand (b) George Caleb Bingham (c) George Catlin (d) John James Audubon
4. What were Nathaniel Currier and James M. Ives noted for?
5. What is folk art?
6. **Thinking Critically** Why do you think many American writers chose historical themes for their works?

American Enterprise

How was the spirit of American enterprise demonstrated in the first half of the 1800s?

VOCABULARY

| American enterprise | mechanical reaper |

A Canal Boom   The *Seneca Chief* was the lead boat in a fleet of boats gathered at Buffalo, New York, on the morning of October 26, 1825. Soon the *Seneca Chief* would begin the first triumphant trip along the Erie Canal to the Hudson River and then south to New York City. Work on the western end of the canal had begun only a little more than 2 years before. Now completed, it was "the longest canal made in the least time with the least experience for the least money . . . of any other in the world," according to one orator on that great autumn day when the fleet set out from Buffalo.

Prominently displayed on the *Seneca Chief's* deck were two kegs, painted red, white, and blue. They contained "pure waters of Lake Erie," which were to be dumped into the Atlantic Ocean when the *Seneca Chief* got to New York City. The Erie Canal was nearly 400 miles (644 km) long, and it took the leading canalboat 8 days to reach New York City. This was much less time than the overland journey took. Because of the Erie Canal, freight rates between Buffalo and New York dropped from $100 to $10 a ton (from $90.70 to $9.07 per t) within a few years. The new canal soon became the main artery of trade between the eastern seaboard and the West.

The success of the Erie Canal set off a great boom in canal building. Before the completion of the Erie Canal, there were fewer than 100 miles (161 km) of canals in the United States. By 1840 more than 3,300 miles (5,310 km) of canals had been built. Canals across several parts of Ohio and Indiana linked Lake Erie and the Ohio River. Another canal connected Lake Michigan and the Mississippi River by way of the Illinois River. The state of New Jersey financed the Delaware and Raritan

Some passengers traveled the Erie Canal but it was mainly built to transport freight.

■ **What is powering the canalboat in this picture?**

Chicago Historical Society, detail

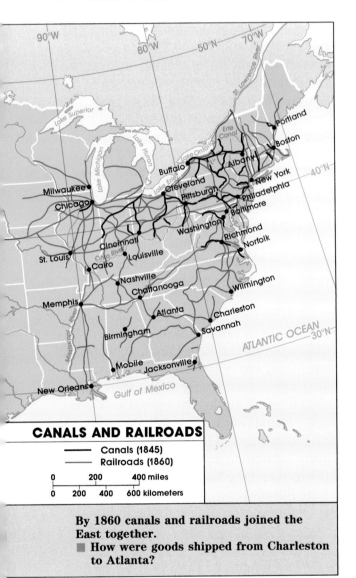

CANALS AND RAILROADS

— Canals (1845)
— Railroads (1860)

0   200   400 miles
0 200 400 600 kilometers

By 1860 canals and railroads joined the East together.
■ **How were goods shipped from Charleston to Atlanta?**

Canal, which, when completed in 1838, linked the waters of the Delaware River and the Atlantic Ocean. These canals were splendid examples of **American enterprise**—that is, the energy and the will of Americans to launch big new projects to benefit them and their country.

Steam Railroads   Canal travel was soon surpassed by the railroads. At first the owners of the Baltimore and Ohio Railroad tried horses and sails to move their cars over rails. In 1830 Peter Cooper

of New York persuaded the owners to try his *Tom Thumb*, the first steam locomotive built in the United States, In its first trial a horse defeated the *Tom Thumb* in a race. Nevertheless, the owners of the Baltimore and Ohio were convinced that the steam locomotive was the best source of power for railroads.

Soon the Baltimore and Ohio, with its steam locomotives, became the first railroad in the United States to carry both passengers and freight. By 1850 there were many others. States, local communities, and private companies financed the 9,021 miles (14,515 km) of railroads built by that time. Railroads had several advantages over canals. Trains were faster than canalboats. Railroad tracks could be laid where it was difficult or even impossible to dig canals. During cold weather, canals might freeze over while railroads could operate in both summer and winter.

Railroads caught the fancy of Americans in ways that canals never could. Canalboats were pulled by horse or mule teams walking on a path beside the canal. Canal travel was smooth and safe but very slow. On the other hand, travel by rail was fast, exciting, and sometimes dangerous. But the danger only added to the fascination of the railroads. As a New York man wrote in his diary in the summer of 1839:

> Imagine a locomotive rushing . . . whizzing and rattling and panting, with its fiery furnace gleaming in front, its chimney vomiting fiery smoke above, and its long train of cars rushing along behind like the body and tail of a gigantic dragon . . . and all darting forward at the rate of 20 miles an hour. Whew!

Steamboats   While steam locomotives sped along the rails, steamboats traveled the rivers of America. The first successful steamboat was built by John Fitch in 1787.

In 1807, Robert Fulton's *Clermont* steamed up the Hudson. Within a few years, steamboats made their appearance on the Ohio and the Mississippi. In 1815 the *Enterprise* steamed from New Orleans, Louisiana, to Louisville, Kentucky, in the record time of 25 days.

Western steamboats were quite different from those on the eastern rivers and the oceans. Western rivers were generally broad and shallow. To navigate in these shallow waters, western boats carried their powerful engines above the waterline. Their huge paddle wheels dipped only slightly into the water to avoid grounding the boat on one of the many sandbars of the western rivers. Steamboats were important to river towns. Without steamboats on the western rivers, Cincinnati, St. Louis, Louisville, Memphis, and Natchez could not have developed as rapidly as they did.

As important as steamboats were, they did not completely replace rafts and flatboats on the western rivers. Steamboats could travel upriver, against the current. But rafts and flatboats could be used for carrying cargo downstream. They were an inexpensive means of shipping. As late as the 1850s many families moved

A steamboat passes St. Louis, Missouri, on the Mississippi River.
■ **How did St. Louis's location give it certain advantages?**

downstream on the Ohio River or the Mississippi River on a slow-moving raft or flatboat.

A Transportation Revolution   Canals, railroads, and steamboats brought about a transportation revolution in the United States. This transportation revolution had a number of effects. For one, it hastened the westward movement of the American people. They could move into western lands more rapidly and easily than their grandparents had moved across the Appalachian Mountains.

Even more important, this revolution made it possible for people in each part of the country to specialize in the manufacture of certain goods. Because it was now easier to exchange goods, no part of the country had to be wholly self-sufficient.

Steamboats carried western corn, wheat, and pork to southern markets, returning with rice, sugar, and hemp. Southern cotton could be carried to New England textile mills by rail or by steamboat. The West and the Northeast exchanged many products by means of the Great Lakes–Erie Canal route. The West produced agricultural goods, and the Northeast made manufactured goods.

The Factory System   Early factories in the United States needed waterpower to turn their machinery. The swift rivers of southern New England proved ideal for this purpose. One such river was the Blackstone, which flowed from Worcester, Massachusetts, to Providence, Rhode Island. By 1840 it provided waterpower for 94 cotton mills, 22 woolen mills, and 34

In an early textile factory, workers operate looms on which cotton cloth is made.
■ **Who are the workers in this factory?**

machine shops and ironworks! With an abundance of waterpower, New England became the first great manufacturing region in the United States.

New Englanders carried the factory system into other parts of the country. By 1850, Ohio was important in the manufacture of woolen cloth. Cincinnati and St. Louis became important manufacturing and commercial centers through the leadership of children and grandchildren of people born in New England. Later others led the way in making Chicago a great commercial and railroad center.

In 1850 the South was still mainly an agricultural region. Still, the spirit of American enterprise was as noticeable there as elsewhere in the United States. Railroads ran through all the southern states. Richmond, Virginia, was the site of a flourishing ironworks. Southern cotton was sent to the northern textile factories and helped to make the North a prosperous industrial region.

Farm Machinery The spirit of American enterprise affected farms as well as factories in the years between 1825 and 1850. In Virginia, Cyrus Hall McCormick perfected a **mechanical reaper** in 1832. His father had tried to develop such a machine for 20 years. The son succeeded in part because he had the help of a black man, Joe Anderson. Before the McCormick reaper came into use, farmers had cut grain by hand at harvesttime. The first mechanical reaper pulled by horses could do the work of five men. Later it was improved even more.

McCormick's reaper was the first of a number of machines that revolutionized farming in the United States. In 1837 John Deere of Illinois and his partner fashioned a steel-bladed plow that was lighter and stronger than the iron or wooden plows

Cyrus McCormick oversees the successful test of the first mechanical reaper. Soon he was selling 1,000 reapers a year.
■ What does a reaper do?

then in use. In 1840 an improved grain drill for planting seed was developed. Later that same year a threshing machine was invented, and in 1850 a mechanical binder proved to be a great help to farmers.

CHECKUP

1. What advantages did railroads have over canals?
2. What were the effects of the transportation revolution in the United States?
3. Why did the factory system develop first in New England?
4. How did the spirit of American enterprise affect farming between 1825 and 1850?
5. **Thinking Critically** How do the events in the first half of the 1800s reflect the growth of the Industrial Revolution in the United States?

Recognizing Attitudes and Emotions

PERSUASIVE WRITING AND SPEAKING

You have just finished reading about the attempts by some people to bring about social change in America. Such people were called reformers. They wanted to better the conditions of life for others. Rights for women, abolition of slavery, and better treatment of Indians and the mentally ill were just a few of their goals.

Many methods were used by reformers to further their causes. They lectured at public meetings, appeared before committees of state legislatures, and wrote articles telling what was wrong and what should be done about it. Not all people wanted social change. Opponents of reform also spoke out and wrote newspaper articles.

The selection below is about the issue of slavery. It was written by abolitionist William Lloyd Garrison, who wanted an immediate end to slavery.

> I will be harsh as truth, and as uncompromising as justice. On this subject, I do not wish to think, or speak, or write with moderation. No! No! Tell a man whose house is on fire to give a moderate alarm; . . . tell the mother to gradually extricate her babe from the fire into which it has fallen — but urge me not to use moderation in a cause like the present. I will not equivocate, I will not excuse — I will not retreat a single inch — AND I WILL BE HEARD.

Dorothea Dix pleaded the cause of the mentally ill and those in prisons. The following passage is part of a speech Dix made before the Massachusetts legislature.

> I come to present the strong claims of suffering humanity. I come to place before the Legislature of Massachusetts the condition of the miserable, the desolate, the

outcast. I come as the advocate of helpless, forgotten, insane, and idiotic men and women; of beings sunk to a condition from which the most unconcerned would start with real horror; of beings wretched in our prisons, and more wretched in our almshouses (poorhouses).

> I must confine myself to a few examples, but am ready to furnish other and more complete details, if required.

SKILLS PRACTICE

In each selection the writer's opinion and attitude toward a major issue of that time is being expressed. On a separate sheet of paper, write an answer to each of the following questions.

1. How does Garrison's use of language show emotion?
2. Why does Garrison use the image of the house on fire?
3. How does Dix describe the mentally ill and the prisoners?
4. Who does Dix consider to be more wretched — the poor or the prisoners?

MAIN IDEAS

1. The 1830s and 1840s witnessed one of the great reform periods in American history.
2. Women's rights, the abolition of slavery, temperance, better treatment for the mentally ill, and free public schools were major areas of interest to reformers at this time.
3. In the arts, American writers and painters began to use American ideas and American scenes rather than relying on European models.
4. The growth of canals, railroads, and factories represented the spirit of American enterprise during the 1830s and 1840s.
5. These developments caused a transportation revolution that speeded up the westward movement of the American people and increased economic specialization in various sections of the country.

VOCABULARY REVIEW

On a separate sheet of paper write **True** if the statement is true and **False** if it is false. Rewrite the false statements to make them true.

1. The Declaration of Sentiments was a statement in support of women's rights.
2. The Concord group was a group of American landscape painters.
3. The reformers of the 1830s and 1840s wanted to make the United States a better place in which to live.
4. Woman suffrage is a term that referred to the mentally ill.
5. Horace Mann was the founder of the Hudson River School.
6. One who advocates equal rights is called an egalitarian.
7. Washington Irving was best known as the author of the *Leatherstocking Tales*.
8. American enterprise may be defined as the energy and will of Americans to undertake new projects.
9. Steamboats on western rivers were different from the steamboats on eastern rivers.

10. Cyrus McCormick's first reaper was known as the *Tom Thumb*.

CHAPTER CHECKUP

1. Why was the Seneca Falls Convention called in 1848?
2. How were educational opportunities for women improved during the 1830s and 1840s?
3. How did Jacksonian democracy and religious beliefs act as sources for reform ideas?
4. What American authors and painters were the first to use American themes?
5. What kinds of songs are considered folk music?
6. What advances were made during the Jacksonian period in transportation and in manufacturing?
7. **Thinking Critically** Would people in your town or city have more likely supported the building of a canal or a railroad in the 1850s? Why?
8. **Thinking Critically** Do you think the presence of slaves in the South helped or hindered the introduction of farm machinery in that region?

APPLYING KNOWLEDGE

1. Imagine that you were going west with your family in the 1830s by way of the Erie Canal. Keep a diary and make entries about your journey for a week. You may use an encyclopedia or other reference book to get further information on early travel by canalboat.
2. Prepare a newspaper editorial or a 3-minute speech about a current issue. You may choose an important issue in your community or one of the following: pollution, nuclear power plants, year-round school, a candidate running for office. Explain why you feel strongly for or against the cause and why you want to persuade others to feel the same way that you do on this issue.

13 *Spanning the Continent* 1820–1853

On to Oregon

How did the Oregon Country become part of the United States?

VOCABULARY

Great American Desert	"Fifty-four forty or fight!"
Mountain Men	49th parallel
Oregon Trail	
provisional government	

Major Long's Mistake Major Stephen Long was chiefly responsible for a great mistake in American geography. In the 1820s this army officer led an expedition in the lands between the Missouri River and the Rocky Mountains. The official maps of the expedition labeled the region the **Great American Desert**. Major Long wrote of this region: "It is wholly unfit for cultivation and . . . uninhabitable by people depending on agriculture for their subsistence."

For 50 years mapmakers copied Long's maps with their misleading labels. Settlers crossed the "desert" without stopping, on their way to the more desirable lands west of the Rockies. Much of the land was a great treeless plain. Today these plains support millions of people. But to those pioneers it must have seemed like an endless desert.

Trails West During Major Long's explorations he discovered routes through the trackless Great Plains. Another army officer, Captain John C. Frémont, also roamed through the West. He and his guide, Kit Carson, discovered suitable routes for the westward migration that would soon follow.

It was Frémont's wife, Jessie Benton Frémont, who carried the story of her husband's explorations to people in the East. She took his official reports of two exploring expeditions of the 1840s and turned them into popular books. Persons planning to venture to the west coast eagerly read the books and studied the maps and the descriptions of the western trails.

By the early 1840s experienced and capable guides were ready to lead wagon trains of settlers and traders over the best routes into the far western lands. Many of these guides were men who had spent their early lives trapping and trading for furs in the Rockies. They have become known in history as the **Mountain Men**.

Mountain Men The Mountain Men were highly resourceful and wise in the ways of the wilderness. Many of them guided exploring parties that were sent out by the army. They led groups that brought goods to trade with the Indians for furs.

During the 1840s, hundreds of families headed west, traveling by covered wagon.
■ **When did Americans settle in Texas?**

EVENTS IN OUR COUNTRY

- 1822 Americans settle in Texas
- 1836 Texas gains its independence
- 1843 Settlers travel the Oregon Trail
- 1844 Polk elected President
- 1846 Mexican War begins
- 1847 Mormons settle in Utah
- 1848 Mexican Cession/Gold discovered in California
- 1850 California becomes a state
- 1853 Gadsden Purchase

1825 1830 1835 1840 1845 1850 1855

EVENTS ELSEWHERE

- 1852 South African Republic established
- 1851 Gold discovered in Australia
- 1846 Potato famine in Ireland
- 1835 Melbourne, Australia, founded
- 1833 Slavery abolished in the British Empire
- 1829 Slavery abolished in Mexico
- 1825 Decembrist revolt in Russia
- 1821 Mexico gains its independence

They also hired out as guides to the wagon trains of pioneers heading west.

Jim Bridger was a famous Mountain Man. He discovered many of the principal landmarks between the Rockies and the Sierra Nevada. Like most of the Mountain Men, Bridger got along well with the Indians. His first wife was the daughter of a chief of the Flathead tribe. They had two children before she died. His second wife was a Ute. She died in childbirth on July 4, 1849. It is said that Jim Bridger raised his motherless baby on buffalo milk.

James Beckwourth was another famous Mountain Man. He was born in Virginia, probably into slavery, but he grew up in St. Louis as a free man. After joining a fur-trading expedition to the Rocky Mountains, Beckwourth lived for 11 years with the Crow Indians. They gave him the name of Morning Star. Later, Beckwourth

became an army scout and discovered a pass through the Sierra Nevada. This route is today called Beckwourth Pass.

The Oregon Country In the late 1700s, American ships visited the Oregon coast. Captain Robert Gray discovered the mouth of the Columbia River in 1792. Little more than 10 years later, the Lewis and Clark expedition gave the United States a further claim to the Oregon Country. In 1811, John Jacob Astor founded Astoria, a fur-trading post near the mouth of the Columbia River. Great Britain also claimed the region. It based its claims on the explorations of Sir Francis Drake in 1579, Captain James Cook in 1778, and Captain George Vancouver in 1792. In 1818, the treaty between Great Britain and the United States that set the northern border of the Louisiana Purchase (see page 328) allowed citizens of both nations to settle in Oregon. But no decision was made about which nation owned the country.

The Oregon Country was much larger than the present state of Oregon. It extended west from the Rocky Mountains to the Pacific Ocean. Its northern boundary was 54°40′ north latitude. This boundary, which touched the southern tip of Alaska, was established by a treaty between the United States and Russia in 1824. In the south the Oregon Country touched the northern border of California. Both American and British fur traders spread the word about the richness of the land.

Christian missionaries also played a prominent part in attracting settlers to Oregon. In 1834, Jason Lee led a party of Methodist missionaries to the Oregon Country. Father De Smet, a Jesuit missionary, also established several missions in Oregon. Marcus Whitman, a young New York doctor, was still another pioneer missionary. In 1836 he and his wife built their

During the 1840s Easterners poured into the fertile Oregon Country.
☐ What fort was built at the point at which the Snake River joins the Columbia River?

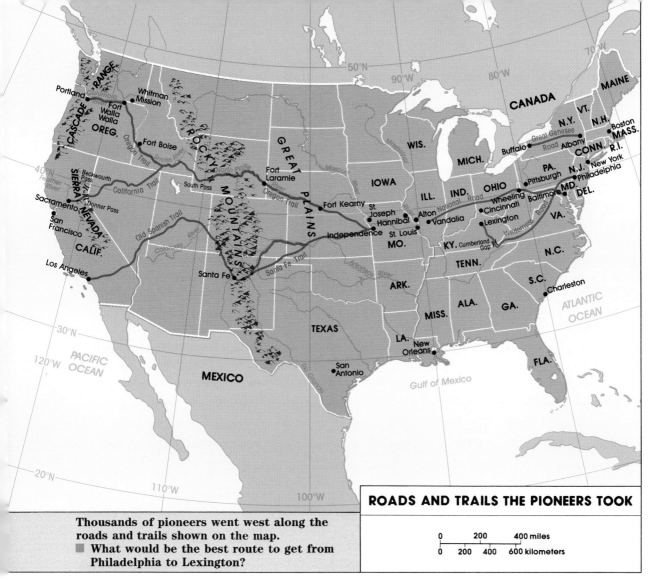

ROADS AND TRAILS THE PIONEERS TOOK

Thousands of pioneers went west along the roads and trails shown on the map.
■ What would be the best route to get from Philadelphia to Lexington?

0	200	400 miles
0	200	400	600 kilometers

mission near the site of present-day Walla Walla, Washington. Narcissa Prentiss Whitman was one of the first white women to settle west of the Rockies.

"Oregon Fever" The reports of the missionaries created great interest in the Oregon Country. By the 1840s the interest in moving to this northwestern region was so intense that it began to be called "Oregon fever." People talked of the great crops of wheat one could raise in Oregon. Stories of the rich soil and the good climate were told. One account declared that

> out in Oregon the pigs are running about under the great acorn trees, round and fat,

and already cooked, with knives and forks sticking in them so that you can cut off a slice whenever you are hungry.

After hearing tales like this, it is no wonder that thousands of people planned to move to the Oregon Country. The first large group to travel the **Oregon Trail** left Independence, Missouri, in the spring of 1843. It included about 1,000 men, women, and children. They had loaded their possessions into huge covered wagons pulled by oxen.

Starting from Independence, the trail to Oregon covered nearly 2,000 miles (3,200 km). The slow-moving caravans went northwest to the Platte River. They followed the river to Fort Laramie in present-day Wyoming. This was a place to stop for rest and for fresh supplies. Then they went on through the Rockies by way of South Pass to the Snake River. Here the settlers could make a choice. Those bound for California turned southwest. Those continuing on the Oregon Trail followed the Snake and the Columbia rivers. The trip took about 6 months.

Setting Up a Government   Some farming had been done in Oregon near the fur-trading posts. However, French Prairie, in the valley of the Willamette (wə lam′ ət) River, was the first area settled solely for farming purposes. By 1841 about 65 American and 61 French-Canadian families were living in the Willamette Valley.

In 1843, settlers began to arrive in large numbers. Among them was George William Bush, a free black man who had fought with Andrew Jackson's army at the battle of New Orleans. Bush, with his wife and five children, arrived in Oregon in 1844. During that same year, American settlers in the Willamette Valley organized a **provisional government**. This was a temporary government set up as a first step toward making Oregon an official territory of the United States. The provisional government passed a law forbidding black people to settle in Oregon. But the law was never seriously enforced. In fact, George William Bush secured a homestead of 640 acres (259 ha) and is today recognized as one of the pioneer settlers of the American Northwest.

Fort Laramie was a busy trading post on the Oregon Trail.
■ **What purpose do you think the three raised structures attached to the fort served?**

National Portrait Gallery, Smithsonian Institution, Washington, D.C., detail

JOHN TYLER
10th President
1841 · 1845

Born: 1790, Greenway, Charles City County, Virginia.
Education: College of William and Mary.
Training: Lawyer, public official.
To presidency from: Virginia.
Position when taking office: Vice President.
Political party: Whig.
Married: (1) Letitia Christian, (2) Julia Gardiner.
Children: Eight sons, six daughters.
Died: 1862, Richmond, Virginia.
Other facts: A tall, thin man, thoughtful and courteous. The first Vice President to succeed to the presidency through the death of a President. Elected a member of the House of Representatives of the Confederate States of America shortly before his death.
During his presidency: Samuel F. B. Morse sent the first message by telegraph from Washington to Baltimore.

The Oregon Question   By 1844 several thousand Americans were living in the region that is today the states of Oregon and Washington. A lesser number of British citizens lived in the same region. Nevertheless, the Americans had made clear their dissatisfaction with joint ownership of the Oregon Country between Great Britain and the United States. "Oregon fever" had brought on an "Oregon question."

Expansion was the chief issue in the presidential election of 1844. John Tyler had quarreled bitterly with the leaders of his own party, so the Whigs made Henry Clay their candidate. James K. Polk of Tennessee was the Democratic candidate. He declared that the United States should have all the Oregon Country that had been jointly occupied up to the 54°40′ boundary with Alaska. **"Fifty-four forty or fight!"** became a slogan of the campaign. Henry Clay avoided the issue of expansion and lost the election.

But two years later, Polk changed his mind. As you will read later in this chapter, the United States was by then involved in a serious dispute that seemed likely to lead to war with Mexico. Faced with this dangerous situation, Polk decided to compromise on the Oregon question. The British, too, were ready to end the dispute. A treaty set the boundary at the **49th parallel** north latitude, an extension of the eastern boundary between the United States and British-controlled Canada. South of this line, only the southern tip of Vancouver Island stayed in British hands. The northern boundary of the United States was now fixed from the Atlantic to the Pacific.

CHECKUP

1. How did the land between the Missouri River and the Rockies get the name *Great American Desert?*
2. What role did missionaries and the Mountain Men play in the settlement of the Oregon Country?
3. Describe the Oregon Trail.
4. How was the Oregon question settled?
5. **Thinking Critically** After hearing the reports, would you have wanted to settle in the Oregon Country? Explain.

Texas: Republic and State

How did Texas become part of the United States?

The Settlement of Texas The first Spanish mission in Texas was established by Father Damian Massanet in 1690. Between this time and the early 1800s, the Spaniards built many missions and presidios in Texas, but few of the settlements survived more than a few years. Some were destroyed in raids by the Comanche or Apache Indians; others were destroyed by the French when they tried to move into East Texas from New Orleans. As a result, Texas was sparsely settled.

By 1830 many settlers had moved to Texas to join Austin's colony. Families had to fit all their belongings into wagons like these.
◼ **What pulled these wagons?**

In 1821, Moses Austin received permission from the Spanish government to bring Americans into Texas. Moses Austin had been a banker and lead mine owner in Missouri. However, he died before he could organize a settlement. His son, Stephen, took over the task of establishing an American colony along the Brazos River.

In the meantime, Mexico won its independence from Spain, and Texas became part of a northern Mexican state. So Stephen F. Austin had to ask the new Mexican government for permission to settle the land that had been granted to his father. The government reaffirmed the grant. In exchange, Austin agreed to bring a certain number of families to settle the land. As part of the agreement, the settlers did not have to pay taxes to the Mexican government for 6 years. However, they were required to become Mexican citizens.

To encourage people to move to Texas, Austin sold the land for a price lower than that of land in the United States at that time. The land was good and had plenty of timber. One landowner wrote that the soil was so rich that "even the weeds grow 20 feet tall." The Brazos River gave the settlers access to the Gulf of Mexico.

By 1825, Austin had assigned tracts of land to 300 families, thus fulfilling his agreement with the Mexican government. During the next 10 years, some 25 land grants were made under conditions similar to Austin's.

Trouble in Texas News of Texas spread. By 1835 the 30,000 Americans in Texas outnumbered the Mexicans living there. Some American settlers had brought slaves with them in spite of Mexican laws against slavery. Moreover, some American communities began to hold

Protestant church services. The increasing number of Americans and their defiance of the law alarmed the Mexican government. Mexico decided to forbid further immigration of Americans to Texas. Some land grants were canceled. Still, the Americans kept coming.

As a result, some Americans in Texas started talking about making their territory either an independent country or a separate state within Mexico. Stephen F. Austin thought they should do neither, but he went to the capital at Mexico City to protest the new policies. When he got there, he was thrown into jail for 8 months. Mexican authorities charged him with secretly working for the **annexation** of Texas to the United States. Annexation is the taking of a country or territory and making it part of one's own country.

At the Alamo General Antonio López de Santa Anna had established himself as dictator of Mexico in the early 1830s. His solution to the problem of Texas was to place the area under military rule. Several armed clashes occurred in 1835 between Mexican soldiers and Texans. Early in the next year, General Santa Anna led his army against the rebellious Texans.

A Mexican army of 4,000 surrounded about 190 Texas volunteers in the Alamo, an old Spanish mission on the outskirts of San Antonio. From February 23 until March 6, 1836, the men in the Alamo held out. By March 6 all of the soldiers were killed. Two slaves, a Mexican servant, a woman, and three children survived.

While some Texans and Mexicans were dying at the Alamo, other Texans were meeting at Washington-on-the-

Texans defended the Alamo. The few survivors included a woman with a newborn infant who was sent to report the news to other Texans.
■ **Do you think this painting was done by an eyewitness?**

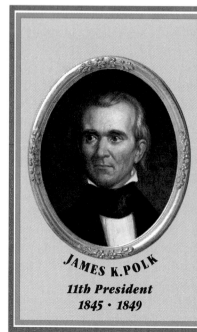

Born: 1795, Mecklenburg County, North Carolina.
Education: University of North Carolina.
Training: Lawyer, public official.
To presidency from: Tennessee.
Position when elected: Private law practice and business.
Political party: Democratic.
Married: Sarah Childress.
Children: None.
Died: 1849, Nashville, Tennessee.
Other facts: Short, slight in build. Served seven terms in House of Representatives. Only former Speaker of the House ever to become President. The first "dark-horse" candidate for President. (A dark-horse candidate is one who is unexpectedly chosen as a compromise between strong candidates.) Declined to seek a second term.
During his presidency: The first baseball game of record took place in Hoboken, New Jersey, in 1846, between the Knickerbockers and the New Yorks.

JAMES K. POLK
11th President
1845 · 1849

Brazos. On March 2, 1836, they declared Texas independent of Mexico. They then set up a temporary government under a constitution modeled on that of the United States. Though it was too late to save the Alamo's defenders, **"Remember the Alamo!"** became the rallying cry for a new Texas army. Within weeks this force was preparing to avenge the Alamo defeat.

Texas Becomes a Republic   Sam Houston commanded the Texas army. Houston was a former governor of Tennessee and a good friend of Andrew Jackson. Before Houston's army went into action, however, Santa Anna's men had wiped out a force of 300 Texans at Goliad. Houston's army soon had its revenge. On April 21, 1836, the army surprised Santa Anna near the San Jacinto (san jə sint′ ō) River. Texans went into battle crying "Remember the Alamo! Remember Goliad!" They quickly defeated the Mexican army and captured General Santa Anna himself.

Following his victory at the battle of San Jacinto, Sam Houston was elected the first president of the **Republic of Texas**. As a prisoner, General Santa Anna signed a treaty recognizing the independence of Texas. Later, however, the Mexican congress refused to approve the treaty. Nevertheless, in 1837, President Andrew Jackson recognized Texas officially as an independent nation.

Texas Joins the Union   Many Texans wanted their republic to be added to the United States. Leaders in the South wanted the same thing. On the other hand, many Northerners opposed the annexation of Texas because it would mean another slave state in the union. Indeed it might mean the addition of even more than one slave state, since Texas was large enough to be divided into a number of states.

The Texas issue, like the Oregon question, came to the fore in the presidential election of 1844. As you know, James K. Polk, the Democratic candidate, spoke out in favor of taking the whole Oregon Country. He also favored the annexation of

Texas. Polk's victory showed that the American people sided with him.

Three days before Polk was inaugurated, Congress voted to admit Texas as a state in the union. However, Americans and Mexicans differed over the boundary between Mexico and the new American state. Mexico claimed the Nueces River as the boundary. The United States said the boundary was the Rio Grande. During the summer of 1845, President Polk angered the Mexican government by sending American troops into the disputed border area.

War with Mexico The Mexican government also sent troops to the disputed area. In April 1846, a force of 1,600 Mexican cavalrymen surrounded 63 American soldiers along the border. Every one of the Americans was killed, wounded, or captured. An angry President Polk told Congress, "Mexico has passed the boundary of the United States, has invaded our territory and shed American blood upon American soil." Congress declared war on Mexico on May 13, 1846.

The Mexican army was poorly trained and poorly equipped. Still, at the beginning of the war, it was larger than the army of the United States. But eager volunteers from the southern states soon increased the size of the American forces. Of the 62,000 volunteers, about 49,000 were from Texas and the states of the lower Mississippi Valley.

During the Mexican War the American navy blockaded both coasts of Mexico. General Zachary Taylor led an invasion

General Winfield Scott led his victorious troops into Mexico City on September 14, 1847. (19°N/99°W; map p. 326)
■ **How does the artist show the people reacting to Scott's army?**

Chicago Historical Society

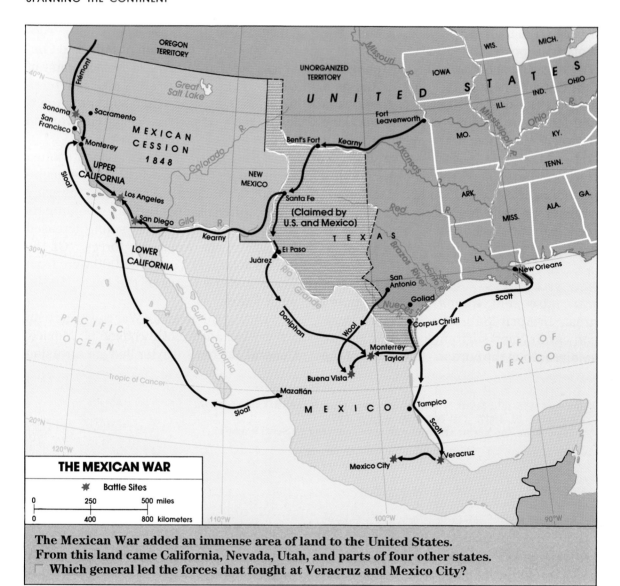

THE MEXICAN WAR

✷ Battle Sites

0 — 250 — 500 miles
0 — 400 — 800 kilometers

The Mexican War added an immense area of land to the United States.
From this land came California, Nevada, Utah, and parts of four other states.
☐ Which general led the forces that fought at Veracruz and Mexico City?

force into northern Mexico, winning victories at Monterrey (mont ə rā′) and Buena Vista (bwā′ nä vē′ stä). General Winfield Scott headed an American force that landed at Veracruz on Mexico's east coast. From there, Scott's soldiers fought their way to Mexico City and captured the capital. Armed with superior guns and led by able officers, the American army was the victor in every battle. The Mexican forces fought bravely, but they were overwhelmed by the Americans. The war lasted less than 2 years.

CHECKUP

1. How did 30,000 Americans become settlers in Texas?
2. Why did Texas declare independence from Mexico?
3. On what issues was James K. Polk's campaign of 1844 based?
4. What were the causes of the Mexican War?

5. **Thinking Critically** Which forms a more logical boundary between Texas and Mexico — the Nueces River or the Rio Grande? Explain.

A Southwestern Empire

What were the results of the war between Mexico and the United States?

"Old Rough and Ready"   Because of his success in the Mexican War, General Zachary Taylor became a presidential candidate in 1848. Running as a Whig, Taylor defeated the Democratic candidate, Lewis Cass. General Taylor's men had called him "Old Rough and Ready" during the Mexican War because he seldom wore an official uniform. Instead, he liked to slouch around in overalls and a farmer's straw hat. This reputation for informality and simplicity helped to make him a popular hero.

The American Revolution had produced George Washington as a military hero and President. The War of 1812 had made Andrew Jackson and William Henry Harrison popular generals and successful presidential candidates. Now the Mexican War had a similar result for General Zachary Taylor.

The Peace Treaty   By far the most significant result of the Mexican War was the expanse of land it brought to the United States. In 1848, representatives of the United States and Mexican governments signed the **Treaty of Guadalupe Hidalgo** (gwä də lüp′ ā hē däl′ gō). In the treaty, Mexico accepted the Rio Grande as the boundary of Texas. Mexico ceded to the United States most of the territory between Texas and the Pacific. Including

Texas, the United States gained nearly half of Mexico's total territory. This expanse of land was even larger than the Louisiana Purchase.

For its part, the United States agreed to pay Mexico $15 million for this land. In addition, the American government agreed to pay claims of American citizens against Mexico up to a total of $3.5 million. Some senators opposed the treaty because they thought it was wrong to take

General Zachary Taylor won fame and popularity during the war with Mexico.
■ How did Taylor's war record help him win the presidency?

Detail, William Garl Brown, Jr./ Chicago Historical Society, 1920.46.

327

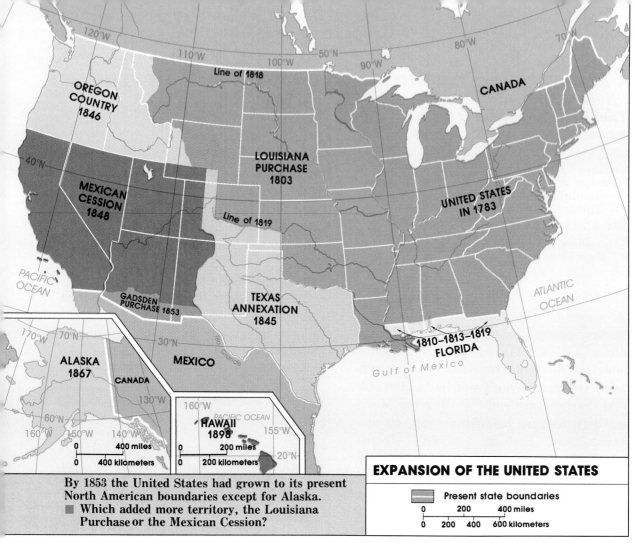

By 1853 the United States had grown to its present North American boundaries except for Alaska.
■ Which added more territory, the Louisiana Purchase or the Mexican Cession?

EXPANSION OF THE UNITED STATES

Present state boundaries

Mexican territory through war. Others opposed the treaty because they feared that the territory would eventually become several new slave states. A few others opposed it because they wanted even more Mexican land added to the United States. After some debate the United States Senate approved the Treaty of Guadalupe Hidalgo.

The land ceded to the United States by Mexico is called the **Mexican Cession**. From this vast area came the states of California, Utah, Nevada, and parts of New Mexico, Arizona, Colorado, and Wyoming. To gain additional land suitable for a southern rail route across the Rockies, the United States paid Mexico $10 million in 1853 for a small strip of land. This is known as the **Gadsden Purchase** because

James Gadsden, the American representative in Mexico, had arranged the purchase. New Mexico and Arizona eventually shared the Gadsden Purchase.

With the Mexican Cession, the United States reached the Pacific Ocean in the Southwest. The 1846 treaty establishing the boundaries of the Oregon Country had brought the United States to the shores of the Pacific in the Northwest. Many Americans in the 1830s and 1840s had said that it was **manifest destiny** for the western boundary of the United States to be the Pacific Ocean. By this they meant that fate had clearly intended our country to stretch from ocean to ocean. In 1848, only 72 years after the Declaration of Independence created a new nation, Americans had achieved this goal.

The Mormons The Mexican Cession included over 500,000 square miles (1,295,000 sq km) of land. Probably no more than 100,000 people lived in this vast area. At least half of these people were Indians. The largest concentration of non-Indian population lived in or near the Salt Lake City area. Nearly all these people were **Mormons**, members of the Church of Jesus Christ of Latter-Day Saints.

The Mormons had originated in western New York State among people who accepted the teachings of Joseph Smith. Smith's teachings were unpopular with many of his neighbors, so the Mormons were forced to move from New York to Ohio, then to Missouri, and finally to Illi-

nois. In Nauvoo, Illinois, a mob killed Joseph Smith, and Brigham Young became the new head of the Mormon church. In 1847 he led the Mormons to the Great Salt Lake. At the time, this area was outside the western boundaries of the United States. However, the Mexican Cession made it part of the territory of the United States.

When the Mormons arrived, the land around the Great Salt Lake was like a desert. They even named their new homeland *Deseret* because of this. Using irrigation, the Mormons built a beautiful city out of this desert. Salt Lake City, or the City of the Saints, as it was called, became a stopping point for travelers on their way to California. In 1850, Congress recognized

The Mormons cross the frozen Mississippi River on the journey that took them to Utah's Great Salt Lake.
▪ **What do you think these people thought as they set out?**

Brigham Young as governor of the Utah Territory, and in 1896, Utah became the forty-fifth state.

California California was the last area in the Americas to be settled by the Spaniards. Soldiers and missionaries were almost equally active in bringing Spanish civilization to the region. The part of the region that the Spaniards called Baja (bä′ hä) California, or Lower California, was settled first. In 1769, Gaspar de Portolá, a soldier, led an expedition from there to Alta California, or Upper California. Gaspar de Portolá and his men built a presidio, or fort, at San Diego. One year later

another presidio was built at Monterey.

Father Junípero Serra (hü nē′ pā rō ser′ rä) led five Franciscan missionaries who were with Portolá's expedition. When Portolá returned to Mexico, Father Serra remained behind. His goal was to bring the Christian religion to the Indians. He founded 9 missions in Upper California before he died in 1784. By 1823 there were 21 missions, stretching from San Diego to San Francisco. Father Serra was lame in one leg, but traveling from mission to mission, he was tireless in supervising the work with the Indians. He was the major force in securing Spain's hold on the lands of Upper California.

Spain sent priests as well as soldiers to explore California's coast.
■ **What groups of people are taking part in this religious service?**

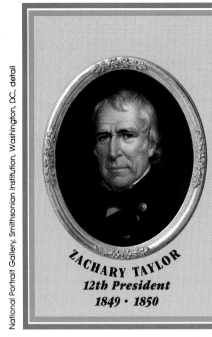

National Portrait Gallery, Smithsonian Institution, Washington, D.C., detail

ZACHARY TAYLOR
12th President
1849 · 1850

Born: 1784, Montebello, Orange County, Virginia.
Education: Private tutors and relatives.
Training: Army officer.
To presidency from: Louisiana.
Position when elected: Major general in United States Army.
Political party: Whig.
Married: Margaret Smith.
Children: Five daughters, one son.
Died: 1850, Washington, D.C.
Other facts: Grew up on the Kentucky frontier. Spent almost all of his adult life in the army. A good military leader who never lost a battle. Called "Old Rough and Ready" by his soldiers. As President, sought advice from others but made his own decisions.
During his presidency: As many as 500 ships were anchored in San Francisco Bay. Most were abandoned as passengers and crew rushed to the goldfields.

When Mexico gained its independence from Spain in 1821, California became a part of Mexico. Not long afterwards, President Andrew Jackson offered to buy all or part of California from Mexico, but he was unsuccessful. When James K. Polk became President, he too tried to buy California. For both Jackson and Polk, a major attraction was the magnificent harbor at San Francisco. They also feared that Mexico was too weak to challenge Russian claims to land on the west coast of North America. Probably no more than 50,000 people lived in California when the Mexican War broke out. Most of these were Indians. Fewer than a thousand settlers from the East lived there.

Nevertheless, these American settlers wanted California to be part of the United States. They took the lead in a revolt against Mexican rule. President Polk may have encouraged this revolt. Captain John C. Frémont may also have had a hand in it. He was in California on an exploring expedition with a small force of American soldiers at the time. On June 15, 1845, the rebels declared their independence from Mexico. The new nation was sometimes called the Bear Flag Republic because a picture of a grizzly bear appeared on its flag.

When the Mexican War began, a small American army commanded by General Stephen W. Kearny invaded New Mexico. Kearny's army captured Sante Fe without a fight and then marched on to California. (See the map on page 326.) Upper California was soon brought under American control with the help of American naval units. When news of the Treaty of Guadalupe Hidalgo came, General Kearny worked to establish a territorial government for California.

Gold! Early in 1848, workers were building a sawmill for John Sutter, an early settler in California, on the American River, near Sacramento. These workers found shiny bits of yellow metal in the stream that supplied the power for the sawmill. Soon the metal was recognized as gold. John Sutter tried to keep the discovery a secret, but the news spread rapidly. Before long, hundreds of Californians were on their way to Sutter's mill.

As the news reached the eastern United States and other parts of the world, the **California gold rush** began. It was 1849 before the real rush developed, so the gold seekers are usually known as **forty-niners.** About 50,000 persons started along the western trails in 1849, nearly all of them hurrying to the goldfields of California. Farmers abandoned their fields, workers flung down their tools, and clerks left their desks. The way was rough, and nearly 5,000 of the gold seekers died without reaching California.

Other eager forty-niners reached California by sea. Some took fast ships around Cape Horn, at the tip of South America, then sailed north along the Pacific Coast to San Francisco. Others sailed to Panama, crossed the isthmus, and continued to California by ship from the Pacific side. This route was shorter and more popular, but it was also more difficult. The land on the isthmus was rough and covered by tropical jungles and swamps. Consequently, the California gold rush stimulated interest in building a canal across the Isthmus of Panama.

A Population Boom By 1850 nearly 100,000 gold seekers had come to California. The mining camps contained a mixture of races and nationalities. One woman wrote home that her neighbors were French, Dutch, Scots, Jews, Italians, Swedes, Chinese, and Indians. Men and women of Spanish, Mexican, Indian, and African ancestry had settled in California even before the discovery of gold. The numbers of all these, except Indians, now increased rapidly.

Most miners were men, though some families had come in search of gold. Whether men, women, or children, they lived at first under primitive conditions. Tents and lean-tos were the usual dwellings. A few miners even made their homes in barrels. Food and other supplies were expensive and hard to get. It was possible to "get rich quick," but most worked hard just to eke out a living. Some of the forty-niners grew discouraged and returned

Prospectors pan for gold in a mountain stream in California.
■ Do you think it would be easy or hard to find enough gold to get rich using this method?

Many miners lived in tents when they arrived in San Francisco.
■ Why did the miners not seek more permanent lodgings in the city?

to their former homes. Nevertheless, enough remained to give California the necessary population to ask for statehood in 1850.

Slavery Expansion?   Not all Americans approved of the rapid expansion of the United States. Many Northerners believed that the annexation of Texas and the Mexican War that followed were plots of Southerners to add more slave territory to the Union. Some Northern leaders demanded that Congress prohibit slavery in the territories gained as a result of the war. Many Southerners were equally determined to make slavery legal in at least part of the Mexican Cession. As you will see, these and other sectional issues came

to a head when California asked in 1850 to be admitted as the thirty-first state in the union.

CHECKUP

1. What were the major provisions in the Treaty of Guadalupe Hidalgo?
2. What did Americans mean by *manifest destiny?*
3. Why were the Mormons concentrated around the Great Salt Lake area?
4. How did California become United States territory in 1848?
5. How did the discovery of gold affect the settlement of California?

6. **Thinking Critically**   What peoples or countries might have been against the doctrine of manifest destiny? Why?

Keeping a Diary

WESTWARD MOVEMENT

Have you ever kept a diary? A diary is a written daily account of what one does and how one feels. On page 310, you read an entry from the diary of a New York man. He had just seen an early railroad train and was excited at the sight.

Below are selections from the diaries of two Americans who made the trip west. One went by ship and the other by wagon train. The first entry is from the diary of Moses Cogswell, a young man from New Hampshire. Cogswell sailed from Boston to California. Like thousands of others, he was headed for California's goldfields. The entry, written a month before the ship docked in San Francisco, told of the long, monotonous voyage.

July 8, 1849

A dead calm sun, exactly overhead. Prospect dark and dreary. Temper cross, body in perspiration. Mind, neither one

Museum of New Mexico detail

thing or another. Occupation, learning Spanish. Companion, sick with the mumps. Food, potted meats and duff [a stiff flour pudding]. Drink, lime juice and rain water. Novelty, a large shark. Ideas, none in the market. Friends, few and far between. Determination, to get gold. Hopes, again to see home . . . if any vessel makes a longer passage than we do, I pity them.

The next entry is from the diary of Susan Magoffin. In 1846, Magoffin and her husband led a trading caravan from Missouri to Santa Fe. Magoffin was then an 18-year-old bride. When she and her husband left Missouri, Santa Fe was part of Mexico. By the time they reached Santa Fe, General Kearny's army had captured the city. Magoffin's diary has this entry for the day of their arrival.

August 31, 1846

I have entered the city in a year that will always be remembered by my countrymen; and under the "Star-Spangled banner," too. The first American lady who had come under such auspices.

SKILLS PRACTICE

Now write your own diary entry, using one of the following situations.

1. Imagine that you are Moses Cogswell and that you have finally arrived in California. It is your first day in the goldfields. Write a diary entry telling how it feels on your first day of searching for gold.
2. Imagine that you are Susan Magoffin and that you are actually on a wagon train. It is the last day on the trail before reaching Santa Fe. Tell how you feel after spending several months on the trail. Tell about your hopes for a new life in Santa Fe.

MAIN IDEAS

1. By the 1840s, increasing numbers of settlers were moving westward in wagon trains across the Great Plains and through the Rocky Mountains.
2. The dispute between Great Britain and the United States over the Oregon Country was settled in 1846 by dividing it along the 49th parallel.
3. Texas won its independence from Mexico in 1836 and became a state in 1845.
4. As a result of the Mexican War, Mexico ceded to the United States a vast expanse of land in the Southwest in 1848.
5. The discovery of gold in California in 1848 brought thousands of people to that region and hastened its development.

VOCABULARY REVIEW

On a separate sheet of paper, write the letter of the term next to the number of its definition.

a. Great American Desert
b. annexation
c. provisional government
d. "Fifty-four forty or fight!"
e. manifest destiny
f. Mormons
g. forty-niners
h. Mexican Cession
i. Mountain Men
j. "Remember the Alamo!"

1. Members of the religious group that settled around the Great Salt Lake
2. The taking of a country or territory and making it part of one's own country
3. Mistaken description of land between the Missouri River and the Rocky Mountains
4. A temporary ruling arrangement
5. Slogan for Americans who wanted all of the Oregon Country
6. Something that many people felt was bound to happen according to fate
7. California gold seekers
8. All the land acquired by the Treaty of Guadalupe Hidalgo
9. A slogan relating to Texas
10. Guides for the western pioneers

CHAPTER CHECKUP

1. Why did pioneers in the West first settle along the Pacific coast rather than in the Great Plains area?
2. What were the main routes to the coast?
3. Compare the ways in which Oregon, Texas, and California were first settled by people of European origin.
4. Why did conflict with other countries arise in the Oregon Country?
5. How did Texas and California win their independence?
6. **Thinking Critically** Besides the Oregon Country and the land in the Southwest, what other areas might the United States have wanted to take under the doctrine of manifest destiny? Explain.
7. **Thinking Critically** Why do you think the United States was able to acquire so much territory in such a short span of time? What does this tell you about the Americans?

APPLYING KNOWLEDGE

1. Make a chart showing important events in the history of Oregon, Texas, and California. Put the following categories on your chart: (a) First American Settlers, (b) Territory, (c) State. Then give the date when each event occurred.
2. On an outline map of the United States, indicate with different colors (a) the Mexican Cession, (b) the Gadsden Purchase, (c) the part of the Oregon Country that was acquired by the United States.
3. Choose a name from the list that follows and find out all you can about that person. Be prepared to report your findings to the class.

John C. Frémont
Jessie Benton Frémont
Narcissa Whitman
Marcus Whitman
Stephen F. Austin
James Beckwourth

How Americans Lived: 1850

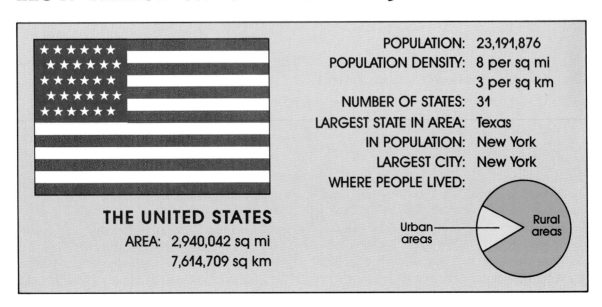

THE UNITED STATES

AREA: 2,940,042 sq mi
7,614,709 sq km

POPULATION: 23,191,876
POPULATION DENSITY: 8 per sq mi
3 per sq km
NUMBER OF STATES: 31
LARGEST STATE IN AREA: Texas
IN POPULATION: New York
LARGEST CITY: New York
WHERE PEOPLE LIVED:

Urban areas · Rural areas

How did life in America vary in 1850?

VOCABULARY

overseer

The box above shows that 23,191,876 people lived in the United States in 1850. How a person lived depended on the section of the country in which the person lived, whether that person was male or female, and whether he or she lived in a city or on a farm. Fewer than one in six Americans were urban dwellers — that is, lived in towns or cities that had a population of more than 2,500.

A Big Eastern City One city dweller in 1850 was Harriet Tubman. She lived in Philadelphia, Pennsylvania, the second most populous city in the United States. She had not been there long, though. Harriet Tubman had been born into slavery on a Maryland plantation. Both sets of her grandparents had been brought in chains to the United States from Africa. From an early age, Harriet Tubman was compelled

to work at various tasks such as maid, children's nurse, field hand, and cook.

In 1849, Harriet Tubman's master died. Rumors said that his slaves were to be sold out of state. Tubman, afraid of what might happen to her, decided to make a break for freedom. She escaped to Philadelphia, where she got a job in a hotel.

Life in Philadelphia had much more variety than life on a Maryland plantation. The city's population was constantly growing and changing. In 1850, more immigrants came to the United States than in any single year before. The total of 370,000 included 164,000 from Ireland, 79,000 from the German states, and 51,000 from Great Britain. Immigrants added many colorful customs to life in Philadelphia and other cities.

Life in Philadelphia in 1850 was also more fast-paced than life on a Maryland plantation. Vehicles drawn by horses and oxen jammed the streets. Their drivers shouted and yelled and cracked their whips. When a fire broke out in the city, volunteer fire companies raced each other to the scene. They often settled with their fists the question of which company got there first.

Chickens and hogs roamed throughout the city. They were the only garbage collection system available in 1850, as they gobbled scraps thrown into the streets. Few American cities had good water systems in 1850, though Philadelphia was an exception. The city's water supply was pumped from the Schuylkill River.

In December 1850, Harriet Tubman set out on what was to be her major work for the next 10 years. She returned to Maryland and guided her sister and two children to freedom. Between periods of employment in the North, Harriet Tubman made some 19 dangerous trips into Maryland. The number of slaves she led from Maryland plantations to freedom is uncertain, but it may have been as high as 300.

A Cotton Plantation Life on a cotton plantation in Mississippi was different from life on a Maryland plantation, where tobacco was the chief crop. Probably fewer than one fourth of the families in Mississippi lived on farms large enough to be called plantations. Life on these plantations — for the white owners — was leisurely and elegant. They generally hired **overseers**, or supervisors, to manage the slaves and take care of business matters.

Tutors came to educate the young sons and daughters of wealthy plantation owners. Still, there was time for plantation boys and girls to learn to ride well. As adults they would be expected to engage in fox hunting with hounds and horses. Such hunts were great social occasions enjoyed by young and old, with visitors from many neighboring plantations.

By 1850, Philadelphia was a busy, commercial city.
■ **What kinds of buildings were found in Philadelphia in 1850?**

337

When the sons of plantation owners reached college age, they often went to a northern school for further education, or perhaps to England. Their return home for vacation or after graduation furnished the occasion for a series of parties. One plantation owner celebrated his son's homecoming with an evening party that included fireworks at 11 o'clock, supper at midnight, and dancing until dawn.

A Small Midwestern City In 1850, Mary Todd Lincoln was also an urban dweller. She was in her early 30s, about the same age as Harriet Tubman. Born in Kentucky, Mary Lincoln lived in Springfield, Illinois, with her husband, Abraham, and their growing family.

Springfield was much smaller than Philadelphia. Yet it was a bustling, rapidly growing community. Thirteen years before, it had become the capital of Illinois.

By 1850, Mary and Abraham Lincoln and their sons Bob and Eddie were living in a two-story white frame house at the corner of Eighth and Jackson streets. The family also had a cow that Abraham Lincoln milked. Not many years earlier this

The Lincoln family lived in this house in Springfield, Illinois, for many years before moving to Washington, D.C., in 1861.
■ Do you think this painting portrays an actual scene from Lincoln's life in Springfield? Explain.

No picture of the Lincolns in 1850 is known to exist. This drawing is from the 1860s.
■ Why is the Lincolns' older son shown wearing a uniform?

neighborhood had been open prairie. Now, frame and brick houses were being built as the population increased.

Like his wife, Abraham Lincoln had been born in Kentucky, but his mother and father had taken him to Indiana when he was a little boy. His family was poor, so he had helped support the other members until striking out on his own at the age of 21. He moved to Illinois and supported himself in various ways while studying law. As a Whig, Abraham Lincoln served several terms in the Illinois state legislature. Between 1847 and 1849 he served one term in the House of Representatives in Washington, D.C. Deciding not to seek reelection, he returned to Springfield to resume his law practice.

Lincoln's office was located on the public square, the center of activity in Springfield. Nearby were the courthouse, the jail, and shops in which blacksmiths, harness makers, and others carried on their trades. Except for a few places where planks had been laid down, the streets were packed dirt. In wet weather the mud was ankle-deep; in dry weather great clouds of dust hung in the air. Through the square there was a constant procession of horses carrying riders or pulling buggies. Oxen hauled creaking carts loaded with wheat, corn, and potatoes. Covered wagons were often seen proceeding farther west.

Though never rich, Abraham Lincoln was able to provide his family with a comfortable existence. In late 1850 the death of their son Eddie brought grief to the Lincoln family. A similar grief was suffered by many American families in those days. For every 1,000 children born in 1850, at least 150 died before they ever reached the age of 1 year.

A Mississippi River Town About 100 miles (160 km) west of Springfield, Illinois, lay the town of Hannibal, Missouri. Living there in 1850 was 15-year-old Sam Clemens. Many years later, Samuel L. Clemens remembered Hannibal as a "sleepy little village." Actually while he was growing up there, it was a small but busy Mississippi River port with a population of about 3,000. It had a number of businesses: two slaughterhouses, four general stores, three sawmills, two planing mills, three blacksmith shops, two hotels, three saloons, a tobacco factory, a hemp factory, a tanyard, and a distillery.

Sam Clemens was a reluctant pupil at the three schools he attended until he was 13. The schools required their students to pay tuition, for there were no free public schools in Hannibal at the time. Clemens also attended a country school during the summers he spent at his uncle John Quarles's farm. It was "a heavenly place for a boy," Samuel Clemens later wrote. And there was always the wide, mysterious Mississippi, an education in itself.

By 1850, Hannibal had become a main stop for many of the forty-niners as they headed west for the goldfields of California. Samuel Clemens later recalled that he and other boys he knew "would have sold our souls" to have gone with the forty-niners. But he was only 13. Besides, his father had died of pneumonia the year before. The boy now had to find a job to help support the family.

Sam Clemens became an apprentice printer at the age of 13. The printing office served as the boy's college. Type was set by hand in those days, so Sam Clemens had to read the written material in order to set it in type. In this way he learned history and read literature.

Still, Sam Clemens found that life in the printing shop was often drudgery. So he fulfilled his boyhood ambition of becoming a Mississippi steamboat pilot. He later became famous under the pen name of Mark Twain. Under that name he wrote *The Adventures of Tom Sawyer, Adventures of Huckleberry Finn,* and other books based on his memories of life in Hannibal, Missouri.

An Indian Village While Mary Todd Lincoln was living much as most other middle-class American women, Cynthia Ann Parker was living a quite different life in the Indian Territory of Oklahoma.

In 1836, Cynthia Ann Parker, then 9 years old, was captured by Comanche Indians when they attacked a settlement in Texas. The Quahadas, one of the Comanche bands, adopted the little girl and treated her as one of their own.

Sam Clemens grew up in the river town of Hannibal, Missouri.
■ **What kind of boat is shown on the Mississippi River?**

In 1850 Cynthia Parker lived in a Comanche village much like this one.
■ What kind of housing did the Comanches use?

By 1850, 23-year-old Cynthia Ann Parker had learned to set up a tepee, to preserve buffalo meat, and to tan and decorate animal skins for clothing. She had married Nocona, a noted Comanche war chief. One of their sons took his mother's family name and was known as Quanah Parker. Like his father, he became a noted chief and tried to unite several Indian tribes in resistance to the advancing tide of settlement. In time, Quanah Parker accepted white civilization and life in the Indian Territory of Oklahoma.

Cynthia Ann Parker refused all efforts to free her from her life with the Indians. The story of the "white Comanche" became a legend in the Southwest. She was living an unusual life in 1850, obviously different from that of most American white women. And yet it was a life much like that led by thousands of other American women — the American Indian women of the Southwest.

CHECKUP

1. How did life change for Harriet Tubman between 1849 and 1850?
2. What was life like on a large cotton plantation in Mississippi in 1850?
3. Compare the lives led by each of the following in 1850: (a) Mary Todd Lincoln, (b) Samuel Clemens, (c) Harriet Tubman.
4. How did the life of Cynthia Ann Parker differ from that of most American women of the time?
5. **Thinking Critically** If you had lived in 1850, in which part of the country would you have wanted to live? Why?

REVIEWING VOCABULARY

1. nationalism   Nationalism is a feeling of loyalty to one's country. What is sectionalism? Did John C. Calhoun take the view of a nationalist or sectionalist in the nullification controversy?

2. nullification   In the dispute over the Tariff of Abominations, John C. Calhoun and other South Carolinians claimed that their state could overturn, or nullify, an action of the federal government. What happened when they tried? Had any state or group of states tried anything like this before? What was the argument of nullification's opponents?

3. reform   In the United States a reform is generally thought of as a change that gives a group a right, a privilege, or a protection that the group was previously denied. List six reforms that were begun in the 1830s and 1840s and the name of the reformer(s) connected with each. Why did some people oppose these reforms? If you had lived at that time, what reforms would you have wanted? Why?

4. American enterprise   The energy and will of Americans to undertake new projects to benefit themselves and their country demonstrated their spirit of enterprise. How did the United States as a country display enterprise in the 1840s? Name two groups or individuals who showed enterprise and explain why. What individuals or companies would you consider enterprising today?

5. annexation   A country may acquire territory by annexation, as was the case when the United States acquired Texas in 1845. What events led to this annexation? How could the United States have avoided war with Mexico?

EXPRESSING YOURSELF

1. Thinking like a President. President Jefferson was amazed when Napoleon offered to sell all of Louisiana to the United States, even though Jefferson only wanted to buy the port of New Orleans. What doubts did Jefferson have about the purchase? Without knowing the future, would you have approved the Louisiana Purchase if you had been the President in 1803? Why or why not?

2. What if. . . ?   Suppose the American invasions of Canada during the War of 1812 had been successful. How would life in North America be different today?

3. In your opinion.   Should the Second Bank of the United States have been rechartered, or was President Jackson right in attacking it as a monopoly? Explain your answer.

4. Who would you rather have been?   If you had lived in the early 1800s, who would you rather have been — a missionary, a pioneer, a reformer, a forty-niner, or a Mountain Man? Why?

5. In what ways. . . ?   How was the annexation of Texas different from the Louisiana Purchase as a way of adding territory to the United States? What are the possible disadvantages of each method?

UNIT 4

The Nation Divides and Reunites

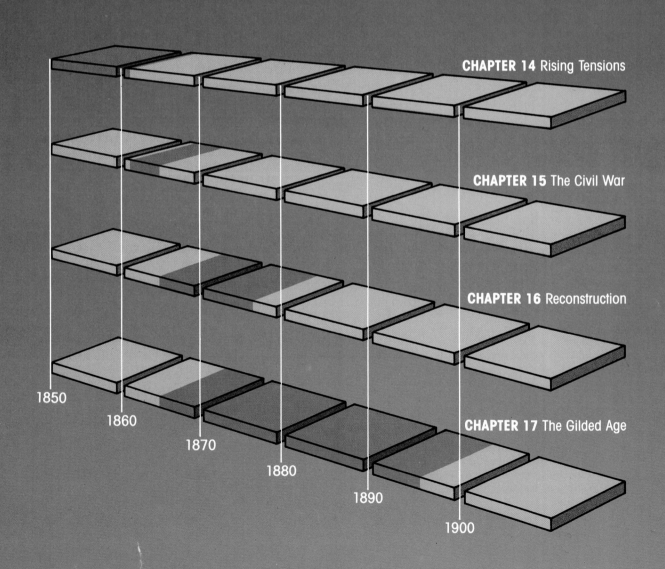

CHAPTER 14 Rising Tensions

CHAPTER 15 The Civil War

CHAPTER 16 Reconstruction

CHAPTER 17 The Gilded Age

1850

1860

1870

1880

1890

1900

14 *Rising Tensions*

1850–1861

Another Compromise

What were the results of the Compromise of 1850?

VOCABULARY	
Seventh of March speech	Fugitive Slave Law
Compromise of 1850	Underground Railroad

Three Great Senators Few of our leaders in government have had more effect on American history than three men sitting in the United States Senate in 1850. One was Henry Clay of Kentucky. Thirty years before, he had helped to arrange the Missouri Compromise, which prevented tension between the North and the South.

Another of the three was John C. Calhoun of South Carolina. Since 1832 he had used his position within the Senate to protect the rights of the South. Daniel Webster was the third great senator. He was as popular in Massachusetts as John C. Calhoun was in South Carolina. Unlike Calhoun, Webster spoke for a strong national government and against the Southern doctrine of states' rights.

Henry Clay, John C. Calhoun, and Daniel Webster were nothing alike. Clay smiled easily, spoke well, and charmed both men and women. Calhoun was very serious and had a brilliant mind. Webster had piercing dark eyes, heavy black brows, and a broad forehead that gave his face an impressive appearance. He was one of the great orators of the day, with a voice that was deep and musical.

For 30 years these three men had served their country. Over that period, they had dealt with the great issues of the times. Now, in 1850, they prepared to deal with an issue that could, if unresolved, bring on a dangerous confrontation between the North and the South. It would be the last time that they would be together. Calhoun, suffering from tuberculosis, would die before the end of the year. Clay and Webster would die in 1852.

The California Question As you learned in Chapter 13, the gold rush brought thousands of people into California. As a result, California was the first territory in the Mexican Cession to ask for admission as a state. Most of the gold seekers in California had come from the free-soil states, where slavery was illegal. Moreover, workers in the goldfields had no desire to face the competition of slave labor. For these reasons, California asked for admission as a free state.

In 1850 there were 15 slave states and 15 free states in the Union. The admission

Henry Clay of Kentucky presents a plan to the Senate that would help resolve the differences between the North and the South. The plan became the Compromise of 1850.
■ When was the Compromise of 1850 approved?

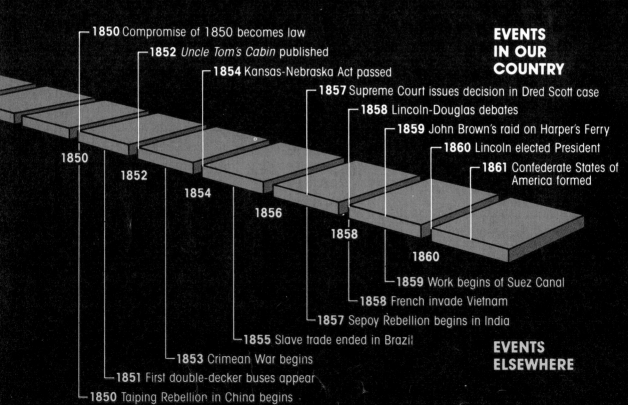

EVENTS IN OUR COUNTRY

1850 Compromise of 1850 becomes law

1852 *Uncle Tom's Cabin* published

1854 Kansas-Nebraska Act passed

1857 Supreme Court issues decision in Dred Scott case

1858 Lincoln-Douglas debates

1859 John Brown's raid on Harper's Ferry

1860 Lincoln elected President

1861 Confederate States of America formed

1850

1852

1854

1856

1858

1860

1859 Work begins of Suez Canal

1858 French invade Vietnam

1857 Sepoy Rebellion begins in India

1855 Slave trade ended in Brazil

1853 Crimean War begins

1851 First double-decker buses appear

1850 Taiping Rebellion in China begins

EVENTS ELSEWHERE

of California would destroy this balance. There were other questions involved, too. The status of slavery in all of the Mexican Cession had not yet been decided. If California became a free state, would this mean slavery would be barred from *all* of the Mexican Cession? To many Southerners, any attempts to bar slavery from the new territories threatened the welfare of the South. They felt that slavery had to expand or the South would die. Many Northerners, on the other hand, felt that slavery could not be allowed to expand into new territory, or the chance to end it altogether would disappear forever.

Clay's Compromise   Southern members of Congress bitterly opposed the admission of California as a free state. Once more Henry Clay began working patiently on a compromise to save the Union. Stephen A. Douglas assisted Clay. Douglas was a young Democratic senator from Illinois. He was nicknamed the Little Giant —"little" because he was well below normal height, and "giant" because of his many accomplishments.

In January 1850, Clay presented his compromise plan in a dramatic speech to the Senate. (See the picture on page 345.) The plan dealt with more than the California question and the status of slavery in the Mexican Cession. In fact, it was an attempt to deal with several unsolved issues between the North and the South. Clay asked both Southerners and Northerners to give in on certain points.

There were six parts to the proposal: (1) California would be admitted to the Union as a free state.
(2) The remainder of the Mexican Cession would be organized into two territories, Utah and New Mexico. Presumably the people of these territories could decide whether they wanted slavery when they applied for admission as a state.
(3) Some land in dispute between Texas and New Mexico would be awarded to New Mexico.
(4) Texas would receive $10 million from the national government for giving up its claims to this land.
(5) The buying and selling of slaves, but not slavery itself, would be prohibited in the District of Columbia.
(6) Congress would enact a strict law requiring that runaway slaves be returned to their masters.

Congress Approves   When Clay's plan came before the Senate, John C. Calhoun made a dramatic appearance. Friends carried him into the meeting room on a stretcher. Too weak to speak himself, Calhoun had a younger Southern senator read his speech. In the speech, Calhoun agreed to the purpose of Clay's bill. However, Calhoun insisted that it should give even more protection to the South. He demanded that the government bring back the political balance between the North and the South and stop tampering with the slavery question.

Senators — indeed, the whole country — waited to hear what Daniel Webster had to say. He was from New England, the part of the country where antislavery feeling was strongest. Many people believed it would be political suicide for Daniel Webster to support the compromise. And yet, in what is called his **Seventh of March speech**, Webster not only approved the compromise but pleaded with the whole country to do the same.

At the beginning of his speech, Webster said:

> I wish to speak today, not as a Massachusetts man, nor as a Northern man, but as an American. . . . I speak today for the preservation of the Union.

Let Northerners make all reasonable compromises with the South, Webster pleaded. Plantations cannot possibly exist in the deserts, plains, and mountains of the Mexican Cession, he argued. Nature would make slavery unprofitable in that region, and Congress would not need to make a law to prohibit it there.

It is doubtful that the compromise would have been approved without Webster's support. As it was, Congress approved the different sections of the compromise, one by one. Most people in the country breathed a sigh of relief as Clay's plan became law in the **Compro-** **mise of 1850**. It appeared that this act had put an end to the controversy between the North and the South. Perhaps John C. Calhoun, the aging and ill South Carolina senator, could see farther ahead than others. When he died a few months later, it is said he murmured with his last breath, "The South, the poor South."

A Disaster for Black People   John C. Calhoun was not alone in seeing future trouble because of the Compromise of 1850. For black people it was no compromise at all. It was a disaster. What did it matter if the slave sales were forbidden in

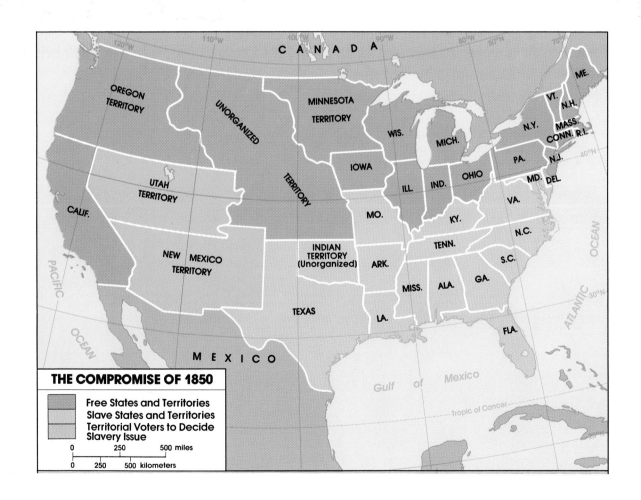

THE COMPROMISE OF 1850

- Free States and Territories
- Slave States and Territories
- Territorial Voters to Decide Slavery Issue

0   250   500 miles
0 250 500 kilometers

the District of Columbia? White families living there could still keep slaves. And Southern officeholders who came to Washington could still bring slaves to serve them in the capital city of a supposedly free, democratic nation.

But the chief threat for black people came from the passing of the **Fugitive Slave Law**, one part of the Compromise of 1850. Slaves who escaped to free soil in the North were no longer safe. They were to be picked up and returned to their masters. The new law provided bounties, or rewards, for the capture of escaped slaves. The law stated, too, that officials in Northern towns and cities had to help in the return of fugitive slaves when asked to do so. Finally, the law said that those people who knew of escaped slaves and did not report what they knew could be fined and even jailed.

Slave owners and many Northerners looked upon the new Fugitive Slave Law as a way of combatting the operations of the mysterious **Underground Railroad**. This was an informal system set up by antislavery people to guide fugitive slaves to safety. It was called "underground" because it was secret and "railroad" because escaping slaves were moved from one "station," or hiding place, to another. Those who guided an escaping slave from one station to another were called conductors.

Effects of the Fugitive Slave Law Before 1850, escaped slaves needed only to get to free soil in the Old Northwest or in Pennsylvania. With the passage of the new Fugitive Slave Law, however, they were no longer safe anywhere in the United States. Furthermore, the new law made it necessary for free blacks in the North and

Runaway slaves walk through the rain on their way to freedom with the help of the Underground Railroad.
■ **What, do you think, is the meaning of the word *underground* in Underground Railroad?**

in the South to carry "freedom papers" proving they were not escaped slaves. Consequently, many escaped slaves and free blacks went to the Canadian province of Ontario, where slavery had been illegal since the late 1700s.

Shortly after her own escape, Harriet Tubman found a home in St. Catherines, Ontario. Here, in the 1850s, she brought the slaves she led to freedom from Maryland. Other American blacks settled in Chatham and Wilberforce, Canada, to avoid the chance of being arrested as fugitive slaves. In addition, by settling there they escaped the kind of racial discrimination they often experienced even in the parts of the United States where slavery was not allowed.

Within the northern United States, a number of fights and riots occurred when slave catchers tried to return blacks to their masters. For example, in 1854 in Boston, slave catchers seized Anthony Burns, an escaped slave. It took marines, cavalry, and artillery to hold back the thousands of people who tried to keep Burns from being returned to his Southern master. The attempt of this angry gathering to free him failed. Nevertheless, a few months after his return to the South, Northern abolitionists purchased Anthony Burns from his master and sent him to freedom in Canada.

Besides guiding slaves out of the South, Harriet Tubman came to their aid in the North. In 1859, along with a crowd in Troy, New York, she helped to free Charles Nalle, a runaway slave who was being returned to the South in keeping with the provisions of the Fugitive Slave Law.

The Fugitive Slave Law was only one part of the Compromise of 1850. But it caused more problems than the other parts of the law had solved. For one thing, more people in the North became abolitionists.

Harriet Tubman (left) led these two people to freedom on the Underground Railroad. ■ Why, do you think, did Tubman choose such dangerous work?

Their negative reaction convinced many people in the South that people in the North did not intend to obey the law.

CHECKUP

1. What part did Henry Clay, John C. Calhoun, and Daniel Webster play in the Compromise of 1850?
2. What were the six provisions of the Compromise?
3. Why did blacks consider the Compromise of 1850 no compromise at all?
4. What was the Northern reaction to the Fugitive Slave Law? What was the Southern reaction?
5. **Thinking Critically** Do you think the Compromise of 1850 benefited the United States? Why or why not?

Tensions Increase

What events increased the tension between the North and the South?

VOCABULARY

Kansas-Nebraska bill	Republican party
popular sovereignty	Dred Scott case
"bleeding Kansas"	

New Leaders President Zachary Taylor died suddenly in 1850. Vice President Millard Fillmore succeeded him. However, the Whigs turned away from Fillmore in 1852. They nominated General Winfield Scott, who, like Taylor, was a hero of the Mexican War. In this election the Whigs, torn between Northern and Southern branches, lost and ceased to exist as a national political party. Franklin Pierce of New Hampshire, the Democratic candidate, was elected President.

A new group of political leaders was emerging on the American scene. Franklin Pierce was the first elected President to be born in the nineteenth century. William H. Seward, a Whig senator from New York, was 24 years younger than Henry Clay. James Henry Hammond, a senator from South Carolina in the 1850s, was 25 years younger than John C. Calhoun.

Stephen A. Douglas, the Little Giant from Illinois, attracted the support of young Democrats as early as 1852. The ambitious Douglas, born in Vermont, had moved west to Illinois at the age of 20. There he rose rapidly in the legal profession and in politics. He married a Southern woman who inherited 150 slaves from her father. Appointed to the Senate in 1847 and reelected in 1852, Senator Stephen A. Douglas had connections with three different sections of the country. Some felt he could be President.

In the election of 1852, the Whigs nominated Winfield Scott for President and the Democrats nominated Franklin Pierce for President.
■ Why, do you think, did each party have a picture of George Washington on the campaign banner?

Born: 1800, Locke, New York.
Education: Largely self-educated.
Training: Lawyer, public official.
To presidency from: New York.
Position when taking office: Vice President.
Political party: Whig.
Married: (1) Abigail Powers, (2) Caroline McIntosh.
Children: One son, one daughter.
Died: 1874, Buffalo, New York.
Other facts: A handsome man more than 6 feet (1.8 m) tall, always well groomed. Apprenticed to a clothmaker at the age of 14; purchased his freedom at 19 for $30. Taught school briefly. Served in state government in New York and in United States Congress. Ran for President in 1856 as a third-party candidate but was defeated.
During his presidency: Elisha Otis invented the first elevator for carrying passengers.

MILLARD FILLMORE

13th President
1850 · 1853

A Controversial Bill In 1854, Douglas presented the **Kansas-Nebraska bill**. Under the bill, two territories, Kansas and Nebraska, would be formed from the Louisiana Purchase land. Both were north of the southern border of Missouri, which was the line drawn by the Missouri Compromise. The compromise had prohibited slavery north of that line. However, Douglas's bill said that the people of Kansas and Nebraska could decide whether they wanted to allow slavery. This would, of course, repeal the Missouri Compromise that had been the law since 1820.

Douglas called this idea **popular sovereignty** — in other words, "Let the people decide." He pointed out that this principle was followed when California asked for admission as a free state. Moreover, as Douglas pointed out, the Compromise of 1850 had left the status of slavery in the remainder of the Mexican Cession to be decided by the people living there.

Some people believe that Douglas sponsored the bill to attract Southern support for another try at the presidency in 1856. Others think that Douglas put forth the bill because it would help in a plan to build a railroad from Chicago to the West Coast. Such a railroad, to be financed partly by the national government, would encourage settlement of the sparsely settled lands north and south of the Missouri River. It would also enable Douglas to profit from his own landholdings along the proposed railway route.

The Kansas-Nebraska bill stirred up a storm of protest in the North. Northerners had come to regard the Missouri Compromise as almost sacred. They were shocked at this attempt to repeal the 34-year-old agreement. Southerners, on the other hand, saw the Kansas-Nebraska bill as an unexpected chance to add another slave state to the Union. The Kansas territory lay west of Missouri, a slave state. Presumably, people sympathetic to slavery would settle in Kansas and vote for its admission as a slave state.

Congress debated the Kansas-Nebraska bill with passion. Some members of Congress, fearing bloodshed, carried revolvers and knives. The halls of Congress mirrored the intense emotions aroused throughout the country for and against the bill. Nevertheless, with President Pierce's support, Douglas got the Kansas-Nebraska bill through Congress. In 1854 the President signed the controversial bill into law. The Kansas-Nebraska Act had two important results. It led to open warfare in Kansas and to the formation of a new political party. In the North and West, the Kansas-Nebraska Act led to a storm of protest. To many people the repeal of the 34-year-old Missouri Compromise to limit slavery was a betrayal.

Warfare in Kansas   Settlers from both the North and South began to pour into Kansas. If the vote of the people was to decide whether Kansas would be a slave territory or free, each side was determined to have the majority. The New England Emigrant Aid Society helped finance settlers who wanted to make Kansas a free territory. In Missouri, organizations were formed to recruit settlers who favored slavery. Many of these people settled along the border between Kansas and Missouri.

In 1855, people living in Missouri crossed the border to vote illegally in the elections for the territorial government.

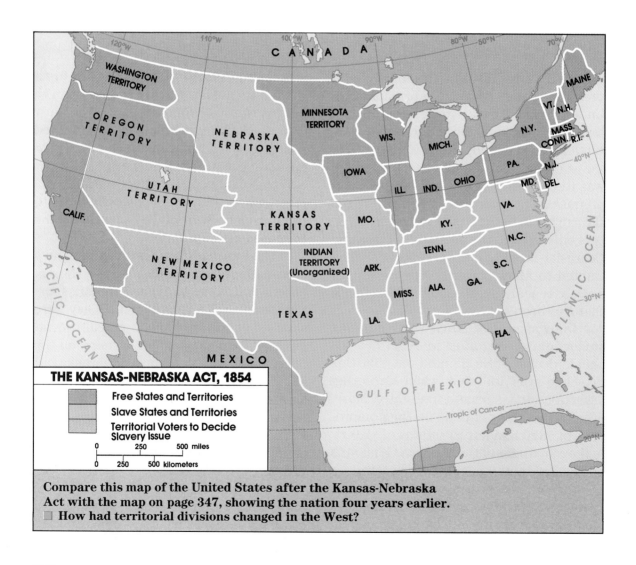

Compare this map of the United States after the Kansas-Nebraska Act with the map on page 347, showing the nation four years earlier.
How had territorial divisions changed in the West?

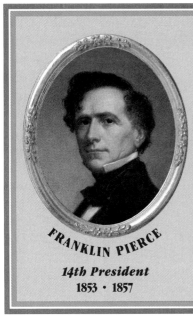

Born: 1804, Hillsborough, New Hampshire.
Education: Bowdoin College.
Training: Lawyer, public official.
To presidency from: New Hampshire.
Position when elected: In private law practice.
Political party: Democratic.
Married: Jane Means Appleton.
Children: Three sons.
Died: 1869, Concord, New Hampshire.
Other facts: Served in New Hampshire state legislature and later in Congress, in both House of Representatives and Senate. At age of 33 the youngest senator when he took his seat in 1838. Rose to rank of general in Mexican War. A dark-horse candidate for President, an office he had not sought. Made no speeches during his campaign.
During his presidency: Japan for the first time opened ports to American ships.

FRANKLIN PIERCE

14th President
1853 · 1857

When the new legislature began to pass proslavery laws, the antislavery settlers decided to set up their own government. With two rival governments vying for control, law and order began to break down. Raids and murders took place. For example, one proslavery group raided the town of Lawrence, destroying some homes and the antislavery newspaper offices there. To strike back at these people, John Brown, a fanatical abolitionist from Ohio, and his sons killed five proslavery settlers in Pottawatomie Creek. The violence and bloodshed led to the territory being called **"bleeding Kansas"** and added to the tensions felt throughout the country.

The Republican Party   Senator Douglas had failed to understand that Northern opposition to the Kansas-Nebraska Act included people from three political parties. In Ripon, Wisconsin, a group of Whigs, unhappy Democrats, and members of a small Free-Soilers party met in a church early in March 1854. They talked about forming a new party. Someone suggested the name

Republican party. Four months later at a meeting in Jackson, Michigan, the name *Republican* was officially adopted.

Across the Northern states more and more meetings took place to protest the Kansas-Nebraska Act. Opposition to the act brought Abraham Lincoln back into politics. In 1856 he helped organize the new party in Illinois and called himself a Republican.

In the election of 1856, the Republicans chose the popular western explorer, John C. Frémont, as their presidential candidate. The Republican slogan of "Free soil, free speech, and Frémont" was shouted and carried on banners, in torchlight parades, and in hundreds of mass meetings. The Republican platform opposed any expansion of slavery and called for the repeal of the Fugitive Slave Law. The Democratic candidate, James Buchanan of Pennsylvania, won the election. Nevertheless, the large popular vote Frémont received in the free states showed that the new Republican party was gaining strength as a political force.

Dred Scott was a slave who sued for his freedom on the grounds that he had been taken by his master into a territory where slavery was prohibited.
■ Why, do you think, did Dred Scott turn to the Supreme Court for help?

The Dred Scott Case Two days after President James Buchanan took office on March 4, 1857, the Supreme Court issued its decision in the **Dred Scott case**. Dred Scott, a slave, had been taken by his master from Missouri, a slave state, to Illinois, a free state. Then Dred Scott was taken to the Wisconsin territory, where slavery was forbidden by the Missouri Compromise. Later his master took him back to Missouri. Some antislavery people helped Dred Scott sue for his freedom on the grounds that he had been taken to live in a territory where slavery was prohibited by law.

The Dred Scott case raised a number of questions. Was a black person a citizen, with the right to sue in a federal court? No, said the majority of the Supreme Court. The Court could have stopped there with its decision, but it decided to go further. Slaves were property, the Court said, and the Fifth Amendment to the Con-

stitution protected property. Congress could not prohibit slavery in any of the territories, and, therefore, the Missouri Compromise of 1820 was unconstitutional.

The justices of the Supreme Court thought their decision would end the controversy over the expansion of slavery into the territories. They were badly mistaken. The Dred Scott decision pleased many Southern Democrats. It seemed to mean that all the territories of the national government were open to slavery and that not even a vote of the people living there could keep slavery out. Most Northern Democrats, however, were angry at the Dred Scott decision. They preferred Douglas's doctrine of popular sovereignty. These differences caused a split in the Democratic party.

Republicans and other opponents of slavery also attacked the Dred Scott decision. Some Republicans announced they would defy the Supreme Court's decision. The Court, they said, had become the ally of Southern slaveholders. This defiance seemed to shock Southern leaders. First, Northerners had refused to obey the Fugitive Slave Law. Now they were defying the Supreme Court of the United States, the highest court in the land. How long, the Southern leaders asked, should the South remain united with the defiant North?

CHECKUP

1. Why did Senator Douglas sponsor the Kansas-Nebraska bill?
2. What were the main provisions of this bill?
3. What were the results of the Kansas-Nebraska Act?
4. How did the Dred Scott decision affect the slavery issue?
5. **Thinking Critically** Do you think it would have been better for Congress or the people of the state to decide whether slavery should be permitted? Explain.

A House Divided

Why did the Southern states secede from the Union?

VOCABULARY

Confederate States
   of America

Seven Debates   In 1858, Senator Stephen A. Douglas ran for another term as senator from Illinois. He seemed certain to be elected. To oppose Douglas, the Republicans nominated Abraham Lincoln. Lincoln boldly challenged the Little Giant to a series of debates. Seven Lincoln-Douglas debates were to be held in the late summer and autumn of 1858, each in a different Illinois city.

Much of the nation was watching what was going on in Illinois that year. Douglas was one of the best-known men in the Senate, and his name was connected to many of the decade's important laws on the slavery issue. Now he was being challenged by the new Republicans.

Although Douglas won the election to the Senate, the debates brought Lincoln to national acclaim. Moreover, in the debates, Lincoln forced Douglas to admit he was not wholly in favor of the Dred Scott decision. This admission would lose

Abraham Lincoln debates Stephen Douglas in Illinois in 1858. Douglas is standing directly behind Lincoln.
■ Why, do you think, was this debate held outdoors?

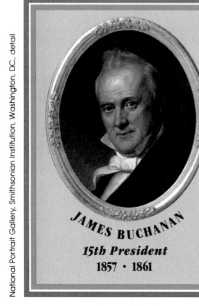

Born: 1791, near Mercersburg, Pennsylvania.
Education: Dickinson College.
Training: Lawyer, public official.
To presidency from: Pennsylvania.
Position when elected: Minister to Great Britain during Pierce's administration.
Political party: Democratic.
Married: The only President never to have married.
Died: 1868, Lancaster, Pennsylvania.
Other facts: A distinguished-looking, white-haired man. Served in mounted troops in War of 1812. Served in both Houses of Congress, where he staunchly supported Andrew Jackson. Held diplomatic posts in Russia and Great Britain. Served as secretary of state under Polk.
During his presidency: Pony express riders carried the mail from St. Joseph, Missouri, to Sacramento, California.

JAMES BUCHANAN
15th President
1857 · 1861

Douglas some Southern support in his campaign for the presidency 2 years later. Southern Democrats would not support any candidate who opposed the Dred Scott decision. Thus the debates widened the split in the Democratic party.

Expansion of Slavery A month before the debates began, Abraham Lincoln made a speech to Illinois Republicans.

> A house divided against itself cannot stand. I believe this government cannot endure permanently half slave and half free.

Lincoln went on to say that it looked as if slavery would become legal throughout the United States. First, the Compromise of 1850 had allowed slavery to exist in the Mexican Cession territory. Second, the Kansas-Nebraska Act allowed slavery in territory where it had been prohibited by the Missouri Compromise. Third, the Dred Scott decision had said the Missouri Compromise was unconstitutional. If so, slavery would be legal in all of the Louisiana Purchase territory, and Congress was powerless to prevent its spread.

Moreover, Lincoln said, the Supreme Court's decision in the Dred Scott case meant something else. Scott had been taken by his master to live in Illinois. But the Court had ruled that this did not make Scott a free man. What was to prevent slaveholders from bringing thousands of slaves into Illinois or any other free state to compete against free labor?

In this speech, Lincoln might also have spoken of other people who wanted to expand slave territory in other directions. Some Southern leaders were urging that the United States buy Cuba from Spain. If Spain refused to sell, these leaders said, the island should be seized by force and made into a slave state. Other people wanted to seize territory in Central America in order to add it to the slave states in the Union. It seemed, indeed, as if slavery was steadily gaining ground in the 1850s.

John Brown's Raid By 1859 there were desperate people determined to end slavery by force, if necessary. John Brown was one of these people. Already he had committed murder in Kansas. "I have only a short time to live — only one death to die," he said then, "and I will die fighting for this (antislavery) cause." After fighting in Kansas, Brown returned to the East.

Eastern abolitionists greeted him as a hero and gave him financial support for his cause. Brown wanted to establish a free state for escaped slaves and free blacks in the mountains of Maryland and Virginia. On October 16, Brown led a group of 18 men, including five free blacks, in a raid on the government arsenal at Harpers Ferry, Virginia. They aimed to seize guns and ammunition stored in the arsenal. They hoped that slaves in the vicinity would rebel against their masters and come to Harpers Ferry for weapons.

Instead, marines commanded by Robert E. Lee of the United States Army surrounded the arsenal. Brown and his men were pinned down in the engine house. When Brown refused to surrender, the marines stormed the engine house and seized

John Brown greets sympathizers as he heads for his own execution.

■ **What, do you think, was the artist's opinion of Brown?**

"The Last Moments of John Brown", by Thomas Hovenden; The Metropolitan Museum of Art, gift of Mr. & Mrs. Carl Stoeckel, 1897

him. He was tried for treason, found guilty, and sentenced to death. His dream of a free state in the mountains ended in a hangman's noose on December 2, 1859.

The reactions to John Brown's deed varied throughout the country. Although most Northerners were shocked by his actions, abolitionists hailed him as a hero of the antislavery cause. This admiration convinced Southerners that the North was determined to destroy slavery.

The Democrats Divide In the presidential election of 1860, the Democratic party split along sectional lines. Northern Democrats chose Stephen A. Douglas as their candidate for President. Southern Democrats chose John Breckinridge of Kentucky. To complicate the voting further, John Bell entered the race as the candidate for the Constitutional Union party. In their platform, they asked people to support the Constitution, the Union of States, and the existing laws.

Lincoln Wins Amid great excitement, the Republicans met in Chicago to choose their candidate. The split in the Democratic party made almost certain the election of the Republican candidate. It turned out to be Abraham Lincoln, who was chosen on the third ballot.

The Republican platform made no threats toward slavery where it already existed. However, it made clear that Republicans would oppose the admission of any new slave states into the Union.

Furthermore, the Republican platform made many other attractive promises. To protect manufacturers and factory workers from foreign competition, it promised high protective tariffs. It promised a railroad to the Pacific and other internal improvements, paid for by the national government. It promised a

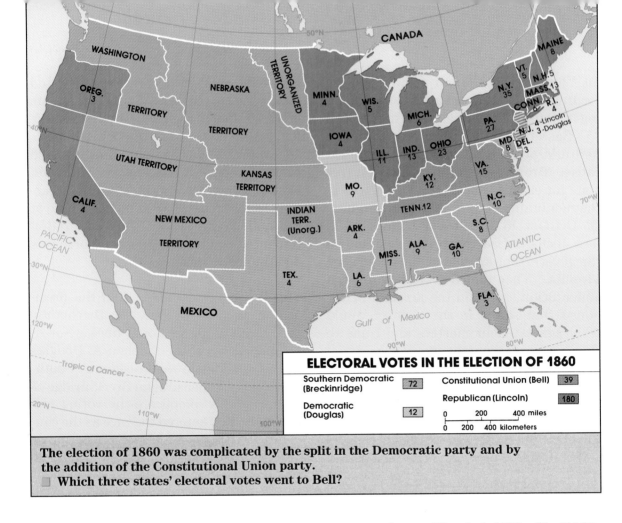

ELECTORAL VOTES IN THE ELECTION OF 1860

| Southern Democratic (Breckinridge) | 72 | Constitutional Union (Bell) | 39 |
| Democratic (Douglas) | 12 | Republican (Lincoln) | 180 |

0   200   400 miles
0   200   400 kilometers

The election of 1860 was complicated by the split in the Democratic party and by the addition of the Constitutional Union party.

■ Which three states' electoral votes went to Bell?

Homestead Act providing free farms from the lands owned by the government.

Lincoln won an easy victory, but it was a sectional victory. Republicans received no electoral votes in ten Southern states. These states had openly threatened to secede if a Republican became President.

Secession Begins   A month after Lincoln's election, a convention in South Carolina voted to take that state out of the Union. Within two months, Mississippi, Florida, Alabama, Georgia, Louisiana, and Texas followed South Carolina's action. The seven states formed the **Confederate States of America**. In February 1861, they named Jefferson Davis of Mississippi their first President.

James Buchanan remained as President of the United States until Lincoln's inauguration on March 4, 1861. He did little to stop the secession of the seven states except to hope that another compromise would be worked out. But no compromise saved the Union this time.

So Abraham Lincoln took his presidential oath "to preserve, protect, and defend the Constitution" with the Union already divided. Seven states had seceded. Eight more were ready to secede.

CHECKUP

1. Why were the Lincoln-Douglas debates significant?
2. What was the aim of John Brown's raid?
3. Why did Lincoln win the presidential election in 1860?

4. **Thinking Critically**   Do you think the Southern states were justified in seceding from the Union? Explain.

North and South in 1860

What social and economic differences existed between the North and the South in 1860?

Free States   In 1860 there were 19 states in which slavery was illegal. These 19, along with the 7 territories and the District of Columbia, had a population of more than 19 million free people. This Northern population differed from that of the South in the number of foreign-born. Most immigrants to the United States settled in the North because they landed at Northern ports. Moreover, they avoided the South because there were fewer jobs there and because of the competition they faced with slave labor.

More than a third of Minnesota's population in 1860 was foreign-born. Many of these people were from Norway and Sweden. New York's foreign-born population was a mixture of European immigrants. One fifth of the population of Massachusetts in 1860 was foreign-born.

Missouri, with 14 percent foreign-born, had a higher percentage than any other state in the South. Louisiana came next with 11 percent, while 7 percent of the population of Texas in 1860 was foreign-born. But they were exceptions in the South. Only a little more than 1 percent of Alabama's population was foreign-born. Arkansas had less than 1 percent.

Slave States   In 1860, "the South" generally meant those 15 states in which slavery was legal. Of these 15, Delaware is not usually thought of as part of the South, though slavery was legal there. Texas and Missouri were perhaps more western than

southern at the time. Nevertheless, they are included as part of the South.

The 15 states of the South had a population of 12,240,000 in 1860. Of these, more than a third were black people. Of the blacks 251,000 were free and 3,950,000 were slaves. Nearly all black people in the South in 1860 had been born there, since importation of slaves had been prohibited after 1808. Similarly, nearly all the white population was native-born. Fewer than 3 percent of white Southerners in 1860 had been born outside the United States. The whites were largely descended from English and Scots-Irish people who had come to America during the seventeenth and eighteenth centuries.

It would be wrong to think of the South in 1860 as a region where all white families owned slaves. Fewer than a third of Southern families owned any slaves. Furthermore, most of the families with slaves owned fewer than ten. This was far less than the number needed to operate a cotton plantation.

Southern farmers without slaves were like Northern farmers in many ways. They often raised some corn and wheat, as Northern farmers did. Moreover, most Southern and Northern farmers lived in simple frame or log houses. But many Southern farmers dreamed of getting more land, buying slaves, and becoming the master of a large plantation.

Plantation Owners   To most Southerners, the plantation owner's life was ideal. A plantation owner had a big house with fine furnishings. The owner's family enjoyed books, music, horses, dancing, good food, and, of course, house servants. Plantation owners as a group had most of the political power in the South. Southern

Cotton plantations like this one on the Mississippi River were dependent on slave labor.
■ How was the cotton harvested?

officeholders usually came from the planter class or followed the wishes of that class. To be counted as a planter, a person had to own at least 20 slaves.

Plantation owners also had great economic power. They provided the money that supported shopkeepers, warehouse owners, lawyers, and cotton merchants. By 1860 the culture and civilization of the South rested on plantation slavery.

Black Southerners   Many black people in the southern United States were descendants of Africans who had developed high civilizations before Columbus discovered America. Some Southern slaves were members of families that had been in America longer than the families of their owners. Conditions of slavery varied widely according to the slave's age, sex, and type of service. Household servants,

for example, were treated better than field hands. Field slaves were working in the fields at dawn and usually stayed there until sunset, with breaks only for meals. On large plantations, an overseer kept watch over the field hands. Some overseers were cruel and used a whip to make the plantation slaves work harder.

Yet most owners treated even their field hands with some care and provided them with a healthful diet. The main reason is that even though masters thought of slaves as property rather than persons, they were very valuable property. A good field hand might cost up to $2,000 to replace. Also, some slaves were skilled at such trades as carpentry, shoemaking, and blacksmithing. They were especially valuable, for their owners could make extra money by hiring them out to other plantation owners.

The Slave System   Even decent treatment by most slave owners, however, could not change the main fact of slavery. That fact was that one human, the master, had nearly total power over another human, the slave. There was no one to control a master's use of force. Even people who thought of themselves as kind masters might whip their slaves to enforce discipline or to set an example. Brutal masters used the lash more often.

The cruelest part of the slave system was the breakup of families through sale. Possibly as many as 3 of every 10 slave couples were separated in this way. One can only imagine the heartbreak involved in the forced separation of husbands from wives and of parents from children.

Yet somehow the black family managed to hold together in slavery. When husband and wife were owned by separate masters on neighboring plantations, the husband would manage to visit his wife and children one or two evenings a week. On many plantations there were several generations of a slave family. Aunts, uncles, cousins, grandparents, and other family members looked after each other.

Slaves managed to preserve not only family life but also parts of their African culture. This they did mainly through songs and storytelling. Also, although most slaves were converted to Christianity, they often maintained some part of their ancient African religions.

Some slaves accepted their tragic lot. Others resisted. Between 1830 and 1860 about 2,000 slaves succeeded in escaping to the North each year, and many other thousands tried. There were more than 200 slave rebellions or plans for rebellion, a few large but most small. Rebellion took special courage, for the price of failure could be torture or death. Most slaves resisted in less dramatic ways. They would work slowly. They would break tools. They would set fire to the toolshed or the barn. They would even allow themselves to become ill or injured so that they could not work.

Free Blacks   The 251,000 free black people in the South in 1860 led uneasy lives. If they traveled, they had to carry papers to prove their freedom. They could neither vote nor hold office, though many were talented and educated people. Law and custom limited their career opportunities. In spite of these restrictions, they had to pay the same taxes as whites, and in some cases, they were even forced to pay additional taxes simply because they were free blacks.

Slaves were sold as property at auctions that attracted big crowds.
■ **Why, do you think, are there more female slaves being sold than male slaves?**

Uncle Tom's Cabin   Only 237,000 free blacks lived in the North in 1860. Therefore, more free black Americans lived in the South in 1860 than in the North. Many Northerners in 1860 had never seen a black person, free or slave. Whatever most Northerners knew about slavery came from what they had read or what they had heard from others.

In the early 1850s one of the most stirring books ever written aroused antislavery feelings in a great many Northerners. The book was ***Uncle Tom's Cabin***. It was written by Harriet Beecher Stowe. Much of what she wrote had been learned from her abolitionist friends. She had seen slavery only once during a short visit to a plantation in Garrard County, in the state of Kentucky.

Nonetheless, Stowe created a moving story about the cruelty of slavery. Among her memorable characters were kindly Uncle Tom, a slave who accepts the indignity of slavery, and the cruel Mississippi slave dealer Simon Legree. Toward the end of the novel, Uncle Tom dies from a beating ordered by Legree. In time, the names of these two characters became **stereotypes**. A stereotype is an exaggerated mental picture of a whole group that is usually based on emotion. Today a Simon Legree is an overbearing boss; an Uncle Tom is a black person who accepts discrimination without protest.

Southerners complained that Harriet Beecher Stowe actually knew very little about slavery. They said that *Uncle Tom's Cabin* contained greatly exaggerated stories of cruelty to slaves. Yet millions of Northerners accepted these stories as the truth. After Mrs. Stowe's book appeared in 1852, many who had been unconcerned about slavery began to oppose it strongly.

Industry and Commerce   The most striking difference between the North and the South in 1860, however, was the amount of industry and commerce. More than 75 percent of all factories in the United States and 70 percent of railroad lines were in the North. Northern banks held 80 percent of all bank deposits. The North had 90 percent of the nation's industrial workers.

By 1860 there were differences in the way of life. Actually, the people of the North and the people of the South were more alike than they were different. But the differences were exaggerated and distorted because neither section had a true picture of the other section. Southerners thought Northern employers were "money

This poster advertises a dramatic production of Harriet Beecher Stowe's *Uncle Tom's Cabin*.
■ **How does the image shown here attempt to appeal to your emotions?**

More than 75 percent of all factories were located in the North in 1860. During the Civil War, the factories were able to produce a large amount of ammunition.

■ What kind of ammunition was produced at this arsenal in Virginia?

grubbers," interested only in profits, and that Northern workers were "wage slaves," laboring in dirty factories. Northerners, for their part, believed that most Southerners were "tyrants," living a life of luxury based on the toil of mistreated slaves.

These basic economic differences led to political disagreements. Southern leaders wanted low tariffs to keep down the cost of manufactured goods. Northern leaders favored tariffs high enough to protect Northern industries from foreign competition. Northern businessmen thought the national government should establish a national banking system. Southerners wanted a national government that would not interfere with the powers of the states.

By 1860, disagreements between the North and the South centered on two questions. First, should slavery be allowed to expand into new territories? And second, are the individual states more powerful than the Union? Southerners generally answered yes. An increasing number of Northerners were answering no.

CHECKUP

1. What were the major differences between the Southern and Northern people in 1860?
2. How were people of the two sections alike?
3. How did slaves show they were unhappy with their existence?
4. Why was *Uncle Tom's Cabin* an important book?
5. **Thinking Critically** Do you think the South's economy could have existed without the slave system? Why or why not?

Understanding a Picture

THE UNDERGROUND RAILROAD

There are many ways to learn about the past. One way is by studying pictures. The painting below is titled the "Underground Railroad." It shows escaping slaves arriving at the farm of Levi Coffin in Newport, Indiana.

The Underground Railroad was not really a railroad at all. It was a network of secret escape routes, set up by antislavery people, to help black slaves flee the South. Many people were involved in this organized attempt to help runaway slaves escape to Canada. Abolitionists, free blacks in the North and South, and slaves all played a part in the system. Escaping slaves were guided to homes or "stations" where they would stay in hiding during the day before traveling to the next station at night.

Once they reached Canada, the slaves were assured of their freedom.

SKILLS PRACTICE

Study the painting. On a separate sheet of paper, write the answers to these questions.

1. How are the slaves in the picture being helped by the abolitionists?
2. By what means of transportation did these escaping slaves get to Coffin's farm?
3. What articles did escaping slaves take with them?
4. What effect, if any, do you think the weather had on these slaves?
5. What, do you think, would happen to these slaves if they were caught?

MAIN IDEAS

1. The Compromise of 1850 settled for a time certain issues between the North and the South, but the Fugitive Slave Law provoked further controversy.
2. The Kansas-Nebraska Act and the Dred Scott decision created new tensions between the North and the South.
3. The agricultural economy of the South and the industrial economy of the North caused political conflict between the two regions.
4. The political conflict was intensified with the dispute over slavery in the territories.
5. Seven Southern states seceded and formed the Confederate States of America after Abraham Lincoln was elected President.
6. These states seceded because they did not want a Republican President and they thought the North wanted to abolish slavery completely.

VOCABULARY REVIEW

On a separate sheet of paper, write **T** if the statement is true and **F** if it is false. If the statement is false, replace the underlined term to make the statement true.

1. Daniel Webster <u>supported</u> the Compromise of 1850 in his Seventh of March speech.
2. The Fugitive Slave Law made it <u>easier</u> for slaves to escape to freedom.
3. <u>Harriet Beecher Stowe</u> was a conductor on the Underground Railroad.
4. The Kansas-Nebraska Act <u>was in agreement</u> with the Missouri Compromise.
5. Popular sovereignty meant that the people <u>in the territories</u> could decide whether they wanted slavery.
6. When Abraham Lincoln and Stephen A. Douglas were candidates for the Senate in 1858, the winner was <u>Douglas</u>.
7. Proslavery and antislavery forces battled for control in <u>Kansas</u>.
8. <u>Dred Scott</u> led the raid at Harpers Ferry.

9. The Confederate States of America was formed <u>before</u> the election of 1860.
10. Most foreign-born people in the United States in 1860 lived in the <u>South</u>.

CHAPTER CHECKUP

1. Why was the Compromise of 1850 needed?
2. Why was the Fugitive Slave Law a disaster for black Americans?
3. What was the Underground Railroad?
4. How did the Kansas-Nebraska Act affect politics in the 1850s?
5. Explain the circumstances and the results of the Dred Scott case.
6. What was the immediate effect of Lincoln's election to the presidency?
7. How was the government of the Confederate States of America like and unlike that of the United States of America?
8. Why were plantations important in the South?
9. **Thinking Critically** If you were living in a territory about to become a state, what reason(s) would you give for prohibiting slavery in your state?
10. **Thinking Critically** Which of the four presidential candidates would you have voted for in the election of 1860? Why?

APPLYING KNOWLEDGE

1. The following headlines might have been found in newspapers of the 1850s. Arrange them in the order in which they happened. Then write one of the stories.

DRED SCOTT DECISION ANNOUNCED
SENATOR CALHOUN DIES
JOHN BROWN HANGED FOR TREASON
STOWE'S BOOK A SENSATION
DOUGLAS INTRODUCES KANSAS-NEBRASKA BILL
BUCHANAN ELECTED PRESIDENT
CLAY SUBMITS COMPROMISE PLAN
SOUTH CAROLINA SECEDES
LINCOLN WINS PRESIDENCY
CONFEDERACY ORGANIZED

15 The Civil War

1861–1865

The War Begins

What were the goals of the North and the South in the Civil War?

VOCABULARY

border states	ironclad
Anaconda Plan	

Lincoln and Davis   Abraham Lincoln traveled by railroad toward Washington, D.C., for his inauguration on March 4, 1861. In order to reach the nation's capital, he had to pass through Maryland, a slave state. Rumors persisted that attempts would be made on Lincoln's life. His advisers urged him to leave the presidential train and enter Washington quietly, in disguise if necessary. Lincoln refused.

Jefferson Davis had served as president of the Confederate States of America for 16 days when Abraham Lincoln was inaugurated as President of the United States. Both men were born in Kentucky. Both left their native state as children. Lincoln's family took him to Indiana, and he himself moved west to Illinois as a young man. After serving for 8 years in the Illinois state legislature and for one term in the United States Congress, Lincoln returned to Springfield, Illinois, to resume his career as a lawyer.

Jefferson Davis's family took him to Mississippi. In that state he and his brothers became plantation owners and had great wealth and prestige. As a young man Jefferson Davis returned to Kentucky for part of his formal education. Then he graduated from the military academy at West Point but served only a short time in the regular army. He commanded a regiment in the Mexican War and earned a reputation for bravery. Later he was a Democratic senator from Mississippi and secretary of war in Franklin Pierce's Cabinet.

The Fighting Begins   Soldiers of the Confederate States of America took over United States forts and arsenals in the South in February and March of 1861. In most cases, the commanders of the forts and arsenals gave up without a fight, but Major Robert Anderson did not. He commanded Fort Sumter in the harbor of Charleston, South Carolina. Confederate guns ringed the harbor.

This was the tense situation that Abraham Lincoln faced when he took office in March 1861. Should he order Major Anderson and his men to leave Fort Sumter or should he try to send in reinforcements? Lincoln knew that Anderson and

Confederate troops fire on the United States fort, Fort Sumter in South Carolina. The conflict marked the beginning of the Civil War.
■ **When did the conflict at Fort Sumter take place?**

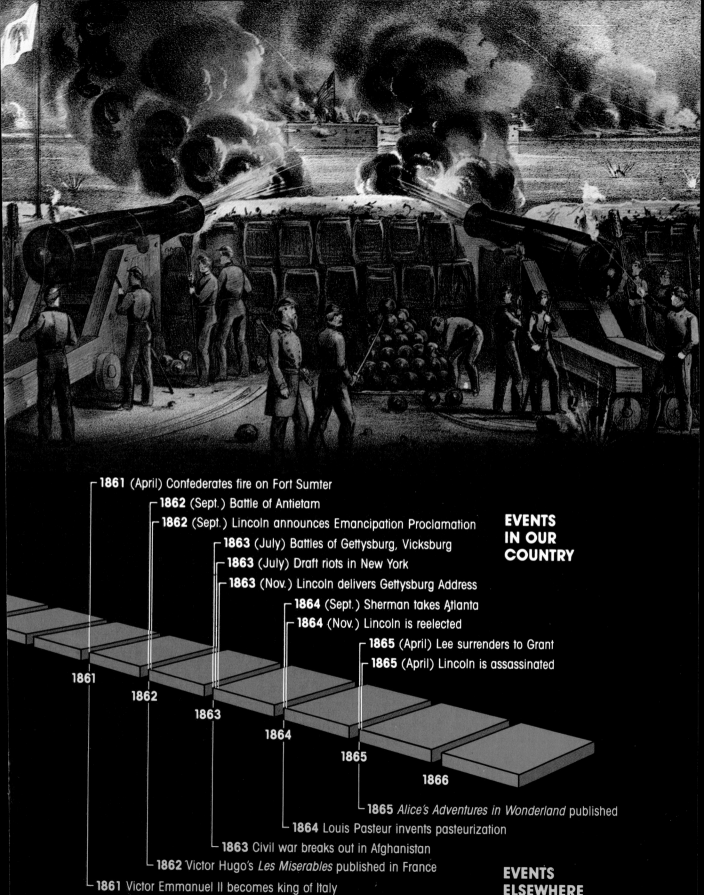

1861 (April) Confederates fire on Fort Sumter

1862 (Sept.) Battle of Antietam

1862 (Sept.) Lincoln announces Emancipation Proclamation

EVENTS
IN OUR
COUNTRY

1863 (July) Battles of Gettysburg, Vicksburg

1863 (July) Draft riots in New York

1863 (Nov.) Lincoln delivers Gettysburg Address

1864 (Sept.) Sherman takes Atlanta

1864 (Nov.) Lincoln is reelected

1865 (April) Lee surrenders to Grant

1865 (April) Lincoln is assassinated

1861

1862

1863

1864

1865

1866

1865 *Alice's Adventures in Wonderland* published

1864 Louis Pasteur invents pasteurization

1863 Civil war breaks out in Afghanistan

1862 Victor Hugo's *Les Miserables* published in France

1861 Victor Emmanuel II becomes king of Italy

EVENTS
ELSEWHERE

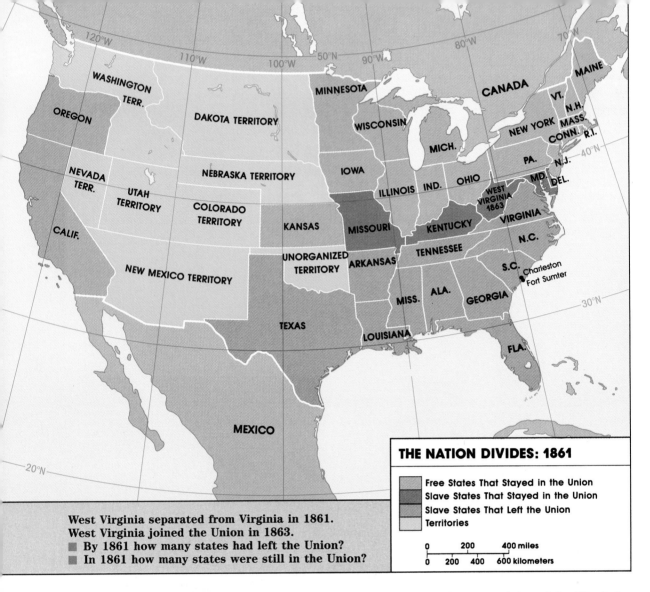

WASHINGTON TERR.
OREGON
NEVADA TERR.
CALIF.
UTAH TERRITORY
DAKOTA TERRITORY
NEBRASKA TERRITORY
COLORADO TERRITORY
NEW MEXICO TERRITORY
UNORGANIZED TERRITORY
KANSAS
MINNESOTA
WISCONSIN
IOWA
MISSOURI
ARKANSAS
TEXAS
LOUISIANA
MISS.
ALA.
GEORGIA
FLA.
TENNESSEE
KENTUCKY
MICH.
ILLINOIS IND. OHIO
WEST VIRGINIA 1863
VIRGINIA
N.C.
S.C.
Charleston
Fort Sumter
CANADA
NEW YORK
PA.
MD
DEL.
N.J.
MAINE
VT.
N.H.
MASS.
CONN.
R.I.
MEXICO

THE NATION DIVIDES: 1861

Free States That Stayed in the Union
Slave States That Stayed in the Union
Slave States That Left the Union
Territories

| 0 | 200 | 400 miles |
| 0 | 200 400 | 600 kilometers |

West Virginia separated from Virginia in 1861.
West Virginia joined the Union in 1863.
■ By 1861 how many states had left the Union?
■ In 1861 how many states were still in the Union?

his men were about to run out of food. At that point, he told South Carolina's authorities that he was sending supplies to the fort but no more soldiers.

The question of peace and war now lay with the Confederates. Jefferson Davis met with his Cabinet. In the discussions, those eager for war won out. Early in the morning of April 12, 1861, a fierce bombardment of Fort Sumter began. Major Anderson surrendered the fort a day later. The Civil War had begun.

With war a reality, President Lincoln asked the North for 75,000 volunteers to put down what he called the "insurrection," or rebellion against the government of the United States. After this, Virginia, Arkansas, Tennessee, and North Carolina left the Union and joined the Confederate States of America. In view of Virginia's strategic location, the Confederates moved their capital from Montgomery, Alabama, to Richmond, Virginia. The two capitals, Richmond and Washington, were less than 100 miles (160 km) apart.

War Goals The goals of the Confederate States were clear. They were fighting for their independence. To achieve independence, they had only to fight on the defensive until the Union realized it was impossible to defeat them. For this main reason, except for two brief invasions of the North, Confederate armies fought mainly a defensive war on their own soil.

The war goals of the Union seemed more difficult to accomplish. The foremost goal was preserving the Union rather than abolishing slavery. There were at least two reasons for this. In southern Ohio, Indiana, and Illinois, there were many people who had economic and family ties with the South. Lincoln and his advisers knew the people in these states would not fight for the abolitionists' goal of freeing the slaves, at least not at the beginning of the war.

Even more important was the need to keep the **border states**, or states between the North and the South, from seceding. In Delaware, Maryland, Kentucky, and Missouri, slavery was legal. If Lincoln announced that the war was being fought to end slavery, some or all of these states might join the Confederacy. As it turned out, none of the four did so. A large number of people in these states did favor the Southern cause. Yet all four furnished more soldiers for the Union than for the Confederacy.

By the end of 1862, it seemed certain that the border states would remain in the Union. After that, abolishing slavery became a second aim of the Union. Even later than that, however, it appeared that the Confederacy might achieve its goal of independence.

Early in the war, a Union regiment practices marching in drill formation—a favorite battle tactic of European armies at the time. The ornate uniforms are imitations of a French style.
Would these borrowed tactics and styles be an advantage or a disadvantage in actual combat? Why?

The Anaconda Plan Early in the war, General Winfield Scott and other Union leaders devised a strategic plan for beating the South. It was called the **Anaconda Plan** after the snake that wraps itself around its victims and crushes them.

The Anaconda Plan had four goals:

(1) To blockade the ports of the Confederacy to prevent trade with Europe
(2) To cut the Confederacy in two by taking control of the Mississippi
(3) To cut the eastern half of the Confederacy in two by advancing up the Tennessee River and then southward into Georgia
(4) To capture Richmond

Bull Run By July 1861, some 30,000 Union troops had gathered around Washington. In western Virginia, Union troops under the command of General George B. McClellan had already won some small battles. Union supporters cried out for more action. "On to Richmond!" they shouted. Northern newspapers urged Lincoln to end the war.

On July 16, 1861, General Irvin McDowell led a Union army south toward Richmond. General P. G. T. Beauregard (bō' rə gärd) commanded a Confederate army stationed at Manassas Junction, Virginia. His troops met McDowell's on the banks of Bull Run, a nearby creek. At first

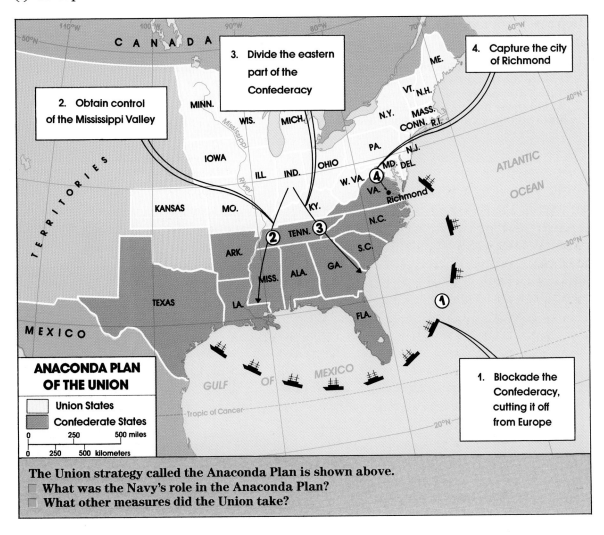

ANACONDA PLAN OF THE UNION

- Union States
- Confederate States

0   250   500 miles
0   250   500 kilometers

The Union strategy called the Anaconda Plan is shown above.
☐ What was the Navy's role in the Anaconda Plan?
☐ What other measures did the Union take?

the Union army drove the Confederates back and appeared to have the battle won. However, one brigade of Confederate troops "stood like a stone wall." They won for their commander, General Thomas J. Jackson, the nickname of "Stonewall" Jackson, and they saved the day for the Confederacy.

At this point in the battle, Confederate reinforcements arrived. Union troops began to retreat. Hundreds of civilians had come south from Washington to watch the battle. They got caught up with the soldiers, turning the whole mass into a disorderly mob. The mob ran until it reached the safety of Washington's defenses.

The disaster at Bull Run showed Union leaders that untrained troops could not be depended on. Therefore, President Lincoln called General McClellan to take command of the Army of the Potomac. That was the name of the Union army gathered around Washington. McClellan spent nearly a year training this army before again invading Virginia.

Grant Fights   While McClellan trained the Army of the Potomac, General Ulysses S. Grant won several victories for the Union in Kentucky and Tennessee. In February 1862, he directed an advance up the Tennessee River. Union gunboats helped capture Fort Henry. This opened the way into central Tennessee.

General Grant's Army of the Tennessee then marched to Fort Donelson, on the Cumberland River. Fort Donelson held out for a time, but Grant finally forced the Confederates to give up. When the fort's commander asked for surrender terms, Grant replied, "No terms except an unconditional and immediate surrender." This made Grant a hero in the North. People began saying that his initials, *U. S.*, stood for "Unconditional Surrender."

After Forts Henry and Donelson had fallen, Grant moved across Tennessee almost to the Mississippi state line. Near Shiloh (shī' lō), Confederate forces made a surprise attack. The battle of Shiloh lasted 2 days, from April 6 to 7, 1862. It was by far the biggest battle of the war up to that time. Though it was counted as a Union victory, "Bloody Shiloh" cost Grant's army 13,000 casualties. The Confederates also lost heavily, with about 11,000 killed or wounded.

Rumors that Grant had mismanaged his army persisted after the battle. Some people demanded that President Lincoln replace Grant as commander of the Army of the Tennessee. Lincoln refused. Shaking his head, the President said, "I cannot spare this man. He fights." Grant not only fought, he won.

Warfare at Sea   While armies fought on land, the United States Navy began to blockade Confederate ports. The blockade kept out supplies the Confederates needed from abroad. Only swift ships known as blockade runners could get through the tightening net of Union vessels. In March 1862, however, it looked as if the Confederates had found a way of breaking the Union blockade. They had captured a Union ship called the *Merrimac* and turned it into an **ironclad** by covering its sides and decks with iron plates 4 inches thick.

With its new armor, the ironclad got a new name—the *Virginia*. Its mission was to break the Union blockade of Virginia's ports. On March 8, 1862, it rammed and sank one blockading vessel, drove another aground, and scattered the remainder of the ships blockading the coast of Virginia. Union guns fired without effect on the iron plates protecting the former *Merrimac*.

The next day a strange-looking vessel challenged the Confederate ironclad. Named the *Monitor*, the Union ship, too, had iron armor. Instead of fixed guns, the *Monitor* had a revolving gun turret that looked like a round metal box stuck on a raft. John Ericsson, a Swedish immigrant, had developed the *Monitor* for the United States Navy.

The *Monitor* and the *Virginia* fired at each other for hours, until all their ammunition was gone. Neither ship won a clear-cut victory, but the *Virginia* finally had to withdraw into the harbor at Norfolk for repairs. Later the Confederates sank the *Virginia* to keep the ship from falling into enemy hands when Union forces captured Norfolk.

Other countries had experimented with ironclad vessels before 1862. However, the *Monitor* and the *Virginia* fought the first battle between ironclads in the world's history. Their meeting proved that such vessels were practical. Even before their battle, the *Virginia* had shown that ships protected by sheets of iron were deadly to wooden vessels. However, the South was not able to use this knowledge because it did not have enough resources to build more ironclad ships. Union vessels, built of wood, maintained their blockade along the coast.

The Peninsular Campaign General McClellan seemed unwilling to order his well-trained Army of the Potomac into battle. He was overly cautious, always believing the opposing Confederate armies to be larger than they actually were. President Lincoln accused McClellan of having the "slows" and finally ordered him to advance on Richmond.

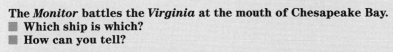

The *Monitor* battles the *Virginia* at the mouth of Chesapeake Bay.
- **Which ship is which?**
- **How can you tell?**

Chicago Historical Society

The State of Kanawha

From the beginning of the United States, eastern and western Virginia were different. Western Virginia was mountainous and there were very few slaves there. The mountain people disliked the rich slave owners of eastern Virginia. It seemed the slave owners always got their way in the state's politics and government.

Virginia seceded from the Union in April 1861. A short time later, representatives of Virginia's western counties met in Wheeling, an Ohio River town in the western part of the state. At the Wheeling Convention, these representatives set up a new state, which they called Kanawha (kə nô′ wə) after another river in the region. Union troops were welcomed in Kanawha, which allied with the North.

The Congress of the United States approved the separation of 48 western counties from the rest of Virginia. In April 1863, Abraham Lincoln issued a presidential proclamation admitting the new state into the Union. By this time however, the new state had the name of West Virginia.

McClellan had a good plan for his attempt to capture Richmond. Instead of moving toward the Confederate capital by land, he had his troops ferried down the Potomac River and into Chesapeake Bay. The Army of the Potomac landed on a peninsula between the York and James rivers. From there McClellan ordered a slow advance toward Richmond.

In the peninsular campaign, as it was called, McClellan's army came within 5 miles (8 km) of Richmond. The army fought one indecisive battle during which Confederate General Joseph E. Johnston received a severe wound. General Robert E. Lee then took over the defense of Richmond. He would command the Confederate Army of Northern Virginia for the next 3 years.

Brilliantly assisted by Stonewall Jackson, General Lee drove McClellan's army back down the peninsula. But in the terrible Seven Days' Battle, from June 25 to July 1, 1862, the Confederates lost twice as many men as the Union army. Still, McClellan continued to retreat. The peninsular campaign was a failure.

CHECKUP

1. Who were the presidents of the Confederacy and of the Union?
2. What was the Anaconda Plan?
3. Where did the fighting begin?
4. What was the peninsular campaign?
5. **Thinking Critically** If you had been Lincoln, would you have sent reinforcements to Fort Sumter or asked the troops there to leave?

Freeing the Slaves

What were the effects of the Emancipation Proclamation?

VOCABULARY

> **Emancipation Proclamation**

The Slavery Issue   Since the beginning of the war, Lincoln had been cautious about including freedom for slaves as a Union war goal. As the war continued, however, antislavery Republicans urged him more and more to do something about slavery. In July 1862, Lincoln announced to the members of his Cabinet that he had decided to issue a proclamation freeing the slaves in the Confederate states. "Wait until the Union wins an important victory," Secretary of State William Seward ad-vised President Lincoln. Otherwise, he said, the proclamation would sound like a desperate effort to escape defeat at the hands of the Confederacy.

Lee Invades Maryland   After McClellan's failure in the peninsular campaign of June 1862, Lincoln replaced him as commander of the Army of the Potomac with General John Pope. Pope, too, was a failure, defeated by Lee's Army of Northern Virginia at the second battle of Bull Run on August 28 and 29, 1862. In September, Lee's confidence in the fighting ability of his army was at its height. It seemed a good time for an invasion of Maryland.

Lee hoped to accomplish two things. An invasion might cause Maryland, and

Both sides suffered a shocking number of casualties at Antietam.
■ Does this picture change or reinforce your answer to the question under the picture on page 369? Why?

perhaps other border states, to secede from the Union. Furthermore, if the Confederates won a victory in Maryland, Great Britain and France might recognize the Confederacy as an independent nation. If this happened, Great Britain might help break the blockade and provide supplies.

To meet the danger in Maryland, President Lincoln put McClellan back in command of the main army in Lee's path. This army halted Lee's invasion in a bitter, bloody battle at Antietam (an tē′ təm) Creek, near Sharpsburg, Maryland, on September 17, 1862. However, McClellan failed to pursue Lee's army fast enough to please Lincoln. For this reason, Lincoln removed McClellan from command for the second and last time.

Emancipation The battle of Antietam could best be described as a draw — neither a victory nor a defeat for the Union or the Confederacy. And yet this indecisive battle had far-reaching consequences. If Lee had won a decisive victory in Maryland, Great Britain and France might have supported the Confederacy. And though it was not a victory for the Union, Antietam gave Lincoln the result he needed before issuing the **Emancipation Proclamation,** his declaration freeing the slaves in the rebelling states.

President Lincoln had followed Secretary of State Seward's advice to delay this announcement as long as possible. Deciding that Antietam had been the "victory" he needed, Lincoln acted. On September 22, 1862, he announced his intention to free all slaves in the rebelling states on January 1, 1863, unless those states would return to the Union before that time.

Slave owners in the unconquered parts of the Confederacy had no intention of freeing their slaves by January 1, 1863. So on New Year's Day, Lincoln issued the Emancipation Proclamation. It proclaimed all slaves "forever free" in those Confederate states still in rebellion. The proclamation had no immediate effect on the slaves in those states, since the Union had no way of enforcing the proclamation. Further, it freed no slaves in the border states nor in those areas of the Confederacy that had been overrun by the Union armies.

Important Consequences Still the Emancipation Proclamation had several important consequences. As Union armies pushed farther into the South, thousands of joyous slave families left the plantations to seek freedom behind Union lines. More than 100,000 former slaves joined the Northern armies after the Emancipation Proclamation. Many free blacks had joined before 1863. One of them, Martin L. Delany, became a major in the Union army. A social reformer, doctor, editor, and world traveler, Delany was the first black officer ever to reach that rank.

The Emancipation Proclamation had important effects on public opinion in the North and in Europe. Most antislavery people in the North welcomed the long-awaited proclamation of freedom. "God bless Abraham Lincoln," wrote Horace Greeley, the antislavery editor of the New York *Tribune*. In Great Britain the common people had favored the Union since the beginning of the war. They greeted news of the Emancipation Proclamation with joy. After that, there was little chance that aristocratic British leaders would risk giving aid to the Confederacy.

Northern Defeats In spite of the Emancipation Proclamation, bad news for the Union came from the eastern battlefields after Antietam. Lincoln continued to search for a man who would lead the

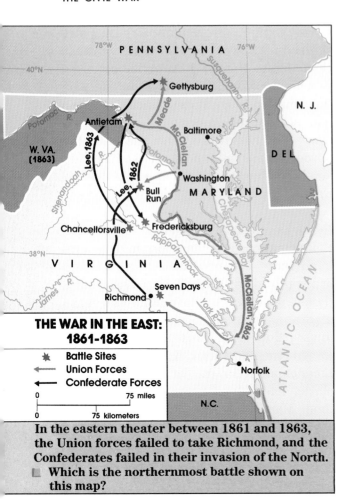

THE WAR IN THE EAST: 1861-1863

- ✹ Battle Sites
- ← Union Forces
- ← Confederate Forces

0 _____ 75 miles
0 _____ 75 kilometers

In the eastern theater between 1861 and 1863, the Union forces failed to take Richmond, and the Confederates failed in their invasion of the North.
■ Which is the northernmost battle shown on this map?

In April 1863, the Army of the Potomac began still another invasion of Virginia. But Hooker had no more success in the spring than Burnside had the previous winter. Lee's Army of Northern Virginia won a battle at Chancellorsville that lasted 3 days, from May 2 to 4, 1863. At the end the Union army began another dismal retreat. The Confederate victory was a costly one, however. One of the 11,000 Confederate casualties was Stonewall Jackson, accidentally shot by his own men. An attempt to save his life by amputating his wounded arm failed, and Jackson died a few days later.

The news from Grant's Army of the Tennessee was nearly as bad as that from the Army of the Potomac. In Mississippi, Grant's men were still trying to take the Confederate stronghold of Vicksburg. In the North, the Congressional elections in the fall of 1862 had gone against the Republicans. Northern Democrats, many of whom opposed Lincoln's policies and the war, gained more than 30 seats in the House of Representatives.

As the bad news continued, Northern opposition to the war mounted. Many people in the North were tired of the war and the awful loss of life it had brought. Few people realized that the momentum of the war was about to change.

Army of the Potomac to victory. For a time he settled on General Ambrose E. Burnside. Under Burnside's command, the Army of the Potomac attacked Lee's army at Fredericksburg, Virginia. The Confederates held a strong position on the south side of the Rappahannock River. Yet Burnside ordered a direct assault.

What took place on December 13, 1862, was a slaughter. The Army of the Potomac lost twice as many soldiers as the Army of Northern Virginia but failed to drive the Confederates from the heights above Fredericksburg. The Union army then withdrew to winter quarters for rest, reinforcements, and more training. General Joseph Hooker, known as "Fighting Joe," replaced the incompetent Burnside.

CHECKUP

1. Why did General Lee invade Maryland?
2. Why was the battle of Antietam important?
3. How did people react to the Emancipation Proclamation?
4. Why did opposition to the war mount in the North in 1862?

5. **Thinking Critically** Why do you think the Emancipation Proclamation freed only those slaves living in the Confederate States?

The Home Fronts

How did the war affect social and economic conditions in the North and the South?

Draft Laws   Both the Union and the Confederacy filled the ranks of their armies in a combination of ways. In the Union army, generous payments were made to men who would volunteer to serve. By 1863, however, more soldiers were needed for fighting. So Congress passed the first **draft** law in United States history. The draft is the process by which men are selected for military service without their expressed consent.

The draft law of 1863 was unfair. Men could hire substitutes or be excused from the draft by paying $300. New York City was the scene of an angry and destructive protest against the draft in July 1863. For several days, mobs ran loose in the city. Nearly 1,000 persons were killed or injured. Elsewhere in the North, minor riots also occurred in protest against the draft laws.

Like the Union, the Confederacy relied at first on volunteers. But since it had a smaller population, it began drafting men nearly a year earlier than the Union. The

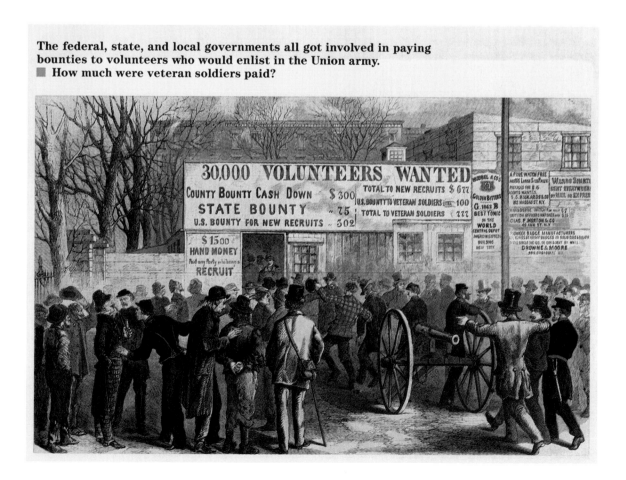

The federal, state, and local governments all got involved in paying bounties to volunteers who would enlist in the Union army.
■ How much were veteran soldiers paid?

Confederate draft act passed in April 1862 also contained injustices. As in the Union, men with money could buy exemption from the draft or hire substitutes to go in their places. Owners of more than 15 slaves and those who supervised the work of that number could claim exemption from the Confederate draft. However, no widespread draft riots took place in the Confederacy. Still, exemptions for the wealthy caused hard feelings there, as they did in the North. Many Confederates said that this was "a rich man's war but a poor man's fight."

The Fighting Forces More than 2.5 million men served in the Union ranks at one time or another during the course of the war. The Confederates had about half that many under arms. To fill the ranks, the Union had two sources that the Confederacy could not or would not use. More than 800,000 immigrants poured into the North during the war. Most of these immigrants were young men. Large numbers of them enlisted in the Union armies. In fact, about one fourth of the Union forces were foreign-born. Even if immigrant ships wanted to dock in Confederate ports during the war, the Union blockade kept them from doing so.

Some Confederate leaders wanted to arm the slaves during the war, but this was never done. Officers in the Confederate army often brought slaves to serve them in camp. Some slaves also were used to dig

The all-black 54th Massachusetts Regiment storms the Confederate stronghold at Fort Wagner, South Carolina.
■ **How can you tell which troops are Confederate troops and which troops are Union troops?**

fortifications and to work in supply trains. Black men were not accepted in the Union army at first, but the situation changed after the Emancipation Proclamation was issued. By the end of the war, at least 200,000 black soldiers were enrolled in the Union army. Hardly a battle was fought in which there were not black troops. Many received medals for their actions on the battlefields, and nearly 40,000 black soldiers died in battle.

Both sides had Native Americans in their armies. The Five Civilized Tribes, living in what is now the state of Oklahoma, even had representation in the Congress of the Confederacy. About 5,500 Indians fought for the Southern cause. A Cherokee chief, Stand Watie, became a brigadier general in the Confederate army. Ely (ēl′ ē) Parker, a Seneca, was one of about 4,000 Indians serving in the Union army. Parker, too, became a brigadier general. As Grant's military secretary, Parker wrote the copies of the surrender terms handed to Lee at the end of the war.

Women and the War   Women in both the North and the South helped their sides in many ways. Southern women managed plantations while their husbands were away. Other women in the South planted crops, worked in the Confederacy's few war factories, and cared for the sick and wounded in Confederate hospitals. Sally Tompkins, who ran a private hospital for the wounded in Richmond, was commissioned a captain—the only woman officer in the Civil War.

Northern women did much the same kind of war work—in factories, on farms, and in hospitals. Louisa May Alcott, the author of *Little Women* and other books, was a nurse during the war. So was Dorothea Dix, who had earlier done so much for the mentally ill. Clara Barton, later a

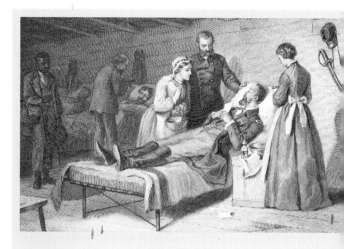

Nurses care for a wounded soldier.
■ What other roles did women play in the Civil War?

founder of the American Red Cross, also cared for the Union's sick and wounded.

Women on each side acted as spies. Belle Boyd, barely 17 at the beginning of the war, became famous as a Confederate spy and messenger. Emma Edmonds served 2 years with the Army of the Potomac disguised as a man.

Financing the War   The Union and the Confederacy used similar methods to finance the war. Both governments sold bonds to their people and to investors in Europe. Both governments collected heavy taxes. Likewise, both issued paper money to help pay wartime expenses. The Union's money was called **greenbacks** because it was printed on green paper. It fell in value and at one time the greenback dollar was worth 39 cents in comparison with gold. Confederate paper money was worth even less. A Confederate paper dollar was valued at only a little more than 1 cent at the end of the war.

In the presidential campaign of 1860, Republicans had promised to raise the protective tariff. With no Southern members

The Confederates issued their own paper money during the Civil War.
■ Why was Richmond printed on the money?

in Congress to oppose the move, the tariff was rasied a number of times during the war. The Union government collected more than $300 million in tariff duties between 1861 and 1865.

The war cost the United States government about $15 billion to save the Union. It also revealed the need for a stronger central banking system. Congress filled this need in 1863 by passing the National Banking Act. It set up the first national system of banking since President Andrew Jackson destroyed the Second United States Bank more than 30 years before.

Most people in the Confederacy suffered badly from shortages in practically everything during the war. Food was plentiful in some parts of the South. However, breakdowns in the transportation system kept food and other supplies from being evenly distributed. The few factories in the South found it impossible to supply both military and civilian populations with shoes, clothing, and other necessities. The tight Union blockade kept drugs and other medicines from reaching the South.

On the other hand, the North remained prosperous during the war. In fact, a great many people made money from the war. The economic problem in the North was rising prices, not shortages. Workers' wages rose less rapidly than prices. In 1864 the organized printers in New York City protested. They asked that their wages be raised to make up for the wartime inflation. "The average value of 16 dollars now paid is really only 8 dollars," they said, "and what printer is expected to support a family on that pittance. . . ?"

CHECKUP

1. Why were draft laws passed during the Civil War?
2. Why did some Americans object to the idea of a draft?
3. How did women help the war effort for the Union and the Confederacy?
4. What economic problems did the North face? The South?
5. **Thinking Critically** Why, do you think, did it cost so much to finance the Civil War?

The Last Years

VOCABULARY

Pickett's charge	Gettysburg Address

Grant and Lee   By 1863 the conflict between the North and the South ranged over a vast area and involved hundreds of thousands of men. New techniques of warfare were being used. European observers came to watch. They were amazed at the skill with which Union and Confederate generals used railroads, telegraph lines, and gigantic supply bases to move and support armies of 60,000 to 100,000 men.

Two opposing generals dominated the last years of this long war. General Ulysses S. Grant made use of the North's superior resources to lead the Union armies to eventual victory. Born in Ohio, Grant had graduated from the military academy at West Point. After serving in the Mexican War, he resigned from the army. In the 1850s he failed at farming and various jobs near St. Louis, Missouri. When the war began, Grant was a 39-year-old clerk in his father's harness shop at Galena, Illinois. Because of his military experience, Grant got a commission as a colonel a few weeks after fighting started.

The Confederacy had given the task of defending its capital at Richmond to General Robert E. Lee and his Army of Northern Virginia. Robert E. Lee's father was Henry Lee, who had won the nickname of "Light Horse Harry" as a cavalry commander in the War for Independence. Later Henry Lee served as governor of Virginia. Robert E. Lee graduated from West Point and served in the Mexican War. Unlike Grant, Lee followed a professional military career afterwards. He was 54 when the war began. The United States War Department had offered him command of the Union armies. Robert E. Lee sadly refused the offer. He felt that his first loyalty had to be to his home state of Virginia. When Virginia joined the Confederacy, so did Robert E. Lee.

Pennsylvania Invaded   In the spring of 1863, General Lee planned another invasion of the North. This time he chose Pennsylvania as his target. Confederate hopes for foreign aid had nearly vanished. And yet a great victory on Northern soil might still convince France or Great Britain that open aid to the Confederate states would be to their benefit. Moreover, a victory in Pennsylvania might drive Northern morale even lower. Finally, Lee's Army of Northern Virginia needed clothes, food,

General Robert E. Lee makes plans for battle.
▪ What features help you distinguish Lee from the other officers?

shoes, horses, and other supplies. General Lee knew his troops could get these things from central Pennsylvania.

In June 1863, Lee's army advanced into Pennsylvania. The Army of the Potomac moved north too, keeping between the Confederate invaders and Washington. At the end of June, Lincoln changed commanders once more. This time he gave command of the army to General George G. Meade. Neither Meade nor Lee had planned to fight a great battle early in July, but on July 1, advance units of the two armies met, almost by chance, near the small town of Gettysburg, Pennsylvania.

Gettysburg   On the first day of the battle, the Confederate troops pushed the Union forces back through Gettysburg. The Union troops dug in on Cemetery Ridge, a long piece of high ground south of the town. During the night Lee and Meade rushed their main armies toward Gettys-

burg. Lee positioned his troops and his headquarters on Seminary Ridge, about a mile northwest of Union lines.

After attempts to outflank the Union Army failed, Lee ordered a frontal attack on Cemetery Ridge. General George E. Pickett of Virginia led the attack, now known as **Pickett's Charge.** On the afternoon of July 3, some 15,000 Confederates marched toward the Union lines across a half mile of open ground as if on parade. Their bravery was wasted. Only a few managed to reach the Union center on Cemetery Ridge, and they were soon driven off by the determined Union defenders.

Other battles of the war had more soldiers taking part. Other battles had a higher rate of casualties. Yet Gettysburg has become the best-known battle of the war. It is also often seen as the turning point. After this battle, Lee ordered his army back to Virginia. Still back on its

Soldiers engage in battle at Gettysburg.   More Americans died in this one battle than in the entire American Revolution.
■ What kinds of battle tactics are the troops using?

home soil, Lee's army fought on for almost 2 more years.

Gettysburg is remembered for another reason. On November 19, 1863, Abraham Lincoln spoke at the dedication of the cemetery there. What he said in the **Gettysburg Address** has been called the perfect expression of the faith of the American people in democracy. (See page 384.)

Control of the Mississippi   Almost from the beginning of the war, Union forces had tried to divide the Confederacy by capturing control of the Mississippi River. In the spring of 1862, a naval force commanded by Captain David Farragut forced New Orleans to surrender. Union gunboats then steamed up the Mississippi, capturing river ports along the way. At Vicksburg, Mississippi, Farragut's fleet was halted by fire from Confederate forts located on a high bluff in front of the city.

Grant swung into action. After his victory at Shiloh, he took Corinth, Mississippi. He then moved south to Vicksburg. That city was so strongly defended it could not be taken by storm. Grant had his army dig in and begin a siege.

The siege provoked terrible hardships among both soldiers and civilians. For 6 weeks the city was under continual bombardment from Union artillery. Women and children were crowded into underground caves. All supply routes into the city were cut by Grant's army. Finally, with food supplies exhausted, the Confederate garrison of 30,000 men surrendered on July 4, 1863, the day after the battle of Gettysburg ended. The surrender of Vicksburg gave the Union complete control of the Mississippi. Texas, Arkansas, and most of Louisiana were now cut off from the other states of the Confederacy by the Mississippi River. The Union was set to complete the Anaconda Plan.

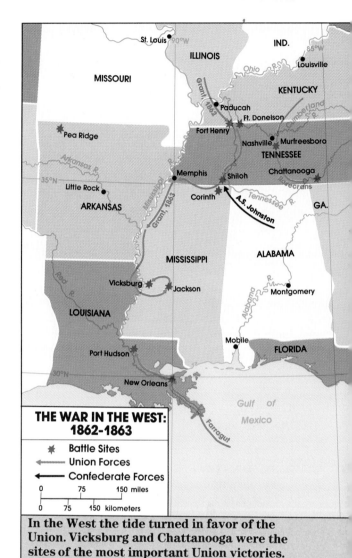

THE WAR IN THE WEST: 1862-1863

* Battle Sites
← Union Forces
◀ Confederate Forces

0   75   150 miles
0   75   150 kilometers

In the West the tide turned in favor of the Union. Vicksburg and Chattanooga were the sites of the most important Union victories.
◼ Where are Vicksburg and Chattanooga located?

The Confederacy Divided   Following the capture of Vicksburg, Grant's army moved to southeastern Tennessee. At Chattanooga a Confederate army commanded by General Braxton Bragg guarded the gap that led through the southern mountains into Georgia. In a series of battles fought during November 1863, the Union army forced its way through the gap in the mountains. This advance made it possible to divide the eastern half of the Confederacy.

The Gettysburg Address

The National Soldiers' Cemetery at Gettysburg was established for the soldiers who lost their lives in the battle there in July 1863. President Lincoln was asked to deliver a few remarks at the dedication. Although he spoke only 3 minutes, his words expressed his profound belief in democracy and the Union.

Four score and seven years ago our fathers brought forth on this continent a new nation, conceived in liberty and dedicated to the proposition that all men are created equal.

Now we are engaged in a great civil war, testing whether that nation, or any nation so conceived and so dedicated, can long endure. We are met on a great battlefield of that war. We have come to dedicate a portion of that field, as a final resting place for those who here gave their lives that that nation might live. . . .

But in a larger sense, we cannot dedicate—we cannot consecrate—we cannot hallow—this ground. The brave men, living and dead, who struggled here, have consecrated it. . . . The world will little note nor long remember what we say here, but it can never forget what they did here. It is for us the living, rather, to be dedicated here to the unfinished work which they who fought here have thus far so nobly advanced. It is rather for us to be here dedicated to the great task remaining before us . . . that we highly resolve that these dead shall not have died in vain —that this nation, under God, shall have a new birth of freedom—and that government of the people, by the people, for the people, shall not perish from the earth.

USING SOURCE MATERIAL
1. Why did Lincoln write the Gettysburg Address?
2. What goal does Lincoln set forth in this speech?
3. Why do you think the last phrase of the address has been called a perfect definition of democracy?

An army commanded by General William T. Sherman accomplished this division in 1864. First, the army fought its way from Chattanooga to Atlanta, Georgia. Atlanta fell to the Union forces in September 1864. Then, Sherman began his "march to the sea." Cutting his army loose from its supply bases, he advanced across Georgia to Savannah, on the Atlantic coast. Sherman's army left a path of total destruction behind it—torn up rail lines, flattened bridges, burned factories and other buildings, and damaged crops. Shortly before Christmas the Union army reached and captured Savannah.

Richmond Falls   Under various commanders the Army of the Potomac had tried to capture Richmond. Early in 1864, Lincoln ordered Grant to come east and take command of all the Union armies. Soon after, Grant ordered another attempt to capture the Confederate capital with the hope this would bring the war to an end.

The Army of Northern Virginia fought off the steady advance of the Union forces toward Richmond. In May 1864 the opposing armies met in the bloody Wilderness campaign. A few days later they fought at Spotsylvania Court House. On June 1 the battle of Cold Harbor began.

In less than a month Grant lost more than 60,000 men as he fought his way toward Richmond, but he kept on attacking. He knew Lee's losses were nearly as great and that the Union could bear such

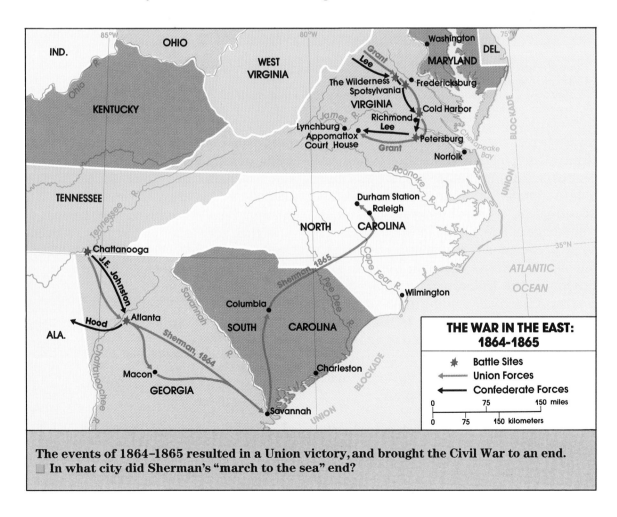

The events of 1864–1865 resulted in a Union victory, and brought the Civil War to an end.
☐ In what city did Sherman's "march to the sea" end?

385

Confederate soldiers sadly roll up their battle flag after Lee's surrender to Grant at Appomattox.
■ How does this artist focus your attention on the flag itself?

losses better than the Confederacy. Still, Grant was unable to defeat the Army of Northern Virginia. Moreover, he was unable to capture Richmond in 1864. Instead of retreating, however, as previous Union commanders had, Grant moved his army south of Richmond. There he besieged the important railroad center of Petersburg. Gradually, the Union army tightened its control of the roads leading into and out of the Confederate capital. In the early spring of 1865, Lee was forced to abandon Richmond. He headed west in an attempt to save his army. Union troops now took control of the Confederate capital.

The Fighting Ends A week later, Lee's hungry, poorly clad, and worn-out army tried to break through the Union lines. The attempt to escape failed as Union troops surrounded the exhausted Confederates at Appomattox Court House, Virginia. There, on April 9, 1865, Lee surrendered his army to Grant and said a touching farewell to his valiant troops.

Other Confederate armies surrendered, one by one. On May 26, 1865, all organized resistance ended.

CHECKUP

1. What was the significance of the battle of Gettysburg?
2. How did the Union plan to divide the Confederacy?
3. What were the results of Sherman's march to the sea?
4. **Thinking Critically** Which part of the Anaconda Plan, do you think, did the most to help the North win the Civil War? Explain.

Wartime Politics

What political opposition did Lincoln face during the war?

Opposing the War   Abraham Lincoln had opposition as he directed the Union's war effort. The opposition came from within his own party as well as from the Democrats. Many Republicans doubted Lincoln's ability to bring the war to a successful conclusion. Lincoln's strongest critics within his own party became known as **Radical Republicans**. As President, Lincoln was able to control them, although they insisted he was too sympathetic toward the South.

Democrats in the Union kept up a vigorous opposition to the Republicans and to many of Lincoln's actions. Stephen A. Douglas died of typhoid fever in the year the war began. Had he lived, he might have kept the Northern Democrats united behind the effort to preserve the Union. As it was, only about a third of the Northern Democrats supported Lincoln's conduct of the war. Known as **War Democrats**, they opposed other Republican policies, such as high tariffs and a central banking system.

By 1864, a presidential election year, the majority of Northern Democrats favored an immediate end to the long war. For this reason, they were known as **Peace Democrats**. Most of the Peace Democrats wanted the Union preserved. But they thought this should be done by discussion and compromise, not by war. A minority of Peace Democrats acted in ways that approached treason. This group of Peace Democrats who opposed Lincoln's policy during the Civil War earned the name of **Copperheads**, after the snake that is said to strike without warning.

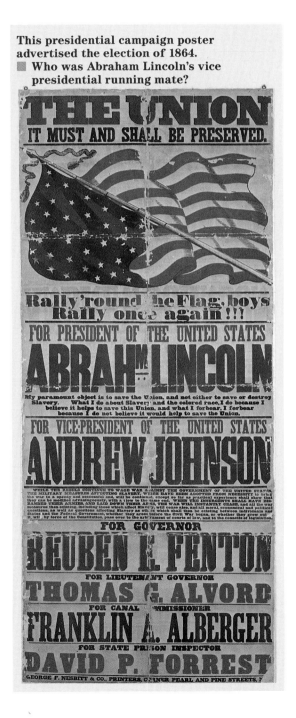

This presidential campaign poster advertised the election of 1864.
■ Who was Abraham Lincoln's vice presidential running mate?

Born: 1809, Hardin County (now Larue County), Kentucky.
Education: Largely self-educated.
Training: Storekeeper, public official, lawyer.
To presidency from: Illinois.
Position when elected: In private law practice.
Political party: Republican.
Married: Mary Todd.
Children: Four sons.
Died: 1865, assassinated at the age of 56 by John Wilkes Booth, a deranged actor.
Other facts: His own description of himself: "in height, 6 feet 4 inches, nearly; lean in flesh, weighing on an average of 180 pounds; dark complexion, with coarse black hair and grey eyes." Traveled by flatboat down the Mississippi when he was 19. Postmaster for 3 years at New Salem, Illinois.
During his presidency: A national income tax was enacted for the first time.

ABRAHAM LINCOLN
16th President
1861 · 1865

National Portrait Gallery, gift of Mr. and Mrs. David A. Morse detail

As president of the Confederacy, Jefferson Davis faced opposition from Confederate state governors and other "states' righters." President Davis favored a strong central government for the Confederacy. At several critical times, Confederate state governors resisted orders from the central government at Richmond. The doctrine of states' rights was, of course, one of the founding ideas of the Confederacy. In fact, some historians have written that the Confederacy died from an overdose of states' rights.

The Election of 1864   The Confederate constitution called for a single 6-year term for its president. So Jefferson Davis did not have to face the task of a presidential election in the middle of the war. This was not the case, though, with Abraham Lincoln. Republicans looked to the War Democrats for support as the election year of 1864 came closer. In fact, the Republican party name was not used that year. A new party, the **Union party**, took the place of

the Republican party. For a time in early 1864 it was not even certain that Lincoln would receive the presidential nomination of the Union party.

At its convention, however, the new party selected Lincoln without great opposition. The party's choice for Vice President was Andrew Johnson. He was a Democrat from Tennessee but had remained loyal to the Union when Tennessee joined the Confederacy. Andrew Johnson was nominated to attract votes from the War Democrats and from the border states.

Peace Democrats nominated General George B. McClellan. In their party platform, the Peace Democrats declared that the war was a failure and should be ended by recognizing the independence of the Confederate States of America. McClellan rejected this part of the Peace Democrats' platform. If he approved, he said, he could not face his old comrades-in-arms. Peace Democrats thought they had a good chance to win. The war seemed to be going badly for the Union in the summer of 1864.

388

John Wilkes Booth shoots Lincoln at Ford's Theater. Booth jumped down to the stage and got away, even though he tripped and broke his leg.
■ What do you see in the picture that might cause Booth to trip?

By election time, however, the war was turning in the Union's favor. Lincoln had advised Northern voters, "Don't swap horses in the middle of the stream." The voters took his advice and returned him to office for a second term. But only a little more than a month after his second inauguration, Abraham Lincoln's life came to a sudden, violent end.

Lincoln's Assassination On the night of April 14, 1865, President and Mrs. Lincoln attended a performance of *Our American Cousin,* a comedy, at Ford's Theater in Washington. An actor named John Wilkes Booth shot Lincoln as the President watched the play. Apparently Booth sought revenge for the South's defeat by shooting the President of the United States. Some of his friends had plotted to shoot the Vice President, the secretary of state, and other leaders at the same time, but only Booth succeeded. Booth escaped to Virginia and was later caught.

Friends carried the wounded Lincoln to a rooming house across from Ford's Theater. There, the morning after Booth's attack, Lincoln died without regaining consciousness. After Lincoln's death, Northerners forgot the cruel things many of them had said about him. Crowds wept as a funeral train returned his body to Springfield, Illinois, for burial. Lincoln had left there only a little more than 4 years before.

CHECKUP

1. Who ran against Lincoln in the election of 1864? Why?
2. What opposition did Davis face as president of the Confederacy?
3. Why was the Union party formed?
4. How did Lincoln die?
5. **Thinking Critically** Do you think it would have been possible to end the war by discussion in 1864? Why or why not?

Using Thematic Maps

PLACE GEOGRAPHY ON THEMATIC MAPS

All maps give different kinds of information about places. Thematic maps show a particular kind of information, such as battles and military action in the Civil War. In this chapter are several thematic maps. Each shows military action in the Civil War.

SKILLS PRACTICE

Use the map below to decide whether the statements are true or false. On a separate sheet of paper, write **True** if the statement is true and **False** if it is false.

1. After leaving Atlanta, Sherman led his troops across Georgia and then northward into South Carolina.
2. The Pee Dee River separates South Carolina and Georgia.
3. After being defeated at Atlanta, General John B. Hood's Confederate forces crossed the Chattahoochee River and retreated into Alabama.
4. Appomattox Court House in Virginia is between the Roanoke River and James River.
5. Norfolk, Virginia, was a major battle site in 1864.
6. The Union blockade was around the city of Charleston.

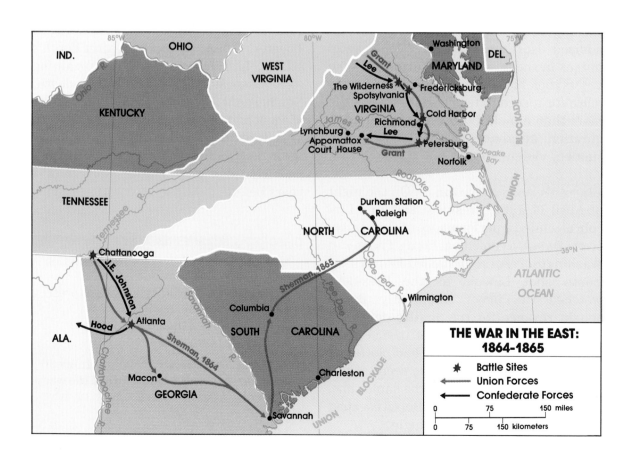

MAIN IDEAS

1. In the Civil War the goal of the North was to preserve the Union, and the goal of the South was to achieve independence.
2. The war that began at Fort Sumter in 1861 lasted 4 years.
3. The Emancipation Proclamation, issued by Lincoln in 1863, freed no slaves immediately but resulted in the enlistment of about 200,000 black soldiers in the Union army. The Emancipation Proclamation freed only those slaves living in the states that were in rebellion with the United States.
4. The battle of Gettysburg is considered the turning point of the war because Lee and his army retreated to Virginia.
5. In the presidential election of 1864, Lincoln faced opposition from Peace Democrats and Radical Republicans.
6. The war ended in 1865 with the surrender of General Lee to General Grant at Appomattox Court House.
7. The Civil War resulted in a tremendous number of casualties for both sides, and it left the South in economic ruin.

VOCABULARY REVIEW

On a separate sheet of paper, write the letter of the best ending for each statement.

1. The border states (**a**) bordered on the Gulf of Mexico, (**b**) included Virginia, (**c**) remained within the Union, (**d**) joined the Confederacy.
2. The Emancipation Proclamation applied to (**a**) only those states still in rebellion against the United States, (**b**) all states in which slavery was legal, (**c**) the border states, (**d**) only Virginia, South Carolina, and Georgia.
3. The Anaconda Plan included (**a**) a naval blockade of Confederate ports, (**b**) releasing snakes in the Appalachian Mountains of the South, (**c**) a refusal to invade Virginia, (**d**) all these things.
4. Draft acts (**a**) took place in the Union but not in the Confederacy, (**b**) took place in both the Union and the Confederacy,

(**c**) were welcomed in both the Union and the Confederacy, (**d**) were fair to rich and poor alike.
5. A greenback was (**a**) a rookie soldier, (**b**) an old gold coin, (**c**) a Confederate sympathizer, (**d**) a piece of Union paper money.

CHAPTER CHECKUP

1. Compare the goals of the Union and the Confederacy at the beginning of the war.
2. Why were the border states important during the Civil War?
3. During what years were the Confederates most successful in the war?
4. Why did the Confederacy expect aid from Great Britain or France?
5. Why was the Civil War criticized as "a rich man's war and a poor man's fight"?
6. How was the Civil War different from earlier wars fought in the United States?
7. Why was Lincoln able to win the election of 1864?
8. **Thinking Critically** Do you think Lincoln was right in trying to save the Union? Why or why not?
9. **Thinking Critically** Why do you think it has been written that the South died from an overdose of states' rights?

APPLYING KNOWLEDGE

1. Make a chart listing the advantages and disadvantages the North and the South faced during the Civil War. Which do you think was most important in helping the North to win the war? Explain.
2. After doing research, prepare either a written or an oral report on one of the following topics:

Famous Generals of the Confederacy
Famous Generals of the Union
Women and the War
The War on the Water
Photography During the War
Medicine and the War
Black Soldiers in the War

16 Reconstruction

1865–1877

Restoring a Divided Nation

What were the differences between Lincoln's and Johnson's plan for Reconstruction and the congressional plan?

Reconstruction	Reconstruction
Lincoln-Johnson	Act of 1867
plan	impeach

From Tailor to President   Persons visiting Andrew Johnson's tailoring shop in Greeneville, Tennessee, in the early 1830s could see the stocky, broad-shouldered tailor sitting cross-legged as he sewed. Andrew Johnson had crossed the mountains to live in eastern Tennessee when he was 17. There he met Eliza McCardle, who was 15 years old at the time. The two were married the following year.

Those early years were hard ones as Johnson struggled to make a living for himself and his family in his Greeneville tailoring shop. He was ambitious and a hard worker. At first, however, his lack of education held him back. He could read only a little and was unable to write more than his name. Anything beyond the simplest arithmetic was a mystery to him.

Eliza McCardle Johnson helped her husband in his tailoring shop. But she helped him with more than his sewing. She taught him to write. As he sewed, she read to him. In the evenings she worked to improve his knowledge of mathematics.

Andrew Johnson began his political career as a friend to working people. First, he was mayor of Greeneville. Later, he became a member of the Tennessee legislature, a United States representative, a governor, and a senator. After the Union army's advance into Tennessee in 1862, Abraham Lincoln made Johnson military governor of that state. During his whole career, Andrew Johnson upheld the Union and opposed the aristocratic slaveholders of the Southern states. Johnson was chosen as Lincoln's Vice President in 1864.

Some Important Questions   Historians call the years from 1865 to 1877 the time of **Reconstruction**. These were the years in which the United States had to rebuild and restore a divided nation.

Reconstruction raised a number of questions. How could the Confederate states be restored to the Union? How could the war damage to the South be repaired? How could 4 million slaves be helped as free persons? Who would control the Reconstruction process — the President or Congress?

Cotton plantations were the basis of the southern economy before the Civil War. After the Civil War the South's economy needed to be rebuilt or reconstructed.
■ When did Reconstruction end?

detail, "The Cotton Pickers," 1876, Winslow Homer, United States, 1836–1910. The Los Angeles County Museum of Arts

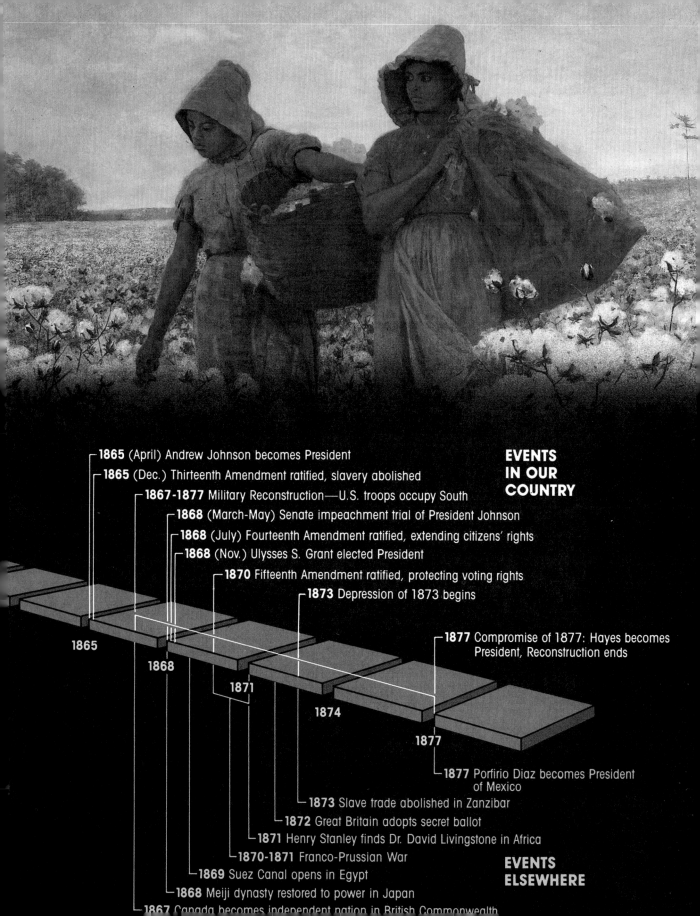

EVENTS IN OUR COUNTRY

1865 (April) Andrew Johnson becomes President

1865 (Dec.) Thirteenth Amendment ratified, slavery abolished

1867-1877 Military Reconstruction—U.S. troops occupy South

1868 (March-May) Senate impeachment trial of President Johnson

1868 (July) Fourteenth Amendment ratified, extending citizens' rights

1868 (Nov.) Ulysses S. Grant elected President

1870 Fifteenth Amendment ratified, protecting voting rights

1873 Depression of 1873 begins

1877 Compromise of 1877: Hayes becomes President, Reconstruction ends

1865

1868

1871

1874

1877

1877 Porfirio Diaz becomes President of Mexico

1873 Slave trade abolished in Zanzibar

1872 Great Britain adopts secret ballot

1871 Henry Stanley finds Dr. David Livingstone in Africa

1870-1871 Franco-Prussian War

1869 Suez Canal opens in Egypt

1868 Meiji dynasty restored to power in Japan

1867 Canada becomes independent nation in British Commonwealth

EVENTS ELSEWHERE

The Lincoln-Johnson Plan   In 1863, Lincoln had announced his plan for restoring the Union.   The first step, according to the President's plan, was for a certain number of men in a Confederate state to take an oath of allegiance to the Union. This number was to be 10 percent of the number that had voted in that state in the election of 1860.   Persons taking the oath of allegiance pledged themselves to support the Constitution of the United States.   They agreed to obey laws passed by the United States Congress and to honor the President's proclamations on slavery. When the 10 percent had taken the oath of allegiance, they could organize a state government.   The President would then recognize it as the true and loyal government of that state.

When Andrew Johnson became President, he followed the 10 percent plan with some additions.   The state governments formed under the plan had to repeal their secession acts. They had to promise that they would make no attempt to pay the Confederate war debt.   Finally, they had to ratify the proposed Thirteenth Amendment to the Constitution, which said: "Neither slavery nor involuntary servitude, except as a punishment for crime whereof the party shall have been duly convicted, shall exist within the United States, or any place subject to their jurisdiction." (See page 211.)

One by one, governments in the former Confederate states carried out the requirements of the **Lincoln-Johnson plan**.   By late fall in 1865, the amendment outlawing slavery had been ratified, and all 11 states had been restored to the Union.   This entitled them to elect members to the Congress of the United States.

Congress Objects   But Congress had its own ideas about Reconstruction.   Some Republican members thought the Lincoln-Johnson plan was too easy on the South. They noted that the old Confederate states,

You can see the shattered ruins of a flour mill in Richmond, Virginia, the Confederate capital, shortly after the end of the Civil War.
■ How would such total destruction make it difficult for the South to recover from the war's effects?

After the Civil War, freed slaves faced many obstacles as they tried to become part of the community.

◼ **What kind of problems are the black Americans facing in this picture?**

acting under the Johnson plan, had chosen as their representatives some of the very people who had been leaders of the rebellion. These included six former members of the Confederate Congress. Perhaps it was understandable that Southern voters would select as leaders the people who had led them in the past. But were former Confederates now to be welcomed into the United States Congress? Were they to be permitted to share in making laws, as though nothing had happened in the preceding 4 years?

Moreover, the newly elected representatives and senators from the South were all Democrats. If they were to join the Northern Democrats already in Congress, the Republican party would lose its majority —and its control of Congress. Republicans were determined to prevent this.

The strongest congressional opposition to the Lincoln-Johnson plan came from a group known as the Radical Republicans. Their goal was to make good at last on the words of the Declaration of Independence, "that all men are created equal." They wanted to raise the freed slaves to full legal equality with whites. This meant that blacks would have the right to vote, would enjoy full civil rights, and would be free from all racial discrimination. Such a sweeping change in Southern society would not be possible, they knew, under the Johnson plan.

Thus, when the newly elected representatives and senators from the former Confederate states arrived in Washington in December 1865, Congress refused to seat them. Instead, the Republicans in Congress offered their own program for restoring the Southern states to the Union. Under the Republican plan, it would be much harder for the Confederate states to resume their places in the Union. For one thing, the Republican congressional plan required the seceded states to approve the Fourteenth Amendment, as well as the Thirteenth, before reentering the Union.

The Fourteenth Amendment in its first section made all persons born or naturalized in the United States "citizens of the

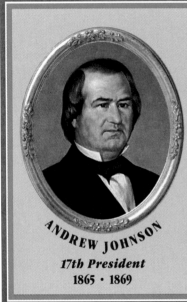

Born: 1808, Raleigh, North Carolina.
Education: Largely self-educated.
Training: Tailor, public official.
To presidency from: Tennessee.
Position when taking office: Vice President.
Political party: Democratic, but elected Vice President on the ticket of the wartime Union party.
Married: Eliza McCardle.
Children: Three sons, two daughters.
Died: 1875, Carter Station, Tennessee.
Other facts: Apprenticed to a tailor at the age of 13. Married at 18 and taught to write by his wife. The only Southern senator who refused to secede with his state. The only President who was impeached. Later became the only former President to serve as a senator.
During his presidency: The United States purchased Alaska from Russia for $7.2 million.

ANDREW JOHNSON
17th President
1865 · 1869

National Portrait Gallery, Smithsonian Institution, Washington, DC., detail

United States and of the state wherein they reside." The first section also prohibited any state from taking away "privileges or immunities" of citizens of the United States. Nor could any state deny to persons within its borders "the equal protection of the laws." Clearly, this section of the Fourteenth Amendment was designed to make black people who were born in the United States citizens. Furthermore, the Fourteenth Amendment attempted to protect them from illegal actions by states or individuals. Thus the amendment was one attempt to help the former slaves in their new status as free people.

Other parts of the Fourteenth Amendment were directed more against Southern Democrats. The second section said that the number of members a state had in Congress could be reduced if that state did not allow any of its adult male citizens the right to vote. In its third section, the Fourteenth Amendment stated that those who had held offices in the South before the war could no longer serve in government if they had taken part in the rebellion. The amendment also said that the United States war debt would be paid. However, the Confederate war debt would *not* be paid. Finally, under the terms of the Fourteenth Amendment to the Constitution, no one who had held slaves would ever be paid for their loss.

Johnson and Congress Struggle President Johnson advised the 11 former Confederate states to reject the Fourteenth Amendment. He particularly opposed the section barring former Southern officeholders from again holding office if they had taken part in the rebellion. Where else, Johnson asked, could the South look for experienced leadership? Moreover, Johnson held that the Southern states had already been restored to the Union by accepting the Lincoln-Johnson plan.

In the summer of 1866, Tennessee ratified the Fourteenth Amendment and returned to the Union. The other ten states of the former Confederacy refused. Radical Republicans declared that these Southern states needed to be treated harshly. For this reason the congressional elections of 1866 were a contest between Johnson's "easy" Reconstruction program and the Radical Republicans' "hard" plan.

President Johnson fought for control over the Reconstruction process. In August 1866 he went on a speaking tour through the North. Hecklers taunted the President almost everywhere he spoke. Angrily, the hotheaded Johnson responded with many angry and ill-considered remarks. He had badly misjudged public opinion among the Northern voters. When the congressional elections were over, the Republicans, led by the Radicals, were still firmly in control of Congress and the Reconstruction process.

Not all Northern voters thought the same way. Still, a large number thought the former Confederate states should be punished. They felt that the South had brought on a long, costly, and bloody war. Some others felt that blacks deserved the same rights as whites and that the Radical Republican program would guarantee equal treatment. Northern industrialists feared that Southern Democrats in Congress would repeal economic benefits favored by the Republicans.

Some Northern business leaders saw a chance to get control of the South's natural resources by supporting a hard Reconstruction program. Republican politicians believed they could stay in power only if they supported the Radical program. That program would deny many white Southerners the right to vote or hold office. It would also permit eligible blacks to vote, and they presumably would vote for Republicans out of gratitude.

This cartoon pictures Johnson as a little boy who has unwisely involved himself in constitutional issues, with disastrous results.
■ **What portion of the Constitution do you think the cartoonist might be referring to in particular?**

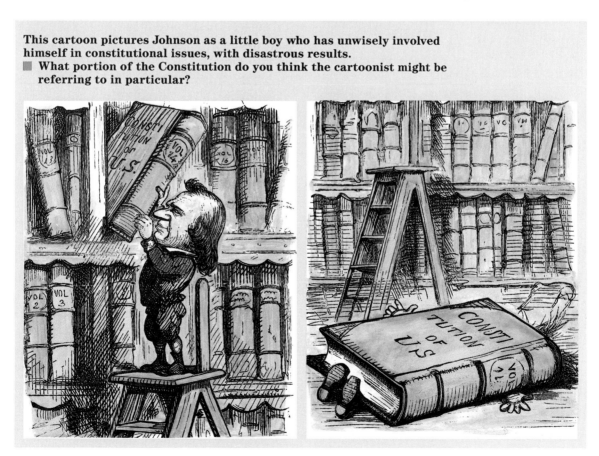

Military Occupation For these reasons, Republicans swept to a big victory in the congressional elections of 1866. The Radicals returned to Washington, set on passing their own Reconstruction bill. President Johnson vetoed it, but on March 2, 1867, Congress easily overrode the veto and passed what was called the **Reconstruction Act of 1867**.

This act divided the former Confederate States of America, except for Tennessee, into five military districts. In each district a United States army general was in charge, with soldiers to carry out his orders. To get out from under military rule, a state had to accept the Fourteenth Amendment and guarantee black men the right to vote. Only then would Congress

A Senate official gives Johnson a summons to appear for his impeachment trial.
■ How do you think Johnson reacted to the news that he would be tried?

agree to accept that state's senators and representatives. United States troops might stay, however, until Congress was satisfied that the state was "reconstructed." In some Southern states, military occupation continued until 1877. The presence of United States troops in those states caused a good deal of resentment toward the federal government.

Johnson Impeached After arranging for military occupation in the South, the Radical Republicans set out to deal with President Johnson. The House of Representatives **impeached** the President— that is, they accused him of "high crimes and misdemeanors" in 11 separate articles. The accusations against him were based on Radical Republican opposition to his policies and on his attempt to fire a member of his Cabinet, not on any actual crimes he had committed. Still, if Johnson were found guilty of these offenses, he would be removed from office.

The Constitution provides that impeachment trials shall take place in the Senate, with senators acting as a jury. When the person on trial is the President, the Chief Justice must serve as the presiding judge. (See page 196.) Johnson's dramatic trial lasted from March 30 until May 16, 1868. Radicals were sure that the necessary two thirds of the senators—36 —would vote for Johnson's conviction. But the final vote was 35 for conviction and 19 for acquittal. Thus the Radicals failed to convict Johnson by the margin of 1 vote. Seven Republicans joined 12 Democrats in voting Johnson not guilty.

Johnson was nearly powerless as he served out the remainder of his term. The Radical failure to remove him, however, had far-reaching effects. It meant that the weapon of impeachment would not be freely or easily used in future conflicts

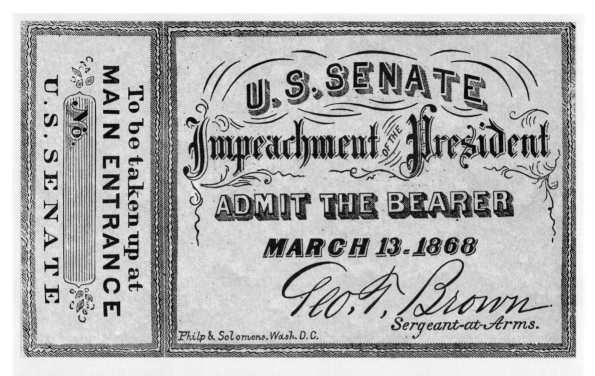

The public was so curious about seeing a President on trial that the Senate had to issue tickets to admit guests to its galleries for the sessions of the trial.
■ Why would so many people want to see this trial?

between Congress and the President. Johnson's fight to save his presidency also helped to ensure the future independence of the executive branch of government.

The Fifteenth Amendment For the presidential election of 1868, the Democrats chose Horatio Seymour, a former governor of New York, as their candidate. The Republicans nominated General Ulysses S. Grant. Grant won a big margin in electoral votes with the help of black voters in the South. This convinced the Radical Republicans that they needed the votes of Southern blacks in future elections. They soon proposed what, in 1870, became the Fifteenth Amendment to the Constitution.

The Fifteenth Amendment forbade any state to deny the right to vote because of "race, color, or previous condition of ser-

vitude." (See page 213.) Black voters in the South supported Grant's reelection to the presidency in 1872. It seemed as if the Radical program for Reconstruction had triumphed completely.

CHECKUP

1. What were the main features of the Lincoln-Johnson plan for Reconstruction?
2. Why did the Radical Republicans gain allies after the election of the first postwar Congress?
3. What were the results of Andrew Johnson's impeachment trial?
4. Why were the Thirteenth, Fourteenth, and Fifteenth Amendments added to the Constitution?
5. **Thinking Critically** Why did the framers of the Constitution make it so difficult to impeach a President?

The Reconstructed South

How did blacks and whites in the South react to Reconstruction?

VOCABULARY

Freedmen's Bureau	scalawag
Black Codes	crop lien system
Amnesty Act	sharecropping
carpetbagger	Ku Klux Klan
	New South

"The Poor South" In 1850, John C. Calhoun had died murmuring, "The South, the poor South." The future he imagined came true 15 years later. In 1865 the South was indeed poor, defeated, and nearly destroyed by war. Confederate dollars and bonds were worthless. Confederate war veterans straggled home, their uniforms in tatters, their feet often bare. Home folks could do little for them but thank them for the sacrifices they had made.

Confederate soldiers often returned home to find destruction of their property.
■ **What has happened to this Confederate soldier's home?**

The war had exhausted white Southerners. For most of them the South was a land of war ruins and war cripples. Their hopes and their fortunes were gone.

For black Southerners, Lincoln's assassination brought sadness and fear. Lincoln had represented the end of slavery and great hope for future progress. But even after Lincoln's death, hope remained. Black people in the South knew they had many friends in Congress and many supporters among the Northern people, both white and black.

The Freedmen's Bureau Months before the end of the war, slaves freed by the Emancipation Proclamation had begun to live a free life. Thousands had enlisted in the Union army. Others stayed in the area where they had served as slaves. In many cases they went to work on land abandoned by their former masters.

In 1865, Congress set up the **Freedmen's Bureau** to help the freed slaves. This was the first time that the national government had given aid to large numbers of people. The Freedmen's Bureau furnished food and supplies for thousands of poor people, both white and black. It found jobs for those without work and homes for those without shelter.

The Freedmen's Bureau organized efforts for the education of the freed slaves. In the 5 years of its existence, the Freedmen's Bureau built 4,300 schools and hired 3,300 teachers. General Oliver O. Howard headed the Freedmen's Bureau. He had fought at Gettysburg and had marched through Georgia with General Sherman. In 1867 he founded Howard University, in Washington, D.C. Hampton Institute, Fisk University, and Atlanta University were also founded during Reconstruction to provide educations for black people.

Setting up schools for freed slaves was just one of the many accomplishments of the Freedmen's Bureau.
■ What is unusual about this classroom and the students who study in it?

Black Codes In spite of aid given by the Freedmen's Bureau, Southern blacks had a rough time after the war. Many white Southerners could not or would not accept the new situation. As a visitor in the post-war South put it, freed blacks "received a hundred blows for every helping hand."

Some of these blows came from the state governments established under the Lincoln-Johnson plan. Legislators in these state governments passed laws that became known as **Black Codes**. The Black Codes differed from state to state. In general, however, they put restrictions on freed blacks that were not applied to Southern whites.

Some of the laws forbade former slaves from moving freely from one place to another. Other provisions of the Black Codes made it illegal for freedmen to possess firearms, to sit on juries, to vote, to hold office, or to change jobs. In some states, blacks were forbidden to own land and to testify against white people in court. Moreover, the Black Codes sometimes applied more severe penalties to black offenders than to whites guilty of the same crimes.

White Southerners declared that these Black Codes were needed to put former slaves back to work and to keep them from roaming restlessly all over the South. Many Northerners believed that the Black Codes were an attempt to restore slavery under another name. As it turned out, these controversial Southern laws

Federal troops stand outside their quarters in occupied New Orleans. How are different groups of local citizens reacting to the presence of United States soldiers in their city?

were one of the main reasons for the Radical Republican victories in the congressional elections of 1866.

Reconstruction Governments Under the Reconstruction Act the army sent some 20,000 soldiers (along with some black militiamen) into ten states of the South. Military governments took the place of the state governments set up under the Lincoln-Johnson plan. Under the direction of the army, new civilian governments were put in charge in these ten states. These Reconstruction state governments then started to repair the war damage and to build a new social and political order in the South. Such a huge task would have challenged the wisdom and skill of the wisest and best leaders.

Some leaders in these new state governments meant well but were lacking in wisdom and experience. Others were corrupt. The third section of the Fourteenth Amendment barred the South's most experienced leaders from participation in government. In 1872, Congress repealed this law by passing the **Amnesty Act**. This allowed all but about 500 former Confederate officials to take part in government.

Carpetbaggers and Scalawags Until 1872, and to some extent even after that, many leaders of Southern state governments were **carpetbaggers**. Carpetbaggers were Northerners who came south after the war. Many of them carried their belongings in luggage made of carpeting. This was the fashion of the times, since carpeting was durable. Some carpetbaggers sincerely wanted to help in the rebuilding of the South. Others were out to profit from the unsettled conditions. Some of these people got leading positions in state governments.

Some white Southerners who worked with the carpetbaggers gained positions of influence in the state governments. Some of these Southerners had the best of intentions. Others simply aimed to gain power for themselves. The old ruling class looked down on these people and called them **scalawags**, a scornful term used to describe mean, runty farm animals.

The new Southern state governments spent money for a variety of purposes, and they spent a lot of it. South Carolina's legislature, for example, spent large sums for rich furnishings in the new state capitol. Louisiana's carpetbag government increased the state debt by $34 million, an immense sum for the time. Still, much of the money spent by carpetbag governments went for good causes. The repair of war damages cost many millions of dollars. Construction of schools for Southern children also cost millions. The carpetbag governments of the Reconstruction period can be credited with creating a public education system for the South.

Black Voters   The Fourteenth and Fifteenth Amendments made it possible for black men to vote and hold office in the South throughout the Reconstruction years. Blacks held every kind of office, from county sheriff to governor and senator. Black voters outnumbered white voters in several states for a time, but only once—in South Carolina—did black people have a majority in a state legislature. Even that was only in one house and for only a few years.

Fourteen blacks served in the United States Congress during the Reconstruction years. Joseph Hayne Rainey of South Carolina was the first black to serve in the House of Representatives. He was a member of that body from 1870 to 1879. Rainey was very effective in speaking for civil rights. He later became an agent for the Treasury Department.

Two black men were chosen as senators from Southern states during Reconstruction. Blanche K. Bruce had been a slave until he escaped to the North. He moved to Mississippi after the war and became a senator in 1874. Pinckney Pinchback was a senator from Louisiana. Pinchback also served briefly as governor of the state of Louisiana.

The Crop Lien System   Of course, most Southerners made their living in other ways than politics after the war. The postwar South had a plentiful supply of land and laborers, both black and white. Yet most small landowners lacked money for seed, tools, and mules to get the land back into production. Plantation owners had somewhat different problems. They had no money to pay people to work on their

Cartoonist Thomas Nast drew this picture of a carpetbagger.
■ **Is Nast's view of this person favorable or unfavorable?**

land, which had formerly been worked by slaves. Often plantation owners sold off part of their land in order to get money.

For plantation owners and small farmers alike, one solution to their problems lay in the **crop lien system**. Through this system, a landowner got seeds, tools, and other necessities from a local merchant. In return, the farmer gave the merchant a first lien on the farm's crop, usually cotton. This meant repaying the merchant first when the year's crop was sold. Often the proceeds did not cover the lien. Consequently, many Southern farmers remained in debt to local merchants until they had to give up their land.

Sharecropping   Another way for Southern farmers to get back into production was by **sharecropping**. Using this method, landowners would get people to

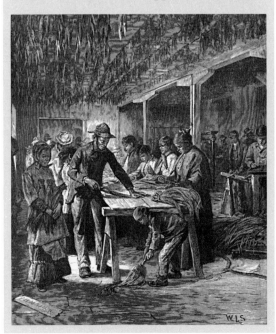

Southern farmers tried to get back into production by lending out land in return for a share of the crops.
■ **What are the sharecroppers harvesting?**

farm their land in return for a share of the crop that was produced. Most landowners insisted that their sharecroppers raise only cotton or tobacco, both good cash crops. This method of farming made it difficult for the postwar South to develop more diversified agriculture.

A great many sharecroppers were freed blacks. (See picture on page 393.) As slaves they had owned no land. The Emancipation Proclamation and the Thirteenth Amendment gave them their freedom but nothing else. Thaddeus Stevens of Pennsylvania, a leader among Radical Republicans in Congress, thought that freed black families should be given 40 acres (16 ha) of land as an economic base. He favored breaking up large Southern plantations in order to distribute this land to freed blacks. But the promise of "40 acres and a mule" for each family of freed blacks never worked out.

Secret Societies   During the early years of Reconstruction, a number of secret societies came into being in the South. Three of these groups were the Order of the White Rose, the Knights of the White Camellia, and, most notorious of all, the **Ku Klux Klan**. In 1866 some Southern war veterans in Pulaski, Tennessee, formed the Klan. It spread rapidly to other Southern states. Klan members met at night, disguised in white hoods and white robes. At first the Klan's goal was to drive carpetbaggers, scalawags, and blacks out of politics. Because Klan members feared the effects that black people's votes would have, the Klan's chief activity became keeping blacks from voting.

Congress responded to the Klan's increasingly violent activities by passing the Ku Klux Klan Act in 1871. This act outlawed the Klan's practices and allowed the President to use military force, if necessary, to stamp them out. President Grant did so, and the Klan's outrages were brought to a halt for a time.

Home Rule Returns   The great majority of Southern whites still resented the fact that blacks had the vote. This was especially true in states where black voters were a majority. In the early 1870s, whites used various means to keep blacks away from the polls. Open threats of violence were common. Even more effective was economic pressure. The war had freed black people, but they still depended on whites for their livelihood. Southern whites warned that they would refuse to hire, rent land to, or give credit to any blacks who dared to vote.

Meanwhile, Congress passed the Amnesty Act of 1872, which restored the vote to all but a handful of whites who had taken part in the rebellion. Together these measures soon produced white voting majorities in the Southern states. Since the carpetbagger governments were Republican, the Democratic party became the white Southerners' instrument for regaining control of their state governments. Democratic voters defeated the Republican carpetbag government in Virginia in 1869. Their resurgence took longer in other states. Nevertheless, white Southern Democrats had taken control of all Southern states by 1877.

With the return of home rule, some Southern leaders tried to make the South an industrial region. By cooperating with Northern industrialists and bankers, Southerners hoped to create a **New South**. By this they meant a land in which manufacturing and commercial interests would play a larger part. In the years following Reconstruction, a number of Southerners began to talk of a New South. The South they envisioned was a prosperous

After Reconstruction, the Southern leaders tried to make the South more industrial. ■ What clues of industry can you find in the picture?

region of cities, factories, and trade, supported by a diversified agriculture. This was a long time coming, however. It would take many years and much more social change before industry was as important in the South as in the North.

CHECKUP

1. How did the future appear for white and for black Southerners at the end of the Civil War?
2. How did the Freedmen's Bureau help Southern blacks?
3. Explain how two systems were used to get Southern agriculture back into production after the Civil War.

4. **Thinking Critically**   Which group do you think white Southerners resented more—carpetbaggers or scalawags? Why?

The End of Reconstruction

What brought Reconstruction in the South to an end?

Union Veterans   Northern soldiers returned to a prosperous land that was almost wholly unscarred by war. Moreover, the United States government gave every veteran $235 in discharge pay, a warm blue uniform, and a ticket to the place where he had joined the army. In the North there were jobs nearly everywhere. Returning soldiers, seeking adventure and opportunity, could go west. Many did.

In 1862, Congress had passed the **Homestead Act**. By this act any citizen or person intending to become a citizen could get 160 acres (65 ha) of government land by meeting certain requirements. Such a person had to be a "head of family" and over 21 years of age. That person had to live on the land continuously for 5 years and pay a fee ranging from $26 to $34.

Women and men who went west as homesteaders faced a solitary life filled with hard work under difficult conditions.
■ What qualities of character does this woman seem to have?

"Homesteader's Wife" by Harvey Dunn; South Dakota Memorial Art Center Collection, Brookings

When these requirements were met, the head of the family owned the land.

The government assumed that anyone being a head of family would be male. Still, there were women who registered for land under the Homestead Act. Many of them got their 160 acres (65 ha) independently, without the aid of men. It is said that these women "sought economic freedom through land ownership . . . sought to earn a living by means other than those of school teacher, maid, or factory worker."

Confederate war veterans were ineligible for the benefits of the Homestead Act until most of them had their citizenship restored by the Amnesty Act of 1872. After that, many of them joined the Union veterans who had already settled on homesteads. Blacks could homestead after the adoption of the Fourteenth Amendment, which made clear their rights as citizens of the United States. Thousands of black families moved west to take up homesteads. Indeed, the Homestead Act was a major reason for the rapid settlement of the Great Plains region after the Civil War. Another reason was the extension of railroad lines. During the Civil War, Congress had passed a number of laws aiding the construction of western railroads.

This kind of economic legislation won widespread support for the Republicans. They were also honored as the party that saved the Union, the party that freed the slaves, and the party of Lincoln. These reasons combined to give the Republicans a slight edge in national politics for years after the Civil War.

Grant's Two Terms   In 1868, General Ulysses S. Grant became another of the war heroes Americans have elected to the presidency. Grant ran the President's office like an army headquarters. Soon after Grant's inauguration he considered annexing the Dominican Republic in the Caribbean Sea.

Grant made some poor appointments to his Cabinet. Though Grant was honest himself, a number of his friends and associates turned out to be corrupt. Several scandals marked Grant's second term as President.

Corrupt Rings   The word *ring* has many meanings. During Grant's two terms as President, however, the word was used to describe a group of people acting outside the law in their own interests. There was, for example, the Whiskey Ring. This was a group of whiskey distillers, most of them in business in St. Louis. For years they worked hand in hand with some corrupt United States officials to keep from paying certain taxes. The Whiskey Ring even got help from Orville E. Babcock, President Grant's secretary. Babcock gave the swindlers advance warning whenever government inspectors were sent to St. Louis from Washington.

The Whiskey Ring was only one of scores of corrupt rings operating in the North at all levels of government. The carpetbagger governments of the South had no monopoly on corruption during these years. Perhaps the most notorious of all the corrupt rings was headed by William Marcy Tweed of New York. The **Tweed Ring** used bribery, graft, and other forms of dishonesty to steal more than $50 million from the city treasury. Eventually "Boss" Tweed was arrested, put on trial for his illegal activities, and found guilty. He fled the United States to escape prison, but was recognized by a Spanish immigration officer. The Spanish official identified Tweed because Thomas Nast's cartoons had made the "Boss" well known all over the world. Tweed was sent back to New York to serve his prison sentence.

Thomas Nast

Millions of Americans know, when they see the figure of a donkey in a political cartoon, that the cartoonist is poking fun at a leader or an idea of the Democratic party. An elephant is just as recognizable as a symbol of the Republican party. But even some of the cartoonists do not know that when they use these symbols, they are borrowing from America's first great political cartoonist, Thomas Nast.

Thomas Nast was born in Germany in 1840. At the age of 6, he came to America with his mother. At 15 he went to work as an engraver, preparing other people's illustrations for printing. By the time he was 23, he was a full-time cartoonist for *Harper's Weekly* magazine. His cartoons in support of the Union cause in the Civil War earned him immediate fame. President Lincoln called him "our best recruiting sergeant" because his work stirred up so much favorable sentiment.

Nast's favorite target of all was "Boss" Tweed of the Tweed Ring. He made Tweed and his henchmen look like the corrupt, self-serving mob that they were. He also made them look ridiculous.

This is the work Nast is best remembered for. But his most lasting contribution to American political life may well be the use of two animals as symbols of our two leading political parties. These symbols are so recognizable that people tend to forget someone had to invent them. But someone did, and that someone was Thomas Nast.

A Disputed Election Just as Ulysses S. Grant began his second term as President in 1873, a depression struck the country. Land and crop prices fell, and thousands were thrown out of work. Still, in spite of this depression and his administration's record of corruption, Grant was unable to understand why the Republicans did not nominate him for a third term in 1876.

Instead, the Republican convention chose Rutherford B. Hayes, the governor of Ohio. Hayes had a reputation for honesty. Moreover, he had reached the rank of major general during the Civil War. The Republicans knew this would make him popular with Union war veterans. The Democrats chose Samuel J. Tilden, the governor of New York, as their candidate. Tilden had won a national reputation by helping to smash the corrupt Tweed Ring.

At first it appeared that Tilden had won the election. He had 250,000 more popular votes than Hayes, and he was just one electoral vote short of a majority. (See pages 201–202, 210–211.) Twenty electoral votes were in dispute, however—19 in three Southern states and one in Oregon. The three Southern states—Florida,

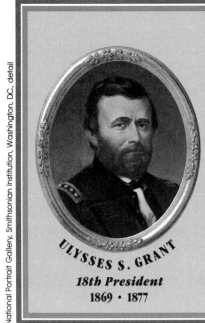

Born: 1822, Point Pleasant, Ohio.
Education: United States Military Academy.
Training: Army officer.
To presidency from: Illinois.
Position when elected: General of the Army.
Political party: Republican.
Married: Julia Dent.
Children: Three sons, one daughter.
Died: 1885.
Other facts: Fought in the Mexican War and served in remote western army posts. Resigned from the army in 1854. Worked at various jobs without much success until Civil War broke out. Lost all his money after leaving the presidency when an investment company he had helped to start went broke. To support his family, wrote his memoirs, which became a financial success.
During his presidency: Joseph Glidden's development of barbed wire solved the problem of fencing the cattle range.

ULYSSES S. GRANT
18th President
1869 · 1877

Louisiana, and South Carolina — were still under military occupation as part of the Radical Republican Reconstruction plan. Each of these states sent two sets of electors for the final count — one set for Tilden, the other for Hayes.

By the time the dispute was settled, it was nearly time to inaugurate a new President. Tensions between Republicans and Democrats had risen to the point that some people feared civil war might break out again. Clearly it was time for a compromise, so Congress appointed a 15-member electoral commission to settle the dispute. A deal was made to make Rutherford B. Hayes President.

To bring about this result, however, Republicans had to make promises to Southern Democratic leaders. For one, soldiers would be withdrawn from those Southern states where they still remained. For another, Hayes promised to pick at least one Southerner for his Cabinet. Finally, leaders of the Republicans in Congress promised to supply money for internal improvements in the South. The day after Hayes took office, he appointed David M. Key of Tennessee to his Cabinet. In April, Hayes ordered the withdrawal of the last troops from the South. These agreements between Republicans and Southern Democrats have sometimes been called the **Compromise of 1877**. It meant the end of Radical Reconstruction.

CHECKUP

1. Contrast the homecoming of the Union war veteran with that of the Confederate veteran.
2. How were Republicans able to remain the dominant political party for a generation following the war?
3. What kind of President was Ulysses S. Grant?
4. Why was the presidential election of 1876 so hotly disputed? How was the dispute settled?
5. **Thinking Critically** What effect do you think the Compromise of 1877 had on Hayes's presidency?

Interpreting Political Cartoons

"BOSS" TWEED

A political cartoon is a drawing that makes a statement about a person, a subject of current public interest, or an important problem. Like a newspaper editorial, it tries to persuade people to see things in a certain way. Sometimes a cartoonist will use a caricature to express a point of view. That is, the drawing will distort or exaggerate a person or thing.

The cartoon below shows Thomas Nast's view of "Boss" Tweed. (Tweed is the fat man on the left. The man beside him, toward the center of the picture, is New York City's mayor. The mayor owed his job to Tweed, who controlled thousands of immigrant voters.) Tweed's powerful New York City political ring swindled millions of dollars from the city trea-

sury. They did this by steering city building contracts to companies that agreed to pay them back part of the contract amount. In 1868 the city began to build a new courthouse. It was supposed to cost $250,000. Three years later the city found that it had spent $8 million — and the building wasn't even finished yet!

SKILLS PRACTICE

Answer the following questions.

1. What question are all the people in the cartoon trying to answer?
2. Who are the people in the background, with their backs to the reader?
3. Why does Nast show all the figures in the cartoon standing in a circle?

WHO STOLE THE PEOPLE'S MONEY?" — DO TELL. N.Y.TIMES. 'TWAS HIM.

MAIN IDEAS

1. After the Civil War, American leaders were confronted with the task of rebuilding and restoring a divided nation.
2. Presidents Lincoln and Johnson favored a Reconstruction plan that treated the Southern states mildly, but the Radical Republicans in Congress favored a plan that would punish the South.
3. The Thirteenth Amendment, Fourteenth Amendment, and Fifteenth Amendment were added to the Constitution with the goal of giving black Americans the same rights enjoyed by white citizens.
4. Blacks in the South had a chance to enjoy new freedoms, get an education, and even win political office during Reconstruction, but they gained little economic power.

VOCABULARY REVIEW

On a separate sheet of paper, write the letter of the term next to the number of its definition.

a. Fourteenth Amendment
b. impeach
c. Black Code
d. carpetbagger
e. Homestead Act
f. Amnesty Act
g. sharecropping
h. Reconstruction
i. Tweed Ring
j. Ku Klux Klan

1. Time of rebuilding after the Civil War
2. A Northerner who went to the South after the war
3. A group of corrupt politicians and businessmen in New York City
4. A way of farming in the South after the Civil War
5. A measure that made native-born Americans citizens
6. A state law restricting freed blacks
7. A secret society whose goal was to maintain white control in the South
8. A law that restored citizenship to most former Confederates
9. To accuse an official of the national government of misconduct
10. A law that made government land available for citizens at low cost

CHAPTER CHECKUP

1. Contrast the Lincoln-Johnson plan with the Reconstruction Act of 1867.
2. Describe the purposes of the Thirteenth, Fourteenth, and Fifteenth Amendments to the Constitution.
3. What were the bad points and the good points of the Radical Reconstruction state governments in the South?
4. Why was a compromise necessary in order to settle the disputed election of 1876?
5. **Thinking Critically** Why were Southerners unable to create the hoped-for "New South" during Reconstruction?
6. **Thinking Critically** Why, do you think, did the years after the Civil War give rise to so much corruption in government, both in the North and the South?

APPLYING KNOWLEDGE

Using information contained in this chapter, write a letter based on one of the following situations.

1. A Northern war veteran describes his plans for reentering civilian life.
2. A Southern veteran writes about his future plans.
3. A former slave tells how the Freedmen's Bureau helped him or her.
4. A white Southerner describes the carpetbag government in his or her state.
5. A New Yorker describes her reaction to one of Thomas Nast's cartoons about "Boss" Tweed.
6. An observer describes Johnson's impeachment trial in a letter to a friend.

17 The Gilded Age

1870–1896

Politics During the Gilded Age

What were some of the features of party politics in the United States during the Gilded Age?

VOCABULARY

Gilded Age	civil service

Two Decades Get a Name   Samuel L. Clemens, better known as Mark Twain, married and settled down in Hartford, Connecticut, in 1872.   One winter night he and his wife invited their neighbors, Mr. and Mrs. Charles Dudley Warner, to have dinner with them.   Warner was a writer, too, though he never became as well known as Mark Twain.   At the time, Charles Dudley Warner was editor of a local newspaper, the *Hartford Courant*.

During the dinner the two men poked fun at the popular novels their wives had been reading.   "Why don't you try to write a better one?" the wives challenged their husbands.   Mark Twain and Charles Dudley Warner accepted the challenge.   The next day they began work together on a novel they called *The Gilded Age*.

The two writers chose the name for their novel carefully.   A thing that is gilded is attractive and shiny on the surface.   Underneath, however, the gilded object may be ugly and cheap.   That is the way the two writers looked at the years in which they lived.   Their novel described the flashy, get-rich-quick society of the United States in the years after the Civil War.   *The Gilded Age* pointed out that underneath the glittering surface lay corruption and false ideals.   Today the novel *The Gilded Age* is all but forgotten.   And yet the name of the novel has lasted.   Historians often call the 20 years between 1870 and 1890 the **Gilded Age**.

Balanced Parties   Leaders of both parties lived up to the compromise that settled the disputed election of 1876.   That is, Republicans in the national government no longer interfered in local affairs in the South.   Democrats had already kept their part of the bargain by allowing the Republican candidate, Rutherford B. Hayes, to become President.

There was little difference between the Democratic and Republican parties during these years.   Nevertheless, the public took an intense interest in politics.   Political speeches and rallies were one of the great forms of public entertainment.   Friends in different parties would even make good-natured bets on the outcome of elections, as if they were sporting events.   Voter turnouts were heavy.   More than 80

During the Gilded Age more people took part in politics than ever before.
The picture on page 413 shows the Democratic convention of 1876.
■ When did Congress pass the Civil Rights Act?

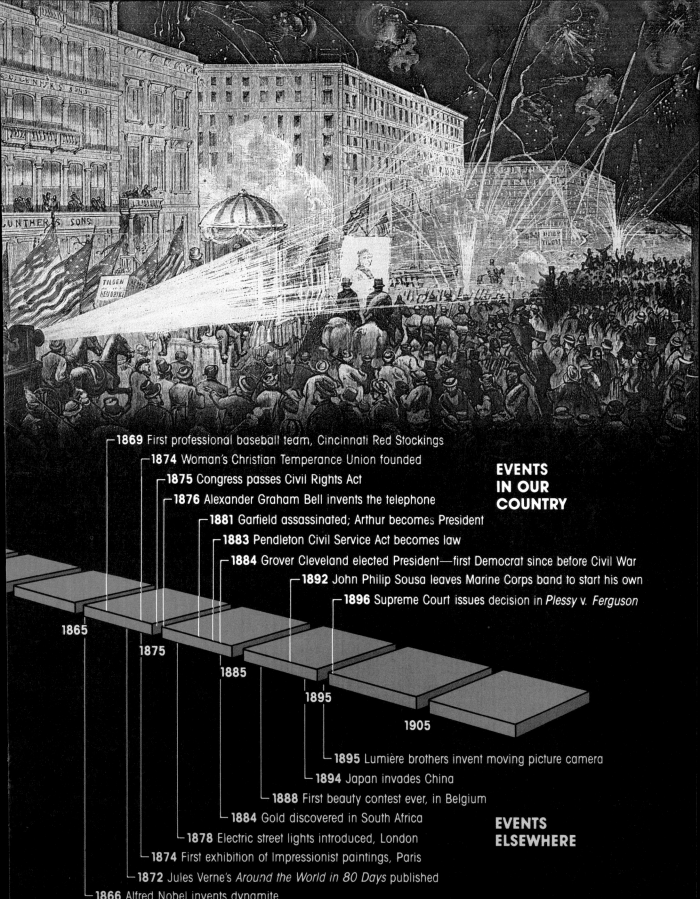

1869 First professional baseball team, Cincinnati Red Stockings
1874 Woman's Christian Temperance Union founded
1875 Congress passes Civil Rights Act
1876 Alexander Graham Bell invents the telephone
1881 Garfield assassinated; Arthur becomes President
1883 Pendleton Civil Service Act becomes law
1884 Grover Cleveland elected President—first Democrat since before Civil War
1892 John Philip Sousa leaves Marine Corps band to start his own
1896 Supreme Court issues decision in *Plessy* v. *Ferguson*

**EVENTS
IN OUR
COUNTRY**

1865
1875
1885
1895
1905

1895 Lumière brothers invent moving picture camera
1894 Japan invades China
1888 First beauty contest ever, in Belgium
1884 Gold discovered in South Africa
1878 Electric street lights introduced, London
1874 First exhibition of Impressionist paintings, Paris
1872 Jules Verne's *Around the World in 80 Days* published
1866 Alfred Nobel invents dynamite

**EVENTS
ELSEWHERE**

percent of all eligible voters cast votes in each presidential election. Today the figure is just a little more than 50 percent.

National elections in the Gilded Age were quite close. Republicans won most of the presidential elections, but the Democrats controlled the House of Representatives. There were few real issues in these elections until the rise of a third party in the early 1890s challenged the Democrats and the Republicans. (You will read about this third party in Chapter 21.) Both the Democratic and the Republican parties became and remained "white men's parties." Gradually, black men were kept from voting and holding office in the southern states, where white Democrats held control. Moreover, women were still denied political rights.

The Hayes Presidency   The scandals of Ulysses S. Grant's administration disgusted many people. The long dispute over the presidential election of 1876 caused much doubt about politicians' honesty. Rutherford B. Hayes, however, conducted himself honorably as President.

Some thoughtful people questioned the wisdom of withdrawing national troops from the southern states. Still, Hayes had made a bargain and he kept his part of it.

Lucy Webb Hayes, wife of the President, was a well-educated woman. Along with her husband she set an example of wholesome respectability. Her critics called her Lemonade Lucy because she refused to serve alcoholic beverages at social occasions in the White House. But this stand won her praise from the Woman's Christian Temperance Union.

President Hayes was conservative in most of his policies, though he did make some weak efforts toward reform of the **civil service**, the system under which people hold jobs in the national government. Since the days of Andrew Jackson, the spoils system had increasingly put unfit people into government jobs. One way to remedy this was to fill these positions through competitive examinations. Still, most politicians wanted to appoint their party workers, and Hayes's attempts at reform failed. In fact, Hayes pleased neither reformers nor conservatives within the Re-

In keeping with the conditions of the Compromise of 1877, federal troops prepare to leave New Orleans.
■ **Is the crowd of citizens to the left friendly or hostile? How can you tell?**

Born: 1822, Delaware, Ohio.
Education: Kenyon College.
Training: Lawyer, army officer, public official.
To presidency from: Ohio.
Position when elected: Governor of Ohio.
Political party: Republican.
Married: Lucy Webb.
Children: Seven sons, one daughter.
Died: 1893, Fremont, Ohio.
Other facts: Practiced law in Cincinnati. Distinguished himself in Civil War. Wounded four times. Rose to rank of major general. Winner in the most disputed presidential election in history. First President to visit the West Coast (San Francisco, 1880). First President to have a telephone in the White House. Declined to seek a second term.
During his presidency: A new transcontinental speed record by rail (3½ days) was set by the Lightning Express.

RUTHERFORD B. HAYES
19th President
1877 · 1881

publican party. As the end of his term approached, the frustrated President announced he would not seek reelection.

The Election of 1880 When the Republican convention met at Chicago in 1880, the fight for the presidential nomination was between Senator James G. Blaine of Maine and former President Grant, who had recently returned from a trip around the world. As the delegates cast ballot after ballot, it became clear that neither Blaine nor Grant could win a majority. To break the deadlock, the delegates compromised. On the thirty-sixth ballot, they picked James A. Garfield of Ohio. Like Hayes, Garfield had been a Civil War general. Chester Arthur, a New York City politician, was chosen as the Republican candidate for Vice President. For years Arthur had been collector of customs for the Port of New York. From this position he controlled many patronage jobs for the Republican political machine in the nation's most populous state.

The Democrats also chose a Civil War general—Winfield Scott Hancock of Pennsylvania—as their presidential candidate. Though the popular vote was very close, Garfield won by a sizable margin in electoral votes.

Garfield and Arthur James A. Garfield was a scholarly man. A graduate of Williams College, he could read and write Latin and Greek. To entertain his friends, he would write Latin with one hand and at the same time write Greek with the other. Yet he was an experienced politician and officeholder, having served for 18 years as a representative from Ohio. Garfield might have been a good President, but he got little chance to show what he could do. On July 2, 1881—less than 4 months after his inauguration—he was shot in the back by Charles J. Guiteau. Guiteau was a disappointed office seeker with a record of unstable behavior.

Garfield lived until September 19. After his death, Guiteau was tried for murder, convicted in spite of his plea of insanity, and hanged on June 30, 1882. By this time Chester A. Arthur was turning out to be an unexpectedly good President.

National Portrait Gallery, Smithsonian Institution, Washington, D.C.. detail

JAMES A. GARFIELD
20th President
1881

Born: 1831, Orange, Ohio.
Education: Williams College.
Training: Teacher, army officer, public official.
To presidency from: Ohio.
Position when elected: Member of Congress.
Political party: Republican.
Married: Lucretia Rudolph.
Children: Four sons, one daughter.
Died: September 19, 1881, about 10 weeks after he had been shot by a disappointed office-seeker in the railroad station in Washington, D.C.
Other facts: Taught Latin, Greek, and other subjects at Hiram College and later became college president. In Civil War, one of the youngest generals in the Union army. A good linguist, campaigned speaking in German before German Americans.
During his presidency: Clara Barton founded the American Red Cross.

Almost overnight he changed from a machine politician to an honest and efficient executive. Garfield's murder by a man who had expected a patronage position caused a great public outcry against the spoils system. Arthur supported a new civil service bill that did much to remedy the evils of the spoils system. This new law set up an impartial Civil Service Commission to administer competitive examinations as a way of finding qualified job candidates. Both Houses of Congress passed this bill, and Arthur signed the Pendleton Act into law in January 1883.

A Democratic President In 1884, Grover Cleveland, the Democratic governor of New York, was elected President, defeating the Republican candidate, James G. Blaine. Cleveland was the first Democrat elected President since James Buchanan in 1856. Like Buchanan, Grover Cleveland was a bachelor when he entered the White House, but in 1886 he married Frances Folsom of Buffalo, New York. Cleveland's bride was the daughter of his friend and law partner. Cleveland was the first and only President to be married in the White House.

Grover Cleveland was one of our hardest-working Presidents. By staying at his desk until 2 or 3 o'clock in the morning, he mastered the details of his job. He improved the civil service and opposed the high protective tariff favored by Republican leaders. In 1888, Benjamin Harrison, the Republican candidate, defeated Cleveland in his try for reelection. However, in 1892, Cleveland won over Harrison and entered the White House for a second term.

CHECKUP

1. How did the Gilded Age get its name?
2. On what matters were Republicans and Democrats in general agreement during the late 1870s and the 1880s?
3. Who were the Republican Presidents during the Gilded Age? Who was the lone Democratic President?
4. **Thinking Critically** If there was little difference between Democrats and Republicans in the Gilded Age, why do you think people were so interested in politics and elections?

Black Americans in the Gilded Age

How did the status of black Americans change during the Gilded Age?

The Civil Rights Act During the era of Reconstruction, many people believed that a new day was dawning for black Americans. Constitutional amendments had ended slavery, made black people citizens, promised them the equal protection of the laws, and given black males the vote. In a final effort to enforce equal treatment of blacks and whites, Congress had passed the Civil Rights Act of 1875. **Civil rights** are the basic rights to which all Americans are entitled. These rights are set forth in several amendments to the Constitution. (See pages 208–210.) Among other things the Civil Rights Act prohibited racial discrimination in places of "public accommodation." These included hotels, railroad stations and passenger cars, steamboats, theaters, "and other places of public amusement."

United States marshalls oversee voting to guarantee that civil rights are upheld.
■ Why, do you think, were soldiers present?

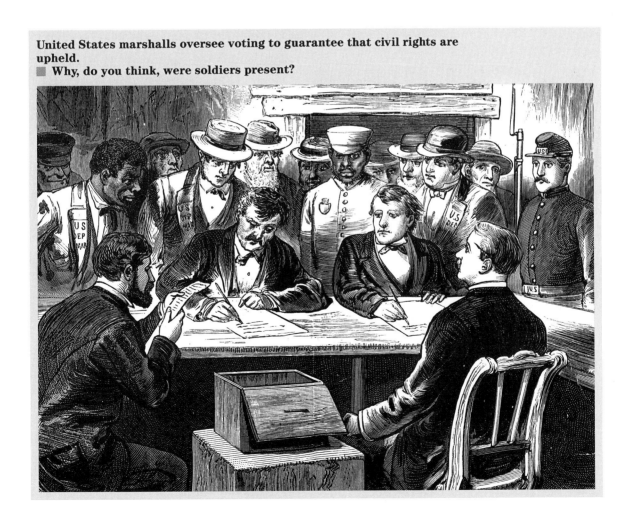

417

Second-class Citizenship Unhappily, Reconstruction turned out to be a false promise. Even before the last federal troops were withdrawn from the southern states in 1877, determined whites were taking away some of the newly won liberties of their former slaves. Then, in 1883, the Supreme Court ruled that the Civil Rights Act of 1875 was unconstitutional. The court said that the Fourteenth Amendment protected citizens only from the actions of state governments, not from the actions of other private citizens. This Supreme Court decision meant that a state could not bar black Americans from using the same hotels, theaters, and other accommodations as whites, but the private owners of those places could.

This Supreme Court decision was in harmony with a new system of relationships between whites and blacks that emerged in the 1880s and 1890s. In this system, blacks were to be **segregated**, or set apart, from whites in nearly all social situations. As part of this development, several southern states began to experiment with laws they hoped would get around the Fourteenth Amendment. Instead of simply prohibiting blacks from using the same facilities as whites — schools, railroad cars, and the like — these laws stated that there should be separate facilities for each race and that these separate facilities should be equal. This system of segregation came to be known as **Jim Crow**, and the laws that enforced it were called Jim Crow laws. The name came from a well-known black character in popular stage performances called minstrel shows. Ironically, the character called Jim Crow — like virtually every other character in the minstrel shows — was usually played by a white actor wearing black makeup.

A Far-reaching Decision In 1896 the United States Supreme Court handed down a historic decision in a case involving a segregation law that had been passed by the Louisiana state legislature in 1890. The law stated:

> All railway companies carrying passengers in their coaches in this state, shall provide equal but separate accommodations for the white and colored races.

A black man named Homer Plessy had taken a seat in a coach reserved for whites. When he refused to leave it, he was arrested. Plessy then sued on the grounds that the Louisiana law violated his rights under the Fourteenth Amendment. Homer Plessy's case against the Louisiana law eventually reached the Supreme Court.

Blacks were driven from whites-only railroad cars all over the country, not just in the South. Such segregation lasted into the middle of the twentieth century.
■ What are the people in back of the seated black man doing?

CHESTER A. ARTHUR
21st President
1881 • 1885

Born: 1830, Fairfield, Vermont.
Education: Union College.
Training: Teacher, lawyer, public official.
To presidency from: New York.
Position when taking office: Vice President.
Political party: Republican.
Married: Ellen Herndon.
Children: Two sons, one daughter.
Died: 1886, New York City.
Other facts: Taught school and studied law. Showed early interest in politics and became leader of Republican machine in New York City. Appointed collector of New York Customs House. Despite reputation as machine politician, served honestly and well as President. Declining health kept him from seriously seeking 4 more years as President.
During his presidency: The Brooklyn Bridge, then the world's largest suspension bridge, was completed in 1883.

In *Plessy* v. *Ferguson* the Supreme Court ruled that the Louisiana law did not violate the Fourteenth Amendment if the separate coaches for blacks and whites were equal. Within a short time after this decision, there were Jim Crow restaurants, Jim Crow washrooms, Jim Crow water fountains, parks, beaches, picnic areas, and more. These facilities could be found all over the South and in parts of the North. And all this was accepted as legal if the facilities were **"separate but equal."** In actual practice the separate facilities were almost never equal. The facilities for blacks seemed to be designed to reinforce the idea that they had become second-class citizens.

Political Rights Meanwhile, southern blacks found their political rights under attack, too. For a few years after home rule was restored in the South, black men had kept voting and holding office. Most black voters favored the Republican party. They thought of it as the party that had won them freedom and the right to vote. This made it hard for black politicians to hold office in the southern states. All these states were under the control of white Democrats.

Still, state legislatures did have a few black Republican members during the Gilded Age. Likewise, there were southern black members in every session of the United States Congress until 1901.

In the 1890s, however, one southern state after another passed laws designed to keep blacks from voting. To do this, they invented a variety of ways to get around the Fifteenth Amendment. So successful were they that one southern state, where 130,000 blacks had been registered voters in 1896, had only 5,300 black voters 4 years later.

At the same time, some southern whites tried to keep black people "in their place" by terrifying them through the horrible practice of **lynching.** A lynching is a murder committed by a mob. During the 1890s, on the average, about three blacks were killed by lynching every week in the southern states.

The Atlanta Compromise   In this worsening situation for blacks, Booker T. Washington made a famous speech in Atlanta, Georgia, in 1895. The occasion was the Cotton States and International Exposition, a miniature world's fair. Washington was the black founder and president of Tuskegee Institute in Alabama, a school for the vocational training of young black men and women. He had already gained national attention for his accomplishments at Tuskegee and for several earlier speeches about relations between the races.

Washington wanted equal rights for blacks as much as anyone did. He knew, however, that whites were not yet ready to agree to this and that they had the power to prevent it. What Washington proposed that September afternoon in 1895 has become known as the **Atlanta Compromise**. Washington advised his fellow blacks to put aside the goals of social and political equality for the present and to concentrate instead on gaining skills that would improve their economic condition. In time, as they gained property, wealth, and experience, they would achieve full equality. Washington urged southern whites to provide economic opportunities to blacks. Do so, he predicted, and "you will find that they will buy your surplus land, make blossom the waste places in your fields, and run your factories." Thus black and white would prosper together in a growing South.

And, Washington concluded, white southerners did not have to fear that this economic cooperation would threaten the separation of the races. Dramatically spreading wide the fingers of one hand, he said, "In all things that are purely social, we can be as separate as the fingers, yet" —at this point he brought his fingers together into a solid fist—"one as the hand in all things essential to mutual progress."

White southerners welcomed Washington's address as a blueprint for race relations in the South. Most blacks also did so at the time. But a number of blacks criticized Washington for accepting, even temporarily, what amounted to second-class citizenship.

W.E.B. Du Bois, an outstanding scholar on the problems of black people in society, agreed only in part with Washington's views. Du Bois felt that the first step toward equality was not economic improvement. The first step was removal of the obstacles that had been thrown up in many states to prevent blacks from voting. In time, the number of people who agreed with Du Bois and criticized Washington would grow.

Booker T. Washington carried his message on the importance of economic advancement to black audiences all around the country.
■ **Why did some blacks disagree with him?**

Like many black families during the exodus of 1879, the Shores family
made a new life for themselves in Nebraska. They are shown here in front
of their sod house and barn.
■ Why would buildings on the plains of Nebraska have to be built from
these materials?

The Exodus of 1879   Not many blacks lived in the northern states during the Gilded Age. For this reason most northerners thought of race relations as only a southern problem. Some blacks did leave the South during these decades. For example, Benjamin Singleton, a former slave, led an emigration of black people from the South to the West in what has been called the **exodus of 1879**.

The exodus of 1879 involved thousands of people. Poor black farmers organized committees, donated their savings, and hired agents to arrange the journey to the West. Most of them settled in either Kansas or Nebraska, where they founded several communities. In most cases the new black residents were accepted, although one group of black emigrants from Mississippi was driven out of Lincoln, Nebraska. On the other hand, Tom Cunningham, a black man, became a police officer in Lincoln. And M.O. Ricketts, a former slave, graduated with honors from the medical school of the University of Nebraska in 1884. Dr. Ricketts was later twice elected to the state legislature of Nebraska.

CHECKUP

1. What evidence was there that black Americans could be considered "second-class citizens" by the end of the Gilded Age?
2. Explain the meaning of the Supreme Court's decisions in the civil rights cases of the 1870s and in *Plessy* v. *Ferguson*.
3. What were the main features of the Atlanta Compromise?
4. **Thinking Critically** Why do you think so many blacks moved west rather than north during the exodus of 1879?

421

Women in the Gilded Age

What were some of the new and changing roles of American women during the Gilded Age?

A Woman for President? Who was the first female candidate for the office of President of the United States? There are at least two claimants to this honor, both well known during the Gilded Age. The earliest was Victoria Woodhull, a lady whose actions created controversy at the time. In 1870, Mrs. Woodhull and her sister were stockbrokers in New York City. They were proud of their success in what was thought of as a man's business. Victoria Woodhull believed women were capable of doing anything. So she announced herself as a candidate for President of the United States in an election that was still 2 years off.

Soon after her announcement, Victoria Woodhull started a weekly newspaper to publicize her candidacy. The newspaper also advocated other reforms she believed in, including women's suffrage, or the right of women to vote. Woodhull tried to get the National Woman Suffrage Association to support her candidacy but was refused. Undaunted, she held her own convention, which declared her to be the presidential candidate of the Equal Rights party. The convention nominated Frederick Douglass for Vice President. The surprised black leader declined the honor, preferring to support Ulysses S. Grant in the election of 1872.

In the unlikely event that Mrs. Woodhull had won the election, her inauguration would have been delayed for 6 months. Only then would she have reached the age of 35, required by the Constitution for a person to assume the presidency. As it turned out, her Equal Rights party was unable to get on the ballot in any state, so she got no votes at all.

Twelve years later a handful of women met in California. They formed the National Equal Rights party and nominated Belva Lockwood, a New York lawyer, for President. Her platform called for equal rights for blacks, women, Indians, and immigrants; regulation of the sale of liquor; uniform marriage and divorce laws in all the states; and universal peace.

Suffrage Denied Belva Lockwood ran a dignified campaign that aroused much public interest. Nevertheless, Susan B. Anthony and many other women's leaders were against her candidacy. They thought

In 1884, Belva Lockwood became the first woman presidential candidate to receive any votes.
▪ Why did Lockwood not vote for herself?

Wyoming, Colorado, Idaho, and Utah granted women the right to vote between 1869 and 1896. These women are preparing to vote in Colorado.
■ **What kind of occasion do the people in this picture think voting in an election is?**

it would bring ridicule to the entire women's suffrage movement. Lockwood did receive 4,140 votes, scattered among six states. None of these votes came from women, for women were still not allowed to vote in a national election.

After the Civil War, Susan B. Anthony and Elizabeth Cady Stanton were shocked that male ex-slaves were given the right to vote, when the right was still denied to women. For the next 50 years, women's organizations made suffrage their chief goal. Their efforts were handicapped for a time by personality and policy clashes, making it difficult to form a united front. For two decades, two different national organizations sought women's suffrage.

Other Reforms   While the right to vote remained the chief goal, women's organizations also worked for other reforms. The temperance movement got new life at the beginning of the Gilded Age through a women's antisaloon crusade that started in Ohio. This led to the formation of the Woman's Christian Temperance Union (WCTU) in 1874. Frances Willard assumed leadership of the organization 5 years later. She committed the organization to a wide range of reforms that appealed to millions of American women.

Women were leaders in bringing the sorry plight of American Indians to the attention of the nation. Early in the Gilded Age, Mary Bonney and Amelia Quinton

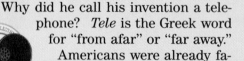

The Telephone

Alexander Graham Bell was born in Scotland. He came to Canada in 1870, and a year later he moved to Boston, where he was a teacher of the deaf. In 1874, Bell conceived a theory for reproducing the human voice by electrical means. Two years later he turned his theory into fact, as the first understandable sentence was transmitted over a short distance. In 1876, assisted by drawings made by Lewis Howard Latimer, a black American electrical engineer and draftsman, Alexander Graham Bell received patents for what he named the telephone.

Why did he call his invention a telephone? *Tele* is the Greek word for "from afar" or "far away." Americans were already familiar with it as part of Samuel F.B. Morse's telegraph. The second part of the word, *phone*, is also Greek. It means "sound" or "speech." Thus *telephone* is a Greek name. It is a better name (or at least shorter) than "an instrument for transmitting speech from far away," which is what it means in English. Can you guess why today we have such a word as *television*?

started the first nationwide organization devoted to improving conditions for the Indians. A few years later, their organization became known as the Women's National Indian Association. This association supported 50 missions working to assist western Indians and convert them to Christianity.

In 1879, Susette La Flesche Tibbles, the daughter of an Omaha Indian chief, made a lecture tour through the East. She used her Indian name, Bright Eyes, and wore Indian costumes when she spoke. The following year, Sarah Winnemucca, daughter of a Paiute chief, met with President Hayes to detail the sufferings of her people. She also published a book, called *Life Among the Paiutes: Their Wrongs and Claims*.

The two young Indian women offered a persuasive argument. They induced many people to support the cause of the American Indian. Among these was Helen Hunt Jackson, a writer whose critical history of the government's shameful treatment of Indians appeared in 1881. This influential book was called *A Century of Dishonor*. Three years later, Mrs. Jackson published *Ramona*, a romantic novel of American Indian and Spanish families' lives in California. It achieved a wide popular success.

Opportunities for Women Going to college was the great adventure for ambitious young women of the Gilded Age. In the Midwest they could go to one of the state universities that were starting to open their doors to women. In the East they could go to one of the new women's colleges offering a liberal arts education similar to that of the men's colleges. From this group of college-educated young women came most of the women's leaders of the next generation.

By the beginning of the Gilded Age, there were three medical schools for women. The University of Michigan's medical school also admitted women along with men. After graduating, however, women had great difficulty in practicing medicine. No established hospital would take them as students, interns, or staff members. The best-trained women in the medical profession had to go to Europe for higher degrees.

For women it was easier to practice law than to practice medicine. Most women lawyers in the Gilded Age were the wives of lawyers. They prepared for admission to the bar by reading law with their husbands. After passing their bar exams, they usually joined their husbands in practice. The early women lawyers were devoted to the cause of women's rights. These lawyers were the first women except for politicians' wives to become active in party politics. This was long before women in most states could vote.

Writing for pay was one way in which women earned money and fame during the Gilded Age. Some of the best women writers of the time produced children's books of high quality. Louisa May Alcott, for example, drew on her own childhood experiences to create realistic youthful characters living in familiar home settings. *St. Nicholas Magazine* for boys and girls printed good books as serials. Mary Mapes Dodge edited the magazine for many years. She insisted on high standards for *St. Nicholas Magazine*, and many of the most capable female and male authors wrote for it.

These students are attending a class at one of the first medical schools for women. Such schools were rare in the nineteenth century, yet even their few graduates had difficulty finding work.
■ Why would a medical school at the time shown here choose to train women separately from men?

Women were hired for the repetitive work of operating the switchboards needed for a new invention, the telephone.
■ Why would an employer in the 1880s want to hire women for this work?

Work for Girls and Women   Teaching was the preferred occupation for women who worked outside the home during the Gilded Age. Indeed, teaching in the elementary schools was on its way to becoming associated primarily with women. At the same time, two inventions created jobs for thousands of girls and women.

A number of people claim to have invented the typewriter. Christopher L. Sholes is generally credited with making the first practical typing machine. By the 1870s, typewriters were being used in thousands of offices. Increasingly, women were being hired as typists. The number of male clerks and stenographers decreased as more women took their place.

From the beginning, women worked at the switchboards made necessary by the invention of the telephone. Thousands of them learned to say "Number, please" as part of their first jobs. Female sales clerks in department stores were replacing male clerks during the Gilded Age, and many women were replacing men in business offices. But the hours for female sales clerks were long, and the pay was low. Moreover, they were given the routine clerical jobs, while male clerks were often promoted to positions as managers.

Jobs in mills and factories were less pleasant, and usually were no better paid. Immigrant girls in particular filled these positions. In the garment trade, **sweatshops** were common. These were shops where workers were employed under unhealthy conditions for long hours at poor wages. Immigrant girls also went into domestic service, working as cooks and maids.

Whether immigrants or native-born Americans, most women during the Gilded Age thought of marriage and a family as their eventual goal. In 1870 there were more than 1.9 million females working at jobs outside their homes. Twenty years later this number had more than doubled, to 4 million. Of this number only about one eighth were married, with a husband present in the home. Nearly three fourths of the females working outside the home in 1890 were young and single.

CHECKUP

1. Name two women who ran for President during the Gilded Age.
2. What reforms occupied the attention of women's organizations during the Gilded Age?
3. Describe opportunities and barriers for women in higher education in the 1870s and 1880s.
4. What kinds of jobs employed hundreds of thousands of women during the Gilded Age?
5. **Thinking Critically** Why do you think four far-western states —Wyoming, Colorado, Idaho, and Utah—were the first states to let women vote?

The Arts in the Gilded Age

How did artists and their works show that there were lasting qualities to the Gilded Age?

VOCABULARY

local colorist

Two Poets   Presidents during the Gilded Age served with little distinction. For black people, the Gilded Age was a time of shrinking opportunities. Though some doors opened for women during the 1870s and 1880s, women failed to win the right to vote. And yet American contributions to the arts were numerous and significant in those years. For example, two of America's greatest poets lived and wrote during the Gilded Age.

Walt Whitman was the older of the two. *Leaves of Grass*, his great collection of poetry, first appeared in 1855, but it was revised and expanded up to the time of Whitman's death in 1892. *Leaves of Grass* reflects the poet's love of life and of America. Some critics disapproved of Whitman's writings. They said that what he wrote was shocking in its subject matter. It also lacked the rhythms and rhymes they expected to find in poetry. Nevertheless, Ralph Waldo Emerson called *Leaves of Grass* "the most extraordinary piece of wit and wisdom that America has yet contributed."

Walt Whitman was a man very much involved with the world. Emily Dickinson was the opposite. Her poems focus on the inner self.

Emily Dickinson lived a normal early life. But as time passed, she became increasingly withdrawn. No one knows when she began writing poetry. Only two of her poems were published before her death in 1886. But she wrote more than 1,700 poems in her Amherst, Massachusetts, home. The manuscripts were preserved by her sister and later published.

Many of these poems are short, made up of just four or eight lines. They often follow the rhythms of the hymns Dickinson and her New England neighbors grew up singing in church. But the poems vary these rhythms with a few startling changes. One Dickinson poem contains the lines, "There is no Frigate like a Book/ To take us Lands away. . . ."

A Trio of Painters   Among the American painters active during the Gilded Age were three masters. One of these, George Inness, was a follower of the Hudson River School in his early career. (See page 305.)

Walt Whitman printed this portrait of himself at the front of *Leaves of Grass*.
■ **Why do you think some people said that Whitman did not "look like" a poet?**

Later, however, he went beyond these painters, developing his own style. His painting *The Coming Storm* is so realistic that viewers might wonder why the boy in the foreground has failed to run for cover. And yet Inness could paint softly. His *June*, finished in 1882, brings thoughts of the beauty seen in that lovely month.

Winslow Homer, another great American painter, went through three different styles and subjects during his career. He first became well known as an illustrator and painter of Civil War scenes. After that, he shifted to landscapes and pictures of rural people working and playing. Like other American painters of the time, Homer traveled abroad. He returned from England in 1882 and took up a third style of painting. This included scenes showing the drama of the sea. *Eight Bells, The Gulf Stream,* and *A Summer Squall* are among Homer's most famous sea pictures.

Thomas Eakins was a third great American painter during the Gilded Age. Eakins had an unusual background for an artist. He had studied anatomy at a medical college. What he learned there made him a master at drawing the human figure at rest or in action. Eakins demonstrated this skill in many fine pictures, including *The Swimming Hole, Between Rounds,* and *Max Schmitt in a Single Scull.*

The Writers Mark Twain not only helped give the Gilded Age its name, but he did his best work during those years. He made Tom Sawyer, Becky Thatcher, Huckleberry Finn, and the Connecticut Yankee

George Inness's painting, *The Coming Storm*, catches the feeling of a muggy summer afternoon.
■ **Why does Inness make the lone human figure in his painting look so small and far away?**

Winslow Homer's painting, _Eight Bells_, shows two sailors using an instrument to measure the position of the sun in order to determine their ship's location. The title refers to the hour—noon—by "ship time."
■ **Why would the sailors want to take this measurement at noon?**

immortal characters. Mark Twain towered over the other writers of the time.

Mark Twain drew on his boyhood experiences on the Mississippi in some of his most popular books. In others he told of his western experiences during the 1860s. For several years he had worked as a newspaper reporter in the mining camp of Virginia City, Nevada, and later in San Francisco. When Twain made use of these backgrounds, his work resembled that of a prominent group of writers of the day, the **local colorists**.

Local colorists were authors who set their tales in a specific region of the United States. They tried to make the scenes, the characters, and the dialogue in their stories typical of that region. Bret Harte became one of the best known of the western local colorists with his stories of the California mining country. Joel Chandler Harris wrote scores of novels and stories of southern life, although he is chiefly identified as author of the Uncle Remus tales. Mary Noailles Murfree became well known under the pen name Charles Egbert Craddock with her first and best book, _In the Tennessee Mountains_, published in 1884. And Sarah Orne Jewett produced hundreds of stories based in the seacoast towns of Maine. Her novel _The Country of the Pointed Firs_ is a classic.

Samantha Allen Speaks Out for Women's Rights

Marietta Holley is largely forgotten today as an author, but her humorous novels were very popular 100 years ago. They dealt with two country characters, Josiah Allen and his wife, Samantha. In the novels, Josiah is pictured as a typical male chauvinist of the time, one who believes that males are always superior to females. Samantha is portrayed as a practical woman whose common-sense arguments for women's rights often leave Josiah speechless.

Josiah Allen believes the only right a woman needs is the right to marry. All women should be put on a pedestal, he says. Samantha, a large woman, wants to know how one as big as she is going to get up on a pedestal in the first place. Then, she asks, how is she going to get down to take care of the children, get back up, then climb down again to prepare supper?

Another time, Josiah says that Samantha's tombstone should read "Wife of Josiah Allen," as was the custom in those

days. A list of his accomplishments could then be put on the tombstone to honor her. Samantha points out that he might die first, in which case she would have "Josiah Allen, husband of Samantha Allen" put on his tombstone. Josiah gets very upset at this. After some thought he announces that if she is going to do that, he is not going to die.

Samantha comments humorously on women's suffrage, temperance, and other issues. In 1892 Marietta Holley wrote *Samantha on the Race Problem*, in which Samantha ridicules white American attitudes toward black people.

The American Publishing Company brought out the first Samantha Allen book in 1873. During the Gilded Age and later, Marietta Holley's Samantha Allen rivaled Mark Twain's Tom Sawyer and Huckleberry Finn in popularity. Samantha's comments helped to advance the ideas of women reformers. In time, her ideas would become everybody's ideas.

Mark Twain had a close association with another classic of the Gilded Age, the *Personal Memoirs of U.S. Grant*. The great general—who was less than a great President—had fallen on hard times in the 1880s. Business losses plunged him into bankruptcy. A series of illnesses and, finally, cancer of the throat brought him near to death. There was a real possibility

that Ulysses S. Grant might die leaving his family in poverty.

Friends came to Grant's rescue. He was taken to a house at Mount McGregor, near Saranac, New York. There, Grant grimly set to work on his memoirs. Mark Twain was then in business as a publisher. He received the final pages of Grant's account only a few days before the tough old general's death. *Personal Memoirs of U.S. Grant* became one of the most successful of all American books. From the sale of the book, Grant's family received nearly $450,000. This sum, a fortune for the time, assured that the general's family would be financially secure in the future.

The Musicians   One of the outstanding musicians of the Gilded Age was John Philip Sousa. When Sousa was only 6 years old, he entered a conservatory to study violin and harmony. He received a solid musical education.

In John Philip Sousa's day, almost every city park contained a bandstand. On summer evenings, crowds of people attended band concerts. Band music fascinated John Philip Sousa. He learned to play all the instruments used in the military bands of the time. In 1880, Sousa became the leader of the United States Marine Corps band. After 12 years in that post, he left the Marine Corps to develop a band of his own.

Sousa turned out to be more than a band leader. He became a composer of marches, a form of music very popular in those days. Sousa's marches are still played today. Among them are "Washington Post March," "Semper Fidelis," "El Capitan," "High School Cadets," and the thrilling "Stars and Stripes Forever." His band toured the United States, played in the capitals of European countries, and made a trip around the world. John Philip Sousa's band and his musical compositions earned for him the title of the March King.

John Philip Sousa's marches came at a time when a great wave of patriotism was covering the scars left by the Civil War. Mark Twain and Charles Dudley Warner were only partly right about the Gilded Age. There was a superficial gilding of life

This poster announced a concert by John Philip Sousa's band.
■ What patriotic symbols can you find in the poster?

during the 1870s and 1880s, but underneath there was strength, not weakness; steel, not tin. During the Gilded Age the United States was laying the foundations for greatness.

CHECKUP

1. How did the poetry of Walt Whitman and Emily Dickinson differ?
2. Give one fact about the paintings of each of the following artists: George Inness, Winslow Homer, Thomas Eakins.
3. For what is musician John Philip Sousa chiefly remembered?
4. **Thinking Critically** Why do you think the writers known as local colorists became prominent at this time in American history?

Distinguishing Between Fact and Opinion

THE GILDED AGE

Some statements people make are statements of *fact*. Others are statements of *opinion*. There are ways to tell the difference. A statement of fact is true—it can be proven. A statement of opinion is what a person thinks or feels. The two statements below show the difference:

1. A touchdown in football counts six points. (Fact)
2. Football is a rougher game than hockey. (Opinion)

You can prove the first statement by reading a rule book or watching the scoreboard at a football game. The second statement is difficult to prove because it says what the person thinks or feels.

SKILLS PRACTICE

Below are facts and opinions about events during the Gilded Age. After reading each statement, mark on a separate sheet of paper whether the statement is fact or opinion. Write **O** for opinion and **F** for fact.

1. In 1876 the United States celebrated the hundredth anniversary of the signing of the Declaration of Independence.
2. A world's fair, held in Philadelphia as part of the celebration, was less interesting than the Cotton States and International Exposition held in Atlanta in 1895.
3. As President, Rutherford B. Hayes was more honest than Chester A. Arthur.
4. After the return of home rule to the South, the Republican party withered and nearly died out in the southern states.
5. Southern states would have been better off if national army troops had remained in the South.
6. The Supreme Court ruled against Homer Plessy in the case of *Plessy* v. *Ferguson.*
7. Booker T. Washington was correct in 1895 when he said economic opportunities were more useful than political rights for black Americans in the South.
8. Thousands of young women got jobs as telephone operators and typists during the Gilded Age.
9. Women were more suitable than men as telephone operators and typists because of their nimble fingers, pleasant voices, and attention to details.
10. Women would have won the right to vote much sooner if they had been able to band together into just one organization.
11. Emily Dickinson would have written better poetry if she had gotten out into the world more.
12. The writings of local colorists were popular in the United States during the last decades of the nineteenth century.

MAIN IDEAS

1. The 1870s and 1880s were sometimes referred to as the Gilded Age because the surface glitter of American society concealed much corruption and ugliness.
2. National elections were close during the Gilded Age because the two major parties were balanced, with few differences after the end of Reconstruction.
3. During the Gilded Age most black Americans were gradually pushed into the status of second-class citizens through custom and by new laws in some states.
4. More and better opportunities in education and careers became available to women, but the right to vote was still to be won.
5. American contributions to literature, painting, and music were substantial during the Gilded Age.

VOCABULARY REVIEW

On a separate sheet of paper, write the letter of the ending that best completes each sentence.

1. The Atlanta Compromise approved (**a**) the goals of the Ku Klux Klan, (**b**) sharecropping and the crop lien system, (**c**) temporary social segregation of blacks and whites, (**d**) the removal of Army troops from the South.
2. The exodus of 1879 referred to (**a**) the departure of carpetbaggers from the South, (**b**) the Cotton States and International Exposition, (**c**) a book written by Ulysses S. Grant, (**d**) a migration of southern black people into Kansas and Nebraska.
3. Civil rights for United States citizens include (**a**) the right to assemble peacefully, (**b**) the right to trial by jury, (**c**) the right of free speech, (**d**) all of these.
4. In *Plessy* v. *Ferguson*, the Supreme Court approved the doctrine of (**a**) civil rights, (**b**) women's suffrage, (**c**) "separate but equal" public facilities, (**d**) none of these.
5. The Gilded Age saw (**a**) the employment of larger numbers of women outside the home, (**b**) the appointment of a woman to the Supreme Court, (**c**) the passage of a national women's suffrage law, (**d**) the nomination of a woman for President by one of the two major parties.

CHAPTER CHECKUP

1. What were the main features of the Atlanta Compromise? Why did Booker T. Washington accept it?
2. Explain how black people became second-class citizens during the Gilded Age.
3. Describe the employment opportunities open to women during the Gilded Age.
4. Explain the chief contributions of each of the following to the arts during the Gilded Age: (**a**) Emily Dickinson, (**b**) Thomas Eakins, (**c**) John Philip Sousa.
5. **Thinking Critically** Why did Booker T. Washington believe that accepting temporary segregation and gaining economic strength was the best way for blacks to pursue equality?
6. **Thinking Critically** Why were lawyers more open than doctors to the ideas of admitting women to their profession?

APPLYING KNOWLEDGE

1. Using information contained in this chapter and in the *Dictionary of American Biography*, do a report on the Civil War activities of each of the men who became President during the Gilded Age.
2. Write a "Help Wanted" advertisement seeking women to work on that "new" invention, the telephone switchboard. Check your local newspaper first to see how "Help Wanted" ads are written today.
3. Have a "literature day" in class. On that occasion read selections from the poetry or fiction of several writers described in this chapter.
4. Prepare a bulletin board with copies of pictures painted by the artists discussed in this chapter.

REVIEWING VOCABULARY

1. popular sovereignty This means letting the people decide, and it sounds like a good idea. What senator proposed this idea in 1854? What act of Congress endorsed it? Where was the idea to be applied? Was popular sovereignty a good idea in that case?

2. emancipation Emancipation is the act of setting someone free. What were the provisions of Lincoln's Emancipation Proclamation? How was it received in the North? In Europe?

3. draft To be drafted is to be selected for military service without one's own consent. Why did both the Union and the Confederacy use the draft during the Civil War? How could some Northerners and Southerners avoid the draft? What were some of the consequences of people's use of these methods to avoid the draft?

4. civil rights The civil rights to which all Americans are entitled are protected against federal action in the first 10 amendments to the Constitution. (See pages 208–210.) These amendments are known as the Bill of Rights. How did the Fourteenth and Fifteenth amendments extend civil rights protection? What rights were protected in the Civil Rights Act of 1875? What happened to that act?

5. sharecropping Sharecroppers grew their crops on land owned by someone else and paid rent to the landowner with a share of the crop. Why did this system come into use in the Southern states after the Civil War? What effect did sharecropping have on the farmers who worked other people's land? What group was particularly affected by sharecropping?

EXPRESSING YOURSELF

1. Who would you rather be? During debate on the Compromise of 1850, would you rather be John C. Calhoun, Daniel Webster, or Henry Clay? Why?

2. Through their eyes. Thousands of people saw Abraham Lincoln and Stephen Douglas debate during the 1858 senate campaign in Illinois. How would one of these debates have sounded to an Illinois citizen? Describe how the two debaters looked and sounded, how they argued their points, and how the audience reacted to their arguments.

3. Thinking like an economist. Economists study the way people make decisions about money and the way money affects other decisions and actions. Suppose you were making an economic analysis of the North and the South just before the Civil War. What points would you consider in your analysis of each region? Which region was better prepared for war? Why?

4. How would you feel? Imagine that you are a Union soldier, and then a Confederate soldier, after one of the following events: (a) the first battle of Bull Run; (b) the Emancipation Proclamation; (c) Pickett's charge at Gettysburg; or (d) Lee's surrender at Appomattox Court House. Describe your feelings.

5. You make the decision. Imagine that you are a senator and so a member of the jury at President Andrew Johnson's impeachment trial. Would you have voted to find Johnson guilty or not guilty of the charges against him? Why?

UNIT **5**

Economic and Social Change

1850

1860

1870

1880

1890

1900

1910

The Indians' Last Stand

Why did warfare break out on the Great Plains?

VOCABULARY

| reservation | Dawes Act |
| nomadic | |

A Bitter Choice   As dawn broke on September 30, 1877, Chief Joseph and his group of Nez Percé (nez pérs) Indians prepared to leave their camp at Snake Creek, near the Bear Paw Mountains in the Montana Territory. Another 40 miles (64 km), just another 40 miles, and they would reach the Canadian border. Then they would be beyond the reach of the United States Army, which was pursuing them.

Before the Nez Percé could break camp, 600 soldiers on horseback appeared on the surrounding hills and began their charge. Quickly the Indian warriors drew themselves into a line of defense. All day the battle raged.

The next day a storm blew in. Cold rains and snow fell for 2 days. The Nez Percé were trapped and greatly outnumbered. Their three remaining chiefs— Chief Joseph, Looking Glass, and White Bird—now had the bitter choice: Should they surrender and give up their independence? Or should they fight on, with defeat almost certain?

The Plight of the Nez Percé   The events that had brought Chief Joseph's people to the encampment at Bear Paw had begun 22 years earlier. The Nez Percé lived in a valley where today's states of Oregon, Idaho, and Washington meet. There they farmed and raised cattle. The Nez Percé lived in groups, or bands, with their own chiefs.

In 1855 the United States government decided to make room for white settlers by requiring the various Indian tribes of the Northwest to move onto **reservations**— public land set aside by the government for the Indians' use. The Nez Percé agreed to accept a reservation of 10,000 square miles (25,900 sq km). In exchange, they received about $200,000 worth of goods.

This agreement lasted just 8 years. In 1863, as more settlers moved in, the United States government decided that the Nez Percé reservation must be cut down from 10,000 to 1,000 square miles (2,590 sq km). Some of the Nez Percé chiefs yielded to government pressure. Five other chiefs, however, refused to move their bands onto the smaller reservation. One of these chiefs was Joseph's father.

Matters stayed that way for the next 14 years. Then, in 1877, the United States Army ordered the chiefs to take their people onto the reservation or face war.

At roundup time a cowhand's riding and roping skills were tested.
■ When was the first successful long drive?

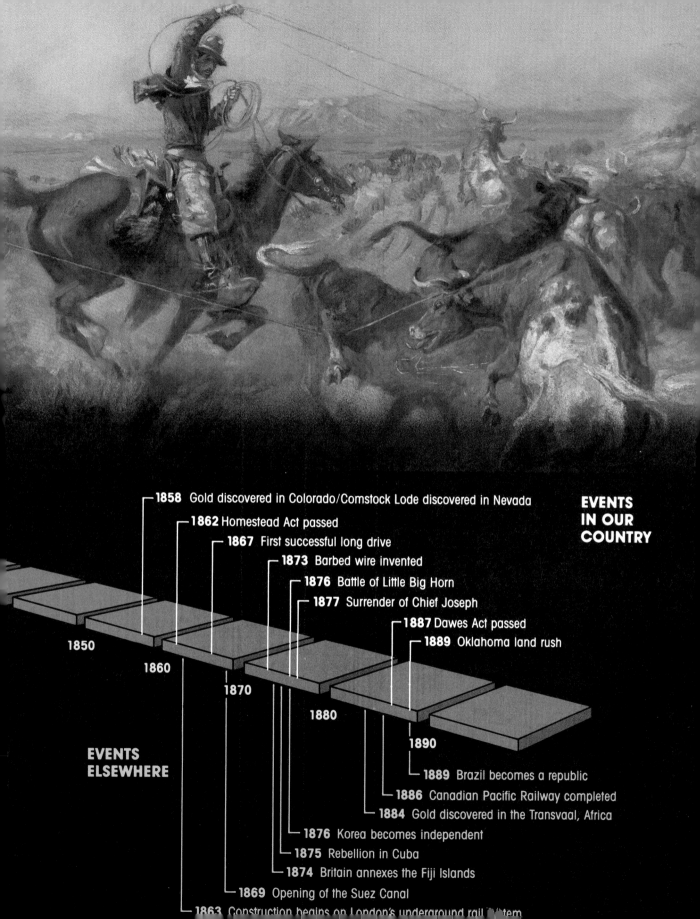

EVENTS IN OUR COUNTRY

1858 Gold discovered in Colorado/Comstock Lode discovered in Nevada
1862 Homestead Act passed
1867 First successful long drive
1873 Barbed wire invented
1876 Battle of Little Big Horn
1877 Surrender of Chief Joseph
1887 Dawes Act passed
1889 Oklahoma land rush

1850
1860
1870
1880
1890

EVENTS ELSEWHERE

1889 Brazil becomes a republic
1886 Canadian Pacific Railway completed
1884 Gold discovered in the Transvaal, Africa
1876 Korea becomes independent
1875 Rebellion in Cuba
1874 Britain annexes the Fiji Islands
1869 Opening of the Suez Canal
1863 Construction begins on London's underground rail system

Chief Joseph was finally forced to move his people onto a reservation.
■ **Do you think this portrait was painted before or after his surrender?**

National Portrait Gallery, Smithsonian Institution, Washington, D.C.

2,000 soldiers and hundreds of civilian volunteers. This force set out to crush the Nez Percé in the summer of 1877.

For the next 3 months, the Indians fled through mountains and thick forests, with the army in close pursuit. From time to time, bitter fighting took place, but each time the Nez Percé slipped out of the army's grasp. Finally, after 3 months, nearly 1,700 miles (2,735 km) of travel, and many battles, the Nez Percé found themselves at Bear Paw on that morning of September 30, 1877.

The Surrender of Chief Joseph　By October 4, Chief Joseph knew his situation was hopeless. Of the 150 warriors who had started out with him in June, only 79 had survived. There was nothing to do but surrender. The next day he did so, with these moving words:

> It is cold and we have no blankets. The little children are freezing to death. My people, some of them, have run away to the hills and have no blankets, no food; no one knows where they are—perhaps freezing to death. I want time to look for my children and see how many of them I can find. Maybe I shall find them among the dead. Hear me, my chiefs. I am tired; my heart is sick and sad. From where the sun now stands, I will fight no more forever.

A Desperate Flight　By that time, Joseph had succeeded his father as chief of his band. Chief Joseph was a peace-loving man. He believed that war would mean disaster for the Nez Percé. With great sadness, he decided that his band must move onto the reservation as ordered.

Before they could do so, warriors from another band of Nez Percé murdered 18 white settlers. Chief Joseph knew what this would mean. The army would surely strike back at all Nez Percé, even his own band who had nothing to do with the killings. His people, fearing for their lives, prepared to flee. There was nothing for the Nez Percé to do now but get ready to fight if attacked.

The Nez Percé numbered only about 150 fighting men and another 550 women, children, and old men. Against them were

Broken Treaties　In the story of the Nez Percé, the fate of nearly all the Native Americans in the West can be seen. First came the arrival of white settlers onto the Indians' ancient lands. A period of conflict between settlers and Indians followed. Pressed by the settlers, the United States government would make a treaty with Indian chiefs, reserving certain areas of land for their people in exchange for signing over the rest. As settlers' demands for land increased, these treaties were often broken. Indians were forced onto even smaller and poorer lands. Many resisted. War between the Indians and the United States Army would follow, and eventually the Indians were defeated.

On the Great Plains   The final chapter of the tragedy of the Native Americans was played out on the vast stage of the Great Plains. This region lies between 100° west longitude and the Rocky Mountains, from Canada all the way to Mexico.

By the 1860s this was the last great unsettled area in the United States. The reason is its climate. The 100° west line of longitude cuts through the center of the Dakotas, Nebraska, and Kansas, and then runs through Oklahoma and Texas. Lands to the east of this line usually receive plenty of rain. To the west, rainfall generally drops below 20 inches (50 cm) a year, in some places even below 10 inches

(25 cm). Wind sweeps over the flatlands, which are bitterly cold in the winter and like a furnace in the summer. This is the region that Major Stephen Long (page 316) called the Great American Desert.

Following the Buffalo   On these dry lands and in the neighboring Rocky Mountains lived about 250,000 Indians. Most of the Plains Indians were **nomadic**, that is, they did not live in permanent villages but traveled across the plains, following the herds of buffalo across the endless grasslands. For these Indians, the buffalo provided food, clothing, tepees, blankets, and tools.

In the late 1700s the Plains Indians started using horses, which had multiplied and spread northward since the Spaniards had brought them to Mexico in the sixteenth century. With horses the Plains Indians became more efficient hunters.

Horses were an important part of the Plains Indians' way of life.
◼ **Why do you think horses were important?**

Gift of Mrs. Wade Plummer, Montana Historical Society

Their warriors also became more efficient fighters, first against each other, later against the whites.

Warfare on the Plains   Until the 1840s the United States government regarded the plains region as one big Indian reservation. Soon, however, the traders, miners, and settlers who crossed the plains demanded protection against the Indians. The government then built army posts along the main trails. It also decided to gather the tribes onto a number of large reservations scattered through the West. This would leave the rest of the land for the whites. At Fort Laramie, Wyoming, in 1851, the Plains Indian chiefs signed treaties agreeing that their tribes would move onto these reservations. The reservation land was to belong to the Indians "forever," and the government guaranteed that no one would disturb their way of life.

The new policy did not last long. In the Colorado Territory "forever" turned out to be 10 years. News of a gold discovery brought thousands of miners into this area in 1858. In 1861 the government forced the Indians to sell most of Colorado. For the next 3 years, there was bloody fighting involving Indians, settlers, and the army. It ended only because nearly all of the Indians were killed. In other parts of the West, the pattern of events was much the same.

Decline of the Plains Indians   The warfare between the Plains Indians and the army and white settlers was not always one-sided. For a time, the Indians were able to hold their own. They were skilled horsemen and fighters. While on horseback, an Indian warrior could fire 20 to 30 arrows in the time it took a soldier or settler to reload his muzzle-loading rifle. In time, however, new weapons like the repeater rifle and the Colt six-shooter shifted the advantage to the whites.

Another thing that weakened the Plains Indians' ability to resist was the destruction of the buffalo herd. The buffalo, you will remember, was the Plains Indians' chief source of food, clothing, and shelter. In 1860 there had been 12 or 13 million buffalo on the Great Plains. During the next 10 years, workers laying railroad track across the plains killed many of these animals. Many more were killed for sport by hunters.

In 1871 the leather made from buffalo hides became fashionable and could be sold in the East for a good profit. Over the next 3 years, 9 million buffalo were killed. By 1878 the great herd was almost wiped out, and by 1900 there were less than 50 buffalo left in the entire country!

A New Policy   In the late 1860s the government announced that all Plains Indians were to be removed to two large reservations. One was in the Black Hills of South Dakota, the other in present-day Oklahoma. Here they were to give up their nomadic ways and become farmers. Worn down by war, the chiefs of the major tribes agreed to this plan in 1867 and 1868.

Some Plains Indians moved onto the two reservations, but many others refused. For the next 7 years, there was war. Finally, after more than 200 battles with the army, the Indians were forced onto the reservations.

For a short period there was quiet. Then in 1874, gold was discovered on the Black Hills reservation of the Sioux (sü) Indians. For a time the army pushed back the thousands of miners who kept trying to enter the reservation. In 1875 the army gave up, and miners poured in.

Angered by yet another broken promise, the Indians took to arms. Many left

Custer's troops fought to the last man near the Little Bighorn. This battle is sometimes called Custer's Last Stand.
■ What does this artist think of Custer? How can you tell?

their reservations and went to the nearby Montana Territory. When they refused to follow the army's order to return, fighting broke out. Now and then, the Indians won a big victory. One came in June 1876, when a large force of Sioux and their Cheyenne allies, under Chiefs Crazy Horse and Sitting Bull, was attacked by Colonel George Custer and his 264 men near the Little Bighorn River in Montana. Custer and his men were wiped out. But within a year Indian resistance on the northern plains was crushed. Most of Sitting Bull's people were captured, and Sitting Bull himself was forced to flee to Canada.

The Dawes Act By 1887 most Plains Indians were living on reservations. In that year, Congress passed the **Dawes Act**, which was aimed at making Indians accept the ways of white Americans. The law permitted the head of each Indian family to own 160 acres (65 ha) of land for farming or twice that much for grazing.

The plan was not successful. For one thing, it tried to force Indians to give up their tribal ways. Most Indians did not want to do this. Also, most Indians were not prepared for farming. They had lived by fishing and hunting. So for the almost 50 years that the Dawes Act was in effect, the standard of living of Native Americans dropped because they could not support themselves by farming.

CHECKUP

1. What events led to the long flight of the Nez Percé?
2. Why were treaties with the Indians broken by the United States government?
3. What developments led to the defeat of the Plains Indians?
4. Why, do you think, was the Dawes Act unsuccessful?
5. **Thinking Critically** Why might a nomad find it difficult to become a farmer?

441

The Mining Frontier

VOCABULARY

"Pikes Peak or Bust!"	Comstock Lode
	vigilante
Centennial State	

The Rush to Colorado Even as the Indians of the plains and the Rocky Mountains were being overcome, other people rushed to take over these areas. First among them were the miners. In Chapter 13 you read how the discovery of gold in 1848 brought thousands to California.

California was only the first of many gold rushes in the West. In the summer of 1858 came the report that gold had been discovered near Pikes Peak in the Colorado Territory. With the melting of the winter snows, the rush to Colorado was on. Within a year 100,000 people set out for the territory with the cry **"Pikes Peak or Bust!"**

A good many of these people gave up and returned home before ever reaching Pikes Peak. For most who made it, a more accurate cry would have been "Pikes Peak *and* Bust!" It turned out that there was little gold or silver there, and what was found was quickly mined out. Many who had rushed to Colorado returned to their homes. Some, however, found work nearby in the new town of Denver. Still others settled down in Colorado to farm or to raise cattle.

Later discoveries of silver and gold in the 1870s brought other miners to the Colorado Territory. In 1876, the population had grown large enough to enable Colorado to become a state. It was known as the **Centennial State** because it entered the Union on the one-hundredth anniversary of the nation.

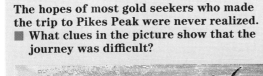

The hopes of most gold seekers who made the trip to Pikes Peak were never realized. ■ What clues in the picture show that the journey was difficult?

A Bonanza! In 1858, the same year gold was found in the Colorado Territory, two Irish immigrants named Pete O'Reilly and Pat McLaughlin made an even greater find in what is now western Nevada. Unfortunately for them, they did not realize it. Neither did Henry Comstock, a lazy, bragging blusterer who had talked them into sharing their claim with him.

O'Reilly and McLaughlin were mining in Six Mile Canyon, on the eastern slope of the Sierra Nevadas, when they hit upon a vein of bluish ore. Two wealthy Californians who saw the ore realized that it was silver. They offered O'Reilly and McLaughlin a few thousand dollars each for their claim. The two miners were glad to sell. Comstock held out for more. When he got $11,000 from the Californians, he was sure he had made the deal of a

Discovery of the Comstock Lode brought a rush of miners to the eastern slope of the Sierra Nevadas.
■ **Can you learn anything from this picture about what life was like in a mining camp?**

lifetime. One can only imagine how all three felt when their discovery turned out to be one of the richest finds in western mining history. It became known as the **Comstock Lode**. A lode is a rich vein of ore lying in the cracks of the rock. The Comstock Lode yielded over $300 million in gold and silver over the next 20 years.

The discovery of this lode touched off the usual rush of miners and others to the region. Thousands staked claims, but only about a dozen became rich. Most of the ore in Six Mile Canyon lay far below the surface. Machinery and expensive mining methods were needed to get it out, and that required a large investment. Thus, it was large mining companies, rather than small individual miners, that took most of the gold and silver from the ground. Indeed, a great many of the people who came to mine on their own wound up working for the mining companies.

The Comstock strike, and others that followed, brought enough people to Nevada for it to become a state in 1864, the year of President Lincoln's reelection.

Boom Towns News of a big strike could turn a mining camp into a good-sized town in days. Hundreds of people would rush in to stake their claims. Then, small-business owners would arrive to sell food, tents, tools, clothing, and other goods to the miners. One such person was Levi Strauss. A 20-year-old immigrant from Germany, Strauss moved to San Francisco and began to manufacture pants made out of a tough cotton fabric called denim. Miners and cattle ranchers bought these pants because of their high quality and durability. By the end of the 1860s, they were considered standard clothing. *Levi's* is a common name for these pants.

Women as well as men arrived. In one mining town a woman from Boston cleared a profit of $11,000 in 1 year by baking and selling pies. Other women ran boarding-houses and small hotels.

As a town grew, a string of wooden buildings began to line the main street. Among them were many gambling houses and saloons. But some of those buildings might also house banks, hotels, newspaper offices, and even theaters.

Levi's were the first denim jeans.
■ To whom did this advertisement appeal?

Mining towns, which sprang up hundreds of miles from settled communities, had no organized law or law officials at first. To deal with the numerous outlaws and thieves, the people of the towns usually made their own laws and formed committees to enforce those laws. The committee members, known as **vigilantes** (vij ə lan′ tēz), would hunt down the worst offenders. Those who were declared guilty of crimes were likely to be hanged, sometimes without even being put on trial. "Frontier justice" was harsh.

The richest mining town in the West was Virginia City, near the Comstock Lode. Mark Twain, the famous American writer, was at that time a reporter for a newspaper in Virginia City. His description of this bustling city gives us something of its flavor during the boom period:

The sidewalks swarmed with people. . . . The streets themselves were just as crowded with . . . wagons, freight teams, and other vehicles. . . . Joy sat on every countenance, and there was glad, almost fierce, intensity in every eye, that told of money-getting schemes. . . . Money was as plenty as dust. . . . There were . . . fire companies, brass bands, banks, hotels, theaters, . . . wide open gambling palaces, . . . street fights, murders, . . . riots, a whiskey mill every fifteen steps, . . . a dozen breweries, and half a dozen jails and station houses in full operation. . . .

Most mining towns blazed brightly for a brief time, and then, like a comet in the sky, were gone. After the gold or silver was mined out, most miners pulled up stakes and moved on. These deserted towns were called ghost towns. Even Virginia City, the richest mining town of them all, was eventually left to gather dust as the rich ore from Comstock Lode dwindled.

Many mining towns in the mid-1800s were lively communities.
■ What kinds of stores were found in this mining town?

Montana Historical Society

The Mining Frontier Moves In the 1860s a number of smaller strikes were made in the mountains of the West. The last great gold rush was in the Black Hills of South Dakota. This rush gave birth to Deadwood, the last and maybe the most colorful of all the mining towns.

By the 1880s the day of the gold rush and the prospectors had passed. Few became rich. But in their search for instant wealth, they helped to settle the West. Each new gold rush brought men and women who ran the stores, farmed the land, and started schools, churches, and newspapers. When the mining frontier passed on, many of these people stayed to raise families and build up the country.

By the 1880s, prospectors with pack horse, pick, and shovel could still be seen wandering the West, but their day had passed. Nearly all mining was in the hands of large companies. Gold and silver continued to be produced in great amounts. Even more important were copper and lead. By 1900, the value of copper mined each year topped that of gold and silver put together. The rowdy, roaring, get-rich-quick days of Deadwood, Silver City, Tombstone, and Last Chance Gulch were gone by then, as were such characters of the mining frontier as Wild Bill Hickok and Poker Alice. But by 1900 the real business of mining the West's treasure had only begun.

CHECKUP

1. With what event is the slogan "Pikes Peak or Bust!" connected?
2. What was the Comstock Lode?
3. How did the discovery of gold or silver affect life in the place of the discovery?
4. Why did ghost towns form?
5. **Thinking Critically** Which group do you think made a greater profit on the mining frontier—the prospectors or the merchants? Why?

445

The Cattle Kingdom

Why did cattle raising become big business?

A Vast Grazing Ground   If thousands were drawn to the mountain regions of the West by gold, many other thousands were drawn to the Great Plains by its grasslands! For hundreds of years the grass of these plains provided food for millions of buffalo. With the buffalo fast disappearing, people realized that cattle could be grazed on this same grass and then sold for good prices.

Thus the cattle kingdom came into being. Its greatest years were between the mid-1860s and the mid-1880s. At its height the cattle kingdom stretched from Texas north to the Canadian border and from Kansas west to the Rockies.

The Growth of Cattle Ranches   Cattle were introduced into the Western Hemisphere by the Spaniards early in the sixteenth century. Over the next 300 years, they multiplied and roamed freely in northern Mexico and Texas. By the middle of the nineteenth century, there were some 5 million head of cattle in Texas alone. These longhorns, as they were called, belonged to no one. They were for the taking. A few bold men did just that, starting large ranches.

The most profitable market for beef, however, was not in sparsely settled Texas

The cowhands in this picture are preparing for a roundup of horses that have spent the winter on the open range.
■ **What roundup activities are shown here?**

detail from "Cowboy Camp During Roundup" by C.M. Russell, Amon Carter Museum

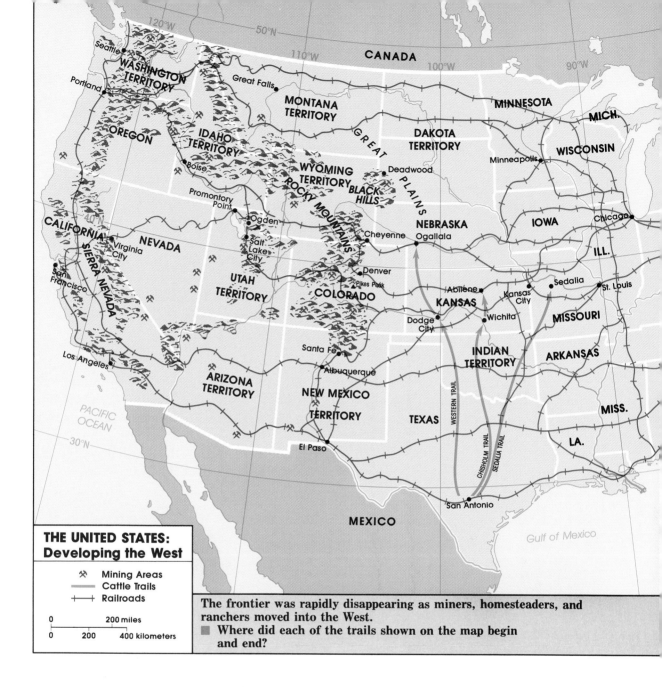

THE UNITED STATES:
Developing the West

⚒ Mining Areas
━━ Cattle Trails
┿┿ Railroads

| 0 | 200 miles |
| 0 | 200 | 400 kilometers |

The frontier was rapidly disappearing as miners, homesteaders, and ranchers moved into the West.

■ Where did each of the trails shown on the map begin and end?

but in the cities of the East. Cattle that brought $3 or $4 each in Texas could be sold for $40 or more in the East. Every Texas rancher knew that; the problem was how to get the cattle there.

Railroads presented the best way. A railroad line had been completed as far west as Sedalia, Missouri, before the Civil War. That was still about a thousand miles (1,600 km) from the Texas ranches. But if the cattle could be herded to Sedalia,

they could be shipped east quickly and cheaply by rail.

The Long Drive   In 1866, the year after the Civil War ended, several Texas ranchers organized the first **long drive**. The plan was to bring the ranchers' herds together and drive them northward to the rail line at Sedalia for shipment east.

Unfortunately, the ranchers chose a poor route. Much of the trail led through

447

wooded areas where it was difficult to control the herd. Parts of the route ran into fenced-in farms and crossed through Indian territory. To add to all the other difficulties, heavy rains turned the cattle trails to mud.

Most of the 260,000 cattle that started the trip died or were lost or stolen. Still, for the cattle that reached Sedalia, ranchers got $35 a head. It was clear that the idea of the long drive was a good one. The only thing that was needed was a better route.

The next year a new route was chosen farther to the west. It ran from Texas across open, unsettled plains to a new rail line running into Abilene, in western Kansas. In 1867, some 75,000 cattle were driven north to Abilene and shipped to Chicago and other cities at a large profit. The long drive was a success, and Abilene became the first great **cow town**. As railroads pushed westward, other cow towns also grew up in Kansas—Wichita, Ellsworth Falls, and Dodge City. During the years of the cattle kingdom, about 6 million cattle were driven to these towns from Texas for shipment.

The Western Cowhand   Out of the cattle kingdom came America's most romantic figure, the cowhand. Celebrated in story and song, the western cowhand captured the imaginations not only of the people in America but also of people all around the world. The cowhand remains a favorite subject for movies, television, and other popular entertainment.

Most cowhands were young men, many of them in their teens. A good number had fought in the Civil War, some on the Union side and some for the Confederates. Perhaps one in every three or four was Mexican. Quite a few others were blacks who had left the South in search of a new life after the Civil War.

These cowhands were photographed around a chuckwagon on the New Mexico range.
■ How does this view of a cowhand's life differ from the view in the painting on page 446?

Image Makers of the West

Few easterners ever saw the West. Their ideas about that region were formed in two ways. Many easterners had read western "dime novels"—paperback adventure stories sold on newsstands for 10 cents — and had seen shows based on western frontier life.

The first dime novel about the West came out in the 1860s. Over the next 30 years, publishers produced more than 2,200 of these stories, each one highly exaggerated. Taking on a half-dozen gunfighters at a time was all in a day's work for characters like Arizona Joe, Denver Dan, and Lariat Lil.

Before long a few westerners saw the possibilities for making money by doing shows for eastern audiences. The first and most famous of these enter-

tainers was William F. "Buffalo Bill" Cody. Cody had worked as a pony express rider, a scout, a cowhand, and a buffalo hunter. After touring small cities and towns for several years with a small show about adventure in the West, Cody created the first great outdoor western show in 1883. Buffalo Bill's Wild West show featured riding and shooting contests, a stagecoach robbery, lots of gunfighting, and plenty of whooping Indians. After performing before huge crowds in the United States for several years, Cody took his show to England, where it was also a big hit.

It was entertainers like Buffalo Bill Cody, together with writers of dime novels, who fixed the image of the cowhand's glamorous life in the minds of many people.

The cowhand on our television screens lives a life of adventure, but a real cowhand's life was a far cry from that. Mostly it was filled with dull routine. For much of the year, the cowhand's main job was to ride back and forth along the boundary of his employer's ranch, keeping cattle from wandering off or being stolen. Twice a year he joined in a cattle roundup. (See the picture on page 437.) The spring roundup was for branding newborn calves with the owner's mark. In the fall roundup, cowhands sorted the cattle by brand and separated those that were ready for market from the herd.

On the Trail Then began the long drive, in which several ranchers might combine their herds. The leader of the drive was the trail boss. For every thousand cattle on the drive, the trail boss took along six cowhands. Two rode at the front of the herd, two in the rear, and one on each side to keep the cattle from wandering off.

Each cowhand might need eight or ten horses, so an extra hand was brought along to take care of them. And, of course, each group needed a cook and a fully equipped chuckwagon.

Once on the trail, cowhands spent up to 18 hours a day in the saddle, day after day, in all kinds of weather. With the herd covering only 15 miles (24 km) a day, the drive lasted 2 to 3 months.

The cowhand's greatest worry was a stampede. Lightning, thunder, or any other noise that frightened the cattle could set them off. It was then that the cowhand called on all his skills. Failure to head off a stampede could mean loss of the herd. It could even mean serious injury or death to himself or his comrades. For this mostly dull and sometimes dangerous work, the cowhand received about $30 a month, or a dollar a day!

Yet, hard as it was, there was something that attracted people to this work. Perhaps the cowhand who set down his recollections of a lifetime explained best what it was:

> All in all, my years on the trail were the happiest I ever I lived. There were many hardships and dangers but . . . most of the time we were solitary adventurers in a great land as fresh and new as a spring morning. . . .

The Open Range   As ranchers learned that their animals could survive the winters on the northern plains, the cattle kingdom moved north. The United States government, which owned the rangeland, charged no rent. Thus, cattle ranchers grazed their herds absolutely free. Little wonder, then, that by 1880, 4.5 million head of cattle grazed on the **open range**.

For a time, cattle ranchers shared the open range, with each honoring the others' claims. After a while, some of the larger operators began to expand their claims to grazing lands and to mark off scarce watering places as their own. This led to many small-scale wars among the cattle ranchers.

Challenges to the free use of the public grasslands came from others as well. By the 1880s, cattle ranchers no longer had the open range to themselves. Sheep-herders and farmers moved in. Before long the cattle owners were battling with these newcomers over use of the land.

Even so, the 1870s and early 1880s were a time of great prosperity for the cattle kingdom. By this time, ranchers had bred the Texas longhorn with eastern stock to produce a better quality of beef. Eastern and European markets paid high prices for these cattle.

Bad Times   This prosperity did not last. Soon there were more cattle than the market demanded. So prices fell sharply. The winter of 1885–1886 was the bitterest in memory. Many cattle died. Then came a hot, dry summer, which killed much of the grass. The winter of 1886–1887, even worse than the previous one, finished off nearly 90 percent of the cattle. Many ranchers were ruined.

This disaster marked the end of open-range ranching. Thereafter, those who raised cattle followed more settled ways. They acquired land of their own and raised smaller herds. The cowhand, master of the open range, became a ranch hand, fixing fences, harvesting hay for winter feed, and doing other chores. By the end of the 1880s, the cowhand had passed into folklore. The day of the cattle kingdom and the Wild West was over.

CHECKUP

1. What problem had to be overcome before cattle ranching could be profitable?
2. What was the long drive?
3. Where were cow towns founded? Why?
4. Why did the prosperous days of the cattle kingdom end?
5. **Thinking Critically** Why would the same cattle bring a higher price in New York than in Texas?

The Farming Frontier

What difficulties did farmers face on the Great Plains?

The Farmers Arrive   Even as cattle ranchers were conducting their first long drives in the 1860s, some farmers were beginning to move onto the Great Plains. This trickle became a flood in the 1870s.

For years, farmers had avoided the area that Stephen Long had called the Great American Desert. Why did they now rush to settle there? There were three reasons. First, there was a change in the weather pattern. For 8 years in a row, rainfall on the plains had been above average. Second, private land companies and railroads, which owned a great deal of land in the West, advertised heavily to attract settlers.

The third reason was that the Homestead Act of 1862 encouraged settlement. In Chapter 16 you read that many veterans of the Union and Confederate armies moved west and acquired land under the terms of the act. Thousands of other Americans got free land, too. A good number of settlers from Germany, Norway, and Sweden also moved to the Great Plains at this time.

Problems the Homesteaders Faced Farmers who settled on the Great Plains found a climate and land different from anything they had known in the East or Europe. Summer temperatures reached 110°F (43°C). There was no wood for buildings, fences, or fuel. The tough **sod,** or the top layer of soil covered with grass, would not yield to the old-style eastern plow.

Lack of water was the biggest problem. One way to get water was to sink a well 200 to 300 feet (60 m to 90 m) deep and

A homesteader with a team of oxen turns over the thick sod of the plains.
■ **How does this painting show the loneliness and isolation of the homesteader's life?**

build a windmill to pump the water to the surface. But at a drilling cost of $2 per foot, plus the cost of building the windmill, few early settlers could afford to have a well to pump much needed water.

Instead, settlers had to learn new ways of farming. They began to use **dry farming**. Dry farming is a method of farming on land that receives little rainfall. Farmers plowed deep furrows in their fields to catch the rain. To keep moisture in the ground, the farmers turned the soil over immediately after a rain. This moved the wet surface soil nearer to the roots while it slowed down evaporation. Farmers also learned to space plants farther apart so the roots would not compete for the scarce water. Finally, they experimented with hardier strains of wheat.

Barbed Wire and Some New Machines

Other problems were solved by inventions. Farmers had to fence in their land to keep range cattle and sheep from trampling their crops, but wood was scarce and expensive on the plains. To fence a 160-acre farm with wood from the East might cost as much as $1,000. In 1873 an Illinois farmer named Joseph Glidden invented barbed wire, and within a few years its cost was low enough for nearly all farmers to use it.

An invention by James Oliver in 1877 helped farmers with their first and hardest task, plowing up the tough prairie sod. This was the chilled-iron plow, made of an extra-strong kind of iron. Mechanical seed drills replaced the backbreaking work of planting seeds in rows.

By the end of the nineteenth century, the Great Plains, once thought of as a desert, was the country's chief producer of grain. Four of America's five leading wheat-growing states in 1900 were wholly or in part on the plains.

Life on the Great Plains

If farming on the Great Plains was difficult, living there was even more so. For most families the first house was made from blocks of sod. After rain or melting snow softened the hard soil, settlers cut the sod into blocks. Piled one upon another, the blocks of sod could make a surprisingly tight building. With their thick walls, sod houses were warm in winter and cool in summer. Still, they were small. They were also dirty, and in rainy weather, they leaked.

Newcomers to the plains found it difficult to adjust to the weather. Summer heat could be nearly unbearable at times. Winter snows and bitter cold could keep people cooped up in their one-room houses for days at a time. Probably the hardest thing about life on the Great Plains was the loneliness. Farms were far apart. For many years there were not even small villages nearby to break up the isolation.

Such conditions might have been easier to bear if settlers could have been sure that their farms would be successful. Of course, there were no guarantees. A few dry years could bring the end of a dream to a farm family. A field filled with golden grain one day could be empty the next, eaten by a swarm of grasshoppers. These insects appeared on the plains every few years in such numbers as to darken the sky. One settler, reporting on the grasshopper plague that swept over a large part of the plains in 1873, wrote:

> So thick were the grasshoppers in the cornfield of which both of us had been so proud, that not a spot of green could be seen. And within two hours . . . not a leaf was left in all that field.

The Oklahoma Land Rush

It may seem a wonder that anyone came to live and farm on the Great Plains. But come they did, and in ever-increasing numbers.

Land seekers used every available form of transportation to rush into Oklahoma on April 22, 1889.
■ **What kinds of transportation can you find in this picture?**

One part of the Great Plains, in fact, was the scene of the most spectacular land rush in the country's history. This was Oklahoma. This land, long known as the Indian Territory, had been set aside for Indian reservations. But settlers who pushed west eyed the land for themselves. The tribes were forced to sell most of it to the United States government. Some 2 million acres (810,000 ha) of it were then divided up into homesteads of 160 acres (65 ha), to be given away beginning at noon on April 22, 1889 — first come, first served.

By the morning of April 22, about 100,000 would-be homesteaders had lined up at the Oklahoma border. With the crack of the starter's gun at noon, the settlers bolted into Oklahoma like locusts descending on a field of wheat. In just hours, nearly all 2 million acres were claimed. New towns sprang up even faster than they had on the mining frontier. At noon on April 22, the town of Guthrie did not exist. Before the sun had set, Guthrie had a population of 15,000. Oklahoma City went from zero population to 10,000 in the same few hours.

Thus, in the last part of the nineteenth century, the promise of land continued to be a powerful lure to the West, just as it had been all through American history. So rapidly was the West settled that in 1890 the Census Bureau announced that there no longer was a clearly defined frontier, the imaginary line that marked off the limit of western settlement. There was still plenty of unsettled land to the east of that line, but by 1890 the last frontier had passed. Americans would have to find their new frontiers elsewhere.

CHECKUP

1. Why did large numbers of farmers move to the Great Plains in the 1870s?
2. What inventions helped the farmers on the Great Plains?
3. How was the settlement of Oklahoma different from that of other states?
4. **Thinking Critically** Why do you think the plains farmers were called sodbusters? Explain.

Skimming

RAPID READING

People use different rates of reading for different purposes. You read a telephone book at a different rate from the one at which you read a textbook. You read an adventure story at a rate different from the one you use for either of the others. You read the directions for assembling a bicycle at still another rate.

The rate you use with the telephone book is called *skimming*. When you skim, you are not concerned with reading all the information on the page but only with finding specific information quickly. Thus, you skim a dictionary or an index to find a certain word. You skim a newspaper to find out whether your favorite team won or lost.

Skimming is useful in studying, too. Suppose you needed to find some very specific information (such as a name, a location, or a date) on a page in this book. You could read the whole page carefully, but skimming is much more efficient. Skimming is also useful for previewing material. Before you start to read a chapter thoroughly, go through its pages quickly. Look for headings, pictures, graphs, maps, and charts. These will give you a general idea of what the chapter covers. This is important because the more you know about what is coming up, the more you will understand about it. In other words, previewing prepares you to get more from the slower, more careful reading that you will be required to do later.

SKILLS PRACTICE

Number a sheet of paper from 1 to 4. Skim the index of your textbook to locate these words and write down the page numbers.

1. Andes Mountains   3. Iron Curtain
2. Incas   4. Sam Houston

Skim the passage below to find the following information:

a. the person who organized the pony express
b. the distance each rider rode
c. the date service began on the pony express
d. the invention that replaced the pony express

The rapid settlement of California created a need for fast mail service across the continent. To meet this need, William H. Russell organized the pony express. The pony express was a system of relay riders on horseback. Stations were set up 15 miles (24 km) apart between St. Joseph, Missouri, and Sacramento, California.

At each station, ponies awaited the rider. The rider was given 2 minutes to transfer himself and the mailbags to a different pony. Then the rider was off again. Each rider usually rode 75 miles (120 km) and then someone else took over. The entire trip, more than 2,000 miles (3,200 km), took about 10 days.

Service on the pony express began on April 3, 1860. It was discontinued 18 months later when telegraph lines between the East Coast and the West Coast were completed. Messages traveled by telegraph across the country in a matter of minutes.

MAIN IDEAS

1. The United States government required various tribes of Plains Indians to move onto reservations to make room for white settlers.
2. Some tribes went to war when their treaties with the government were broken and they were forced to give up their land.
3. The discovery of gold and silver brought people to the West, which led to the growth of towns, cities, and states.
4. Ranchers moved to the Great Plains because grazing lands were plentiful and cattle raising was very profitable.
5. Farmers who settled on the Great Plains had to learn different methods of farming to grow crops in this dry region.

VOCABULARY REVIEW

On a separate sheet of paper, write **T** if the statement is true and **F** if it is false. If the statement is false, replace the underlined term to make the statement true.

1. Public land set aside for <u>cattle ranchers</u> to use was called a reservation.
2. The first shelter for most white settlers on the Great Plains was a <u>tepee</u>.
3. Most Plains Indians were <u>nomadic</u>.
4. "Pikes Peak or Bust!" was a slogan of miners bound for <u>Nevada</u>.
5. The Comstock Lode was the richest <u>ore</u> find in western mining history.
6. <u>Oklahoma</u> is called the Centennial State because it became a state in 1876.
7. Groups who enforced the law in early mining towns were known as <u>vigilantes</u>.
8. Abilene, Kansas, was the first great <u>mining camp</u>.
9. <u>The Homestead Act</u> was aimed at making the Plains Indians accept the ways of white Americans.
10. Cowhands on the long drive drove cattle north from <u>Texas</u> to railroad lines in Kansas and Missouri.

CHAPTER CHECKUP

1. Why were the Plains Indians forced to change their way of life?
2. How did the discovery of gold and silver change the West?
3. What is the source for each phrase?

   "I will fight no more forever."
   "Pikes Peak or Bust!"
   "The Great American Desert"

4. Compare the life of a cowhand in the 1860s with that of a cowhand in the 1880s. Explain why a change took place.
5. What effect did the growth of farming have on cattle ranching?
6. Describe some of the hardships the farmers on the Great Plains faced.
7. **Thinking Critically** Was the United States government's policy of awarding land in the Oklahoma Territory fair? Why or why not?
8. **Thinking Critically** Why would private land companies and railroads want to attract people to the West?

APPLYING KNOWLEDGE

1. You own cattle and want to hire cowhands. Write an advertisement describing the job. Include hours of work, duties, and pay.
2. For a time, Chief Joseph agreed that the Nez Percé should move to the reservation. Some of his followers agreed with this view; others opposed it. Take either point of view and write an argument to convince the others.
3. Describe the conflict between the Native Americans and the army from the point of view of
   a. an easterner who has moved west to start a farm.
   b. a 13- or 14-year-old Indian who has lived on the plains all his or her life.
   c. an army private who is assigned to protect white settlers.

19 Industrial Growth

1860–1900

Carnegie and Steel

How did Andrew Carnegie rise from being a poor immigrant to become one of the richest men in America?

Bessemer process

The Carnegies Immigrate to America
Making a living in Dunfermline (dən fėrm′ lən), Scotland, was not easy for William Carnegie. Carnegie was a skilled worker, a handloom weaver of linen cloth. Just about the time his first child, Andrew, was born in 1835, the first power loom in Dunfermline was put into operation. Other power looms followed, putting hundreds of handweavers like William Carnegie out of work.

In 1848, William and Margaret Carnegie and their two sons, Andy and Tom, left Scotland to seek new opportunities in America. Arriving in New York, they continued on to Pittsburgh, Pennsylvania.

It was necessary for both parents and 13-year-old Andy to find work immediately. Andy's first job was as a bobbin boy in a textile mill. When the bobbins, or spools, on the spinning machines were full of cotton thread, Andy replaced them with empty ones. The job required no skill, and it paid accordingly: $1.20 a week.

An Ambitious Young Man After a short while at his job and others like it, Andy became a messenger in a Pittsburgh telegraph office. When he was not delivering telegrams, he watched the telegraph operators at work. Soon, Andy mastered that skill, and at the age of 16 he was hired as an operator at $4 a week. In a short time he became one of the best in the country. In the evenings Andy went to school to learn bookkeeping, and on his own he read the important English, Scottish, and American writers of the day.

In 1853, Andrew Carnegie caught the eye of Thomas A. Scott, a leading official of the Pennsylvania Railroad Company. Scott hired the young man as his personal telegrapher and secretary. His starting pay was $35 a week. "I couldn't imagine what I could ever do with so much money," Carnegie later recalled.

For the next 12 years, Andrew Carnegie worked for Scott and the Pennsylvania Railroad Company. As his responsibilities increased, his income did, too. He invested it wisely, usually with Scott's advice. By the time he was 33 years old, Andrew Carnegie had an income of $50,000 a year. He could easily have retired from work, but that did not fit in with the ambitious young man's plans. Amer-

The rise of industry in the United States was closely linked to new uses for iron and steel.
■ When did Carnegie enter the iron business?

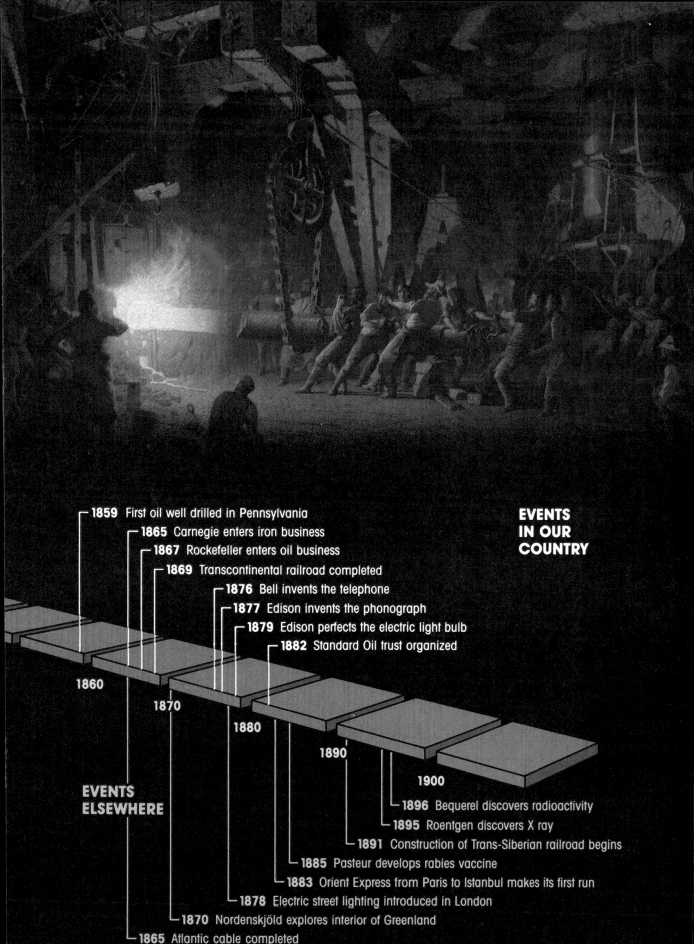

EVENTS IN OUR COUNTRY

1859 First oil well drilled in Pennsylvania
1865 Carnegie enters iron business
1867 Rockefeller enters oil business
1869 Transcontinental railroad completed
1876 Bell invents the telephone
1877 Edison invents the phonograph
1879 Edison perfects the electric light bulb
1882 Standard Oil trust organized

1860
1870
1880
1890
1900

EVENTS ELSEWHERE

1896 Bequerel discovers radioactivity
1895 Roentgen discovers X ray
1891 Construction of Trans-Siberian railroad begins
1885 Pasteur develops rabies vaccine
1883 Orient Express from Paris to Istanbul makes its first run
1878 Electric street lighting introduced in London
1870 Nordenskjöld explores interior of Greenland
1865 Atlantic cable completed

ica was just entering a period of great economic expansion, and Carnegie was determined to have a role in it.

The Iron Business   Carnegie saw his opportunity in the iron business. Pittsburgh, located close to the coalfields of Pennsylvania, was one of the leading centers of America's iron industry. The demand for weapons and other war goods during the Civil War and for rails for the railroads had given the industry a big boost. In 1865, Carnegie left the Pennsylvania Railroad and soon after entered the iron business. He invested in one company that made iron rails and in another that made locomotives. But his shrewdest move was to buy the Keystone Bridge Company, a builder of iron bridges.

"I saw," said Carnegie later, "[that with railroads growing] it would never do to depend further upon wooden bridges for permanent railway structures." Using the best materials and design, the Keystone Bridge Company became the leading builder of iron bridges.

Steelmaking   Carnegie soon decided to shift from iron to steelmaking and devoted all his efforts to it. The advantages of steel over iron had long been known. Steel is stronger, easier to work with, and less likely to break under stress. But until the middle of the nineteenth century, making steel was slow and expensive. It took several weeks just to turn 50 pounds (23 kg) of iron into steel. Then an American named William Kelly and an Englishman named Henry Bessemer, working independently, discovered how to make steel quickly and cheaply. This new method, later called the **Bessemer process**, revolutionized the steel industry. (See the picture on page 457.) By the 1870s, English steel mills using this process turned 30,000 pounds (13,600 kg) of pig iron into steel in a matter of minutes.

A visit to a steel mill in England convinced Carnegie that the future of industrial growth was in steel. By this time, railroads had reached into upper Michigan and Minnesota, where large deposits of rich iron ore had been found in the 1840s.

Carnegie's company supplied the steel for the Eads Bridge over the Mississippi River at St. Louis, Missouri.
■ How do you think the Eads Bridge, finished in 1874, helped St. Louis to grow?

It was now possible to bring this ore by ship across the Great Lakes and then by rail to Pittsburgh. In 1873, Carnegie began to build a steel plant near Pittsburgh. Two years later the J. Edgar Thompson Works, the largest steel plant in America, opened. Carnegie named the plant for the president of the Pennsylvania Railroad, figuring that this bit of flattery would win the railroad's business. He was right.

The Thompson steel plant opened in 1875. That was a depression year in America. Nonetheless, Carnegie's company prospered. An excellent salesperson, Carnegie convinced many railroad companies of the advantages of steel rails over iron. Among other things, steel rails lasted 20 times longer than iron ones. Orders poured in.

Carnegie was hardly alone in the steel business in the United States. In fact, in 1880 there were more than 1,000 companies, large and small, that made iron or steel. Many companies, however, were unable to compete and went out of business. Carnegie bought up a number of others. By the 1890s the Carnegie Steel Company made nearly as much steel as all the remaining companies put together.

Reasons for Carnegie's Success Carnegie's success in business can be attributed to the following factors.

(1) *Efficiency* Carnegie was always ready to use the newest and most efficient methods to make steel. This helped him to keep costs down. He lowered costs still more by buying and running his own iron and coal mines. He also bought the railroads and ships to carry these materials to his mills.

(2) *Reinvesting profits* Carnegie put most of his profits back into the business. That is how he could buy the newest machines and buy his own iron-ore mines.

Steel made Andrew Carnegie one of the richest men in the nation.
■ How is Carnegie's office different from the office of a business executive today?

(3) *Skilled management* Carnegie was an excellent judge of talent. He chose the ablest men he could find to run his companies. He once joked that his tombstone should read, "Here lies the man who was able to surround himself with men far cleverer than himself."

(4) *Foresight and imagination* Carnegie was able to see changes coming and adjust to them. For example, the 1880s were boom years for railroad building. In that decade some 70,000 miles (112,630 km) of track were laid. Carnegie's company made most of these rails and profited greatly. But Carnegie also realized that the railroad boom would end. And he saw that there would soon be a great demand for steel in the construction of the nation's

One of the Carnegie Steel Company's biggest steel mills was at Homestead, Pennsylvania.
■ **What do you think working here would have been like?**

growing cities. So in 1887, even as orders for rails kept pouring in, Carnegie shifted much of his production from steel rails to steel beams for buildings. As a result, when the demand for this steel became strong, he was far ahead of his rivals.

Growth of the Steel Industry Led by Carnegie, the steel industry in the United States grew rapidly. In 1867, when Carnegie was just beginning in the iron business, fewer than 20,000 tons (18,140 t) of steel were produced in the United States. In 1875, the year his new steel plant opened, United States production still trailed far behind England. Twenty-five years later, United States steelmakers turned out more than 10,000,000 tons (9,070,000 t) of steel, more than any other country. And Andrew Carnegie's mills made more steel than any other company in the world.

In 1901, Carnegie decided to sell his steel business to a new corporation formed by the great American banker J.P. Morgan. The new firm was the United States Steel Corporation. For his companies, Carnegie received nearly a half-billion dollars. He spent the rest of his life giving away most of his fortune to a variety of worthy causes.

Andrew Carnegie's achievements in the steel industry were an important factor in America's industrial growth. The two advanced side by side. Just as Carnegie rose to become the world's greatest steelmaker during the last 30 years of the nineteenth century, so the United States rose to become the world's greatest producer of manufactured goods.

CHECKUP

1. Why did Andrew Carnegie's family leave Scotland?
2. How did the young Andrew Carnegie prepare himself to get ahead?
3. Why did Carnegie shift from iron to steel?
4. What were four factors that led to Carnegie's success?
5. **Thinking Critically** Why do you think many of Carnegie's competitors went out of business?

460

Railroads

How did the railroads contribute to the growth of the American economy?

Railroad Networks Expand   One of the main factors in America's change from an agricultural economy to an industrial society was the railroad. In Chapter 12 you read about the first railroads in the United States. By the start of the Civil War, there were 30,000 miles (48,270 km) of railroad track in the country. In the last 40 years of the century, railroad networks expanded greatly. By 1900 the United States had more than six times as much track — 193,000 miles (310,000 km). (See the map on page 447.) Before the Civil War most of the tracks were in the Northeast. By 1900, railroads reached into every corner of the country.

To encourage railroad building, especially in areas where few people lived, the federal and state governments helped the railroad companies with loans and with gifts or grants of land or money. Such grants are called **subsidies**. Railroad companies received more than 180 million acres (72.9 million ha) of land from the federal and state governments.

Not all railroad companies received government help, however. In fact, most of the railroads built in the United States were built without any government aid.

The Transcontinental Railroad   The most spectacular railroad building took place in the West. In 1862, Congress passed a law designed to fulfill the dream of linking the Atlantic and Pacific coasts by rail. At that time, railroads reached only a third of the way across the vast

This poster announces the opening of the nation's first transcontinental railroad in 1869.

■ What advantages of railroad travel does this poster point out?

The first transcontinental railroad was completed when rail lines from east and west came together at Promontory Point, Utah (41°N/112°W; map p. 447).
■ How was this event celebrated?

continent. Under this act of Congress, a new company called the Union Pacific was to start building westward from Omaha, Nebraska. This railroad would link up with one being built eastward from Sacramento, California, by a second company, the Central Pacific. Altogether the new line would run for nearly 1,800 miles (2,896 km), almost entirely through unsettled territory. For each mile of track that was laid, a company would receive a gift of 10 square miles (26 sq km) of land, which was later increased to 20 square miles (52 sq km), plus a large loan of money. With such rich incentives, each company raced to lay all the track it could.

The transcontinental railroad was the grandest construction project of the age. At one time more than 20,000 workers were employed, most of them Chinese, Mexican, and Irish immigrants. The difficulties they faced were enormous. To build around and sometimes through the mountains, Chinese workers on the

Central Pacific had only pickaxes and shovels. Crews laying track across the plains even had to face Indian attacks. Under the blazing summer sun and in the below-zero cold and snows of winter, the work went on.

After 7 years the two lines met at a tiny place called Promontory Point, Utah. On May 10, 1869, a ceremony was held to mark the historic occasion. Leland Stanford, president of the Central Pacific, drove a golden spike into the final railroad tie, and the telegraph flashed the news to a cheering nation: "One, two, three—done!" Actually, the message should have been, "One, two, three, four—done!" On his first swing, Stanford missed everything, bringing howls of laughter from the watching work crews.

In the next 15 years, three more transcontinental rail lines were built, all with subsidies from the federal government. A fifth, built without federal subsidies, was completed 10 years after that.

Railroads Help to Settle the West
Transcontinental railroads contributed to the rapid settlement of the West. Railroad companies wanted people to move west and use their rail lines for shipping crops and for travel. Also, as the population in the West increased, railroad landholdings became more valuable. Therefore, railroad companies promoted western settlement by advertising in the eastern United States and in Europe as well. Many thousands of the people who settled in the American West were influenced to do so by the railroads.

Railroads led to rapid settlement in other ways as well. Without railroads it would have been impossible to have large-scale farming in the West, for there would have been no way to ship crops to market. Also, railroads made moving west faster and safer than ever before.

Railroads and the Economy Railroads contributed to the growth of the industrial economy in many ways. The railroad industry was the largest employer in the United States. In 1900 more than 1 million people worked for railroads. Railroads also created a demand for other goods. In 1880, for example, three fourths of all the steel made in the United States was used to make steel rails. Thus the steel industry was given a great boost by the railroads. Most important, railroads carried raw materials and finished goods cheaply from one part of the country to another. Railroads also helped some businesses grow. Here is an example of how this happened.

Suppose A and B are manufacturers of stoves. Their cities are 100 miles (160 km) apart. Company A sells its stoves for $60 each, including a small profit. Company B, which is more efficient, can sell a stove of the same quality for $40.

When transportation was by horse-drawn wagon, we'll say that shipping one stove cost $1 a mile. You can see that each company will sell its stoves in its own city. Even though Company B's stoves are cheaper, they cannot compete with Company A's stoves in A's city, for it will cost $100 to ship them there.

But see what happens when the railroad arrives and lowers the cost of shipping. One stove can now be shipped, let us say, at 10 cents a mile. Now Company B can sell stoves in A's city more cheaply than A can ($40 for the stove plus $10 for shipping). Company A will now be forced out of business.

Since Company B is selling more stoves, it can afford newer and better machinery. That will lower its costs. It will also be buying larger amounts of raw materials and therefore can buy them at a lower price. Down comes the price still more, perhaps to $30 a stove. Company B might also be able to get lower rates from the railroads because it is such a big customer. Now B can compete in cities still farther away. As it takes over the markets of other stove makers, Company B will grow still larger.

CHECKUP

1. What help did railroad companies receive from governments when they built their lines?
2. What problems confronted the workers who built the first transcontinental railroad?
3. Give two ways in which railroads contributed to the settlement of the West.
4. Name three ways in which railroads helped to bring about the growth of an industrial economy.
5. **Thinking Critically** Why do you think the federal government encouraged railroad building with subsidies?

People, Money, and Resources

VOCABULARY

capital	board of directors
corporation	electricity
dividend	

A Strong Foundation The steel industry and the railroads were two factors that led to America's industrial growth in the late nineteenth century. But there were a number of other factors. One was that a foundation had already been laid before the Civil War. You read earlier how a factory system was established and spread through the Northeast. By the time of the Civil War, textiles, shoes, and many other goods were being made in factories. You also learned how the construction of canals, steamboats, and finally railroads created a transportation system that could move these goods swiftly and cheaply.

The Civil War gave a boost to manufacturing. Not only was iron needed for weapons, but with more than 2 million men under arms, there was a great demand for uniforms, boots, and other supplies. Thus at the end of the war, factories all over the North stood ready to manufacture all sorts of goods. After the Civil War the United States was ready to embark on an age of industrial expansion.

Resources and Population Another factor leading to industrial growth in the United States was its wealth of natural resources. In Pennsylvania, West Virginia, Ohio, Kentucky, and Illinois were large deposits of coal, the main source of fuel in industrial countries at the time. Later, other large coal deposits would be found in the western states. Between 1865 and 1900, coal production rose from 3 million tons (2.7 million t) to nearly 200 million tons (180 million t).

In this chapter, you have read about the great discoveries of iron ore in Michigan and Minnesota. In the West, the mining frontier produced not only gold and silver but also such important metals as copper, lead, and zinc. As a result, in just 15 years America's output of lead ore increased threefold, and the output of copper

Oil was a big factor in the industrial growth of the United States.
■ Why was this well called a gusher?

ore increased eightfold. Oil, which was used for lighting and lubrication (its use as a fuel would come later) was found in Pennsylvania in 1859 and later in Ohio and West Virginia. Thus there was plenty of oil even before the great discoveries in Texas and other states of the West and the South.

A third important factor in America's industrial growth was its rapidly increasing population. Between 1860 and 1910, America's population tripled. This meant there were more people to buy the products of its factories. Just as important, the population increase provided an abundant supply of labor to make those products. A large part of the increased population were immigrants, and it was they and their children who made up the majority of the workers in America's mines and factories.

Capital   A fourth important factor in America's industrial growth was **capital**, or money that is invested in factories, machines, or other businesses. Building factories, buying machines, mining ores, and laying railroad track take a great deal of money. A growing number of Americans had some capital to invest, but few could set up a large business by themselves.

Capital to start large businesses also came from foreign countries. Just as Americans sought profitable investments in American industry, so did wealthy people, companies, and banks in countries such as England and France. All in all, ten times as much capital was invested in American industries in 1900 — from all sources — as was invested just 35 years before.

Those people who wished to start new companies often made use of the form of business organization known as a **corporation**. A corporation — like the joint-stock company that you read about in Chapter 4 — makes it possible to pool the

Trading the stock of corporations became a big business in New York.
■ What do all these men have in common?

capital of many individuals. The corporation sells stock, or shares of ownership, in the business to these people. If the business does well, stockholders receive a **dividend**, or a share of the profits. If it does poorly, stockholders may lose the money they invested, but they cannot be held responsible for the corporation's losses beyond that amount.

To protect their investment, stockholders elect a **board of directors**, or a group of people who make the major decisions about how a corporation will be run. The board of directors then chooses the officers of the corporation — president, vice president, secretary, and treasurer. The corporation's officers manage the day-to-day operation.

The corporation was already in wide use in America before the Civil War. After the war most of the large businesses that speeded America's industrial development were corporations.

New Inventions   Yet another important factor contributing to America's industrial growth was the work of a number of outstanding inventors. Americans had always been an inventive people, but the last half of the nineteenth century was an especially inventive time. One way to show this is by looking at figures from the United States Patent Office. This is the office where inventors register their inventions. In 1850 the Patent Office issued 883 patents for inventions. Forty years later the number leaped to 25,313.

Most of the thousands of new inventions made only minor adjustments to the machines used to make or do things — a better valve here, a new gear there. Taken together, they added up to big gains in efficiency and cost. In some cases, a single invention led to great gains by itself. George Westinghouse's invention of the air brake in 1869 made it safe for trains to travel faster and stop quickly.

A few inventions were so important that they created whole new industries and changed the way people lived, worked, and communicated with each other. One example was Alexander Graham Bell's invention of the telephone in 1876. The emperor of Brazil, trying out Bell's invention when visiting the United States, shouted in amazement, "It talks!"

Less than 15 years later, a half-million phones were in use in the United States, and thousands of women were working as telephone operators. Christopher Sholes's invention of the typewriter in 1867 also changed the way people worked. Within a half-dozen years, the Remington Company was producing typewriters in large numbers. This machine changed office work in the United States, and it also provided new job opportunities for women.

Thomas Alva Edison   The man whose inventions most changed the way Americans lived was Thomas Alva Edison. Edison was an endlessly curious person. Illness kept his school career from starting until he was 8 years old. It ended just 3 months later when his father could no longer pay the school fees. Young Edison's mother, a former schoolteacher, taught him a few subjects at home, but for the most part the boy educated himself.

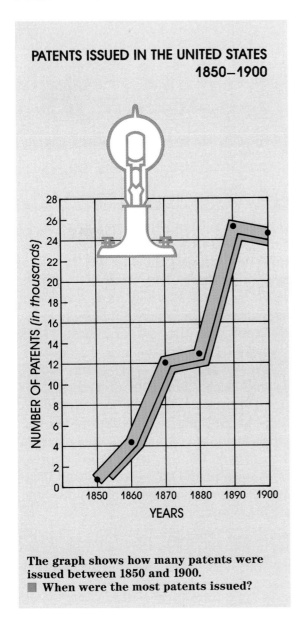

The graph shows how many patents were issued between 1850 and 1900.
■ When were the most patents issued?

466

A Giant Birthday Party

The year 1876 marked the one-hundredth anniversary of the Declaration of Independence. To celebrate the event, the United States gave itself a birthday party in Philadelphia, the birthplace of the nation. The party was a world's fair called the Centennial Exhibition. Those who planned the exhibition determined that it would be the biggest, fanciest, and most awe-inspiring show on earth, fit for a glorious and growing nation.

The Centennial Exhibition was just that. Main Hall, which stretched for a third of a mile (.5 km), was the world's largest building. In Machinery Hall stood a symbol of the new industrial age—a giant steam engine, 40 feet (12 m) tall, which supplied the power that ran 800 other machines in the hall. All in all, there were some 200 buildings

sprawled over several hundred acres. Fifty countries entered exhibits, making this one of the largest world's fairs.

The most popular building was Machinery Hall. There one could see all the latest machines and inventions from all over the world—everything from the typewriter and the telephone to the Westinghouse air brake and the railroad sleeping car. Americans noted with pride that machines from their own country compared well with those from the most advanced countries in the world.

The Centennial Exhibition opened on May 10, 1876, and ran for 6 months. During that time 10 million people—more than one in every five Americans—visited the exhibition. It was one of the most successful birthday parties of all time.

He read all the science books he could. At the age of 10, he set up a laboratory in the basement of the Edison home. There he spent many hours on experiments.

Two years later, Edison got a job selling newspapers and candy on a train. He persuaded the train conductor to let him set up a chemistry lab in the baggage car. That venture ended when some chemicals spilled and set fire to the wooden floor of the car.

While still a teenager, Edison learned to operate a telegraph. It was in this work that his curiosity began to turn to **electricity**, a form of energy. By 19, he was already thinking of a career as an inventor. That was not as wild an idea as it might sound. At the time, there were only about

Thomas Edison in his New Jersey laboratory.
■ Why do you think Edison chose to be photographed in this setting?

200 trained engineers in the United States, and very few of these engineers knew much about electricity.

For the next few years, Edison worked for a company on the New York Stock Exchange. The company received prices of stocks on a machine called a stock ticker and reported the prices to customers. Edison came up with inventions that improved the stock ticker and was able to sell his inventions for $40,000. He was then able to quit his job and, at the age of 23, give his full attention to inventing in his Newark, New Jersey, shop.

During the next 5 years, Edison averaged about 40 inventions a year. One was

the mimeograph machine. He also figured a way to send four messages at once over a single telegraph wire.

The Wizard of Menlo Park In 1876, Edison built a larger laboratory at Menlo Park, New Jersey. He hired a team of people to help him in the business of inventing. He expected, he said, to turn out "a minor invention every 10 days and a big thing every 6 months or so." And he did. The next year Edison invented the phonograph and created another entirely new industry.

Already known as the Wizard of Menlo Park, Edison set out to build a practical electric light bulb. After countless experiments he succeeded in 1879. Three years after that, he built the first central power plant for producing electricity and carrying it into homes and offices. This was the Pearl Street power station in New York City. Again, an entire new industry was created, and the way people lived, worked, and relaxed was changed. Numerous other inventions followed, including the motion-picture machine and the storage battery. Each of these inventions, and others as well, led to new industries.

CHECKUP

1. What natural resources found in the United States were important for industrial expansion?
2. In what two ways did population growth help industrial expansion?
3. Why is capital an important factor in helping industries to grow?
4. Name five inventions and explain how they contributed to industrial growth in the late 1800s.
5. **Thinking Critically** Thomas Edison once said, "Genius is only 1 percent inspiration and 99 percent perspiration." What does this statement mean?

The Oil Industry

VOCABULARY

tycoon	rebate
oil refinery	trust

John D. Rockefeller   The final factor that contributed so greatly to America's industrial growth was the rise of a number of able business leaders. They came from many backgrounds, but all had imagination, an ability to organize, a willingness to take risks, and a driving ambition to win wealth and power. Those business leaders who achieved exceptional wealth and power were called **tycoons**. Andrew Carnegie is one good example. Another is John D. Rockefeller. What Carnegie was to steel, Rockefeller was to oil.

John D. Rockefeller was born in 1839 in upstate New York. Serious-minded and religious, he decided early in life on a business career. After high school he studied bookkeeping at a small business college in Cleveland, Ohio. In 1859, at the age of 20, he and a friend went into business, trading in grains and meat. The business was successful from the start, thanks to Rockefeller's shrewdness and his attention to detail. He boldly borrowed from banks to expand the business. When the Civil War broke out, the firm was in a position to make large profits selling supplies to the Union army.

Black Gold   By this time, Rockefeller had become interested in the new but booming oil industry. People had long known of areas in western Pennsylvania where oil seeped through rock and floated on the creeks. A few people bottled and sold the oil as medicine, but otherwise it had no value. In the 1850s, Benjamin Silliman, a chemistry teacher at Yale University, showed that "Pennsylvania rock oil" could be purified and made into usable products, such as kerosene, for lighting lamps. (Interestingly, at this time no one knew of any use for one of the other products that came from refining oil, and it was thrown away. That product was gasoline.)

Silliman's findings showed that oil could be valuable if someone could find a way to get it out of the ground in quantity. In 1859, Colonel Edwin L. Drake drilled the first oil well at Titusville, Pennsylvania, and a new industry was founded. People flocked to the region to drill for oil. It was the gold rush all over again, except that this time the treasure was black gold, or oil. The crude oil was shipped to nearby Cleveland, where a few men had started **oil refineries**. At an oil refinery, crude oil is purified and made into usable products.

Eliminating the Competition   Oil refining was the part of the oil business that John D. Rockefeller entered in 1867, at the age of 27. His was one of perhaps 30 refineries that competed with each other in Cleveland.

The entire oil industry — from drilling to refining to distributing the kerosene to customers — was marked by fierce competition. Rockefeller saw that if he could gain control of refining, he could control the whole industry. He would be able to name the price he would pay the drillers for their crude oil. He could also name the price at which he would sell the refined oil to distributors. In 1870, Rockefeller formed the Standard Oil Company with the aim of gaining control of the refining business. Within 2 years he was able to buy out most of the other oil refineries in

Cleveland. A few years after that, he reached out to gain control of large refineries in New York, Philadelphia, Baltimore, and Pittsburgh.

How did Rockefeller accomplish this? For one thing, he was an efficient producer. Like Andrew Carnegie in steel, he plowed back profits into the business to pay for expansion. He used the latest methods and machinery. He saved money by manufacturing his own barrels, building his own warehouses, and buying his own pipelines, which carried oil from the wells to his refineries. Thus he was able to refine oil more economically.

Rockefeller was also able to ship his oil for less money. As the largest shipper of oil, he forced railroads into secret deals to give him **rebates** — that is, to pay back to him a portion of the freight rates they charged him. Thus, in Ohio, Rockefeller could ship oil for only 10 cents a barrel,

whereas his competitors had to pay 35 cents. After a time, he demanded that the railroads also give him a share of the freight charges his competitors paid! The railroads had to agree or lose Rockefeller's business.

With such advantages, Rockefeller could sell oil for less than his competitors. He gave other companies a choice: sell out to him at a fair price, or be driven out of business. Standard Oil was quite willing to sell oil at a loss for as long as it would take to drive another company out of business. With methods such as these, Rockefeller gained control of 90 percent of the refining business in the United States by 1879. Thus he virtually had a monopoly of the oil industry.

The Trust In 1882, Standard Oil adopted a new form of organization called a **trust**. A trust is a group of corporations

Oil refineries have been located in New Jersey since the beginning of the industry. This refinery is one of the many that belonged to Rockefeller.
■ Why do you think this oil refinery was located near the water?

run by a single board of trustees. In the Standard Oil Trust, owners of shares in Standard Oil and 39 other oil companies agreed to exchange their stock for trust certificates. The voting rights that went with the stock were held in trust by a small group of people called a board of trustees. The board of trustees controlled and managed Rockefeller's 39 companies. They saw to it that the companies cooperated with each other instead of competing. They limited production and charged high prices. The resulting profits were shared by the original stockholders.

The Standard Oil Trust was so successful that other industries soon formed trusts. Businesses grew bigger. In 1900 two thirds of all manufactured goods in the United States were being produced by a handful of giant corporations.

The Benefits — and Dangers — of Big Business

Large businesses could bring important benefits to the American people. They were often able to make goods more efficiently, at a lower cost than small companies could. This was important for several reasons. It meant that American goods could compete in foreign markets against goods made in other countries. Selling more goods abroad meant more jobs for American workers. At home, big businesses could sell their goods for less.

But did they? Sometimes, yes. Even while making large profits, John D. Rockefeller passed on his lower costs to the buyers. Many trusts and monopolies, however, did not. In fact, one of the main reasons for forming the trust was to raise prices without fear of competition. This, then, was one reason why many Americans in the late 1800s became concerned about the growth of big business.

There were other reasons. Big corporations threatened to put an end to both

This cartoon portrays Rockefeller piling up money because of his control of the oil business.
■ What does the globe represent here?

competition and opportunity in business. People also feared big business's growing power in politics. By the last part of the century, therefore, there was a growing popular demand to control the growth and the behavior of big business.

CHECKUP

1. List the methods Rockefeller used to gain control of the oil industry.
2. What benefits did large-scale businesses bring to the American people?
3. Why did Americans become concerned about the growth of big business?

4. **Thinking Critically** How do rebates today differ from the ones that Rockefeller received from the railroads?

Framing Questions

SETTING PURPOSES FOR READING

Have you ever seen a pamphlet that gives information in the form of questions and answers? Presenting information in this way takes advantage of two important facts about reading. First, you get more out of reading when you read for a purpose, that is, for specific information. Second, the best way to get specific information is to ask a question that directs you to it.

How does reading for a purpose help you get more from your reading? Notice how this question has set a purpose for reading what comes next. Reading for a purpose helps you focus on the material. When you know what you are reading for, you concentrate better. You read more efficiently because you are looking for specific information to answer your question. You can better understand what you are reading and recall what you have read.

What can you do when a purpose has not been set for you? You can set one for yourself. In this textbook you have noticed headings and subheadings in heavy type. These headings are signals to tell you what lies ahead. To set purposes for your reading, simply turn these headings into questions. When you frame questions, you create your own study guide. For example, in the subheading "The Carnegies Immigrate to America," on page 456, these are some questions that might come to mind: Who were the Carnegies? Why were they important? Why did they come to America? What did they do in America? When did they come to America?

SKILLS PRACTICE

On a separate sheet of paper, make up some questions from the subheadings below. Some subheadings may lead to four or five good questions, whereas others may lead to only one or two.

1. Reasons for Carnegie's Success
2. Growth of the Steel Industry
3. Railroad Networks Expand
4. The Transcontinental Railroad
5. Railroads Help to Settle the West
6. Railroads and the Economy
7. New Inventions
8. Black Gold
9. The Trust
10. The Benefits — and Dangers — of Big Business

To practice your skills, do the same for the next chapter. First use your skimming skill to preview the chapter. Then write out your questions. When you start reading for the answers to those questions, you will find that you are reading with a better focus, greater efficiency, and more understanding. It will also be easier to recall what you have read.

MAIN IDEAS

1. Andrew Carnegie became a successful steelmaker by using efficient production methods, reinvesting profits, and hiring talented people to manage his companies.
2. Transcontinental railroads transported settlers to the West and allowed raw materials and goods to be shipped economically across the country.
3. Industrial growth in the United States was encouraged by improved transportation, an abundant supply of natural resources, increasing population, capital for investment, new inventions, and bold business leaders.
4. In the late nineteenth century, many large companies formed trusts and monopolies to eliminate the competition, thus increasing their profits.

VOCABULARY REVIEW

On a separate sheet of paper, write the letter of the best ending for each sentence. Choose your answer from the terms following each sentence.

1. Bell and Edison were famous _____. (**a**) investors (**b**) inventors (**c**) business leaders
2. When railroads returned money to Rockefeller in secret deals, he received _____. (**a**) dividends (**b**) stock (**c**) rebates
3. The Bessemer process is used to make _____. (**a**) textiles (**b**) steel (**c**) oil
4. A gift of financial aid from the government to a person or company is a _____. (**a**) rebate (**b**) stock (**c**) subsidy
5. Money invested in a business is called _____. (**a**) deposit (**b**) capital (**c**) resource
6. One who invests money in a corporation to own part of it receives _____. (**a**) stock (**b**) rebates (**c**) inventions

7. An inventor is given the exclusive right to his invention for a certain time through a _____. (**a**) share (**b**) profit (**c**) patent
8. Having complete control of the supply of certain goods is a _____. (**a**) trustee (**b**) monopoly (**c**) corporation
9. A form of business organization that allows a company to control many other companies is a _____. (**a**) refinery (**b**) patent (**c**) trust
10. A form of business organization that makes it possible to pool the capital of many individuals is a _____. (**a**) subsidy (**b**) refinery (**c**) corporation

CHAPTER CHECKUP

1. What factors led to industrial growth in the United States in the late 1800s?
2. How did the Civil War affect industrial growth?
3. How did railroads affect the economy?
4. Does a patent encourage or discourage inventions? Explain.
5. Describe the steps that Rockefeller took to create a monopoly.
6. **Thinking Critically** Can a country without its own natural resources become industrialized? Explain.
7. **Thinking Critically** Compare the advantages and disadvantages of a corporation and of individual ownership of a business.

APPLYING KNOWLEDGE

1. Make a diagram of the organization of a corporation. Show the board of directors, the corporation's officers, and the stockholders. If you need more information, see page 465.
2. List all the electrical appliances in your home. Ask your parents to check off the ones in their homes when they were growing up. Ask your grandparents or other older people to check off the ones they had as children.

20 Cities and Immigrants 1880–1915

Urban Growth

Why did cities grow rapidly in the late 1800s?

VOCABULARY

| architect | skyscraper |

Birth of the Skyscraper When the Home Insurance Company hired William Le Baron Jenney to design a new office building in Chicago in 1882, the company did not know he was about to change the face of the American city. Jenney was an **architect**—a designer of buildings. He was born in 1832 and had studied in Boston and in Paris, France. At a time of rapidly growing cities, Chicago was one of the fastest growing cities in the country. Not even a great fire in 1871, which left much of the city in ashes, slowed Chicago's growth for long. Its population, which was 290,000 in 1870, had already reached a half million by 1880. New buildings were being built.

William Le Baron Jenney and other architects who designed office buildings had to consider two main requirements. One was that the buildings had to be very tall. This was necessary because of the high price of land in the downtown area. The other was that there had to be plenty of window space to allow daylight into the offices, since electric lighting was not in wide use at the time.

The problem in those days was that the whole weight of a building, including the floors and the inner walls, was supported by its outside walls. Therefore, the taller a building, the thicker its walls had to be at the bottom. And if many spaces had to be left for windows, the walls would have to be even thicker. As a result, few office buildings were more than five or six stories high.

Jenney's solution was to design the new building with a skeleton of iron and steel—the same steel that Carnegie and others were making into rails for the railroads. This strong metal skeleton, rather than the outer walls, would carry the weight of the building. With this design Jenney could make his building taller without making the lower walls so thick.

Jenney's Home Insurance building was completed in 1885. It was 10 stories high, taller than all but a few buildings of the time. More important, Jenney had developed a design that would one day allow the construction of buildings many times higher than the Home Insurance building. These very tall buildings seemed to touch, or scrape, the sky. The modern **skyscraper** had been born.

One of the many United States cities that experienced rapid growth in the late 1800s was Atlanta, Georgia, a center of trade and transportation.
■ What was the peak year of immigration?

EVENTS IN OUR COUNTRY

1880 Decade of great urban growth begins
1882 Chinese Exclusion Act passed
1885 First modern skyscraper
1889 Jane Addams opens Hull House
1890 Riis publishes *How the Other Half Lives*
1907 Peak year of immigration

1880
1885
1890
1895
1900
1905
1910

EVENTS ELSEWHERE

1913 Bohr develops theory of atomic structure
1912 First Balkan War begins
1910 Mexican Revolution begins
1905 First motor buses in London
1897 Famine in India
1891 Famine in Russia
1887 France unites holdings in Indochina

Louis Sullivan   If Jenney was the father of the modern skyscraper, Louis Sullivan helped make the design America's greatest contribution to architecture. Sullivan was 24 years younger than Jenney. Like Jenney, he was born in Massachusetts, studied there and in Paris, and moved to Chicago to embark upon his career. By the time he was 26, Sullivan was one of that city's most successful architects.

The Flatiron Building in New York City was one of the first skyscrapers.
■ How is this building different from the other buildings around it?

Sullivan believed that the American city should develop its own kind of architecture, different from anything else in the world. The new American building, he wrote, "must be tall, every inch of it tall. . . . It must be every inch a proud, soaring thing." Following Jenney's work, Sullivan designed a number of tall buildings, not only in Chicago but also in New York, Buffalo, and St. Louis. He became the most important American architect of his time. As a result of the work of Sullivan and his followers, the look of the American city was changed forever.

Americans Move to the City   Skyscrapers were evidence that in the last half of the nineteenth century America was becoming urban. In 1790, when the first census was taken, only 1 American in 20 lived in a city. Even in 1860, only 1 in 6 did. But 40 years later, the number was 1 in 3. In 1860 only 16 cities had a population of 50,000 or more. By 1910 there were more than 100.

Some of these cities were truly huge. New York's population, which was a half-million people in 1850, grew to 3.4 million in 1900. Philadelphia went from 121,000 to 1.5 million in that time, and Chicago from 29,000 to 1.3 million.

The greatest single decade of city growth was the 1880s. In that 10-year period some cities doubled and even tripled their populations. Kansas City, Missouri, went from 60,000 to 132,000; Omaha, Nebraska, from 30,500 to 140,000; and Minneapolis, Minnesota, from 47,000 to 164,000. Places that were hardly larger than villages and small towns at the start of the decade were busy cities by its end. Birmingham, Alabama, went from 3,000 to 26,000; Duluth, Minnesota, from 3,300 to 33,000; and Seattle, Washington, from 3,500 to 42,000.

Reasons for Growth   Location had a good deal to do with the growth of these cities. Many were on important water routes. Fine harbors for oceangoing ships fostered the growth of some important commercial and shipping centers. These trade centers included cities such as New York, Boston, Philadelphia, and Baltimore on the Atlantic seaboard, New Orleans along the Gulf of Mexico, and San Francisco and Seattle on the Pacific coast. Other cities, located on inland rivers and canals, served as collecting and processing points for goods produced in the countryside. St. Louis on the Mississippi River and Buffalo at the western end of the Erie Canal are examples.

As important as water transportation was to the growth of cities, railroads became even more important in the last half of the nineteenth century. For example, the location of Minneapolis on the Mississippi River had always given the city good water transportation. But the great growth of Minneapolis came in the 1880s when railroads tied the city to the rich wheatlands of the West and made it into a center for flour milling. In the same way, Chicago increased greatly in size when it became a major railroad center.

Railroads not only made some cities larger, they also created new ones. Kansas City, Missouri, was founded when a railroad company decided to run a line through that town rather than through nearby Fort Leavenworth.

The Industrial Revolution contributed to the growth of cities. People flocked to cities for jobs in the new factories. Many cities owed their growth to a single large industry. In Pittsburgh and Birmingham it was steel. In Cleveland it was oil refining. Milwaukee had beer; Omaha had meat packing; Minneapolis and St. Paul had wheat milling. After the

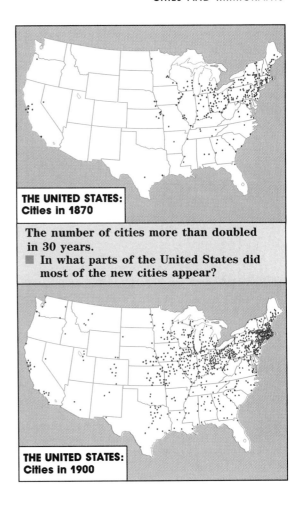

THE UNITED STATES: Cities in 1870

The number of cities more than doubled in 30 years.
■ In what parts of the United States did most of the new cities appear?

THE UNITED STATES: Cities in 1900

turn of the century, Detroit began producing automobiles. Of course, very large cities like New York, Philadelphia, and Chicago, had many industries — they were centers for railroads, manufacturing, banking, and trade.

Mass Transportation   Transportation developments in the late nineteenth century changed not only the size of the cities but also their shape. Early cities were "walking cities"—that is, most people traveled to work and other places on foot. In a walking city, factories and warehouses, shops, and offices were in the center of the city, and most people lived near their place of work. Even the owners usually lived close to their factories. A

With the introduction of electric streetcars, like these in San Francisco, California, people began to move out from the center of the cities.
■ What other changes would streetcars cause in the cities?

walking city almost never measured more than 3 or 4 miles (5 or 6 km) from one end to the other—about the distance a person might walk in an hour. When population increased in the walking city, more people simply crowded into the existing space.

Then in the mid-1800s the street railway, or horsecar, made its appearance. These cars, drawn by horses along a track, could carry people about twice as fast as they could walk. Horse-drawn cars were the first step in the development of mass transportation.

In the late 1880s electric streetcars, or trolley cars, replaced the horsecars. Streetcars made it possible for people to live farther from the center of the city. Cities spread out. By 1900 larger cities might measure 8 or 10 miles (13 or 16 km)

from one end to another. People who could afford it began to move out from center of the city. Poorer workers and newcomers to the city were left to occupy the older downtown neighborhoods.

1. What changes in design and materials made it possible to have taller office buildings?
2. Compare the size of America's urban population in 1790 and 1900.
3. Give three reasons why cities changed in the late nineteenth century.
4. How did mass transportation change cities?
5. **Thinking Critically** How did skyscrapers change the way people lived and worked?

People in the Cities

Leaving America's Farms   In 1860 about 6 million people lived in America's cities. In 1900, some 30 million did. Where did these millions of new city dwellers come from? One main source was America's countryside.

During the late 1800s, 40 percent of the townships in the United States saw their population decline. Most of this decline took place because many rural people moved to the cities. All in all, between 1880 and 1910 about 11 million people who were born in rural areas moved to cities. The traffic was almost entirely one-way — for every 20 who left the farm for the city, only 1 city dweller moved to a farm. In some parts of New England and the Midwest, entire villages were abandoned.

A small but growing part of this movement was made up of black people leaving the rural South. At first, black farm families moved into southern states, where there had been a large number of free blacks before the Civil War. In the late nineteenth century, however, southern blacks began to move to northern and western cities.

Why did farm people go to the city? There were several reasons. For one thing, during the last three decades of the 1800s, farm prices had been low, and farmers had had a hard time making a living. Many even lost their farms.

Perhaps more important was the hope of escaping the long hours, the hard work, and the loneliness of farm life. Kate Sanborn, a New England woman who lived on a farm, explained what life was like on many eastern farms:

> It's all work, with no play and no proper pay. . . . and how can the children consent to stay on, starving body and soul? *That* explains the 3,318 abandoned farms in Maine at present. And the farmers' wives! What monotonous, treadmill lives! Constant toil, with no wages, no allowance, no pocket money, no vacations, no pleasure trips to the city nearest them. . . . Someone says that their only chance for social life is in going to some insane asylum!

By comparison, the city seemed a place of glamour and excitement. There were theaters, sports, and various other entertainments. There were shops with goods from around the world. There were variety and crowds and the latest marvel of the age, electric lighting. (Even as late as the early 1930s, some 90 percent of America's farms still had no electricity.)

Perhaps most important of all was economic opportunity. Some people, no doubt, had a view colored by popular literature, with its stories of winning fame and fortune in the city. Most people, however, were more realistic. They hoped simply for jobs that would give them a little better way of life.

A Rising Tide of Immigrants   Another main source of population for America's growing cities was Europe. Immigrants from Europe's farms and villages had been swelling the population of American cities since the 1820s. In the 1840s and 1850s alone, more than a million Irish arrived.

479

They were fleeing a terrible **famine**, or a very great shortage of food, as well as harsh British rule. Altogether, about 2 million Irish came to the United States between 1820 and 1860. Another 1.5 million immigrants came from Germany, and three quarters of a million more were from England, Scotland, and Wales. Thousands of others arrived from France, the Netherlands, and the Scandinavian countries.

Those who had been skilled workers —tailors, carpenters, weavers, and the like—found a demand for their services in the cities and settled there. Most of the immigrants, though, were farmers. To them, America promised plentiful land and a good life in farming. Although thousands did become farmers, the great majority of these immigrants, too, wound up in the cities.

Most immigrants were far too poor to buy a farm. They had to find work quickly, and they could do this in the cities. Because they were unskilled, all they had to sell was their muscle power. They took whatever work they could get at whatever pay they were offered.

Prosperity and Freedom The wave of immigration before the Civil War was just the beginning. Between 1865 and 1914, 25 million immigrants entered the United States. Most were from Europe, but some came from Asia and from other countries in the Americas.

For the first part of this time period, most immigrants came from the same

Loaded down with family possessions, European immigrants come ashore in New York.
■ **How might a photograph of this scene present a different view?**

Hot Dogs

Among the foods Germans brought to America was the meat sausage. In St. Louis in the 1880s, one of these German immigrants, Antoine Feuchtwanger, began to sell these sausages to the public in a new way — in a roll. Feuchtwanger came from Frankfurt, Germany, and was therefore known as a Frankfurter. So his new sausage sandwich came to be called that, too.

As America's first hot "fast food," frankfurters were popular at picnics, baseball games, beaches, and wherever else people went for outdoor entertainment. It was at baseball games that the frankfurter began to be called a hot dog. The change came in two steps. In a New York baseball park in the 1890s, vendors called attention to their hot fast food by shouting, "Get your red hots! Red hots!" For a time, frankfurters were called red hots. The change from *red hots* to *hot dogs* came about 10 years later. T.A. Dorgan, a very popular newspaper cartoonist, had eaten many red hots at ball games. But one day in 1906 he was suddenly struck by how much the frankfurter looked like the long body of a dachshund, a short-legged German dog. German sausage, German dog; red hots, hot dog — it clicked. He drew a cartoon showing the red hot as a dachshund in a bun and called it "Hot dog!" And it has been called by this name ever since.

countries in northern and western Europe as had the earlier immigrants. Beginning in the 1880s, however, large numbers began to arrive from eastern and southern Europe. These included people from Russia, Poland, Austria-Hungary, Italy, Greece, and Romania. Immigration from this part of Europe came to be called the **New Immigration**, and the name given to immigration from the countries in northern and western Europe was the **Old Immigration**. By the 1890s the number of New Immigrants entering the United States each year passed the number of Old Immigrants. In 1907, the peak year of immigration, 80 percent of the 1.2 million people who left their countries to enter the United States were New Immigrants.

These immigrants came to America for many different reasons. Most were peasants — poor farming people. In their countries, population was growing fast, and there was simply not enough land to go around. Some young men left so they would not have to serve in the army. Many thousands, like the Poles and the Slovaks, were being forced to live under foreign rule. Armenians fled Turkish persecution. More than a million Jews fled persecution in Russia.

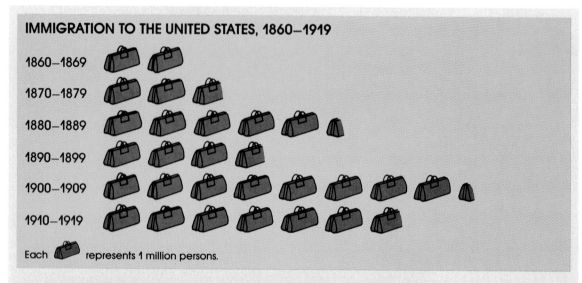

IMMIGRATION TO THE UNITED STATES, 1860–1919

1860–1869

1870–1879

1880–1889

1890–1899

1900–1909

1910–1919

Each represents 1 million persons.

This pictograph shows the number of immigrants who entered the United States between 1860 and 1919.
■ In which decade did the largest number arrive?

Mary Antin was one of those Jews whose family fled Russia. In her autobiography she described what it was like to experience a **pogrom**. A pogrom is an organized massacre of people. In Russia pogroms of the Jews were usually encouraged by the government.

> They [the peasants] would set out to kill the Jews. They attacked them with knives and clubs and scythes and axes, killed them or tortured them, and burned their homes.

In 1891, when Mary was 10, her father went to America. After 3 years he had saved enough to send for his wife and six children. Once in America, Mary enjoyed the benefits of a free public education. She later went on to college and became a social worker and a writer. When she wrote her autobiography, she called it *The Promised Land,* for she believed that her life story proved "what a real thing is this American freedom."

Not all who came to America in the New Immigration planned to stay. Some —perhaps as many as one in three— came to earn money to return and buy farmland in their native country.

The New Immigrants New Immigrants poured into cities in even greater numbers than did the Old Immigrants. They found jobs in the new factories of industrial America. They worked in steel mills, meat-packing plants, and textile factories. They made cigars in crowded workshops or sometimes in their own homes. Some women worked as **domestics**, or household servants. Others labored in the garment industry.

By 1910, foreign-born people made up 40 percent of New York City's population, 36 percent of Chicago's, and 34 percent of San Francisco's. Together with their children these people made up more than three fourths of the population of those cities, and of Detroit and Cleveland as well. More Italians lived in New York City than in Rome, and more Greeks lived there than in any city in Greece except Athens. More Poles lived in Chicago than in any Polish city except Warsaw. In a strange twist of history, the rapid growth of urban America at this time was largely the result of the arrival of European peasants!

Immigrants from Asia added to the foreign-born population of several western cities. Chinese had been arriving on the West Coast since the days of the California gold rush. Many thousands of them were hired to build the Central Pacific Railroad in the 1860s. The Chinese population spread throughout the West in both large and small cities, and large neighborhoods of Chinese people formed in Los Angeles and San Francisco.

Japanese immigrants did not arrive much before the end of the century. They came in smaller numbers, about 70,000 in all. Most Japanese immigrants took up farming or fishing, but some found work in industry or opened small shops in some of the cities of California.

Many American cities now had a foreign flavor. The New Immigrants, like earlier immigrants, sought the comfort and security of living with people of the same nationality. They clustered in neighborhoods where they continued to speak their own languages, follow their familiar customs, and wear their traditional dress. These neighborhoods became known by such names as Little Italy and Greektown. Foreign-language newspapers appeared by the dozen.

Out of both choice and necessity, immigrants lived at first in separate city neighborhoods, like San Francisco's Chinatown (left) and New York's Little Italy (right).
■ **What would be the advantages of living in such a neighborhood?**

Employment   There was a popular saying about America in Europe: "The streets are paved with gold." One person wrote that upon arrival in the United States, immigrants quickly learned three things:

> First, that the streets were not paved with gold; second, that the streets were not paved at all; and third, that they [the immigrant workers] were expected to pave them.

Immigrants of the late nineteenth and early twentieth centuries were mostly unskilled workers. Fewer than 1 in 10 had a trade, or work skill. Fewer still could speak English. Add to this the discrimination they often met, and it is not hard to understand why immigrants wound up with the hardest and lowest-paid jobs. These immigrants, along with the descendants of black slaves, provided much of the physical labor that built modern America.

In particular, immigrants from southern and eastern Europe filled the bottom ranks of heavy industry. In the Carnegie steel mills in Pittsburgh, for example, more than 11,000 of the 14,000 common laborers in 1907 were from eastern Europe. Irish, Chinese, Mexican, and Italian immigrants dug tunnels and laid track for the railroads. The women did domestic work and held jobs in canneries, mills, and clothing factories. Their hours were long and their wages were low.

Even so, most immigrants found themselves better off in America than they had been in the Old Country. And in time, many were able to improve their positions. As new waves of immigrants arrived and took the poorest jobs, the earlier immigrants who had held these jobs moved up the ladder. Many immigrants and their children were also able to learn skills and to advance.

Immigrants provided much of the labor for such jobs as laying the cities' new trolley tracks.
■ **Why would immigrants have good luck finding this kind of job?**

A Presidential Veto

The Chinese Exclusion Act was passed in 1882. On March 16, 1896, Senator Henry Cabot Lodge of Massachusetts proposed a bill in Congress to further restrict immigration by prohibiting all people who could not read or write from entering the country. The bill was passed by Congress but vetoed by President Grover Cleveland. In the following document Cleveland states his reasons for the veto.

A century's stupendous growth, largely due to the assimilation and thrift of sturdy and patriotic adopted citizens, attests the success of this generous and free-handed policy, which, while guarding the people's interests, exacts from our immigrants only physical and moral soundness and a willingness and ability to work. . . .

The best reason that could be given for this radical restriction of immigration is the necessity of protecting our population against degeneration and saving our national peace and quiet from imported turbulence and disorder.

I can not believe that we would be protected against these evils by limiting immigration to those who can read and write in any language twenty-five words of our Constitution. In my opinion it is infinitely more safe to admit a hundred thousand immigrants who, though unable to read and write, seek among us only a home and opportunity to work, than to admit one of those unruly agitators and enemies of government control, who can not only read and write but delights in arousing by inflammatory speech the illiterate and peacefully inclined to discontent and tumult. Violence and disorder do not originate with illiterate laborers. They are rather victims of an educated agitator. The ability to read and write as required in this bill, in and of itself, affords, in my opinion, a misleading test of contented industry and supplies unsatisfactory evidence of desirable citizenship or a proper apprehension of the benefits of our institutions. . . .

USING SOURCE MATERIAL

1. How did Lodge's bill propose to test a person's ability to read and write?
2. According to Cleveland, what type of person causes violence and disorder?
3. Do you think immigration to the United States should be limited today? Give reasons to support your answer.

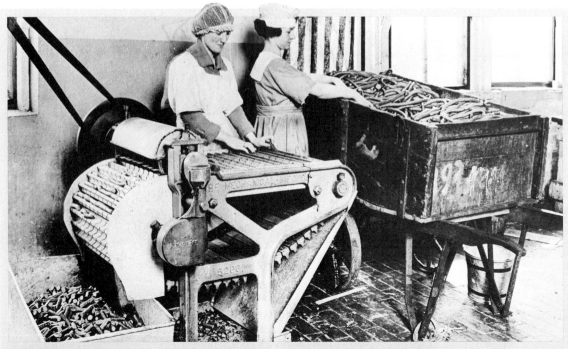

Canneries provided jobs for immigrant women, though the work was often seasonal.
■ What can you conclude from this picture about safety on the job for cannery workers at this time?

Reactions to Immigration Some Americans grew worried about the large number of immigrants entering the United States. These Americans disliked and feared the foreign ways of the newcomers. Would these new immigrants adopt American ways and values? Or would they weaken the character of America? Further, America was, for the most part, a Protestant country. These new immigrants were mainly Roman Catholic, Greek and Russian Orthodox, and Jewish. Some American workers complained that the immigrants worked for low pay and would either take away their jobs or lower the wage level for all. All in all, said those who believed these things, America could be preserved only by limiting the number of foreigners entering the United States or by ending immigration altogether. Those who favored this course were known as **nativists**.

Nativism won its first victory in the Chinese Exclusion Act of 1882. This was an act of Congress that ended further immigration of Chinese people. Nativists were not able to limit the flow of European immigrants at that time. However, their demands continued to be heard, and they would finally succeed in the 1920s.

CHECKUP

1. Why did urban populations increase in the late 1800s?
2. How did the New Immigration differ from the Old Immigration?
3. What kinds of employment did the immigrants find?
4. Why did some Americans worry about the large number of immigrants entering the country?
5. **Thinking Critically** What arguments might have been made in favor of large-scale immigration?

486

Urban Problems

How did Americans try to deal with the problems created by rapid urban growth?

Growing Pains   With populations doubling and even tripling in a decade, how could cities hope to keep up with the need for services? The answer was that, try as they might, they could not. Take street paving, for example. In 1890, after 10 years of mushrooming growth, not a single one of Minneapolis's 200 miles (320 km) of streets had been paved. Only 100 miles (161 km) of New Orleans's 500 miles (805 km) were paved. In Chicago, the nation's second largest city, two thirds of the streets were still dirt in 1900.

One can imagine the difficulty of getting around on such streets, whether by horse and wagon, by bicycle, or on foot. In dry weather, wagons raised clouds of choking dust. In rainy weather, the streets became rivers of mud.

Crowded cities meant crowded buildings. And since most of these buildings were made of wood, the chance of a fire sweeping away a whole section of a city was great. Many cities experienced that fate. The worst fire of the century occurred in Chicago in 1871. Within days, a third of the city —17,000 buildings —was destroyed, more than 300 persons were dead, and 90,000 were left homeless.

A third of Chicago was destroyed by a fire in October 1871.
■ **How does this fire scene differ from what you might see around a large fire today?**

487

Crime increased in the crowded cities. Robbery, assault, and even killing were on the rise. In some notorious sections, like Hell's Kitchen in New York and the Barbary Coast in San Francisco, laws were rarely obeyed.

Yet another serious urban problem was **sanitation** — making clean and healthful conditions. When cities were smaller, garbage was thrown into the streets and alleys, sometimes to be eaten by pigs that were permitted to roam freely. In the mushrooming cities of the late 1800s, other means were needed to get rid of the garbage that piled up and dirtied both the air and the water. Outhouses and cesspools were no longer sufficient for disposing of sewage when hundreds of people lived in a single building.

Jacob Riis photographed this tenement courtyard at New York's Baxter Street.
■ **What do you think a typical day was like for the children pictured here?**

Tackling the Problems To cope with such problems, cities had to change their ways. They had always depended upon volunteer fire fighters to battle the blazes and on volunteer police to protect the population against crime. Now they began to organize professional fire departments, train fire fighters, and buy fire engines that could pump water to the roofs of most city buildings. They organized professional police departments to protect citizens. They arranged to collect garbage on a regular schedule.

Sometimes, though, in trying to solve one problem, cities made another problem worse. In 1900 most cities had built water systems that piped water into homes and offices. They also built underground sewage systems to replace outdoor toilets and cesspools. The problem was that the sewage pipes often led into the same lakes and rivers from which the city drew its water supply. It was little wonder, then, why such diseases as typhoid fever and cholera became widespread.

The Housing Problem The city's greatest failure was its inability to provide good housing for its people. The housing problem was especially bad in large cities.

New York, the biggest city, had the biggest problem. There the poor, especially the immigrants, were packed into **tenements**. These were mostly four-to-six-story wooden apartment buildings, often in run-down condition. As the population increased, each building had to house more people. For example, a five-story tenement at 36 Cherry Street was already crowded with 500 people in 1865. Twelve years later, 800 lived in the same building.

Jacob Riis A newspaper reporter named Jacob Riis (rēs) did more than any other person to make Americans aware of

Members of this family earned a living by making artificial flowers in their apartment.
■ How would you describe living conditions in this family's apartment?

what life in a tenement was like. Riis was an immigrant himself. He came to America from Denmark in 1870 at the age of 21. He tried his hand at such jobs as farming, coal mining, brickmaking, and peddling before landing a job with a New York newspaper in 1877. For the next 15 years, Riis worked as a police reporter for two of the city's great newspapers, the *Tribune* and the *Evening Sun.*

Time and again his reporting on accidents and crime brought him into the city's slums. The young reporter became outraged by the conditions he saw there. He began to write articles about the life of the poor, and especially of children in these slums.

In 1890, Riis wrote a book called *How the Other Half Lives.* At one point he invites the reader to enter a typical tenement with him:

> . . . the hall is dark, and you might stumble over the children pitching pennies back there. . . . Here where the hall turns and

dives into utter darkness is a step. . . . All the fresh air that ever enters these stairs comes from the hall door that is forever slamming, and from the windows of dark bedrooms. . . . The sinks are in the hallway, that all tenants may have access —and all be poisoned alike by their summer stenches.

In many of these buildings, there was no running water. To get water for cooking or bathing, tenants had to take their buckets to a public pump in the street. Toilets were in outhouses in the backyards. Riis reported how diseases raced unchecked through the tenements, taking a high toll among children. Of 138 children born in one tenement, 61 died at an early age, most of them before they were a year old.

Through his writings Jacob Riis got the tenement block known as Mulberry Bend torn down and replaced by a park. But there were hundreds of tenement blocks in New York City, with 2.5 million people living in them.

Jane Addams and Hull House The plight of the city's poor stirred the consciences of many. Some reformers took on the task of making life better for them. One of the most famous of these was Jane Addams. She was born into a prosperous family in a small Illinois town in 1860. She was part of the first generation of American women to attend college. After her graduation Jane Addams looked for a career in which she could be of service to others. She found it on a trip to England. There, in London, she visited what was known as a **settlement house**. In this building, services of various kinds were provided for the poor people of the neighborhood.

On her return to America, Jane Addams resolved to open a settlement house. She and a college friend, Ellen Gates Starr, rented an old, run-down mansion in a poor section of Chicago. The old building was repaired and in 1889, Hull House was opened to the people of the neighborhood. Most of them were poor Italian, Greek, Polish, Jewish, and Russian immigrants.

Helping the Urban Poor Hull House served as a neighborhood center. Here the poor received medical care, got help in finding jobs, and took lessons in English. There was a kindergarten class for the young and there were social clubs for the elderly. Young people took lessons in music and drama, and learned job skills as well. Jane Addams and her fellow settlement workers lived among the people they were serving. They respected the immigrants' customs and values even as they helped them move into the mainstream of American life.

Hull House became a model for settlement houses in other cities. Some 70 others were established in cities such as New York, Boston, and Detroit in the 1890s and early 1900s.

Settlement houses showed what could be done to help the urban poor. Yet the settlement houses alone could not possibly take care of the millions of needy people. It was clear that many more changes would be needed for America to cope with the problems accompanying its tremendous growth.

Governing the Cities City governments were poorly suited to cope with the problems of growth. In fact, one observer called city governments in the United

Jane Addams helped found Hull House, a settlement house that provided many services for the poor in Chicago.
■ **Who provides such services today?**

States "the worst in Christendom—the most expensive, the most inefficient, and the most corrupt."

The problem was that these governments were designed in an earlier age, when cities were smaller and problems were simpler. Mayors had little power because in earlier times it was thought unwise to give much power to one person. What power there was in government usually lay with the city council. This body was made up of 12 to 24 people, each of whom was mainly interested in his own neighborhood rather than in the needs of the city as a whole. Yet there were great tasks to be done—roads to be paved; street railways to be built; public buildings to be constructed; gas, water, and electricity to be provided; and the health of the people to be protected.

The Political Machine   Stepping into this situation was the **political machine**. *Machine* was simply the name given to a political organization that ran smoothly, from the political workers at the bottom to the boss at the top. The machine elected its friends. In awarding contracts for paving roads, constructing city buildings, and providing public utilities, officials acted as the boss told them to. Those who received the contracts paid the machine and the boss handsomely. There were always people who were willing to offer thousands in payoffs in order to make millions in profit.

The machine was able to elect its people because it won the support of immigrants. From the boss to the workers, the machine understood the problem of immigrants when few others seemed to care. It met the newcomers at the boat and helped them find their first jobs. It provided them with food and coal in hard times. It helped out when their children had

Politics in the early 1900s was often controlled by the political machine.
■ Who supported the political machines?

brushes with the law. It joined their ethnic celebrations. It helped them with their citizenship papers. In return, the grateful immigrants gave the machine their support on election day. From the point of view of the immigrants, casting their ballots for the machine candidates was a fair exchange.

CHECKUP

1. Name four problems faced by the growing cities of the late nineteenth century.
2. Who was Jacob Riis?
3. How did Jane Addams try to help the urban poor?
4. List the points in favor of and against the political machine in the late 1800s.
5. **Thinking Critically** Do you think the positive actions of the political machine outweighed the negative? Explain.

Making Inferences

DRAWING CONCLUSIONS FROM EVIDENCE

Read the following paragraph and answer the questions below on a separate sheet of paper.

One can imagine the difficulty of getting around on such streets, whether by horse and wagon, by bicycle, or on foot. In dry weather, wagons raised clouds of choking dust. In rainy weather, the streets became rivers of mud. Whatever the weather, the long skirts that women wore were constantly getting dirty.

1. Is this paragraph about a city of today?
2. Are the streets paved or unpaved?
3. What problems might a horse-drawn wagon have after several days of rain?

Nowhere above does it state that the place is not a city of today or that the streets were unpaved. You probably figured out those facts by using clues, or bits of evidence, you found in the paragraph. You also brought to your reading the knowledge that a heavy wagon will sink in mud. That information helped you to answer the third question.

The process of drawing conclusions from bits of evidence is called *making inferences*. It is an important learning skill. It helps you make the most of the information you have. When you make inferences, you combine the new information with what you already know to draw conclusions. The more evidence you have and the more information you bring to your reading, the more likely it is that you will make correct inferences.

SKILLS PRACTICE

Read the following document carefully. It is New York's Regulations for Teachers in 1872.

1. Teachers each day will fill lamps, clean chimneys and clean wicks.
2. Each teacher will bring a bucket of water and a scuttle of coal for the day's session of school.
3. Make your pens carefully. You may whittle nibs for the individual tastes of the pupils.
4. Men teachers may take one evening a week for courting purposes, or two evenings a week if they attend church regularly.
5. After ten hours in school, teachers should spend the remaining time reading the Bible or other good books.
6. Women teachers who marry or engage in unseemly conduct will be dismissed.
7. Each teacher who smokes, uses liquor in any form, frequents pool or public halls, or gets shaved in a barber shop, will give good reason to suspect his worth, intentions, integrity, and honesty.
8. Each teacher should lay aside from each pay a goodly sum of his earnings for his benefit during his declining years so he will not become a burden on society.
9. The teacher who performs his labors faithfully and without fail for five years will be given an increase of twenty-five cents per week in his pay providing the Board of Education approves.

Now, on a separate sheet of paper, write one thing you can infer from the regulations about each of the following subjects.

1. Differences in attitude toward female and male teachers
2. Freedom of teachers to do as they wished outside of school
3. Teachers' salaries
4. Retirement pay for teachers
5. Care of school buildings

★ ★ ★ ★ ★ ★ ★ ★ ★ **CHAPTER 20 REVIEW** ★ ★ ★ ★ ★ ★ ★ ★ ★

MAIN IDEAS

1. Location, job opportunities, and the development of mass transportation contributed to the growth of cities in the late 1800s.
2. The movement of American farm people to the city and the arrival of immigrants from other countries led to a dramatic increase in the urban population.
3. Overcrowded cities created health and safety problems.
4. To solve these problems, cities developed professional fire and police departments, regular garbage collections, and underground sewage systems.
5. City political machines gave immigrants aid in exchange for their votes.

VOCABULARY REVIEW

On a separate sheet of paper, write **T** if the statement is true and **F** if it is false. If the statement is false, replace the underlined term to make the statement true.

1. An office or business building of many stories with a skeleton of iron and steel is called a <u>tenement.</u>
2. People who design office buildings are called <u>social workers.</u>
3. In the late 1880s, city transportation was improved by the introduction of <u>electric streetcars.</u>
4. In the late 1880s, people coming from eastern and southern Europe to the United States were called the <u>Old Immigration.</u>
5. Many Jewish immigrants from Russia had experienced massacres called <u>pogroms.</u>
6. In the late 1800s a major urban problem was <u>sanitation.</u>
7. Americans who felt that immigration should be greatly reduced were known as <u>political bosses.</u>
8. A city building where various services were provided for the poor was a <u>settlement house.</u>
9. A political machine got votes for its candidates by helping <u>immigrants.</u>
10. During the 1880s, great population gains were made in <u>rural</u> areas.

CHAPTER CHECKUP

1. How did the location of a city influence its growth?
2. Why did immigration to the United States increase in the late 1800s?
3. Why did immigrants settle in neighborhoods where people of their own nationality lived?
4. List the problems growing cities faced in the late 1800s and their solutions. Which of these problems do we still have today?
5. **Thinking Critically** Why do you think richer people moved out of the center of the cities after the arrival of streetcars?

APPLYING KNOWLEDGE

1. Most people in the United States are either immigrants or the descendants of immigrants. Find out the background of your own family. List the countries your grandparents, great grandparents, or earlier ancestors came from. Then compare your list with the lists of your classmates. How many different countries have you and your classmates listed? Make a class list of these countries or regions.
2. Describe what you think were the attitudes of the following people toward immigrants: (**a**) an employer looking for cheap labor, (**b**) an American concerned about keeping his job, (**c**) a nativist, (**d**) the boss of a political machine in a big city.

493

CHAPTER 21 *Workers and Farmers Seek Reforms*

1865–1900

Industrialism and the Workers

How did industrialism change the ways of work?

VOCABULARY

labor union	blacklist
strike	

A 10-year-old Worker Samuel Gompers learned at first hand about unions and employers early in his working career. Samuel was born in England in 1850. He attended school for a few years but had to drop out to help bring in income for his family. He took up his father's trade, cigar making. At the age of 10, Samuel was a full-time member of the English working class. Samuel was paid a wage of sixpence (then about twelve cents) a week.

In 1863 the Gompers family moved to the United States. They hoped to escape a life of poverty in England. As it turned out, they simply exchanged their London slum for one on New York's Lower East Side. In their cramped apartment, Samuel and his father rolled tobacco leaves into cigars from early morning until night. After a year, Samuel began to work in the cigar-making shops of New York City. The hours were long and the pay low, but Samuel liked his job.

Belonging to a Union In 1864 the cigar makers formed a **labor union.** A labor union is an organization formed by a group of workers to bargain for higher pay and better working conditions. The 14-year-old Samuel joined the union, though he did not take an active part in it. One day his union called a **strike**—that is, they stopped working in an attempt to gain better wages and working conditions. But the strike was unsuccessful, and the workers finally returned to their jobs without gaining anything.

For Samuel Gompers, however, that was not the end of the matter. Gompers's employer fired him and others who had taken part in the strike. The employer also sent the names of the strikers to other employers, warning them against hiring these troublemakers. Such a list of names is known as a **blacklist.**

For a year and a half, Samuel Gompers could not work at his trade in New York. He took what jobs he could find in small cigar-making shops in New Jersey. Being blacklisted was one part of Samuel Gompers's education on unions.

He also learned a lot working in the factory. In cigar factories, workers sitting at long tables did all the work by hand. In

During the Pullman strike the United States cavalry escorts a train loaded with meat as it moves out of the Chicago stockyards past angry strikers.
■ **When did the Pullman strike occur?**

494

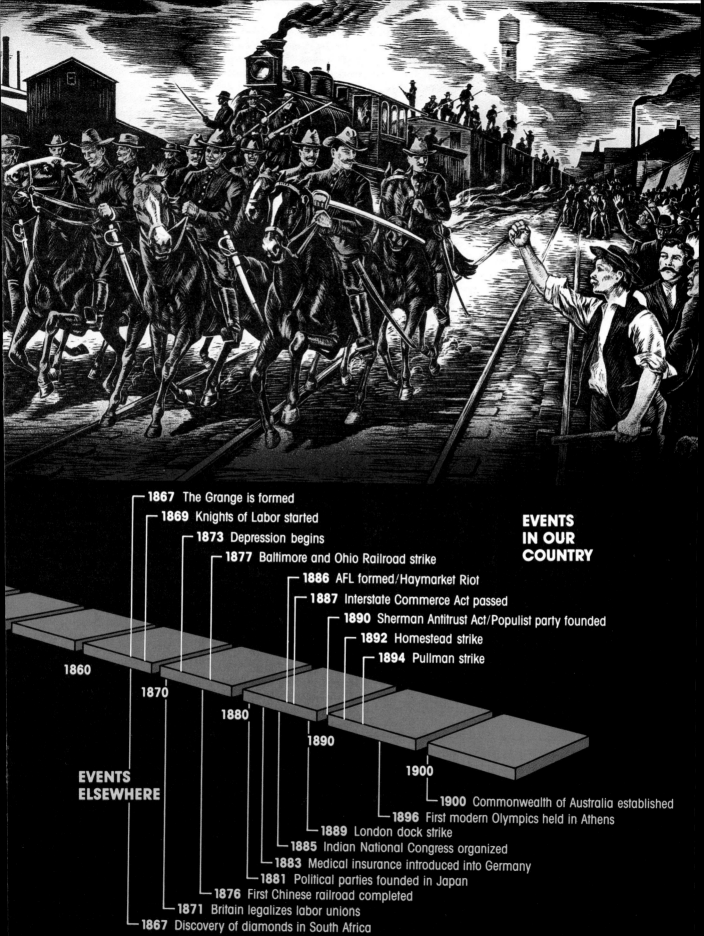

EVENTS IN OUR COUNTRY

1867 The Grange is formed
1869 Knights of Labor started
1873 Depression begins
1877 Baltimore and Ohio Railroad strike
1886 AFL formed/Haymarket Riot
1887 Interstate Commerce Act passed
1890 Sherman Antitrust Act/Populist party founded
1892 Homestead strike
1894 Pullman strike

1860
1870
1880
1890
1900

EVENTS ELSEWHERE

1900 Commonwealth of Australia established
1896 First modern Olympics held in Athens
1889 London dock strike
1885 Indian National Congress organized
1883 Medical insurance introduced into Germany
1881 Political parties founded in Japan
1876 First Chinese railroad completed
1871 Britain legalizes labor unions
1867 Discovery of diamonds in South Africa

Samuel Gompers was determined to prove that labor unions could bring about better working conditions.
■ Do you think Gompers looks more like a union member or a businessman?

a number of such shops, workers took turns reading aloud. Other workers chipped in money from their own wages to pay the reader for the time lost. As the workers rolled the cigars, they discussed political, social, and economic questions.

It was in these discussions that Gompers first began to think seriously about the problems of labor in an industrial society. He wondered how workers could protect themselves and improve their work conditions. He finally concluded that workers would make gains by organizing themselves into unions.

Gompers began to take an active part in the cigar-makers' union. He organized a new branch and was elected its president at the age of 25. Gompers then turned his efforts to making the national cigar-makers' union stronger.

Machines Replace Skilled Workers Gompers and others came to their conclusions about unions because industrialism had made great changes in the way people worked. In earlier times, goods such as clothing, shoes, and furniture were made by skilled workers in their own homes or in small shops. These workers took pride in the products they made, and they were respected for their skills. Often they worked for themselves, setting their own hours. If they worked for someone else, their employer was usually a skilled worker, too. Employers and employees had a close working relationship. They worked out agreements about wages and conditions of work. Employers also knew their employees' families and showed concern for their welfare.

All this changed as small workshops gave way to factories. No longer did one worker make a product from beginning to end. Instead, the work was broken down into many separate steps. Each step was done by a different worker who always did the same task. For example, in a shoe factory, a worker might stitch soles or nail heels — over and over, all day long. The routine became dull and monotonous. It was hard to take pride in one's work.

In many fields, machines began to do the jobs that skilled workers had done before. "You can take a boy fresh from the farm," said one worker with 30 years experience, "and in 3 days he can manage a machine as well as I can." Many machines were run by young boys and girls, some of them only 7 or 8 years old. Young women from the farms of the nearby countryside were also hired. So, too, were unskilled immigrants. All were paid very low wages. Skilled workers could not compete with goods made by lower-paid workers in factories. Many had to give up their trades. Some became factory workers.

Industrialism changed the America of the 1800s in many ways. For instance, at the start of the century, 9 of every 10 Americans made their living by farming, and many of the others were self-employed. By the end of the century, half of all American workers worked for wages.

Working Conditions In the factories of the nineteenth century, working conditions were poor. Buildings were dimly lighted and badly ventilated. Hours were long. It was not unusual for workers to put in 12 to 15 hours a day. They were often not protected from dangerous machinery. A single slip, a moment of inattention, could cost a life or a limb.

Work was even more dangerous for the millions who worked in the mines, on railroads, and in lumbering. In 1891, on railroads alone, more than 7,000 workers were killed and another 33,000 were injured. By 1900 the United States had one of the highest accident rates among industrial countries. Each year, more than 20,000 workers were killed and 10 times that number were injured. There was no pay for those who were unable to return to work, no health insurance, and no pension for the family of a worker who was killed.

Children were widely employed in factories in the late 1800s. The children shown below in a textile factory probably worked at least 12 hours a day, 6 days a week.
■ What kinds of safety hazards can you find in the photograph?

A sweatshop operator threatens a young woman at a sewing machine.
■ Why, do you think, is the operator threatening the woman?

Women and Children   Women worked the same long hours and under the same unsafe conditions as men. Women made up 20 percent of the work force in manufacturing near the end of the century. They made up the largest part of the work force in the garment industry — the making of dresses and other clothing. However, the female workers usually received less pay than the male workers.

Children made up another important part of the industrial work force. Nearly a quarter-million children worked in factories and mines in the 1880s. Within 10 years that number more than doubled. Boys and girls between 10 and 14 years of age worked 10 to 12 hours a day. In the South especially, where new textile factories were opening in the 1890s, the number of child workers shot upward. Children

under 10 years old worked the 12-hour night shift in some southern cotton mills. Their bosses kept the children from falling asleep at their machines by throwing cold water on them from time to time.

One reformer of the time expressed the unfairness of child labor in these bitter lines:

> The golf links lie so near the mill
> That almost every day
> The laboring children can look out
> And see the men at play

Many workers lived in company towns, where employers owned the homes and the stores. At times the employers even paid the workers in scrip (paper money issued by the company). It could be used as money only in company towns.

As companies grew larger, employers no longer knew those who worked for them. Many began to think of their workers simply as a cost of production. One New England manufacturer said that he felt the same about his workers as he did about his machines. "So long as they can do my work for what I choose to pay them, I keep them, getting out of them all that I can." When factories built up a surplus of goods from time to time, many owners thought nothing of laying off workers for months.

CHECKUP

1. What early experiences taught Samuel Gompers about labor unions?
2. How did the increased use of machines affect skilled workers?
3. Describe the working conditions in factories.
4. What changes occurred in the employers' attitude toward workers?
5. **Thinking Critically** How do you think industrialism affected family life?

Workers Organize

What did workers do to improve their working conditions?

The First Unions How could workers improve their situation in an industrial society? Certainly not by acting alone. An individual worker, especially one who was unskilled and could be easily replaced, had no chance to bargain for better wages or better hours with an employer. Some workers began to see that if they banded together in a union, they might make employers listen to their demands. If the employer refused to bargain with them, they could strike.

These were the views held by Samuel Gompers. That is why he became so active in his cigar-makers' union in the 1870s. By that time, unions had already been on the scene in America for many years. In the 1820s and 1830s, workers formed a number of **trade unions**. A trade union is one whose members work at a single skilled trade, such as printing, baking, or carpentry. However, these early trade unions were weak and unsuccessful. Only a few struggled on into the 1860s.

In 1866 an ironworker named William Sylvis tried to bring all trade unions together into a single organization, the National Labor Union (NLU). The NLU favored an 8-hour day. They also talked about workers owning factories and mines and being their own employers. NLU leaders proposed many long-range social reforms, but they were opposed to using strikes to achieve these reforms.

Most workers, however, were interested in more immediate goals, such as better wages and hours. After Sylvis died in 1869, the NLU became involved in politics and was reorganized as the National Labor Reform Party. When its candidates were defeated in the election of 1872, most of its members left.

The Depression of 1873 The 1870s were troubled times for workers. A depression began in 1873 and lasted for 6 years. Workers lost jobs. Others had to accept pay cuts. There was much frustration and anger.

Faced with the fifth wage cut in 3 years, Baltimore and Ohio Railroad workers walked off the job in 1877. The strike spread to railroad lines as far west as St. Louis. In some cities, violence occurred. Dozens were killed or injured, and property worth millions of dollars was destroyed. President Rutherford B. Hayes was forced to call out federal troops to restore order.

The Knights of Labor During this time, another labor organization was slowly growing. This was the **Knights of Labor**. The organization was started in 1869 to unite "all who toiled" — skilled and unskilled, men and women, black and white — into one big union. Even employers could join. The only people who could not join were professional gamblers, liquor dealers, bankers, and lawyers.

The Knights of Labor wanted equal pay for men and women, an 8-hour working day, health and safety measures in factories and mines, and an end to child labor. Like the National Labor Union, the Knights of Labor opposed strikes. They favored some long-range social reforms.

At a Knights of Labor convention, delegate Frank Farrell (left) introduces Terence Powderly.
■ **What kind of reaction is Powderly getting from the audience?**

One, for example, was a demand for free public land for settlers in the West.

Terence V. Powderly The Knights of Labor grew rapidly after Terence V. Powderly became its leader. Powderly had not even known about unions until he was 21 years old. He was born in Pennsylvania in 1849, the son of poor Irish immigrants. At 13 he left school to start working. Some years later, while working in a machine shop in Scranton, Pennsylvania, he heard a leader of the coal miners give a talk about unions. Powderly joined the union of skilled machinists, and soon afterwards was elected president of his local branch.

Powderly's union activities got him in trouble with his employer. When the depression of 1873 hit, Powderly was one of the first to lose his job. He was also blacklisted and could not find work for some time. A year later, he was shocked at the sight of the charred bodies of coal miners who had been killed in a mine explosion. These experiences, he related later, led him to resolve "to improve the conditions of those who work for a living."

Powderly then became a member of the Knights of Labor. He was a dynamic speaker and inspired many others to join the group. In 1879 he was elected to head the union. He took office with the pledge, "Labor first, last, and all the time."

Boycotts and Strikes Powderly did not want the Knights of Labor to strike. He thought unions were not strong enough to win strikes. He favored the use of **boycotts** instead. A boycott is an organized campaign in which people refuse to buy goods or services from or have any dealings with a particular group or company. The Knights of Labor used boycotts successfully a number of times.

The union also used the strike, despite their leader's opposition to it. In fact, successful strikes led to the biggest period of growth for the Knights of Labor. After one successful strike against a powerful railroad, membership jumped from 100,000 to 700,000 in a year.

The strike was a two-edged sword, however. When the group lost a big strike later on, workers dropped out almost as rapidly as they had earlier joined.

The Haymarket Riot The Knights of Labor suffered a crippling blow in 1886. During a strike for an 8-hour workday at the McCormick Company in Chicago, workers clashed with police. One worker was killed and several others were injured. **Anarchists** — people who wanted to do away with all government — called a protest meeting at Haymarket Square the next day. The protest meeting was orderly. As police moved in to maintain order, someone—no one knows who—threw a bomb, killing seven people. Eight anarchists were tried and convicted; four were executed.

Although the Knights of Labor had nothing at all to do with the protest meeting at Haymarket Square, they became connected with violence in the minds of many Americans. Public opinion turned against the union. More members dropped out. Although the Knights of Labor continued to exist for a number of years, they were never effective after the Haymarket Riot.

Gompers and the AFL Like many other members of trade unions, Samuel Gompers's cigar makers were also members of the Knights of Labor. But Gompers and the trade unionists did not share many of Powderly's beliefs. They had no patience with the vague, long-term reform goals of Powderly's group. They believed that unions should seek gains for their members in the present, rather than try to reform society in a distant future. Unions should concentrate on "bread-and-butter" issues such as wages, hours, and safety in the workplace. Gompers also believed that the strike was an important weapon for labor. Gompers was not afraid to use the strike when necessary.

During a strike in Chicago in 1886, a bomb explodes at a mass meeting. Though anarchists were convicted for the crime, many people blamed the Knights of Labor.
■ Why, do you think, did the public blame the Knights of Labor?

The best chance for success, Gompers said, was in organizing skilled workers. A strike of skilled workers would be more successful than one of unskilled workers, who could easily be replaced by an employer. The workers should be organized by their special skills. Workers who did the same kind of work in the same industry were more likely to share the same problems, agree on common goals, and stick together to reach them.

In 1886, Gompers and other trade union leaders organized the **American Federation of Labor** (AFL). Members were not individual workers. The AFL was a union of unions. It helped individual unions to attract new members, and it also settled conflicts that arose between the different unions that belonged to it. Gompers was elected the first president of the AFL. He was reelected every year except one until his death in 1924.

Opposing the Unions Employers resisted unions every step of the way. Their views were summed up by a mine owner:

> I . . . will employ no one that belongs to any labor organization, and will at once discharge . . . any man who has anything to do with any labor organization.

Companies used blacklists and other methods to keep unions from getting started. Workers who went on strike risked their jobs, for employers might hire others to take their place. Some companies even hired private armies to do battle with striking workers.

A strike in 1892 showed how bitter the struggle between workers and employers had become—and how hard it was for unions to win. In that year, the Carnegie steel plant at Homestead, Pennsylvania, announced a wage cut. The ironworkers' union went out on strike. The company brought in 300 armed men from a detective agency to battle the strikers. Men on both sides were killed. After several months, the strike was broken and the union crushed. The company took back only 10 percent of the strikers. The rest were fired.

The Pullman Strike Two years later, the unions suffered another setback. Then workers for the Pullman Palace Car Company in Illinois went on strike. This company manufactured railroad cars. George Pullman, the owner, cut wages an average of 25 percent in 1 year when busi-

During a strike workers of many ethnic groups joined together to fight for better conditions.
■ **How can you tell that people of many different ethnic groups joined this picket line?**

During the Pullman strike in 1894 United States troops used violence to control the crowd.
■ What forms of physical force can you find in the picture?

ness slowed down. However, he refused to lower the rent he charged workers who lived in his company-owned houses. When several workers went to see him about this, Pullman fired them. Angry workers went on strike. They were joined by members of the American Railway Union, a union of railroad workers. In Chicago, the railroad workers refused to handle trains that included Pullman cars. Railroads came to a standstill.

The United States government stepped in. Trains carried the mails, so the government went to a federal court to get an **injunction**. An injunction is a court order that tells people that they can or can not do something. In this case the injunction ordered the workers to stop interfering with the mails. President Grover Cleveland also sent 2,000 troops to Chicago to see that the order was obeyed. This act touched off violence. When the strike leaders refused to obey the injunction, they were arrested. The leader of the

American Railway Union, Eugene V. Debs, spent 6 months in jail. Under the protection of the federal troops, train service was restored. The strike was broken.

Despite such setbacks, organized labor made steady gains. By 1904, union membership rose to 2 million workers. The AFL accounted for most of these people. Under Gompers's leadership, labor unions came to be accepted.

CHECKUP

1. Why were trade unions formed?
2. What means did Terence Powderly favor to advance the cause of labor?
3. How did the Haymarket Riot affect the Knights of Labor?
4. Why were the McCormick Harvester and Pullman strikes regarded as setbacks to labor unions?
5. **Thinking Critically** Which do you think is the more effective action—the boycott or the strike? Explain.

503

The Farmers Organize

How did industrialism affect the farmers?

VOCABULARY

Grange	Sherman
cooperative	Antitrust Act
Interstate	
Commerce Act	

Mary Lease Speaks for the Farmers

At a gathering of Kansas farmers in 1890, a tall slim woman rose to address them with these words:

> We were told two years ago to go to work and raise a big crop, that was all we needed. We went to work and plowed and planted; the rains fell, the sun shone, nature smiled, and we raised the big crop they told us to; and what came of it?

All of her listeners, she was aware, knew the answer all too well.

> Eight-cent corn, ten-cent oats, two-cent beef, and no price at all for butter and eggs—that's what came of it. Then the politicians said we suffered from overproduction.

The speaker was Mary Lease. She knew about the hardships of western farmers firsthand. The daughter of Irish immigrants, she had moved to Kansas from the East at age 20, taught school briefly, and married a young pharmacist. The couple decided to try their hand at farming. For 10 years they struggled. Finally the debts, the falling prices, and the loneliness of farm life were just too much. The Leases gave up.

Mary Lease then took up the cause of the debt-ridden farmers of Kansas, even though she was no longer one of them. As a public speaker she had a deep, powerful voice, and as her words show, she knew how to express her thoughts. When farmers decided to form a political party to seek solutions to their problems in 1890, they welcomed Mary Lease's help. That year she made 160 speeches. Two years later, in the presidential election, she traveled through the West and the South seeking support for the party's candidates. In one state she spoke to eight different groups in a single day.

She was not always favorably received. A southern newspaper wrote that "the sight of a woman traveling around the country making political speeches . . . [is] simply disgusting." Such comments, however, did not stop Mary Lease.

The Farm Problem

Mary Lease was one of hundreds who spoke out about the economic problems many farmers faced in

Mary Lease of Kansas was an effective spokeswoman for the hard-pressed farmers of America.
■ Why, do you think, would Lease speak out for the farmers?

New machines and improvements to old machines brought about a dramatic rise in crop production. This steam-powered machine threshed thousands of bushels of wheat daily.
■ How was the wheat transported to the barn?

the 1880s and 1890s. For two centuries, part of the American dream had been to farm one's own land. Millions were now doing that; but something had gone wrong with the dream.

Most of the problem resulted from the industrialism that was changing so much else in American life. Before industrialism, most farms in the United States, except for some southern cotton and tobacco plantations, were small. The farm family raised a variety of crops and animals for its own needs, and sometimes a little more for sale. Farmers did not plant many acres.

Inventions such as the mechanical reaper began to make changes as early as the 1830s. In the last half of the nineteenth century, improvements on tools and machines, and the invention of new ones frequently made it possible for a farmer to plant and harvest many more acres. For example, a single farmer could produce nearly 20 times as much wheat with a day's labor in the 1890s as he could produce 50 years earlier.

New machines, however, were expensive. It only paid to use them on large farms. So farmers bought more land. They also specialized in a single crop, which they sold for cash. As a result, farming became more and more a growing business enterprise.

The Business of Farming   Farmers, like other business people, now had to consider several factors if they were to succeed. One was the price they got for their product. A second was the cost of producing it. A third was the cost of shipping it to market. In the last part of the nineteenth century, all three factors and more worked against the American farmer.

Take the first factor, price. Price is largely set by supply and demand. A poor

The Farmers' Department Store

While city dwellers shopped in large department stores, most farm families in the late nineteenth century were limited to the country store. There, choices were few and prices were often high. A growing number, however, had already begun to buy goods in a different way — by mail order.

Mail-order merchants at first relied upon advertisements in the small newspapers and magazines that many farmers bought. By the 1890s, however, the larger companies such as Montgomery Ward and Sears, Roebuck and Company were sending out catalogs that described thousands of items for sale.

The illustrated catalog quickly became the farmers' department store. For weeks after it arrived, family members feasted their eyes on items from watches and clothing to baby carriages, bicycles, sewing machines, and farm wagons.

Buying from catalogs became widespread in rural areas after 1900. Sears, Roebuck and Company printed 300,000 catalogs in 1897, but 30 years later the company distributed 65 million! By then, Sears was the largest retail seller of goods in the world.

Not only were mail-order catalogs found in nearly every farm home, but in many one-room schoolhouses, children practiced reading and spelling from the catalogs. For practice in arithmetic, they filled out make-believe orders and added up the cost of the items. To some the catalog was known as "the wish book," to others simply as "the big book." By any name, mail-order catalogs helped to bridge the gap between city and country and to make farmers' lives better.

Chas. A. Stevens & Bros.

Cloaks Suits and Furs

The Most Perfect in style, finish, fit, workmanship and materials.

We Employ One Agent in every locality to show Fashion Plates and Samples and take orders for our goods. Write for special circular about this.

Stevens' Fall Catalogue

NOW READY. EVERY WOMAN WANTS IT

More than one million women watch for this announcement and write as soon as they see it. It is the only catalogue published that contains just what you want. It is the catalogue that sells more ladies' fine Cloaks, Suits and Furs than all other catalogues combined. The cause of this most wonderful business lies within the garments themselves. Wear one Stevens garment and you will understand why the army of women who will have no other grows so rapidly.

The Catalogue is Free. Write for it To-Day

We prepay express charges everywhere and guarantee very best values in America, which means about *half the usual prices* asked in many localities.

CHAS. A. STEVENS & BROS., 109 to 115 State Street, Chicago

harvest reduces supply and causes prices to rise. A good harvest increases supply and causes prices to fall. But in the late nineteenth century, trains and steamships began to carry crops swiftly and cheaply from one part of the world to another. Thus, grain grown on newly opened farmlands in the Soviet Union, Canada, Australia, and several South American countries competed with grain grown on the Great Plains. Price was now determined by supply and demand in the whole world, not just in the United States. The international economy was growing.

Most farmers did not understand the full meaning of that fact. They had always lived by the simple idea that the harder they worked and the more crops they grew, the more money they would earn. And so in the late nineteenth century, American farmers tripled the production of wheat and corn, and more than doubled the production of cotton. That increased world supply, and prices fell still more.

As for costs of production, the price of farm machinery was high. Taxes on land and farm buildings were high. And when the farmers borrowed money to buy more land or to see them through hard times, they found that interest rates were high, too. Charges of 17 to 25 percent a year were common in the West. In the South, where many farmers had to buy supplies on credit from storekeepers, interest ran from 40 to 100 percent a year.

Transportation costs, the third factor in determining whether or not farmers would make money, were also high. Railroads set freight rates low on routes where there was competition, and high where there was none. The latter was usually the case in farming country. One railroad charged five times as much to carry freight west of Chicago as to carry it east of that city. West of Chicago, there was no competition; east of Chicago, there was. Some farmers had to pay to the railroads half what they received for their crops. They also paid high charges for storing their crops in warehouses and grain elevators. Many of these were owned by the railroads.

A final problem that farmers experienced is harder to pinpoint but just as important. It was the feeling that they were not sharing in the progress of the nation. They felt left behind. Once they had been the ideal citizens, the backbone of the republic. Now they felt that city folks looked down on them as "hicks" and "hayseeds."

The Grangers   Faced with these many problems, farmers began to organize. In 1867, Oliver H. Kelley, a clerk in the

At an outdoor meeting in Illinois in 1873, members of the Grange talk over their problems.
■ What kinds of problems do you think they were discussing?

United States Department of Agriculture, founded an organization commonly called the **Grange**. The purpose of the organization was to bring farm families together for social and educational gatherings. Soon, however, farmers were talking about their common problems and how to deal with them.

In a number of midwestern states, Grangers — members of the Grange — pooled their money and formed **cooperatives**. A cooperative is an organization that is owned and operated for the benefit of those who use its goods and services. Grangers set up factories to make farm machinery, built their own warehouses, and formed their own insurance companies. Grangers also got the legislatures in Illinois, Iowa, Minnesota, and Wisconsin to pass laws regulating railroad rates. These laws were known as Granger laws.

The Granger movement did not prosper for long, however. A number of the cooperatives failed, because the farmers lacked the necessary capital and business experience. With the return of better crop prices in the late 1870s, interest and membership in the Grange fell.

Regulating Interstate Commerce

The Granger laws, too, became less effective as the result of several later decisions of the Supreme Court. In the most important of these, the Court said that a state's Granger law could apply only to traffic that was entirely within that state. Once the traffic crossed state lines, it was interstate commerce, or trade between two or more states. Under the Constitution, only Congress had the power to regulate interstate commerce. This Supreme Court decision was made in 1886.

The following year, Congress used that power and passed the **Interstate Commerce Act**. This law forbade railroads to charge unfair rates, give rebates to favored shippers, and charge more for short distances than for long ones. The law also set up an Interstate Commerce Commission (ICC) to see that the law was carried out. The Interstate Commerce Act was an important first — it marked the first time the federal government attempted to regulate privately owned business. However, Congress did not give the ICC enough power to enforce the law. So the agency became ineffective.

Regulating the Trusts

An attempt to stop the growth of trusts and monopolies proved no more effective. This was the **Sherman Antitrust Act** of 1890. The Sherman act declared that trusts and other ways of restricting trade were illegal. The purpose of the law was to break up the trusts so that small business owners would have a chance to compete in industry.

However, the law's wording was vague, and companies found ways to get around it. When the government did occasionally charge a business with wrongdoing, the courts usually sided with the business. The number of trusts and monopolies continued to grow.

CHECKUP

1. How did machines change farming?
2. Name three economic factors that determined whether a farmer would succeed in business.
3. What steps did the Grange take to improve the farmers' situation?
4. What two laws did Congress pass to regulate large businesses, and how effective were they?
5. **Thinking Critically** Why was it difficult for a farmer to plan what his yearly income would be? Is this still true today?

The Populist Movement

What reforms did the Populists propose?

Farmers Enter Politics The 1880s were hard times for the farmers. Many had to give up their farms. One response to the hard times were the **Farmers' Alliances**, which were organized throughout the West and the South. More than 2.5 million farmers joined. They believed that neither of the main political parties — Republicans or Democrats — would help farmers. So in 1890 the alliances entered politics. The Farmers' Alliances elected many people to local and state offices, and to the United States Congress. It was in this election campaign that Mary Lease made the speech you read earlier in this chapter.

Encouraged by this success, the alliances, together with some reformers and labor leaders, formed a national party, which they called the People's party, or **Populist** party. At its convention in 1892, the new party chose General James Weaver of Iowa, a Civil War veteran, to run for President.

The Populist Platform The bitterness and despair of Populists can be seen in the language of their **platform**, or statement of party goals.

> We meet in the midst of a nation brought to the verge of moral, political, and material ruin. . . . Corruption dominates the ballot box. . . . The fruits of the toil of millions are boldly stolen to build up colossal fortunes for a few. . . .

The platform added that "government injustice" had turned the population into "two great classes — tramps and millionaires."

The platform went on to propose major social and political changes. They included

- government ownership of railroads, telegraphs, and telephones, which would be run "in the interests of the people."
- secret ballot in voting.
- a shorter workday for those laboring in factories and mines.
- government-run savings banks where people could safely deposit money without using the hated privately owned banks.

The People's party is in a leaky balloon, patched together with groups.
According to this cartoonist, what was the People's party platform?

509

Born: 1837, Caldwell, New Jersey.
Education: Public school to age 14. Later read law.
Training: Lawyer, public official.
To presidency from: New York.
Position when first elected: Governor of New York.
Political party: Democratic.
Married: Frances Folsom.
Children: Three daughters, two sons.
Died: 1908.
Other facts: A big, good-humored man who weighed 260 pounds (118 kg) when he became President. Called "Uncle Jumbo" by his relatives. The only President married in the White House. Daughter Esther was the only child of a President to be born in the White House. The only President to serve two terms that were not successive.
During his presidency: The Statue of Liberty was unveiled in New York Harbor.

GROVER CLEVELAND
22nd and 24th President
1885 • 1889, 1893 • 1897

- a graduated income tax. Those with large incomes would pay a greater percentage of their earnings than those with small incomes.
- direct election of senators by the voters. At that time senators were chosen by the state legislatures.
- **initiative** and **referendum**. The initiative allows the people themselves to propose a law by signing a petition. If enough people sign, the legislature must examine the proposal and vote on it. The referendum allows the people to vote directly on a proposed law. Their vote is final.
- free coinage of silver.

The last proposal, the free coinage of silver, needs explanation. Until 1873 the United States government had minted both silver and gold dollars. In that year the government stopped making silver coins. At just about that time, much silver was found in new mines in Nevada and Colorado. Populists wanted the government to allow silver to be coined again. The idea was that if *both* gold and silver dollars circulated, there would be more dollars available to buy the same amount of goods. Therefore prices would rise. Farmers would receive higher prices for their crops and could pay their debts more easily. Not surprisingly, silver mine owners also wanted the government to buy silver and coin it.

In the 1892 election the Populists made a good showing for a new party. President Benjamin Harrison, a Republican, was seeking reelection against the Democrat Grover Cleveland, a former President himself. Cleveland was elected, but Populist James Weaver received a million votes (about 9 percent of all the votes cast) and carried four western states. Populists also elected three governors and a number of United States senators and representatives.

The Depression of 1893   No sooner did Grover Cleveland become President for the second time, in 1893, than a depression began. Banks and businesses failed.

Farm prices dropped still further and more farmers lost their farms. In the cities, 20 percent of the workers were unemployed, and many who still had jobs took wage cuts. Anger and frustration built up. There were hundreds of strikes. Many were accompanied by violence. The largest was the Pullman strike that you read about earlier.

Like many other Americans of the time, President Cleveland held to the belief that there was nothing government could or should do in a depression. The job of helping those who were suffering from unemployment belonged to private charities and local government, he said. Not everyone agreed. Charities and local governments were running out of money. Some proposed that the federal government hire unemployed men to build roads. But this proposal was never seriously considered.

Cleveland also strongly opposed coining silver. Most business people shared this opposition. They said that coining silver would cheapen the dollar and be bad for business. Bankers said it would be unfair to be paid back in dollars worth less than the ones they had loaned out. Many wage earners also were opposed to coining silver and adding to the money supply. They feared that if prices rose, their wages would buy less.

With each passing month of hard times, the money question came to overshadow all others. The country was divided on the question. Westerners and southerners in the President's own Democratic party disagreed with him. They favored silver.

Gold or Silver? For the presidential election of 1896, the Republican party chose William McKinley of Ohio as its candidate. The Republican party came out firmly against the free coinage of silver. It favored the **gold standard**—that is, that the money supply of the country should be based on gold only.

Even in the best of times, farm families had to work hard—as this painting suggests—to make a living from the soil.
■ **What kind of house is this farm family living in?**

Born: 1833, North Bend, Ohio.
Education: Miami (Ohio) University.
Training: Lawyer, public official.
To presidency from: Indiana.
Position when elected: United States Senator.
Political party: Republican.
Married: (1) Caroline Lavinia Scott, (2) Mary Lord Dimmick.
Children: Two daughters, one son.
Died: 1901, Indianapolis, Indiana.
Other facts: Recruited and commanded an Indiana regiment in Civil War. Called "Little Ben" by his men because he was 5 feet 6 inches (170 cm) tall. While he was President, electric lights were installed in the White House.
During his presidency: James Naismith, a physical-education teacher at what is now Springfield (Massachusetts) College, started the game of basketball, using two peach baskets and a soccer ball.

BENJAMIN HARRISON
23rd President
1889 · 1893

At the Democratic convention, those who favored silver were in the majority. The debate in the convention over the money question produced the party's candidate for President, William Jennings Bryan of Nebraska. Born and raised in Illinois, Bryan had moved to Nebraska to open a law practice with a college friend. He soon became active in politics. He was an excellent speaker with a clear voice that carried a great distance. That was an important quality for a speaker in the days before microphones. In 1890 he was elected to Congress and served two terms.

By 1894 Bryan had decided to seek the presidency. To become better known, he spent the next 2 years touring the country, making speeches. Still, by the time of the Democratic convention in 1896, few thought the 36-year-old Bryan had much chance for the nomination. He was too young and too inexperienced, said the party leaders, to become the Democratic candidate for President.

But Bryan had planned carefully. As he rose to make his speech in favor of

silver, a friend passed him a note that read, "This is a great opportunity." Bryan scribbled a quick reply: "You will not be disappointed."

What followed was one of the most famous speeches in American history. Bryan declared that he was speaking for the small farmers of the nation who "are fighting in the defense of our homes, our families, and prosperity."

> You come to us and tell us that the great cities are in favor of the gold standard; we reply that the great cities rest upon our broad and fertile prairies. Burn down your cities and leave our farms, and your cities will spring up again as if by magic; but destroy our farms and the grass will grow in the streets of every city in the country.

At the end of what has become known as the "cross of gold" speech, Bryan challenged the opponents of silver with these words:

> Having behind us the producing masses of this nation and the world, supported by

the commercial interests, the laboring interests, and the toilers everywhere, we will answer their demand for a gold standard by saying to them: You shall not press down upon the brow of labor this crown of thorns, you shall not crucify mankind upon a cross of gold.

With that, the convention went wild. The Democrats had found their leader. They supported the free coinage of silver, and William Jennings Bryan was named their candidate for President.

The Election of 1896   Populists now faced a problem. To join the Democrats in support of Bryan would mean the end of the Populists as a separate party. But if they had their own candidate, that would split the free-silver vote and give the election to the Republicans. In the end, the Populists supported Bryan.

The campaign of 1896 was one of the most dramatic in our history. Bryan, the youngest man ever to run for President, traveled 18,000 miles (28,800 km) and gave 600 speeches. He was the first candidate ever to wage this kind of active campaign. On the other hand, contributions from business people and bankers who feared free silver gave the Republicans the largest amount of campaign funds ever collected up to that time. In some businesses, employers ordered their workers either to vote for McKinley or lose their jobs.

Bryan won support from the farmers of the South and the West, but he did not do well among either workers or the urban middle class. McKinley won the election.

Soon after the 1896 election, the economy improved. Poor harvests in Europe led to higher farm prices. Gold was found in Alaska, adding to the money supply. Business picked up. Farm protest quieted down, and the Populist party lost its appeal. It broke up into small factions, and

After his dramatic "cross of gold" speech, William Jennings Bryan is carried off the floor of the convention hall on the shoulders of his supporters.
■ Do you think a political speaker today would be whisked off on the shoulders of the supporters?

soon the party disappeared from the political scene.

The Populists, however, made an important contribution. They were the first American party to favor using the power of the federal government to deal with social and economic problems. Many of their ideas in time became law.

CHECKUP

1. Why did farmers enter politics?
2. List five goals of the Populist party.
3. What was the issue regarding silver in the 1896 election?
4. Who were the candidates in that election, and who won?
5. **Thinking Critically** Why do you think they called themselves the People's party?

Writing a Description

MORE VIVID WRITING

When you write a description, you want the reader to *see* exactly what you are describing. You also want the reader to be interested in what you write. One way to make your writing more interesting and vivid is to use adjectives and adverbs. Study the following example:

a. The boy worked at the factory.
b. The young boy worked long hours at the noisy, windowless factory.

Which sentence is more interesting and vivid? In the first example you were given information. In the second a picture was created for you through the use of adjectives.

Another way to make your writing more interesting and vivid is to vary sentence beginnings. Try to begin one sentence with a phrase or clause that answers *who*. Begin another with a phrase or clause that answers *when*. Other sentences could tell *where, why,* or *how*. Often it won't be possible to use *all* these sentence beginnings in every paragraph. By this rule you'll vary your writing.

SKILLS PRACTICE

Read the following paragraph.

> In the early morning the young lad trudges wearily to the badly ventilated factory. Because his family needs his income, he cannot go to school. He spends twelve hours each day at a large noisy machine. Next to him, another exhausted boy is about to fall asleep. By throwing cold water on him, the foreman keeps the boy awake.

On a separate sheet of paper, list all the adjectives and adverbs. For example, in the first sentence these words are *early, young, wearily, badly,* and *ventilated*. Then write the phrase or clause from each sentence that tells *who, when, where, how,* or *why*.

Study the picture on this page, and note as many details as you can. Using the suggestions above, write a paragraph describing the picture for someone who cannot see it.

MAIN IDEAS

1. Poorly ventilated buildings, dangerous machinery, low wages, and long working days were some of the problems workers faced in an industrial society.
2. Workers joined labor unions in an effort to get higher wages and organized boycotts and strikes to improve their working conditions.
3. Farmers in the late 1800s produced more than ever before, but they earned less because of the low prices of farm products and the high costs of machinery and transportation.
4. Farmers and reformers founded the People's, or Populist, party to seek remedies for their social and economic problems through politics.
5. The free coinage of silver was a major issue in the election of 1896.

VOCABULARY REVIEW

On a separate piece of paper, write the letter of the vocabulary word next to the number of its definition.

a. anarchist
b. blacklist
c. strike
d. boycott
e. trade union
f. Grange
g. cooperative
h. initiative
i. platform
j. referendum

1. The names of workers who were not to be given jobs.
2. A social organization for farm families
3. A statement of a political party's goals
4. An organization of skilled workers
5. The stopping of work to get an employer to agree to workers' demands
6. An organization that buys and sells for the benefit of its members
7. The right of the people to vote directly for or against laws
8. The refusal to deal with a particular group or company
9. A person who wants to do away with government
10. The right of the people to introduce new laws

CHAPTER CHECKUP

1. What problems or abuses were each of the following laws supposed to correct? **(a)** Sherman Antitrust Act **(b)** Interstate Commerce Act **(c)** Granger laws
2. What were the advantages of industrialism? What problems did industrialism create?
3. List the advantages and disadvantages of belonging to a union in the late 1800s.
4. What effect did the Haymarket Riot and the Pullman strike have on union membership? Why?
5. What problems did farmers face in the 1880s and 1890s?
6. Explain how supply and demand affect the prices of goods.
7. Why did the Populists lose their appeal to voters?
8. **Thinking Critically** Compare the AFL with the Knights of Labor.
9. **Thinking Critically** Why do you think third parties find it difficult to get their candidates elected in the United States?

APPLYING KNOWLEDGE

1. In an encyclopedia or other reference book, find the origin of Labor Day. Be prepared to report your findings to the class.
2. In an almanac find the number of people in the labor force for the past 10 censuses. Make a line graph to show how the number of workers has changed.
3. In your library look up the story of Jacob Coxey and Coxey's army. How is this story related to the depression of the 1890s?

How Americans Lived: 1900

THE UNITED STATES

AREA: 2,969,834 sq mi
7,691,870 sq km

POPULATION: 75,994,575
POPULATION DENSITY: 26 per sq mi
10 per sq km
NUMBER OF STATES: 45
LARGEST STATE IN AREA: Texas
IN POPULATION: New York
LARGEST CITY: New York
WHERE PEOPLE LIVED:

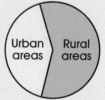

Urban areas | Rural areas

How did life in urban America differ from life in rural America in 1900?

VOCABULARY

vaudeville　　　life expectancy

During the last half of the nineteenth century, the United States became an increasingly industrial and urban nation. Although more than half of the American population still lived on farms, in villages, and in small towns, the number of people living in cities was increasing rapidly.

By 1900, the ways of life in urban and rural America had grown apart in many respects. One example of the growing differences was shown in leisure time.

Leisure Time in a Small Town Sinclair Lewis was a famous American writer in the 1920s and 1930s. His best-known books, such as *Main Street* and *Babbitt*, were about small-town America. It was a subject that Lewis knew firsthand, having grown up in the small town of Sauk Centre,

Minnesota. In 1900, when Harry Sinclair Lewis was 15 years old, Sauk Centre had a population of about 2,200. Main Street would not be paved for another 24 years, and residents of Sauk Centre walked on wooden sidewalks.

Within 10 miles (16 km) of Sauk Centre were more than 30 lakes. These lakes were year-round playgrounds for young people like Harry Lewis. (It was only in later years that he started using his middle name.) In warm weather the young people swam, fished, and floated on rafts they had made from logs. There was duck hunting in autumn, and ice skating in winter. On the nearby hills, many young people sledded.

Although it was small, the town of Sauk Centre offered both its young and adult residents a good many public entertainments. In 1900, many professional entertainers toured America's small towns. At the Sauk Centre opera house, residents could watch a play, listen to a lecture, hear a dramatic reading, or attend a concert. The concert might be anything

HOW AMERICANS LIVED: 1900

from a choral group or military band to a single performer playing tunes on musical glasses. The opera house was also the site of occasional sporting events, such as wrestling matches.

Entertainments such as these were not late-night activities. In Sauk Centre, as in nearly all other small towns in 1900, there were no streetlights. People were usually in bed by 9:00 or 10:00 P.M. and up again at 4:00 or 5:00 A.M.

Then there was the circus. A writer who grew up in a small midwestern town later recalled, "From the time the 'advance man' flung his highly colored posters over the fence till the coming of the glorious day, we thought of little else." With its acrobats, animal acts, clowns, and death-defying feats on the trapeze and the high wire, the circus gave the people of Sauk Centre and of a hundred other villages and towns across the country their most exciting day of the year.

Mostly, however, residents of Sauk Centre provided their own entertainment. There were frequent dances: school dances, a fireman's dance, and special dances run by the town's social clubs. Even people like Harry Lewis who could not dance went along anyway to look on. And there were picnics, county fairs, and gun-shooting contests. Baseball was popular among Sauk Centre residents. During the warm weather, one could always find neighborhood games going on.

Leisure Time in the City By 1900, city people had more leisure time than ever before. This was due to the invention of labor-saving machinery. In 1860 the average worker was on the job 6 days a week and put in 66 hours of labor. In 1900 the number of hours per week for the average worker was under 60. Many city dwellers worked 5½ days a week, or even 5 days.

How did city people use their new leisure time? Certainly they provided some of their own entertainment, just as rural dwellers did. Young people skated and sledded in winter, and in summer one could find a baseball game on nearly every vacant city lot. However, as cities became more crowded, there were fewer empty lots. Local governments found it necessary to create playgrounds as special areas for recreation.

The most popular sport in America in 1900 was bicycling. Probably 2 million Americans owned bicycles in that year. Both men and women bicycled, sometimes

In areas where winters were cold, ice skating was a popular pastime in both small towns and cities.
■ What is unusual about how skaters dressed in 1900?

together on a "bicycle built for two." Cycling was especially popular in the cities because the streets were paved. In 1900, many bicyclists were members of cycling clubs. These groups put pressure on local and state government to provide more paved roads.

However, by 1900, entertainment in cities was becoming more and more an organized activity — even a business. City people were becoming spectators rather than participants. Professional baseball was already a big business in 1900. Occasionally, crowds as large as 50,000 watched National League teams play. In 1901, a new league, the American League, was formed, and 2 years later the champions of each league played in the first World Series. (The Boston Red Sox defeated the Pittsburgh Pirates.) College football

was also a popular sport. In addition to the thousands who watched the games, millions more followed them through the sports page of their newspapers — a feature that had been added to the papers in the 1880s.

Those who lived in large cities could choose from many stage plays, musical comedies, and concerts every night of the week. In 1900 the most popular theater entertainment was the **vaudeville** show. Vaudeville shows were variety shows that included song-and-dance acts, comedy, magic shows, animal acts, and juggling.

In 1900 there was even something new called the moving picture. Thomas Edison had invented the moving picture in the 1880s. For the next 10 years or so, curious Americans put their nickels in a "peep-show" machine to see the flickering

At the turn of the century, bicycling was the favorite sport of Americans.
■ **Why do you think bicycling is so much more popular in Europe than in the United States?**

The peep show was the forerunner of motion pictures.
■ **How was the machine operated?**

images. By 1900 a few promoters were using moving-picture projectors to put these images onto a large screen in front of seated audiences. It was a hint of things to come.

Medical Care in a Rural Area There were also growing differences between rural and urban America in the kind and quality of medical care available.

What kind of training did the country doctor of 1900 have? If he was an older man (nearly all doctors were men), he had learned medicine as a young man by working a year or two for a doctor—who himself had probably learned medicine the same way. No license was needed to practice medicine, and there were no examinations to pass. Young doctors in 1900 were more likely to have gone to medical school—but not to college. Normally, one went straight from high school to medical school. Most medical schools were little more than two or three classrooms, with no laboratories. The course of study was 2 years. Students spent half of each year attending lectures and the other half getting on-the-job training in a hospital.

In small towns, villages, and farm areas, patients did not visit doctors. Doctors visited patients. There was no good medical reason for going to a country doctor's office, for he had little special equipment there. A doctor could carry all his instruments and medicines in his small black bag.

A Country Doctor Sinclair Lewis's father's career as a doctor in small-town Minnesota was typical. Dr. Edwin Lewis began his practice of medicine in Ironton. Dr. Lewis visited all his patients in their homes. For house calls less than 3 miles away, he usually walked. For those more than 3 miles distant, he rode on horseback. Once a week Dr. Lewis visited the neighboring town of Melrose, which had no doctor of its own.

After moving to Sauk Centre, Dr. Lewis opened an office on the town's main street. However, he continued to visit most of his patients in their homes. The main change from his Ironton days was that he now traveled by horse and buggy rather than on horseback.

The country doctor was truly a family doctor. That meant that he attended not only the sick person but also everyone else who was in the household. He checked the pulse, looked at the tongue and throat, observed the general appearance, and asked questions about each person's health. Although mercury thermometers had been invented some years before, the average doctor considered them unnecessary and rarely used them.

For many sick patients there was little that a doctor could do to help them. In the first place, not one doctor in a thousand could perform the scientific tests that would show whether the patient had an infection, such as tuberculosis or pneumonia, two of the most feared killers of the time. Second, there were no medicines to combat infections. For fever, pain, or general weakness, doctors ordered bed rest and a tonic.

In rural areas, a doctor was often paid for his services "in kind." This meant that patients might pay him with firewood, oats for his horses, bushels of wheat, or even days of work in his field or stable. Few country doctors in rural America earned large incomes in 1900.

Medical Care in the City   City doctors had a number of things in common with country doctors in 1900. City doctors, too, were mainly family doctors; and they had no better medicines than did the country doctor. However, by 1900, some important differences between medical practice in the city and the countryside had appeared.

One difference was in training. An increasing number of city doctors had gone to college and had studied basic science before going to medical school. And at least at some of the better medical schools, scientific training was increased.

A country doctor (left) in the mountains of eastern Tennessee attends to a young patient in her home. A surgeon (right) performs an operation in a city hospital.
■ **What are the major differences between the two pictures?**

Although city doctors treated many of their patients in their homes, a growing number were keeping office hours by 1900. This was mainly so that they could make use of new medical equipment, such as the X-ray machine. Wilhelm K. Roentgen, a German physicist, discovered X rays in 1895. He called the rays *X rays* because he did not understand what they were.

Also, there were enough patients in the city to allow some doctors to specialize in certain illnesses. By 1900 a number of them were doing so. This meant that patients who could afford it could receive treatment from a doctor familiar with the latest methods for their special health problems.

Every city had at least one hospital, but that was not an advantage to most city dwellers. This was because in 1900, hospitals were mainly for the poor. Patients were treated by doctors who donated their time or by young medical students getting their training. As the patients got better, they were expected to work in the wards, helping others.

People who could afford private doctors did not use hospitals. Women nearly always gave birth in their own homes. In 1900, even major surgery, such as removing an appendix, took place in the patient's home. In fact, nearly 20 years later, a magazine for doctors carried an article explaining how to hook up an automobile battery to a portable electric light for nighttime surgery in the patient's home.

Even with the improved medical knowledge of 1900, however, common diseases still took many lives. The highest death rate was among infants less than 1 year old. The second largest was among children from 1 to 5 years old. They usually died from such diseases as measles, whooping cough, scarlet fever, and diphtheria. In 1900 there were nei-

X rays are used to help detect abnormalities such as broken bones or lung disease.
■ What part of the body is this doctor observing?

ther cures nor vaccines for these diseases. Overall, the average **life expectancy** was 47 years. This is a far cry from today's life expectancy in America—70 years for men and 77½ years for women.

CHECKUP

1. What did people in rural areas do for recreation in 1900?
2. How did leisure-time activities differ for a city dweller?
3. Compare the ways that doctors in rural and urban areas performed their duties in 1900.
4. Why was life expectancy in 1900 so much different from what it is today?
5. **Thinking Critically** What advances have been made in medicine since 1900?

REVIEWING VOCABULARY

1. subsidy From the 1850s through the 1870s, the United States government gave millions of dollars in subsidies to railroad companies. These subsidies helped pay the costs of building railroads in the West. How could the government justify giving the taxpayers' money to a private railroad company?

2. capital Large amounts of capital were needed to build America's businesses. Which industry or industries would you consider to have been good investments for capital in the late 1800s? Which would be good today? Give reasons to support your answers.

3. platform Through its platform a political party seeks to win the support of as many voters as possible. Name at least five proposals that might be included in a party platform for a presidential election today.

4. cooperative In the late 1800s midwestern farmers formed cooperatives to improve their economic situation. What were the advantages and disadvantages of belonging to this type of organization?

5. initiative The Populists wanted the initiative so that people could introduce new proposals for laws to the legislature by signing a petition. Why would the Populists be in favor of this reform? What did the Populists hope to accomplish with the initiative?

EXPRESSING YOURSELF

1. What do you recommend? You are a Nez Percé warrior accompanying Chief Joseph. The date is October 2, 1877. Chief Joseph has asked your advice: Should the Nez Percé surrender and give up their independence? Or should they fight on when defeat is almost certain? How would you advise him? Give reasons to support your answer.

2. What do you do next? You have traveled 1,960 miles (3,136 km) from Boston to Denver, Colorado, to try your luck at mining. After 3 months you have still found no gold or silver. What do you do next? What are your choices?

3. In your opinion. Thomas Edison's inventions changed the way Americans lived. In your opinion, which of his inventions caused the greatest changes? Explain.

4. What if . . . Until 1882 nearly anyone who wanted to come to the United States from another land was allowed to do so. In that year the Chinese Exclusion Act was passed. What if all immigration to the United States had been stopped at that time? How would the United States be different today?

5. Convince the voters. Nearly all voters at the end of the 1800s were either Republicans or Democrats. Suppose you were James Weaver. What arguments would you use to persuade people to leave their party and to support you and the Populists? What would you say to the farmers? To the industrial workers?

UNIT 6

Becoming a World Leader

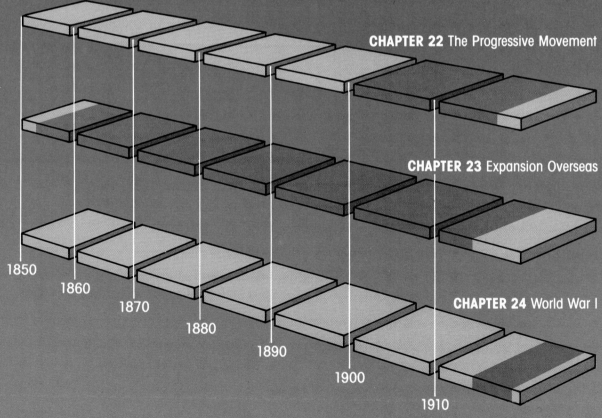

CHAPTER 22 The Progressive Movement

CHAPTER 23 Expansion Overseas

CHAPTER 24 World War I

1850

1860

1870

1880

1890

1900

1910

22 *The Progressive Movement*

1900–1917

Working for Reform

What were the main reforms proposed by the Progressives?

VOCABULARY

public utility	muckraker
direct primary	commission government
recall	city manager
Progressive movement	

La Follette Fights the Machine The turning point of Robert La Follette's career was probably the day of his meeting with Senator Philetus Sawyer. La Follette had recently been defeated for reelection to Congress, where he had served three terms. He had come home to Madison, Wisconsin, to practice law.

Sawyer was a millionaire, a United States senator, and the boss of the Wisconsin Republican party. He was involved in a lawsuit in which he stood to lose $300,000. The judge in the trial was Robert La Follette's brother-in-law. According to La Follette, Sawyer offered him a bribe "to fix things" with his brother-in-law. La Follette angrily refused the bribe and told the public what had happened. With that, Philetus Sawyer vowed that La Follette, a Republican, would never again have the support of the party.

That meeting took place in 1891. For the next 9 years, Robert La Follette learned what it meant to have a political party controlled by one man. In 1896 he decided to seek the Republican nomination for governor. Denied the backing of the regular organization, La Follette built support of his own. He championed popular issues such as regulating the railroads and the **public utilities** — those companies that sold water, gas, and electricity to the public. He also won support from many young Republicans who were unhappy with the party machine.

At the party's convention, La Follette thought a majority of the delegates were for him. They were at first, but Sawyer's forces bribed enough of them to win the nomination for their own man. In 1898 the organization again blocked La Follette's bid for the nomination.

La Follette's Reforms After that, La Follette added to his list of reforms the **direct primary**. In a direct primary, voters in each party choose the party's candidates directly, instead of having a convention of delegates choose them.

Robert La Follette was finally nominated and elected in 1900, and he was reelected twice. During his three terms as

Robert La Follette speaks at a county fair in 1897. After becoming governor, he was successful in reforming Wisconsin's state laws.
■ Why was a fair a good place to make a speech?

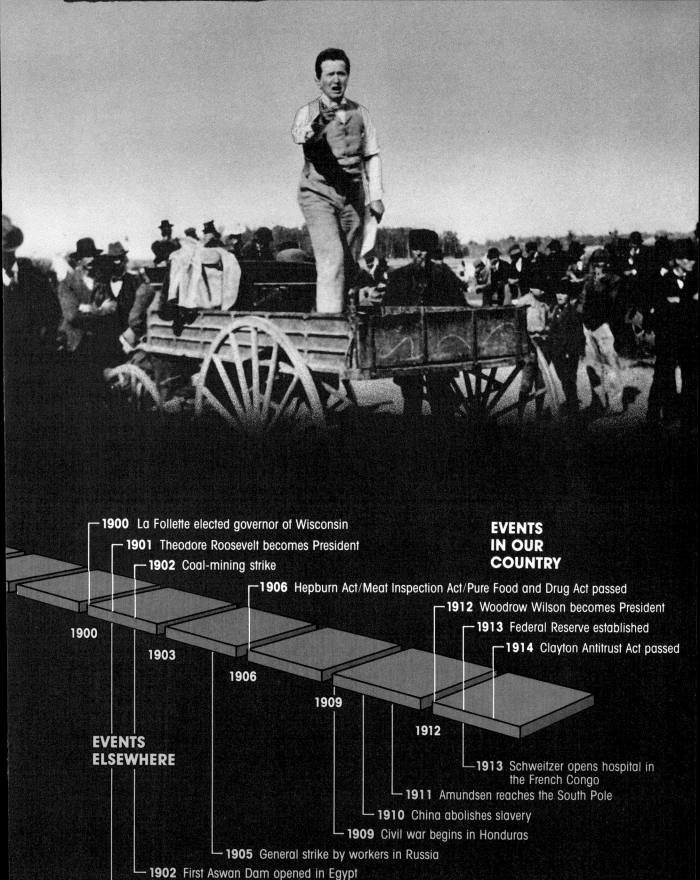

EVENTS IN OUR COUNTRY

1900 La Follette elected governor of Wisconsin
1901 Theodore Roosevelt becomes President
1902 Coal-mining strike
1906 Hepburn Act/Meat Inspection Act/Pure Food and Drug Act passed
1912 Woodrow Wilson becomes President
1913 Federal Reserve established
1914 Clayton Antitrust Act passed

1900

1903

1906

1909

1912

EVENTS ELSEWHERE

1913 Schweitzer opens hospital in the French Congo
1911 Amundsen reaches the South Pole
1910 China abolishes slavery
1909 Civil war begins in Honduras
1905 General strike by workers in Russia
1902 First Aswan Dam opened in Egypt
1901 First Nobel Peace Prize awarded

governor of Wisconsin, the legislature passed many reform laws. It adopted the initiative, the referendum, the direct primary, and the **recall**. By using the recall, voters may remove an official from office. All these measures were meant to take away some power from the political bosses and return it to the people.

The legislature also passed a workmen's compensation law, which made payments to those hurt on the job. It created commissions to regulate railroad and utility rates. It taxed the railroads on the value of their properties so that for the first time they paid a fair share of taxes. It adopted a state income tax. It made a start on conserving the state of Wisconsin's natural resources.

La Follette believed in using experts in government instead of politicians. Madison, the state capital, was also the home of the state university, and Governor La Follette called in professors to study problems and give him advice. He appointed university experts to office. When he set up commissions to regulate business or do other special jobs that required detailed knowledge, he hired experts to serve on them. La Follette's reforms and his use of experts came to be known as the Wisconsin Idea. The program spread across the nation. Soon many other states also had reform governors.

Later, "Fighting Bob" La Follette was elected to the United States Senate, where he served for 19 years. In a poll in 1959, the United States Senate named him one of the five greatest members ever to serve in that body.

Florence Kelley Combats Child Labor

For Florence Kelley the turning point came much earlier in life. In 1871, when she was 12, her father took her to visit a glass factory. Mr. Kelley thought the up-to-date method of production would impress her. What struck Florence, however, and what she remembered all her life, was the sight of boys who were younger than she was, working by the hot furnaces. The welfare of children became a lifelong interest of Florence Kelley.

In 1891 she started working at Hull House, Jane Addams's settlement house in Chicago. Florence Kelley made studies of the working conditions of women and children in the neighborhood. Her work led the Illinois legislature to pass a law in 1893 prohibiting child labor and setting an 8-hour day for women. Kelley was given the job of enforcing the law, but she was given no real power to do so. Four years later she was still reporting the large number of accidents that happened when tired child workers got caught in machinery. Bitterly, Kelley wrote that "killing children by machinery has not yet been made a crime in the state of Illinois."

Soon afterwards, Florence Kelley became head of an organization devoted to putting an end to child labor. She played an important part in getting almost every state to adopt a child labor law between 1900 and 1914.

Only such state laws could be applied to businesses that operated entirely within a state. Under the Constitution, the United States government could make laws to regulate business only in dealings that went across state lines. But in a time when businesses were growing larger, more and more big companies were hiring children as workers. Kelley therefore took the lead in forming a national committee to seek a federal child labor law. Because of the work of this committee, Congress twice passed child labor laws. Each time, however, the Supreme Court ruled them unconstitutional. Not until the 1930s was there finally a federal child labor law.

Florence Kelley (second from left), who had been chief factory inspector for Illinois, poses with others who had also served as factory inspectors.
■ **What, do you think, was the duty of a factory inspector?**

Florence Kelley also championed laws to limit working hours and set minimum wages for women. Many states adopted such laws between 1900 and 1915.

The Progressive Movement Robert La Follette and Florence Kelley worked in different fields, but they had much in common. They were both concerned about the problems and the injustices that had developed as America became a more industrialized society. They both believed that dedicated, trained people could find ways to make things better. And both believed that government could and should be used to remedy these problems and injustices.

La Follette and Kelley were part of a large number of men and women who became interested in reform — changing things for the better — around the turn of the century. They included business people and teachers, doctors and lawyers, social workers and clergy. In politics they were Republicans, Democrats, and independents. These people came to be known as Progressives. They made up the **Progressive movement**, a wave of reform that swept the country in the early 1900s.

Progressives sought some of the same changes Populists had, such as the initiative, referendum, and direct election of senators, but the two movements were quite different. Populists were from farms and small towns. Their programs reflected the interests of rural America. Most Progressives were city dwellers. They focused on problems of urban and industrial life. Some were mainly concerned with improving housing or health. Others sought to get rid of sweatshops. Some worked to give the people a greater say in government and to make government, especially in the cities, more honest and efficient. Still others wanted to limit the power of great corporations and regulate them in the public interest.

MᶜCLURE'S
MAGAZINE

Christmas
1903

NINE SHORT STORIES
Pictures in Color

The Story of
Rockefeller

OPENING OF
THE SECOND PART OF
THE HISTORY
OF STANDARD OIL

By
Ida M. Tarbell

John La Farge on the Hundred
Greatest Pictures, and
Other Features

S. S. McCLURE CO., NEW YORK AND LONDON

Ida Tarbell, one of the muckrakers, wrote articles on the history of Standard Oil Company, for *McClure's Magazine*.
■ Who was exposed by Tarbell's articles?

The Muckrakers   A group of writers played an important role in the Progressive movement. In popular magazines and books, they called attention to what was wrong and stirred the public to action. President Theodore Roosevelt once said that they were like a character in a well-known novel who spent all his time raking up the muck, or dirt, on the floor. The image stuck, and thereafter these writers were known as **muckrakers**.

One of the muckrakers was Lincoln Steffens, who exposed the corruption of governments in many American cities. Another was Ida Tarbell. She spent 5 years gathering facts on the methods John D. Rockefeller used to drive out competition so that he could create a monopoly.

Johnson Reforms Cleveland   Those who knew Tom Johnson during his business career would not have guessed he would one day be the greatest reform mayor in America. Johnson was a millionaire. He had made his money in steel mills and in street railways in Indianapolis, Detroit, and Cleveland. During the first 40 years of his life, he showed no interest in politics. He seemed content to expand his street-railway business and add to his personal fortune.

Then Johnson read a book called *Progress and Poverty,* in which Henry George, an economist, wrote about poverty and its causes. Johnson was moved by this book. He began a new career as a reform politician.

In 1901, Johnson was elected mayor of Cleveland. One of the first things he did was open up government to the people. He held public meetings in a circus tent. There, citizens and city officials discussed ideas for dealing with Cleveland's problems. For many years, those with friends in government had paid lower taxes than other citizens. Johnson put a stop to that practice. He got the city council to tax the utility companies and to make the street-railway companies lower their fares.

Johnson knew that few politicians had the knowledge to run a department of public health, to plan housing and parks, or to manage a school system. So he brought in experts to run the city departments. By the time Tom Johnson left office in 1908, the muckraker Lincoln Steffens called Cleveland "the best-governed city in the United States."

Cleveland was but one of many cities in which reform forces won control of the government. In Detroit, New York, San Francisco, and other cities, strong reform mayors fought corruption.

Tom Johnson (right), brought honest, efficient government to the city of Cleveland.
■ **What public office did he hold?**

New Forms of City Government Progressives brought about two changes in the form of city government. The first came about by accident. In 1900 a hurricane and tidal wave destroyed much of Galveston, Texas. The outdated and inefficient city government could not cope with the emergency. Therefore the state appointed a commission of five experts. Each commissioner took over one or more city departments, such as the police, fire, and water departments. Together, the commissioners ran the city. The people of Galveston were so pleased with the results that they changed their form of government permanently. Thus **commission government** was born. By 1914 more than 400 cities had adopted it.

The second new form of government was the **city manager** system. Under this system, elected commissioners appointed an expert, who used modern business methods to run the city. This took much of the politics out of city government and bypassed the political machine. The city manager system was first used in Staunton, Virginia, in 1908. It soon spread to other small and medium-sized cities.

The Wisconsin Idea Spreads Wisconsin was only one of a number of states in which Progressives brought reform. In Oregon, New York, Missouri, California, Iowa, New Jersey, and other states, Progressive governors battled the political machines and cleaned up corruption. Many states adopted the initiative, referendum, direct primary, and direct election of senators. In 1913 the Seventeenth Amendment provided for the direct election of senators in all states.

Progressive states set up commissions like those in Wisconsin to regulate rates charged by railroads and public utilities. They also adopted many of the laws that

In 1912, almost 15,000 women and their children marched down Fifth Avenue in New York City to support women's suffrage. This was 8 years before the passage of the Nineteenth Amendment.
■ What did this amendment provide for?

Florence Kelley championed. In addition to child-labor and maximum-hour laws, those states provided for workmen's compensation and gave pensions to families of workers who were killed or seriously injured on the job.

During the Progressive Era, women made important gains in their effort to win the right to vote. Four states had given women the right to vote by 1896, but not another state was added to the list for the next 13 years. Starting in 1910, however, the women's movement began to achieve success. In the next 5 years, seven more states granted women full voting rights.

1. Name and explain five reforms that came about in Wisconsin under the leadership of Robert La Follette.
2. For what reforms did Kelley work?
3. How did the Progressive movement differ from the Populist movement?
4. Explain the contribution that each of the following made to the reform movement: Lincoln Steffens, Ida Tarbell, Tom Johnson.

5. **Thinking Critically** Which groups of people might have been opposed to the Progressives' reforms? Why?

The First Modern President

What were Theodore Roosevelt's main accomplishments as President?

VOCABULARY

arbitration	conservation
Square Deal	Bull Moose party

A Man with a Zest for Living   Progressivism arrived on the national level with the presidency of Theodore Roosevelt. As a youth growing up on Long Island, New York, he was sickly and weak. Still, Teddy, as his family called him, had an iron will. Through exercise and determination he grew strong. When he went to college, he took up boxing — even though he was so nearsighted he could hardly see without his glasses.

Roosevelt read widely, a habit he continued throughout his life. He was one of the best-read and best-informed persons ever to serve as President. He also wrote a dozen books, on subjects from botany to American history. He had a zest for living and seemed to be interested in just about everything.

A Career in Politics   What most interested Roosevelt, however, was politics and power. Very early in his life, he decided that he wanted to be "a member of the governing class." He joined the local Republican club in New York and was soon chosen to run for the state legislature. He won and at 23 was its youngest member.

It was at this time that Roosevelt, who came from a well-to-do family, gained his first understanding of the life of the working poor. While investigating working and housing conditions among New York's immigrants, Roosevelt visited workers who were making cigars in their own homes. He later wrote:

I have always remembered one room in which two families were living. . . . There were several children, three men, and two women in this room. The tobacco was stowed about everywhere, alongside the foul bedding, and in a corner where there were scraps of food. The men, women, and children in this room worked by day and far on into the evening, and they slept and ate there.

In 1884, Roosevelt's wife died, just 2 days after giving birth to their first child. On the same day, his mother died. Roosevelt was shattered. He gave up politics and left New York. He bought a ranch in the Dakota Territory. For the next 2 years this eastern city dweller lived the life of a ranch hand.

For two years, young Teddy Roosevelt lived on a ranch in the Dakotas.
■ **How is Roosevelt dressed?**

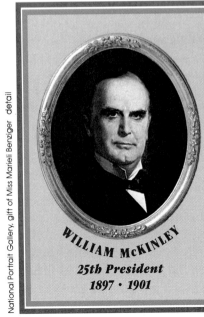

Born: 1843, Niles, Ohio.
Education: Attended Allegheny College, but illness forced his withdrawal from school.
Training: Lawyer, public official.
To presidency from: Ohio.
Position when elected: Governor of Ohio.
Political party: Republican.
Married: Ida Saxton.
Children: Two daughters, who died in infancy.
Died: September 14, 1901. Shot 9 days earlier by an anarchist at the Pan-American Exposition in Buffalo, New York.
Other facts: In the Civil War, served for a time under Colonel Rutherford B. Hayes, another future President. Devoted to his invalid wife. The first President to use the telephone extensively in his campaign.
During his presidency: Thousands of Americans rushed to the Klondike region of Canada in search of gold.

WILLIAM McKINLEY
25th President
1897 · 1901

In 1886, Roosevelt returned to the East and politics. He ran for mayor in New York City but was defeated. He was later appointed to the United States Civil Service Commission, on which he served 3 years. Then he served as the police commissioner of New York City and, after that, as assistant secretary of the navy in Washington, D.C. Roosevelt left this position to serve as a lieutenant colonel in the Spanish-American War, as you will read in the next chapter.

The White House   Returning from the war as a national hero, Roosevelt was elected governor of New York. He proved to be an effective reform governor. He was so effective, in fact, that the boss of the state's Republican party wanted to get rid of him. He arranged for Roosevelt to be nominated for Vice President in 1900. William McKinley was the party's choice for a second term as President. One Republican leader who was unhappy with the nomination of Roosevelt warned, "Don't you realize that there's only one life between this madman and the White House?"

McKinley and Teddy Roosevelt were elected. Only a few months after President McKinley began his new term, he was shot by a crazed man. He died soon afterward. Thus at the age of 42, Theodore Roosevelt became the youngest President of the United States. "Now look," said the Republican leader who had warned about Roosevelt, "that . . . cowboy is in the White House."

Regulating Big Business   Like other Progressives, Roosevelt believed that government must play a larger role in regulating big business. Early in his presidency he took action against the Northern Securities Company. This company, formed in 1901, controlled all the long-distance railroad lines in the northwestern part of the country. With no competition, it could charge customers whatever it wished.

Roosevelt said the company violated the Sherman Antitrust Act (see page 508). The Supreme Court agreed and ordered that the company be broken up. This was the first time the antitrust law had really been enforced. Roosevelt later brought action against Standard Oil, the American Tobacco Company, and more than 40 other large business combinations.

These actions earned Roosevelt the nickname the Trustbuster. Roosevelt himself would have been the first to say that the name was not accurate. He was not against all big businesses. In fact, he felt that growth was a perfectly natural development in modern business. There was a difference, however, between "good trusts" and "bad trusts." The latter were the ones that had been formed by illegal methods or that took unfair advantage of the public. Bad trusts, said Roosevelt, should be broken up. The others should be regulated by the federal government.

The Coal-Mining Strike   In another early action, Roosevelt used his power as President to settle a strike in the coal-mining industry. Mining was probably the most dangerous job in America. Every year, explosions and cave-ins took the lives of several thousand workers. Black lung,

a disease caused by coal dust settling into the lungs, shortened the lives of thousands of other miners. Hours were long and the work was backbreaking. For their labor, coal miners averaged only about $600 a year. A miner's income was far less than the amount an average-sized family needed to live on in 1900.

In the spring of 1902, miners asked the owners of the coal mines for a wage increase, an 8-hour workday, and recognition of their union. The owners refused, and the men walked out. The strike dragged on into the fall with neither side budging. Owners would not even talk with union leaders.

With winter nearing and with some cities fearing a fuel shortage, the President stepped in. He called representatives of both sides to the White House and asked them to settle their differences. The miners were willing, but the owners were not. One owner still refused to talk to the union leader. Roosevelt later wrote that "if it wasn't for the high office I hold, I

The coal miners' strike of 1902 lasted from May to October. People across the country lined up to buy baskets of coal.
■ How do you think the coal will be used?

The Day the Air Age Began

Of the many inventions in the early 1900s, few would prove as important as the airplane. Yet oddly enough, the first flight of an engine-powered flying machine passed almost unnoticed.

The inventors of this airplane were Orville and Wilbur Wright, owners of a small bicycle shop in Dayton, Ohio. In the late 1890s the Wright brothers became interested in the possibilities of flying. After trying out their theories with large box kites and gliders, they built a passenger-carrying glider in 1900. To test it, the Wrights chose the beach at Kitty Hawk, North Carolina. The glider worked beautifully. For the next 2 years, the brothers experimented with different wing shapes and made other improvements. Finally they added a small gasoline engine.

On December 17, 1903, with Orville at the controls, they made the first successful flight—12 seconds long! Taking turns, the Wrights made three more flights that day. The longest lasted 59 seconds, during which the plane traveled 852 feet.

The Wright brothers were now ready to tell the world. But the world did not seem ready to listen. In the next 2 days, only six newspapers in the country carried the story!

The nation's press had missed the significance of what had happened at Kitty Hawk on December 17, 1903. For that was the day the age of air travel began.

would have taken him by the seat of the breeches and . . . chucked him out the window."

Roosevelt eventually succeeded in getting the two sides to agree to **arbitration**. This meant that a third party would listen to both sides and propose a fair settlement, which the owners and the miners would have to accept. The strike then ended.

Roosevelt was not the first President to step into a major strike. Earlier Presidents, however, had sided with business and had sent in troops to break the strikes. Roosevelt was the first to take into account labor's viewpoint and to insist on a settlement fair to both sides.

This was in line with Roosevelt's idea that government should use its power to see that everyone—business, labor, and the public—was treated fairly. Government should make certain that everyone received a **Square Deal**, said Roosevelt. This term became his slogan.

Further Reforms   In 1904, Theodore Roosevelt was elected by a landslide to a full term as President. He promptly sought stronger laws to regulate the

Born: 1858, New York, New York.
Education: Harvard College.
Training: Writer, public official.
To presidency from: New York.
Position when taking office: Vice President.
Political party: Republican.
Married: (1) Alice Lee, (2) Edith Carow.
Children: Four sons, two daughters.
Died: 1919, Oyster Bay, New York.
Other facts: An energetic man who loved the outdoors. Hiked, swam, rode horseback, and boxed. The youngest man (42 years, 10 months) to become President. The first President to ride in an automobile (1902), to go underwater in a submarine (1905), and to ride in an airplane (1910).
During his presidency: An earthquake struck San Francisco in April 1906, destroying most of the city and killing some 700 people.

THEODORE ROOSEVELT
26th President
1901 · 1909

railroads. The Interstate Commerce Act of 1887 had never been effective. Pressed by the President, Congress passed the Hepburn Act in 1906. This law gave the Interstate Commerce Commission new powers to set rates.

Roosevelt also induced Congress to pass the Meat Inspection Act. Conditions in the meat-packing business in the United States were disgraceful. The plants were filthy. Companies passed along spoiled and diseased meat to consumers. In 1906 a writer named Upton Sinclair wrote *The Jungle,* a novel exposing these conditions. The book caused a sensation. After reading it, Roosevelt sent investigators to find out whether Sinclair's charges were true. Roosevelt then used his influence with Congress to pass a law that required federal inspection of meat before it could be sold. Another new law — the Pure Food and Drug Act — required truthful labeling of medicines.

Conservation Roosevelt gave strong support to **conservation**, or the protection of natural resources. The conserva-

tion movement had begun in the late 1800s. Forests were being cut down at a shocking rate, and practices in both the lumbering and mining industries were wasteful. Acting under a law of Congress, Roosevelt set aside 150 million acres (60.7 million ha) of land to add to the national forests. This was three times as much land as had been set aside by all earlier Presidents combined. He also saw to it that the government held on to millions of acres of mineral-rich land for the future. Most important of all, he brought the need for conserving our natural resources to the attention of the people.

Taft Becomes President Following his victory in the 1904 election, Roosevelt had announced that "under no circumstances will I be a candidate for or accept another nomination." Now, in 1908, many supporters urged him to run again. He was still very popular, and he probably could have been reelected. Roosevelt, however, was determined to keep his word, and he refused all urgings that he run again.

Born: 1857, Cincinnati, Ohio.
Education: Yale College, Cincinnati Law School.
Training: Lawyer.
To presidency from: Ohio.
Position when elected: Secretary of war.
Political party: Republican.
Married: Helen Herron.
Children: Two sons, one daughter.
Died: 1930, Washington, D.C.
Other facts: Weighed more than 300 pounds but played tennis and golf and was an excellent dancer. Threw out the first ball at the beginning of the major-league baseball season in 1910, starting a practice that lasted many years. The only person to have served both as President and as Chief Justice.
During his presidency: Robert E. Peary led the first expedition to the North Pole (1909), and Roald Amundsen's expedition resulted in the discovery of the South Pole (1911).

WILLIAM H. TAFT

27th President
1909 · 1913

At the same time, the President wanted to be sure that his policies would be continued. He believed the best person to do this was his friend William Howard Taft, who was the secretary of war. With Roosevelt's support, Taft won the Republican nomination and the election. His Democratic opponent was Willian Jennings Bryan of Nebraska. It was Bryan's third attempt to win the presidency.

Taft's Record   Taft was no doubt sincere when he promised to carry out Roosevelt's policies. Indeed, progressivism did make some gains under Taft. Congress passed a new law further strengthening the Interstate Commerce Commission. Congress approved and sent on to the states for their approval one constitutional amendment for an income tax and another for the direct election of senators. These became the Sixteenth and Seventeenth Amendments in 1913. The President also started almost 80 new antitrust suits, nearly twice as many as Teddy Roosevelt had begun.

Yet Progressives distrusted Taft. He ignored them in making appointments to office. At the start of his term, he asked Congress to lower the tariff. Instead, Congress passed a bill to raise it. Taft signed the bill into law anyway, even though Progressives urged him to veto it. Then he further angered Progressives by calling that law "the best tariff bill that the Republican party ever passed." On conservation, another favorite cause with Progressives, Taft's clumsy handling of the issue made it appear that he was against conservation when he was really in favor of it. Before long, Taft and the Progressives in his party were criticizing each other.

A Cooling Friendship   Meanwhile, the friendship between Roosevelt and Taft had cooled. Roosevelt felt that Taft had failed to keep his promise to carry out Roosevelt's policies. Taft felt that Roosevelt was criticizing him unfairly.

In 1912, Roosevelt announced that he would battle Taft for the Republican nomination. "My hat is in the ring," proclaimed the former President. Roosevelt was still popular with the public, but Taft supporters controlled the Republican convention. When Taft got the nomination, Roosevelt and many of his Progressive followers walked out of the convention.

The Bull Moose Party A short time later, Roosevelt supporters formed a new party and nominated their hero for the presidency. Roosevelt accepted, saying that he felt "as fit as a bull moose." The name of the party was the Progressive party, but many people called it the **Bull Moose party**.

The platform of the new party aimed to make political life more democratic. It favored the initiative, referendum, direct primary, and woman suffrage. It prom-

ised an 8-hour day, minimum wages for women, a federal child labor law, workmen's compensation, and unemployment insurance.

The split between Taft and Roosevelt supporters gave the Democratic party a golden opportunity. The party nominated Governor Woodrow Wilson of New Jersey for President in 1912.

Progressivism and Civil Rights Although progressivism was making life more democratic for white Americans, it brought few changes for black people. By the early 1900s a number of black leaders were becoming impatient with Booker T. Washington's advice against pressing for social equality too quickly.

One of these leaders was W. E. B. Du Bois, a Harvard-trained social scientist. Du Bois and several other black leaders met at Niagara Falls, Canada, in 1905. They issued a declaration demanding full political and civil rights for blacks immediately. In 1910, Du Bois and others in the so-called Niagara Movement joined forces with a group of prominent people — blacks and whites — who had recently formed the National Association for the Advancement of Colored People (NAACP). For the next quarter of a century, Du Bois was a strong voice for black rights as editor of the NAACP's magazine, *The Crisis*.

Taft is pictured here as the crown prince, perched on King Teddy's shoulder.
■ Is this before or after their split? Explain.

CHECKUP

1. What steps did President Theodore Roosevelt take to regulate big business?
2. How did he settle a strike in the coal-mining industry?
3. What did Roosevelt do concerning conservation of natural resources?
4. How did the split between Roosevelt and Taft help Woodrow Wilson get elected?
5. **Thinking Critically** How do you know Roosevelt was a popular President?

The Wilson Presidency

What reforms were passed during Woodrow Wilson's presidency?

A Boy Who Dreamed of Glory   The story of Woodrow Wilson's youth, one person wrote, "is the story of a boy who dreamed of winning glory by great speeches that would move people. . . ." Many a young person has no doubt shared that dream. Few, however, could have worked with such determination as Woodrow Wilson did to make it come true.

Woodrow Wilson was born in Virginia in 1856. As a teenager he memorized the speeches of great orators and delivered them in a forest or in an empty building. He continued to develop his skill with language in college, becoming not only a fine speaker but an excellent writer as well. His goal in life, he wrote a friend, was to have "a commanding influence in the councils . . . of my country."

From Professor to Governor   Wilson became a college professor and later president of Princeton University in New Jersey. His chance to enter politics came in 1910. The Democratic party in New Jersey was marked by scandal. It needed a candidate for governor whose honesty was beyond question. Wilson was a perfect choice. He was nominated and elected.

Wilson became one of the leading Progressive governors in the nation. He stood up to the Democratic machine and refused to support its boss for the United States Senate. Under his leadership, New Jersey adopted far-reaching reforms. These included a direct primary law, workmen's compensation, regulation of utilities and railroads, and a law to clean up corrupt election practices. This record won attention and helped Wilson win the Democratic nomination for President in 1912.

Wilson's Views on Trusts   In the campaign of 1912, Wilson and Roosevelt were the two chief candidates, with Taft trailing far behind. One of the main issues on which Wilson and Roosevelt differed was the method of handling the trusts. You

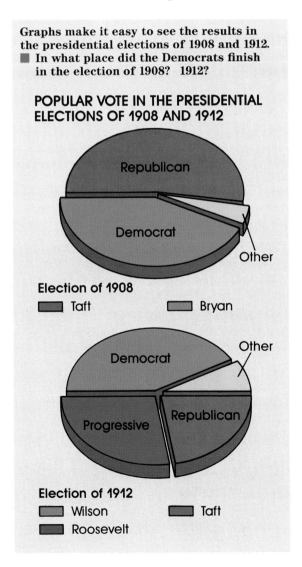

Graphs make it easy to see the results in the presidential elections of 1908 and 1912.
■ In what place did the Democrats finish in the election of 1908? 1912?

POPULAR VOTE IN THE PRESIDENTIAL ELECTIONS OF 1908 AND 1912

Republican

Democrat

Other

Election of 1908
■ Taft   ■ Bryan

Democrat

Other

Progressive   Republican

Election of 1912
■ Wilson   ■ Taft
■ Roosevelt

Woodrow Wilson, shown here with his first wife and their three daughters, became governor of New Jersey in 1910.
■ When did Wilson become President?

imported items. It was the first law to lower the tariff since the Civil War.

It was expected that lowering the tariff duties would result in less income for the United States government. To make up for this loss, Congress added an income tax to the law. The income tax was made possible by the Sixteenth Amendment, which had been added to the Constitution earlier that year.

Reforming the Banking System   Next, Wilson asked Congress to reform banking. The banking system then in effect had been designed 50 years earlier. Since that time, the country's needs had changed greatly. Furthermore, control of banking lay in the hands of a few powerful bankers. Wilson and many Progressives believed it was wrong for a few individuals to have such power over the economy.

With Wilson's leadership, Congress created the **Federal Reserve System**. The law divided the country into 12 banking districts, with a Federal Reserve Bank in each district. The Federal Reserve Bank did not do business with the public. It provided certain services for the private banks in its district, and it had power to regulate certain practices.

Heading the whole system was a Federal Reserve Board in Washington, D.C. Its members were appointed by the President. Through their decisions they could affect the supply of money in circulation and the rate of interest that borrowers would pay. Thus they had a large influence on the economy of the nation. As a result, banking in the United States remained a private business, but the federal government now supervised it.

Dealing with the Trusts   During the 1912 elelction, Wilson had promised to break up trusts. As President, he found it

have already learned that Roosevelt did not believe that a company was automatically bad because it was big. In fact he felt that large business combinations were a natural development of modern business. Roosevelt believed that the correct way for the federal government to deal with them was to accept them but regulate them so they would serve the public interest.

Woodrow Wilson, on the other hand, believed that all trusts were bad because they shut out competition. He said that government should break up trusts and prevent new ones from forming. His strong belief in competition also led Wilson to favor lowering the tariff. Congress passed the Underwood Tariff Act in 1913. This law lowered the tariff on hundreds of difficult to devise a law that would do this. The result was that he proposed two separate laws.

One was the **Clayton Antitrust Act**. This law prohibited companies from gaining control of other companies in the same industry. It also stopped them from engaging in certain business practices *if* these practices reduced competition. That was a big if, however. In most cases, it was hard for the government to prove that a company's practices had really reduced competition. Usually the courts sided with business.

The second law was the Federal Trade Commission Act. This law was close to Roosevelt's views about how to deal with trusts. It created a federal commission to regulate big business. The President ap-

pointed five commissioners. These commissioners had the power to investigate businesses and order them to stop "harmful practices," such as false advertising. But telling a trust not to do certain things was very different from breaking it up. All in all, Wilson found that regulating the trusts was a difficult problem. Of all the reforms that Wilson supported, he was least successful in this area.

Wilson's Other Reforms President Wilson backed several laws to help farmers. The Federal Farm Loan Act of 1916 provided low-interest loans to farmers. Another measure set up a network of trained agricultural agents to advise farmers on the growing and marketing of crops.

The President also supported two important laws involving labor. One was the Adamson Act. This set an 8-hour workday for railroad employees. This was the first time the federal government had made a law about the length of the workday in a private business. A second law was the Keating-Owen Child Labor Law of 1916. This law attempted to end child labor by punishing companies that used it. Any product made by children under 14, said the law, could not be shipped across state lines. However, in 1918 the Supreme Court ruled this law unconstitutional.

Rating the Progressives How successful were the Progressives? Did they really accomplish their goals of achieving greater democracy, regulating business in the public interest, and protecting people against the ills of an industrial society?

The record is mixed. City governments became more honest and provided better services to their citizens. Yet political machines and bosses did not disappear. They often found ways to use the

Wilson considered all trusts bad.
■ What, do you think, is the message this cartoon is trying to convey?

Major reforms were enacted when Wilson was President. Here Wilson signs the first federal child labor act, later declared unconstitutional.
■ Why, do you think, are people standing around Wilson?

new laws to regain power. Businesses continued to grow bigger and more powerful, despite state and federal laws aimed to curb them. Women and child labor laws made a start toward protecting workers in an industrial society, but their effect was limited.

Still, the Progressive movement brought about important changes. It showed how experts could make government better and more efficient. It firmly established the idea that government had a responsibility to deal with large social problems. It established the principle that business had responsibilities to the public. And finally, it established the idea that the federal government should play an active role in improving American life.

Those changes would become the foundation for much that followed in the twentieth century.

CHECKUP

1. How did Wilson's views on trusts differ from those of Roosevelt?
2. How does the Federal Reserve System influence the economy?
3. How did the Clayton Antitrust Act and the Federal Trade Commission Act attempt to deal with trusts?
4. What important changes did the Progressive movement bring to American life?
5. **Thinking Critically** How do lower tariffs and antitrust laws encourage competition in business?

Taking Notes

THEODORE ROOSEVELT

As you read textbooks, you will find it helpful to take notes on the material. Writing down important information in this shortened form helps you in three ways. First, it gets you to think about which facts are more important and which are less important. Second, it helps you remember what you read. Third, it helps you review quickly what you read.

What should you include in your notes and what should you leave out? A simple rule that will help you make that judgment is to keep in mind the purpose of your reading. For example, read the following paragraph.

> Theodore Roosevelt's colorful personality brought him a great deal of newspaper coverage. His Rough Rider hat and large gleaming teeth became familiar to millions through newspaper photographs and political cartoons. Roosevelt skillfully used this press coverage to win support for his proposals. Often, he went to the people to get Congress to act. An example occurred in 1906. Certain leaders of Congress were blocking Roosevelt's bill for federal inspection of meat. Roosevelt had a report about the unsanitary conditions in meat-packing plants. He gave part of it to the newspaper. When people read it, they were outraged. Roosevelt then warned the congressmen who were blocking the bill that if Congress did not act, he would publish the rest of the report, which was even more shocking. The public, he warned, would blame the congressmen who opposed it. With that, the leaders dropped their opposition and the Federal Meat Inspection Act was passed.

It may be interesting that Roosevelt often wore cowboy hats and that he had large gleaming teeth. If your purpose in reading the para-

graph is to get information for a report on "Clothes That Presidents Wear," or "The Dental Features of Presidents," those are facts you would want in your notes. But if your purpose for reading is to understand the Progressive era, or presidential power, your notes would probably look like this:

> TR—colorful personality—much newspaper coverage. TR used press to pressure Cong.—example: 1906—Cong. block bill to inspect meat. TR gave press part of report on unsanitary cond.—public outraged—TR threatened to publish the rest—leaders gave in—passed Fed. Meat Inspec. Act.

SKILLS PRACTICE

To get some practice in note taking, turn to page 532 and take notes on the section "Regulating Big Business."

MAIN IDEAS

1. Most Progressives wanted the government to regulate big business, break up trusts, and reform the banking system.
2. In a number of cities, reform movements took power out of the hands of political bosses and gave it to trained experts.
3. During the Progressive era, many states passed laws to protect workers.
4. Theodore Roosevelt began the tradition of an active federal government led by a strong chief executive.
5. Roosevelt used arbitration to settle the coal-mining strike, tried to break up trusts, and supported laws regulating railroad rates and food inspection.
6. During Wilson's administration, tariffs were lowered, the banking system was reformed, and a federal commission to regulate big business was established.

VOCABULARY REVIEW

On a separate sheet of paper, write the word or phrase from the list that best completes each sentence.

public utility	commission
banking	direct primary
city manager	recall
muckraker	conservation
Progressive	arbitration

1. Voters in each party select their party's candidates in a _____.
2. The Bull Moose party was a nickname for the _____ party.
3. A company that sells water, gas, or electricity is a _____.
4. An elected official may be removed from office before his or her term is over by _____.
5. The creation of the Federal Reserve System brought about reforms in _____.
6. The form of government first used in Galveston, Texas, was the _____.

7. To protect the nation's natural resources, Theodore Roosevelt had an active program of _____.
8. A writer of the early 1900s who exposed abuses in business and government was called a _____.
9. The process of having a third party settle a disagreement between employers and employees is called _____.
10. An expert hired to run a city is called a _____.

CHAPTER CHECKUP

1. Who were the Progressives?
2. How did the muckrakers help to bring about reforms?
3. What reforms were made in city governments in the early 1900s?
4. Why was Roosevelt called the Trust-buster?
5. What did Roosevelt mean by the Square Deal?
6. Why was the Bull Moose party formed?
7. List two reforms brought about by each of the following. (a) La Follette (b) Roosevelt (c) Taft (d) Wilson
8. **Thinking Critically** Explain how the direct primary and the recall gave more power to the people.
9. **Thinking Critically** Which reform made by the Progressives do you think has had the most lasting effect?

APPLYING KNOWLEDGE

1. Draw up a list of reforms you would support for your community. Choose one, write about the problem, and tell how it might be solved.
2. The Food and Drug Administration established by Theodore Roosevelt still exists. Find out about its activities. What drugs have been outlawed? What rules are there about labeling food?

23 Expansion Overseas

1853–1914

America Looks Outward

Why did Americans become interested in overseas expansion in the late 1800s?

VOCABULARY

overseas empire	imperialist

To the Philippines Sailing by the light of a pale moon, the United States Pacific fleet entered the quiet waters of Manila Bay in the Philippine Islands. It was midnight on April 30, 1898. Farther down the bay, closer to the shore, the Spanish fleet lay waiting. Commodore George Dewey, commanding the American fleet, knew that fighting would begin at dawn.

Dewey's force was a small one, six warships in all. But all of them were armored and fitted with modern rapid-fire guns that could hit a target more than 5 miles (8 km) away.

At 61, George Dewey was a part of the old navy as well as the new. Born in Montpelier, Vermont, in 1837, he entered the United States Naval Academy in 1854. During the Civil War he served in the Union fleet that won control of the Mississippi River from Confederate forces. In the years that followed the war, the navy entered a long period of decline. Old wooden ships were not replaced, even though some European countries were building steel ships. During this period, Dewey said that America's navy was the "laughingstock of the nations." By the 1890s, however, new steel ships were entering service in the navy.

By 1898, George Dewey had risen to the command of America's small Pacific fleet. Trouble was then starting with Spain, and Dewey's fleet was ordered to Hong Kong, a British possession on the coast of China. This put the American ships only 1,000 miles (1,600 km) from the Philippine Islands, which were under Spanish control. On April 25, 1898, the order came from Washington: "Proceed at once to the Philippine Islands."

The Battle of Manila Bay At 4:00 A.M. on May 1, Dewey's men were awakened for coffee. As the American fleet steamed farther into the bay, Spanish guns on shore opened fire. The shells fell harmlessly into the water. By 5:40 A.M. the American ships had closed to within 3 miles (4.8 km) of the Spanish fleet. Turning to his captain, Dewey ordered: "You may fire when ready, Gridley."

It was a one-sided contest. Spain's ancient wooden vessels were no match for America's steel ships. By noon, the Spanish surrendered. They had lost 8 ships

The painting shows the American fleet, under Dewey, defeating the Spanish at Manila Bay in the Philippines. (14°N/121°W; map, p. 555)
■ Why was this an easy battle for the Americans?

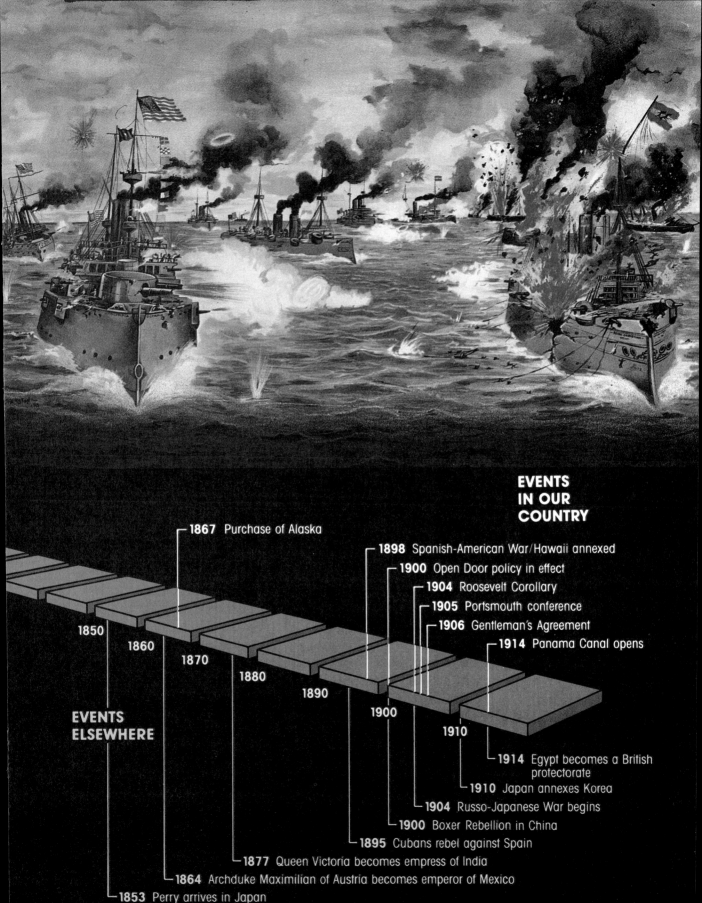

EVENTS
IN OUR
COUNTRY

1867 Purchase of Alaska

1898 Spanish-American War/Hawaii annexed

1900 Open Door policy in effect

1904 Roosevelt Corollary

1905 Portsmouth conference

1906 Gentleman's Agreement

1914 Panama Canal opens

1850

1860

1870

1880

1890

1900

1910

EVENTS
ELSEWHERE

1914 Egypt becomes a British
protectorate

1910 Japan annexes Korea

1904 Russo-Japanese War begins

1900 Boxer Rebellion in China

1895 Cubans rebel against Spain

1877 Queen Victoria becomes empress of India

1864 Archduke Maximilian of Austria becomes emperor of Mexico

1853 Perry arrives in Japan

Commodore George Dewey enters Manila Bay on his warship, the *Olympia*.
■ What tells you this is a warship?

and 381 men; Dewey had lost not a ship nor a man in the brief encounter. Manila Bay was Dewey's, and within a year all the Philippine Islands became American territory.

Changes in American Thinking Adding land to its holdings was nothing new for the United States. In the first half of the nineteenth century, large territories were added by purchase, by diplomacy, and by war. But all that land was on the North American continent and had bordered the United States. The Philippines lay across the Pacific Ocean, some 7,000 miles (11,200 km) from the western coast of the United States. At the time Dewey set sail for Manila Bay, most Americans had never heard

of the Philippines. Probably not 1 person in 100 could have pointed to them on a map.

How did it come to pass, then, that the American flag was raised over this land in 1898? For the answer, we must look at changes that had been taking place in America and in American thinking. During the years after the Civil War, most Americans showed little interest in affairs outside their own borders. Restoring the Union, settling the West, and adjusting to industrialization took up the country's energies. One New York newspaper in the 1880s even called on the government to bring home its ministers—representatives to other countries—and abolish the foreign service!

However, some Americans had reasons for urging their country to look outward. The great production of America's farms, factories, and mines caused some people to believe that the United States was producing more goods than its people could consume. If Americans were to continue to be employed and if farms and businesses were to keep on making profits, the United States would have to find markets in other lands for its goods. Bankers and investors also looked abroad for opportunities to invest in railroads, mines, factories, and other businesses.

Other people thought the United States should expand its influence in the world. They watched with envy as Great Britain, France, Germany, and other European countries created **overseas empires**—that is, extended their control over distant lands. The United States was also a great power, they declared. It, too, should have colonies. People who held this view were called **imperialists.**

Looking to the Pacific Some Americans had been looking outward for many years. Merchants from Philadelphia, New

York, Boston, and other ports in the Northeast had been sending trading ships to China since the 1780s.

In the 1850s, trade also began with Japan. For more than 200 years, Japan had shut itself off almost completely from contact with other lands. In 1853, Commodore Matthew Perry arrived in Japan with a fleet of four warships. Perry carried a letter from the President of the United States, asking that trade be opened between the two countries. The Japanese were distrustful, and Perry went home empty-handed. He returned the next year, however, and this time a trade treaty was signed. The Japanese agreed to open several ports to American trading ships.

Trade with the Far East led to American interest in the islands of the Pacific. By the late nineteenth century, steam engines were rapidly replacing sails on oceangoing ships. Steamships making long trading voyages from the United States to the Far East or to Australia needed island stopovers where they could take on a new supply of coal. For the same reason, the new steam warships needed island bases.

Thus the United States became interested in Samoa, a group of islands in the South Pacific about 2,500 miles (4,000 km) from Australia. In 1878, local rulers gave the United States the right to build a naval base in Samoa. Britain and Germany also had claims in the islands. Arguments among the three countries almost led to war. In 1899, however, it was agreed that Samoa would be divided between the United States and Germany, with Great Britain receiving land in Africa and elsewhere in the Pacific.

Americans in Hawaii Imperialists were even more interested in another territory in the Pacific. This was Hawaii, a

In 1853, Commodore Matthew Perry arrived in Japan. His visit helped open Japan for trade with the United States.
■ How did Perry travel to Japan?

group of islands about 2,000 miles (3,200 km) southwest of San Francisco. Polynesian peoples from the South Pacific had been living on these islands for hundreds of years when the English explorer Captain James Cook first came upon them in 1788. From then on, whalers and trading ships sailing between Asia and the United States used the islands as a stopover for taking on fresh food and supplies.

In the 1820s, missionaries went to Hawaii to convert its people to Christianity. Soon, other Americans went to live there. In 1835 an American company started a sugarcane plantation in Hawaii. Before long, planters were recruiting people from China, Japan, and other lands in Asia to work on these plantations. Later, planters raised pineapples as well as sugarcane. The American sugar planters grew rich

Hawaii's Queen Liliuokalani ruled her country for 2 years.
■ What is she wearing that shows she was a queen?

and powerful. Hawaii had a native king, but the real power to govern passed into the hands of the planters.

In 1875 the United States agreed to allow Hawaiian planters to ship sugar into the country without paying a tariff. In return, Hawaii promised never to allow any country other than the United States to control its territory. Twelve years later King Kalakaua (kä lä′ kä′ ü ä), the ruler of Hawaii, gave the United States the right to build a naval base at Pearl Harbor. The United States and Hawaii were drawing closer together.

Hawaii Is Annexed Meanwhile, sugar-cane growers in Louisiana were unhappy about the competition with Hawaiian sugar. In 1890 they got Congress to impose a new tariff duty on Hawaiian sugar. The tax made Hawaiian sugar more expensive than sugar grown in the United States. Sales dropped, and the islands faced hard times.

Americans in Hawaii had an answer to this problem: Let the United States annex Hawaii. Once it was part of the United States, the sugar tariff would no longer apply.

In 1891, Queen Liliuokalani (lē lē ü ö kä lä′ nē) became Hawaii's new ruler. She had a different answer to the problem. She believed in "Hawaii for the Hawaiians." In 1893 she scrapped the old constitution and announced a new one that would take away power from the legislature, which Americans controlled, and give it to herself.

Fearing a loss of both their power and their property, the sugar planters decided to overthrow the queen. To help them, the American minister to Hawaii sent in marines from American ships in the harbor. The queen was removed from power. Then the victorious planters formed a republic and asked that it be made part of the United States. American imperialists were delighted. It appeared that Hawaii was about to come under the control of the United States.

President Grover Cleveland, however, opposed imperialism. He sent a representative to Hawaii to find out what had happened there. When the report came back that Americans had been behind the revolt and that American armed forces had wrongly been used, Cleveland refused to go along with annexation. For the next 5 years, the islands remained an independent republic under the control of the American planters. Hawaii was finally annexed during the war with Spain in 1898. It became our fiftieth state in 1959.

Alaska Is Purchased

The United States had also acquired land in the North Pacific. In 1867, Secretary of State William Seward had had a chance to add a large new territory to the United States. This came about when Russia offered to sell the North Pacific region known as Alaska. Seward was very much in favor of expansion. However, he had some trouble in getting Congress to agree to make the purchase. Few people had any idea of Alaska's great wealth of natural resources. Some members of Congress called this northern land "Seward's Icebox" or "Seward's Folly."

Finally, however, Congress agreed to buy Alaska for $7.2 million. It turned out to be as great a bargain as Louisiana had been. In 1896, gold was discovered in the Yukon Territory, and the Alaskan gold rush was on. Large deposits of oil and gas have been found in more recent years. In 1959, Alaska became the largest state in the Union.

President Johnson and William Seward were ridiculed for the purchase of Alaska. ■ What, do you think, does the penguin and the person on the left represent?

The Venezuela Boundary Dispute

Closer to home, the United States was flexing its muscles. For many years, Venezuela and Great Britain had argued over the boundary between Venezuela and the British colony of Guiana in South America. When gold was discovered in the area, the argument became more heated. Venezuela asked the United States to step in and arbitrate the dispute. The British, however, felt their claim was right. They refused to settle the matter by arbitration.

In 1894, President Cleveland's secretary of state, Richard Olney, told the British that the Monroe Doctrine gave the United States the right to step into any dispute between European and South American countries when it threatened the peace of the Western Hemisphere. When Britain rejected Olney's claim, American anger rose and there was talk of war. The British were startled by this reaction. They had no desire to go to war with the United States over an unimportant territory thousands of miles away. In 1897 they agreed to arbitration. Two years later the matter was settled. American influence in Latin America was increased, and the Monroe Doctrine was given new importance.

CHECKUP

1. How did American thinking about an overseas empire change in the late 1800s?
2. What brought about United States contact with the following areas in the Pacific? (a) China (b) Japan (c) Samoa
3. How did Hawaii come to be a part of the United States?
4. Why did the United States intervene in a boundary dispute in South America?
5. **Thinking Critically** Do you think Cleveland was right in refusing to annex Hawaii after the revolt? Explain.

War and Empire

What were the results of the war with Spain in 1898?

VOCABULARY

yellow journalism	Teller Amendment
diplomacy	Rough Riders
"Remember the Maine!"	

Rebellion in Cuba   It was the war with Spain in 1898 that announced America's arrival as a world power. The war broke out over events in Cuba, an island 90 miles (144 km) off the southern coast of Florida. This island, together with Puerto Rico, some 500 miles (800 km) east of Cuba, were all that was left of Spain's once-great empire in the Americas.

The people of Cuba had tried many times to rid themselves of Spanish rule, but each time they had been beaten down. In 1895, Cubans once more rose up against Spain. In hit-and-run attacks, rebels swept down from their camps in the mountains to burn sugar plantations and sugar mills. To crush the uprising, Spain sent a tough general by the name of Weyler (we' ē ler) to Cuba. Weyler's plan was simple and cruel. Rebels were receiving food and supplies from people living in the countryside. By cutting off this support, General Weyler believed he could end the rebellion. He ordered thousands of Cubans moved off the sugar plantations and farms and herded them into a few towns surrounded with barbed wire. Spanish troops then burned plantations, crops, and buildings.

Meanwhile, death stalked the towns Weyler had turned into concentration camps. More than 100,000 Cubans died of starvation and disease. Weyler's nickname, "the Butcher," was well deserved.

Yellow Journalism   Americans followed the events in Cuba through their newspapers. Two New York newspapers, Joseph Pulitzer's *World* and William Randolph Hearst's *Journal*, were locked in a war of their own. Each sought to be the largest-selling newspaper in America. To win readers, they made use of sensational headlines and exaggerated news stories. Such reporting came to be called **yellow journalism.**

The war in Cuba was just what the *World* and the *Journal* needed to sell newspapers. Pulitzer and Hearst each tried to outdo the other in printing the most shocking tales of Spanish cruelty, often with little care for truth. Each hoped that the United States would go to war with Spain

President McKinley is trying to restrain the forces that are using yellow journalism. ■ What is the figure on the left holding?

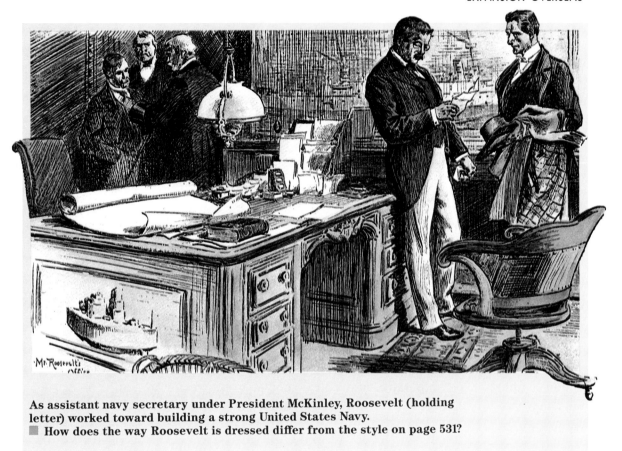

As assistant navy secretary under President McKinley, Roosevelt (holding
letter) worked toward building a strong United States Navy.
■ How does the way Roosevelt is dressed differ from the style on page 531?

over Cuba. On one occasion, Hearst sent a
famous artist named Frederic Remington
to Cuba to send back drawings of the cruel
warfare on the island. After a short time
Frederic Remington sent a telegram to
Hearst: "Everything is quiet. There is no
trouble here. There will be no war. I wish
to return." Hearst replied: "Please remain. You furnish the pictures and I'll
furnish the war."

Sympathy for the Rebels   Stories of
the cruelty in Cuba stirred the conscience
of the American people. There was growing talk of America's "responsibility" to
step in and stop the killing. In Congress,
there was open sympathy for the rebels.
Some officials, including Assistant Secretary of the Navy Theodore Roosevelt,

urged that the United States join the
fight. Roosevelt's aim was not only to help
Cuba but to gain colonies through war.
Congress passed a resolution favoring the
Cuban side, but President Cleveland ignored it. He believed both sides were at
fault in Cuba.

President William McKinley, however, opposed war. He hoped to end the
violence and Spanish misrule through
diplomacy, that is, through peaceful
negotiations between the governments involved. The President protested to Spain
about General Weyler's "uncivilized and
inhuman" conduct. A new government in
Spain removed Weyler in 1897. When
Spain's rulers spoke of possibly granting
Cuban self-rule within the Spanish empire,
it seemed that war might be avoided.

"Remember the *Maine!*" Then came two events in February 1898 that pushed the United States toward war. The first involved a letter that the Spanish minister to the United States wrote to a friend in Havana, Cuba. The letter was stolen by a Cuban rebel and published in the New York *Journal*. In the letter the minister, Dupuy Delôme (dü pü ē′ dē lōm′), called McKinley "weak" and said the President would do anything, including going to war, to be popular with the public. Americans were angered by this insult to their President.

The second and more important event came a week later. The United States had sent the battleship *Maine* to Cuba to protect Americans because riots had broken out in Havana. The ship was lying at anchor in Havana Harbor on the night of February 15 when suddenly an explosion ripped it apart. The ship sank, and 260 American sailors serving on the *Maine* lost their lives.

No one has ever discovered who caused the explosion. Most Americans, however, immediately blamed the Spaniards and demanded action. The *Journal's* headline read: "WAR! SURE! MAINE DESTROYED BY SPANISH." Soon the war cry "**Remember the *Maine!*"** could be heard from coast to coast.

The United States Goes to War Ten days after the explosion, Assistant Secretary of the Navy Theodore Roosevelt sent a cable to Commodore George Dewey.

> Keep full of coal. In the event of declaration of war by Spain, your duty will be to see that Spanish squadron does not leave the Asiatic coast . . . . then [prepare for] offensive operations in Philippine Islands.

McKinley could no longer resist the public pressure for action. On April 11, 1898, he laid the question before Congress. One week later, Congress passed a

A mysterious explosion destroys the *Maine* in Havana harbor. This event was one of the causes that touched off the Spanish-American War.
■ Havana is the capital of what country?

Chicago Historical Society

resolution that recognized Cuban independence and allowed the President to use armed force if necessary to make the Spaniards leave the island. One part of this resolution was the **Teller Amendment**. It said that the United States would not seek to take Cuba for itself.

Spain replied by declaring war on the United States on April 24. The next day, Congress declared war on Spain. The Spanish-American War had begun. Commodore Dewey steamed out of Hong Kong Harbor bound for Manila Bay.

Manila Surrenders The war in the Pacific was over quickly. A few weeks after Dewey's smashing victory at Manila Bay, Filipinos led by 29-year-old Emilio Aguinaldo (ā mē′ lyō   ä gē näl′ dō), rose up against Spanish rule. They had done this 2 years earlier, but the Spaniards had put down their revolt at that time.

Now the rebels declared independence and set up a new government. They won several victories over the Spaniards. Rebels already controlled much of the land and had surrounded Spanish forces in Manila by the time American troops arrived. Americans joined in the siege. Manila surrendered on August 12. Meanwhile, United States forces also captured the Spanish-controlled islands of Wake and Guam (gwäm) in the Pacific.

Success in Cuba The American navy was equally successful in the Atlantic. Near the end of May, Spain's Atlantic fleet sailed into the harbor of Santiago, the main Spanish military post in Cuba. American warships quickly took up positions just outside the harbor.

The American army's first efforts were disorganized. It had trouble matching men with the right equipment. In its main training center at Tampa, Florida,

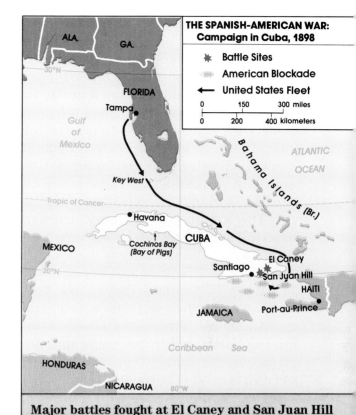

THE SPANISH-AMERICAN WAR: Campaign in Cuba, 1898

* Battle Sites
* American Blockade
← United States Fleet

Major battles fought at El Caney and San Juan Hill were important to the outcome of the war.
From which city did the United States fleet set sail?

thousands of men drilled under the hot sun in woolen winter uniforms.

In late June, about 17,000 Americans made the crossing from Tampa to Cuba. They landed on the southern coast of the island, a few miles east of Santiago. Although Spain had about 200,000 troops in Cuba at the time, Spanish generals did not take advantage of their number. The Americans landed without a fight.

During the following days the army fought and won battles at El Caney and San Juan (sən hwän) Hill. Among the soldiers at San Juan Hill was Lieutenant Colonel Theodore Roosevelt. When the war started, Roosevelt resigned from his desk job with the navy to take part in the fighting. Roosevelt was an officer in a cavalry regiment known as the **Rough Riders**.

The regiment was an odd collection of cow-hands, ranchers, miners, Native Americans, and eastern college students.

With American troops pinned down by enemy fire, Teddy Roosevelt ordered a charge up San Juan Hill. Amid a hail of bullets, the Rough Riders advanced up the hill. They were joined by two regiments of black soldiers from the regular army. Despite heavy casualties the Americans took the hill.

The victories at El Caney and San Juan Hill opened the way to Santiago. Admiral Cervera, commander of the Spanish fleet, knew his position was hopeless. If he stayed in Santiago Harbor, the fleet would face a rain of shells from American guns on shore. If he made a dash for open sea, he would surely be caught and destroyed by the waiting United States fleet. Cervera wished to surrender, but his government foolishly ordered him to fight. On July 3 the Spanish fleet sailed out of the harbor to its doom. In 4 hours, Admiral William Sampson's American fleet sank or ran aground every one of Spain's ships.

The United States Gains an Empire Three weeks later, on July 25, American troops under General Nelson A. Miles landed in Puerto Rico. They met little opposition and soon took the island.

By August 12 the war was over. In the final peace treaty, Spain agreed to leave Cuba and to hand over Puerto Rico to the United States. The United States also acquired the Philippine Islands and Guam. Thus in less than 4 months of fighting, the United States gained an empire. No wonder John Hay, one of the imperialists, called the Spanish-American War "a splendid little war."

Other Views Not all Americans favored having an overseas empire. For several months the issue was debated in the

Black American soldiers fought bravely beside Roosevelt's Rough Riders in Cuba. Roosevelt's success at San Juan Hill was due in part to the support of two black cavalry regiments — the Ninth and Tenth.
■ Which side was wearing red pants?

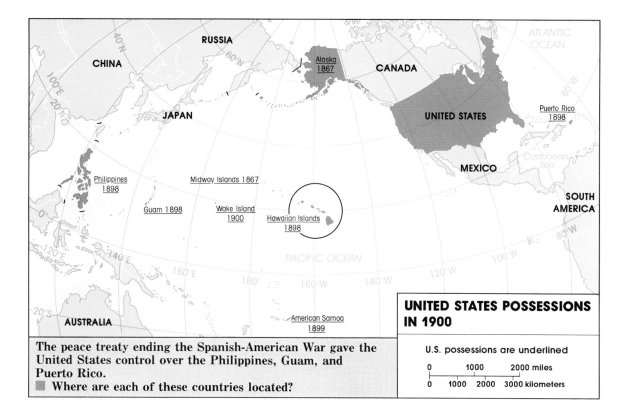

RUSSIA

CHINA

Alaska 1867

CANADA

JAPAN

UNITED STATES

Puerto Rico 1898

ATLANTIC OCEAN

Philippines 1898

Midway Islands 1867

MEXICO

Caribbean Sea

Guam 1898

Wake Island 1900

Hawaiian Islands 1898

SOUTH AMERICA

PACIFIC OCEAN

AUSTRALIA

American Samoa 1899

UNITED STATES POSSESSIONS IN 1900

The peace treaty ending the Spanish-American War gave the United States control over the Philippines, Guam, and Puerto Rico.
■ Where are each of these countries located?

U.S. possessions are underlined

0   1000   2000 miles

0   1000   2000   3000 kilometers

Senate and throughout the land. Americans had once had to fight for independence from colonial rule, said some. Was it right, they asked, for the United States now to take other lands as colonies? They declared that ruling other peoples without their consent went against the ideas of the Declaration of Independence. These critics added that it was unwise to try to rule a people having a different culture from our own.

In the end, however, national pride won out. The United States Senate approved the peace treaty, and America had an empire.

Many in the Philippine Islands thought that the end of Spanish rule would be the start of Philippine independence. When they found this was not to be, the Filipinos under Aguinaldo rose up against the Americans. It took 70,000 American troops nearly 3 years to put down the rebellion at a cost of $600 million—more than the cost of the war with Spain. In the bitter guerrilla warfare, American troops sometimes used the same harsh treatment against the Filipinos that the Spaniards had used against the Cubans.

CHECKUP

1. What activities by the Spanish in Cuba in the mid-1890s aroused the sympathy of Americans?
2. How was the United States pushed toward war with Spain in February 1898?
3. List the terms of the peace treaty ending the Spanish-American War.
4. Why did some Americans oppose the building of an overseas empire?
5. **Thinking Critically** Do you think the United States should have granted the Philippines and Puerto Rico their independence? Why or why not?

American Interests in Asia

How did the United States seek to expand its influence in Asia?

VOCABULARY

sphere of influence	Boxer Rebellion
Open Door policy	Gentlemen's Agreement

The Open Door Policy One reason imperialists wanted to keep the Philippine Islands was that they are close to China. China, with its 400 million people, it was believed, would become a great market for American goods. The imperialists also saw great investment opportunities in developing China's natural resources and in building its railroads.

As it happened, that door was fast closing to Americans at the very time the United States gained the Philippines. All through the nineteenth century, European powers had taken advantage of the weakness of the Chinese government to create **spheres of influence** in China. A sphere of influence is an area of a country where another nation has gained special trading privileges and other rights solely for itself. The nation that secures those rights will then usually keep out traders and investors from other countries. After Japan defeated China in a war in 1895, more spheres of influence were carved out.

American businesses asked the United States government to do something to keep them from being shut out of China. In 1899, therefore, Secretary of State John Hay sent messages to each of the great trading powers. He asked them to agree to an **Open Door policy** in China. This meant that all nations should have an equal opportunity to trade anywhere in China, even within another country's sphere of influence.

None of the six governments that Hay wrote to was really happy with his idea. However, none flatly said, "No." So Hay announced to the world that all six had "accepted" his proposal.

The Boxer Rebellion Business people, missionaries, and others usually came to live in their country's sphere of influence, bringing with them their foreign ways. Many Chinese objected to this. Thousands of them joined secret societies whose goal was to drive the "foreign devils" out of China. The largest society was one whose Chinese name meant "Righteous and Harmonious Fists." Westerners called them Boxers because they practiced exercises that looked as if they were boxing.

In June 1900 the Boxers rose up in rebellion. They killed hundreds of foreigners as well as hundreds of Chinese Christians, and they destroyed a great deal of foreign property. The Boxers also laid siege to the hundreds of foreigners in the capital city of Peking (pē kingʹ).

An international army from eight countries, including the United States, was sent to rescue their citizens. The army arrived at Peking and defeated the Boxers.

The United States feared that some countries would use the **Boxer Rebellion** as an excuse to carve out more spheres of influence for themselves in China. Secretary Hay stated that the United States was against such threats to China's independence. He persuaded the powers to accept money from China instead of territory to pay for the losses caused by the Boxers. China agreed to pay $330 million. The United States received $24 million but returned $20 million to be used to send Chinese students to school in America.

American forces mount an attack in Peking during the Boxer Rebellion.
These Americans were part of a six-nation international army that rescued
foreigners trapped in China. (40°N/104°E; map, p. 555)
■ What tells you that the Americans were undefeated in this battle?

War Between Japan and Russia   Until the middle of the 1800s, Japan had isolated itself from the rest of the world. After Commodore Perry opened Japan to foreign trade, that country imported not only Western goods but Western ideas. Within a few decades, the Japanese government had been modernized, and the Japanese economy had become industrialized. By 1900, Japan was an important power on the continent of Asia.

Like the other powers, Japan sought to extend its control over other lands. It soon became a rival of Russia for control of Korea and of Manchuria, an area of northeastern China. (See the map on page 555.) In 1904, Japan and Russia entered into a war.

Japan had the better of the fighting, both on land and on sea. But after a year, Japan began to run out of money and resources. The Japanese government asked President Theodore Roosevelt to help arrange a peace.

Roosevelt Steps In   Roosevelt agreed to try to end the war. He hoped for a peace that would leave neither country with too much power. He knew that if one became too powerful, that country might take over more of China and end the Open Door policy. In 1905, Roosevelt brought representatives of Japan and Russia together at the Portsmouth Naval Shipyard in Kittery, Maine. With great skill, he got the two sides to agree to peace.

Through his peacemaking efforts, Roosevelt had hoped to win greater influence for the United States with Japan. In fact, however, the opposite occurred. Japan did get control over Korea and a sphere of influence in half of Manchuria. But many Japanese thought their country should have received more land. Further, many expected that Russia would be made to pay a large amount of money to Japan for Japan's loss of life and property during the war. When the treaty gave Japan no money, the Japanese public blamed President Roosevelt.

The Gentlemen's Agreement   Relations between the United States and Japan were worsened by the poor treatment of Asian immigrants in California, including the Japanese. Californians feared that Asian immigrants working for low pay would take away jobs from Americans. They passed state and local laws that discriminated against Asians. In 1906 the San Francisco school board ruled that Asian children could not go to the regular public schools with whites. This was a blow to Japanese pride, and Japan protested.

President Roosevelt was concerned about further damage to America's relations with Japan. He invited San Francisco's mayor and members of its school board to the White House and got them to cancel their order to segregate the Asian children. At the same time, Roosevelt got the Japanese government to agree not to let more workers leave Japan for the United States. This arrangement was known as the **Gentlemen's Agreement**.

Unfortunately the agreement did not end discrimination against Asians on the West Coast. Lawmakers in California, Washington, and other states passed laws forbidding people of Japanese descent to

On its world cruise from 1907 to 1909, the "Great White Fleet" visited ports on four continents.

own land. These laws were meant to keep them from owning farms. Asians were also forbidden from holding certain jobs.

Tour of the Great White Fleet   President Roosevelt did not want Japan or anyone else to think that he had settled the school board incident out of fear. Roosevelt believed the United States should have a powerful navy. During his presidency, more modern ships were added to the navy. The President announced that the new American fleet—16 modern battleships—would sail around the world and make friendly calls at the ports of many nations. He called the tour a goodwill

Other nations were impressed with the strength of the United States Navy.
■ **How did the fleet show the world that the United States was a great power?**

cruise. His purpose, however, was to make a dramatic show of America's new naval strength.

The fleet sailed down and around the coast of South America, visiting the major ports. Then it sailed across the Pacific to Hawaii, New Zealand, and Australia.

During its 14-month voyage, the Great White Fleet, as it was called, visited many countries. Everywhere, including Japan, it received a warm welcome. Thousands of Japanese school children welcomed the fleet by waving American flags and singing "The Star-Spangled Banner."

The ships returned to the United States shortly before the end of Roosevelt's second term. The tour succeeded as he had hoped. It showed American goodwill, and it showed off American military power.

CHECKUP

1. Why did John Hay promote the Open Door policy?
2. What was the Boxer Rebellion?
3. How did President Roosevelt try to improve relations between Japan and the United States?
4. What was the Gentlemen's Agreement?
5. **Thinking Critically** Would you consider the Open Door policy successful or unsuccessful? Explain.

559

Controlling the Caribbean

" . . . Carry a Big Stick"   Theodore Roosevelt was fond of quoting a West African saying: "Speak softly and carry a big stick; you will go far." To Roosevelt this meant that the United States should be prepared to use force in dealing with other countries to achieve its goals. Nowhere was this policy followed more openly than on the islands in, and the lands around, the Caribbean Sea. In the Caribbean area, Roosevelt rarely spoke softly, but he did carry a big stick.

The pattern of American control of the Caribbean area was set in Cuba. In entering the war against Spain, Congress had promised not to annex Cuba. That promise was kept. However, American troops remained on the island for 3 years. The United States helped build schools and restore the Cuban economy.

In 1902 the United States and Cuba signed a treaty, and American troops left. However, the treaty placed certain limits on Cuba's independence. It required Cuba to give naval bases to the United States. It also gave the United States the right to send troops into Cuba to preserve Cuban

President Theodore Roosevelt used "big stick" diplomacy in his dealings with Latin American countries.
■ What do the small figures in the cartoon represent?

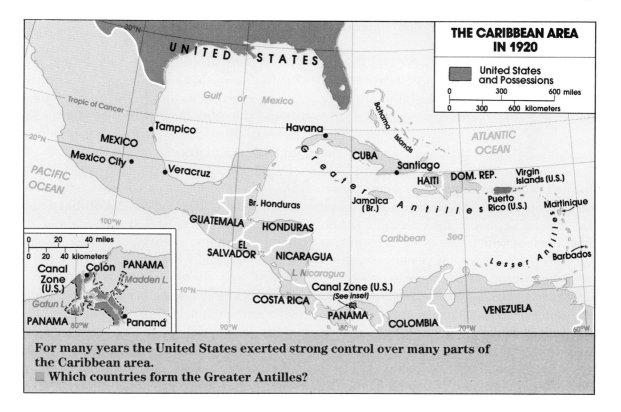

THE CARIBBEAN AREA IN 1920

United States and Possessions

For many years the United States exerted strong control over many parts of the Caribbean area.
Which countries form the Greater Antilles?

"independence." In fact, American troops did return in 1906 when there was a threat of civil war in Cuba. They remained for 3 years, and a few years later they returned yet another time. Thus, though the island of Cuba was not a colony of the United States, it was not completely independent either. A country in such a position is called a **protectorate**.

Puerto Rico, a smaller island with a smaller population, was a different case. The island remained under military control until a civil government was established in 1900. In 1917 it became a territory of the United States, and all Puerto Ricans were granted United States citizenship. The President appointed officials to run the government. In 1950, Congress permitted Puerto Rico to draw up its own constitution and elect more of its own officials. Whether Puerto Rico will become the fifty-first state is still a matter for debate.

The Roosevelt Corollary Several Latin American countries were not paying off large debts they had incurred by borrowing from Europeans. Roosevelt believed that the countries had an obligation to pay their debts. At the same time, he did not wish European countries to use military force to collect what was owed them. Roosevelt feared that they might use the debts as an excuse to take control of a small country and gain a foothold in the Western Hemisphere.

In 1904, Roosevelt announced his solution to this problem. The United States, he said, would see that Latin American countries paid their debts, preserved order, and protected life and property. If necessary, the United States would act as a police power and **intervene**, or step in, to do this.

This plan came to be known as the **Roosevelt Corollary**, or addition, to the Monroe Doctrine. That doctrine, you will remember, said that foreign countries might not intervene in the countries of the Western Hemisphere. Under the Roosevelt Corollary, the United States would keep other countries from intervening— by intervening itself.

United States Intervention The Roosevelt Corollary was first used in 1905 in the Dominican Republic, a small nation on an island in the Caribbean Sea. The Dominican Republic had a debt of $32 million, most of which was owed to countries in Europe. These European countries were threatening to use force to collect the debts. President Theodore Roosevelt got the Dominican Republic to agree to allow the United States to take over the collection of **customs duties**. These are taxes that are paid on imported goods. Half the duties were then used to pay off debts; the

This cartoon uses two symbols of the United States—the eagle and the flag—to show the spread of American influence.
■ Over what three places is the United States flag flying?

other half of the duties went to help run the government.

American customs collectors, backed by the power of the United States government, remained for many years. Like Cuba, the Dominican Republic was not a colony. But it was no longer completely independent either.

The Roosevelt Corollary helped turn the Caribbean Sea into an "American lake." Using the Roosevelt Corollary, the United States controlled the actions of many countries in the region. Under Presidents Taft and Wilson, intervention in the affairs of these countries increased. Often, United States Marines were sent into the region and they remained for many years. These interventions in the Caribbean area led to a great deal of ill will toward the United States.

Planning a Canal A big reason why the United States wanted to control the Caribbean was to protect a future canal across Central America. Such a canal would eliminate the need to go around the tip of South America and would take nearly 8,000 miles (12,800 km) off the trip between New York and San Francisco. Trade would increase, and the United States Navy could travel quickly from one ocean to another.

The idea of a canal was not a new one. In the 1880s Colombia granted a French company the sole rights to build a canal across Panama, which Colombia controlled. The company failed to carry out its plan but hoped to sell to the United States the rights to build a canal.

Many members of Congress favored a canal site farther north, in Nicaragua. However, at the time the site was under discussion, a volcano in Nicaragua erupted. A Nicaraguan postage stamp featuring the volcano had been issued before the volcano erupted. To persuade Congress to turn down the Nicaraguan route, the leading stockholder in the French company that controlled the Panama route sent a copy of the stamp to every member of Congress. The threat that an active volcano might pose to the canal was a factor in swinging members of Congress in favor of the Panama route.

In 1903, representatives of the United States and Colombia worked out an agreement. The United States would rent a strip of land across Panama, a part of Colombia, and would build a canal there. In return, Colombia would receive the sum of $10 million, plus a yearly payment of $250,000 for 99 years. The United States would pay the French company $40 million for the building rights.

However, Colombia's senate refused to approve the treaty. Its members didn't see why the French company that failed should get $40 million when Colombia, the owner of the land, got only $10 million. They thought Colombia should get at least $25 million.

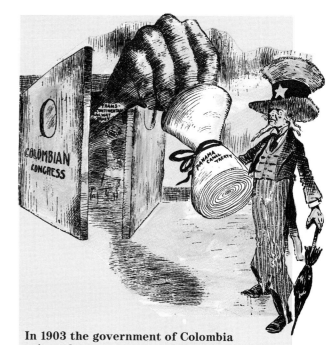

In 1903 the government of Colombia rejected a treaty with the United States concerning a canal across Panama.
▨ What symbol represents the United States?

In the early 1900s a volcano was pictured on a Nicaraguan postage stamp. The volcano was in the area of a possible site for a canal across Central America.
▨ Has this stamp been used?

A Revolt in Panama Probably an agreement could have been worked out with a bit of patience. But Roosevelt was eager to "make the dirt fly"—that is, to start building a canal. He was angered by Colombia's refusal, and accused them of bad faith. A revolt of Panamanians, who also wanted a canal built, allowed the impatient Roosevelt to have his way.

Panamanians had revolted unsuccessfully against Colombian rule many times. This time they succeeded. President Roosevelt knew of the plan in advance. He sent a United States warship into the area. The presence of this warship prevented Colombian troops from landing in Panama to put down the uprising. The revolt occurred on November 3, 1903. It lasted hardly a day and was practically bloodless. Without the loss of a single life, Panama won its independence.

A Slice of History

A Doctor Helps Build a Canal

The Panama Canal was the greatest engineering achievement of the age. Everything about it was colossal. One person figured out that if all the earth removed from the canal's path was loaded onto railroad cars, the cars would circle the globe four times. Fifty million sacks and barrels of cement went into making the canal locks. This was enough cement to build a wall 8 feet (2.4 m) wide, 12 feet (3.7 m) high, and 300 miles (480 km) long!

Yet for several years an obstacle no larger than a half inch stood in the way of this colossal work. That obstacle was the mosquito, the carrier of deadly yellow fever and malaria. In the unsuccessful attempt by the French to build a canal in the 1880s, many workers had died from these diseases.

The job of ridding Panama of yellow fever and malaria was given to Colonel William C. Gorgas (gôr′ gəs), an army medical officer. Earlier, Gorgas had wiped out yellow fever in Havana, Cuba, in just a few months. There he directed squads of workers to clean out every gutter, drain, and other place with standing water where mosquitoes could breed.

At first, those in charge of the canal project refused to believe there was any connection between mosquitoes and disease. They denied Gorgas the supplies and workers he needed. Later, a new chief engineer who supported Gorgas was appointed. Within 2 years, Colonel Gorgas stamped out yellow fever in the Canal Zone and began to bring malaria under control as well.

Three days later, the United States recognized the new Republic of Panama. Within 2 weeks the new government signed a treaty with the United States. The United States was allowed to rent — "forever" — a strip of land 10 miles (16 km) wide in which to build its canal that would link the Atlantic and the Pacific oceans.

Throughout Latin America there was widespread resentment over the treaty. Latin Americans felt that their powerful northern neighbor had bullied and cheated the country of Colombia. In 1913, President Woodrow Wilson urged Congress to apologize and make a cash payment to Colombia, but Congress refused. In 1921, Congress tried to make up for the damage in relations by voting a payment of $25 million to Colombia. In 1978, the United States Senate ratified a treaty turning the Panama Canal over to Panama on December 31, 1999.

The building of the Panama Canal was one of the great engineering feats of all time. Millions of cubic yards of earth were moved.
■ Was part of the canal built through a mountainous area?

Digging the Canal   Bad relations or not, work on the canal went forward. At first, the principal task was to control disease in Panama's tropical climate. As soon as yellow fever was curbed, the digging of the canal began in earnest.

In 1907, Colonel George Goethals (gō′ thəlz), an army engineer, was put in charge of the huge construction project. The canal's route of 50 miles (80 km) ran through jungle, swamps, and mountainous land. Over 40,000 workers were employed in building what was called "the big ditch." Most of the workers came from the West Indies. By hand labor, dredges, and steam shovels, millions of cubic yards of earth were moved. In August 1914, 10 years after the first shovelful of earth was turned, the first ship passed through the new Panama Canal. Although the United States controlled the canal, it was open to ships of all nations.

CHECKUP

1. Why did Cuba become known as an American protectorate?
2. What was the Roosevelt Corollary, and where was it first used?
3. How was the United States able to gain control of land for a canal across Central America?
4. What difficulties had to be overcome in building the Panama Canal?
5. **Thinking Critically** Why do you think the United States was more successful in extending its influence in the Caribbean region than in Asia?

Outlining

HAWAII

Outlining is a special form of note taking. It helps you organize information. A good outline helps you see at a glance how facts and ideas are related to each other.

Most outlines are made up of three parts. First are the main topics or ideas. These brief statements have a Roman numeral in front of them. Next are the subtopics, which support the main topics. They are labeled with capital letters. Third are the details, which tell about each subtopic. They are indicated with Arabic numerals.

To create a good outline, start by previewing what you are reading. Note the headings in heavy type. They will give you ideas about possible main topics. Often you can use these headings themselves as the main topics. For example, suppose you are going to outline the story of how Hawaii became part of the United States, pages 547–548. Start your outline by writing the title at the top of your paper. Surveying pages 547–548, you see two headings that you can use as main topics.

> HAWAII
> I. Americans in Hawaii
> II. Hawaii is annexed

As you read, you find that the first paragraph deals with the background and early history of the territory. That can be used for a subtopic under main topic I.

> HAWAII
> I. Americans in Hawaii
>   A. Background and early history

Information about early inhabitants, Captain Cook's discovery, and Hawaii as a stopover for whalers and trading ships are all details about subtopic A. Label these details with Arabic numerals. Your outline will look like this:

> HAWAII
> I. Americans in Hawaii
>   A. Background and early history
>   1. Early inhabitants — Polynesians
>   2. Cook discovers Hawaii in 1788
>   3. Hawaii becomes stopover for ships

As you continue, you find information about Americans arriving in Hawaii. Some came as missionaries. Later, many became sugar planters and pineapple growers. In time, they became rich and powerful and controlled Hawaii's government. That gives you your second subtopic and supporting details:

>   B. Americans arrive in Hawaii
>   1. 1820s — missionaries
>   2. 1835 — sugar planters; later pineapple growers

The rest of your outline for main topic I would look like this:

>   C. U.S. and Hawaii draw closer
>   1. 1875 — U.S. allows sugar to be imported without tariff
>   2. 1875 — Hawaii promises not to let others control its lands
>   3. 1887 — U.S. gains right to build naval base at Pearl Harbor

SKILLS PRACTICE

Following this format, complete the outline on how Hawaii became part of the United States on a separate sheet of paper. Start with main topic II, "Hawaii Is Annexed."

MAIN IDEAS

1. In the late 1800s, Americans began to look outside the country for investment opportunities and new markets for goods.
2. Imperialists believed that the United States should have colonies and develop an overseas empire.
3. American anger over Spanish cruelty in Cuba, combined with the sinking of the *Maine* and American nationalism led the United States into war with Spain in 1898.
4. The United States came out of its involvement in the Spanish-American War with an overseas empire.
5. With the Open Door policy, the United States tried to preserve trading opportunities with China and to keep that country from being carved up by other powers.
6. Under Presidents Roosevelt, Taft, and Wilson, the United States government intervened in the affairs of many countries in the Caribbean area.

VOCABULARY REVIEW

On a separate sheet of paper, write **T** if the statement is true and **F** if it is false. Then rewrite each false statement to make it true.

1. Imperialists were opposed to extending control over distant lands.
2. Venezuela asked the United States to arbitrate its dispute with Germany concerning its boundary lines.
3. Yellow journalism was the reporting of events in such a way as to make the stories more sensational.
4. "Remember the *Maine!*" became a slogan after the battleship was blown up at Manila Bay.
5. The Boxer Rebellion came about as an effort to get foreigners out of Japan.
6. George Dewey led a cavalry regiment known as the Rough Riders.
7. The United States government pressed for the Open Door policy so that it could have an equal opportunity to trade with China.

8. The Gentlemen's Agreement allowed Japanese children in the United States to attend public schools if Japan would prohibit more workers from leaving Japan for the United States.
9. The Roosevelt Corollary encouraged European countries to intervene in the Western Hemisphere.
10. Customs duties are taxes that are paid on goods imported from another country.

CHAPTER CHECKUP

1. List the reasons for favoring imperialism and the reasons for opposing it. Which side would you agree with?
2. What countries or territories came under control of the United States in the 1800s?
3. Why did sugar planters in Hawaii want the United States to annex Hawaii?
4. What led to the Spanish-American War?
5. Why did the United States become concerned with affairs in Asian countries?
6. What effect did the Roosevelt Corollary have on relations between the United States and the nations in the Caribbean?
7. Why was the building of the Panama Canal important to the United States?
8. **Thinking Critically** Do you think the press has a responsibility to report only the facts to its readers, or should it also express opinions?
9. **Thinking Critically** Do you think one country has the right to intervene in the affairs of another country? Explain.

APPLYING KNOWLEDGE

1. In your library, find out the status of Puerto Rico and of the Philippines today with regard to the United States.
2. Read about Walter Reed. Find out how his activities affected the building of the Panama Canal.
3. Investigate the recent change in the status of the Panama Canal. Find out if all Americans were in favor of this change.

24 *World War I*

1914–1919

Europe Goes to War

Why did World War I break out in 1914?

VOCABULARY

militarism	Western Front
mobilize	

A Day for Celebrating   There was a joyous air in the Bosnian town of Sarajevo (sär′ ə ya′ vō) on the morning of June 28, 1914. Bosnia was a territory of the Austro-Hungarian Empire, but most of its people were Serbs. On this day, Sarajevo would be celebrating the victory, many years before, of the Serbian people over the Turks. To mark the occasion, there would also be a visit from Archduke Franz Ferdinand, the heir to the Austro-Hungarian throne, and his wife, Sophie. The day was a special one for the royal couple, too; it was their fourteenth wedding anniversary.

Austria-Hungary was a large hodge-podge of an empire in central and eastern Europe. It was made up of Austrians, Hungarians, Czechs, Slovaks, Slovenes, Serbs, Italians, Croatians (krō ā′ shənz), Poles, and others. Many of these peoples did not want to be part of the Austro-Hungarian Empire. They wanted to live in independent countries of their own. For example, the Serbs in Bosnia wanted their territory to become part of the neighboring country of Serbia. Naturally, Austria-Hungary wanted to keep control of Bosnia. In fact, one of the reasons for the visit of Archduke Franz Ferdinand was to soothe the Serbs in the empire.

Death in Sarajevo   A group of seven young men in Sarajevo that morning had other ideas. They were members of a secret society called Union or Death. Its goal was to unite Bosnia with Serbia. Armed with guns and homemade bombs, the men scattered through the crowd to wait for the archduke's procession.

Shortly after 10:00 A.M. the archduke's motorcar rolled down the street past the first member of the group. He froze. The second, a few steps away, threw a bomb that barely missed the car but injured a dozen spectators. The next four also had opportunities but failed to seize them.

The seventh man, Gavrilo Princip (prēn′ tsēp), did not fail. The driver of the archduke's car made a wrong turn, bringing it down the street on which Princip was standing. As the car came within 5 feet (1.5 m) of him, Princip fired two shots, killing both the archduke and his wife.

Those two shots set off a chain of events that led to one of the most destructive wars in history. Nearly every country

This painting, depicting trench warfare of World War I, shows an American infantry fighting in France.
■ What type of weapon are these soldiers using?

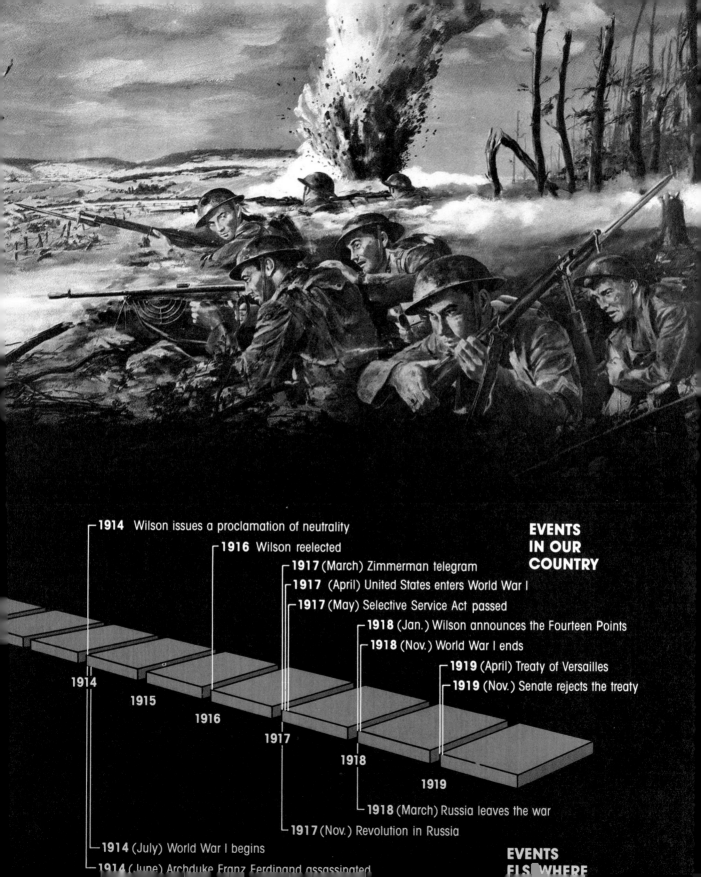

EVENTS IN OUR COUNTRY

- **1914** Wilson issues a proclamation of neutrality
- **1916** Wilson reelected
- **1917** (March) Zimmerman telegram
- **1917** (April) United States enters World War I
- **1917** (May) Selective Service Act passed
- **1918** (Jan.) Wilson announces the Fourteen Points
- **1918** (Nov.) World War I ends
- **1919** (April) Treaty of Versailles
- **1919** (Nov.) Senate rejects the treaty

1914
1915
1916
1917
1918
1919

- **1918** (March) Russia leaves the war
- **1917** (Nov.) Revolution in Russia
- **1914** (July) World War I begins
- **1914** (June) Archduke Franz Ferdinand assassinated

EVENTS ELSEWHERE

Shortly after this picture was taken, Archduke Franz Ferdinand and Countess Sophie were killed by a Serbian in Sarajevo. (43°N/18°E; map, p. 584) ■ In what year did this take place?

in Europe became involved in what soon came to be called the Great War, but is known today as World War I. Before it was over, 10 million soldiers and 10 million civilians were killed. About 20 million more soldiers were badly injured. In countries such as France and Germany, a whole generation of young men was completely wiped out. Property worth billions of dollars was destroyed.

How could the killing of two people in a distant corner of Europe lead to such horrifying results? To understand this, we must understand what had been happening all over Europe during the previous 35 years.

Imperial Rivalries The late nineteenth century was the great age of imperialism, or empire building. European powers added to their colonial holdings by raising their flags over many lands. Russia and Austria-Hungary, two of the great land powers, extended their control over neighboring peoples. Britain, France, Germany, Italy, and others added to their empires or created new ones by carving out colonies in Asia and Africa.

Colonies were important to European countries for several reasons. Industries in these countries were producing many kinds of manufactured goods. The colonies provided raw materials for the industries and were markets for the manufactured goods. Bankers could invest in colonies and get a good, safe return on their money. Also, exercising control over others gave a satisfying feeling of power and pride to the peoples and governments of the imperialist countries. The race for colonies led to growing rivalry among the European powers.

Nationalism and Armies Among the great powers of Europe, nationalism was on the rise. Nationalism is a very strong feeling of loyalty toward one's country. Nationalism was also strong among the subject peoples of Austria-Hungary. Many people were fiercely proud of their national heritage and expressed their loyalty to it. Sometimes, however, nationalism turned into a chip-on-the-shoulder attitude toward others and added fuel to old grudges and hatreds. Such strong feelings could easily lead to war.

The rise of nationalism and the drive for colonies was accompanied by **militarism**, that is, an emphasis on armies, navies, and military power. Each country believed that a large army was an expression of national greatness. It also provided the means to protect oneself against others. Britain, an island nation, had the world's largest navy. Germany had an army of 4.5 million soldiers; France, an army of 4 million; and Russia, an army of more than 6 million. Europe was an armed camp.

The Growth of Alliances Countries did not depend only upon their own armies and navies to protect themselves. They formed alliances with others. By 1914 there were two major alliances in Europe. Germany, Austria-Hungary, and Italy formed the Triple Alliance. The other major alliance was the Triple Entente (än tänt'), made up of Russia, France, and Great Britain. There were other alliances, too. Great Britain promised to protect Belgium from attack. Russia was the protector of Serbia.

With rivalries growing, nations arming themselves heavily, and a system of alliances involving every major power, peace in Europe rested on shaky ground. In fact, between 1900 and 1914, war almost broke out five different times. No wonder an American visiting Europe said that the continent was like a powder keg. "It requires only a spark to set the whole thing off," he predicted.

The shots fired in Sarajevo provided that spark. Austria-Hungary blamed Serbia for the death of its future emperor and declared war. Russia **mobilized**, or assembled, its army and prepared for war to protect Serbia. Germany knew what that would mean. If Russia attacked Austria-Hungary, Germany was bound by treaty to come to its ally's defense. That would automatically bring in France on the side of *its* partner, Russia. Germany would then face the situation it most dreaded, a war on both its eastern and western borders.

Germany, therefore, jumped the gun and declared war on both Russia and France. Germany's armies crashed into

Mounted troops of Austria and Germany take part in training exercises in 1909.
■ How does this differ from training today?

neutral Belgium, hoping to circle around the main French armies and knock France out of the war quickly. This brought Belgium's protector, Great Britain, into the war. In just a week's time, much of Europe was at war.

Later that fall, Turkey joined Germany and Austria-Hungary. These countries formed the Central Powers. Russia, France, and Great Britain were known as the Allies. Bulgaria joined the Central Powers in 1915. Italy, which had held back from joining the Central Powers, also entered the war in 1915 but on the side of the Allies. The lineup of sides was completed, and the continent of Europe was in flames.

A New Kind of Warfare Germany's big plan to quickly defeat France almost succeeded. However, German troops were stopped just 15 miles (24 km) from Paris in the battle of the Marne. A French plan for a quick knockout of Germany was no more successful. With that, fighting in the west settled into a stalemate.

In those first months of the war, the loss of life was staggering. Each side lost a half-million men. The main reason was a new weapon, the machine gun. A single gun could mow down hundreds of soldiers crossing an open field. Armies, therefore, had to learn to fight defensively. A soldier's shovel proved to be as important as his gun, as each side dug trenches, or long ditches, for protection. The men lived in these muddy trenches for months at a time, through rain and miserable cold. All the while, huge guns fired across the battle

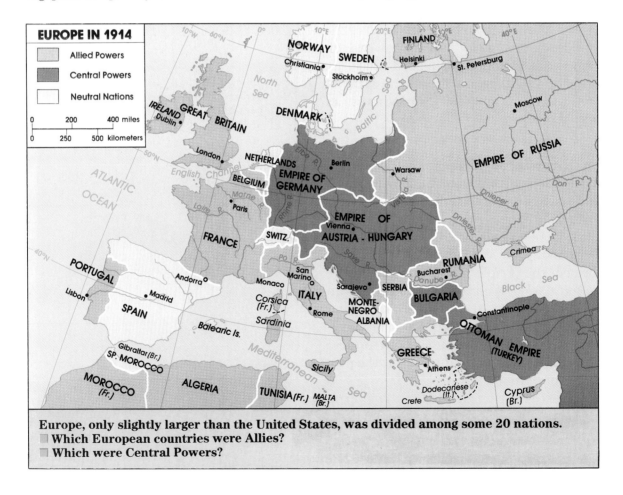

EUROPE IN 1914

Allied Powers
Central Powers
Neutral Nations

Europe, only slightly larger than the United States, was divided among some 20 nations.
 Which European countries were Allies?
 Which were Central Powers?

From 1914 to 1918, armies on both sides of the Western Front lived in trenches, or ditches. There was a line of front trenches, followed by networks of supply and command trenches.
■ **What item of furniture do these soldiers have?**

lines without letup. This line of trenches, running 400 miles (640 km) across Belgium and France, was known as the **Western Front**. Along this line, the French and German armies pounded away at each other. Thousands of soldiers died in battle, yet neither side made significant gains.

On the Western Front   In trench warfare a typical battle consisted of soldiers of one side rushing out—"going over the top"—and trying to break through the enemy's line of trenches. If they succeeded, they could pour men through the gap and attack the enemy's line of trenches from the rear. But barbed wire, machine guns, and poison gas made such attempts costly. In 1915 alone, the French lost 1.5 million men. For 3½ years, battle lines on the Western Front hardly moved.

On the Eastern Front, fighting between Russia and the Central Powers was equally fierce. The Russian armies defeated the Austro-Hungarian forces in a number of battles. On the other hand, German armies were successful in taking over huge chunks of Russian territory. In fact, German troops came within 20 miles (32 km) of Moscow, the capital city.

CHECKUP

1. What happened in Sarajevo in June 1914?
2. Why were European countries competing for colonies at this time?
3. What were some results of the rise of nationalism in Europe?
4. How was the warfare of World War I different from that of earlier wars?
5. **Thinking Critically**   Do you think the Central Powers and the Allies would have gone to war even if the archduke and his wife had not been killed? Give reasons for your answer.

America's Reaction

Why did the United States enter the war in 1917?

VOCABULARY

| international law | *Lusitania* |
| submarine | *Sussex* Pledge |

A Call for Neutrality   Americans were shocked by the news that Europe was at war. Most, however, shared the view expressed by one newspaper: "Luckily we have the Atlantic between us and Europe. It is their war, not ours." President Wilson also said that this was a war "with which we have nothing to do." The President asked that all Americans be neutral "in thought as well as in action."

Being neutral in thought was hard for many. Nearly one in every three Americans either was born in Europe or had parents born in Europe. Many had relatives in the countries now at war. A good many Americans of German background sided with Germany. Many Irish Americans were opposed to anything that was British.

Most Americans, however, leaned toward Great Britain and the Allies. Not only were many Americans of British origin, but they spoke the same language and shared many traditions. Many high officials in the United States government were pro-Ally. Also, Germany's invasion of neutral Belgium, with widespread destruction, turned a great many Americans against Germany. Still, for all these feelings, nearly all Americans wanted the United States to remain neutral and stay out of the fighting.

Violating America's Rights   As the war progressed, Americans found it more and more difficult to follow a neutral course. The reason had to do with the violation of America's neutral rights on the seas. As a neutral nation, the United States had certain rights under **international law**. International law is the body of rules that countries agree to follow in controlling their relations with each other. One right held by neutral nations was to trade with both sides, except in weapons and similar war goods. But part of the war plan of each side was to keep supplies from reaching its enemy.

The British, with the largest navy in the world, used several means to do this. They dropped explosive devices called mines in the North Sea, making it dangerous for any ship to try to sail to German ports. They also announced a blockade of

In 1915, three thousand women met in Washington, D.C., and organized the Women's Peace Party.
■ What do the signs refer to?

Members of a German U-boat crew watch a British ship go down after being torpedoed.
■ How did some British soldiers escape the sinking vessel?

all German ports. This meant that no ship, no matter what it was carrying or what country it was from, would be allowed to enter the ports. The British navy stopped and searched American ships on the high seas for war goods. This was legal under international law, except that the British used their own definition of war goods. Their list included anything they thought might be of help to the enemy such as oil, metals, even cotton and food. British warships sometimes forced American cargo ships into British ports for weeks at a time.

These actions angered people in the United States. President Wilson protested them strongly. The British continued them but were careful not to go so far with their actions as to cause a break in relations with America.

Submarine Warfare   Britain's powerful navy kept German warships bottled up in port for most of the war. Germany, therefore, could not use its surface fleet to keep supplies from reaching its enemy. To do this, the Germans came to rely on a new weapon, the **submarine**. The submarine, a warship that could operate underwater, was also known as the "U-Boat," a short form of its German name; *Unterseeboot.* It proved to be a very effective weapon. However, it could only be effective by breaking the rules of war agreed upon under international law.

The reason was this: International law required that before sinking an enemy merchant or passenger ship, the commander of a warship must allow time for passengers and crew to get off safely. Passengers and crew were considered to be civilians, and civilian life was to be spared.

These rules were made in an age when all warships were fast, heavily armed surface vessels. Giving warning before sinking a merchant ship or passenger ship cost nothing but a little time. Because the safety of passengers was assured, even citizens of neutral countries had the right to travel on ships of warring nations. The submarine, however, was a small weak vessel that depended upon surprise. If it came to the surface to give warning, it could easily be sunk by its intended victim. Yet firing its torpedoes without warning was almost certain to take the lives of innocent civilians — including people from neutral nations.

On February 4, 1915, Germany declared the waters around the British Isles to be a war zone. German submarines would sink without warning all enemy ships in that zone, including passenger and merchant ships. The German government warned neutral ships that they entered the war zone at their own risk. "It may not always be possible to save crews and passengers," said the German announcement. President Woodrow Wilson was shocked and angry. The United States, he told the German government, would hold Germany responsible for any loss of American lives or American ships.

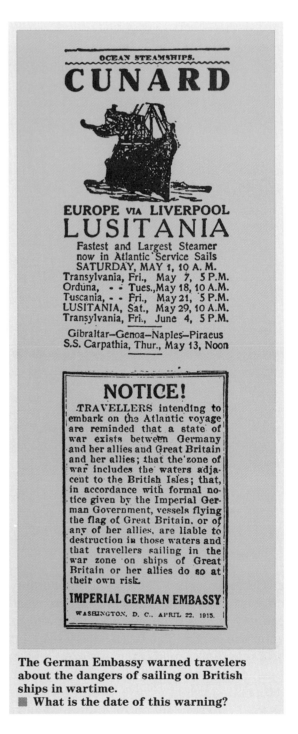

The German Embassy warned travelers about the dangers of sailing on British ships in wartime.
■ What is the date of this warning?

The *Lusitania* Is Sunk   Wilson did not have to wait long for his words to be tested. On May 7, 1915, the British passenger liner ***Lusitania*** was torpedoed without warning off the southern coast of Ireland. Within 15 minutes the ship sank, carrying 1,198 passengers—128 of them Americans—to a watery grave.

The sinking of the *Lusitania* led to a major crisis between the United States and Germany. Some enraged Americans, including former President Theodore Roosevelt, called for war. But President Wilson followed a more cautious course. He demanded that Germany apologize, make payment to the families of the victims, and end its use of the submarine.

Germany replied, correctly, that the *Lusitania* had been carrying arms and ammunition. The Germans also pointed out that they had placed ads in New York newspapers warning Americans to stay off the ship. Wilson, however, declared that none of this excused the loss of life. He insisted that Germany yield.

After a time, Germany accepted responsibility for the loss of American lives and agreed to pay damages. It also promised not to sink unarmed passenger ships without warning. This outcome was regarded as a victory for President Wilson.

The *Sussex* Pledge That was not the end of submarine warfare, however. The German pledge covered only passenger ships. Over the following months, German submarines sank many British and French merchant ships.

Then in the spring of 1916, a German submarine torpedoed the French passenger ship *Sussex*, injuring several American passengers. This time, Wilson warned that if Germany continued to attack ships without warning, the United States would break off diplomatic relations. This would be a most serious step because it was just one step short of war.

The Germans were eager to keep the United States out of the war. As a result, Germany gave in and issued the ***Sussex* Pledge**. German submarines would no longer torpedo either passenger ships or merchant ships without warning. Once again, it appeared that President Wilson had won a victory for American principles without going to war.

Preparedness A growing number of Americans came to believe that while the United States must work for peace, it must also prepare for the possibility of war. They favored a program of preparedness. Supporters of preparedness said that to defend the country, the army and navy had to be built up.

A good many Americans disagreed with this idea. Instead of keeping us out of war, they said, having a larger army and navy would tempt the United States to get involved in the war. Moreover, argued some, preparedness would just put money into the pockets of those who profited from war.

Wilson Wins a Second Term In 1916, Wilson sought a second term as President. His Republican opponent was Charles Evans Hughes, a justice of the Supreme Court and a former Progressive governor of New York. Wilson had won the support of many Progressives through his championing of Progressive laws in his first term. Now his supporters came up with the slogan "He kept us out of war." The slogan proved to be effective, and Wilson was the winner in a close election.

Wilson knew that the longer the war in Europe dragged on, the harder it would be to keep America from being drawn into it. Earlier he had tried several times to get the two sides to end the war. Following his reelection in 1916, he tried once more. Neither side, however, was ready to settle for anything less than a clear victory.

In January 1917, Wilson made a speech before the United States Senate in which he gave his own ideas on a fair peace settlement. He called for a "peace without victory," one with neither a winner nor a loser. "Only a peace between equals can last," he said. The President also came out in favor of a general association of nations to keep the peace.

A Fateful Decision   Even before Wilson's speech, however, Germany's leaders had made a fateful decision. They felt they had reached a turning point because Russia, faced with a revolution at home, was about to withdraw from the war against Germany. The German leaders believed that Germany could win the war if it could cut off all supplies from the United States to the Allies. They believed they now had enough submarines to do this. Therefore, Germany announced that it

would no longer be bound by the *Sussex* Pledge. All ships, including those of neutral nations, that entered the waters around the British Isles beginning January 31 would be torpedoed without warning.

Germany knew that this action would probably bring the United States into the war. However, German leaders believed it would take a year before American military forces could go into action in Europe. By then, the submarine warfare, combined with an all-out attack on the Western Front, would have knocked out the British and the French.

President Wilson promptly broke off diplomatic relations with Germany. Still, he hoped to avoid war. However, events soon forced him to act.

The Zimmerman Telegram   In February, German submarines sank three American ships. Then came startling news

Posters on a campaign truck in 1916 urge the reelection of Woodrow Wilson while stressing his achievements.
■ What was the name of Wilson's running mate?

At a special session on April 2, 1917, President Woodrow Wilson asks Congress to declare war on Germany.
■ Where does the Congress of the United States meet?

from the British government. Some British agents had intercepted a secret telegram from Germany's foreign secretary, Arthur Zimmerman, to the German minister in Mexico.

Should war break out between Germany and the United States, the German diplomat was instructed by Zimmerman to offer Mexico the opportunity to ally itself with Germany. In exchange for Mexico's support, Germany would help Mexico "to reconquer the lost territory in Texas, New Mexico, and Arizona." This was the territory taken over by the United States after the Mexican War. (See page 339.) When the United States government released this telegram to the newspapers on March 1, the American public was furious. Especially angry were the people of the Southwest. Then in March, German submarines sank five more American ships.

The United States Goes to War   Wilson could delay no longer. On April 2, 1917, he called Congress into session and asked it to declare war on Germany. He said:

The world must be made safe for democracy. . . . We have no selfish ends to serve. We desire no conquest, no dominion. We seek no . . . material compensation for the sacrifices we shall freely make. We are but one of the champions of the rights of mankind.

On April 6, 1917, Congress declared war on Germany. The United States had entered the Great War.

CHECKUP

1. Why did most Americans lean toward the Allies from the very outbreak of the Great War?
2. In what ways did the British violate America's neutral rights on the seas?
3. Why did German submarine warfare make it more difficult for the United States to stay neutral?
4. How did the Zimmerman telegram help bring the United States into the war?
5. **Thinking Critically**   If Germany had continued to observe the *Sussex* Pledge, do you think the United States would have entered the war? Why or why not?

579

Waging the War

What steps did Americans take to win the war?

VOCABULARY

Selective Service Act	convoy
ration	armistice

Filling the Ranks Now came the gigantic task of gearing up for war. The first step was to create an army. Americans had a long tradition of being opposed to a large standing army. At the time America entered the war, the regular army numbered only 75,000 men. In May 1917, Congress passed the **Selective Service Act**. This law required men between the ages of 21 and 30 to register for the draft. Later the age limits were widened to 18 and 45.

Before the war ended, 24 million men had registered, and nearly 3 million were drafted. Another 2 million volunteered or were in National Guard units called up for duty. Altogether more than 4.8 million Americans entered the service. This number included thousands of women who enlisted in the Nurse Corps of the army and the navy.

A New Role for Government On entering the war, the United States was shocked to learn that the Allies were short of ammunition, clothing, and food. America would have to supply food and other supplies not only for its new army but for the Allies as well.

Throughout American history, decisions about what and how much to produce had always been made by private businesses. They decided on the basis of the demand for the goods and the opportunity for profit. Now, however, the federal government took on a greater role. To increase industrial production and cut down waste, the government created the War Industries Board. President Wilson picked Bernard Baruch, a Wall Street financier, to head the board. The War Industries Board had sweeping powers. If there was not enough steel for both trucks and guns, the board decided how many of each should be made and which companies should make them. The board could also set prices for government purchases of supplies.

Urged on by the War Industries Board and by large government contracts, factories ran day and night. Shells, rifles, uniforms, and other military supplies poured out of America's factories.

These women are working in an ammunition factory in Connecticut during World War I. Many took jobs outside the home for the first time in order to work in defense industries. ■ Why are most of these workers women?

A Need for Workers   With more than 4 million men in uniform, there was a shortage of workers for making steel, running railroads, digging coal, and operating machines.   To make the best use of the workers that remained, the government created the War Labor Board.   The labor board saw to it that workers were available where they were needed.   The board also urged management to recognize unions and bargain fairly with them.   In return, it won from labor leaders such as Samuel Gompers of the AFL a "no strike" pledge. Gompers and his union strongly supported the war effort.

Two groups helped to fill the gap created by workers leaving for the service.   A million additional women took jobs outside the home during the war.   They did work that had never before been open to them.   They made guns and ammunition, drove trucks, operated streetcars, and supervised assembly lines.

A second large new group of industrial workers was made up of southern blacks. Hundreds of thousands left the rural South for jobs in the factories of northern cities. In some communities the newcomers met with hostility, as they crowded into whatever housing was available.   These families were part of the first great wave of black migration from the South.

Increasing Food Supplies   To increase production of food and also to cut down consumption at home, the government created the Food Administration.   President Wilson appointed Herbert Hoover to head it.   Wilson could not have found a better person for the job.   Herbert Hoover was born and raised on a small Iowa farm.   He was orphaned at the age of 10.   He worked his way through Stanford University, where he studied engineering, and became a mining engineer.

Herbert Hoover, head of the Food Administration, also directed relief programs in Europe.
■ What was the purpose of relief programs?

Hoover's work took him to distant lands—Australia, Russia, Africa, Latin America, and China.   He was among the Americans trapped in Peking, China, during the Boxer Rebellion of 1900.   His skills as an engineer and an organizer of large projects made him a millionaire before he reached the age of 40.

Hoover was living in London when the war in Europe broke out.   He quickly offered his services to do welfare work among the victims of war.   As head of the Belgian War Relief, he organized the feeding of 10 million starving Belgian and French people.

When the United States entered the war, Herbert Hoover lent his brilliant organizing talents to his own country.   Under Hoover the Food Administration encouraged farmers to grow more by offering a high price for all the wheat they could produce.   Hoover also got Americans to cut down consumption of food by observing "wheatless Mondays" and "meatless Tuesdays." Americans were also urged not to waste food. When eating apples, they were told to be "patriotic to the core." The government also **rationed,** or limited the consumption of, certain goods, such as sugar, so that there would be enough for the troops.

Safeguarding Shipping   All the goods of America's farms and factories would be of no help in the war effort if they could not be delivered safely to Europe. When the United States entered the war, German submarines were sinking ships twice as fast as they could be replaced.

Admiral William Sims of the United States Navy proposed the use of a **convoy** system. In a convoy, freighters and troop carriers travel in a large group, escorted on all sides by destroyers. These are small, fast warships that are equipped to fight off submarines.

Sims had to spend several weeks convincing the British navy that his convoy plan would work. Then he had to win over his fellow admirals in the United States Navy. They wanted to hold back their warships for other possible naval action. But Sims finally convinced them that convoying was an essential task.

Convoys proved to be very successful. In just 6 months, shipping losses were cut by two thirds. Most important, not a single one of the 2 million American troops that were ferried to Europe was lost to the submarines.

Pershing Heads the Army   The job of shaping the draftees and volunteers into a fighting army went to General John J. Pershing. Pershing had had a varied career in the army. He had spent boring years in isolated outposts in the West. He had taught military science at the University of Nebraska and at West Point. He had served behind a desk in Washington and had fought in Cuba and the Philippines during the Spanish-American War. His commanding officer in the fighting in Cuba said he was "the coolest man under fire I ever saw."

Pershing got his nickname, Black Jack, from commanding for a time the Negro Tenth Cavalry, an outstanding unit. He and these troops liked and respected each other, and Pershing carried his nickname proudly throughout his career.

In 1917, with more than 30 years of service, Pershing wanted a bigger challenge. He was quite open about his ambitions. When the United States broke off relations with Germany, Pershing told a group of newspaper reporters:

> That means that we will send an expedition abroad. I'd like to command it. Each of you must know some way in which you can help me. Now tell me how I can help you so that you can help me.

As it turned out, Pershing needed no help from the reporters. He had already come to the notice of President Wilson. One month after the United States entered the war, Pershing was called to the White House. "General, we are giving you some very difficult tasks these days," said the President. "Perhaps so, Mr. President," replied Pershing, "but that is what we are trained to expect." That is all that was said. A few weeks later, Wilson appointed Pershing to command the American Expeditionary Force (AEF).

The Yanks Are Coming   The first American soldiers set foot in France in June 1917. Their numbers, however, were small and increased slowly through the fall and winter. Not until the spring of 1918, a

On June 26, 1917, the first American troops arrived in France. It was nearly a year before large numbers of American troops arrived in Europe.
■ How did these troops get from the United States to France?

year after the United States entered the war, did large numbers of American soldiers arrive. Then they came in a flood.

A sizable number of these troops were black Americans. Altogether nearly 370,000 blacks were in the service. Although they, too, were part of the fight to "make the world safe for democracy," they faced discrimination at every turn. However, they fought hard and courageously. Many were honored by the French government for their bravery under fire.

Russia Leaves the War American forces arrived none too soon. Events in

the east had changed the military picture dramatically. The war had gone badly for Russia. Its government was very inefficient. Its army was plagued by shortages of guns, ammunition, clothing, and food.

In March 1917 the Russians overthrew their tsar, or emperor, and set up a democratic government. That government was in turn overthrown by the Communists 6 months later. Communist leaders were determined to get Russia out of the war even if it cost territory. They made peace with Germany in March 1918.

With Russia's withdrawal from the war, Germany could shift troops from the

Eastern Front to the Western Front. Bolstered by these new arrivals, German forces began a great offensive in the spring of 1918. Once again, as in the early weeks of the war, they hammered French and British troops back toward Paris. But this time, when Allied armies rallied to check the German advance, American troops were at their side.

American Troops in Action   Americans saw their first important action of the war in May, when they captured the town of Cantigny (kän tēn yē′) at one end of the Allied line. In June some 30,000 American troops helped the French turn back a German drive at Chateau-Thierry (sha tō tye rē′), some 56 miles (90 km) from Paris. Then, despite heavy losses, Pershing's troops took Belleau (be lō′) Wood.

In July and August came what many believe was the turning point of the war. The Germans attacked once more along the Marne River. With 85,000 American troops holding down one end of the line, the Allies stopped the Germans. Then the Americans started a counterattack. General Pershing later wrote that this attack "turned the tide of the war."

From this point on, it was the Allied and American forces that were on the offensive. In early September, American troops, now more than half a million strong, drove back the Germans at Saint-Mihiel (san mē yel′). Later that month the Americans fought a bloody battle in the Argonne Forest, again pushing the Germans back. By the end of September 1918, more than 1.2 million American troops were in action.

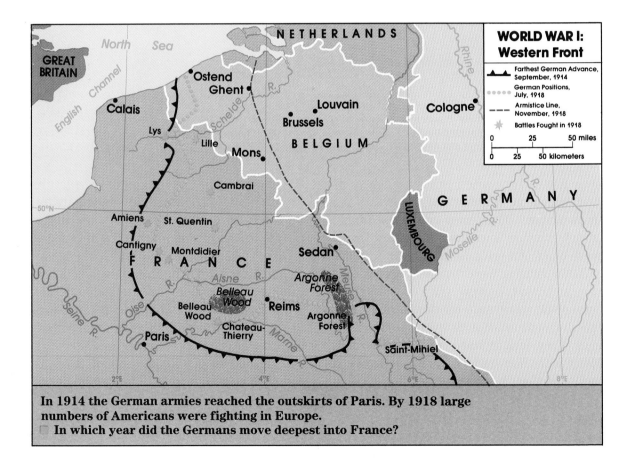

In 1914 the German armies reached the outskirts of Paris. By 1918 large numbers of Americans were fighting in Europe.
◻ In which year did the Germans move deepest into France?

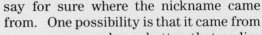
Doughboys

Fighting men pick up nicknames easily, especially in wartime. During the War for Independence, there were minutemen. By the 1830s, marines were being called "leathernecks," from the black leather collar that was part of their uniform. And in the Civil War, Northern soldiers were called "blues" and Southern soldiers "grays," after the colors of their uniforms.

In World War I the nickname for an infantryman, or foot soldier, was "doughboy." No one can say for sure where the nickname came from. One possibility is that it came from a brass button that earlier soldiers wore on their uniforms. The buttons were called doughboys because they had the same shape as biscuits by that name that used to be served to sailors. Another explanation is that the infantry used to wear white belts that they cleaned with a kind of clay, or "dough." Whatever the origin of the word, just about everyone called an infantryman a doughboy.

The Great War Ends The Central Powers now knew their cause was hopeless. One by one they surrendered—Bulgaria in September, Turkey in October, Austria-Hungary in November. Germany finally asked for an **armistice**, or cease-fire, and at exactly 11:00 on the morning of November 11, 1918, the shooting stopped. The Great War was over.

The United States had played an important part in achieving the victory over Germany. It had provided food and supplies when they were desperately needed. The British and French had suffered terrible losses during 4 years of fighting. Their troops were tired and discouraged. The arrival of fresh troops from America gave a great lift to Allied morale and helped the British and the French to fight on. In the end, it was the knowledge that several million more American troops could be thrown into battle that convinced the Germans they could not win.

CHECKUP

1. What steps were taken to produce war goods?
2. How did the government increase the production of food and curb consumption at home?
3. In getting goods and troops to Europe, how was the threat of submarine warfare met?
4. In what ways did the American Expeditionary Force help win the Great War?
5. **Thinking Critically** Why do you think Germany asked for an armistice while its army still held territory in France?

Making the Peace

Why did the United States fail to approve the Treaty of Versailles?

VOCABULARY

Fourteen Points self-determination	League of Nations reparations

Wilson's Peace Program President Wilson had called the Great War the "war to end all wars." In January 1918, Wilson outlined a peace known as the **Fourteen Points**. He asked for the following:

(1) An end to secret treaties

(2) Freedom of the seas

(3) Free trade among nations

(4) A reduction in the size of armies and navies

(5) A move toward ending colonialism

(6) The removal of German troops from Russia

(7) The removal of German troops from Belgium

(8) The removal of German troops from France and the return of Alsace-Lorraine to France

(9) Changes in Italy's borders according to the nationalities of people living in border areas

(10) Limited self-government for the peoples of Austria-Hungary

(11) The removal of German troops from the Balkans with Serbia gaining access to the sea

(12) Independence for Turkey but with the opportunity for other groups under Turkish rule to have self-government

(13) Independence for Poland

(14) Creation of association of nations

A goal of several of the Fourteen Points was for each nationality group to be able to live in its own country, under a government chosen by its own people—in short, to be able to practice **self-determination**. Wilson's fourteenth point was, to him, the most important one. The President called for all countries of the world to form the **League of Nations**. The foremost goal of this international organization would be to insure that the nations of the world would never again wage war against one another.

Allied Powers Have Other Plans Europe's victorious powers, however, had other plans. Each country—France, Great Britain, and Italy—burned with revenge and wanted to punish Germany.

Each, fearing for its future security, wanted to leave Germany too weak ever to make war again. Each wanted to take over territory that was part of Germany or Austria-Hungary, to take over Germany's colonies, or do both. And each wanted to make Germany pay for the entire cost of the war. Such payments are called **reparations**, since they are for repairing the damage caused by the enemy.

The Paris Conference Paris, France, was chosen as the place where delegates from 32 nations would meet in January 1919 to draw up a peace treaty. President Wilson decided to attend himself. No President had ever gone to Europe during his term of office. But Wilson felt that only he could get his goals written into the treaty. All the major decisions at the conference were made by the Big Four—Wilson and the prime ministers of Great Britain, Italy, and France.

The peace treaty was completed 4 months later. It was signed in the Palace

In 1919, world leaders met at the Palace of Versailles near Paris, France, to sign a peace treaty ending World War I.
■ Why, do you think, was it called the Treaty of Versailles?

of Versailles (ver sī'), and was therefore called the Treaty of Versailles. But it was not the "peace without victory" that Wilson had hoped for. It was a victor's peace, dictated to defeated Germany. Nor was it a peace based completely on the Fourteen Points. Wilson had to accept many compromises. France not only recovered territory lost to Germany in an earlier war, but it also occupied valuable mining areas in Germany. Great Britain and France took over many of Germany's overseas colonies. Germany was allowed to keep only a small army and a small navy. Finally, the treaty laid the entire blame for the war on Germany and required that it pay reparations to the Allies. The amount was a staggering $56 billion.

Wilson did win on a number of points. Many boundaries in Europe were redrawn. The Polish and Czech peoples each got their own country. Serbs were united in a new country, Yugoslavia, though this country contained other national groups as well. Most important to Wilson, the countries who drew up the peace terms accepted his plan for the League of Nations. They made the international peace-keeping organization a part of the Treaty of Versailles.

The Task of Winning Approval   Wilson now faced the task of winning his country's approval of the peace treaty. The Constitution requires that a treaty must be approved in the United States Senate by a two-thirds vote.

The most controversial part of the treaty was the plan for the League of Nations. A number of senators had already announced that they opposed having the United States join the League of Nations. They said that this would break America's long tradition of isolation. Among them

Defending the League

To gain public support for the League of Nations, Wilson decided to go on a speaking tour. He made 37 speeches during his 8,000-mile (12,800-km) trip, including a stop (shown above) at San Diego, California. On September 25, 1919, he appeared before a group of citizens in Pueblo, Colorado. That night the President collapsed from fatigue. Soon thereafter he suffered a stroke and was left partly paralyzed. This is part of the speech he made in his last public appearance.

In the Covenant [Pledge] of the League of Nations the moral forces of the world are mobilized. . . . And what do they unite for? They enter into a solemn promise to one another that they will never use their power against one another for aggression; that they never will impair the territorial integrity of a neighbor; that they will never interfere with the political independence of a neighbor; that they will abide by the principle that great populations are entitled to determine their own destiny and that they will not interfere with that destiny; and that no matter what differences arise amongst them they will never resort to war without first having done one or other of two things — either submitted the matter of controversy to arbitration . . . or submitted it to the consideration of the council of the League of Nations. . . .

You will say, "Is the League an absolute guarantee against war?" No; I do not know any absolute guarantee against the errors of human judgment or the violence of human passion, but . . . I ask you this: If it is not an absolute insurance against war, do you want no insurance at all? . . . The arrangements of this treaty are just, but they need the support of the combined power of the great nations of the world. And they will have that support. Now that the mists of this great question have cleared away. . . , I believe that men will see the truth, eye to eye and face to face. . . .

USING SOURCE MATERIAL

1. What promises do the nations belonging to the League have to make?
2. Why are there no guarantees against war?
3. If you had been Wilson, what arguments would you have used to persuade the American people to support the League of Nations?

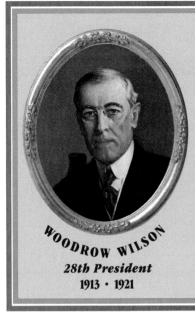

Born: 1856, Staunton, Virginia.
Education: Princeton University.
Training: Lawyer, teacher, university president, public official.
To presidency from: New Jersey.
Position when elected: Governor of New Jersey.
Political party: Democratic.
Married: (I) Ellen Louise Axson, (2) Edith Bolling Galt.
Children: Three daughters.
Died: 1924, Washington, D.C., following a stroke in 1919 that made him an invalid.
Other facts: An outstanding scholar. A professor at Bryn Mawr, Wesleyan, and Princeton. Also coached the football team at Wesleyan. Became president of Princeton University. The first President to hold a doctoral (Ph.D.) degree.
During his presidency: The United States purchased Denmark's Virgin Islands for $25 million.

WOODROW WILSON
28th President
1913 · 1921

were William Borah of Idaho, Robert La Follette of Wisconsin, and Hiram Johnson of California.

Other senators would approve the league only if certain of its powers were changed. These foes of Wilson were led by Republican Senator Henry Cabot Lodge of Massachusetts. Lodge pointed out that the Constitution of the United States gives Congress the sole power to declare war. But Article X of the league's constitution said that the league would protect member countries against attack. Did not this require the United States to go to war, even without Congress' approval? Wilson said it did not. But Lodge and others wanted that guaranteed in writing. Wilson refused to compromise.

The Senate Votes Down the Treaty In September 1919, Wilson took his case directly to the people. In 3 weeks his train took him to 29 cities. In Pueblo, Colorado, the health of the 63-year-old President gave out. He collapsed and was rushed back to Washington. There, on October 2, he suffered a stroke.

With President Wilson's illness went the last hope for his cause. The forces that favored United States entry into the League of Nations were now without a leader. In November 1919, the Senate voted against the Treaty of Versailles, with the League of Nations. Several months later, supporters of the League of Nations tried again to win a majority vote in the Senate for the treaty. More senators voted for the treaty this time, but there still were not the two thirds of the members required for approval.

CHECKUP

1. Name five of Wilson's Fourteen Points.
2. What peace terms did Europe's victorious powers want?
3. Name three countries that gained their independence as a result of the Treaty of Versailles.
4. Why did Wilson fail to win approval for the peace treaty?
5. **Thinking Critically** If you had been a senator in 1919, would you have voted for or against the treaty? Explain.

Recognizing Propaganda

WORLD WAR I POSTERS

"Propaganda," someone has written, "is a good word with a bad reputation." One dictionary defines it as "the spreading of ideas, information, or rumor for the purpose of helping or injuring . . . a cause. . . ." The purpose of propaganda is to influence people to believe certain ideas or to follow certain courses of action.

Attempts to influence can take many forms, such as symbols, slogans, cartoons, and posters. When Smokey the Bear warns people to be careful with matches because "only you can prevent forest fires," that is propaganda. Smokey is a symbol that uses a slogan.

In this case the propaganda is truthful. It promotes a good cause. Why then does the world *propaganda* have a bad reputation? The answer is that in the twentieth century, some groups and governments have used propaganda to spread lies and to promote evil causes. Adolf Hitler, the dictator of Nazi Ger-many, rose to power in the 1930s by using propaganda. He once wrote, "The great masses of the people will more easily fall victims to a great lie than a small one."

SKILLS PRACTICE

During World War I, propaganda was used by all sides. Posters were an effective way of appealing to the public. Study the posters below and answer the questions on a separate sheet of paper.

1. What is the message of the poster on the right?
2. What emotion are the posters trying to arouse in the American people?
3. How does the poster on the left try to appeal to all Americans?
4. Why do you think posters like these were effective propaganda during World War I?
5. Are posters still being used as propaganda today? Explain.

590

★★★★★★★★★ CHAPTER 24 REVIEW ★★★★★★★★★

MAIN IDEAS

1. Among the causes of the Great War that started in Europe in 1914 were nationalism, militarism, and a web of alliances, but the spark that set off the war was the murder of the Archduke Franz Ferdinand.
2. The sinking of American ships by German submarines was a major factor in the United States entering the war in 1917 on the side of the Allies against the Central Powers.
3. American troops and supplies helped bring about an Allied victory in 1918.
4. The Treaty of Versailles placed the blame for the war on Germany, forced Germany to give up territory, reduced its military forces, and made it pay for the cost of the war.
5. President Wilson persuaded the countries represented at the peace conference to create the League of Nations, but he could not persuade the Senate that the United States should join.

VOCABULARY REVIEW

On a separate sheet of paper write the letter of the term next to the number of its definition.

a. armistice **f.** reparations
b. convoy **g.** ration
c. self-determination **h.** submarine
d. mobilize **i.** *Sussex* Pledge
e. nationalism **j.** Western Front

1. To assemble armed forces for war
2. Strong feelings of loyalty to one's country
3. A group's ability to live in its own country under a government of its own choosing
4. A line of trenches running across Belgium and France
5. A warship that operates underwater
6. A group of ships escorted for safety by destroyers
7. An agreement by the German government that its submarines would not torpedo ships without warning
8. A cease-fire
9. To limit the consumption of certain goods
10. The payment for damages caused by war

CHAPTER CHECKUP

1. How did each of the following help bring on the Great War? (**a**) alliances (**b**) nationalism (**c**) militarism
2. What effect did the Zimmerman telegram have on American public opinion?
3. Name three agencies that were set up to aid the war effort on the home front.
4. How did women's roles change during the war? What other social changes occurred at this time?
5. Who were the Big Four?
6. How did Wilson's views on peace differ from those of the European victors?
7. **Thinking Critically** Why might the Treaty of Versailles be called "a victor's peace"? Give several reasons to support your answer.
8. **Thinking Critically** Why do you think Wilson called World War I "the war to end all wars"?

APPLYING KNOWLEDGE

1. Find out the origin of Armistice Day. By what name is it called today?
2. In your library, look up the stories of two heroes of World War I, Sergeant Alvin York and Captain Eddie Rickenbacker. Write a paragraph about each, telling what he did.
3. Find out where the Tomb of the Unknown Soldier is and why it was built. Report your findings to the class.
4. Draw your own poster to encourage Americans to support the war effort in 1917.

REVIEWING VOCABULARY

1. arbitration   President Theodore Roosevelt persuaded both sides in the coal strike of 1902 to agree to arbitration. What is the advantage of using arbitration to settle a dispute? When are both sides in a dispute more likely to agree to arbitration? Explain.

2. conservation   Today we are all aware of the need for conservation. In the early 1900s, however, conservation was a fairly new idea. What did President Roosevelt do to advance the cause of conservation? Why is conservation of our natural resources important?

3. imperialist   American imperialists in the 1890s wanted to create an overseas empire. Why would an imperialist have reason to be pleased by 1900? How did the imperialism of European powers contribute to the outbreak of World War I? What were the advantages of belonging to an empire? The disadvantages?

4. protectorate   In the early 1900s, Cuba, Panama, and the Dominican Republic became *protectorates* of the United States. What does that term mean? Look at the map on page 561. Why did the United States seek to turn these and other countries in the Caribbean region into United States protectorates?

5. self-determination   One of Woodrow Wilson's Fourteen Points was the principle of self-determination. Name three countries that were formed after World War I largely on the principle of self-determination. Why were some of the Allies not in favor of applying this principle to all peoples? What other countries would have been against it?

EXPRESSING YOURSELF

1. What evidence would you need?   You are helping Florence Kelley try to convince your state legislature to pass a child labor law. Several legislators say they see no need for such a law. What evidence would you show them to persuade them to vote for your bill?

2. Through other eyes.   A citizen of the Philippines Islands is listening to the United States Senate debate the peace treaty with Spain in 1899. A senator turns to this person and asks what he or she thinks about the part of the treaty that deals with the Philippines. How might he or she respond?

3. What if . . . ?   The Panama Canal is a narrow waterway across Central America that connects the Atlantic and Pacific Oceans. What if there were no canal? How would the United States and other countries be affected?

4. In your opinion.   During World War I each side tried to keep supplies from reaching its enemy. Ships of the United States and other neutral countries risked being seized by British warships or sunk by German submarines. In your opinion, should President Wilson have ordered American ships not to carry goods to either side in order to avoid any such incident? Why or why not?

5. In what ways . . . ?   The United States has just entered World War I. In what ways can you help your government win the war? In what ways will your life change as a result of the war?

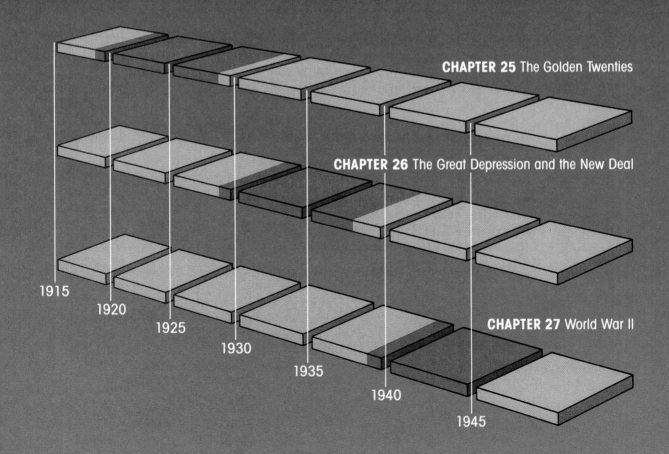

1915

1920

1925

1930

1935

1940

1945

CHAPTER 25

The Golden Twenties

1919–1929

A Time of Prosperity

How did the mass production of automobiles and other goods increase American prosperity?

VOCABULARY

| assembly line | consumer credit |
| consumer goods | |

A Born Tinkerer   What was it, a man asked Henry Ford in 1908, that made him tick? What was the ambition that drove him? Ford was already a successful manufacturer of cars and a millionaire. Ford replied that his "life desire" was to produce cars at the rate of one a minute.

In 1908 that seemed impossible. More than 1,400 cars a *day?* Why, many of the 60 or so automakers of that time didn't make that many in a *year!* Even if a car maker could produce more, who would buy them? Cars were expensive.

Still, if anyone could achieve the goal, it was Ford. No one had contributed more to the business of making automobiles. Ford was born on a farm near Dearborn, Michigan, in 1863. He hated farm life. What interested him was machinery. He was a born tinkerer. One day he was given a watch. By the next morning he had taken it apart and put it together again.

At 16, Henry moved to Detroit to become a machinist. For the next dozen years, he worked in various machine shops. He seemed to drift along with no goals other than to tinker with watches and engines. Eventually he took a job as a mechanic with the electric company.

A "Horseless Carriage"   European inventors were experimenting with a new product, the automobile. In 1892, American brothers J. Frank and Charles Duryea invented the first American automobile. It was a carriage powered by a 1-cylinder gasoline engine.

The Duryea's invention fired Ford's imagination. For the next 4 years, he spent his spare time building his own "horseless carriage" in a shed behind his home. He made most parts by hand, including the 2-cylinder gasoline engine. The machine, mounted on bicycle wheels, had no brakes. It could only go forward.

At two o'clock in the morning on a spring day in 1896, Ford took his invention out for a trial run. The gasoline engine sputtered and the ride was jerky, but it worked! In the next few years, Ford built several cars. Soon he was driving them in daylight, much to the amusement and puzzlement of the people of Detroit.

In the 1920s, prosperity blossomed. *Boomtown*, Thomas Hart Benton's painting, captures the spirit of that period.
■ What industry is depicted in this painting?

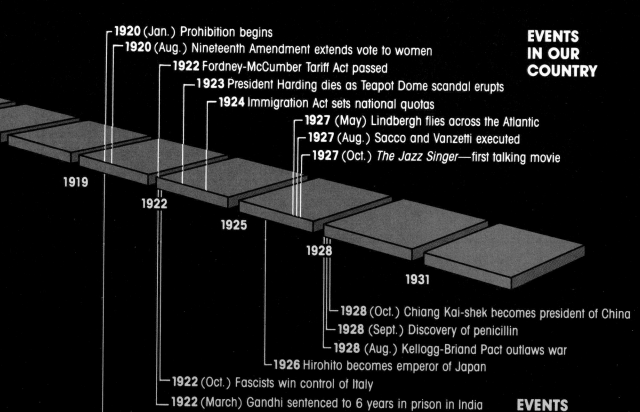

1920 (Jan.) Prohibition begins
1920 (Aug.) Nineteenth Amendment extends vote to women
1922 Fordney-McCumber Tariff Act passed
1923 President Harding dies as Teapot Dome scandal erupts
1924 Immigration Act sets national quotas
1927 (May) Lindbergh flies across the Atlantic
1927 (Aug.) Sacco and Vanzetti executed
1927 (Oct.) *The Jazz Singer*—first talking movie

1919

1922

1925

1928

1931

1928 (Oct.) Chiang Kai-shek becomes president of China
1928 (Sept.) Discovery of penicillin
1928 (Aug.) Kellogg-Briand Pact outlaws war
1926 Hirohito becomes emperor of Japan
1922 (Oct.) Fascists win control of Italy
1922 (March) Gandhi sentenced to 6 years in prison in India

Birth of the Model T   In 1903, Ford and several investors formed the Ford Motor Company. At first, like Ransom Olds, David Buick, and other carmakers of the time, Ford built racing and luxury cars. After a few years, however, he came up with a simple yet revolutionary idea. Instead of producing cars for the rich, he would build a car so inexpensive that ordinary people could afford to buy it. To keep down costs, the car would be simple in design, and it would be available in only one color — black.

Thus was born the famous Model T — the car Americans affectionately called the Tin Lizzie. Introduced in 1908, the Model T sold for $850, far less than other cars at the time. Ford sold nearly 6,000 cars the first year. Six years later the Ford Motor Company made a quarter of a million Model Ts and still could not keep up with the demand. Ford was the biggest car manufacturer in the world.

More Efficient Factories   Meanwhile, Ford steadily made his factories more efficient. In the early days, a few skilled workers—jacks-of-all-trades—assembled each car. Then Ford hired engineers to study the assembly process and break it down into the different small, simple steps that made it up. He assigned separate workers to do each of these steps. As he explained:

> The man who puts in a bolt does not put on the nut; the man who puts on the nut does not tighten it. On operation number 34 the budding motor gets its gasoline. . . . On operation number 44 the radiator is filled with water, and on operation number 45 the car drives out.

Ford achieved a big breakthrough in 1914 when he introduced the moving **assembly line** to car making. "We began taking the work to the [workers], instead of the [workers] to the work," he later wrote.

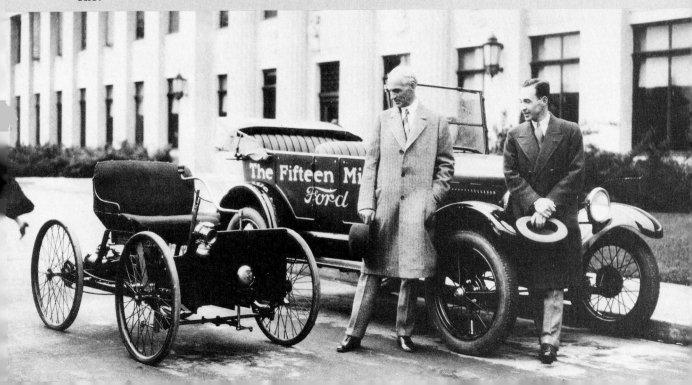

Henry Ford and his son, standing beside the 15 millionth Ford automobile, look fondly at the first one.
■ How does the newer car differ from the older one?

Heavy parts were put on a moving belt, which was driven by an electric motor. Workers remained in one place, performing their tasks on each partly built car as it passed slowly by. This saved more motions and was even more efficient. In just a few months, Ford cut the amount of time needed to make a single Model T from 14 hours to 93 minutes.

Putting America on Wheels   As production leaped ahead, Ford kept lowering the price of his car. And as he lowered the price, he sold still more cars. In 1916 he sold nearly 600,000 Fords at $360 each — less than half the price of 8 years earlier. By that time a new car rolled off Ford's assembly lines every 3 minutes.

In 1920, Henry Ford got his life desire. Ford factories produced a car every minute of the working day. Even that amazing record paled next to the one Ford Motor Company achieved 5 years later — one car every 10 seconds! By then, Ford lowered the price of the Model T to $260.

By the 1920s, other carmakers were also using the methods pioneered by Ford. General Motors went further than Ford and gave the public a large choice in models and colors. Millions of Americans owned cars.

The Automobile Brings Changes   The automobile changed the way people worked and played. People could live farther from their places of work than before. This speeded the growth of suburbs around large cities. People could shop in places far from their own neighborhoods — even as far away as neighboring cities. They could travel long distances to places of interest, or perhaps even to places that were not special at all. "Going for a spin" in the family car became a favorite form of entertainment for many Americans.

In the 1920s, newspaper and magazine advertisements helped create a huge market for cars.
■ What features does this ad emphasize?

The automobile had a good deal to do with making the 1920s a decade of prosperity. (See the picture on page 595.) Auto factories employed hundreds of thousands of workers. Hundreds of thousands more worked to make the steel, glass, rubber, paint, and other materials that went into making cars. New businesses such as gas stations, tourist cabins, and roadside restaurants sprang up. Local, state, and federal governments spent billions of dollars on roads, bringing profits to construction companies and jobs to many workers. Altogether, according to a reasonable estimate, the automobile industry created about 4 million jobs.

The Growth of Industries   No industry benefited more from the automobile than did the oil industry. In 1901, drillers struck oil at Spindletop, Texas, and opened a whole new era. This discovery was followed by others in Texas, California, and other western states. By 1930 the oil industry had become 16 times larger than it was in 1901. The automobile, with its demand for billions of gallons of gasoline, made this growth possible — and made it necessary.

The boom times of the 1920s were the result of more than just the automobile. Other industries contributed. Construction of new homes, office buildings, and factories reached an all-time high in the 1920s. The electrical industry also grew rapidly. In 1900 only a few city homes and apartments had electricity. By 1930

This picture was used to illustrate a magazine advertisement promoting electric refrigerators.
■ What did people use before the invention of the electric refrigerator?

nearly all did. That in turn gave a big lift to the manufacture and sale of such new electric household appliances as refrigerators, washing machines, vacuum cleaners, irons, and toasters. These appliances proved to be great time-savers for the household chores that at the time were seen as the exclusive responsibility of women.

A Flood of Consumer Goods   In the 1920s, America's factories poured out **consumer goods** — things that people want and use. Manufacturers increased productivity by installing new electrical machinery. They also followed Henry Ford's example and used moving assembly lines and other time-saving methods.

Manufacturers and store owners made use of two "inventions" of earlier times to help sell this flood of goods. One was advertising. Although a few products had been advertised for many years, advertising became big business in the 1920s. In that decade, companies spent $3 billion on advertising. Advertising created a desire for goods.

The second invention, **consumer credit**, made it possible to satisfy that desire. Using consumer credit, buyers could enjoy the use of a product immediately while paying only part of its price at the time of purchase. The rest was paid for in small monthly installments. Half of all consumer goods and 60 percent of all cars were bought "on time" — that is, using credit — during the 1920s. People who could never before afford to make such major purchases were now able to do so.

Prosperity — But Not for All   Not all Americans shared in the prosperity of the 1920s. In such "sick" industries as coal mining, cloth manufacturing, and shipbuilding, many workers were laid off.

The high cost of tractors and other farm machinery was one reason many farmers found themselves in debt at a time when most Americans were relatively well off.
■ **How was plowing done before tractors were used?**

Moreover, while skilled workers generally did well, the wages of the unskilled rose little, if at all. Unskilled workers included most blacks, Mexican Americans, and recent immigrants. Black people continued to leave the rural South for the cities of the North and West.

Most farmers also missed out on the prosperity of the 1920s. To produce more crops during World War I, farmers had borrowed money to buy more land. The land was expensive at the time, and payments were high. Farmers didn't mind, however, because they were receiving very good prices for their crops. After the war, crop prices fell. Still, farmers had to make the same high payments on the money they had borrowed to buy their land. Other costs remained high, too. Many farmers went deep into debt. A good many farmers lost their farms to foreclosure when they failed to pay those debts.

Even with these and other exceptions, the 1920s were good times for the country as a whole. Americans enjoyed the highest standard of living the world had ever known. Economic experts saw no reason why good times should not continue. It was, said some, a golden age. America had entered the New Era.

CHECKUP

1. What methods used by Henry Ford led to his success in making automobiles?
2. What changes did the automobile bring to the way Americans lived?
3. What ideas were used widely in the 1920s to increase the sale of goods?
4. What groups did not share in the prosperity of the 1920s?

5. **Thinking Critically** In what ways can the creation of a large new industry affect other parts of the economy?

Social Tensions and Social Change

VOCABULARY

Red Scare	prohibition
radical	Harlem Renaissance
quota	

A Rise in Prejudice   American society underwent some important changes in the 1920s. The nation also experienced many tensions. World War I had stirred feelings of hatred and intolerance for the enemy. These feelings did not die out when the war ended. With the enemy defeated, some people's feelings of hostility were turned against other targets—racial and religious minorities, political ideas, and immigrants to the United States.

Many blacks had served their country in the war "to make the world safe for democracy." They expected that when they returned home they would enjoy the rights of Americans more fully. But in the South, where most blacks lived, the threat of violence was never far below the surface. In 1919, the first postwar year, more than 70 blacks were lynched. Many of them were war veterans.

Black people who went north during and after World War I also met with racial prejudice as they competed with whites for jobs and housing. In 1917, whites in East St. Louis, Illinois, attacked blacks, touching off a riot that took the lives of 39 blacks and 10 whites. Two years later in Chicago, white youths killed a young black who was swimming in an area that whites had reserved for themselves. For 6 days, rioting raged in Chicago. Thirty-eight people were killed, more than 500 were injured, and 1,000 more were left homeless as their houses burned.

Marcus Garvey   The rough treatment directed at black people gave rise to black protest and resistance. One of the most widely followed black leaders was Marcus Garvey, who had been born in Jamaica. Garvey founded the Universal Negro Improvement Association. He preached a message of racial pride and even of racial superiority. He wrote about the achievements of the people of Africa in past times. He said that blacks should return to Africa to create their own society.

Garvey asked his followers to donate money so he could buy ships that would carry them back to Africa. The ships that Garvey bought, however, were broken-down tubs, unfit for an ocean voyage. Garvey was sent to jail for using the United States mail to defraud, or trick, people into giving money to his "back to Africa" movement. Many of his followers, however, believed he was really sent to prison for his ideas. After 2 years, Garvey was freed and deported, or sent out of the country, to his native Jamaica. Although some important black leaders like W.E.B. DuBois did not agree with Garvey, he gave hope and pride to many black people.

The Red Scare   In 1917, as you read earlier, Communists overthrew the government of Russia. Soon after that, they proclaimed the goal of spreading communism throughout the world. In 1919 a handful of people created the American Communist party. In that same year a small band of anarchists set off a number of bombs in an attempt to advance their idea that all governments should be abolished. Some Americans thought these scattered acts of terrorism were the start of a campaign to overthrow the United States government. They began to see every problem in American life, such as labor strikes, as the work of Communist plotters. This fear of Communist plots came to be called the **Red Scare**.

Some people who believed in this threat wanted the government to crack down on these radicals. **Radicals** were people who proposed to alter drastically, or even to overthrow, the American political or economic system. More than half the states passed laws that would punish radicals for their beliefs. In Washington, D.C., Attorney General A. Mitchell Palmer added to the Red Scare by talking about plots to destroy America. On New Year's Day 1920 Palmer directed raids on private homes and meeting places in 33 cities. Police rounded up about 6,000 people.

Palmer claimed that these people were a danger to the country. Most, however, were guilty of nothing more than being foreign-born. Nearly all were later released. Palmer did, however, arrange to send nearly 500 back to the countries they had come from.

Sacco and Vanzetti In time the Red Scare ended. But strong feelings continued against foreigners and radicals. In 1920, Nicola Sacco and Bartolomeo Vanzetti were accused of killing a man who had been carrying a factory payroll in Massachusetts. Both were Italian immigrants. Both were also anarchists.

The evidence against them was not very strong, but they were found guilty

Ben Shahn's "Bartolomeo Vanzetti and Nicola Sacco." From the Sacco-Vanzetti series of twenty-three paintings (1931–32). Tempera on paper over composition board. 10½ × 14½. Collection, The Museum of Modern Art, New York. Gift of Abby Aldrich Rockefeller

The case of Sacco and Vanzetti aroused interest all over the world. Many people believed the two anarchists had been denied a fair trial.
How can you tell these men are under arrest?

Lindbergh Flies Across the Atlantic

On May 21, 1927, the crew of a fishing boat in the Atlantic was startled to hear the pilot of a low-flying airplane call out, "Which way to Ireland?" If these men did not know who the pilot was, they were among the few in Europe and America who didn't. For Charles A. Lindbergh had captured the imagination of millions with his attempt to become the first flier to cross the Atlantic alone without stopping.

Lindbergh was a tall, shy 25-year-old with experience as an airmail pilot and stunt flier. When a wealthy New Yorker announced a prize of $25,000 for the first person to fly the Atlantic, Lindbergh was determined to try for it. With help from a group of St. Louis business executives, he bought a single-engine plane which

he named the *Spirit of St. Louis*.

For weeks Lindbergh prepared for his flight. He figured out almost to the exact gallon the amount of gasoline he would need to reach Paris, France.

Finally, on May 19, 1927, word came that bad weather over the Atlantic had cleared. The next morning, Lindbergh took off from a New York airfield. He took no parachute and no radio. For the next 33½ hours, millions followed the flight of the so-called Lone Eagle through special reports in the newspapers and over radio. Finally, at 10:21 P.M. on May 21, 1927, the *Spirit of St. Louis* touched down in Paris, France. "Lucky Lindy" had done it—and in doing so, he became the greatest hero of the decade.

anyway and sentenced to death. Many believed that Sacco and Vanzetti did not get a fair trial. All appeals failed, and in 1927 they died in the electric chair.

Limiting Immigration For many years a movement to limit the number of immigrants entering the United States had been growing. In 1924, Congress passed a law which limited the number of people from Europe who could enter the United States in any given year to 150,000. Each country in Europe was assigned a **quota**—that is, a share of the total number. The law was designed so that countries in southern and

eastern Europe, where the new immigrants came from, got much smaller quotas than the countries of northern and western Europe. Asian and African nations got no quotas at all.

The new immigration laws did not apply to people who lived in the Western Hemisphere. Immigration from Canada, Mexico, and some other Latin American lands increased during the 1920s.

The Ku Klux Klan Revives One especially ugly expression of the desire to "save" America from foreign influences and radical ideas was the Ku Klux Klan

(KKK). The original Ku Klux Klan had abused blacks in the South during Reconstruction. (See page 404.) The new Klan was started in 1915. It was still anti-black, but it was now also anti-Catholic, anti-Jewish, and anti-immigrant. Using threats and violence, Klan members tried to drive these groups from their communities.

The KKK grew rapidly. By 1924 it claimed more than 4 million members. The Klan had great influence in several state legislatures in the Midwest. Klan members boldly held marches in the streets of many towns and cities, including the nation's capital.

By 1925, however, Americans began to turn against the Klan's use of threats and violence. Klan membership and influence fell sharply within a few years.

Women Gain More Independence

Among the most important changes in American society were changes affecting women. The role women played in the war effort brought wider support to the movement for women's suffrage. That movement was crowned with success in 1920, when the Nineteenth Amendment to the Constitution was approved. Women gained the vote in time to cast ballots in the presidential election of that year.

Many new inventions cut down the time needed for housework. Women were more likely than ever to take jobs outside the home. Women had long worked in factories, and in household jobs as cooks, servants, and so forth. Now more of them found work as schoolteachers and nurses, in offices and at department-store counters. By 1930, women made up 22 percent of the work force.

Women, especially young women, sought the same freedoms that men had. This desire to break away from traditional roles was signaled by dramatic changes in their appearance and behavior. To the horror of many parents, young women bobbed, or cut short, their hair. They wore knee-length skirts. They danced new dances like the Charleston. These young women were called flappers.

These changes were not true of all women—not even a majority. For most women, life continued much as it had before the 1920s. This was especially the case in small towns and rural areas.

Movies, Sports, and Cars

Many Americans began to live differently. The home became less important as the center of family life. Three things took people out of the home more and more: moving pictures, sporting events, and the car.

Moving pictures had grown steadily in popularity since their invention in the 1890s. By the 1920s, going to the "movies"

For many young women in the 1920s, bobbed hair became a mark of independence.
■ What styles today have the same impact?

was America's favorite form of entertainment. Actors like Rudolph Valentino, Mary Pickford, and Charles Chaplin became idols to millions. In 1927 came the first talking picture, *The Jazz Singer.* "Talkies" revolutionized the moving-picture industry. Movies soon became even more popular. By 1930, about 100 million people went to the movies every week.

The 1920s were also a golden age for sports. Large crowds turned out to watch their favorite college football and professional baseball teams. Nearly 100,000 people packed Soldiers' Field in Chicago to watch Jack Dempsey and Gene Tunney fight for the heavyweight boxing championship. Every sport had its own heroes.

In baseball it was the Babe — George Herman Ruth, the great home run slugger. In college football, it was Red Grange of Illinois and the Four Horsemen of Notre Dame. Bobby Jones in golf and Bill Tilden and Helen Wills in tennis became sports legends. Gertrude Ederle became the first woman to swim the English Channel.

Most important, the car undercut the home as the center of family life. Sons and daughters were forever asking to borrow the car for the evening — or so it seemed to many parents. Dinner, once the time when the whole family ate together, became simply the third meal of the day, eaten whenever and wherever it was convenient to do so.

Sports heroes attracted more notice in the 1920s than ever before. ■ What changes made this nationwide attention possible?

Sports Heroes of the 1920's

The Radio Craze   One new form of entertainment promoted family togetherness. That was the radio. Soon after the first commercial station, KDKA of Pittsburgh, Pennsylvania, took to the air in 1920, a radio craze swept the country. By 1923, some 500 radio stations were broadcasting. In 1926 the first nationwide radio network, the National Broadcasting Company, was founded.

By the end of the decade, nearly half of all American families owned a radio. Families gathered around the radio to listen to their favorite programs — music, comedy shows, adventure programs, and the evening news. By broadcasting sporting events, the radio promoted the great interest in sports in the 1920s.

Prohibition   Still another important change in American society in the 1920s was **prohibition**. This was the effort to forbid the sale and drinking of alcoholic beverages. The effort to control drinking in America went back nearly a hundred years, to the 1830s. Women and religious groups had taken the lead. They argued that liquor was the cause of crime, family breakup, and other social evils. From the 1870s on, the leading organization in fighting "Demon Rum" was the Woman's Christian Temperance Union (WCTU).

The prohibition movement made headway in the twentieth century. By the time of World War I, about half the states had banned the sale of liquor and beer. Most of these were rural states. In 1919 the Eighteenth Amendment was added to the Constitution, prohibiting the manufacture, sale, or transportation of liquor throughout the United States. Thus began what many Americans called the Noble Experiment.

Prohibition did result in a decline in drinking. But it led to some other results

KDKA in Pittsburgh, on the air in 1920, was the nation's first commercial radio station. ■ How would a station today be different?

that were unfortunate. Millions of people simply refused to obey the law. Some bought liquor from bootleggers — people who made it illegally or smuggled it into the country. Some bought liquor at speakeasies — bars where alcoholic beverages were sold illegally. Some brewed their own liquor at home.

Without public support, enforcement of prohibition was nearly impossible. The federal government assigned 2,000 agents to enforce the law. It would have taken a hundred times that many to prevent liquor from illegally entering the country along the thousands of miles of border and coastline. Further, bootleggers and speakeasies were often able to operate because they "bought protection" from the law by paying off dishonest public officials and police officers.

Perhaps worst of all, prohibition contributed to the growth of organized crime. Bootlegging was a $2 billion-a-year business, and rival crime organizations fought

THE TWENTIES

No decade has been given more names than the 1920s. Some called these years the Golden Twenties, thinking of the prosperity they brought. To others this was "the dry decade"—the era of prohibition.

One of the labels most often given to this decade is the Roaring Twenties. The decade was "roaring," many believed, because everything was wide open—bootleggers, gangsters, and lawbreakers were everywhere. "Roaring" also referred to the noises—the roar of machines in factories, of cars and trucks in traffic, and of crowds at sporting events. Another name for the 1920s is the Jazz Age. Jazz is a style of music created by black people in the South, es-

pecially in New Orleans, in the late nineteenth century. A blend of African and European influences, jazz is America's special contribution to the world of music. By the 1920s, jazz was popular in much of the United States. Both black and white musicians played jazz. It became a symbol of the free and easy spirit.

Of course, no single label can capture a decade. Certainly to quiet, conservative Calvin Coolidge, the 1920s was not the Jazz Age. People who lost farms or held low-paying jobs didn't think of the era as the Golden Twenties. Yet each of the labels attached to the 1920s does show us something about the flavor of those years.

The Smart Set

Edited by George Jean Nathan and H.L. Mencken.

"The Diamond as Big as the Ritz"
By F. Scott Fitzgerald

it out on the streets for control of this business in several American cities.

By the end of the 1920s, it was clear that prohibition was not working. In 1933 the Twenty-first Amendment to the Constitution was adopted, repealing the Eighteenth Amendment.

Literature of the 1920s   The 1920s produced some of America's greatest literature. Many of the writers of the time were disillusioned by World War I. They felt that the dying and suffering of millions

had all been for nothing. This was the theme of Ernest Hemingway in two of his greatest novels, *The Sun Also Rises* and *A Farewell to Arms*.

Other writers focused on what they saw as shortcomings in American society. Sinclair Lewis wrote about the narrowness of small-town life in *Main Street* and *Babbitt*. Flappers and speakeasies were the subject of much of F. Scott Fitzgerald's writing. But Fitzgerald also criticized the emphasis on material success that he saw in the 1920s.

National Portrait Gallery, Smithsonian Institution

New York City poets of the 1920s: Edna St. Vincent Millay (left) wrote about love, death, and the yearnings of youth in Greenwich Village. Countee Cullen (right) wrote about the way black Americans were treated.
■ **How were most black Americans treated in the 1920s?**

The decade also produced important poetry. Robert Frost's poems dealt with the more traditional side of American life. Those of Edna St. Vincent Millay, however, spoke with the voice of the modern world. "I burn my candle at both ends," she wrote of the decade's pursuit of pleasure.

Black poets like Langston Hughes, Claude McKay, and Countee Cullen spoke of the despair of black people in white America. "If We Must Die" and "To My White Friends," two of McKay's poems, told how it felt to be discriminated against.

The writings of these and other black writers were part of an important body of literature that came out of Harlem, New York's large black community, during the 1920s. This flowering of black literature was part of a larger black cultural movement that is called the **Harlem Renaissance**, a revival of cultural and intellectual life centered in Harlem. Much of this black literature dealt with the African roots of American blacks. And much delivered the message of racial pride. "I am a Negro — and beautiful," read a line in one of Langston Hughes's poems.

CHECKUP

1. In what ways did racial prejudice show itself following World War I?
2. How did each of the following contribute to tension in the early 1920s: (a) the Red Scare, (b) Sacco and Vanzetti, (c) the Ku Klux Klan?
3. How did life change for women in the 1920s?
4. What effects did the following items have on American life in the 1920s: (a) sports, (b) radio, (c) prohibition?
5. **Thinking Critically** What evidence might support the claim that many of the social tensions of the 1920s grew out of World War I?

The Political Scene

What were the main developments in politics and foreign affairs during the 1920s?

Harding and Normalcy   By the time of the 1920 election, the American people had grown tired of World War I, the League of Nations, and Woodrow Wilson's idealism. They wanted to get back to normal living and to enjoy the fruits of the nation's material progress.

Warren Harding of Ohio, the Republican candidate for President, caught the national mood perfectly. Americans, said Harding, wanted "not heroics but healing, not nostrums but normalcy." Harding was elected by one of the largest margins ever.

The federal government had grown greatly during wartime. As President, Harding aimed to reduce both federal spending and federal power. He especially believed that government should not interfere with business through regulation. If business were allowed to manage its own affairs, he felt, the country would prosper. Harding summed up his beliefs when he said, "What this country needs is less government in business and more business in government." His ideas were very different from those of the Progressives, who believed that government should regulate business in the public interest.

Harding supported most of the goals of business. To protect American products from foreign competition, he favored a high tariff. In 1922, Congress passed the Fordney-McCumber Tariff Act. This law set tariff duties higher than they had ever been before.

A Time of Corruption   Harding was a friendly, likable man. With his strong, handsome face and silver hair, some said that he "looked like a President." But he had serious weaknesses. He was a poor judge of people. And he could not say no to friends.

For a few top positions in his Cabinet, Harding chose people of great ability. He made Herbert Hoover his secretary of commerce. Charles Evans Hughes, a former governor, Supreme Court justice, and candidate for President, became the secretary of state. Andrew Mellon became secretary of the treasury. He was a millionaire banker and industrialist.

For too many other posts, though, Harding chose his old Ohio pals and card-playing friends. They turned his administration into one of the most corrupt in American history. Attorney General Harry Daugherty, an Ohio friend, took bribes to give pardons, paroles, and liquor

Attorney General Harry Daugherty tries to hide the skeletons in his closet.
■ Who is the shadowy figure on the left?

Born: 1865, Corsica (now Blooming Grove), Ohio.
Education: Ohio Central College.
Training: Newspaper editor and publisher.
To presidency from: Ohio.
Position when elected: United States senator.
Political party: Republican.
Married: Florence Kling DeWolfe.
Children: None.
Died: 1923, in San Francisco, California, while returning from a trip to Alaska.
Other facts: A friendly, generous man, but weak-willed. A good speaker. Editor and an owner of a newspaper, the *Marion Star*. A compromise choice for the Republican presidential nomination. The first President to visit Alaska.
During his presidency: The Unknown Soldier of World War I was buried at Arlington National Cemetery.

WARREN G. HARDING

29th President
1921 · 1923

permits. (Certain businesses were given these permits to produce alcohol for manufacturing, research, and medicinal purposes.) Daugherty was tried, but was able to avoid a jail term. Charles Forbes, head of the Veterans Administration, sold $250 million worth of government property to private buyers at ridiculously low prices in exchange for payments from the buyers. Forbes did go to jail for his crimes.

Teapot Dome   The biggest of the Harding scandals came to be called **Teapot Dome**. Teapot Dome was a hill in Wyoming, under which lay a large deposit of oil. The federal government owned this land. When Wilson was President, he had reserved the oil there and at Elk Hills, California, for the use of the United States Navy. President Wilson put these sites under navy control.

When Harding became President, he made an old friend, Albert Fall, secretary of the interior. Fall got the President to transfer control of Teapot Dome to his department. Then, in exchange for a large

bribe, Fall allowed several oil companies to drill oil wells there. The companies made fortunes before the scheme was discovered. Fall became the first Cabinet secretary to be sent to jail.

In August 1923, while on a trip to Alaska and the West Coast, Harding became ill suddenly and died. None of these scandals had yet come to light, and the people mourned Harding as a good and beloved President. Before he died, however, Harding had begun to learn how his friends had betrayed him and the public. Speaking to a friend, Harding said, "In this job I am not worried about my enemies. I can take care of them. It is my friends who are giving me trouble."

Coolidge Follows Harding   Vice President Calvin Coolidge was vacationing at his father's farm in Vermont when news of Harding's death reached him. Late at night, by the light of a flickering kerosene lamp, Coolidge was sworn in as Harding's successor by his father, a local justice of the peace.

Born: 1872, Plymouth, Vermont.
Education: Amherst College.
Training: Lawyer, public official.
To presidency from: Massachusetts.
Position when taking office: Vice President.
Political party: Republican.
Married: Grace Goodhue.
Children: Two sons.
Died: 1933, Northampton, Massachusetts.
Other facts: A shy, close-mouthed man with a dry wit. Practiced law in Northampton, Massachusetts. Held local and state offices. Elected governor of Massachusetts in 1918. The first President whose inaugural address was broadcast by radio. After his retirement from public service, wrote a daily newspaper column.
During his presidency: The first women governors, Nellie Tayloe Ross of Wyoming, and Miriam A. Ferguson of Texas, took office in 1925.

CALVIN COOLIDGE
30th President
1923 · 1929

The setting was a fitting place for Coolidge's term to begin. To most people, Coolidge stood for the simple values of rural America—thrift, honesty, and hard work. He was one of the few Presidents in our history to save money from his presidential salary. He won the people's trust by removing many of Harding's corrupt friends from office.

Coolidge was a colorless man. He earned the nickname Silent Cal because he said so little in public. But silent or not, he seemed to be what the public wanted. In 1924 he ran for election with the slogan "Keep Cool With Coolidge." Times were prosperous, and Coolidge won easily.

Coolidge's Policies   Coolidge shared Harding's views on government, economy, taxes, and business. He kept government spending down. During Harding's and Coolidge's terms, the national debt was reduced from $24 billion to $16 billion.

Coolidge and Treasury Secretary Mellon favored cutting taxes on high incomes. They said this would free money for investment, making the economy grow and creating jobs. Congress followed their advice and lowered taxes on the wealthy. It also cut business taxes.

Coolidge also believed that government should not interfere with the dealings of business. "The business of America is business," he said. In the Progressive era, Presidents Roosevelt, Taft, and Wilson had used the antitrust laws to break up trusts. They had given new power to the Interstate Commerce Commission and created new agencies like the Federal Trade Commission to regulate business. Coolidge did nothing like this.

Big Business Gets Bigger   With the government ignoring the antitrust laws, big business got bigger. There were thousands of **mergers**, in which two or more companies combined to form a single company. More and more of American business was being controlled by fewer and fewer large firms. By 1929 nearly half the business wealth in the country was owned by just 200 companies. The other half was shared by nearly 400,000 smaller companies. In some industries, competition had just about disappeared.

Few Americans seemed to mind. Times were good, and most believed that business enterprise had made them so. Goods, goods, and more goods flowed from the factories to an eager consuming public. The United States, it was said, was the first country in the history of the world to solve the problem of scarcity of goods. It was only a matter of time before the nation's plenty would be enjoyed by every last American.

Labor Unions Decline The story of American labor unions in the 1920s was quite different. During World War I the government had backed their efforts to or-ganize workers, and union membership had risen. So had wages. Right after the war, however, unions lost strikes in such industries as steel, coal, and textiles.

In the next few years, unions lost other big strikes in the meat-packing and railroad industries. As a result, most of labor's wartime gains were wiped out.

During the 1920s, employers used the blacklist and other means to keep labor unions out of their companies. Some companies also offered new benefits to their workers, such as paid vacations, health care, and recreational programs. In this way, employers spread the benefits of capitalism to their workers while also weakening the appeal of labor unions. For these and other reasons, unions lost members in the 1920s.

This painting, by American artist Georgia O'Keefe, shows factories along the East River in New York City.
■ Why, do you think, were these factories built along the river?

An Agreement on Reducing Navies
Although the United States did not join the League of Nations, it promoted steps to maintain world peace. In 1921 the United States took the lead in heading off a naval arms race among several countries. It invited the leading naval powers to attend a conference in Washington, D.C.

Secretary of State Hughes startled the conference with a bold proposal. Each country, Hughes said, should build no new warships for the next 10 years. They should also scrap some ships already in service. In 1922, Japan, Great Britain, the United States, France, and Italy signed a treaty accepting Hughes's plan.

The *Myoko*, Japan's first warship since naval disarmament, is shown during a launching ceremony.
■ **What does *to launch a ship* mean?**

The Kellogg-Briand Pact In 1928 the United States and France invited countries to sign a treaty agreeing not to use war "as an instrument of national policy," and to settle disputes by peaceful means.

The treaty was called the **Kellogg-Briand Pact**. Frank Kellogg was secretary of state under President Coolidge. Sixty-two countries signed the Kellogg-Briand Pact. If it had worked, it would have meant the end of war among these countries. But the treaty had no enforcement provisions. It was nothing more than a statement of good intentions.

Relations with Latin America The United States also took steps to improve its relations with Latin American countries. These countries resented United States interference in their affairs.

In 1917, Mexico adopted a new constitution. Under it, the government was to take over ownership of mines and oil owned by foreign companies. American companies owned many of these properties. They appealed to the United States government to protect their interests. For several years, relations between Mexico and the United States grew steadily worse.

Still, neither country wanted war. In 1927, President Coolidge appointed Dwight Morrow the new ambassador to Mexico. Morrow helped arrange a compromise between the Mexican government and the American businesses.

In 1928 the United States also agreed that it would no longer use the Roosevelt Corollary as a reason for intervening in Latin America. When rebels fought the government in Nicaragua in 1927, Coolidge sent in marines. This time the United States arranged to end the fighting and to hold an election. Even though the side favored by the United States lost, the marines were withdrawn.

The War Debts During World War I the United States lent billions of dollars to the Allies. After the war, these countries said that the United States should not demand repayment. America, they said, should treat these loans as its contribution to the war effort. The Allies held that they had made their contribution in blood and destroyed property.

The United States, however, insisted that the debts be repaid. The Allies could use the reparation payments they were receiving from Germany to help pay the debts. This insistence caused some bad feelings between the United States and European countries. If the Allies had to use their money to pay war debts, they argued, they would have less money to buy American goods. During the 1930s nearly every country stopped paying its war debts.

Hoover Becomes President In 1927, Calvin Coolidge caught the country by surprise with a one-sentence announcement: "I do not choose to run for President in 1928." The Republican party then turned to Herbert Hoover as its candidate.

Democrats countered with Alfred E. Smith, a reform governor in New York. It would have been hard to find a greater contrast between two candidates. Both had started life as poor boys, but Hoover was raised on an Iowa farm, and Smith grew up in New York City. Hoover had a career as a mining engineer and business executive. Smith was a career politician. Hoover was a Quaker. Smith was a Catholic, the first of his faith to run for the presidency. On prohibition, Hoover was a "dry." Smith was a "wet"—that is, he favored repeal of the prohibition amendment. Smith seemed to stand for everything that rural and small-town Americans were against. Hoover won the election of 1928 by a wide margin.

In 1928 the rival candidates were Herbert Hoover and Alfred E. Smith.
■ Which man was the candidate of the Republican party? Of the Democratic Party?

In one of his speeches during the campaign, Herbert Hoover said:

> We in America are nearer to the final triumph over poverty than ever before in the history of any land; . . . given a chance to go forward with the policies of the last 8 years, we shall soon, with the help of God, be in sight of the day when poverty shall be banished from this nation.

Most Americans shared Hoover's belief that prosperity could be made permanent. Who could know that Hoover's words would soon be used to mock him?

CHECKUP

1. What policies did President Coolidge follow?
2. What steps were taken in the 1920s to maintain world peace?
3. Who were the candidates in the presidential election of 1928, and how did they differ?
4. **Thinking Critically** What evidence might support the claim that President Harding was a poor judge of people?

Making Tables and Graphs

PRESENTING STATISTICAL INFORMATION

During the 1860s about 2,314,000 immigrants came to America. For the next two decades, immigration rose, climbing to 2,812,000 in the 1870s and 5,246,000 in the 1880s. After slipping to 3,687,000 in the next 10-year period, immigration reached 8,795,000 in the first decade of the new century. Thereafter, it fell to 5,735,000 between 1911 and 1920 and to 4,107,000 in the next 10-year period. From 1931 to 1940, immigration plunged to just 528,000.

Did you find it difficult to absorb all that information? Sometimes when statistical information is presented in sentence form, it is hard to picture clearly. That is why tables and graphs are so useful. They allow us to present statistics in a manner that is easy to read and understand.

To make a table showing the information above, you would set up two columns. The one on the left would be for decades: 1861–1870, 1871–1880, and so on. The one on the right would be for the number of immigrants in each decade. So, for the years from 1861 to 1880, your table would look like this:

Decade	Number of Immigrants
1861–1870	2,314,000
1871–1880	2,812,000

SKILLS PRACTICE I

Copy the table that was started above. Using the statistical information in the paragraph quoted at the beginning of this page, complete the table up to 1940.

The information in your table can also be shown effectively on a line graph. Using a sheet of graph paper, place points along the bottom line for the decades. The first point will be for 1861–1870, the next point for 1871–1880, and so on. On the vertical line to the left, enter points for the number of immigrants. Moving upward, the first point will be 1 million people, the second point 2 million people, and the third point 3 million people.

For 1861–1870, follow the line for that date upward, past 2 million but below 3 million. Place a dot on the line about where you think 2,314,000 should be. Next, follow the line for 1871–1880 upward, placing a dot about where you think 2,812,000 should be. Now connect the dots. So far, your line graph should look like the graph below.

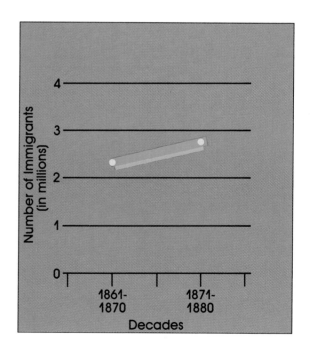

SKILLS PRACTICE II

Using the information in the paragraph quoted at the beginning of this page, complete the line graph to 1940. Remember to connect the dots at the end of your work.

MAIN IDEAS

1. American manufacturers produced record numbers of cars, household appliances, and other consumer goods in the 1920s.
2. Minority groups felt increased prejudice and were among those who did not share fully in the prosperity of the 1920s.
3. A fear of foreign influence led to the Red Scare after World War I and to laws restricting immigration.
4. Cars, movies, and sporting events made the home less important as the center of family life in the 1920s.
5. Many of the Progressives' attempts to regulate business were reversed during the presidencies of Harding and Coolidge.

VOCABULARY REVIEW

To fill the blank in each statement, unscramble the words that follow it. Write your answers on a separate sheet of paper.

1. During the 1920s a revival of arts and culture begun in the black community in New York City was called the _____.
   LAMHRE NSNIAACEERS
2. A hill that lay over a large oil deposit in Wyoming gave its name to a scandal during the Harding administration, known as _____.
   ETTPOA MDEO
3. An arrangement in which workers construct a car or other product by adding parts as it is carried along a moving belt is an _____.
   BAESLMYS NLIE
4. The 1920s saw the manufacture of a flood of items that people wanted or needed for their own use—that is, of _____.
   EOUCMRSN OSOGD
5. When people buy goods with a small payment at the time of purchase and pay the rest in monthly installments, they are using _____.
   OMRECSNU DIETRC

CHAPTER CHECKUP

1. How did the mass production of inexpensive automobiles affect American life?
2. How did consumer credit affect the buying habits of Americans?
3. Which industries and groups of people missed out on the prosperity of the 1920s?
4. How did communists and anarchists become linked in many Americans' minds?
5. What were the desirable and the undesirable effects of prohibition?
6. What were the attitudes of Presidents Harding and Coolidge toward business?
7. **Thinking Critically** Why do many people mistakenly think of Henry Ford as the inventor of the automobile?
8. **Thinking Critically** Were the arguments made by the Allies for not paying their war debts good arguments? Why or why not?

APPLYING KNOWLEDGE

1. Find out why the following people were the subject of many newspaper articles in the 1920s. Then write a sentence about each one that tells why he or she was famous.

Adm. Richard Byrd	Babe Ruth
Miriam A. Ferguson	Al Capone
Gertrude Ederle	Bessie Smith
Charles Lindbergh	Gene Tunney
Ernest Hemingway	Bobby Jones
Rudolph Valentino	Rudy Vallee

2. Look up and read one poem by Langston Hughes and one by Robert Frost. How do the subjects of these poems differ?
3. Find a photograph, drawing, or map of your town or city before the coming of the automobile. Compare it with your community today.
4. Between 1908 and 1925, the price of a Model T Ford actually fell from $850 to $260. Can you think of any products whose prices have fallen a great deal in your lifetime? Name one, and find newspaper or magazine ads from a few years ago and today to show the fall in prices.

26 The Great Depression and the New Deal 1929–1938

The Great Depression

What were some of the causes of the Great Depression?

Crash! The New York Stock Exchange is one of the world's great marketplaces. This is the **stock market**—the place where shares of stock in America's largest corporations are bought and sold. On Thursday, October 24, 1929, the stock market opened as usual at 10:00 A.M. Within minutes, however, it was clear that this would be no ordinary day. Stock prices were tumbling. Panic set in. People scrambled wildly to sell their shares before prices went still lower. At the close of business, a record number of shares had been traded. Those workers who kept the records of sales were hours behind in recording them.

On Friday and Saturday the price of stocks remained steady. But on Monday the slide began again. Then on Tuesday, October 29—Black Tuesday—everything fell apart. Prices plunged. Some stocks could not be sold at any price. In the end, 16 million shares were sold, and billions of dollars in values were wiped out. People who were wealthy only a week before lost everything.

This was the beginning of the stock market crash of 1929. It was also the beginning of the Great Depression.

A Craze to Get Rich Why did the stock market crash happen? As you learned in the last chapter, business boomed in the 1920s. Many corporations made large profits. People who owned stock, or shares of ownership, in these profitable companies also did well. They received high dividends, or earnings, from their investments. Other people wanted to buy these shares. With so many people wanting to buy, the price of stocks went up.

As stock prices rose, some people thought they could use the stock market to get rich. Their idea was simple. They forgot about dividends and the true value of a company. They just bought stocks. With stock prices going up, they thought there would always be someone else to buy the stocks from them at a higher price. This kind of buying, with the hope of a quick profit, is called **speculation**. In fact, it is hardly different from gambling.

Worse still, some people speculated with borrowed money. They bought stock on margin. This meant that they paid as

Isaac Soyer called this bleak scene of city life during the Great Depression *Employment Agency.*
■ What do you think these people are waiting for?

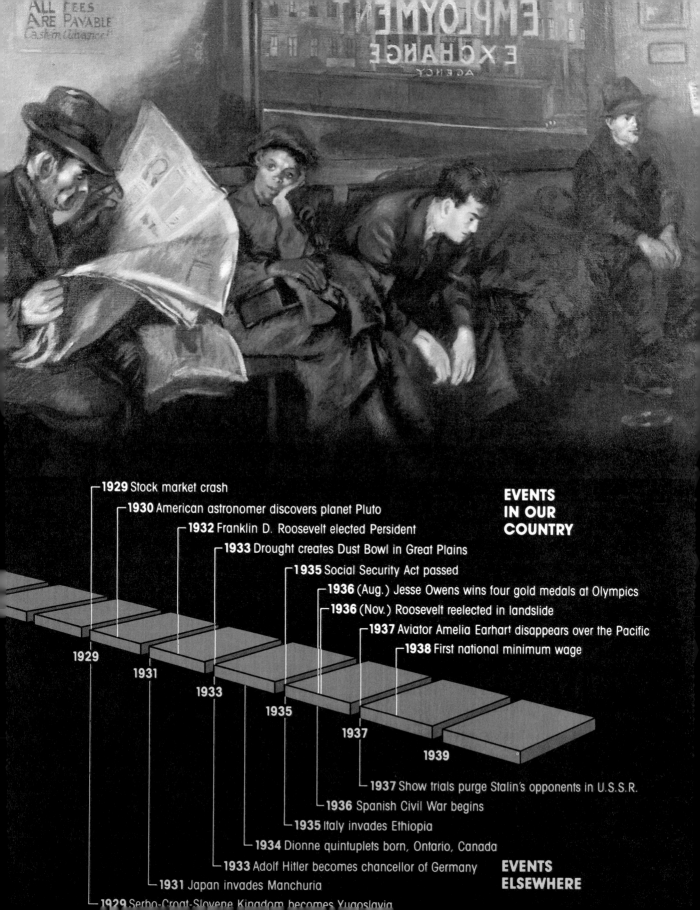

ALL FEES
ARE PAYABLE
Cash in Advance!

EMPLOYMENT
EXCHANGE
AGENCY

**EVENTS
IN OUR
COUNTRY**

1929 Stock market crash

1930 American astronomer discovers planet Pluto

1932 Franklin D. Roosevelt elected Persident

1933 Drought creates Dust Bowl in Great Plains

1935 Social Security Act passed

1936 (Aug.) Jesse Owens wins four gold medals at Olympics

1936 (Nov.) Roosevelt reelected in landslide

1937 Aviator Amelia Earhart disappears over the Pacific

1938 First national minimum wage

1929   1931   1933   1935   1937   1939

1937 Show trials purge Stalin's opponents in U.S.S.R.

1936 Spanish Civil War begins

1935 Italy invades Ethiopia

1934 Dionne quintuplets born, Ontario, Canada

1933 Adolf Hitler becomes chancellor of Germany

1931 Japan invades Manchuria

1929 Serbo-Croat-Slovene Kingdom becomes Yugoslavia

**EVENTS
ELSEWHERE**

little as 10 percent of the price of the stock in cash. When the stock's price went up and they sold it, they would pay off the loan out of their profit. Few margin buyers thought about how they would pay off their loans if stock prices went down.

Only about 1 in every 100 Americans owned stock in the 1920s. Less than half of these people, along with some banks, engaged in speculation. But there were enough speculators to send stock prices rapidly upward, beginning in 1927. In the months that followed, people talked about "getting rich quick."

The Downward Plunge   All speculative crazes come to an end sooner or later. This one did in September 1929. For the next month, stock prices drifted downward. Some investors realized that the boom was over and decided to sell their stocks. Now there were more sellers than buyers. Prices slipped a little further. That led other shareholders to decide to

sell. Down went the prices still more. Soon speculators who had bought on margin were forced to sell to pay off the loans they had taken out. By then the prices of stocks were tumbling.

This is what happened on October 24 and again on October 29. The downward plunge continued. In 3 weeks, investors lost $30 billion. Speculators were not the only ones who went broke. The bankers and stockbrokers who had lent them money were also big losers.

Even that was not the end of it. Stock prices continued downward for 3 more years. A share in United States Steel Corporation, which cost $262 before the crash, brought just $22 in 1932. By that time some stocks were worth nothing at all.

A Depression Spreads   The stock market crash of 1929 was followed by a depression that spread over the country. The crash was not, however, the main cause of this depression. That cause lay in certain

On the day the stock market crashed, hundreds of frightened people crowded around the New York Stock Exchange on Wall Street.
■ **What is a stock exchange?**

weaknesses of the American economy, weaknesses that were hidden during the prosperous 1920s. A basic trouble was that Americans could not consume as much as they produced. Wages of workers increased in the 1920s, but production of goods increased even more. Even with consumer credit, ordinary people did not have enough money to buy all the cars, refrigerators, washing machines, and vacuum cleaners that were made.

Nor could all the goods be sold abroad. The high tariff prevented Europeans from selling much that they produced to the United States. Europeans could not earn money to buy American goods. And after making payments on their war debts, some European countries could not afford to buy any goods.

By early 1929 the economy was slowing down. Car sales were off. Home-building was down. Sales of consumer goods were dropping. Store **inventories** —the supplies of unsold goods—began to pile up. Stores cut back on their orders to factories. Factories cut down on production and laid off workers.

With ordinary people unable to buy all the goods American industry was producing, the economy depended heavily on the willingness of the well-to-do to buy and spend. This is where the stock market crash entered the picture. The people who lost money in the crash had nothing left to spend. Even well-to-do people who were not "in the market" were frightened by the crash. Fearing that bad times might be coming, they stopped spending and investing. That simply helped to bring on the bad times they feared.

The crash contributed to the depression in other ways, too. Banks that had lent money to speculators or had invested in stocks lost a great deal of money. If people asked for their savings back all at

Apple selling provided the only income for some people during the Great Depression.
■ How much did apples sell for?

once, the banks would be in trouble. That is what happened. Between the years 1929 and 1932, more than 4,000 banks failed. When a bank failed, its depositors lost all their savings.

Conditions Get Worse   Soon after the stock market crash, President Hoover met with leaders of business and industry. He called on them to keep people employed and not to cut wages. He urged cities, states, and businesses to go ahead with their plans for new construction. Hoover's idea was to keep people earning money. They could then continue to buy goods and keep others working.

Many companies did try at first to keep employment and spending up. But business got worse. Factory managers began to lay off some workers and to cut the wages of others. Workers without jobs could not buy goods, so still more factories had to cut their output. Thousands of firms, large and small, went out of business. Meanwhile, cities and states all over the nation were running out of money. They had to put off building roads, schools, and other needed improvements.

Unemployment spread. In 1930, some 4 million people were out of work. The number rose to 8 million in 1931. In 1932, 13 million—one in every four workers—were without jobs. In Cleveland, half of the work force was unemployed. In several cities the proportion was even higher. (See the picture on page 617.)

With no money and no place to live, many people "took to the road" or "rode the rails"—that is, hopped onto freight trains. They went from city to city looking for work. At one time, more than 2 million Americans were wandering in this way.

By this time the depression had become the worst ever in American history. It would be known to future generations as the Great Depression.

Desperate People In the cities, soup kitchens were set up. People patiently stood in line for hours for some free bread and a cup of watery soup. Small groups of desperate people could always be found near the back doors of restaurants, searching through the barrels of garbage for food.

New York City politicians hand out loaves of bread and cans of milk to some of the many people in need of food.
What are the milk crates made of?

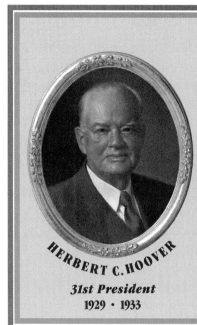

Born: 1874, West Branch, Iowa.
Education: Stanford University.
Training: Mining engineer, public official.
To presidency from: California.
Position when elected: Secretary of commerce.
Political party: Republican.
Married: Lou Henry.
Children: Two sons.
Died: 1964.
Other facts: Orphaned at age 9. Worked his way through college. Directed mining projects in many countries. Was in China during Boxer Rebellion and supervised building of defenses. Organized food relief in Belgium during World War I and directed relief programs in Europe following World War II. In the late 1940s, headed a commission to streamline government.
During his presidency: Amelia Earhart made the first solo flight by a woman across the Atlantic Ocean.

HERBERT C. HOOVER

31st President
1929 · 1933

On the edge of cities and in empty lots, clusters of shacks sprang up. One-room shacks made from wooden packing cases, cardboard, and flattened tin cans housed whole families. Those who blamed the President for the sad state of affairs called these clusters of shacks "Hoovervilles." Others, sleeping on park benches, called the newspapers with which they covered themselves "Hoover blankets."

Farmers were worse off than ever. Farm prices had not been good in the 1920s. Between 1929 and 1932, they collapsed altogether. A bushel of wheat that sold for $1.03 in 1929 brought only 33 cents in 1932. Cotton, selling for 19 cents a pound in 1929, cost 6 cents a pound in 1932. The price of corn was so low that farmers burned it for fuel rather than sell it. Many farmers who could not pay their debts lost their farms.

Fighting the Depression President Hoover tried to fight the depression. Under one program, the federal government helped farmers by buying and storing some of their crops. This did not succeed in keeping farm prices from falling further. Hoover also proposed the Reconstruction Finance Corporation (RFC) in 1931. The RFC made loans to banks, insurance firms, farm mortgage associations, and railroads to keep them going.

Still, Hoover drew the line at involving the federal government in the economy much more than that. He was opposed to having the federal government provide direct relief — that is, money or jobs — to the unemployed. He believed that providing relief was the job of private charities and local and state governments. If the federal government provided relief directly to the needy, these citizens, Hoover felt, would become too dependent on the government. They would lose their self-reliance. Private charities, however, had never before had to cope with so many needy people. They did not have enough money to do the job. And many city governments did not have the money to help.

In May 1932, many World War I veterans marched on Washington, D.C., to demand immediate payment of a promised bonus.
■ How do you think the veterans felt?

The Bonus Army   World War I veterans had been promised a bonus, or sum of extra money, for service to their country. The bonus was to be paid in 1944. The depression threw many of these men out of work. They felt they should get their bonuses right away, when they needed them most. More than 15,000 veterans marched on Washington, D.C., to make their demands heard. In tents and hastily built shacks, they camped near the Capitol.

When Congress refused their demands, most of the veterans gave up and returned home. About 2,000 veterans, wives, and children remained, though.

Fearing they would cause trouble, President Hoover ordered the army to remove them. Led by General Douglas MacArthur, soldiers used tear gas to drive out the campers and then set their shacks afire. Pictures of the fleeing veterans appeared in papers all over the country. President Hoover's popularity sank lower than ever.

Getting Ready for the 1932 Election
Faced with the worst depression in the nation's history, Republicans knew they had an uphill fight to win the 1932 election. They picked Hoover to run again. The Democratic choice was Governor Franklin D. Roosevelt of New York.

The day after the Democratic convention in Chicago chose Roosevelt as its candidate, he made a dramatic break with tradition. Until then, candidates had not attended conventions. It was customary for a delegation from the party to call on the candidate at his home and tell him of his nomination — which he had known about all the time, of course. But Roosevelt flew from Albany, New York, to Chicago to accept the nomination in person.

He intended his trip to be a symbol. "Let it be from now on the task of our party to break foolish traditions," he said to the wildly cheering convention.

CHECKUP

1. What caused the stock market crash of 1929?
2. What were some of the weaknesses in the American economy that helped bring on the Great Depression?
3. How were businesses and farmers affected by the depression?
4. What steps did President Hoover take to fight the Great Depression?
5. **Thinking Critically** How are overproduction and unemployment related to each other?

The New Deal

What were some of the New Deal measures to deal with the Great Depression?

Another Roosevelt Judging by his family background and upbringing, Franklin D. Roosevelt seemed a most unlikely person to be breaking with traditions. The Roosevelts had lived in America for nine generations, since the middle of the seventeenth century. Franklin grew up with all the advantages of wealth. He attended private schools and traveled to Europe eight times before he was 14 years old. He was a distant cousin of President Theodore Roosevelt, and he married the President's niece, Eleanor. But unlike Theodore, who headed a Republican administration, Franklin was a Democrat.

Franklin Roosevelt had entered politics in 1910 as a Democratic member of New York's state legislature. He then served in Woodrow Wilson's administration as assistant secretary of the navy. Mainly because he carried the famous Roosevelt name, the Democratic party nominated him for Vice President in 1920. The Roosevelt name proved to be of little help, however, in the first postwar election. That was the year of Republican Warren Harding's landslide victory.

Roosevelt's life was changed when he was stricken with polio in 1921. For many months he was bedridden. Never again was he able to walk without the aid of crutches and braces. At the age of 39, his political career seemed ended. But with help from his wife, Franklin Roosevelt fought back. Some believe that this experience gave him a deeper understanding of less fortunate people who had to struggle every day with life's setbacks.

After several years of rebuilding his muscles, Roosevelt renewed his activity in politics. Eleanor attended meetings for him and helped to keep his name before the public. In 1928, Roosevelt was elected

Franklin D. Roosevelt poses with his wife and his mother on inauguration day, 1933. ■ In what year was he first elected President?

623

governor of New York. He proved to be able and popular, and in 1930 he was re-elected by a large margin.

The Election of 1932 Franklin Roosevelt was conservative in many ways. However, during this terrible depression he believed that times called for change and for new ideas. When campaigning for the presidential nomination in 1932, he said:

> The country demands bold, persistent experimentation. It is common sense to take a method and try it. If it fails, admit it frankly and try another. But above all, try something.

In accepting the Democratic nomination, Roosevelt told the delegates, "I pledge you, I pledge myself, to a new deal for the American people." The phrase **New Deal** came to stand for his administration.

President Hoover believed that his own policies were best for the nation. He warned that if Roosevelt and the Democrats were elected, "the grass will grow in the streets of a hundred cities, a thousand towns; the weeds will overrun the fields of millions of farms." But the American people wanted a change. In the election of 1932, Roosevelt got 23 million votes to Hoover's 16 million. Roosevelt was the victor in 43 of the 48 states.

Dealing with the Banking Crisis By the time Roosevelt was inaugurated on March 4, 1933, the depression had worsened. Unemployment climbed toward the 15-million mark. Despite this, Roosevelt struck a note of confidence as he addressed the nation by radio. "This great nation will endure as it has endured, will revive and prosper," he said. He assured his listeners that "the only thing we have to fear is fear itself." He said that the nation wanted "action, and action now." (See Primary Source Reading, facing page.)

President Roosevelt's first action dealt with the banking crisis. As the depression continued, more and more banks had failed, and people who had deposited money in the banks lost all their savings. By early 1933, people were in a panic. They rushed to banks to take out their savings. This caused still more banks to run out of money and close.

Hours after taking the oath of office, President Roosevelt declared a **bank holiday**. All banks in the country would be closed. He then called Congress into a special session to pass an emergency banking bill. The bill provided that government experts would examine the records of each bank and allow only the healthy ones to reopen. It was passed and signed into law in just 8 hours.

Hundreds of worried depositors, fearing a bank failure, wait to withdraw their savings. ■ What is the name of the bank shown in the photograph?

FDR's First Inaugural Address

Franklin D. Roosevelt took office on March 4, 1933, at one of the gloomiest times in the nation's history. Banks were closing all over the country. Thousands of farmers were going broke. Record numbers of Americans were out of work. Millions were ready to give up hope. The new President knew that the times called for dramatic action. In his first inaugural address, he promised just that kind of action. He stepped to the microphone on that March day and brought to the American people a message of hope.

This is preeminently the time to speak the truth, the whole truth, frankly and boldly. Nor need we shrink from honestly facing conditions in our country today. This great nation will endure as it has endured, will revive and will prosper. So, first of all, let me assert my firm belief that the only thing we have to fear is fear itself — nameless, unreasoning, unjustified terror which paralyzes needed efforts to convert retreat into advance. . . .

I am prepared under my constitutional duty to recommend the measures that a stricken nation in the midst of a stricken world may require. These measures, or such other measures as the Congress may build out of its experience and wisdom, I shall seek, within my constitutional authority, to bring to speedy adoption.

But in the event that the Congress shall fail to take one of these two courses, and in the event that the national emergency is still critical, I shall not evade the clear course of duty that will then confront me. I shall ask the Congress for the one remaining instrument to meet the crisis — broad executive power to wage a war against the emergency, as great as the power that would be given to me if we were in fact invaded by a foreign foe.

USING SOURCE MATERIAL

1. What kind of fear was Roosevelt referring to in the first paragraph?
2. What are the "two courses" Roosevelt refers to at the opening of the third paragraph?
3. What does Roosevelt compare the emergency to at the end of the third paragraph? Why do you think he chose this comparison?

On Sunday evening, March 12, Roosevelt spoke to the American people over the radio in the first of his many **fireside chats**—radio reports to the American people. In a reassuring voice he explained what the government was doing about the banking crisis. "I can assure you," he said confidently, "that it is safer to keep your money in a reopened bank than under your mattress."

When the banks opened Monday morning, people were again standing in line. This time, however, most of them were putting money in. In a few days, most of the banks were open again. The banking crisis had passed.

Later, Congress approved insurance for deposits up to a certain amount. Even if a bank should fail, depositors would be able to get their money back.

The First Hundred Days Franklin D. Roosevelt—FDR, as the newspapers began to call him—moved quickly to follow up this first success. In the spring of 1933, he sent to Congress a flood of ideas for dealing with the depression. Congress acted on them in record time. In the first hundred days of the New Deal, 15 major laws were passed. Most of them dealt with the three R's of the New Deal—relief, recovery, and reform. Relief meant providing immediate help for the millions in need. Recovery meant helping businesses, farmers, and workers recover from the depression and get back to prosperity.

President Franklin Roosevelt talks to the nation in one of his fireside chats.
■ **How can you tell that this is a radio broadcast?**

A Civilian Conservation Corps (CCC) crew works on a land conservation project.
■ What is the bulldozer in the background used for?

Reform had to do with long-term change. The aim of reform was not only to prevent future depressions but also to better the lives of all Americans.

One of the first and most successful programs of the hundred days was the Civilian Conservation Corps (CCC). This program combined unemployment relief and conservation. The CCC hired 250,000 men between the ages of 18 and 25 to work on conservation projects in rural areas. They were all from needy families. These young men built wildlife shelters, fought forest fires, built reservoirs, stocked streams with fish, and planted trees. For this they received, in addition to room and meals, $30 a month. Of this amount, they were required to send $25 home to their families. Recruits could stay in the CCC for up to 2 years. Before the program ended in 1942, more than 2.5 million young men took part in it.

Other New Deal programs provided money and jobs for the unemployed. Under the Federal Emergency Relief Act (FERA), Congress sent $500 million to the states to give to the needy. The Public Works Administration (PWA) spent $3 billion over several years to hire people to build roads, bridges, dams, and government buildings. This was the first time the federal government had hired the unemployed directly. In still another program, the New Deal created temporary jobs for 4 million people to get them through the winter of 1933–1934.

Programs like the CCC, the FERA, and the PWA had several aims. By giving money to the needy and jobs to the unemployed, these programs provided relief. They also provided an inexpensive way to make many needed public improvements. And they were also meant to aid recovery, for as the people who received the money spent it, they would create jobs for others.

Aid for Agriculture

The New Deal's main effort to assist the farmers was the Agriculture Adjustment Act (AAA). Overproduction had caused farm prices to fall. Would not cutting down production cause farm prices to rise again? This was the idea behind the AAA.

In this program the government paid farmers *not* to plant crops on a part of their fields. Another program helped farmers get low-interest loans to meet their mortgage payments. This would help them keep their farms.

Businesses were proud to display the blue eagle, the emblem of the NRA.
■ **Why was "We Do Our Part" an appropriate slogan for the NRA?**

Helping Business and Workers

The main effort to bring about recovery in industry was the National Industrial Recovery Act (NIRA or NRA). Employers claimed that companies would hire back workers and start up production if they were allowed to ignore the antitrust laws. Then instead of having to compete, they could cooperate. They could prevent overproduction by agreeing to produce only a certain amount. They could prevent price-cutting and insure a profit by agreeing on how much to charge. The NRA gave business the right to do these things. In exchange, business was required to do certain things for its workers. Companies had to pay a fair minimum wage, agree on maximum hours, end child labor, and allow their workers to form unions.

The NRA was hailed as a great experiment when it first went into effect in June 1933. Parades and rallies were held to whip up public support. Businesses that pledged cooperation displayed the NRA symbol — a blue eagle with the words *We Do Our Part*.

Still, industrial recovery was disappointing. In a short time, both business and labor were complaining that the program did not work well for them. By the spring of 1935, the NRA was failing. The Supreme Court ended it by declaring that the law was unconstitutional.

The Tennessee Valley Authority

The most sweeping reform of the hundred days was the creation of the Tennessee Valley Authority (TVA). This was an attempt to plan the economic development of a whole region. The Tennessee Valley runs through parts of seven states in the Southeast. The 3.5 million people living in this region were among the poorest in the country. Their land was worn out by erosion. Frequent floods added to their misery.

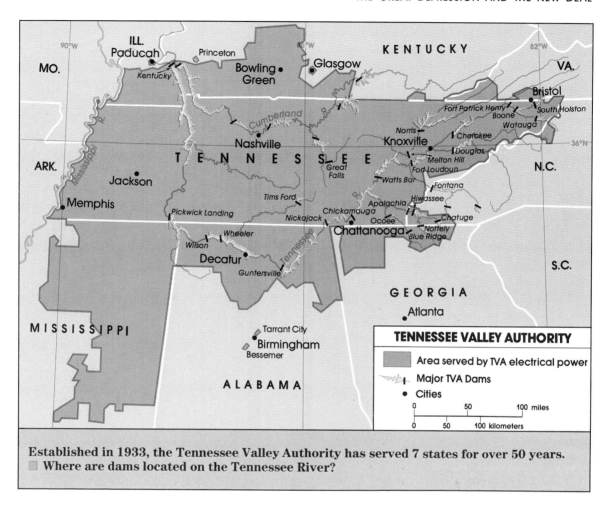

Established in 1933, the Tennessee Valley Authority has served 7 states for over 50 years. Where are dams located on the Tennessee River?

To control flooding, the Tennessee Valley Authority built 20 dams on the Tennessee River and the streams and small rivers that feed it. At many of these dams, waterpower produced electricity at low rates for the whole area. The TVA also planted millions of trees to help keep the soil from eroding or washing away during rainstorms.

The TVA was a remarkable success. Cheap electricity attracted businesses to the region. The standard of living was raised. Even so, critics said that the government should not be in the business of producing electricity. They felt that the government was competing unfairly with private electric companies.

Americans Approve The first 2 years of the New Deal brought encouraging signs. The number of unemployed people, though still high, had been reduced by 4 million. Farmers were doing better. New laws regulated the activity of the stock market and reformed the banking system. Perhaps most important, people seemed to have renewed faith in their government's ability to help them.

Not everyone agreed that FDR was on the right track, however. Some people believed that the New Deal was moving too slowly and not doing enough to restore prosperity. Others felt that it was changing too much too quickly. The second group included many business leaders.

They complained about the growth of government and government regulations.

In 1934, however, the majority of Americans gave a clear signal that they approved of the New Deal. In the congressional elections of that year, they elected more Democrats to Congress than had ever been elected in the nation's history.

Another New Law Encouraged by this show of support, Roosevelt proposed many other new laws in 1935 and 1936. One of these laws set up the Works Progress Administration (WPA). The WPA was an emergency program that gave jobs to 35 million unemployed persons. During the next half-dozen years, the WPA built or improved thousands of school buildings, more than 800 airports, and 500,000 miles (800,000 km) of roads.

The WPA also hired writers, actors, artists, and musicians. It brought art, theater, and musical concerts to people in large and small communities.

Social Security President Roosevelt regarded the **Social Security Act** as the most important new law of his administration. For the first time, the government provided help for people in their old age. During their working years, workers would be required to make contributions to a special insurance fund. These contributions were matched by employers. When the workers retired, they would receive monthly payments from this fund.

An artist working for the WPA painted this mural portraying workers on a WPA construction project. The entire mural now covers a wall in the headquarters of the United States Department of the Interior, in Washington, D.C.
■ What were the construction workers building?

The law had two other parts. One provided help for workers who became handicapped and could no longer work, and for children with no means of support. The other provided for unemployment insurance. Workers who lost their jobs would receive payments for a number of weeks while they looked for work.

The Wagner Act   Another major law, the Wagner Act, dealt with labor relations. You will recall that one part of the NRA gave workers the right to form unions. But the Supreme Court ruled that the NRA was unconstitutional, and the law was thrown out.

President Roosevelt then gave his backing to a bill sponsored by New York

Senator Robert Wagner. This bill guaranteed workers the right to join unions and practice **collective bargaining**. In collective bargaining a union represents the workers and bargains for them with the employer for better wages, hours, and working conditions. The Wagner Act also prohibited employers from interfering with the efforts of workers to form unions.

The Election of 1936   When Roosevelt ran for reelection in 1936, he could point to many gains in the fight against the Great Depression. He and the Democratic party overwhelmed the Republican party and its candidate, Governor Alfred Landon of Kansas. Roosevelt won more than 60 percent of the votes and carried every state except Maine and Vermont.

At the start of his second term in 1937, FDR was at the height of his popularity. Yet hardly a year later the New Deal was in retreat, and Roosevelt was on the defensive against his critics. What had happened to reverse the President's fortunes?

The Supreme Court Controversy   The President himself created opposition to his administration by trying to change the membership of the Supreme Court. That Court had declared other New Deal programs unconstitutional besides the NRA. Roosevelt feared that if the Court went on to declare such laws as the Wagner Act and the Social Security Act unconstitutional, much of the New Deal would be undone.

All the justices on the Supreme Court were elderly. Roosevelt believed that many of them held old-fashioned ideas about the Constitution. He asked Congress to pass a law giving him power to appoint one new justice for every old one who did not retire at the age of 70. This would have allowed Roosevelt to appoint 6 new justices immediately.

President Roosevelt's plan for expanding the Supreme Court by six justices inspired this cartoon.
■ Why do the six new justices all look alike?

Roosevelt's proposal led to a storm of protest. He was accused of trying to pack the Court with his own supporters. The plan made Roosevelt appear power-hungry. Furthermore, the Court undercut Roosevelt's arguments when it ruled that both the Wagner Act and the Social Security Act were, in fact, constitutional. The court-packing plan was not adopted and Roosevelt lost much public support.

Decline of the New Deal Then, late in 1937, the economy went into a tailspin again. Farm prices fell, and unemployment climbed. Many critics blamed this slowdown on New Deal policies. Opposition grew in Congress, and from that time on, few Roosevelt proposals were enacted. Still, Roosevelt's foes were unable to do away with the earlier reforms.

The last important New Deal social reform approved by Congress was the Fair Labor Standards Act of 1938. This law created the first national minimum wage, set the maximum number of work hours that could be required of a worker at 40 per week, and abolished child labor. But by the end of 1938, the New Deal was for all intents and purposes over.

CHECKUP

1. How did President Franklin Roosevelt deal with the banking crisis?
2. What was done under the Social Security Act?
3. What factors brought the New Deal to an end?
4. **Thinking Critically** Explain how each of the following New Deal programs provides at least one of the New Deal's three R's, *relief, recovery,* or *reform:* CCC, FERA, PWA, AAA, NRA, TVA, WPA, Social Security Act, Wagner Act, Fair Labor Standards Act of 1938.

Hard Times

What was life like for Americans during the Great Depression?

Getting Along Most Americans were scarred by the Great Depression in one way or another. Millions who had once earned a living for their families now felt shame and a loss of self-respect because they could not find jobs. Millions more who still had jobs lived in constant fear of losing them. With the future so uncertain, young people postponed marriage. Families cut down expenses. They did without the daily newspaper, put off repairs on the car, and decided against using the doctor or the dentist. They found inexpensive ways to entertain themselves. Families gathered around the table to play the newest game, Monopoly. Or they listened to the radio, which brought entertainment into their homes. The main expense for entertainment outside their homes was the 15¢ admission to the movies. Some 85 million Americans went to the movies every week and, at least for a while, escaped from the realities of the depression.

With few jobs available, young people stayed in school and continued their education. A special New Deal program, the National Youth Administration, provided part-time work for many students.

Alexandre Hogue painted this view of a farming region that was devastated by drought.
■ Why might the family have abandoned this farm?

Dallas Museum of Art, Dallas Art Association Purchase.

The Plight of the Farmers   Poverty in rural America was just as serious. Hundreds of owners of small farms lost their land, their buildings, everything. By the end of the Great Depression, nearly half of all farmers in the United States were tenant farmers — people who worked land that belonged to someone else. In the South, sharecroppers and migrant workers struggled along on an income less than $300 a year.

Among the people hit hardest were those who lived on the western part of the Great Plains. This belt of land stretches from South Dakota through Kansas, Colorado, and Oklahoma, and on down to the plains of Texas and northeastern New Mexico. For several years this region experienced terrible droughts. The soil turned to dust. Beginning in 1933, high winds swept the dust across the open plains, whipping it into great clouds that darkened the sky. One observer reported:

> When the wind died and the sun shone forth again, it was on a different world. There were no fields, only sand drifting into mounds . . . In the farmyard, fences, machinery, and trees were gone, buried. The roofs of sheds stuck out through drifts deeper than a man is tall.

That winter, dust from western farms settled on the snow that covered New England farms 1,000 miles (1,600 km) away.

Dust storms continued for several years, giving to the region the name **Dust Bowl**. One farmer, watching a storm from his window, said that he was "counting the Kansas farms as they came by."

With their farms gone, thousands of people piled their old trucks and cars high with mattresses, furniture, pots and pans,

Families from all over the Dust Bowl packed their belongings and headed for California to start new lives.
■ **How was this family traveling to California?**

and a suitcase or two, and headed west. There they hoped to make a fresh start. Many wound up in California and became migrant workers, living in roadside camps.

Blacks and the New Deal   Black people were hit especially hard by the Great Depression. In good times they could at least get certain low-level jobs that whites did not want. But in the depression even these jobs were in demand, and many of them went to whites. The unemployment rate among blacks was twice that of whites.

About 80 percent of black Americans still lived in the South, most of them in rural areas. There, two thirds of the black farmers who raised cotton made no money at all from their crops. Many of them survived mainly by raising vegetables and hunting rabbits and other small game.

Overall, however, the relief and welfare programs of the New Deal helped millions of black Americans. In addition, President Roosevelt appointed a number of blacks to important positions in government. He named William Hastie to a federal judgeship and Robert Weaver to an important post in the Department of the Interior. Mary McLeod Bethune became a special adviser on minority affairs. These officials and others came to be known as the Black Cabinet. They often met together and spoke up for the interests of black people.

Eleanor Roosevelt also worked to end discrimination against blacks and other minorities. In 1939 the Daughters of the American Revolution refused to let a black opera singer, Marian Anderson, sing in the concert hall they owned in Washington, D.C. Mrs. Roosevelt promptly resigned from the organization and arranged for Anderson's concert to be given on the steps of the Lincoln Memorial. More than

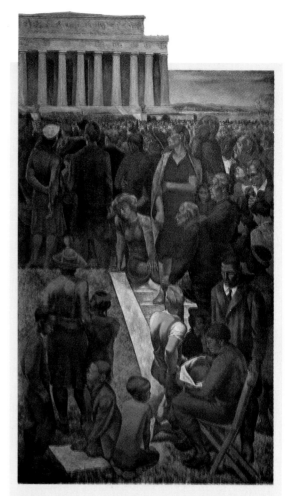

Thousands of people heard Marian Anderson sing at the Lincoln Memorial in 1939.
▪ What was rare about this crowd in 1939?

75,000 people attended to show their support. Some regard the Anderson concert as one of the first modern civil rights demonstrations.

Most black people clearly felt they had gained from the New Deal. In 1928 the great majority of black voters supported the Republican party. But in 1936 a large majority voted for the Democrats.

Mexican Americans in the Depression
The number of immigrants from Mexico had grown in the 1920s. Most worked on farms in the Southwest.

Some federal and state officials decided to reduce the number of people seeking jobs by sending Mexicans back to

Mexico. From 1930 to 1940, between a quarter million and a half million Mexicans—no one knows for sure how many—were forced to go back to Mexico. Most of these people were Mexican citizens. Some of the younger people, though, had been born in the United States and were American citizens.

Indians in the Depression   Of all the minorities, Native Americans had the hardest time during the Great Depression. Their unemployment rate was three times that of the nation as a whole. They had lower incomes than other Americans—an average of only $48 a year. Moreover, they received less schooling and died younger than other Americans. Most New Deal relief and recovery programs did not help them.

The New Deal did, however, make an important change in government policy toward the Indians. The old policy of breaking up Indian lands and giving the land to individual Indians to farm had proved to be a failure. It was also destroying Indian culture. The Indian Reorganization Act of 1934 ended the breakup of Indian reservations into small pieces of land. It also allowed tribes to have more say over their future, and so allowed them greater cultural pride.

Women in the Depression   Women, too, could point to some gains during the New Deal. President Roosevelt appointed Frances Perkins as secretary of labor. She was the first woman Cabinet officer. Secretary Perkins was responsible for the report that led to the Social Security Act. Eleanor Roosevelt worked tirelessly to advance women's rights. Partly due to her influence, President Roosevelt appointed more than 100 women to high positions.

Frances Perkins was secretary of labor throughout Roosevelt's presidency. She was the first woman to serve in the Cabinet.
■ What kind of job do the men in this photograph have?

For the great majority of American women, however, nothing much changed during the Great Depression and the New Deal. They continued to face job discrimination. For example, women made up 80 percent of the schoolteachers but less than 2 percent of the principals and school superintendents. In some school systems, women teachers who married were forced to give up their jobs. In general, women continued to earn less money than men for the same type of work.

Labor in the Depression   During the Great Depression, one of the big changes in America was the growth of unions. The American Federation of Labor had long been based on the idea of trade unionism. (See page 499.) Trade unions, however, left out the millions who worked on factory assembly lines and in other jobs that did not call for special skills. Some union leaders thought workers in the same industry, whatever their jobs, should be brought into one union, called an **industrial union**. John L. Lewis, head of the United Mine Workers, was one leader who favored this course.

Most AFL leaders were opposed to industrial unionism. In 1935, Lewis and others broke away from the AFL and formed what later came to be called the **Congress of Industrial Organizations** (CIO). They organized workers in America's basic industries — steel, autos, rubber, textiles, and so on. Usually, employers did not agree to recognize these unions and bargain with them until after long and bitter strikes. In some such strikes, the workers introduced a new tactic: the sit-down strike. Workers would stay in the plant during their strike instead of picketing outside. This prevented the company from bringing in strikebreakers to replace union members.

The Butler Institute of American Art, Youngstown, Ohio.

The 1930s were important years for labor unions. They gained the right to strike.
■ **Which person in the painting shows the workers' right to strike?**

By the end of the 1930s, some 8.5 million American workers belonged to unions —an increase of 100 percent in just 5 years. All of America's major industries had been unionized.

CHECKUP

1. Why was the western part of the Great Plains hit so hard by the depression?
2. What steps were taken to help black people under the New Deal?
3. How did other minority groups fare under the New Deal?
4. What changes came about in labor unions during the 1930s?
5. **Thinking Critically** Why do you think hard times were especially hard for members of minority groups during the Great Depression?

Using the Dictionary

DEFINITIONS

Many words have more than one meaning and can be used in different contexts. Think of all the ways you can use the word *run*. You run, or move rapidly, from one place to another. Politicians run for office. Workers run machines. A person who spends more than he or she earns will soon run into debt. A baseball player crossing home plate scores a run. Some dictionaries have more than 50 definitions of the word *run*.

When you look up a word in a dictionary, you can expect to find many definitions. The one you will want is the one that will make sense in your sentence. For example, look at this sentence using the word *platform*. "The Republican party platform in 1924 favored high tariffs, lower taxes, and a continuation of prohibition." Here is one dictionary's entry for the word *platform*.

   plat·form (plat′ fôrm), *n.* **1.** a raised level surface or structure formed with planks,

boards, or the like. **2.** the walk between or beside the tracks of a railroad station. **3.** *U.S.* the floor beyond the inside doors at either end of a railroad passenger car; vestibule. **4.** a piece of raised flooring, in a hall or in the open air, from which a speaker addresses his audience. **5.** a plan of action or statement of the beliefs of a group, especially a statement of the beliefs of a political party at a convention where a candidate is nominated.

How many definitions of *platform* do you see? Which is the definition intended by the sentence?

SKILLS PRACTICE I

A number of terms used in Chapter 26 are listed below. After each term are descriptions of two or three people who might mean very different things when they use that term. Find these words in your dictionary. Then, on a separate sheet of paper, write the definition that each of these people would most likely have in mind.

   1. Depression (an economist, a psychiatrist, a road engineer)
   2. Strike (a gold miner, a baseball player, a labor union organizer)
   3. Crash (an airplane pilot, a stockbroker, an uninvited guest)
   4. Cabinet (a carpenter, the President of the United States)
   5. Stock (a cattle rancher, an investor, a department store manager)

SKILLS PRACTICE II

Select four of the words above and use them in sentences. Make sure your sentences show that you understand the definition you are using for each word.

MAIN IDEAS

1. A stock market crash, largely caused by reckless speculation, ushered in the worst depression in the nation's history.
2. In his first hundred days in office, Franklin D. Roosevelt sent Congress a flood of proposals for relief, recovery, and reform, and Congress quickly adopted them.
3. By providing social security, unemployment insurance, and jobs for the unemployed, the federal government accepted responsibility for the welfare of citizens.
4. Despite the success of a number of its programs, the New Deal failed to bring an end to the Great Depression.

VOCABULARY REVIEW

Write the sentences below on a separate sheet of paper and fill in the blanks. To help you, the first letter of the word or words to be filled in is shown.

1. Stocks are traded in a s_____ m_____.
2. If a corporation earns profits, d_____ may be paid on its stock.
3. The supply of merchandise, or goods, a store has on hand to sell is its i_____.
4. When nominated for President, Franklin D. Roosevelt promised "a N_____ D_____ for the American people."
5. The 4-day period in 1933 during which all banks were closed for inspection was called a b_____ h_____.
6. A drought on the Great Plains caused a large part of that region to become known as the D_____ B_____.
7. Roosevelt called each of his radio reports to the American people a f_____ c_____.
8. The program that provided funds for workers who retired or became handicapped was called s_____ s_____.
9. When union representatives negotiate with employers on wages and working conditions, they are involved in c_____ b_____.
10. In the 1930s, John L. Lewis and others organized workers into i_____ u_____.

CHAPTER CHECKUP

1. How did each of the following help bring on the Great Depression: (**a**) speculation, (**b**) overproduction of goods, (**c**) a high tariff, (**d**) surplus farm crops?
2. What does it mean to say that Roosevelt's New Deal programs dealt with *relief, recovery,* and *reform*?
3. What were the provisions of the Wagner Act and the Fair Labor Standards Act of 1938?
4. Why did Roosevelt want to change the number of Supreme Court justices? What was the result of his proposal?
5. How did the CIO differ from the AFL?
6. **Thinking Critically** How did Hoover's approach to the Great Depression differ from Roosevelt's?
7. **Thinking Critically** Why were the American people ready to accept a strong role for government in the economy during the New Deal?
8. **Thinking Critically** Why did the American people reelect Roosevelt overwhelmingly in 1936, even though the depression was still going on?

APPLYING KNOWLEDGE

1. Find out how the Twentieth Amendment to the Constitution changed elections. Be prepared to report your findings to the class.
2. In your community, interview people who lived through the Great Depression. Ask them what they remember about it. Record your information. Compare it with the information your classmates collect.
3. Two songs that were popular during the Great Depression are "Brother, Can You Spare a Dime?" and "Happy Days Are Here Again." Find the words to the songs. If you or any of your classmates play musical instruments, perhaps you can give a performance of one of the songs. What point is each song trying to make?

27 *World War II*

1939–1945

The Rise of the Dictators

How did World War II get started?

A General Offers a Challenge To the representative from Virginia, the witness's ideas about the use of airplanes in war were untested theory, and he said so. The witness was General William "Billy" Mitchell of the Air Service of the United States Army. Mitchell had claimed that with an airplane he could "destroy or sink any ship in existence." Now, in 1921, he was testifying before a committee of Congress. Making a claim was one thing, said the doubting lawmaker. Proving it was another. This was the chance Mitchell had waited for. "Give us the warships to attack and come watch it," he challenged.

Mitchell had joined the army at the age of 18. He became interested in airplanes and in 1916 learned to fly. After watching British night bombers take off for strikes behind enemy lines in World War I, Mitchell wrote: "I am sure the future will see operations conducted in this way by thousands of planes." He himself later led two such operations.

After the war, General Mitchell tried to persuade top military leaders that the airplane would change warfare. The target, he said, would no longer be the enemy's armies but its industries, supplies, transportation, and cities. By dealing crippling blows beyond the battlefield, airplanes would leave armies helpless. As for battleships, the airplane made them outdated. To develop air power for the next war, Mitchell said, an air force command separate from the army and the navy was needed.

Most generals and admirals, however, saw the airplane as just another weapon to be used by the army and the navy in their regular operations. Unable to persuade his superiors, Billy Mitchell took his case to the public. He gave speeches, wrote magazine articles, and testified before Congress. Now, in 1921, he would have the chance to prove his case.

A German battleship that had been surrendered after World War I was towed to a point about 60 miles (100 km) off the Virginia coast. The battleship was supposed to be unsinkable. With members of the Cabinet and Congress watching, Mitchell's planes swooped down and dropped their bombs. Some 20 minutes later, the battleship lay at the bottom of the ocean.

American bombers take off from an airfield in England, bound for German-held territory.
■ Why are the farmers with haywagons so close to the planes?

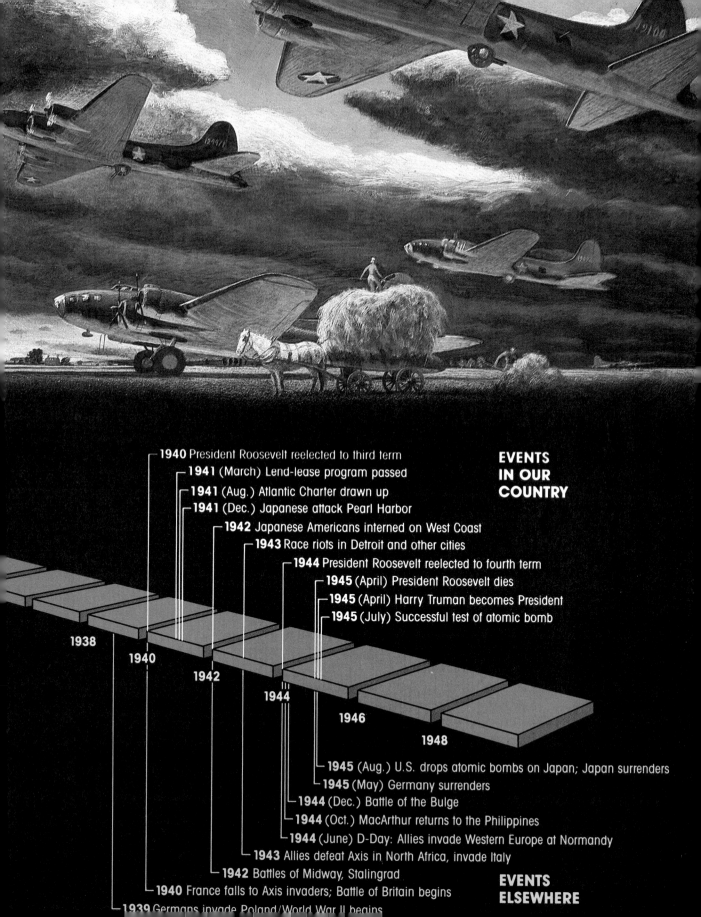

EVENTS IN OUR COUNTRY

1940 President Roosevelt reelected to third term
1941 (March) Lend-lease program passed
1941 (Aug.) Atlantic Charter drawn up
1941 (Dec.) Japanese attack Pearl Harbor
1942 Japanese Americans interned on West Coast
1943 Race riots in Detroit and other cities
1944 President Roosevelt reelected to fourth term
1945 (April) President Roosevelt dies
1945 (April) Harry Truman becomes President
1945 (July) Successful test of atomic bomb

1938
1940
1942
1944
1946
1948

1945 (Aug.) U.S. drops atomic bombs on Japan; Japan surrenders
1945 (May) Germany surrenders
1944 (Dec.) Battle of the Bulge
1944 (Oct.) MacArthur returns to the Philippines
1944 (June) D-Day: Allies invade Western Europe at Normandy
1943 Allies defeat Axis in North Africa, invade Italy
1942 Battles of Midway, Stalingrad
1940 France falls to Axis invaders; Battle of Britain begins
1939 Germans invade Poland/World War II begins

EVENTS ELSEWHERE

Mitchell Fails to Convince Many military leaders still were not convinced. The test had not taken place under true battle conditions, they noted. Mitchell, regarded as a troublemaker, was sent on a long inspection tour of other countries. In 1924, after visiting Asia, Mitchell wrote a report predicting a Japanese attack on the American naval base at Pearl Harbor, Hawaii. Waves of planes launched from aircraft carriers would strike some morning at about 7:30, he wrote. The army said Mitchell's report was "unsound" and put it aside. Mitchell kept criticizing the leadership of the army and the navy publicly. In 1925 he was suspended from duty. A year later he resigned from the army. He died 10 years later, in 1936.

Democracy Loses Out At least part of Billy Mitchell's message was eventually heeded by the United States. The nation did not spend much for arms in the 1920s and 1930s, but the army and the navy did begin to give greater attention to the need for bombers and aircraft carriers. It was a good thing they did, for in the 1930s the world was once again becoming a dangerous place. In many countries, democracy was being replaced by **totalitarian** governments — governments with total power over the people. In a democracy, government is the servant of the people. Under a totalitarian government the people exist to serve the state. Free elections, free speech, free press — all are ended.

Most totalitarian governments were headed by a **dictator**, or an all-powerful ruler. Such dictators rose to power by promising jobs and national glory to the people. They glorified war and force.

Fascists, Nazis, and Communists Italy faced depression and unemployment after World War I. The government was

Benito Mussolini and Adolf Hitler destroyed democracy and set up dictatorships in their countries.
■ **What country did each man head?**

weak. Many Italians also felt that their country did not receive all it should have from the peace treaty. Taking advantage of these grievances, a teacher, writer, and soldier named Benito Mussolini (bə nē′ tō mü sə lē′ nē) and his Fascist (fash′ ist) party took power in 1922. Calling democracy "a rotting corpse," Mussolini established a dictatorship in Italy.

In Germany a weak democratic government that had been set up after the war could not weather the storm of the depression. Many Germans also felt bitter about the peace terms that had been forced on their country in the Treaty of Versailles. Adolf Hitler, a former army corporal, blamed Germany's defeat on enemies within the country — weak old leaders, Communists, and, especially,

Jews. Hitler was a man consumed by hatred. One historian has written, "He hated the Jews, he hated democracy, he hated the Christian religion in which he was reared. . . . " In the 1920s he developed a twisted philosophy that proclaimed the German people to be a "master race" who would one day control all of Europe.

In the 1920s few Germans paid much attention to Hitler and his followers, called Nazis. With the start of a depression in 1930, however, his message began to attract Germans. In 1933, Adolf Hitler became chancellor, or prime minister, of Germany. Within a year he threw out the German constitution and made himself dictator. He began to build up Germany's military forces, even though this had been forbidden by the Treaty of Versailles. He also took Germany out of the League of Nations. And he introduced laws that took away most legal rights of German Jews.

Following the Communist revolution of 1917, Russia changed its name to the Union of Soviet Socialist Republics (U.S.S.R.), or the Soviet Union. Its head, V. I. Lenin, proclaimed the Communist goal of worldwide revolution. After Lenin's death in 1924, Joseph Stalin succeeded him as the Soviet dictator.

On the other side of the world, generals and admirals were gaining control of the government in Japan. Japan was a growing industrial nation. To get the coal, oil, and other raw materials it needed, and also to win glory, Japan's military sought control of eastern Asia.

The Axis Powers Japan was the first of these countries to break the peace. In 1931 its army invaded Manchuria, a northern province of China. In less than a year, Manchuria was brought under Japanese control. The League of Nations made only a weak protest. Japan responded by withdrawing from the league.

Four years later, in 1935, the Italians under Benito Mussolini invaded the North African country of Ethiopia. The invasion brought an immediate appeal from Ethiopia to the League of Nations. Again the league failed to stop an attack. Ethiopia was soon conquered, and Mussolini pulled Italy out of the league. It was now plain to see that the world organization could not curb aggression.

In 1936 it was Hitler's turn. He sent German troops into the Rhineland, a part of Germany that bordered on France. Under the Treaty of Versailles, the Rhineland was to have remained **demilitarized** —that is, no soldiers or weapons were to be stationed in the area. Again nations protested, but again to no avail.

Until 1936 each of these militaristic nations acted on its own. In that year,

The military leaders of Japan wanted their country to control eastern Asia.
◾ Did the person who draw this cartoon support, or oppose, Japan's actions?

Mussolini and Hitler signed a treaty of alliance. Mussolini boasted that from that moment on, the world would turn on the axis between Rome and Berlin, the capitals of the two countries. For this reason, Italy and Germany were called the **Axis powers**. Later that year the two countries signed a treaty of cooperation with Japan. Eventually the three became military allies as well, forming a Rome-Berlin-Tokyo axis.

America Tries to Stay Neutral Americans watched these events with growing concern. They were determined to have no part of another war. Americans had shed their blood in the last one, yet the world was no safer for democracy. Furthermore, with the coming of a worldwide depression, European countries had stopped paying their war debts to the United States. That led to more bad feelings between the former allies.

Between 1935 and 1937, Congress passed several laws intended to keep America from being drawn into war. These laws were called the **Neutrality Acts**. One law prohibited the sale of arms to countries at war. Another forbade Americans to lend money to warring countries or to travel on their ships. A third law said that countries at war could not buy goods from the United States on credit. They had to pay for the goods in advance and then carry them away in their own ships.

The Good Neighbor Policy Meanwhile, the United States attempted to improve relations with the other countries of the Western Hemisphere. President Hoover had made a start on this with a goodwill tour of Latin America. President Roosevelt continued these efforts. His policy, he said, would be one of "the good

On his return from Casablanca, President Roosevelt (left) stops to visit Brazil's President Getulio Vargas (holding cane). ▪ What tells you they are getting along fine?

neighbor—the neighbor who . . . respects himself, and because he does so, respects the rights of others."

United States troops were withdrawn from Nicaragua and from Haiti, the last two Latin American countries in which they had been stationed. The United States also gave up its right to intervene in Cuba, which it had been allowed to do by a 1903 treaty. And it joined other Western Hemisphere countries in agreeing that "no state [nation] has a right to intervene in the internal or external affairs of another." From these changes the United States reaped a harvest of goodwill. When war finally came, almost every country in the hemisphere stood side by side with the United States.

The Road to War   Meanwhile, the armies of the dictators continued to march. In 1937, Japan started a full-scale war against China. Japanese planes destroyed railroads, supplies, and cities, just as General Mitchell had predicted. In Europe, Hitler pushed ahead with his goal of conquest. He claimed that his only aim was to bring together all German people under one flag. In 1938, Nazi troops took over the German-speaking country of Austria without a fight.

Later that year, Hitler demanded that Czechoslovakia hand over a part of its country — the Sudetenland (sü dāt′ ən land).

About 3 million German-speaking people lived there, along with many others. Czechoslovakia prepared to fight. The leaders of France and Britain knew that if war came, their countries would be drawn in. In September 1938 they met with Hitler in the German city of Munich and bowed to his demands. Left alone, Czechoslovakia had no choice but to yield. We know today from German records that if Britain and France had not given in, German generals were planning to remove Hitler from power.

Hitler had told Great Britain and France that the Sudetenland would be the

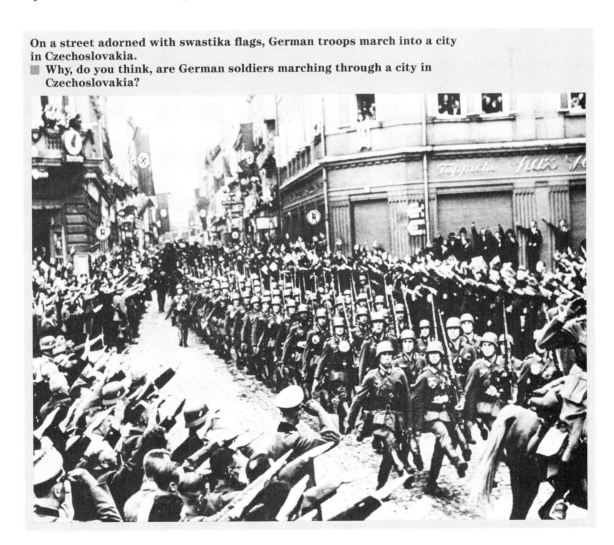

On a street adorned with swastika flags, German troops march into a city in Czechoslovakia.
■ Why, do you think, are German soldiers marching through a city in Czechoslovakia?

The German invasion of Poland included the first aerial bombing of cities in history. Warsaw and other cities were devastated.
■ **What was the purpose of such attacks on civilian targets?**

last territory he would demand in Europe. But 6 months later his armies seized the rest of Czechoslovakia without firing a single shot.

Britain and France now saw that they would have to rearm quickly. When Hitler demanded territory from Poland and threatened to attack, Britain and France promised to come to Poland's aid. Hitler was not to be stopped, however. First he made sure that if Britain and France went to war against Germany, the Germans would not have to fight the Soviet Union at the same time. In August 1939, Germany and the Soviet Union—who had been sworn enemies—stunned the world by signing a treaty in which they agreed not to attack each other. In a secret part of the deal, they also agreed to divide Poland between them, and Germany agreed to let the

Soviets take over the Baltic countries of Estonia, Lithuania, and Latvia.

Now the way was clear. On September 1, 1939, German planes, tanks, and troops attacked Poland. Two days later, Britain and France declared war on Germany. World War II had begun.

CHECKUP

1. How did the totalitarian governments that came to power in the 1930s differ from democratic governments?
2. What aggressive actions had Japan, Italy, and Germany taken by 1936?
3. What did Congress do to try to keep the United States out of war?
4. What events brought on war in Europe?
5. **Thinking Critically** Why, do you think, did so many people in Germany, Italy, and Japan support dictators?

The United States Enters the War

What finally brought the United States into World War II?

France Falls   Hitler's armies moved with such swiftness and force in September 1939 that their attack was called a **blitzkrieg**, which is German for "lightning war." Planes struck at cities, railroads, and highways as well as at Polish troops. Tanks rolled over Polish positions before Poland's army could adjust. In less than a month, Poland fell. Soon after, the Soviet Union invaded Finland and took a large piece of that nation.

During the fall and winter, a quiet settled over the battlefronts. But in the spring of 1940, Nazi armies struck again with fury. In April they invaded Denmark and Norway. In May, Hitler's armies attacked the Netherlands and Belgium without warning and conquered both countries in a few days. From Belgium the Germans wheeled into northern France. The sudden attack trapped the British and French armies with their backs to the sea, at a place called Dunkirk. Waves of bombers and fighter planes battered the troops. They were saved only by the greatest rescue operation in history. In boats of every size and description, people from English coastal villages crossed the English Channel and ferried the soldiers to England.

There was now no way to save France. Early in June, Italy invaded France from the south. On June 22, 1940, France surrendered. Britain now stood alone, the last democracy among Europe's major powers.

The American Response   The speed of Hitler's victories in Europe shocked Americans. At President Roosevelt's urging, the Congress spent billions of dollars to build up the country's military strength. It also passed the country's first peacetime draft law.

Meanwhile a debate grew over aid to Britain. On one side were the people who said that the best way to protect the United States was to help Britain with all possible aid short of going to war against the Axis powers. This was President Roosevelt's belief. On the other side were the people who said that helping Britain probably

Members of the America First Committee opposed American involvement in the war. How are these women showing their opposition to the war?

would draw the United States into war. Those who held this view were called **isolationists**. The leading isolationist group was the America First Committee. Its speakers, such as Charles A. Lindbergh, argued that the United States should stay out of the conflict and create a "Fortress America" that the Axis would not attack.

As the country rearmed, the presidential election of 1940 took place. Roosevelt ran for a third term — something no President had ever before won — and was reelected easily.

Lend-lease By the end of 1940, Britain was running out of money with which to buy arms from the United States. President Roosevelt proposed that the United States lend Britain the weapons it needed. Congress passed this program, called **lend-lease**, in the spring of 1941. By summer the United States, still officially neutral in the war, was also sending lend-lease aid to the Soviet Union. This was because Hitler, ignoring the treaty he had signed in 1939, suddenly attacked the Soviets on June 22, 1941.

Later that summer, President Roosevelt and Winston Churchill, the British prime minister, met on a ship off Newfoundland. There they drew up the **Atlantic Charter**, a statement of shared aims for the postwar world. The two agreed that their countries would work for the defeat of "Nazi tyranny," for a lasting peace, and for the right of all peoples to choose their

The Japanese surprise attack on the naval base at Pearl Harbor, Hawaii, on December 7, 1941, brought the United States into the war. (21°N/158°W; map, p. 657)

own form of government. By this time, American naval vessels were protecting American and British merchant ships as they carried war goods across the Atlantic Ocean. In the fall these American warships and German submarines were firing at each other. The United States was edging closer and closer to war.

The Attack on Pearl Harbor When war came, however, it was not in the Atlantic but in the Pacific. In Asia, Japanese armies had been on the move for several years. When they marched into Indochina in July 1941, Roosevelt stopped all American trade with Japan. This included the sale of oil, which Japan needed badly. Tensions rose between the two countries.

That fall, representatives from each side tried to settle their differences. Japanese military leaders, however, had already decided on war. In the predawn hours of Sunday, December 7, 1941, bombers and fighter planes took off from Japanese aircraft carriers and headed for the American naval base at Pearl Harbor, in Hawaii. At 7:55 A.M.—almost precisely the time that Billy Mitchell had predicted 17 years earlier—they struck. Catching the American forces completely by surprise, the Japanese planes dealt a crippling blow to America's Pacific fleet and air force. They sank or damaged 19 warships, including 8 battleships. They destroyed 150 planes, more than half of the air force in the Pacific. Only luck happened to

■ Does this painting show Pearl Harbor during, or after, the Japanese attack?

Born: 1882, Hyde Park, New York.
Education: Harvard College.
Training: Lawyer, public official.
To presidency from: New York.
Position when elected: Governor of New York.
Political party: Democratic.
Married: Eleanor Roosevelt, a distant cousin.
Children: Five sons, one daughter.
Died: 1945, Warm Springs, Georgia, 3 months after the beginning of his fourth term.
Other facts: Served as assistant secretary of the navy under Wilson. Crippled by polio at age 39. The first President to appear on television. The only President to serve more than two terms.
During his presidency: Grand Coulee Dam on the Columbia River in Washington was completed. It is still the largest concrete dam and the greatest single source of waterpower in the United States.

FRANKLIN D. ROOSEVELT

32nd President
1933 · 1945

spare the American aircraft carriers. They were at sea when the Japanese attack came. There were more than 4,000 American casualties in the Pearl Harbor attack. More than 2,300 were known to be dead, and nearly 1,000 more were missng and presumed dead. Almost 1,200 more were wounded.

The next day, Congress declared war on Japan. Three days later, Germany and Italy joined their Axis partner and declared war on the United States.

The Grand Alliance On New Year's Day, 1942, the United States broke a tradition that extended back to the Revolutionary War by making an alliance with other nations. On that day, 26 countries including the United States signed the Declaration of the United Nations. They pledged to fight against the Axis powers until victory was gained and the countries that had been conquered were liberated.

The Allies who would carry most of the fighting were, of course, the United States, the Soviet Union, and Great Britain. It was also clear that the role of the United States would be far larger than it had been in World War I. The Americans would supply most of the military equipment for the Allies. They would also have to build a great fighting force of their own. Eventually, more than 15 million men and women served in the United States armed forces during the war. An even greater number than that would serve in war-related industries and activities at home.

CHECKUP

1. How did the Germans conquer most of Europe during the first year of the war?
2. What was the major argument of the isolationists?
3. What steps did President Franklin D. Roosevelt take to prepare the United States for war?
4. **Thinking Critically** Why do you think the Japanese wanted to risk bringing the United States into the war?

A World at War

VOCABULARY

pacifist	concentration camp
D-day	Holocaust
genocide	island-hopping

A Grim Outlook For the first six months after the United States entered the war, the outlook for the Allies was grim. In the Pacific, Japan marched from one success to another. By the summer of 1942, its armies controlled large parts of China, the Southeast Asian mainland, the Philippines, the Dutch East Indies, and nearly every island in the western Pacific. In addition, the Japanese navy in February crushed a combined United States-British fleet in the battle of the Java Sea.

On the other side of the world, the outlook for the Allies was equally poor. In Europe, German armies had taken Greece and Yugoslavia in 1941 and had driven hundreds of miles into the Soviet Union. In North Africa, German and Italian armies under General Erwin Rommel, "the Desert Fox," pushed British forces back across the desert into Egypt. The Axis forces were just a victory away from smashing through to the Suez Canal and to the oil fields of the Middle East.

Europe First The United States had to develop a plan for fighting a war in both Asia and Europe. From the beginning, America's military leaders decided on a strategy of "Europe first." The main effort would be to defeat Germany.

The first task was to bring German submarines under control. For the first year of the war, submarines sank Allied ships faster than they could be replaced. To combat the submarines, naval vessels and airplanes convoyed ships. Scientists also developed new antisubmarine weapons. Meanwhile, lights burned at night in American shipyards, where ships were being turned out in record numbers. By 1943 the Allies were winning the battle of the Atlantic.

In the fall of 1942, the tide of battle on land also began to turn in favor of the Allies. On the eastern front the Soviets held firm at Stalingrad and then counterattacked. Hitler's armies were defeated with the loss of a quarter of a million German soldiers and the capture of another 100,000. The Soviet Union's casualties were even higher, including countless civilians. The battle of Stalingrad was one of the decisive battles in history. From then on, the German armies in the Soviet Union fell back.

General Dwight Eisenhower In the west, Allied armies also took the offensive. Commanding the American forces in Europe was a man from a family of **pacifists** — people who oppose war. Dwight Eisenhower had never been in combat himself, but he turned out to be one of the great generals of the war.

Dwight Eisenhower was born in Texas and grew up in Abilene, Kansas. Dwight, or Ike, as he was nicknamed, went to the United States Military Academy at West Point, much to the distress of his pacifist family. In the peacetime army of the 1920s and 1930s, Eisenhower rose slowly, but he impressed the army's top leaders. When the United States entered World War II, General George C. Marshall, chief of staff of the army, promoted Eisenhower over 366 senior officers. Marshall appointed him to command American forces in Europe. Eventually Eisenhower would assume command of all Allied troops in western Europe.

The United States, Great Britain, and the Soviet Union had decided on a strategy to defeat the Axis powers: First they would drive the Axis forces out of North Africa, then they would invade Italy, and finally attack German-occupied France.

Eisenhower's first job was to plan the invasion of North Africa. In November 1942, some 300,000 Allied troops landed in Morocco and Algeria. Only days before the landing, more than 1,600 miles (2,600 km) to the east, British field marshal Bernard Montgomery had won a brilliant victory at El Alamein (el al ə mān') in Egypt and had begun to drive the Axis armies back to the west. Caught between the British and the advancing Americans, the Axis forces in North Africa surrendered to the Allies in May 1943.

The Advance into Europe Two months later, Allied forces from North Africa invaded Sicily, an Italian island in the Mediterranean Sea. After 38 days of fierce fighting, the island fell to the Allies. During this time the Italian people drove the dictator Mussolini from power. Near the end of the war, he was captured and executed by Italian patriots.

Sicily was the jumping-off place for an invasion of southern Italy on September 3, 1943. Within a week, the new Italian government not only surrendered but changed sides and joined the Allies. German troops, however, quickly occupied most of Italy. Allied armies could move north only slowly and at great cost.

Dwight Eisenhower, commanding general of the Allied forces, gives last minute encouragement to a group of soldiers.
■ **What tells you these soldiers are about to go into battle?**

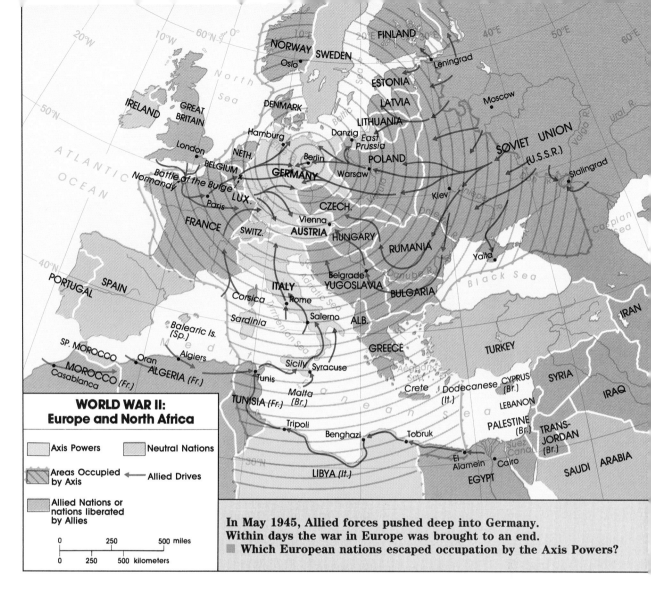

WORLD WAR II:
Europe and North Africa

- ☐ Axis Powers
- ☐ Neutral Nations
- ▨ Areas Occupied by Axis   ← Allied Drives
- ☐ Allied Nations or nations liberated by Allies

0   250   500 miles
0   250   500 kilometers

In May 1945, Allied forces pushed deep into Germany. Within days the war in Europe was brought to an end.
■ Which European nations escaped occupation by the Axis Powers?

Growing Allied air power carried the war home to the German people. (See the picture on page 641.) By early 1944, fleets of British and American bombers attacked German cities almost around the clock. Only occasional bad weather spared German factories, railroads, oil refineries, and civilian populations from the pounding. The enemy's ability to supply its armies was slowly being destroyed. Never did General Billy Mitchell appear to be more of a prophet.

The Normandy Invasion All the while, the Allies continued to build for **D-Day** — the date that would be chosen for the inva-

sion of western Europe. Mountains of supplies and thousands of planes and ships were assembled in England for this operation. Before dawn on June 6, American, British, Canadian, and French troops in southern England crossed the English Channel and landed on the beaches of Normandy in France. This force of 176,000 soldiers was supported in the D-Day landings by 4,000 ships and 11,000 planes overhead. It was one of the greatest military operations in history. The invasion of Europe had begun.

Within a few weeks, the invasion force reached a total of about 1 million men. In late July they broke through the German

653

The largest fleet ever assembled approaches Normandy on D-Day, June 6, 1944.
■ **Why, do you think, are the soldiers using field glasses?**

defenses and pushed inland. Before the end of August, Paris was freed. By the end of September, French and Belgian soil was all but cleared of German troops. In eastern Europe, Soviet troops were clearing their land of Hitler's armies as well.

In December 1944 the Germans threw everything they had into a last desperate effort to avoid defeat. In the Battle of the Bulge, they attacked westward into Belgium and Luxembourg with the aim of splitting the Allied armies. Though German troops created a bulge about 60 miles (100 km) deep in the Allied line, they could not break through the line. The German threat ended, and Allied armies went back on the attack.

In March 1945 the Allies crossed the Rhine River. British and American forces advanced toward Berlin from the west; Soviet troops poured in from the east. In

April, American and Soviet troops met in northern Germany. A week later the Soviet army entered Berlin. Germany surrendered on May 8—V-E (Victory in Europe) Day. Hitler's dream of an empire that would last a thousand years lay in ashes. Hitler himself escaped punishment by committing suicide before he could be captured.

Concentration Camps Late in 1942, confirmed reports had reached the Allies that Hitler and his Nazis were engaging in one of the most monstrous crimes in human history. They intended to exterminate the entire Jewish people, simply because they were Jews.

The killing of an entire ethnic, national, or religious group is known as **genocide**. Throughout Nazi-occupied lands, Jews were rounded up, packed onto freight

654

trains, and shipped hundreds of miles to any one of a dozen **concentration camps** in Poland, Austria, and Germany. These camps were set up for the imprisonment and slaughter of human beings. Every day the Nazis marched thousands of prisoners to their deaths, usually in gas chambers. Other prisoners were forced to work themselves to death doing slave labor.

In the final months of the war, Allied troops came upon the grisly evidence of this Nazi madness. Even men who had been hardened by years of combat grew sick at the sight of the torture rooms, the gas ovens, the mass graves, and the starving, half-dead survivors.

Altogether, at least 6 million Jews had been put to death. And Jews were not Hitler's only victims. As many as 6 million others, including Poles, gypsies, and political foes of the Nazis, were also killed. This mass killing of prisoners by the Nazis came to be called the **Holocaust**.

After the war, the Allies put some top Nazis on trial at Nuremberg, Germany, for their war crimes. Ten were hanged.

Two Crucial Battles In the Pacific the Japanese tide was first checked and then reversed in two big naval battles in 1942. In the first a British-American force met the Japanese in May in the battle of the Coral Sea. This battle introduced something new into naval warfare. Ships of the opposing navies did not fire on each other —in fact, they were not even in sight of

The Germans rounded up millions of innocent civilians, including most of Europe's Jews, and shipped them off to concentration camps.
■ **What might these people think is going to happen to them?**

each other. All the fighting was done by planes launched from aircraft carriers. Neither side could claim complete victory in this battle, but Japan's advance toward Australia was halted.

The second battle occurred in June near Midway Island in the central Pacific, not far from Hawaii. The United States Navy had intercepted Japanese messages stating that an invasion fleet was headed toward Midway. The Americans, under the command of Admiral Chester W. Nimitz, were ready and handed the Japanese a stinging defeat.

From One Island to the Next From that time on, Japan was thrown on the defensive. In August 1942, American marines landed on Guadalcanal (gwäd əl kə nal'), one of the Solomon Islands, near Australia. Fierce fighting raged for 6 months, but the United States troops took the island. For the next 2 years, Allied forces, mainly American, fought their way back through the islands of the Pacific toward Japan. Allied sea, air, and land forces attacked only certain islands while bypassing and cutting off the supplies of other Japanese-held islands. This strategy was called **island-hopping**.

In the central Pacific, naval and marine forces under Admiral Nimitz advanced in this manner through the Gilbert, Marshall, and Mariana islands. The Japanese defended every island fiercely. Allied forces suffered heavy losses, but they proved equal to the task. By the fall of 1944, the southern part of Japan was within range of land-based bombers operating from the islands of Guam (gwäm) and

Smoke rises from the United States aircraft carrier *Yorktown* after Japanese bombers attacked the ship at the battle of Midway Island.
■ What advantages and disadvantages would each kind of vessel—ship and airplane—have in battle against the other?

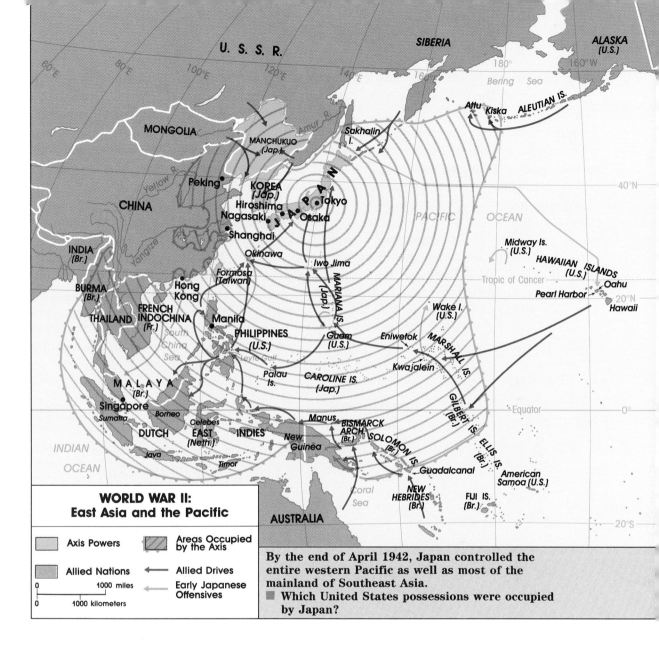

WORLD WAR II:
East Asia and the Pacific

Axis Powers

Areas Occupied
by the Axis

Allied Nations

Allied Drives

Early Japanese
Offensives

0   1000 miles

0   1000 kilometers

By the end of April 1942, Japan controlled the
entire western Pacific as well as most of the
mainland of Southeast Asia.
■ Which United States possessions were occupied
by Japan?

Saipan (sī pan′). The following spring the
Allies captured the islands of Iwo Jima
(ē′ wō jē′ mə) and Okinawa (ō ki nä′ wə).
This brought American air bases within
750 miles (1,200 km) of Tokyo. American
planes rained destruction on that and
other Japanese cities almost daily.

General Douglas MacArthur   Meanwhile, a second fighting force in the southwest Pacific advanced toward Japan. This
force was under the command of General
Douglas MacArthur. Unlike his former

aide Dwight Eisenhower, Douglas MacArthur was raised to be a military man from
birth. His father was a general who had
commanded American forces in the Philippines after the United States acquired
those islands from Spain. At West Point,
MacArthur made the best 4-year record in
the history of the academy. During World
War I he fought with reckless courage and
rose to the rank of general. Under President Hoover, MacArthur became chief of
staff, the youngest man ever to hold the
army's highest position.

MacArthur retired from the United States Army in the 1930s. He was in the Philippines helping to train an army and design a defense for the islands when war threatened. President Roosevelt recalled him to active duty and made him commander of the combined American and Philippine force.

"I Shall Return" MacArthur's troops were hopelessly outnumbered and outgunned when Japan invaded the Philippines in December 1941. Several months later, as his army retreated, MacArthur escaped to Australia on a submarine. "I shall return," he vowed.

Starting in late 1942, General MacArthur moved northward from Australia toward Japan. In a series of brilliant campaigns, Allied forces island-hopped closer to the Philippines. On October 20, 1944, Americans landed on the island of Leyte (lā′ tē) in the Philippine Islands. Wading ashore, General MacArthur announced dramatically, "People of the Philippines: I have returned."

Just 3 days later, Japan made a desperate attempt to stop the American advance. It threw most of its remaining warships into battle against American ships and planes in the Leyte Gulf in what was the largest battle in naval history.

General MacArthur (left) wades ashore at Leyte Island, returning to the Philippines. With him are members of his staff and Filipino officers.
■ Why do MacArthur and the others have to wade ashore?

Japan's navy was crushed, and Japan was through as a naval power.

As Japan was being driven back toward its home islands, the United States had a change in leadership. President Roosevelt had been elected to a fourth term as President in 1944. Even then, his health was failing. On April 12, 1945, while vacationing at Warm Springs, Georgia, he suffered a stroke and died almost instantly. Vice President Harry Truman became President.

The Atomic Bomb   It fell to President Truman to make one of the most historic decisions of the war and perhaps of all human history. That was the decision to drop an atomic bomb on Japan.

In 1939 the famed scientist Albert Einstein wrote a letter to President Roosevelt. Scientists, he told the President, had learned how to split the atom, releasing unimaginable energy. This made possible the building of the most destructive weapon the world had ever known.

Roosevelt promptly organized a top-secret effort to build an atomic bomb. This effort was known as the Manhattan Project. The United States was fortunate to have some of the Axis countries' best scientists working on the Manhattan Project. Dozens of them had fled fascism or Nazi persecution in their homelands. The list included Enrico Fermi of Italy; Niels and Aage Bohr of Denmark; Leo Szilard, Edward Teller, and Eugene Wigner, all of Hungary; and Otto Frisch of Austria.

On July 16, 1945, on a desert near Alamogordo (al ə mə gôr′ dō), New Mexico, the first atomic bomb in history was tested. The test was a success. The bomb was ready.

Many of President Truman's scientific advisers urged him to use the bomb against Japan. Some, however, disagreed. They feared that unleashing this

Albert Einstein's research and writings helped scientists develop the Atomic bomb.
■ Was this photograph taken early, or late, in Einstein's career?

new force might have terrible consequences for the future of humankind. No one really knew what those consequences might be. In the end, Truman made his decision on military grounds. Military leaders believed that the Allies would have to invade Japan to defeat it. Such an invasion could cost at least a half-million American casualties — counting those killed and wounded. Truman decided that if the atomic bomb could end the war quickly, it should be used.

World War II Ends   On July 26 the President warned Japan to surrender or face "prompt and utter destruction." When no reply came, a lone American bomber dropped an atomic bomb on the Japanese city of Hiroshima (hi rō shē′ mə) on August 6. The bomb wiped out nearly the whole city. At least 70,000 people were

The atomic bomb unleashed a destructive power unlike anything the world had ever seen before.
■ Why did the Japanese decide to surrender after being hit with two such explosions?

killed instantly; tens of thousands of others later died from the aftereffects of the blast. A new and dangerous era of human history had been ushered in by the dropping of the atomic bomb. Two days later the Soviet Union entered the war against Japan. When Japan still did not surrender, a second bomb was dropped; this time on the city of Nagasaki (näg ə säk′ ē) on August 9. Five days later, Japan gave up. The formal surrender was signed a little more than 3 weeks later, on September 2, 1945.

The war had been costly. The loss of human life was appalling. Of the American forces alone, more than 400,000 were dead. Altogether, World War II took perhaps 60 million lives around the world. Large parts of Europe and Asia lay in ruins. People could only hope that somehow, out of the death and destruction of war, a better world would come.

CHECKUP

1. Why was the outlook grim for the Allies in the first year of war?
2. What was the Allied strategy in Europe?
3. What was the Allied strategy for the war in the Pacific?
4. What events in World War II occurred at each of the following places: El Alamein, Normandy, Stalingrad, the Coral Sea, the Leyte Gulf, Hiroshima?
5. **Thinking Critically** What effect do you think the knowledge of Hitler's Holocaust might have had on relations between ethnic, racial, and religious groups in the postwar world?

The Home Front

How did the war affect Americans at home?

VOCABULARY

| total war | relocation center |

Total War   In 1939, before the start of World War II, a United States government report declared:

> War is no longer simply a battle between armed forces. . . . It is a struggle in which each side strives to bring to bear against the enemy . . . the power of every . . . resource at its command. The conflict extends from the soldier in the front line to the citizen in the remotest hamlet. . . .

That prediction turned out to be accurate. In no other war was the whole population of the United States so fully involved as in World War II. In no other war were the country's material resources so completely devoted to the goal of victory. Homemakers saved cooking fats to be made into explosives. Schoolchildren collected scrap iron and newspapers for recycling. Everywhere, people sacrificed willingly. Those few who chose not to or neglected to were harshly reminded by others, "Don't you know there's a war on?" This is what was meant by **total war**.

These young people helped the war effort by planting their own vegetable gardens.
How did the popularity of gardens at home help the war effort thousands of miles away?

661

A Production Miracle American industry held one of the keys to victory. A government agency, the War Production Board (WPB), helped organize the change-over from peacetime manufacturing to making goods for war. The WPB also saw that war industries received the raw materials they needed. Production of refrigerators, stoves, washing machines, and other consumer goods was halted. In Detroit, Michigan, automobile factories stopped making cars and turned out airplanes, tanks, and military trucks. In hundreds of cities and towns across the United States, factories ran 24 hours a day. Scientists, meanwhile, developed substitutes for scarce materials. With the Japanese army in control of the sources of natural rubber in the Far East, scientists developed synthetic rubber.

The result was a production miracle. In 1939 the United States built fewer than 6,000 planes. When President Roosevelt set a goal in 1940 of 50,000 planes a year, there were many doubters. A top Nazi general sneered, "The Americans can't build planes, only electric ice boxes and razor blades." But Americans proved him wrong. By 1944 the United States was producing not 50,000 planes a year but nearly *double* that number. In fact, in that year the United States produced twice as many goods as the Axis powers combined. World War II was won on the production lines at home as well as on the battlefields.

Rationing With the United States helping to feed, clothe, and arm its allies as well as its own armed forces, some goods were in short supply at home. To make sure that everyone got a fair share of these scarce goods, the government rationed them, that is, limited the amount that each person could buy.

The Office of Price Administration (OPA) issued small books of ration stamps. For a long list of items, including

Ration stamps were needed to buy a whole range of goods, from gasoline to groceries, during World War II. Books of such stamps were carefully guarded family possessions.
■ How did rationing help assure the fair distribution of scarce goods?

SOLDIERS *without guns*

Some women, like these pilots (left), served in the armed forces during World War II. Millions of other women entered the civilian work force for the first time and served on the home front.
■ What does the slogan on the factory poster (right) mean?

sugar, coffee, butter, meat, canned goods, fats and oils, fuel oil, gasoline, tires, and shoes, a buyer had to produce ration stamps as well as money. The OPA also set the prices of all goods except agricultural products.

Millions of Jobs The demand for goods created millions of jobs. At the same time, the armed forces took more than 15 million people out of the labor force. The result was that in just a few years the nation went from high unemployment to full employment. In fact, in some industries and in farming there was a labor shortage. Incomes rose, as workers received added pay for working overtime. Farmers shared in the general prosperity as prices for their crops rose.

Wartime created new opportunities for women. Six million additional women entered the work force—an increase of 50 percent in just a few years. Many worked at jobs that before had been closed to them. They worked in steel mills and in shipyards. They operated cranes, moved freight on the docks, and cut trees in the forests. In many defense factories, nearly half the workers were women. Some 300,000 women worked in the aircraft industry alone.

Anthropologist Margaret Mead estimated that at least 3 million of the 6 million women who were added to the work force at the time of World War II would never have held jobs otherwise. Still, the experience introduced many of these women to a new and different economic role.

Blacks in the War Just before the country entered the war, A. Philip Randolph, head of the Brotherhood of Sleeping Car Porters, threatened to lead 150,000 blacks in a march on Washington unless the President moved against racial discrimination in industry. This prompted President Roosevelt to issue an order banning discrimination in defense plants. This order improved work opportunities for blacks. So did the mounting demand for workers in wartime industries. Many blacks left the South for jobs in the war factories of the North.

As in World War I, the arrival of large numbers of blacks in northern cities led to racial tensions. In 1943 there were race riots in a number of cities. The worst was in Detroit, where 34 people died. In many areas, black people continued to meet with discrimination.

Benjamin Davis, the first black American general, decorates his son, a combat pilot. ■ Why are all the servicemen in this picture blacks?

In the military, too, discrimination against blacks was still the rule rather than the exception. A million black men and women served in the armed forces, but nearly all of them were in segregated units. Nonetheless, the barriers of race appeared to be weakening. The marine corps for the first time accepted black volunteers, and some 17,000 black marines proudly served in the war. Many more blacks in the armed forces rose to become officers than in World War I. More than 80 black fighter pilots were decorated for their actions in combat.

Although they were still denied equal rights, blacks made their contribution to the war effort on the home front and in battle. The contribution of a black doctor named Charles Drew saved thousands of lives. Dr. Drew developed the blood bank, in which blood was collected and stored for the use of those who had been wounded in battle.

The wartime experience of black Americans was a revelation. Many who served in France and Great Britain encountered for the first time societies where racial prejudice was not so pronounced as it was at home. Even blacks who moved north in search of jobs found a less segregated world than they had known. Finally, Hitler's vicious persecution of minorities forced many Americans of all races to admit once and for all that racial prejudice was not compatible with American ideals. All of this laid the groundwork for one of the most important developments of the postwar years, the civil rights movement of the 1950s and 1960s.

Japanese Americans One minority group, the Japanese Americans, fared badly during the war. Most Japanese Americans lived on the West Coast. Many residents there had long held a prejudice

General Mark Clark presents heroism awards to the Japanese American 442nd Combat Team. ■ Why did some Americans find this regiment's achievements surprising?

against this minority. To this prejudice was now added the fear that people of Japanese ancestry might help the Japanese enemy in an attack on the land along the Pacific Coast.

A demand arose for people of Japanese ancestry to be removed from the West Coast of the United States. Some military and political leaders joined the chorus, and President Roosevelt bowed to the pressure. In February 1942 he ordered the army to move some 110,000 people of Japanese background to **relocation centers** farther inland.

These relocation centers were crowded, hastily built camps where the residents lived behind barbed wire and under armed guard during the war. Some 70,000 of the 110,000 who were forced to give up their homes, businesses, and jobs had been born in the United States and were American citizens.

The whole episode was a shameful one, not fitting for a democratic society. There was never any evidence of disloyalty on the part of the Japanese Americans. In fact, when it was finally decided to accept Japanese Americans into service in 1943, thousands of them signed up. One of their groups, the 442nd Regimental Combat Team, was the most decorated combat force in the army. Its motto, "Go for broke," accurately described the reckless bravery of its members in combat in Italy and France. After the war some of the Japanese Americans were eventually paid by the government for the loss of their property. The payments they received, however, covered no more than 20 percent of their losses.

CHECKUP

1. How was World War II different from earlier wars?
2. How did American industry help the Allies win World War II?
3. How did the United States government meet the problem of shortages of many kinds of goods?
4. What contributions did black Americans and Japanese Americans make to the war effort?
5. What obstacles did black Americans and Japanese Americans face during World War II?
6. **Thinking Critically** Were women and minority group members better off or worse off during World War II than they had been before?

Understanding Authors' Points of View

COMPARING POINTS OF VIEW

When two people write about the same event, they may study the same evidence and look at the same documents, newspapers, diaries, and letters. Yet they can arrive at totally different conclusions. How is that possible?

It is possible because each writer has a point of view. Perhaps the writers are working in different time periods. Perhaps they come from different backgrounds. Most likely they have had different experiences. They may have different ideas about society and about which things are most important. In other words, they weigh evidence differently.

Here are two passages about the relocation of Japanese Americans during World War II. The first passage was written by John J. McCloy in 1942, just after the removal was completed. McCloy was assistant secretary of the army, and it was the army that carried out the removal.

> I wonder if anyone realizes the skill, speed and humanity with which the evacuation of the Japanese has been handled by the Army on the West Coast? I am struck with the extreme care that has been taken to protect the persons and goods and even the comforts of each individual. Certainly an organization that can do a humane job like this and still be a fine fighting organization is unique—and American. I hope other countries that have similar problems will not overlook how an answer has been found in this country.

More than 30 years later, two historians, Leonard Dinnerstein and David M. Reimers, wrote about the same event this way:

> The hasty removal meant considerable hardship and suffering. Given only five days' notice of the evacuation, those interned could take only what they could

carry; the government took over and held in storage all other belongings. In addition to the financial losses the conditions in the relocation centers were miserable. At first, the Japanese were placed in temporary quarters, including a hastily converted race track, which lacked basic facilities. Eventually, the government built ten camps, but they were mostly located in barren desert country, hot in the summer and cold in the winter. The surroundings were drab and unattractive, complete with barbed wire, military police, and, in some cases, machine guns. One Nisei intern later wrote of the camp in Arizona, "I must say this scorching Hell is a place beyond description and beyond tears."

SKILLS PRACTICE

Compare the writers' points of view in the two passages. How might McCloy's position have influenced his point of view? Dinnerstein and Reimers wrote 30 years later. How might the passage of three decades have affected their point of view?

MAIN IDEAS

1. Dictators who glorified the use of force and war threatened world peace in the 1930s.
2. The United States tried to stay on a neutral path, but after Hitler's German troops overran Europe in 1940, the United States gave massive aid to Britain.
3. The United States entered World War II in December 1941 after Japan attacked Pearl Harbor in Hawaii.
4. World War II started badly for the United States in both Asia and Europe, but within a year the United States and its allies were on the offensive in both regions.
5. World War II ended in 1945 after two atomic bombs were dropped on Japan.
6. World War II was won on the production lines as well as on the battlefields.

VOCABULARY REVIEW

Using a separate piece of paper, match the terms with the phrases below.

a. blitzkrieg
b. concentration camps
c. demilitarize
d. dictator
e. Holocaust
f. isolationists
g. Neutrality Acts
h. pacifists
i. rationing
j. totalitarian

1. Describing a form of government that has total power over its people
2. A person who has total power in governing a country
3. To remove armed troops from a region
4. Laws intended to keep the United States out of war
5. A German word meaning "lightning war"
6. People who wanted the United States to keep out of affairs of other countries
7. Places where Hitler's government imprisoned and killed Jews
8. People opposed to all war
9. Limiting the sale of articles in short supply so that they can be shared fairly
10. The attempt by Hitler and his government to exterminate the Jewish people

CHAPTER CHECKUP

1. What was the Good Neighbor policy? What countries did it affect?
2. How did economic conditions and increasing nationalism lead to the rise of dictatorships in Europe?
3. Why did Adolf Hitler sign a pact with the Soviet Union in 1939? Did he keep his agreement?
4. How did the American view of the war in Europe change after the fall of France?
5. What action did the United States government take toward Japanese Americans living on the West Coast? Why?
6. **Thinking Critically** How did the activities of Italy, Germany, and Japan in the 1930s show the weaknesses of the League of Nations?
7. **Thinking Critically** Why did President Truman decide to drop the atomic bomb on Japan? Why did some of his advisers oppose that decision? Who do you think was right—Truman or the advisers who opposed it?
8. **Thinking Critically** Why do you think Japanese Americans were treated differently from German Americans and Italian Americans during World War II?

APPLYING KNOWLEDGE

1. Interview your grandparents and other people of their generation. Find out what they can recall about what they were doing at the time of the announcement of the attack on Pearl Harbor, and what they thought and felt about the news.
2. From interviews and from books about World War II, find out how civilians helped the war effort. Learn about (**a**) victory gardens, (**b**) air-raid wardens, (**c**) war bonds, (**d**) collecting paper, rubber, and scrap metal.
3. In your library, find the story of Anne Frank, a young girl who lived in Europe during World War II. Report to the class on her experiences.

How Americans Lived: 1950

THE UNITED STATES

AREA: 2,974,726 sq mi
7,704,540 sq km

POPULATION: 150,697,361
POPULATION DENSITY: 51 per sq mi
20 per sq km
NUMBER OF STATES: 48
LARGEST STATE IN AREA: Texas
IN POPULATION: New York
LARGEST CITY: New York
WHERE PEOPLE LIVED:

Rural areas / Urban areas

How did the use of leisure time change in 1950?

At the midpoint of the twentieth century, the American people were prospering. After providing for the necessities of life, they had more spending money left over than ever before. Thanks to the great inventiveness and productivity of American industry, they also had more free time than ever before. In 1900 the average **workweek** was just under 60 hours. In 1950 it was about 40 hours. In the home the electric vacuum cleaner, the washing machine and clothes dryer, and the steam iron cut down the amount of time spent on housework. So did the new frozen foods, which could be cooked in minutes.

The Age of Television How did Americans use their new leisure time in 1950? A good part of it was spent in front of a small box that brought flickering images on a bluish screen into their living rooms. In 1950 the age of television was just bursting upon America. Back in 1946, at the end of World War II, television had been only a novelty. There were about 7,000 sets in the entire country—about 1 for every 20,000 people. Telecasts were shown only between 5 P.M. and 10 P.M. In that year, barely a few thousand people in just five cities could watch heavyweight boxing champion Joe Louis defend his title against challenger Billy Conn.

Just 4 years later, in 1950, millions watched the New York Yankees defeat the Philadelphia Phillies in the World Series. There were television sets in nearly 4 million homes—1 for every 40 people. And Americans were buying new TV sets at the rate of 20,000 a day! Ten years later, Americans would own 50 million television receivers.

In just a few years, television had changed the entertainment habits of Americans. People went out in the evening less and less. Instead, they spent their leisure time watching television.

The average American watched 3 hours of television every day — more than 20 hours a week. On Tuesday evening most sets were tuned to comedian Milton Berle's show. He soon came to be called Mr. Television. Westerns were also a favorite. Most Americans couldn't seem to get enough of programs about frontier outlaws and pioneers in the Wild West.

Television Takes Over Meanwhile, other forms of entertainment suffered. Since the 1930s "big bands" such as those of Benny Goodman, Harry James, the Dorsey brothers, and Count Basie had toured the country, playing in theaters and dance halls. In 1950 they were playing to smaller and smaller audiences, as people stayed home to watch television.

The moving picture industry was also hit hard by the competition of television. In 1946 an average of 82 million Americans went to the movies each week. In 1950 the number fell to 60 million. The movie industry tried to fight back with ads such as

these: "Don't be a living room captive." "Step out and see a great movie!" In 1952 the industry introduced the wide screen in the hope of bringing people back to the box office. Another 10 years would go by before Hollywood studios stopped fighting television and began to make movies for showing on TV screens.

TV's Effect on the Family Noting how whole families gathered to watch evening programs, some observers suggested that television was becoming an important force for drawing families together once again. Others, however, pointed out that in earlier days, families had provided their own entertainment. They talked with each other. They joined in games, songs, and storytelling. Now, few words passed among them as they watched the entertainment provided by the television.

In fact, television was undermining even family mealtime conversation. In 1954 the frozen "TV dinner" was introduced in markets around the country. At

In 1950, television was a new and fascinating form of entertainment.
■ What differences do you see in the way this family is dressed and the way a family today would probably be dressed to watch television?

about the same time came the "TV table," a small metal tray on folding legs. Now in some homes, family members sat in front of the television, eating their separate dinners on their separate tables, and hardly exchanging a word.

More Leisure Time   Americans also spent much of their free time playing and traveling. In earlier days, time off from work — and there was not much of that — was thought of as a time for rest to prepare for the next day's work. By 1950, that attitude had changed dramatically. Now, time off from work was thought of as time for enjoyment. For example, in the 1950s, Americans spent as much money on lei-sure goods as they did on housing. Five million people had fishing licenses back in 1933. Just 20 years later, 15 million did. The number of hunting licenses increased similarly. The boating industry also boomed in the 1950s. By the middle of the decade, there was one boat for every 30 Americans. Americans were not only working fewer hours in 1950, they were also getting longer vacations. Before World War II, fewer than half of all American companies gave their workers paid vacations. By the early 1950s, nearly all of them did. Most of these vacations were at least 2 weeks long. There were also many more "long weekends" of 3 and sometimes 4 days.

This advertisement shows how the automobile helped to make leisure time enjoyable for many. Entire families, including pets, could go on vacations together.
■ What do you think this family is about to do?

After World War II, most people who traveled overseas went by airplane rather than by ship.
■ What does the circle in the symbol on the door stand for?

Millions of Travelers   To a growing number of Americans in 1950, a vacation meant going someplace, not relaxing at home. Millions picked up, packed into the family car, and traveled. By the middle of the 1950s, about 70 million Americans — nearly 1 in every 2 — took at least one automobile vacation each year. Many spent part of their vacations in a state or national park. Others went from city to countryside or from countryside to city. Everywhere Americans were on the road. Hotels, motels, gas stations, and restaurants did a growing business.

A smaller but growing number of Americans in 1950 were using their vacations to travel to other countries. In the past this kind of travel had been only for the rich. But the millions who saw wartime service overseas had stirred up an interest in foreign travel. Higher income, lower transportation costs, and faster travel made it possible for many ordinary people to visit other lands.

The airplane was the most important factor. Before the war nearly all overseas travelers went by steamship. In 1950, for the first time, air passengers outnumbered those who traveled by sea. In that year more than 670,000 Americans traveled to other countries. Just a few years later the number passed 1 million, and it has continued to rise.

CHECKUP

1. How did the average workweek change between 1900 and 1950?
2. How did the coming of television affect American family life?
3. By 1950, how had vacations changed from earlier times?
4. What businesses grew and profited from Americans' vacation activities?
5. **Thinking Critically**   What effects might television have had on aspects of life not mentioned here, such as education and politics?

REVIEWING VOCABULARY

1. consumer goods A vast increase in the manufacture and sale of consumer goods contributed to the prosperity of the 1920s. List five examples of consumer goods that many people bought in the 1920s. Then explain how advertising and consumer credit helped to increase the sales of these and other consumer goods at that time.

2. collective bargaining The Wagner Act of 1935 guaranteed workers the right of collective bargaining. Explain what collective bargaining is, and who takes part in it. What evidence can be found after 1935 to support the idea that, by guaranteeing collective bargaining, the Wagner Act gave a great boost to the growth of labor unions?

3. totalitarian By the 1930s, early attempts at democracy were being replaced in a number of countries by totalitarian governments. Such a government was usually headed by a dictator. How did totalitarian governments react to the idea of individual rights and freedoms? How did they react to the idea of equal rights for all citizens?

4. isolationist President Roosevelt and the isolationists had very different views on American foreign policy. What did isolationists believe? Would an isolationist have favored or opposed Roosevelt's lend-lease policy? The Atlantic Charter?

5. Holocaust The word is an old one. It means both *destruction* and *sacrifice*. Since World War II, it has come to have a special meaning. What does the word refer to now, and why? How does this Holocaust differ from similar large-scale destructions in the past?

EXPRESSING YOURSELF

1. In what ways . . . ? In every year of the 1920s, 2 million to 3 million Americans bought new cars. How did the increased use of cars change life in an average American city or town? Write 3 paragraphs, devoting each to one change.

2. Thinking like an economist Congress is considering a high tariff law that will sharply reduce the amount of goods imported from foreign countries. Congressional leaders want to know if this is likely to affect the sale of American goods to these same countries. What would you tell them, and why?

3. You report the story You are a newspaper reporter during the Great Depression. Your editor wants you to write a story on how the depression has affected one family in your town or neighborhood. Talk to an older adult—perhaps a grandparent—about memories of the depression. Then write a story, based on those memories, as if the events happened only yesterday.

4. What if . . . ? In June 1940 France surrendered, leaving only Great Britain in all of Europe to fight against Nazi Germany. What if the United States had decided not to help Great Britain, and the British had been forced to surrender? What might this result have meant in a few years for the United States?

5. Consider the pros and cons It is July 1945. President Truman has just learned that scientists have successfully tested an atomic bomb. In preparing to decide whether to use this new weapon against Japan, he asks you to draw up a list of reasons for and against doing so. What reasons will you present to the President?

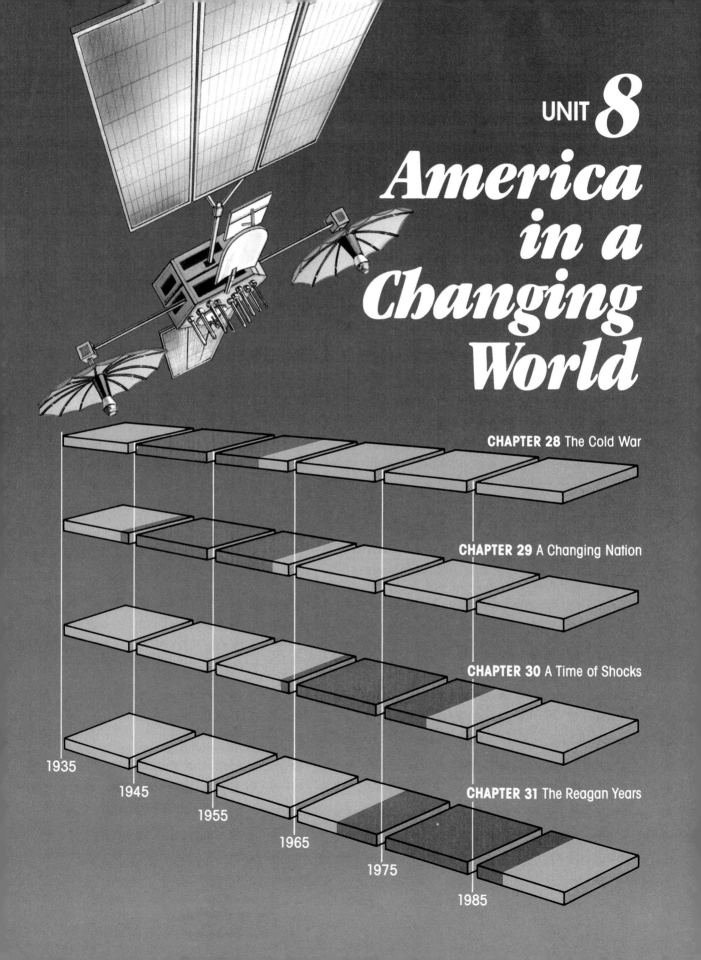

UNIT **8**

America in a Changing World

CHAPTER 28 The Cold War

CHAPTER 29 A Changing Nation

CHAPTER 30 A Time of Shocks

CHAPTER 31 The Reagan Years

1935
1945
1955
1965
1975
1985

CHAPTER 28 The Cold War

1945–1962

An End to Wartime Cooperation

What was the result of the end of wartime cooperation between the Allies?

Truman Becomes President "Last night the moon, the stars, and all the planets fell on me," Harry Truman told reporters on April 13, 1945. He was describing how he felt after learning that President Roosevelt had died suddenly, and that he—Harry Truman of Missouri, Vice President of the United States—was now President.

Harry Truman had never expected to wind up in the White House. He was born in Independence, Missouri, in 1884. After graduating from high school, he held a few minor jobs before taking over the operation of the family farm outside of town.

During World War I, Harry Truman served in France with the United States Army and rose to the rank of major. Six weeks after he returned home, he married Bess Wallace, whom he had known since childhood. Truman and a friend became partners in a men's clothing store, but after a few years the business failed. Mean-while, Truman became involved in local politics. He held local office until 1934, when he was elected to the United States Senate. His reputation for hard work and loyalty to his party earned him the Democratic nomination for Vice President in 1944. And now, less than a year later, he was President. The burden of making decisions that would affect the whole world rested on him.

Fortunately, Truman was able and willing to make decisions. On his presidential desk he placed a sign that said "The buck stops here." He also had a favorite saying for officials who were afraid to make decisions for which they might be criticized. "If you can't stand the heat," Truman said, "get out of the kitchen."

The United Nations One of President Truman's first acts was to welcome delegates from 50 nations to a conference in San Francisco on April 25, 1945. Early in the war the United States, Great Britain, and the Soviet Union had agreed that an international organization should be formed after the war to keep the peace. Since then, many of the details had been worked out. Those who gathered in San Francisco drew up the final charter, or constitution, of the **United Nations**. In 2

The United Nations built its permanent headquarters beside the East River in New York City.
■ What do the flags represent?

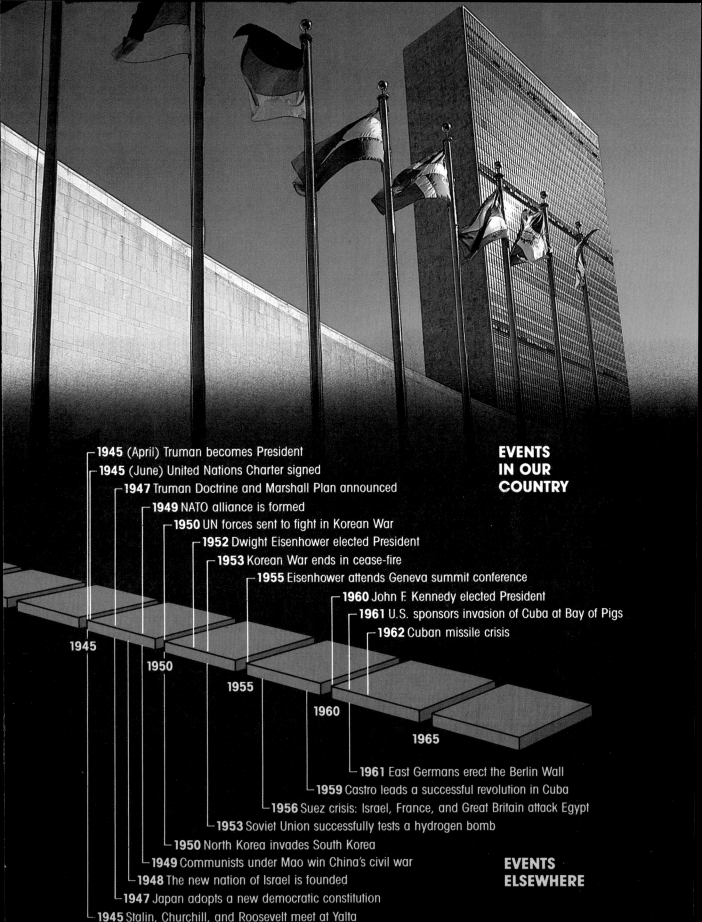

EVENTS IN OUR COUNTRY

- **1945** (April) Truman becomes President
- **1945** (June) United Nations Charter signed
- **1947** Truman Doctrine and Marshall Plan announced
- **1949** NATO alliance is formed
- **1950** UN forces sent to fight in Korean War
- **1952** Dwight Eisenhower elected President
- **1953** Korean War ends in cease-fire
- **1955** Eisenhower attends Geneva summit conference
- **1960** John F. Kennedy elected President
- **1961** U.S. sponsors invasion of Cuba at Bay of Pigs
- **1962** Cuban missile crisis

1945

1950

1955

1960

1965

EVENTS ELSEWHERE

- **1961** East Germans erect the Berlin Wall
- **1959** Castro leads a successful revolution in Cuba
- **1956** Suez crisis: Israel, France, and Great Britain attack Egypt
- **1953** Soviet Union successfully tests a hydrogen bomb
- **1950** North Korea invades South Korea
- **1949** Communists under Mao win China's civil war
- **1948** The new nation of Israel is founded
- **1947** Japan adopts a new democratic constitution
- **1945** Stalin, Churchill, and Roosevelt meet at Yalta

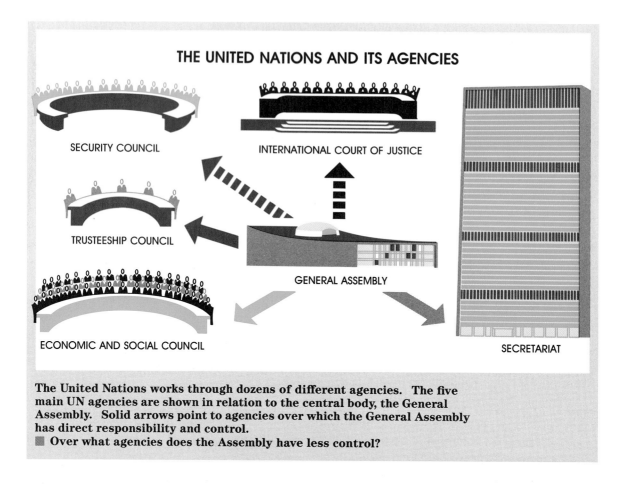

THE UNITED NATIONS AND ITS AGENCIES

SECURITY COUNCIL

INTERNATIONAL COURT OF JUSTICE

TRUSTEESHIP COUNCIL

GENERAL ASSEMBLY

ECONOMIC AND SOCIAL COUNCIL

SECRETARIAT

The United Nations works through dozens of different agencies. The five main UN agencies are shown in relation to the central body, the General Assembly. Solid arrows point to agencies over which the General Assembly has direct responsibility and control.
■ Over what agencies does the Assembly have less control?

months their work was done. All 50 nations signed the completed charter.

The main bodies of the new international organization were the General Assembly and the Security Council. In the General Assembly every nation, regardless of size, had an equal voice. (See the diagram above.) However, the General Assembly had no power to act on important issues. That was left to the Security Council, a group of 11 members that dealt with major questions like threats to world peace. The council had 5 permanent members — the United States, Great Britain, the Soviet Union, France, and China. Each of these nations could veto a decision of the council. Other countries would take turns filling the remaining 6 seats. (Later the total membership of the council was raised to 15.) Other parts of the United Nations included the International Court of Justice, the Economic and Social Council, and the Secretariat, which handled the day-to-day business of the organization.

Decisions at Yalta Even as the United Nations charter was being signed, disagreements were arising between the wartime allies. Most of the big decisions President Truman had to make grew out of the breakdown of cooperation with America's wartime ally, the Soviet Union. That cooperation had reached its high point in February 1945. By then the end of the war in Europe was in sight. The Big Three leaders of the Allies — President Roosevelt, British Prime Minister Winston Churchill, and Soviet Premier Joseph

Stalin—met at Yalta in the Soviet Union to make decisions about the postwar world.

All three leaders wanted a peace that would end Germany's power to make war. They agreed that until a final peace treaty was made, Germany would be divided into four parts, or zones. Each of the Big Three powers would send an army to occupy one zone, with a French army occupying the fourth. The German capital of Berlin, located inside the Soviet zone, would also be divided into four parts.

The three leaders agreed on free elections in the Eastern European countries, which Soviet troops were then occupying. In addition, Stalin promised to enter the war against Japan within 3 months after Germany's final defeat. In return the Soviet Union would get control of certain territories in Asia.

Soviet Actions By the time Harry Truman became President, it was clear that the Soviet Union was not keeping its word about free elections. In Poland, the Soviets placed a Communist government in power against the wishes of the people. Over the next 3 years, they did the same in other Eastern European countries — Czechoslovakia, Romania, Bulgaria, and Hungary.

The Soviets justified their action by pointing out that Germany had invaded their country twice in a generation, at a cost of millions of Soviet lives. Each time, they said, the invasion route had been through Poland and Eastern Europe. To protect themselves in the future, the Soviets declared, they must have "friendly governments" on their borders. To Stalin this meant Communist governments. The United States, Great Britain, and other countries, however, saw Stalin's moves in Eastern Europe as an effort to expand the Soviet empire and to spread communism.

Europe's Iron Curtain In Germany, cooperation ended soon after the war. A part of the Yalta agreement stated that the four occupying powers — Great Britain, France, the United States, and the Soviet Union — would run Germany as a single economic unit. This meant that goods and money would move freely from one zone to another. The Soviets, however, kept their zone separate from the others. The Soviets also cut off their zone of occupation in Berlin from the other three.

In March 1946, Winston Churchill delivered a speech at Westminster College in Fulton, Missouri. He said that the Soviets had lowered across the center of Europe from the Baltic Sea to the Adriatic Sea, an **iron curtain**, cutting off Eastern Europe and its people from Western Europe. From behind this iron curtain came reports of denial of freedom, persecution of church leaders, prison camps, and death.

Thus, less than a year after the victory over Hitler, the great alliance was in shreds. Each side filled the air with charges and threats. Each side used every means short of actual fighting to advance its own goals and to harm the interests of the other side. This struggle came to be called the **cold war**.

CHECKUP

1. What are the main bodies of the United Nations?
2. What did the Big Three leaders agree to at Yalta?
3. What happened in Poland and other countries of Eastern Europe that led to a split between the United States and the Soviet Union?
4. **Thinking Critically** What did Winston Churchill mean when he said, "an iron curtain has descended" across Europe? Why did he choose that phrase?

Cold War and Hot War

In what ways did the United States try to contain Soviet influence during the cold war?

Containment   To keep the Soviet Union from getting control of more territory, the United States followed a policy called **containment**. This meant that wherever the Soviet Union pressured to expand its territory or influence, the United States would use equal pressure to contain or limit it, doing so by using diplomatic, economic, or military means.

One region in which the Soviets were trying to make gains was the eastern Mediterranean. In Greece they backed the Communist side in a civil war. In neighboring Turkey the Soviets tried to get the government to give them a share of control over the Dardanelles. This narrow waterway connects the Black Sea to the Mediterranean Sea. (See the map below.) Control of this entrance to the Mediterranean had been a goal of Russia's leaders for more than 200 years. The Soviets also demanded that Turkey allow them to build naval bases in that region. If the Soviet Union succeeded in its aims in Greece and Turkey, it would control the whole eastern end of the Mediterranean Sea.

The Truman Doctrine   President Truman decided to act. In March 1947, he asked Congress to send $400 million in military aid to Greece and Turkey. He also declared that the United States would support peoples who were resisting attempts by Communists to take over their countries. This policy became known as the **Truman Doctrine**. Strengthened by this American aid, both Greece and Turkey were able to defend themselves. Soviet expansion and Communist influence in the region were contained.

The Marshall Plan   The countries of Western Europe also needed help, but of a different kind. Their economies had not recovered from the ruin of war. Poverty was widespread. Many feared that this poverty would be a breeding ground for communism. These countries needed money not for weapons but for farm equipment, factories, and machines to get their economies going again.

In June 1947, Secretary of State George C. Marshall proposed that the United States provide this help. President Truman backed the idea, which became

The Sea of Marmara and the two straits of the Bosporus and the Dardanelles connect the Black and Aegean seas.
☐ Why are the two straits considered strategic waterways?

known as the **Marshall Plan**. Congress passed it in 1948. In the next 3 years, the United States put $12 billion into the Marshall Plan. By 1950 the countries of Western Europe were back on their feet.

Blockade and Airlift The United States, Great Britain, and France decided to combine their three occupation zones in Germany into one and allow the unified zone to have its own government. The Soviets were opposed. In June 1948 they blocked all roads, railroads, and canals connecting Berlin, which lay deep within their occupation zone, to the western part of Germany. The Soviet aim was to make the Western powers give up their plans for a separate West German government or else be forced out of Berlin.

President Truman never considered getting out of Berlin. "We are going to stay, period," he said. To keep food, fuel, and other supplies flowing into the city, the United States organized an airlift. For the next 10 months, American and British pilots flew cargo planes into West Berlin. At the height of the airlift, planes landed with supplies every 3 or 4 minutes. Meanwhile in the United States, Congress enacted a new peacetime draft to rebuild the army, which had been mostly disbanded after World War II.

The Berlin airlift was successful. The Soviets called off the blockade in May

Children watch as a plane bringing supplies to West Berlin descends toward the airport runway.
■ Why might these children be happy to see the plane?

The Third World

The term *Third World* was coined at the height of the cold war. The United States and the Western democracies stood on one side, and the Soviet Union and its satellites in Eastern Europe stood on the other. People called the first group of nations the Western World, or Free World, and the second group the Communist World.

During these same years, the colonial empires of Great Britain, the Netherlands, and France crumbled. Dozens of countries in Asia and Africa became independent. These emerging nations did not consider themselves

a part of the cold war struggle. Because they were not a part of the Free World and not part of the Communist World, it was said that they formed the Third World.

In later years the term *Third World* took on a new meaning. Today a Third World country is one with an underdeveloped economy. Thus almost all the countries of Africa, Asia, South America, and Central America, and many countries in the Middle East are called Third World countries — whatever their feelings may be about the Free World and the Communist World.

1949. That fall the Federal Republic of Germany (West Germany) came into being, with a democratic government, in the American, British, and French occupation zones. Soon after, the Soviets created the German Democratic Republic (East Germany) with a Communist government. Thus what was at first the temporary division of Germany became permanent.

NATO   Many leaders in the United States and Western Europe feared that the Soviet Union might decide to use its military power in Europe. President Truman believed that the best way to curb the Soviets was for all the countries to stand together. Truman said that the United States would be willing to help defend Western Europe. In April 1949 the United

States, Canada, and ten other countries formed the **North Atlantic Treaty Organization**, usually referred to as **NATO**. The NATO countries agreed that an attack on any one of them would be considered an attack on all.

Four other countries have joined the alliance since then. West Germany joined in 1955 and began to rearm. The Soviets responded by linking most of the Communist countries of Europe in a military alliance of their own. This alliance was called the Warsaw Pact, after the Polish capital city where it was organized.

In NATO's first year, President Truman nominated General Dwight Eisenhower to be the alliance's first commander. Eisenhower promptly went to Europe to start the work of organizing

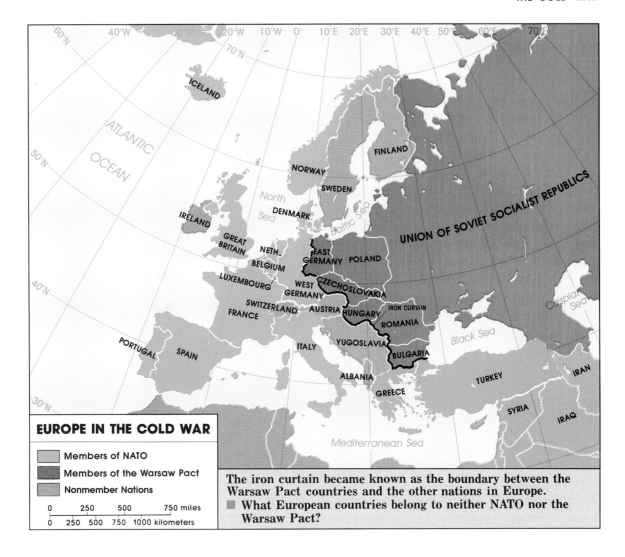

EUROPE IN THE COLD WAR

- Members of NATO
- Members of the Warsaw Pact
- Nonmember Nations

| 0 | 250 | 500 | 750 miles |

| 0 | 250 | 500 | 750 | 1000 kilometers |

The iron curtain became known as the boundary between the Warsaw Pact countries and the other nations in Europe.

■ What European countries belong to neither NATO nor the Warsaw Pact?

the military forces of the NATO countries into a common defense.

Prompt action was even more necessary after September 1949. In that month came the startling news that the Soviets had successfully tested an atomic bomb.

Gains for Democracy Japan, unlike Germany, was not divided after the war. The United States had the only occupying forces in Japan. General Douglas MacArthur, who was in charge of American forces in Japan, actually governed the country for several years. He carried out important reforms. MacArthur ordered some large landholdings divided among poor farm workers. He saw to it that women gained rights. In 1947, Japan adopted a new constitution, which made the country a democracy. The constitution promoted civil rights and gave women the right to vote for the first time. In 1951 the United States and other countries signed a treaty with Japan, ending the occupation. As the years went by, Japan and the United States were drawn closer together by shared commercial interests and a shared opposition to the Soviet Union.

Elsewhere in Asia the postwar years saw the end of Europe's colonial empires.

One after another, Asian lands that had been ruled by European countries for centuries became independent. Many started out with democratic governments, although these were often changed later.

The United States was in favor of these colonies becoming independent and ruling themselves. It welcomed these countries into the family of nations. In fact, the United States set an example for other countries by granting independence to its own colony, the Philippines. In 1934, Congress had passed a law promising the Philippines their independence in 10 years. The war delayed this timetable, but on July 4, 1946, the United States made good on its word. The Philippines became independent, with an elected president and an elected legislative body.

Communists Take Over China   During these years the United States was also concerned about the spread of communism in Asia. In China two groups had been fighting for control of the country since 1927. The Nationalists, led by Chiang Kai-shek (chyäng′ kī shek′), controlled the government. The Communists, led by Mao Zedong (mou′ dzü′ dùng), sought to overthrow the Nationalists. During World War II, the two sides had worked together to defeat Japan, but afterwards they began to fight again. The United States supported Chiang and the Nationalists. The Soviet Union backed Mao Zedong and the Communists.

Despite American aid, the Nationalists lost ground. Chiang and his generals made serious military mistakes, and corruption in the government caused much of the population to turn against them. Meanwhile, the Communists promised land reform, meaning that they would take land away from the big landowners and give it to the peasants who had worked on

the land. In 1949, Mao's forces drove the Nationalists off the mainland of Asia onto the nearby island of Formosa, now called Taiwan (tī wän′). That fall, Mao Zedong proclaimed a new Chinese government, the People's Republic of China.

A 1949 street demonstration in China celebrates Mao Zedong and the success of the revolution by Chinese Communists.
■ Why is Mao idealized here?

The Division of Korea   One of the wartime agreements of the Allies was that the Asian land of Korea, long ruled by Japan, should be a free and independent country. At the end of World War II, the United States and the Soviet Union agreed that their troops would take over Korea from the surrendering Japanese army. The Soviets would occupy the area north of 38° north latitude (the 38th parallel). American troops would move into Korea south of that line.

This division was supposed to be temporary, but the cold war made it permanent. The United Nations called for elections to unify the country, and in 1948 an election under UN supervision was held in the south. The Soviets, though, would not allow the United Nations to run an election in the north. In North Korea the Soviets set up a separate Communist government called the People's Republic of Korea. They also trained and equipped a strong North Korean army. Then the Soviet Union withdrew its troops. Soon afterwards, the United States also pulled its troops out of the area now called the Republic of Korea, or South Korea. Each government in Korea claimed to be the rightful government for the whole country.

American soldiers serving in Korea found an environment that was sometimes familiar and sometimes strikingly unfamiliar.
■ What type of terrain is shown here?

War in Korea   On June 25, 1950, the North Korean army invaded South Korea. President Truman believed that North Korea could not be allowed to get away with this aggression. He ordered American naval and air forces to help South Korea. He also asked the United Nations to take action. The Security Council did so, calling on member nations to come to South Korea's aid. The Soviet Union probably would have vetoed this action of the Security Council, but its representatives were not present. The Soviet delegation had walked out in protest a year earlier when the United Nations refused to turn over China's seat to the government of the new People's Republic.

Eventually, 19 members of the United Nations sent troops to help the South Koreans. The United States sent the largest number by far. General Douglas MacArthur was named commander of all UN forces in Korea.

At first everything went North Korea's way. Communist troops drove the UN forces back to Pusan, at the southernmost tip of South Korea. Finally in August the

UN line held firm. Then in mid-September, General MacArthur staged a brilliant surprise landing by sea at the Yellow Sea port of Inchon, far behind the North Korean line. At the same time, UN troops to the south went on the attack. North Korean troops retreated. UN forces drove the troops back across the 38th parallel, overran most of North Korea, and pushed on toward the Yalu River, North Korea's border with China. By fall, victory and the reunification of the two Koreas seemed assured.

China Enters the War Then came a sudden new development. In October, China began warning the UN troops not to move any closer to its borders. General MacArthur, who believed the Communist warning to be a bluff, ignored it. He assured President Truman that the UN forces could easily handle any Chinese troops that might attack. But MacArthur had made a serious error in judgment. In late November 1950 a quarter-million Chinese troops poured across the Yalu. They drove the UN army back near the 38th parallel, where the UN forces finally held.

General MacArthur now wanted to bomb China, blockade its coast, and transport Chiang Kai-shek's armies from Formosa to the mainland to fight the Communists. President Truman and his military advisers, however, disagreed.

Truman and MacArthur first met when the President flew to Wake Island in 1950. A later meeting was not so cordial. (19°N/167°E; map, p. 773)
■ How do the two men seem to be getting along here?

DIVISION OF KOREA

- North Korea
- South Korea
- ----- Cease-fire line July 1953

CHINA

NORTH KOREA

Pyongyang

Cease-fire line July 27, 1953

Seoul
Inchon

Ullung I.

SOUTH KOREA

Pusan

Cheju I.

Hiroshima

JAPAN

MANCHURIA

U.S.S.R.

Sea of Japan

Yellow Sea

Korea Strait

The end of the war left Korea divided into Communist and non-Communist countries.
☐ What line of latitude passes through the border between North and South Korea?

They did not want to widen the war. They believed MacArthur's policies "would involve us in the wrong war, at the wrong place, at the wrong time, and with the wrong enemy." MacArthur continued to insist on his views. When he challenged Truman publicly, the President removed him from command.

Many Americans agreed with MacArthur, and when he returned to the United States in April 1951 he got a hero's welcome. In a speech before Congress, he told his listeners of his belief: "In war there is no substitute for victory." Still, enthusiasm for a war with China dimmed soon, and President Truman was given credit for holding fast to his power as civilian commander-in-chief.

The war now settled into a **stalemate**, that is, a situation in which neither side could win. Peace talks, started in 1951, soon stalled.

The Korean War Ends Many Americans were frustrated. In the presidential election of 1952, they turned against the party in power, the Democrats. The Republican nominee was Dwight Eisenhower, the popular war hero, and he won easily. During the campaign, Eisenhower had promised, if elected, "I will go to Korea." People hoped that he would find a way to end the war. President Eisenhower did go to Korea immediately after his election. Still, the war continued for another 7 months.

In the summer of 1953, the two sides finally agreed to a cease-fire. The boundary between North Korea and South Korea was set very close to where it had been when the war started. To many Americans this was an unsatisfactory end to a war that had cost nearly 54,000 American lives. American efforts had, however, succeeded in stopping North Korea from taking over South Korea by force.

CHECKUP

1. How did the Truman Doctrine and the Marshall Plan serve as the two main parts of American containment policy in the late 1940s?
2. What was the purpose of the North Atlantic Treaty Organization (NATO)?
3. What changes took place in the government of China after World War II?
4. What action did the United States take after the North Korean army invaded South Korea?

5. **Thinking Critically** What risks were involved for China and for the United States in China's entry into the Korean War?

Containment and Coexistence

How did President Eisenhower seek to keep the peace while continuing to contain Soviet influence?

Curbing Communism in Southeast Asia
The policy of containment was continued in the 1950s under President Eisenhower. Soviet expansion in Europe had been checked. But Eisenhower and Secretary of State John Foster Dulles were concerned about the spread of communism in Southeast Asia. Dulles believed that if one Southeast Asian country fell to communism, nearly all the others would also fall. He thought that an organization like NATO was needed for this region of the world.

In 1954 the United States, Great Britain, and France, with Australia and New Zealand, joined three Southeast Asian countries — Pakistan, Thailand, and the Philippines — to form the Southeast Asia Treaty Organization (SEATO). This treaty was different from the NATO treaty. Although members agreed to help each other in case of attack, they did not promise to go to war to do so.

A Relaxation of Tensions During the 1950s, cold war tensions relaxed a bit. Three things took place in 1953 to bring about this development. One was the end of the fighting in Korea. The second was the death of Soviet dictator Joseph Stalin. The new leaders of the Soviet Union were more willing to try to reach an agreement with the leaders of the West. The third event was the development of a hydrogen bomb by the Soviet Union, matching the bomb the United States had built a year earlier. Now both sides had a weapon a thousand times more powerful than the bomb that wiped out Hiroshima. As President Eisenhower said, nuclear war would be suicide for the human race. Soviet leaders spoke of the need for **coexistence**, that is, living together in peace.

In 1955, President Eisenhower met with leaders of the Soviet Union and other countries in Geneva, Switzerland, in a **summit conference**. This is a meeting of the top leaders of the world's major powers. For the first time since the wartime conferences 10 years before, heads of the United States and Soviet governments met face-to-face. They talked about ways to prevent an arms race between the two countries. Although no agreements were reached, each side was convinced that the other really wanted to avoid war. This desire to work for peace came to be called "the spirit of Geneva."

The U-2 Incident During the following years, contacts between the two countries increased. Another summit conference was scheduled for Paris in May 1960. But just 2 weeks before the summit meeting, an American military airplane flying over the Soviet Union was shot down. As the plane crashed to the ground, hopes for the summit conference crashed with it.

The airplane was a high-flying American spy plane called a U-2. The captured pilot admitted he had been spying on Soviet military bases. Arriving in Paris, the Soviet premier, Nikita Khrushchev (nə kēt′ ə krush chôf′), demanded that the United States stop such flights and apologize. President Eisenhower said the U-2 flights would be stopped, but he refused to apologize. Khrushchev left Paris, and the summit was cancelled.

Francis Gary Powers, pilot of the U-2 spy plane, was put on trial by the Soviets and sentenced to 10 years in prison.

■ Why, do you think, did this trial take place in the Soviet Union?

The Middle East   Another region of concern to the United States was the Middle East. Geographically, this area is important as a link that connnects three continents—Africa, Europe, and Asia. Its vast deposits of oil make it important economically as well. Following World War II, strong feelings of nationalism had been awakened among the Arab peoples of this region. These feelings were heightened by the creation of the new state of Israel. In the late 1800s, Jews from Europe started a movement to set up a Jewish nation in their old, biblical homeland of Palestine. Jewish settlement in Palestine grew in the early 1900s. Before World War II, the Jewish population reached nearly a half million. Arabs living in Palestine became alarmed. Palestine had been their home for generations. They feared that the coming of more Jews would lead to a separate Jewish state.

The Founding of Israel   After World War II, Jews who escaped the Holocaust were determined to have a homeland of their own. Thousands went to Palestine. In 1947, the United Nations voted to divide Palestine into two countries, one Arab and one Jewish. Jews accepted the plan, but Arabs opposed it. Finally, on May 14, 1948, Jews proclaimed the founding of their new nation, which they called Israel. Immediately, neighboring Arab countries sent their armies to join the Arab population of Palestine in fighting Israel. Israel, backed by aid from the United States, managed to hold its own in the fighting.

After 8 months, both sides accepted a bid by the United Nations to stop the war. Dr. Ralph Bunche, an American, headed the United Nations team that worked out the truce, or cease-fire. Dr. Bunche was later awarded a Nobel Peace Prize for his work in the Middle East.

All Westerners were forced to leave the area during the Suez War.
■ **What type of terrain is this?**

The Suez War   In the 1950s, Colonel Gamal Abdel Nasser (gə mäl′ äb′ dəl nas′ ėr) came to power in Egypt. He wanted to end Western influence in his country and was determined to destroy Israel. Starting in 1955 he encouraged raids across the border into Israel. The next year he seized control of the Suez Canal from Great Britain.

Israel wanted to end the raids on its land. The British and the French wanted to regain control of the canal, through which much of their trade flowed. The three countries agreed on a plan. In October 1956, Israeli forces launched an attack against the Egyptians. In 4 days they smashed Nasser's armies and swept across the Sinai (sī′ nī) Peninsula to the Suez Canal. British and French troops also landed to take control of the canal.

Both the Soviet Union and the United States opposed this action. The two countries supported a United Nations resolution that stopped the fighting and got the three invading armies to withdraw. A UN peacekeeping force took their place.

The Eisenhower Doctrine   President Eisenhower feared that the Soviet Union might gain influence in the Middle East after the Suez war. In 1957 he announced a policy that extended containment to this region. Eisenhower said that the United States would defend countries in the Middle East against armed attack by Communist countries. The United States also offered economic help to the countries of the region. This policy became known as the **Eisenhower Doctrine**.

The Eisenhower Doctrine was used for the first time in 1958. Lebanon was threatened with revolution by forces backed by both the Soviet Union and Egypt. The Lebanese government asked for help. President Eisenhower sent United States marines into Lebanon, and the rebellion quickly ended.

CHECKUP

1. How did the United States try to check the spread of communism in Southeast Asia?
2. What was the spirit of Geneva?
3. What was the U-2 incident, and what effect did it have on Soviet-American relations?
4. In what ways did the United States become involved in the Middle East in the 1950s?
5. **Thinking Critically** Why did the Middle East come to be considered an important region for the security of the United States and its allies in the 1950s?

New Threats, New Hopes

How did President Kennedy extend or modify the containment policy of Truman and Eisenhower?

President Kennedy   President Eisenhower was succeeded in the White House by John F. Kennedy. Kennedy had long been interested in international affairs. In 1940, while he was still a student in college, he wrote a thesis about why England was not prepared for World War II. This thesis was published as the book *Why England Slept.* Shortly before the United States entered that war, Kennedy joined the navy. In 1943 the torpedo boat he commanded was sunk by a Japanese warship. Kennedy swam 3 miles (5 km) to an island, towing an injured crew member by holding a strap of the man's life jacket in his teeth. In later years, when asked how he became a war hero, Kennedy replied, "It was involuntary. They sank my boat."

After the war, John F. Kennedy was elected to Congress, where he served for the next 14 years. He continued his interest in foreign affairs, supporting the Marshall Plan and NATO. In 1960, Senator Kennedy received the Democratic nomination for President. In an extremely close election, he defeated the Republican candidate, Vice President Richard Nixon.

President Kennedy's inaugural address dealt mainly with foreign affairs. He made clear that he would continue the policy of containment. "Let every nation know," he said, " . . . that we shall pay any price, bear any burden, meet any hardship, . . . in order to assure the survival and the success of liberty." At the same time, Kennedy declared that he wanted to find peaceful solutions to problems. "Let us never negotiate out of fear," said the new President. "But let us never fear to negotiate."

Presidential candidates John Kennedy and Richard Nixon took part in four televised debates during the 1960 election campaign. Some 70 million people watched.
■ Why had such debates never been held before?

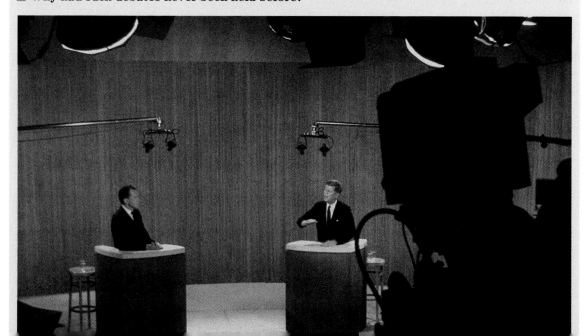

Peace Corps volunteers often learned even more than they taught. This volunteer works with men in Ecuador.
■ **What would this young man have had a chance to learn in Ecuador?**

The Peace Corps President Kennedy brought several new ideas to American foreign policy. One that turned out to be extremely successful was the **Peace Corps**. Under this program, American men and women with skills in such varied fields as medicine, carpentry, teaching, farming, and engineering volunteered to go to Third World countries seeking help in these areas.

The Peace Corps members lived among the people, learning to understand their language and to appreciate their ways. The Americans helped farmers increase their crops, assisted in building water and sewage systems, taught basic skills, and in other ways helped to raise standards of living. Within 4 years the United States government was sending 10,000 volunteers to serve in 46 countries. Peace Corps volunteers created much goodwill toward the United States.

The Alliance for Progress Another of Kennedy's programs was the **Alliance for Progress**. This was a plan for build-

ing up the economies of countries in the Western Hemisphere, helping their poor people, and making democratic government stronger. Latin American governments, the United States government, and private investors joined to provide the needed capital. In 1961 all the countries of the hemisphere except Cuba joined the alliance. During the next 4 years, Latin American countries put $22 billion into the program, and the United States added another $4 billion.

The results, however, were disappointing. Although the economies of some countries did grow, the military and upper classes that controlled those countries' governments dragged their feet on reform. The poor remained poor, and the governments did not become more democratic. Later, Congress cut United States spending for the alliance.

The Bay of Pigs In January 1959 a Cuban revolution led by Fidel Castro overthrew the dictator who ruled Cuba. At first, many Americans were friendly toward Castro. But when he executed political opponents and seized American-owned property in Cuba, opinion turned against him. Castro also developed close ties with the Soviet Union. Thousands of Cubans became **exiles,** people driven or forced to flee their home country for political reasons. Most settled in the United States. Many of these exiles were determined to return and overthrow Castro.

In 1960, President Eisenhower approved a secret plan to train and arm these exiles for an invasion of Cuba. Our government believed that the Cuban people would support the invaders and rise up against Castro.

Kennedy learned of this plan after becoming President. He had doubts about its wisdom, but he allowed it to go forward. However, he ruled out the use of United States troops and planes. In April 1961 about 1,400 anti-Castro Cubans landed at the Bay of Pigs on the southern coast of Cuba. It became clear very quickly that the United States government and the Cuban exiles had misjudged the situation badly. There was no popular uprising. Within a few days, all the invaders were killed or captured. This misadventure was a serious setback for the United States in Latin America and the rest of the world. At the same time it drove Castro more firmly into the Soviet camp.

The Berlin Wall Tensions between the Soviet Union and the United States increased after a meeting between President Kennedy and Premier Khrushchev a few

The Berlin wall went up virtually overnight in August 1961. This young boy on the West Berlin side only pretends to want to get over the wall.
■ What message did construction of the wall send to the whole world?

months later in Vienna, Austria. The Soviets had never given up the goal of getting the Western powers out of Berlin. The wartime allies had never agreed on a peace treaty with defeated Germany. When Eisenhower was President, Khrushchev threatened that his country would make a separate peace treaty with East Germany. He said that would end any rights that the Western powers had to be in Berlin. Eisenhower declared that the Western nations would not accept this and would remain in West Berlin, and Khrushchev dropped the threat.

Khrushchev now made the same threat to Kennedy, and Kennedy gave the same reply. The United States would not abandon the people of West Berlin. The two sides disagreed on other issues as well. It was a grim President Kennedy who returned to Washington. Determined to show the Soviet Union that the United States would stand firm, he doubled the number of men drafted. The President also asked Congress to increase spending for weapons.

One reason the Soviets wanted the Western powers out of Berlin was that more than 4,000 people were escaping each week from Communist East Germany into the West. Many of these slipped out by way of West Berlin. This fact told the world that life behind the iron curtain was hardly the paradise that Soviet propaganda made it out to be.

On the morning of August 13, 1961, Berliners awoke to find that the East German government was putting up a barbed wire fence between East Berlin and West Berlin. Later a cement-block wall replaced the fence. Guards with "shoot-to-kill" orders patrolled the wall. The wall made escape from East Berlin nearly impossible, but it was also a reminder to the world of the differences between a Communist state and a free society. Kennedy sent American troops into West Berlin as a sign that the Western powers would remain in Berlin. Gradually, tensions eased in Germany. The Berlin wall, however, stands to this day.

The Cuban Missile Crisis   A year later, the Soviet Union offered a still more serious challenge to the United States. In October 1962 an American spy plane took photographs showing that the Soviets were secretly building missile bases in Cuba. From these bases, missiles could carry nuclear bombs to much of the eastern and southern United States. For several days, President Kennedy discussed possible moves with his advisers. Then he went on television to inform the American people of the threat. He ordered the navy to stop any ship bound for Cuba with weapons. He demanded that Khrushchev remove the missiles already in Cuba and tear down the missile bases.

President Kennedy showed the American people photographs of the missile bases that had been taken by U-2 planes in surveillance flights over Cuba. These photographs clearly showed that the bases were being built with great speed, and that they held more than just defensive weapons. No one was quite sure what the Soviet Union was trying to gain by building the bases, but they were certainly meant to be some kind of challenge to the United States.

For 6 days the world stood on the brink of war. No one knew whether the Soviet ships on their way to Cuba would challenge the navy's blockade. American planes carrying live nuclear bombs took off and awaited orders. Behind the scenes, messages passed back and forth between Kennedy and Khrushchev. As the Soviet ships neared the blockade, Khrushchev decided

During the tense days of the missile crisis in Cuba, American troops were on alert in nearby Florida and all over the world.
■ Why are the soldiers on the right dressed in camouflage uniforms?

not to challenge the United States. The ships turned back. The crisis was over. In the end the Soviet Union removed the missiles and bases. In return the United States promised not to invade Cuba.

Steps to Avoid War   One result of the Cuban missile crisis was that both sides realized they must avoid such dangerous showdowns. In 1963 they installed a **hot line**—a special communications system between the White House and Moscow—so that the leaders could talk immediately in a crisis. In the same year, the United States and the Soviet Union—along with Great Britain—worked out a treaty to ban the testing of nuclear weapons above the ground, underwater, and in outer space. Underground tests were still allowed. More than 100 nations joined in signing the treaty to ban testing.

In a speech that year, President Kennedy summed up the new awareness of the danger of nuclear war and of the need for the two sides to work for peace. "Our most basic common link," he said, "is that we all inhabit this small planet. We all breathe the same air. We all cherish our children's future. And we are all mortal."

CHECKUP

1. What new ideas did President Kennedy bring to foreign policy?
2. Why was the Bay of Pigs affair a setback for the United States?
3. Why was the Berlin wall built?
4. How was the 1962 Cuban missile crisis resolved?

5. **Thinking Critically**   What do you think would happen if the Soviets or the East Germans took the Berlin wall down today?

693

Reading for Sequence

THE COLD WAR

Understanding sequence—the order in which events occur—is necessary to understand history. That is because events almost always depend on earlier events. For example, take these three events:

Columbus discovers America.
The English start colonies in America.
American colonies rebel against England.

Clearly the founding of colonies in America depended on someone first discovering the land. The revolution could happen only after there were colonies to rebel. Without knowing the correct sequence of these events, you could make neither head nor tail of the early years of America's history.

Sequence is not the same as cause and effect. Just because one event occurred before another does not mean that the first event caused the second event to happen. Columbus did not cause the English to start colonies in America a hundred years later. But the two events are related, and knowing their sequence helps you to understand the ways in which they are related.

As you read, it is important to recognize the sequence of events. Writers provide various aids to help you follow sequence. Of course, the best aids are dates. But be alert also for signal words that tell *when* something happened. Some common signal words are *first, later, then, next, earlier, finally, during this time,* and so on.

SKILLS PRACTICE I

Read the sections under the headings "War in Korea," "China Enters the War," and "The Korean War Ends," on pages 683–685. Locate and write down all the signal words for sequence, including dates, that you can find in those sections.

SKILLS PRACTICE II

Even when there are no signal words, you will be able to put events in the correct order by reading carefully. For example, these four events are listed in the order in which they are mentioned under the heading "Soviet Actions," on page 677.

1. Soviet troops placed a Communist government in power in Poland.
2. Soviet troops placed Communist governments in power in other countries of Eastern Europe.
3. Germany invaded the Soviet Union twice through Poland and Eastern Europe.
4. The wars cost millions of Soviet lives.

Read the section under the heading "Soviet Actions," on page 677. On a separate sheet of paper, copy the four events listed above in the order in which they actually occurred.

MAIN IDEAS

1. Less than a year after their victory over the Axis powers, the United States and the Soviet Union were involved in a cold war.
2. To keep the Soviet Union from expanding the territory under its control, the United States adopted a policy of containment.
3. The United States under President Truman expressed its commitment to the security of Western Europe through the Truman Doctrine, the Marshall Plan, and participation in the NATO alliance.
4. When Communist North Korea invaded South Korea in 1950, United Nations forces, most of which were supplied by the United States, came to the aid of South Korea.
5. President Eisenhower carried on Truman's policy of containment, but also sought to promote peaceful coexistence in meetings with Soviet leaders.
6. During John F. Kennedy's presidency, the United States and the Soviet Union disagreed over events in Berlin and Cuba.

VOCABULARY REVIEW

On a separate sheet of paper, write the number of the statements below. Next to each number write the word or phrase that best completes the statement.

Peace Corps	Alliance for Progress
cold war	Truman Doctrine
NATO	summit conference
containment	Marshall Plan
United Nations	iron curtain

1. The organization founded in 1945 to help keep the peace was the _____ .
2. Winston Churchill accused the Soviets of lowering an _____ _____ across Europe.
3. By 1946 the United States and the Soviet Union were engaged in a conflict called the _____ .
4. To prevent the spread of communism, the United States adopted a policy of _____ .

5. United States military aid to Greece and Turkey was called for under the terms of the _____ .
6. The United States helped the countries of Western Europe recover from the effects of war through the _____ .
7. The United States joined with countries of Western Europe in a defense alliance called _____ .
8. In 1955, President Eisenhower met with the leaders of the Soviet Union and other countries at Geneva in a _____ .
9. American volunteers who went to underdeveloped countries to help people were members of the _____ .
10. A program started by President Kennedy to help countries in the Western Hemisphere was called the _____ .

CHAPTER CHECKUP

1. What areas of the world were affected by each of the following: (**a**) the Truman Doctrine, (**b**) the Marshall Plan, (**c**) the Alliance for Progress, (**d**) the Eisenhower Doctrine?
2. What changes occurred in Japan after World War II, and how were they different from the changes in Germany?
3. What part did the United Nations play in the Korean War?
4. Explain the background and the outcome of the following: (**a**) the Bay of Pigs invasion, (**b**) the Cuban missile crisis.
5. **Thinking Critically** How did President Truman's views on the Korean War differ from General MacArthur's, and why was Truman able to make his views stick?

APPLYING KNOWLEDGE

1. List the countries that are in the North Atlantic Treaty Organization today. Locate each on a globe or world map.
2. Several United Nations agencies are usually referred to by abbreviated names. Find out the full title and responsibilities of each of the following agencies: (**a**) UNESCO, (**b**) UNICEF, (**c**) WHO.

29 A Changing Nation

1944–1963

The Consumer Society

What were the major factors contributing to prosperity in postwar America?

GI Bill of Rights	**Sunbelt**
Green Revolution	

Wartime Housing   Before World War II, the company of Levitt & Sons of Long Island, New York, was not much different from a thousand other builders of homes. The company was started during the Great Depression. By the end of the 1930s, it was building about 50 homes a year on Long Island. This area was a suburb of New York City, and homes there were fairly expensive. Levitt & Sons, like other home builders in those days, built only a few houses at a time.

Then came the war. With building materials and labor in short supply, the construction of private homes fell off sharply. There was, however, a great need for temporary low-cost housing near the nation's mushrooming military bases and booming war industries. The Levitt company won a contract to build such housing at the naval base in Norfolk, Virginia. To complete the construction of 2,300 dwell-ing units quickly and efficiently, Levitt adopted some of the mass-production methods of factories.

Homes for Veterans   When the war was over, there was a mood of uncertainty in the country. Some feared a return to the depression of the 1930s. Many builders were cautious about starting too many new homes. Some builders, like Levitt, saw the situation differently. Millions of war veterans would be returning home and starting families. They would need housing. Furthermore, Congress had passed a law in 1944 called the Servicemen's Readjustment Act, or the **GI Bill of Rights**. One part of this law allowed veterans to borrow money at low interest rates to buy homes. Other government programs begun during the New Deal also made borrowing for home buying easier. Levitt saw a great demand for inexpensive homes, suitable for families that were just starting out.

Levitt bought 1,400 acres (567 ha) of land near the town of Hicksville, Long Island. Hicksville is a few miles east of Queens, a part of New York City. Land near Hicksville was cheaper than land in the city. That would help keep down the cost of a house. Levitt also knew that the

William Levitt built several Levittowns in the northeastern United States in the years after World War II.
■ **How might people personalize their homes?**

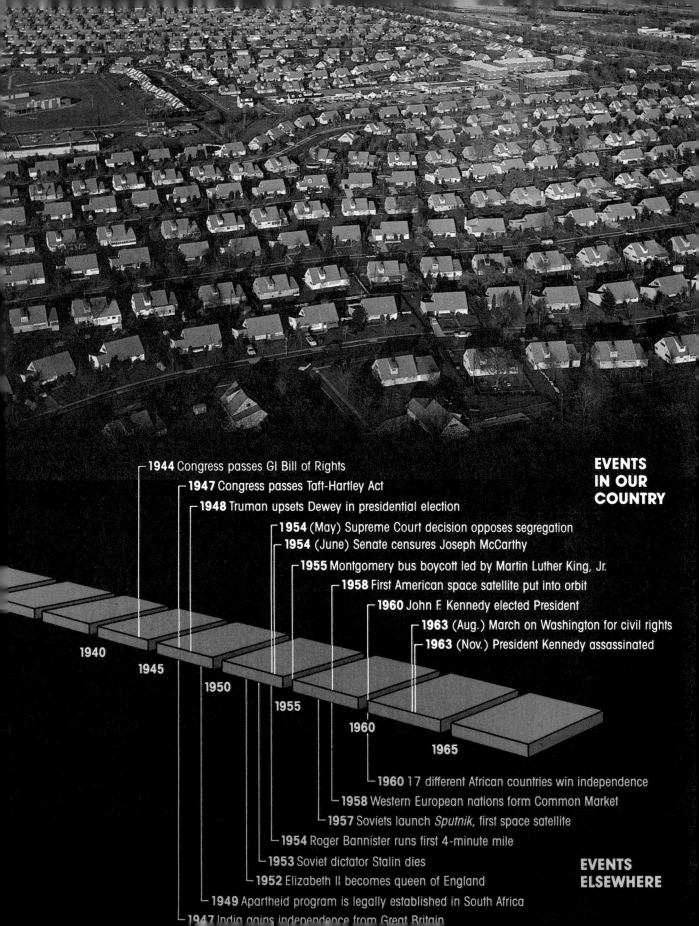

1944 Congress passes GI Bill of Rights

1947 Congress passes Taft-Hartley Act

1948 Truman upsets Dewey in presidential election

1954 (May) Supreme Court decision opposes segregation

1954 (June) Senate censures Joseph McCarthy

1955 Montgomery bus boycott led by Martin Luther King, Jr.

1958 First American space satellite put into orbit

1960 John F. Kennedy elected President

1963 (Aug.) March on Washington for civil rights

1963 (Nov.) President Kennedy assassinated

1940

1945

1950

1955

1960

1965

1960 17 different African countries win independence

1958 Western European nations form Common Market

1957 Soviets launch *Sputnik*, first space satellite

1954 Roger Bannister runs first 4-minute mile

1953 Soviet dictator Stalin dies

1952 Elizabeth II becomes queen of England

1949 Apartheid program is legally established in South Africa

1947 India gains independence from Great Britain

**EVENTS
ELSEWHERE**

suburbs had been growing for many decades. To many people the suburbs meant a better life — open space, clean air, and a good environment for raising a family.

Building Whole Communities Levitt's plan was to build not just a handful of homes but an entire community. Levittown, as the community was called, would have 6,000 one-family houses plus its own shopping centers, parks, schools, and churches. Each house would come complete with kitchen appliances and would have a front yard and a back yard. Veterans would rent for a year at $65 a month. After that they could buy the house for $8,000. No down payment would be needed, and the monthly payment would actually be lower than the rent. Levittown was a bold experiment in mass production.

Building began in 1947. To keep costs down, Levitt applied the mass-production methods it had developed at the Norfolk navy base. All the houses had to be the same. The housing site became a huge assembly line. Work crews, each with its own specialty, went from house to house, putting in plumbing, installing stairs, and nailing on shingles. At each house, trucks dropped off the exact materials the next work crew would need — pipes, roofing materials, paint. Soon the company was building 150 houses a week. By the end of 1949, Levittown was completed, and every one of its houses was rented or sold.

Levitt went on to build other Levittowns. (See the picture on page 697.) One in Bucks County, Pennsylvania, near Philadelphia, had 17,000 homes. A third, in New Jersey, had 12,000. These communities made Levitt the largest home builder in the East. Meanwhile, other builders were using Levitt's idea in Park Forest, Illinois; Orange County, California; and

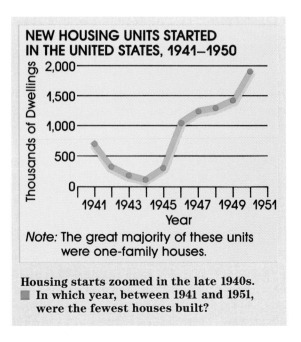

NEW HOUSING UNITS STARTED IN THE UNITED STATES, 1941–1950

Note: The great majority of these units were one-family houses.

Housing starts zoomed in the late 1940s. In which year, between 1941 and 1951, were the fewest houses built?

dozens of other places all over America. In fact, the postwar years marked the start of the greatest period of home building in American history.

An Increasing, Shifting Population This building boom was connected to three major developments in postwar America. First, there was a great increase in population. The growth of America's population had slowed down sharply during the Great Depression and the war. After the war, however, there was a "baby boom." This created a demand for housing.

Second, the building boom was connected to great shifts of population within the United States. The first shift was away from the farm. In 1940 nearly 1 in every 4 Americans lived on a farm. Thirty years later, fewer than 1 in 20 did.

This shift resulted mainly from advances in agriculture known as the **Green Revolution**. American scientists developed new varieties of rice, wheat, soybeans, and corn that produced many times more food than older varieties had. With better fertilizers, better insect control, and more efficient farm machinery, production increased dramatically. In 1950 a single farm worker could raise enough food to feed 15 people. In 1970 the same worker could feed 45 people. Fewer people were needed on farms, and millions of people left the land.

A second great population shift was from the city to the suburbs. You have read something about this shift already. After World War II about a million people each year joined the movement to the suburbs. By the early 1960s more Americans lived in the suburbs than in cities. Cars and new roads made it possible for people to live in the suburbs and work in the cities. In time, business and industry moved to the suburbs. Huge shopping centers were also built there. Soon many people were working in the suburbs as well as living there.

Suburbs grew so rapidly that by the 1960s and 1970s some suburbs had become like the cities their residents had sought to escape. It was often hard to tell where the city ended and the suburbs began. Traffic jams were a part of every rush hour. Noise and pollution increased. So did crime and taxes. At the same time, suburbs offered fewer cultural experiences, such as museums, plays, and concerts, than did cities.

Shifts Between the North and the South A third population shift was from the northern and eastern parts of the United States to the West and the South. This area, roughly the southern third of the country, came to be known as the **Sunbelt**. Its climate is sunny and warm much of the year, and winters are mild. People moved to the Sunbelt for various reasons. Many of these people were senior citizens

The Sunbelt, with its warm climate and mild winters, has attracted many older Americans.
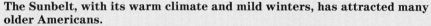 **What other features attracted people to the Sunbelt?**

who wanted a warmer climate. Younger people were attracted by the different style of living in this region. As the textile industry moved south and the oil, gas, space, and defense industries in the Sunbelt states grew, people were drawn there by job opportunities.

As a result, towns sprang up in California and Florida in areas where orange trees had grown only a few years before. New cities — called "boomtowns" like the mining towns of the Old West (pages 443–445) — appeared in Arizona, New Mexico, Texas, and the Gulf Coast states. Small cities became great ones. By 1984, six of the ten largest cities in the United States —Los Angeles, Houston, Dallas, San

Diego, Phoenix, and San Antonio —were in the Sunbelt. The states in the Sunbelt had become the fastest-growing areas of the country.

A fourth major population shift was the movement of black Americans from the South to the North. As late as the 1930s, about 80 percent of the black population still lived in the southern states. So great was the migration during and after World War II that by 1960 more than half the black population lived outside the South. Most lived in cities of the North, the Midwest, and the West. This was the only population shift that did not create a demand for the construction of new housing. Most blacks moved into older housing in the central cities.

Housing developments such as this one in Texas appeared in many new cities in the Sunbelt.

■ **What materials are these houses made of?**

The Demand for Consumer Goods

The third major development in the building boom was the period of prosperity that the United States experienced from 1945 to 1970. It was the longest period of sustained prosperity in the nation's history. This prosperity was based mainly on the demand for consumer goods.

During the war, Americans had made good money but found few things to spend it on. They put their money into savings or bought United States war bonds. At the end of the war, therefore, they had saved billions. When factories again started to make cars, stoves, refrigerators, and other goods, consumers snapped them up as fast as they came off the assembly lines. This postwar demand for goods lasted for several years, providing high employment and good wages.

The baby boom also created a demand for consumer goods, from food and clothing to washing machines and toys. Later, as the postwar babies became teenagers, it meant a demand for such goods as hi-fis and stereos, records, and tape recorders.

Jobs were plentiful in the prosperous years after World War II.
■ How can you tell that these workers are enjoying prosperity?

necessity. In the prosperous 1920s, auto manufacturers considered it a good year when their industry sold 3 million cars. In most years in the 1950s and 1960s, they sold twice that many.

New consumer goods created whole new industries. In 1946 only 6,000 television sets were made in America. By 1950 American manufacturers were producing more than 7 million sets a year. Television created jobs for people who made the sets, sold them, repaired them, and created programs for them.

Purchases of consumer goods were made easy by plenty of consumer credit. In 1950 the newest thing in consumer credit, the credit card, was introduced at gas stations. Credit cards spread quickly to other businesses.

In addition to the growing market at home, the United States found a large market overseas for its goods. Europe's economies were shattered by the destruction of World War II. For many years, therefore, United States factories would be the chief suppliers of goods to that continent.

Thus, despite several recessions, the country was producing twice as many goods and services in 1970 as in 1945. Americans were earning more money and enjoying more goods than ever before.

More Goods, More Jobs   The growing population meant that city and state governments had to spend more for schools, roads, hospitals, and police and fire services. This meant still more jobs. More jobs meant more people who could afford to buy homes. And that, in turn, meant more sales of kitchen appliances, lawn mowers, and tool kits.

As people moved to the suburbs, owning a car became more and more of a

CHECKUP

1. Why was there a building boom in the United States after World War II?
2. Why did suburbs grow dramatically in the years after World War II?
3. How did improvements in agriculture lead to a growth in urban population?
4. What were some of the reasons for the growth of the Sunbelt?
5. **Thinking Critically**   Why was the period following World War II a time of prosperity?

Postwar Politics and Policies

What were the major domestic events of the presidency of Harry S. Truman?

A Smooth Changeover   When the fighting ended in World War II, Americans everywhere wanted to get back to normal living quickly. Most of the 12 million men and women still in the service were eager to return home. Factory owners wanted to shift their operations back to making peacetime products.

Considering the size of the task, the changeover from wartime to peacetime progressed fairly smoothly. Within a year, 9 million men and women exchanged their uniforms for civilian clothes. The GI Bill of Rights not only aided veterans in buying homes, but also helped them go to college, train for jobs, and start businesses. Eventually, 8 million veterans took advantage of the opportunity for advanced education. Both they and the nation benefited from the knowledge and skills they gained. Factory owners, too, made the return to civilian production quickly. Less than 5 months after the shooting stopped, 90 percent of the war industries were back to making peacetime goods.

Rising Prices   The main problem of the early postwar years turned out to be **inflation**, or rising prices. Factories could not keep up with the demand for consumer goods. When demand is greater than supply, prices rise. In addition, workers wanted wage increases to make up for the rise in living costs. There were many strikes. When employers agreed to raise wages, they covered their higher costs by charging more for their products. This raised the cost of living, leading to still more demands for higher wages.

President Truman tried to hold down inflation by continuing wartime price controls, but prices rose anyway. In 1946 nearly all price controls were removed. Prices continued to rise for a time before finally leveling off.

The Taft-Hartley Act   By the fall of 1946, frustration over strikes, shortages, and rising prices was high. Many angry Americans felt that labor unions had grown too powerful. In elections that November, they gave the Republicans control of both houses of Congress for the first time since the beginning of the Great Depression. In 1947, that Republican Congress passed the Taft-Hartley Act. This law outlawed the **closed shop**. A closed shop is a workplace in which the company

In 1946, workers in a Connecticut city demonstrate during a labor dispute.
■ Why are they demanding wage increases?

One newspaper got the results of the 1948 presidential election wrong in its early editions. President Truman was amused by the blunder.
▪ What newspaper made this mistake?

agrees to hire only people who already belong to a union. The new law also allowed the President to stop certain strikes. When the President felt that a strike threatened the country's welfare, he could call for an 80-day cooling-off period. President Truman vetoed this bill, but Congress passed it over his veto.

President Truman had many other disagreements with Congress. He sought laws to protect the civil rights of blacks and other minorities. As you know, civil rights are rights guaranteed to all Americans by the Constitution. The right to vote and the right to a fair trial are examples of civil rights. Truman also asked for laws to prevent racial discrimination in hiring. Congress did not act on his proposals. On his own, however, Truman gave orders to end segregation in the armed forces.

The Election of 1948   In 1948 the Democrats nominated Harry Truman to run for a full term as President. His opponent was Thomas E. Dewey, a successful and popular governor of New York. Some of Truman's decisions had made him unpopular with various groups of voters. Most people — including most Democrats — expected the Republicans to win easily after 16 years of Democratic rule.

Harry Truman surprised them all. He took his campaign directly to the people. Truman traveled 31,000 miles (50,000 km) and made more than 350 speeches. People admired the President's down-to-earth manner. By comparison, Dewey avoided talking about issues and seemed stiff and formal. On election day, Truman had the support of farmers and organized labor, and he won.

Born: 1884, Lamar, Missouri.
Education: High school.
Training: Farmer, soldier, public official.
To presidency from: Missouri.
Position when taking office: Vice President.
Political party: Democratic.
Married: Bess Wallace.
Children: One daughter.
Died: 1972, Kansas City, Missouri.
Other facts: Operated the family farm for 15 years. Joined the National Guard and served in Europe in World War I. Held local offices in Missouri and elected to United States Senate, where he won a reputation as an investigator of waste and corruption in defense spending. Enjoyed playing piano and taking early morning walks.
During his presidency: The atomic age began with the testing of an atomic bomb at Alamogordo, New Mexico, in July 1945.

HARRY S. TRUMAN
33rd President
1945 · 1953

The Fair Deal   After his victory, President Truman called for laws that would bring New Deal reforms such as social security and the minimum wage to Americans still not covered by them. He also called for new programs in education, health care, agriculture, and low-income housing. Truman called his program the Fair Deal.

Congress gave Truman some of what he asked for. It extended social security coverage to 10 million more workers, and it raised the minimum wage. It also passed a housing act under which the federal government cleared slums and built housing for low-income families. But Congress turned down Truman's other ideas.

Cold War Politics   During the years of the cold war, some Americans began to question whether communism was spreading at home. In 1946, officials in Canada discovered a Soviet spy ring that was stealing atomic secrets. Were Communists and their sympathizers in the United States also in positions where they might harm

the nation? In 1947, responding to growing pressure from people in the government and outside it, President Truman ordered a check on the loyalty of all federal employees. In the next 4 years, more than 3 million federal workers were investigated. Most were cleared, but 212 were fired as possible "security risks."

Meanwhile, committees of Congress and of several state legislatures looked for evidence of Communist influence. A new Red Scare was building throughout the country. The attorney general of the United States warned that Communists "are everywhere—in factories, offices, butcher shops, on street corners, in private business. . . ." The charge that Communists had become well established caused great worry.

McCarthy's Rise and Fall   Republican Senator Joseph R. McCarthy of Wisconsin took advantage of these fears to gain fame and power. Early in 1950 he rocketed to public attention with the claim that there were more than 200 "known Communists"

COMMUNIST PARTY ORGANIZATION U.S.A-FEB. 9, 1950

In the 1954 congressional hearings, Senator Joseph McCarthy makes a charge of Communist influence in the United States Army.   Seated at the table is Joseph Welch, the army's chief lawyer.
■ Why were millions of Americans able to watch the hearings?

in the State Department.   For the next 4 years, McCarthy held the headlines with charges that there were Communists in universities, in government, in business, and even in the military.   He accused Presidents Roosevelt and Truman of "20 years of treason."   He called George C. Marshall, the great wartime general and author of the Marshall Plan, a traitor.   Senator McCarthy never proved any of his charges.   Still, many people, worried by communism, believed at first that he was doing patriotic work.

In 1954 a Senate committee investigated McCarthy's charge of Communist influence in the United States Army.   The committee's hearings were televised.   Millions of Americans saw McCarthy in action for the first time.   His actions and methods caused him to lose a lot of support.   Later that year the Senate **censured**, or condemned, him for his behavior.   McCarthy's influence fell sharply after that.   When the Democrats took control of the Senate in 1957, Senator McCarthy lost his committee chairmanship.   Joseph McCarthy died later that year.

CHECKUP

1. What troubles did inflation cause in the years just after World War II?
2. What were some of the provisions of the Taft-Hartley Act?
3. How successful was President Truman in getting his Fair Deal program enacted by Congress?
4. Why did Senator Joseph McCarthy become well known in the early 1950s?
5. **Thinking Critically**   Why did prices rise soon after World War II ended?

The Eisenhower and Kennedy Years

How did both President Eisenhower and President Kennedy carry on the New Deal policies of their predecessors, and how did they modify those policies?

VOCABULARY

space satellite	urban renewal
New Frontier	assassination

Eisenhower's Program The fall of Senator Joseph McCarthy came while Dwight D. Eisenhower was President. McCarthy had once said that President Eisenhower had allowed himself to be tricked by Communist lies. That was a charge that few Americans believed. Eisenhower was one of the best-liked and most trusted Presidents in history. During his campaigns for election, millions expressed their feelings by wearing "I Like Ike" buttons.

When Eisenhower was finishing his wartime service in Europe, few Americans knew anything about his political beliefs. Like other generals in our history who have risen to positions of political power, he was wise enough to keep his politics to himself as long as he was in uniform. Neither party knew just where he stood, but both knew that he would make an attractive candidate. A group of Democrats had

Republican presidential candidate Dwight Eisenhower is greeted by enthusiastic crowds during the 1952 election campaign.
■ Why, do you think, was Eisenhower a favorite of the people?

Born: 1890, Denison, Texas.
Education: United States Military Academy.
Training: Army officer.
To presidency from: New York.
Position when elected: General of the army at the time of his nomination.
Political party: Republican.
Married: Mamie Doud.
Children: Two sons.
Died: 1969, Washington, D.C.
Other facts: Served as an army officer in Panama, the Philippines, and the United States. Commanded Allied forces for the invasion of Europe in World War II. Later became president of Columbia University, and then commander of NATO forces in Europe. The first President licensed to pilot an airplane.
During his presidency: The crippling disease infantile paralysis was conquered when Dr. Jonas Salk invented an antipolio vaccine.

DWIGHT D. EISENHOWER

34th President
1953 · 1961

tried to convince him to run against Truman in 1948. In 1952 the Republicans had more success.

At the time Ike was serving in Europe again, as supreme commander of NATO's forces. He resigned from that job in June 1952 and announced that he was a candidate for the Republican nomination for President. The Democrats were divided that year. Unable to choose from among the announced candidates, they drafted Governor Adlai Stevenson of Illinois at their convention. Stevenson was a graceful, witty speaker and a man of considerable intelligence. Still, he was no match for the appealing general. Ike was swept into office, winning the electoral votes of 39 states.

The Republican party also gained control of both houses of Congress in the 1952 elections. Those contests, however, were much closer than the presidential election. The Republican majority in the House of Representatives was just 7 seats. In the Senate the two parties were tied,

which meant the Republican Vice President would deliver any tie-breaking votes. The country had backed Ike overwhelmingly. It had backed the rest of his party less decisively.

Eisenhower called his program Modern Republicanism. Although some members of his party wanted to repeal the reforms of the New Deal, Eisenhower accepted them. During his two terms of office, Congress again raised the minimum wage and brought millions of additional workers into the social security system. Eisenhower favored both actions. He also created the Department of Health, Education, and Welfare. This new department was so named because it brought together all the programs of the federal government that dealt with the health, education, and welfare of Americans. To head the new department, President Eisenhower named Oveta Culp Hobby of Texas. Hobby was only the second woman to serve in the Cabinet. During these years the federal government also provided increased funds for

The interstate highway system, begun in 1956, was built by the states, using large contributions of federal money and assistance.
■ How do the highway overpasses help the flow of traffic on the main highway?

medical research, hospitals, and urban renewal. In addition, Eisenhower proposed the Federal Highway Act of 1956, under which most of today's interstate highway system was built.

On the other hand, Eisenhower wanted to lessen the involvement of the federal government in many areas. Soon after taking office, he removed the last of the federal controls over prices and wages that had been put into effect during the Korean War. He opposed New Deal programs like the Tennessee Valley Authority. (See page 628.) He believed that private companies, rather than the government, should develop electric power. He also favored less government regulation of business and industry.

In 1955, President Eisenhower suffered a serious heart attack. At first, few people thought he would be well enough to run for a second term of office. But he made a strong recovery. In 1956 he was reelected in a landslide, receiving 57 percent of the vote.

The Space Age Opens   The space age began during Eisenhower's presidency. On October 4, 1957, the Soviets put the world's first **space satellite**, which they called Sputnik, into orbit around the earth. One month later they launched Sputnik 2, which carried a live dog. This Soviet achievement was a blow to American prestige. It appeared that the Soviets had beaten America at its own game— science and technology. More importantly, Soviet success in putting a space satellite into orbit around the earth increased concern for America's security against attack.

President Eisenhower and Congress responded by providing more funds for America's space program and by setting up the National Aeronautics and Space Administration (NASA) to direct it. They also adopted the National Defense Education Act (NDEA). One aim of this act was to produce more scientists and science teachers by providing funds for their training.

Meanwhile the United States speeded up its space efforts. In 1958 the first American satellite was lifted into orbit. Still, the United States would remain behind the Soviet Union in the space race for some time. In 1961, Yuri Gagarin, a Soviet military officer, became the first person to orbit the earth.

The Election of Kennedy   In 1960, John F. Kennedy won the presidency in the closest race of the twentieth century so far. He won by 118,000 popular votes—a bare one tenth of 1 percent more than his Republican opponent, Vice President Richard Nixon, received. This was the first "television election"—the first campaign to be waged mainly on television and the first that was probably decided by it. Kennedy and Nixon engaged in a series of four televised debates. Before the debates, polls showed Kennedy trailing by a wide margin. Voters were favorably impressed, though, by the showing the senator from Massachusetts made in the debates. Afterward, Kennedy pulled even with Nixon. He became the first Roman Catholic President and, at 43, the youngest man ever elected to that position.

The New Frontier   During his campaign, John F. Kennedy often spoke of the need to "get the country moving again." The American frontier and its challenges had disappeared long ago, he said, but the challenges America now faced offered "a

John F. Kennedy is shown with his family in 1960.
■ How is Kennedy in this picture noticeably different from the last 6 or 7 Presidents you have read about?

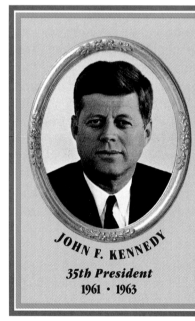

Born: 1917, Brookline, Massachusetts.
Education: Harvard College.
Training: Author, public official.
To presidency from: Massachusetts.
Position when elected: United States senator.
Political party: Democratic.
Married: Jacqueline Bouvier.
Children: One daughter, two sons.
Died: November 22, 1963, shot by an assassin in Dallas, Texas.
Other facts: As naval officer in South Pacific in World War II, decorated for heroism. Served in both houses of Congress. Received Pulitzer Prize for his book *Profiles in Courage*. The first Roman Catholic to become President.
During his presidency: A civil rights march brought 200,000 people to Washington, D.C., in a demonstration of the demands of black people for equal rights.

JOHN F. KENNEDY
35th President
1961 · 1963

New Frontier." The term **New Frontier** became the slogan of John F. Kennedy's presidency.

Soon after taking office, Kennedy called on Congress to pass a number of laws to improve the economy and to help the less fortunate. At the time, the unemployment rate stood at over 8 percent. He recommended funds to retrain unemployed workers and to help depressed areas. He also asked for an increase in the minimum wage. Congress approved these requests. The lawmakers also supported the President's proposal for money for **urban renewal**, which was a program to restore run-down areas in America's inner cities.

President Kennedy was not able, however, to get Congress to enact two other programs. The first was a plan to provide medical care for the aged through the social security system. The second would have provided money to help local school districts build schools and pay teachers' salaries, and it also would have provided help to needy college students.

The young President was a strong supporter of the space program. In 1961 he proposed that the United States

should commit itself to achieving the goal, before this decade is out, of landing a man on the moon and returning him safely to earth.

Congress supported this call with funds for the space program.

President Kennedy Is Assassinated
On November 22, 1963, Kennedy went to Dallas, Texas, to deliver a speech. Crowds lined the streets to greet the President's motorcade as it passed by. Kennedy rode in an open car. Suddenly, shots rang out. Two bullets struck the President. By the time he could be brought to a hospital, Kennedy was dead. He was the fourth American President to die by **assassination**, as murder of a political figure or for a political purpose is called.

Within hours, police arrested a 24-year-old man named Lee Harvey Oswald and charged him with the crime. Two

On the plane that will carry the body of the murdered President Kennedy back to Washington, D.C., a Texas judge administers the oath of office to the new President, Lyndon Baines Johnson.
■ What office did Johnson hold prior to being President?

days later, as Oswald was being moved from one jail to another, a Dallas nightclub owner named Jack Ruby stepped out from behind a group of reporters and shot Oswald. Millions of shocked Americans watched the murder of Oswald on their television sets.

A special commission headed by Chief Justice Earl Warren was appointed to get to the bottom of the Kennedy assassination. After a 9-month study, the group concluded that Oswald had acted alone. But doubts remained. Some people said that the commission had failed to follow all the leads and had left many questions unanswered. In 1979 a committee of the House of Representatives conducted another study of Kennedy's murder. One group of experts used a new method to analyze a tape recording that contained the sounds of the gunshots. They con-

cluded that the shots came from more than one rifle. Other experts disagreed with these findings. Where did the truth lie? And if there was more than one rifle, who fired it? Each new answer seemed only to produce a puzzling new question.

CHECKUP

1. Why did Eisenhower call his program Modern Republicanism?
2. Why was the launching of Sputnik a blow to America? How did the United States react?
3. What different signals did Kennedy's New Frontier program send to American businesses?
4. **Thinking Critically** In what ways, for better and for worse, has television changed national political campaigns in the United States since the end of World War II?

The Struggle for Equal Rights

What major steps were taken to advance the civil rights of blacks and other minorities in the 1950s and early 1960s?

VOCABULARY

VOCABULARY

Brown v. Board of Education of Topeka	**nonviolent resistance**
	sit-in

Continuing Segregation   Like most black Americans of his day, Thurgood Marshall had personal experience with segregation. The grandson of a slave, Marshall was born in Baltimore, Maryland, in 1908. In 1930 he was denied admission to the law school of the University of Maryland because of his race. Instead he attended the

Thurgood Marshall (center) led the NAACP legal team in arguing the *Brown* case. He later became a member of the Supreme Court. ■ How can you tell that these lawyers won their case?

law school at all-black Howard University in Washington, D.C. After his graduation he went to work for the National Association for the Advancement of Colored People (NAACP) and soon became head of its legal department. The NAACP was the leader in the struggle against practices and laws that denied blacks their full rights as Americans.

In the 1930s and 1940s, the NAACP and Thurgood Marshall won many important cases in the courts. Still, segregation remained. A half century earlier, in the case of *Plessy* v. *Ferguson*, the Supreme Court had adopted the "separate but equal" rule (page 419). Most northern states did not have the Jim Crow laws that prevailed in the South, but segregation existed in the North as well. Unwritten laws, or custom, kept blacks living in separate neighborhoods, eating in separate restaurants, bathing at separate beaches, and in countless other ways living their lives apart from whites.

In practice, separate facilities were almost never equal. School buildings for black children, for example, were often old, poorly equipped, and supplied with out-of-date books. Even if the facilities were exactly equal, Marshall pointed out, "the very fact of segregation establishes a feeling of humiliation and deprivation in the group considered to be inferior."

Attacking School Segregation   To end segregation, Marshall and the NAACP decided they must attack the "separate but equal" rule head-on. The case they chose for this involved an 8-year-old black girl named Linda Brown in Topeka, Kansas. Linda lived just five blocks from a public school. This school, however, was for whites only. Linda had to go to an all-black public school more than 20 blocks away. With help from the NAACP, Linda's father sued to allow his daughter to attend the all-white school. The case made its way through the courts to the Supreme Court of the United States. Handling the case for the NAACP, Marshall argued that the Court should reverse the decision reached in the case of *Plessy* v. *Ferguson*.

In May 1954 the Supreme Court gave its historic decision in the case of ***Brown* v. *Board of Education of Topeka***. "We conclude," the Court wrote, "that in the field of public education the doctrine of 'separate but equal' has no place. Separate educational facilities are inherently [that is, by their very nature] unequal." The Court soon followed up this historic decision with an order that desegregation of public schools should begin promptly.

Resistance to Desegregation   Following the Brown decision, some states and cities promptly obeyed the order of the Su-

preme Court and ended school segregation. Much of the white South, however, resisted change. White citizens' councils were formed to fight desegregation. They threatened blacks and whites who challenged segregation with the loss of their jobs. The Ku Klux Klan came to life again, threatening violence to stop desegregation. Southern leaders and officials threw roadblocks into the path of desegregation.

In Arkansas the governor used National Guard troops to keep nine black students from entering Little Rock's Central High School. To enforce the desegregation order of the Court, President Eisenhower had to send federal troops to Little Rock. Even so, desegregation in the South went at a snail's pace. Six years after the Supreme Court ruled segregated schools unconstitutional, 99 percent of the black students in ten southern states were still in segregated schools.

Elizabeth Eckford, a black student, is heckled by a group of whites in Little Rock as she tries to enter a previously all-white high school.
■ **How do you think Eckford feels?**

Montgomery's blacks helped each other out during the bus boycott. Anyone who had a car or could get one would go to a meeting place like this to offer rides to black workers who needed them.
■ What is the range of ages of the people shown in the picture?

The Montgomery Bus Boycott With change coming only slowly through the courts, black people turned to more direct ways to end Jim Crow laws and practices. In Montgomery, Alabama, in December 1955, a black woman named Rosa Parks boarded a bus at the end of a day's work and took a seat near the front. At that time, buses in Montgomery, as in nearly all other southern cities, were segregated by law. Whites sat in the front, and blacks sat in the back. On that December day, all the seats in the bus were soon filled. When a white man entered, the driver ordered Parks to give him her seat and move to the back. Rosa Parks refused, and the driver had her arrested.

Montgomery blacks then began a boycott of the city's buses, refusing to ride them. The boycott was led by a young minister named Martin Luther King, Jr. Dr. King believed that blacks should refuse to obey unjust laws. But he also believed that as Christians they had to do so without violence and without hate. "If we are arrested every day," he told his followers, ". . . if we are trampled over every day, don't let anyone pull you so low as to hate them. We must use the weapon of love." Even after he was jailed for a while and after his home was bombed, King told his followers to stick to the path of **nonviolent resistance**, and they did.

Meanwhile the NAACP and Thurgood Marshall challenged Montgomery's bus law in the courts. A little more than a year after Rosa Parks was ordered to give up her seat, the Supreme Court ruled that Montgomery's bus segregation law was unconstitutional.

The victory over segregation in Montgomery made Dr. King a national figure. In 1957 he helped to form a new organization called the Southern Christian Leadership Conference (SCLC) to fight for civil rights. The SCLC adopted King's philosophy of nonviolent resistance.

714

Sit-ins   King's example and leadership inspired black college students in the South to stage **sit-ins** to force department stores to desegregate their lunch counters. In a sit-in, students took seats in a section reserved for whites. They expected to be treated roughly, but they were committed to nonviolence. Some carried small cards in their pockets with reminders, such as these:

Don't strike back or curse if abused.
Don't laugh out.
Show yourself courteous and friendly at all times.
Sit straight and always face the counter.
Remember love and nonviolence.

Eventually, police would arrest the students taking part in the sit-ins. Blacks would then boycott the stores. Faced with the loss of business in other parts of their stores, many owners gave in and desegregated their lunch counters. The first sit-in was in 1960. In the next several years, thousands of students, both black and white, took part in sit-ins. By 1963 these demonstrations led to the desegregation of lunch counters, hotels, and theaters in 300 southern cities.

Freedom Riders   Still other nonviolent fighters for civil rights chose as their target the segregated bus stations of the South. Blacks and whites called Freedom Riders rode together from town to town on interstate buses. Inside the bus stations they refused to obey the signs that marked the segregated waiting rooms, water fountains, and toilets. Often they were met by riots and beatings. Their quiet dignity won attention and support for their cause.

In May 1961, United States Attorney General Robert F. Kennedy called on the Interstate Commerce Commission to ban segregation in stations used by interstate buses. A few months later, the commission did so.

President Kennedy Acts   Still, progress came slowly. In the fall of 1962, President Kennedy had to send 5,000 troops to the all-white University of Mississippi to protect the right of James Meredith, a black air force veteran, to attend the school. In Birmingham, Alabama, the following spring, nonviolent marchers led by Dr. King were met by violence. (See the Primary Source Reading on page 716).

In June 1963, President Kennedy decided to give a televised address to the nation on the subject of civil rights. Although the year marked the one-hundredth anniversary of the Emancipation Proclamation, black people were still being denied the full measure of rights that America promised to all its citizens. "Are we to say to the world," Kennedy asked, "and, much more importantly, to each other that this is a land of the free except for Negroes?" The President announced that he would ask Congress to pass a strong civil rights bill.

Sit-ins like this brought about the desegregation of lunch counters.
■ How old are these participants?

Letter from Birmingham Jail

Martin Luther King, Jr., was arrested in April 1963 in Birmingham, Alabama, for leading protest marches and sit-ins against segregation. While King was in jail, a group of local white religious leaders issued a statement opposing his tactics. King responded to the group with an open letter.

My Dear Fellow Clergymen:

While confined here in Birmingham city jail, I came across your recent statement calling my present activities "unwise and untimely."

. . . Frankly, I have yet to engage in a direct action campaign that was "well timed" in the view of those who have not suffered unduly from the disease of segregation. For years now I have heard the word "Wait!" . . .

Perhaps it is easy for those who have never felt the stinging darts of segregation to say, "Wait." But when you have seen vicious mobs lynch your mothers and fathers at will and drown your brothers and sisters at whim; when you have seen hate-filled policemen curse, kick, and even kill your black brothers and sisters; when you see the vast majority of your twenty million Negro brothers smothering in an airtight cage of poverty in the midst of an affluent society; when you suddenly find your tongue twisted and your speech stammering as you seek to explain to your six-year-old daughter why she can't go to the public amusement park that has just been advertised on television, and see tears welling up in her eyes when she is told that Funtown is closed to colored children, and see ominous clouds of inferiority beginning to form in her little mental sky, and see her beginning to distort her personality by developing an unconscious bitterness toward white people; when you have to concoct an answer for a five-year-old son who is asking, "Daddy, why do white people treat colored people so mean?"; . . . when you are forever fighting a degenerating sense of "nobodiness"—then you will understand why we find it difficult to wait.

USING SOURCE MATERIAL

1. What is King trying to achieve by listing so many abuses in one long sentence in the last paragraph?
2. Why do you think King includes the stories of the six-year-old girl and the five-year-old boy in this list?

Over 200,000 people marched on Washington, D.C., to support civil rights in 1963.
■ What is the name of the tall structure in the background?

A March on Washington, D.C. Civil rights leaders decided to hold a march on Washington, D.C., to urge Congress to pass the bill. On August 28, 1963, more than 200,000 Americans, black and white, gathered at the Washington Monument and the Lincoln Memorial. Dr. King gave a moving speech. "I still have a dream," said Martin Luther King. "It is a dream deeply rooted in the American dream."

> I have a dream that one day . . . the sons of former slaves and sons of former slave-owners will be able to sit down together at the table of brotherhood. . . .

The rally ended with the singer Mahalia Jackson leading the singing of "We Shall Overcome," a hymn that had become the anthem of the civil rights movement.

Still, as the one-hundredth year after the Emancipation Proclamation drew to a close, Kennedy's civil rights bill had not been passed by Congress. And with the death of the President who proposed it, the task of getting that bill through Congress and enacted into law would have to be carried by a new President, Lyndon Johnson.

CHECKUP

1. What far-reaching decision affecting public schools was made by the Supreme Court in 1954?
2. What was the immediate effect of this decision?
3. Why did a bus boycott take place in Montgomery, Alabama?
4. In what other ways was the struggle for civil rights for black people carried on in the 1950s and early 1960s?
5. **Thinking Critically** Why were freedom rides and sit-ins effective in ending segregation?

Reading a Mileage Chart

FINDING ROAD MILES

In this chapter you read that the number of cars bought by Americans increased. You also read that the population shifted from one part of the United States to another. With this movement of people, cars became more and more of a necessity. People used cars to get from the suburbs to jobs in the cities. With better roads and highways, people were able to travel easily by car from one city to another.

When you travel by car, you want to know the distance between places. A mileage chart is a quick and easy way to tell distance. The chart below shows the number of road miles between some cities in the United States.

Suppose you want to find the distance between St. Louis and Miami. Put a finger of your left hand on *Miami* on the left side of the chart. Now find *St. Louis* at the bottom of the chart. Put a finger of your right hand on *St. Louis*. Move both fingers, one across and one up, until they meet, at 1265. That is the number of road miles between the two cities.

SKILLS PRACTICE

Use the mileage chart below to answer the following questions.

1. How many miles is it from Denver to New Orleans?
2. Which city is closer to New York, Seattle or San Francisco?
3. Which two cities are closest together?
4. Which two cities are farthest apart?
5. How far would you have to drive from Chicago to Kansas City?

	Boston	Chicago	Dallas	Denver	Kansas City	Los Angeles	Miami	New Orleans	New York	St. Louis	San Francisco	Seattle	Washington, D.C.
Boston		990	1805	1990	1420	3085	1565	1550	215	1160	3190	2950	445
Chicago	990		960	995	510	2120	1370	945	790	285	2195	2020	705
Dallas	1805	960		780	495	1425	1370	505	1565	650	1785	2165	1375
Denver	1990	995	780		600	1170	2135	1295	1760	875	1270	1385	1645
Kansas City	1420	510	495	600		1610	1530	830	1185	255	1890	1925	1050
Los Angeles	3085	2120	1425	1170	1610		2820	1920	2765	1820	390	1180	2725
Miami	1565	1370	1370	2135	1530	2820		870	1300	1265	3160	3425	1115
New Orleans	1550	945	505	1295	830	1920	870		1320	710	2295	2695	1115
New York	215	790	1565	1760	1185	2765	1300	1320		950	2930	2825	220
St. Louis	1160	285	650	875	255	1820	1265	710	950		2140	2175	805
San Francisco	3190	2195	1785	1270	1890	390	3160	2295	2930	2140		825	2875
Seattle	2950	2020	2165	1385	1925	1180	3425	2695	2825	2175	825		2845
Washington, D.C.	445	705	1375	1645	1050	2725	1115	1115	220	805	2875	2845	

MAIN IDEAS

1. The 25 years following World War II marked the longest period of prosperity the United States has ever known.
2. This prosperity was based mainly on the demand for consumer goods.
3. Four great shifts in population occurred in the years after World War II: away from farms, from cities to suburbs, from the North to the Sunbelt, and—for many black people—from the South to the North.
4. Truman's Fair Deal, Eisenhower's Modern Republicanism, and Kennedy's New Frontier continued the policies of the New Deal while modifying some of them.
5. Americans began exploring space in the late 1950s and early 1960s.
6. During the 1950s and early 1960s, progress was made toward desegregating American society, but much remained to be done.

VOCABULARY REVIEW

On a separate sheet of paper, write the letter of the best ending for each sentence. Choose your answer from the terms following each sentence.

1. The Green Revolution brought about advances in _____. (a) education (b) agriculture (c) war
2. Help in getting an education, buying a home, and starting a business was made available under the GI Bill of Rights to _____. (a) farmers (b) immigrants (c) war veterans
3. The area in the United States that is known as the Sunbelt is in the _____. (a) North and the West (b) North and the East (c) South and the West
4. When there is inflation, the cost of living _____. (a) rises (b) drops (c) is unchanged
5. A business that has a closed shop hires only members of a _____. (a) union (b) minority shop (c) family
6. When Senator McCarthy was censured by the Senate, he was _____. (a) praised (b) condemned (c) investigated
7. Sputnik, which was sent up by the Soviets, was the world's first _____. (a) jet plane (b) space satellite (c) missile
8. To get department stores to desegregate lunch counters, both black and white college students took part in _____. (a) riots (b) sit-ins (c) road marches
9. The case of *Brown* v. *Board of Education of Topeka* resulted in the order to desegregate _____. (a) buses (b) public beaches (c) public schools
10. In dealing with segregation, Martin Luther King, Jr., was committed to a policy known as _____. (a) containment (b) nonviolent resistance (c) open door

CHAPTER CHECKUP

1. How did the rapid growth in population help create new job opportunities?
2. What brought about rising prices in the years following World War II?
3. What did the Taft-Hartley Act do?
4. What did President Eisenhower and Congress do in response to the Soviets' launching of their Sputnik satellite?
5. **Thinking Critically** Why do you think Senator Joseph McCarthy's accusations about Communists in government received so much attention?
6. **Thinking Critically** What are the advantages and disadvantages of nonviolent resistance as a means for social change?

APPLYING KNOWLEDGE

1. If any of your grandparents or other members of your family are veterans of World War II, ask them if they benefited from the GI Bill of Rights and, if so, in what way. Report your findings to the class.
2. Find out about the acts of courage of the following people in their efforts to gain civil rights for all: (a) Rosa Parks, (b) James Meredith, (c) Martin Luther King, Jr.

CHAPTER 30 *A Time of Shocks*

1964–1980

Lyndon Johnson and the Great Society

What were the major programs and goals of President Johnson's Great Society?

VOCABULARY

Civil Rights Act of 1964	Great Society ghetto

A Rising Politician   At the time of John F. Kennedy's death, Congress had passed few of the major laws he had asked for. The task of getting Kennedy's program passed fell to his successor, Lyndon B. Johnson. It could not have been left in more skilled political hands. No one knew better how to get a bill through Congress.

Even as a child, Lyndon Johnson had been fascinated by politics. His father served for a time in the Texas state legislature, and young Lyndon often went to the state capitol with him to watch the lawmakers in action. He also loved visiting the voters in his father's district during election campaigns.

After graduating from college and teaching for a year, the 24-year-old Johnson went to Washington to serve as secretary to a Texas representative. In 1937 he won election to Congress himself. After 11 years in the House of Representatives,

Johnson was elected to the Senate in 1948 by the narrow margin of 87 votes. Fellow senators quickly recognized his talents. In just 4 years, Democratic senators elected him their leader. In this position, he became one of the most powerful men in Washington, D.C.

Johnson tried for the Democratic nomination for President in 1960, but he lost out to John F. Kennedy. When Kennedy invited him to run as the vice presidential candidate, Johnson accepted. Three years later Johnson was President.

The Civil Rights Act of 1964   While the country was still grieving over Kennedy's death, Johnson was able to get several of the late President's ideas passed into law. In urging Congress to pass Kennedy's civil rights bill, he said, "No memorial . . . could more eloquently honor President Kennedy's memory." Because of Johnson's able work with Congress, this bill became the **Civil Rights Act of 1964**.

The law made racial discrimination illegal in hotels, restaurants, and other businesses that serve the public. It also gave the federal government more power to speed up the desegregation of public schools and other public institutions.

Large demonstrations, such as this one in Washington, D.C., were frequent sights in the 1960s. Groups demonstrated over many issues.
■ Why do many large demonstrations take place in Washington, D.C.?

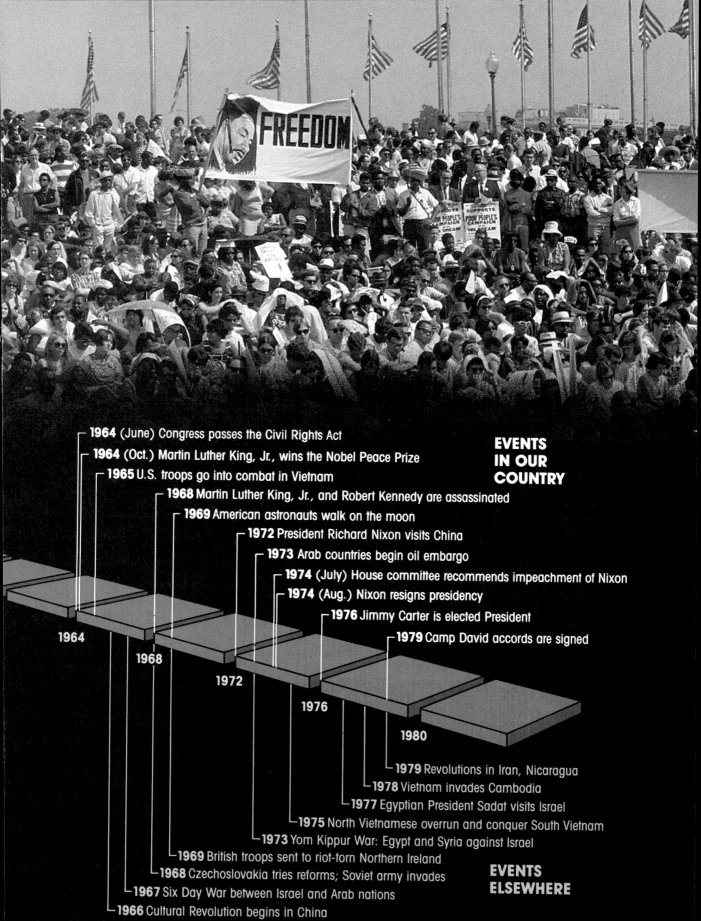

EVENTS IN OUR COUNTRY

- **1964** (June) Congress passes the Civil Rights Act
- **1964** (Oct.) Martin Luther King, Jr., wins the Nobel Peace Prize
- **1965** U.S. troops go into combat in Vietnam
- **1968** Martin Luther King, Jr., and Robert Kennedy are assassinated
- **1969** American astronauts walk on the moon
- **1972** President Richard Nixon visits China
- **1973** Arab countries begin oil embargo
- **1974** (July) House committee recommends impeachment of Nixon
- **1974** (Aug.) Nixon resigns presidency
- **1976** Jimmy Carter is elected President
- **1979** Camp David accords are signed

1964
1968
1972
1976
1980

EVENTS ELSEWHERE

- **1979** Revolutions in Iran, Nicaragua
- **1978** Vietnam invades Cambodia
- **1977** Egyptian President Sadat visits Israel
- **1975** North Vietnamese overrun and conquer South Vietnam
- **1973** Yom Kippur War: Egypt and Syria against Israel
- **1969** British troops sent to riot-torn Northern Ireland
- **1968** Czechoslovakia tries reforms; Soviet army invades
- **1967** Six Day War between Israel and Arab nations
- **1966** Cultural Revolution begins in China

In 1964, President and Mrs. Johnson visited poor families in Appalachia to learn about their situation and what the government could do to help.
■ Why, do you think, would these people be happy to see the President?

As a result, schools in the South were desegregated more rapidly. In addition, the act prohibited race and sex discrimination in hiring, and it attempted to protect the voting rights of blacks. These last parts of the law proved difficult to enforce. Still, this act was the most important civil rights law since Reconstruction days.

The Great Society Less than a year after becoming President, Lyndon Johnson ran for a full 4-year term. He overwhelmed his Republican opponent, Senator Barry Goldwater of Arizona, by more than 16 million votes and carried all but five states.

In addition to getting Kennedy's proposals enacted, Lyndon Johnson put forth his own program. "We have the opportunity," he said, "to move not only toward the rich society but the **Great Society**." To Johnson, the Great Society was one that cared for its aged and underprivileged, one that broadened opportunities for all, and one that promoted racial justice. Achieving these goals would call for an increased role for the federal government.

As part of his Great Society program, Lyndon Johnson called for a "war on poverty." Congress allotted money to local communities to provide relief and jobs for the poor. It set up a food stamp program for needy families. It started the Job Corps to help workers train for better jobs and to help high school students find summer work. It created Head Start, an education program for preschool children. Another program, Volunteers in Service to America (VISTA), was a kind of Peace Corps at home. It enlisted volunteers to help people in poor areas improve their living conditions. Other programs helped low-income tenants with rent payments and built more public housing.

There were other programs in the Great Society. Medicare provided health care for the aged through the Social Security system. Through a program of aid to education, schools for the first time received large amounts of federal money. In addition, cities received help for improving public transportation and for rebuilding old neighborhoods. States received money to help build new hospitals. Not since the New Deal had so many important laws been passed in such a short time.

The Space Program   The government also provided added support for the space program. That program had already passed two important milestones. In 1961, Alan Shepard became the first American to enter space when he rode a rocket 117 miles (188 km) into space from Cape Canaveral, Florida. In 1962, John Glenn became the first American to orbit the earth. These achievements were part of a series of launches called Project Mercury.

Astronaut John Glenn made history when he became the first American to orbit the earth. ■ **What is the name of Glenn's spacecraft?**

Now the space program pressed on with the next steps toward putting a man on the moon. Project Gemini, another series of launches, included a "space walk." This program was followed by Project Apollo. Apollo included a launch in 1968 in which a team of astronauts orbited the moon and returned to earth safely. In 1969 another Apollo mission landed people on the moon for the first time. (See page 732.)

A Change in Immigration   Congress also passed a new immigration law in 1965. The act changed the old quota system, which had favored immigrants from northern and western Europe. Immigration from countries outside the Western Hemisphere was limited to a total of 170,000 a year, with no more than 20,000 from any one country. Another 120,000 could enter the United States from countries in the Western Hemisphere.

After this law went into effect, the main sources of immigration to the United States changed. Since 1965 most immigrants have come from Mexico and from such Asian countries as the Philippines, Korea, and Vietnam.

More Blacks in Government   Even after the Civil Rights Act of 1964, southern blacks found it difficult to vote. Local officials used various methods to keep blacks from registering. Therefore, President Johnson got Congress to pass the Voting Rights Act of 1965. This law said that when local officials refused to do the job of registering voters fairly, federal officials would step in and do it.

This law proved to be effective. In less than a year, the number of southern blacks who were registered to vote jumped by 40 percent. Soon more blacks were seeking office. Within 20 years, some 5,400 blacks held office in the United States, and half of them were in the South. Blacks became mayors of such great cities as Cleveland, Atlanta, New Orleans, Detroit, Los Angeles, Chicago, and Philadelphia.

In addition, President Johnson appointed blacks to major posts in the federal government. Robert Weaver, a housing expert, became the first black Cabinet officer when he was named to head the new Department of Housing and Urban Development. Thurgood Marshall was named to the Supreme Court, the first black to serve on that body.

Rioting in the Ghettos   The civil rights movement brought great changes to much of the United States and especially to the South. Still, the laws of the 1960s had little to do with the daily problems of millions who lived in black **ghettos** of northern, midwestern, and western cities. A ghetto is a section of a city in which members of a minority group live. The reality of the lives of ghetto residents was crowded, run-down housing, and high unemployment, especially among young people.

Many ghetto dwellers felt they were treated unfairly by their landlords, merchants, and the police. In 1965, anger boiled over in Watts, the black ghetto of Los Angeles. For 6 days, black residents rioted, burning property and looting stores. Before the riot finally ended, 28 black people were dead, hundreds of white-owned buildings were destroyed, and the homes of many black residents lay in ashes.

Watts turned out to be but the first of many ghetto riots. Between 1965 and 1967 there were riots in more than 70 cities. Those in the summer of 1967 were the worst in United States history. In Detroit, block after block was destroyed.

After the Detroit rioting, President Johnson appointed a special commission to study the causes of the riots. The commission was headed by Governor Otto Kerner of Illinois. The report of the Kerner Commission warned, "Our nation is moving toward two societies, one black, one white — separate and unequal."

President Johnson tried to get Congress to pass additional civil rights legislation. But by this time, resistance among many whites to more civil rights laws was growing. This resistance was called *white backlash.* Congress did pass a Fair Housing Act in 1968, forbidding discrimination in renting or selling houses. But it did not pass any other civil rights laws.

In April 1968, Martin Luther King went to Memphis, Tennessee, to support a sanitation workers' strike. Many workers believed they were being paid poorly because they were black. Only a few years before, King had received the Nobel Peace Prize as a champion of nonviolence. At Memphis he urged the workers to seek their goals without practicing violence. On April 4, Dr. King was shot and killed by a hidden sniper. During the next week, blacks in more than 100 cities exploded in anger at the killing of this great leader.

CHECKUP

1. What did the Civil Rights Act of 1964 provide for?
2. What advances were made in the space program during Johnson's presidency?
3. How was immigration changed by the law passed in 1965?
4. Why did riots occur in many cities in the middle years of the 1960s?
5. **Thinking Critically**   Why would achieving the goals of the Great Society require the federal government to play a larger role?

Vietnam

What were the reasons for and the results of United States involvement in Vietnam?

VOCABULARY

domino theory	**Vietnamization**
Gulf of Tonkin Resolution	

Turmoil in Indochina   During Lyndon Johnson's presidency the United States became heavily involved in a war thousands of miles from home. The war deeply divided the American people. It was not a war that Johnson wanted. Yet step by step, the decisions he made drew the United States further into it. And in the end, the war in Vietnam (vē et näm′) destroyed his presidency.

The Southeast Asian countries of Vietnam, Laos (lä′ ōs), and Cambodia (kam bō′ dē ə) are part of an area once called Indochina. Indochina was a French colony from the mid-1800s to World War II, when the Japanese took it over. After the war, France tried to regain control. But the people of Indochina wanted to be free of foreign rule. Ho Chi Minh (hō chē min′), a Vietnamese Communist, was a leader of the independence movement. His group, the Vietminh (vē et min′), fought against the French for the next 8 years, from 1946 to 1954. Ho's rebels received aid from the Soviet Union and Communist China. The United States helped the French with millions of dollars in arms and supplies.

In the spring of 1954, the Vietminh delivered a crushing defeat to the French armies. The following month the major European powers and representatives of the peoples of Indochina met in Geneva, Switzerland. They agreed that the French would withdraw from Indochina and that the area would be divided into three countries — Laos, Vietnam, and Cambodia. Vietnam would, temporarily, be further divided into two parts. Communists led by Ho would control North Vietnam, the area north of 17° north latitude. South Vietnam, the part south of 17°, would be controlled by an anticommunist government. After 2 years, Vietnam would hold national elections to unite the country under a single government.

The elections never took place. The South Vietnam government was headed by a strong anticommunist named Ngo Dinh Diem ([ə]ngō din dyem). Fearing that the Communists would win the election, Diem refused to go through with it. Instead, he declared South Vietnam to be an independent country, with himself as its president.

Ho Chi Minh battled the French and set up a Communist government in North Vietnam.
■ **How would you describe Ho from the photograph?**

In Support of South Vietnam The United States became the chief supporter of the anticommunist South Vietnamese government. This was during the height of the cold war, and the policy of the United States was to contain Soviet communism and influence. President Eisenhower likened the countries of Southeast Asia to a row of standing dominoes. If one was knocked over, the others — Cambodia, Laos, Thailand, Burma, Indonesia, and the rest — would each fall in turn. If the United States was to contain communism, it must keep the first domino, South Vietnam, from falling. This belief came to be known as the **domino theory**.

Following this idea, the United States sent millions of dollars in military aid and supplies to South Vietnam. President Eisenhower also sent 600 Americans to help train South Vietnam's troops. The Soviet Union and China, meanwhile, continued to aid North Vietnam.

Unfortunately, Diem's government began to lose the support of the people in South Vietnam. Communist guerrillas called Vietcong (vē et kông′) moved into the countryside. North Vietnam sent supplies to the Vietcong by way of the Ho Chi Minh Trail. This "trail" was actually a system of roads and trails built or improved by the North Vietnamese. The Ho Chi Minh Trail went through Laos and Cambodia to several places in South Vietnam. By the early 1960s, while John F. Kennedy was President, some of North Vietnam's troops had also moved south to fight beside the Vietcong. Kennedy increased American aid during his 3 years in office. He also sent more military and civilian advisers. By the end of 1963, there were nearly 17,000 American advisers in South Vietnam.

American military advisers in Vietnam were soon followed by American combat troops. Many villages were destroyed in the fighting.
■ **What do you think might have happened in this village?**

Some of them were accompanying South Vietnamese troops into battle.

By the time Lyndon Johnson became President, the South Vietnamese were almost completely dependent on American military and economic aid. Still the fighting went badly for them. A new government of military leaders replaced that of Diem, but this did not help. President Johnson's advisers warned that without a great increase in American help, South Vietnam would lose.

The Gulf of Tonkin Resolution   In August 1964 the United States Navy reported that North Vietnamese torpedo boats had fired on two American destroyers in the Gulf of Tonkin (tän′ kin) off North Vietnam. President Johnson asked Congress to approve a resolution allowing him to "take all necessary measures" to turn back "any armed attack against the forces of the United States and to prevent further aggression." This resolution was known as the **Gulf of Tonkin Resolution**. Congress passed it overwhelmingly.

American involvement now increased rapidly. In February 1965, Johnson ordered American bombers to start bombing North Vietnam. In April he ordered American troops into combat. More men were drafted into the army. By 1968, more than 500,000 American troops were in Vietnam.

Opposition to the War Grows   All through 1966 and 1967 there were many predictions of victory. But victory did not come. At first a majority of the American people supported America's involvement. As the war dragged on, however, and the number of American dead and wounded mounted, opposition grew. In the beginning, opponents of the war were mostly young people. Later they included people of all ages. These opponents held large

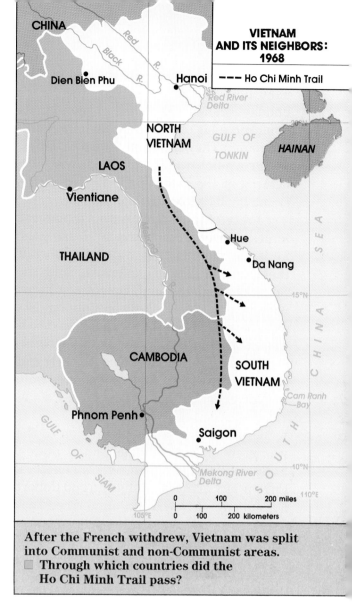

After the French withdrew, Vietnam was split into Communist and non-Communist areas.
☐ Through which countries did the Ho Chi Minh Trail pass?

protest marches in Washington, D.C., and in many other cities.

Many of these opponents believed that the war was a civil war between the Vietnamese people and should be settled by them. Other Americans objected to supporting the South Vietnamese government, which was a dictatorship. Although many thousands of young men volunteered for service, other thousands went to prison or moved to other countries rather than fight in what they believed was an unjust war. The war in Vietnam had greatly divided the American people and Johnson was losing support.

The Tet Offensive   At the end of January 1968, on the Vietnamese New Year's holiday called Tet, the Communists launched a big offensive throughout South Vietnam. They attacked 30 major cities, taking a number of them. There was even fighting at the gates of the United States embassy in Saigon, the capital city.

United States and South Vietnamese forces recovered and hit back. During the following months, they wiped out most of the gains of the Tet offensive, and the North Vietnamese and Vietcong suffered very heavy losses. Yet the Communists still controlled much of the countryside. It was clear that the United States government's rosy statements about an early end to the war with the Communist forces were not correct.

A Troubled Period   Opposition to the war grew stronger in the United States. Early in 1968, two Democratic senators, Eugene McCarthy of Minnesota and Robert F. Kennedy of New York, announced that they would oppose Lyndon Johnson for the party's nomination for President. At the end of March, President Johnson told the nation in a televised speech that the United States would stop bombing North Vietnam and would seek to settle the war through peace talks. He ended the speech with the surprise announcement that he would not run for reelection.

The nation was in for further shocks. In June 1968, Senator Robert Kennedy was shot and killed by a Jordanian immigrant who opposed Kennedy's support for Israel. This was just 2 months after Martin Luther King, Jr., had been gunned down and less than 5 years after the assassination of Senator Kennedy's brother, President John F. Kennedy.

In the summer of 1968, Democrats met in Chicago to choose their candidate. With antiwar demonstrators battling police outside the convention hall, the Democrats chose Vice President Hubert H. Humphrey to run for President. Meanwhile the Republican party chose former

Fighting reached the streets of Saigon, the southern capital, during the Communists' 1968 Tet offensive.
■ **Why are some of the soldiers walking and others riding?**

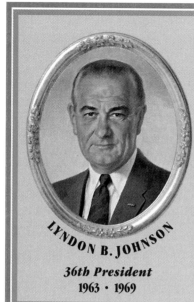

Born: 1908, near Stonewall, Texas.
Education: Southwest Texas State Teachers College.
Training: Teacher, public official.
To presidency from: Texas.
Position when taking office: Vice President.
Political party: Democratic.
Married: Claudia "Lady Bird" Taylor.
Children: Two daughters.
Died: 1973, San Antonio, Texas.
Other facts: A star debater in high school. Taught public speaking and debating as a high school teacher. Entered politics as secretary to a Texas congressman. At age 44 became leader of his party in the Senate, the youngest man ever chosen for that position.
During his presidency: In 1965 the federal government for the first time embarked on a major program of aid to elementary and secondary schools.

LYNDON B. JOHNSON

36th President
1963 · 1969

Vice President Richard Nixon to run again. Humphrey had long been a popular Democrat, but he lost support because the public connected him with Johnson's war policies. A third-party candidate, Governor George Wallace of Alabama, drew millions of votes by appealing to people who opposed the civil rights movement. In November, Nixon won by a narrow margin.

Vietnamization During the presidential campaign, Nixon promised to end the war in Vietnam "with honor," while assuring that South Vietnam would remain independent and non-Communist. In 1969 he announced his plan to do this. He called his plan **Vietnamization**. The United States would train and equip South Vietnamese troops to take over the fighting. This would free American troops to withdraw gradually from Vietnam. Meanwhile, the United States would provide air support for the troops and would renew the bombing of North Vietnam. President Nixon announced that the first 25,000 troops would leave Vietnam by the end of August 1969.

During the next 3 years, the United States slowly wound down the war. By the end of 1972, fewer than 25,000 American troops remained in Vietnam. At the same time, the United States Air Force continued its heavy bombing of North Vietnam.

Moving into Cambodia Meanwhile, President Nixon ordered bombing attacks on Vietcong supply lines and bases in Cambodia, a neutral country. The President kept these bombings secret from Congress and the American public. Then in April 1970 he revealed that he had sent troops into Cambodia to search out and destroy Vietcong bases there.

The news that the war had been widened led to new and angrier protests at home, especially at colleges. At Kent State University in Ohio, National Guard troops shot and killed four students during an antiwar demonstration. Police killed two students in another protest at Jackson State College in Mississippi.

Meanwhile, Congress cut off funds for any further operations in Cambodia. Congress also voted to repeal the Gulf of

South Vietnamese refugees run for waiting helicopters after the fall of Saigon to the Communists.
■ Why, do you think, did these people want to leave Saigon?

Tonkin Resolution. But neither of these actions could now have any effect on the United States involvement in Vietnam.

The War Ends   In 1972, Nixon sent an adviser to meet secretly with representatives from North Vietnam. These meetings led to a cease-fire in January 1973. The United States agreed to pull its forces out of Vietnam. The North Vietnamese agreed to return all American prisoners of war. Less than 2 months later, the last American troops left Vietnam. The war had cost more than 57,000 American lives. Another 300,000 Americans had been wounded.

Vietnamization succeeded in getting American troops out of Vietnam. It did not succeed in keeping South Vietnam independent. Fighting between North and South Vietnam broke out again. In the spring of 1975, South Vietnamese forces suddenly crumbled, and North Vietnamese troops overran the country. At the same time, Communists in Cambodia took control of that country. Thousands of refugees fled from South Vietnam, with more than 100,000 coming to America.

CHECKUP

1. How did Vietnam come to be divided along the 17° north latitude line?
2. How and why did the United States become the chief supporter of the government of South Vietnam?
3. What was the Gulf of Tonkin Resolution, and why was it passed?
4. In what ways did the war in Vietnam divide the American people?
5. What happened after American troops withdrew from Vietnam?
6. **Thinking Critically**   Why did more Americans oppose United States participation in the Vietnam War after the Tet offensive?

The Rise and Fall of Richard Nixon

What were the main successes and failures of Richard Nixon's presidency?

Reducing Tensions   When Richard Nixon became President, he said that the great powers were moving "from an era of confrontation"—that is, facing each other with hostility—"to an era of negotiation." During the cold war, Nixon was known as a strong anticommunist who was against compromising with the Soviet Union. However, Nixon surprised his critics by negotiating with Communist countries. He and his national security adviser, Henry Kissinger, sought to reduce tensions with the Soviet Union and lessen the chances of nuclear war. This policy was called **détente** (dā tänt′), from a French word that means "relaxing of tensions."

In 1969 the United States and the Soviet Union started talks aimed at limiting nuclear arms. The meetings were called the Strategic Arms Limitation Talks (SALT). After more than 2 years, the two sides agreed to put a limit on building offensive weapons for 5 years. In 1972, President Nixon went to Moscow to sign this agreement, which became known as the SALT I treaty. Nixon and the Soviet leader, Leonid Brezhnev (brezh′ nef), also signed agreements to cooperate in health research, the exploration of space, and protection of the environment. Though the SALT I treaty did not end the arms race, it was a step forward.

A New China Policy   No action of President Nixon's surprised more people than his reversal of United States policy toward the People's Republic of China. Throughout the 1950s and 1960s, the United States regarded Mao Zedong's government as an enemy and had no dealings with it. We continued to recognize the Nationalist government on Taiwan as the legal government of China. The People's Republic of China was equally hostile toward the United States.

During these same years, however, relations between China and the Soviet Union, the two large Communist countries, chilled. By the late 1960s, China felt that the Soviet Union, not the United States, was its greatest enemy. It sought to improve relations with the United States. Nixon had been one of the strongest foes of the Chinese Communists. He decided, how-

In 1972, President Nixon and Soviet leader Brezhnev made an agreement on arms limits. ▪ Do you think they held their sensitive discussions in this setting?

The Moon Landing

"Tranquility Base here. The *Eagle* has landed." The words of Commander Neil A. Armstrong crackled across 240,000 miles (384,000 km) of space to planet Earth. The date was July 20, 1969, the time 4:17 P.M., Eastern Daylight Time. Some 6½ hours later, Armstrong stepped out of the landing craft *Eagle* and onto the surface of the moon. Back on Earth a billion people watched the scene on television.

The next day, Armstrong and Edwin E. "Buzz" Aldrin, Jr., explored the moon's surface, collected moon rocks, and performed experiments.

After 21½ hours they rejoined astronaut Michael Collins on the orbiting space

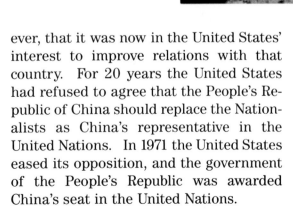

capsule for the return of Apollo 11 to Earth.

The space voyage of Armstrong, Aldrin, and Collins was one of the greatest feats of exploration in history. It was also one of the great feats of science. For 8 years, thousands of scientists, engineers, and workers had teamed up to make their moment of triumph possible.

The moon landing was a victory for the United States in the space race with the Soviet Union. Commander Armstrong, however, viewed this space achievement in broader terms. As he first set foot on the moon, he said, "That's one small step for a man, one giant leap for mankind."

ever, that it was now in the United States' interest to improve relations with that country. For 20 years the United States had refused to agree that the People's Republic of China should replace the Nationalists as China's representative in the United Nations. In 1971 the United States eased its opposition, and the government of the People's Republic was awarded China's seat in the United Nations.

A few months later, in February 1972, President Nixon visited Beijing (bā jing'), the capital of the People's Republic of China. There he and the Chinese leaders took the first steps toward restoring normal relations between the two countries. They agreed to allow cultural exchanges and a limited amount of trade. They continued to disagree on the future of Taiwan. While agreeing that Taiwan was part of China, the United States defended the right of the Nationalists to rule it. Following this "opening up" of China, many Americans and Chinese traveled to each other's countries to visit, study, and do business.

War in the Middle East   The Middle East continued to be a threat to world peace in the 1960s and 1970s. With Egyptian President Gamal Abdel Nasser calling on Arabs to wage a "holy war" against Israel, fighting once again broke out in June 1967. Israel was victorious in the Six Day War against Egypt, Jordan, and Syria. Israeli forces captured the Sinai Peninsula and the Gaza Strip from Egypt, drove the Syrians off the Golan Heights, and gained control of the West Bank of the Jordan River.

Despite a cease-fire, real peace was nowhere in sight. By the late 1960s the Arab states were being rearmed by the Soviet Union, their chief supplier of weapons. The United States, meanwhile, provided Israel with jet planes and other weapons.

When Nixon became President, the United States tried to improve its relations with the Arab nations. Although still supporting Israel, the Nixon administration said it would follow a more "even-handed" policy between Israel and the Arabs, not favoring one over the other. Nixon had several reasons for this policy. First, he hoped to use American influence to prevent another war, for there was danger that the superpowers might be drawn into such fighting. Second, because Arab countries supplied Western nations and the United States with much of their oil, it was important to assure that this supply would continue and that the large investment of American oil companies in the region was protected.

On October 6, 1973, the Jewish holy day of Yom Kippur, Egypt and Syria suddenly attacked Israel. Using arms supplied by the Soviets, they were able to drive back the Israelis, who suffered heavy losses in troops and weapons. Then an emergency shipment of arms from the

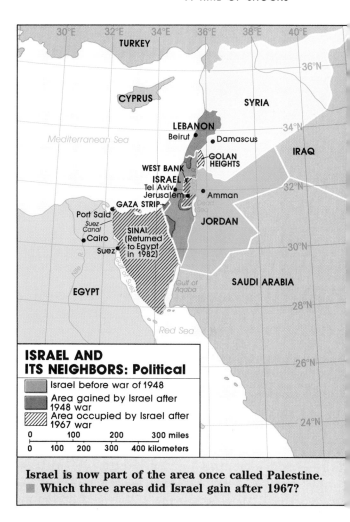

ISRAEL AND ITS NEIGHBORS: Political

- Israel before war of 1948
- Area gained by Israel after 1948 war
- Area occupied by Israel after 1967 war

0   100   200   300 miles
0 100 200 300 400 kilometers

Israel is now part of the area once called Palestine. Which three areas did Israel gain after 1967?

United States helped the Israelis turn the tide of battle. Israeli forces drove into Egypt before the Soviet Union, the United States, and the United Nations induced them to accept a truce. During the following months, Henry Kissinger, who was now secretary of state, played a key role in getting Israel and Egypt to pull back their forces. United Nations troops were placed between them.

An Oil Embargo   To punish the United States for helping Israel, some Arab countries placed an embargo on oil shipments to the United States and several other Western countries during the war. The

An Iranian youth tends his grazing herd near one of the many pipelines that carry oil from vast oil fields to ports in the Middle East.
■ What kind of animals are these?

These problems were accompanied by inflation. Heavy government spending for the war in Vietnam and for new social programs helped cause a big rise in prices. In 1971, Nixon tried to end inflation by putting a 90-day freeze on wages and prices. This freeze was followed by wage and price controls like the ones used during World War II. These measures slowed inflation for a time, but when the controls were removed a year later, prices started to climb again.

Revenue Sharing and Busing   President Nixon also proposed a plan to share the federal government's revenues with the states. Under this plan, which was quickly adopted by Congress, the federal government each year gave a sum of money to each state to use as it saw fit in dealing with its problems. The President also proposed, and Congress enacted, laws to start cleaning up air and water pollution. However, Nixon was not in favor of many of the social programs that had been begun under Lyndon Johnson's Great Society, and he tried to reduce federal support for social programs.

By the time Nixon took office, great progress had been made in desegregating schools in the South. In some parts of the North, however, progress was slow. There, no Jim Crow laws existed. But some city school boards kept schools segregated by drawing school district boundaries along racial lines. To end segregation, federal courts, therefore, began to order the busing of students from one school district to another. Many people favored busing as a tool to end segregation, but many others were opposed. President Nixon was one of these opponents. He asked Congress to stop the courts from ordering busing. Congress refused, however, and court-ordered busing continued.

fighting ended in November, but they kept the embargo on for another 4 months, causing shortages of gasoline and heating oil. Meanwhile, the Arab countries and other oil-producing countries raised oil prices sharply, from $2 to $11 a barrel, in less than a year. These countries were members of the Organization of Petroleum Exporting Countries (OPEC), which they had formed with the aim of getting better prices for their oil. The embargo gave them their opportunity.

A Slowing Economy   During President Nixon's first years in office, the economy slowed down. Unemployment rose. Most people did not realize it at the time, but this slowdown marked the end of the 25-year era of prosperity that followed World War II. For the next decade, there would be little growth in the economy, and the problem of unemployment would continue.

The Watergate Break-In   In 1972, Richard Nixon ran for reelection against Democratic Senator George McGovern of South Dakota. The President's foreign-policy successes won him much support. Nixon won one of the greatest presidential election victories in history, carrying every state but Massachusetts.

Less than 2 years after his victory, Nixon resigned from office. His troubles began before the 1972 election when five burglars were caught breaking into the offices of the Democratic National Committee in the Watergate complex, a group of apartment and office buildings in Washington, D. C. Police learned that the five were working with two other men who had ties to Nixon's reelection campaign committee and to the White House. The burglars were looking for documents that would help bring about the defeat of the Democrats in the fall campaign.

President Nixon was not involved in the plan for the break-in. Still, when he learned what happened, he tried to cover up the connection between the people in his administration and the crime. He blocked an FBI investigation, and he approved the payment of "hush money" to the burglars so they wouldn't talk. The President told his staff to stonewall investigators — that is, to tell them nothing. Under the law, such attempts to block justice are crimes.

All this was done secretly. Publicly, the President dismissed the matter as a "third-rate burglary." He said his administration had nothing to do with it. However, a few newspaper reporters began to dig up the facts. Then in January 1973, the five Watergate burglars and the two men who directed them were tried and found guilty. Six of the men stuck to their story that they had acted on their own. But the

The Watergate is a modern office and apartment complex in Washington, D.C. It gave a name to the scandal that started when burglars broke into Democratic party offices there.
■ Where do people who live and work in the Watergate park their cars?

seventh admitted to Judge John Sirica that the burglary had been approved by people high up in the White House. The Senate set up a committee, headed by Senator Sam Ervin of North Carolina, to investigate. Still denying any connection with Watergate, Nixon appointed a law professor, Archibald Cox, as a special government prosecutor to investigate.

The Senate Hearings   The televised Senate hearings began in May 1973. John Dean, a former Nixon aide, told the committee that Nixon officials were connected with the Watergate burglary and other illegal activities aimed at opponents of the President. Dean said that the President had taken part in covering up the facts.

Who was telling the truth? For a time it seemed there might be no way to find out. Then a witness revealed that Nixon had secretly tape-recorded all conversations in his White House office. Everyone realized that the tapes probably held answers to the key questions: What did the President know? When did he know it? Was Dean's testimony truthful?

For the next year, there was a tug-of-war over the tapes. On one side were the Senate committee, special prosecutor Cox, and Judge Sirica. On the other side was President Nixon. Nixon claimed that a President had a right to keep his records confidential. He called this right "executive privilege." He ordered Cox, his own appointee, to stop asking for the tapes and other records. When Cox continued to press for them, Nixon ordered him dismissed. This touched off such a storm of public criticism that Nixon finally turned over a few tapes to Judge Sirica. This did his cause no good, for one of the tapes had a gap of 18½ minutes. Experts said the tape had been deliberately erased.

The special Senate committee set up to investigate the Watergate scandal began to hold hearings in the spring of 1973. Much of the nation watched the proceedings daily on television.
■ What are the people on the floor in the foreground doing?

Born: 1913, Yorba Linda, California.
Education: Whittier College.
Training: Lawyer, public official.
To presidency from: New York.
Position when elected: Member of a New York City law firm.
Political party: Republican.
Married: Thelma "Pat" Ryan.
Children: Two daughters.
Other facts: A naval officer in the Pacific in World War II. Served in both houses of Congress. As Vice President under Eisenhower, toured nearly 60 countries. Defeated in run for presidency in 1960 but elected in 1968. Only President ever to resign from office. Did so when faced, in 1974, with almost certain impeachment for his part in Watergate scandal.
During his presidency: The Twenty-sixth Amendment to the Constitution lowered the voting age from 21 to 18.

RICHARD M. NIXON
37th President
1969 · 1974

Agnew Resigns   In the midst of all these troubles, Americans received another shock to their faith in their government. A separate investigation turned up evidence that Vice President Spiro Agnew had taken bribes as governor of Maryland and had also cheated on his income taxes. Agnew then resigned from office.

Under the Twenty-fifth Amendment to the Constitution, which had been added in 1967, President Nixon named Gerald Ford to serve as Vice President. Ford was a leading Republican member of the House of Representatives, so both houses of Congress readily gave him the required majority approval.

Nixon Resigns   Meanwhile, the Watergate cover-up was falling apart. In the spring of 1974, former Attorney General John Mitchell, two of Nixon's closest aides, and four other White House officials were charged with obstructing justice and with **perjury**, or lying under oath. They were later convicted and sent to prison.

The House Judiciary Committee began hearings on whether Nixon should be impeached—that is, officially charged with high crimes that could lead to his removal from office. The committee demanded more tapes. Nixon refused to turn them over. Instead, he gave the committee transcriptions, or written copies, of some of the tapes. But the copies left out the material the committee was seeking. The Judiciary Committee then recommended that the House of Representatives impeach Nixon for obstructing justice and misusing presidential power.

A few days later, the Supreme Court ruled unanimously that President Nixon had to give up the tapes. Nixon now admitted that the tapes showed he had been part of the cover-up. Faced with almost certain impeachment and possible conviction, Nixon resigned as President on August 9, 1974. Gerald Ford became President. He was the first person to serve in that office who had not been elected either President or Vice President.

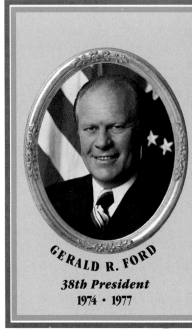

Born: 1913, Omaha, Nebraska.
Education: University of Michigan.
Training: Lawyer, public official.
To presidency from: Michigan.
Position when taking office: Vice President.
Political party: Republican.
Married: Elizabeth "Betty" Bloomer.
Children: Three sons, one daughter.
Other facts: A star football player in high·school and college. Coached boxing and was an assistant football coach for 3 years at Yale. A naval officer in World War II. Served 13 terms in House of Representatives. Became Vice President by action of the President and Congress under the Twenty-third Amendment after resignation of Spiro Agnew in 1973.
During his presidency: The United States in 1976 observed the bicentennial of the Declaration of Independence with celebrations in many communities.

GERALD R. FORD

38th President
1974 · 1977

Ford Succeeds Nixon   On taking office, Gerald Ford told the American people, "Our long national nightmare is over. Our Constitution works." Ford was referring to the system of checks and balances in the American government. A President had abused the power of his office; the courts and Congress had risen up to check him. The Constitution did, indeed, work.

President Ford himself did much to restore public confidence in the government. He was an open, honest, and friendly man. Still, he angered many people when he granted Richard Nixon a full pardon for any crimes he might have committed as President. Ford said it was important for the nation to put Watergate behind it and to look ahead to dealing with its problems. Many Americans, however, felt that if Nixon had broken the law, he should stand trial like any other citizen. In the end, more than 50 people in the Nixon administration were fined or sent to jail for their part in Watergate.

Two major reforms of Ford's presidency grew out of the abuses of the Watergate scandal. Congress passed a new Privacy Act and amended the 8-year-old Freedom of Information Act. These laws allowed citizens to examine all but the most sensitive government documents, and to view and correct any information about themselves in government files. Congress also passed an Election Reform Act that called for public funding of presidential elections.

CHECKUP

1. What change did President Nixon bring about in our policy toward China?
2. What events in the Middle East brought on an oil embargo?
3. What was the purpose of each of the following programs: (**a**) revenue sharing, (**b**) busing?
4. What event started Watergate?
5. Why did the House of Representatives try to impeach President Nixon?
6. **Thinking Critically**   What do you think would have happened if President Nixon had not resigned and the impeachment proceedings against him had continued?

The Carter Administration

What were President Carter's main achievements in foreign policy?

solar energy	human rights
Camp David accords	SALT II
	hostage

A President from Georgia In 1976, Gerald Ford decided to seek a full term as President. The Democrats chose a former governor of Georgia as their candidate. He was James Earl Carter, Jr., who preferred to be known as Jimmy Carter. An outsider to Washington politics, Carter campaigned as one who wanted to restore the people's faith in their government after Watergate. Continued unemployment and the pardon of Nixon were some reasons why Ford lost the support he needed. In a close election, Carter won the presidency.

President Carter appointed to his Cabinet and other high offices more women and members of minority groups than had any other President. He also took steps to protect the environment and reform the civil service system. However, Carter was not able to get Congress to accept a great many of his recommendations.

Providing for Energy When Carter took office in 1977, the country was importing half the oil it consumed. Carter wanted to make the country less dependent on foreign oil. He proposed programs for conserving oil and gas, increasing the use of coal and nuclear power, and experimenting with **solar energy** — that is, energy from the power of the sun. Congress, however, passed only a weak version of the President's energy plan.

Meanwhile, an accident occurred in 1979 at the nuclear power plant at Three Mile Island near Harrisburg, Pennsylvania. No one was injured, but experts agreed that a disaster was barely avoided. Increasing public opposition to nuclear energy, along with high construction costs, led power companies to put aside plans to build new nuclear plants. America would continue to depend mainly on oil, gas, and coal for its energy.

The cooling towers of the Three Mile Island nuclear plant overlook homes in a peaceful neighborhood near Harrisburg, Pennsylvania.
■ What features of Three Mile Island are recognizable?

The Problem of Inflation   During President Carter's term, inflation became a more serious problem. From 1977 to 1981, oil-exporting countries raised the price of oil by a staggering 250 percent. That added to the cost of many other goods and services. Labor unions, trying to keep up with the cost of living, sought higher wages for their members. Businesses raised prices.

President Carter tried several ways to deal with inflation, but nothing worked. By 1980 the annual rate of inflation had climbed to more than 12 percent. Meanwhile, interest rates rose sharply, and economic growth slowed down.

The Panama Canal Treaties   The control of the United States over the Panama Canal and the Canal Zone had been a sore point with the people of Panama for many years. After anti-American riots in Panama in 1964, President Johnson opened talks with Panama to work out a new treaty. These talks continued under Presidents Nixon, Ford, and Carter. Finally, two treaties were agreed upon. Under them the United States and Panama would run the canal jointly until the year 1999. After that the canal would be turned over to Panama. The United States would keep the right to defend the canal.

Some Americans complained that the United States was giving away the canal. Still, the Senate approved both treaties in 1978 by the required two-thirds vote.

The Camp David Accords   For 30 years, Arab countries had been united in their determination to destroy Israel. But in 1977, President Anwar Sadat (än′ wär sə dät′) of Egypt offered to make peace.

Talks between Sadat and Israeli Prime Minister Menachem Begin (mə näk′ əm bā′ gin) started but then stalled. Fearing that the chance for peace might slip away, President Carter invited Sadat and Begin to meet with him at Camp David, the presidential vacation home in Maryland. After 2 weeks of difficult negotiations, the three

President Carter clasps hands with President Sadat of Egypt and Prime Minister Begin of Israel at the signing of the Camp David accords.
■ **What nations do the three flags represent?**

Born: 1924, Plains, Georgia.
Education: United States Naval Academy.
Training: Naval officer, farmer.
To presidency from: Georgia.
Position when elected: Private citizen.
Political party: Democratic.
Married: Rosalynn Smith.
Children: Three sons, one daughter.
Other facts: During 7 years in the navy, served on battleships and submarines. Helped develop the first nuclear-powered submarines. Resigned from navy after his father's death to manage family farm and peanut warehouse. Governor of Georgia from 1971 to 1975. After his term as President, taught and wrote. Enjoyed the hobby of woodworking.
During his presidency: The Panama Canal Zone, governed by the United States since 1903, became a part of Panama.

JAMES EARL CARTER
39th President
1977 · 1981

produced the **Camp David accords**. These agreements provided a set of principles on which peace between Israel and Egypt would be based, and held out hope of general peace in the Middle East.

In March 1979, Israel and Egypt signed the peace treaty. Israel returned the Sinai Peninsula to Egypt. Egypt recognized the state of Israel and agreed to normal relations between the two countries.

Unhappily the Camp David accords did not lead to general peace in the region. Many Arab countries were angry with Egypt for making peace with their common enemy. The Palestine Liberation Organization (PLO), an armed group of Palestinians based outside of Israel, continued to demand a return to their homeland and the destruction of Israel. And in 1981, Sadat was assassinated by a group of soldiers in his own army who were fiercely opposed to his policies.

Unrest in Central America Carter believed that the United States should promote **human rights** around the world. This policy meant that we should not support governments that prevented free speech, denied fair trials, and killed or jailed political opponents. Unfortunately, many governments, both Communist and non-Communist, did just those things.

In Central America, President Carter found it difficult to stick to this human rights policy. In most countries of this region, governments were controlled by a handful of wealthy families who owned most of the land. These families did little for the masses of peasants and city dwellers who lived in poverty.

In several Central American countries, rebels used guerrilla warfare against their governments in the 1970s. The rebels usually included both Communists and non-Communists. Often the rebels received support from the Communist government of Cuba. The governments that were under attack used ruthless methods against the rebels and against anyone else who dared to criticize them. Thousands were killed or imprisoned and tortured.

Carter did not want to support governments that denied human rights to their people. Yet rebel victory might lead to the

741

spread of communism in the region. So the United States gave military and economic aid to the governments while trying to get them to stop their violations of human rights.

In Nicaragua in 1979, rebels calling themselves Sandinistas succeeded in overthrowing a government led by a dictator named Anastasio Somoza. Somoza's family had ruled Nicaragua for more than 40 years, and had built a fortune of hundreds of millions of dollars at the expense of that country's people. At first the Sandinistas included both Communists and non-Communists. The United States hoped that the new government would be democratic and that it would not try to stir up more revolution in the region. It did not turn out that way, as Communists gained the upper hand in the Nicaraguan government.

Before long the Sandinistas, along with Cuba, were aiding guerrillas fighting

A large crowd of Nicaraguans in Managua celebrate the end of their revolution in 1979. Why, do you think, was this a happy time?

the government in neighboring El Salvador. There the government had made some efforts to give land to poor farmers. But at the same time the army and private "death squads" roamed the country, killing not only rebels but also thousands of innocent victims. Again President Carter tried to get the government to change its behavior while providing arms and military advisers to train government troops to fight the rebels.

SALT II In 1979, American and Soviet negotiators agreed on a new treaty to limit the arms race. The treaty was called **SALT II.** The SALT II agreement attempted to establish equality in missile systems between the two countries. When SALT II was sent to the Senate for approval, however, there was opposition. Some senators felt that it favored the Soviets and that it would be difficult to monitor the Soviets' missiles.

Any chance that the Senate might approve SALT II was taken away in December 1979 when the Soviet Union invaded Afghanistan, an Asian neighbor. To protest the Soviet action, President Carter withdrew SALT II from the Senate. He also cut off grain sales to the Soviet Union, and he announced that the United States would boycott the 1980 Olympic Games in Moscow. None of these acts caused the Soviet Union to pull its army out of Afghanistan. However, Soviet soldiers were resisted by Afghan fighters, who took to the mountains and continue to fight the Soviet soldiers.

Elsewhere in Asia, Carter followed the course begun by Nixon toward improving relations with China. In 1979, for the first time in 30 years, the United States sent an ambassador to the People's Republic of China, and the Chinese sent an ambassador to the United States.

American Hostages in Iran   In the oil-rich nation of Iran, the United States had long supported a pro-Western ruler named Shah (Emperor) Mohammad Reza Pahlavi (pä′ lə vē). The shah was trying to turn his ancient land into a modern industrial and military power. He met great opposition from traditional Moslems. The clergy believed the shah's modernization went against Moslem teachings. The shah added to his problems by using secret police to torture and murder his opponents.

In January 1979 the shah was driven from his throne. A new government headed by a Moslem religious leader, or ayatollah (ī ə tō′ lə), named Ruhollah Khomeini (rü ō′ lə kō mā′ nē) took power. This government was anti-American because of American support of the shah.

For a time the shah lived in Mexico and then in Panama, safe from the demand of Iran that he be returned to that country to stand trial for crimes against the people. Then in October 1979, President Carter allowed the shah to enter a hospital in the United States for the treatment of cancer. A few days later, on November 4, angry students seized the American Embassy in Iran's capital city of Tehran. The students took more than 50 Americans in the embassy as **hostages**. They refused to release these prisoners unless the United States handed over the shah.

The United States refused to yield. The shah returned to Panama and later went to live in Egypt, where he died some months later. Iran finally released the Americans after 444 days in captivity.

The day of the hostages' release was also Jimmy Carter's last day as President. American voters, dissatisfied with Carter's mixed record and angry over his inability to free the hostages, had rejected Carter's bid for reelection in 1980. On January 20, 1981, about a half-hour before the

Americans who had been held hostage in Iran stop in West Germany on their way home.
■ What time of year did this take place?

plane carrying the hostages took off from Tehran, the American people watched Ronald Reagan take his oath of office as President. Reagan had promised to lead the country in a new direction in the 1980s. President Reagan would now try to fulfill that promise.

CHECKUP

1. What problems inside the United States confronted President Carter?
2. How was the status of the Panama Canal changed?
3. What steps did President Carter take to bring peace to the Middle East?
4. Why were Americans taken hostage in Iran?
5. **Thinking Critically** Why was it difficult for the United States to follow a foreign policy in Central America based on human rights?

Classifying

GROUPING ITEMS AND IDEAS

Classifying means "grouping things according to what they have in common." For example, look at this list.

airplane
covered wagon
Model T
The *Clermont*
transcontinental railroad

These five items have been taken from different periods in history. You will quickly see, though, that they have something in common. They are all means by which people travel from one place to another. They could be classified as means of transportation.

Often, items or things will fit more than one classification. For example, here is a list of laws and programs mentioned in Chapter 30.

Civil Rights Act of 1964	VISTA
Voting Rights Act of 1965	Medicare
Fair Housing Act of 1968	Job Corps

You might classify all these items under the heading *Laws and Programs of the Johnson Presidency*. Three of these items — the Civil Rights Act of 1964, the Voting Rights Act of 1965, and the Fair Housing Act of 1968 — could be classified as civil rights laws. You might put VISTA and the Job Corps under the heading *Aid to the Needy*.

Why classify? Classifying helps you to see connections. Making connections helps you to understand and to remember.

SKILLS PRACTICE

On a separate sheet of paper, draw a 6-column grid with the headings shown below. Classify items 1–20 by writing the number of each item under the correct heading. Some items may fit under more than one heading. If you need help, skim back through Chapter 30.

1. Apollo
2. Medicare
3. Archibald Cox
4. Tet offensive
5. Martin Luther King, Jr.
6. Head Start
7. "executive privilege"
8. Camp David accords
9. Mercury
10. Richard Nixon
11. human rights
12. Vietnamization
13. Food stamp program
14. John Glenn
15. Ho Chi Minh Trail
16. Kerner Commission
17. Cape Canaveral
18. John Sirica
19. Thurgood Marshall
20. Panama Canal treaties

a. Space Program	b. Vietnam War	c. Watergate	d. Civil Rights Movement	e. Johnson's "Great Society"	f. Carter's Foreign Policy

MAIN IDEAS

1. Under President Lyndon Johnson's leadership, Congress enacted the most sweeping reforms since the New Deal, with programs in education, Medicare, and food stamps, among others.
2. Important gains were made in civil rights during the 1960s, yet many black Americans continued to live in poverty.
3. The United States became heavily involved during the 1960s in a costly and unpopular war in Vietnam.
4. President Richard Nixon's foreign policy brought improved relations with the Soviet Union and the People's Republic of China.
5. President Nixon's part in the Watergate scandal wrecked his presidency and caused him to resign from office.
6. President Jimmy Carter negotiated a peace between Egypt and Israel, promoted human rights around the world, encouraged democracy in Central America, and worked for new limitations on strategic arms.

VOCABULARY REVIEW

On a separate sheet of paper, write the letter of the term next to the number of its definition.

a. ghetto
b. Vietnamization
c. Civil Rights Act of 1964
d. domino theory
e. Camp David accords
f. détente
g. Great Society
h. SALT II
i. Gulf of Tonkin Resolution
j. Medicare

1. A law that, among other things, prohibited racial discrimination in businesses serving the public
2. An act that gave the President authority to take military action in Vietnam
3. A plan that permitted American troops to withdraw gradually from Vietnam
4. The arms limitation treaty negotiated during Carter's presidency

5. What Johnson called his reform program
6. A crowded area where minorities live
7. A relaxing of tensions between the United States and Communist countries
8. The agreements establishing peace between Egypt and Israel
9. The idea that the fall of one Southeast Asian country to communism would cause others to fall
10. An act providing health care for the aged

CHAPTER CHECKUP

1. What effect did the Voting Rights Act of 1965 have?
2. How did the continuing war in Vietnam affect Lyndon Johnson's political career?
3. Tell what each of the following stands for: (a) OPEC, (b) SALT, (c) VISTA.
4. Tell how each of the following terms was related to the Watergate affair: (a) executive privilege, (b) hush money, (c) stonewall, (d) "third-rate burglary," (e) 18½-minute gap.
5. **Thinking Critically** What were the main effects of rising oil prices on life in the United States?

APPLYING KNOWLEDGE

1. Interview family, friends, and others to learn how the Vietnam War affected their lives. You may also use your library for finding out about this period.
2. Find out what you can about the many ways in which Americans conserved oil during and after the embargo.
3. Find out when and why the Twenty-fifth Amendment was added to the Constitution.
4. Make a time line in which you show the important steps in the United States space program from 1957 to 1969.
5. Find out what the rates of inflation and unemployment are in the United States today.

31 *The Reagan Years*

1981–1988

Tax Cuts, Weapons Programs, and Budget Deficits

What changes did Ronald Reagan want to make as President?

VOCABULARY

federal budget	budget deficit
New Federalism	national debt
missile	tax loophole
Strategic Defense Initiative (SDI)	trade deficit
	space shuttle

The Great Communicator   Ronald Reagan was born in small-town America before radio and television broadcasting existed. Still, no President of the United States had ever made more effective use of these instruments of mass communication to win support for himself and his ideas. Reagan was able to reach the presidency by using the skills he had developed during earlier careers in front of the microphone and the camera. During Reagan's presidency, many people who marveled at these skills of his referred to him as the Great Communicator.

Ronald Reagan was born in 1911 in Tampico, Illinois. His father was a struggling shoe salesman. The family moved frequently from one small Illinois town to another. Between the ages of 6 and 10, Ronald Reagan attended a different school

each year. After high school he attended Eureka College, a small school near Peoria, Illinois. Graduating during the Great Depression, he managed to find work as a radio announcer.

For 5 years Reagan was a sports announcer for a station in Des Moines, Iowa. Then in 1937 the handsome young Reagan left for Hollywood and landed a job as a movie actor. During the next 2 decades, he appeared in 53 movies. He also served as president of the Screen Actors Guild, the union of movie actors. Still later, Reagan moved into television, serving as the host of a series sponsored by General Electric Corporation.

A New Career in Politics   Ronald Reagan and his family had been Democrats, and during the Great Depression he had been a strong supporter of President Franklin Roosevelt's New Deal. In the late 1950s, however, Reagan's political views became more conservative. He soon switched to the Republican party.

Reagan was already known to millions of Americans as a movie and television personality, but he won attention as a possible candidate for office when he made a nationally televised speech in support of

A boom in such new high technology industries as computers was one of the features of the economic recovery in the mid-1980s.
■ What are these American workers making and testing?

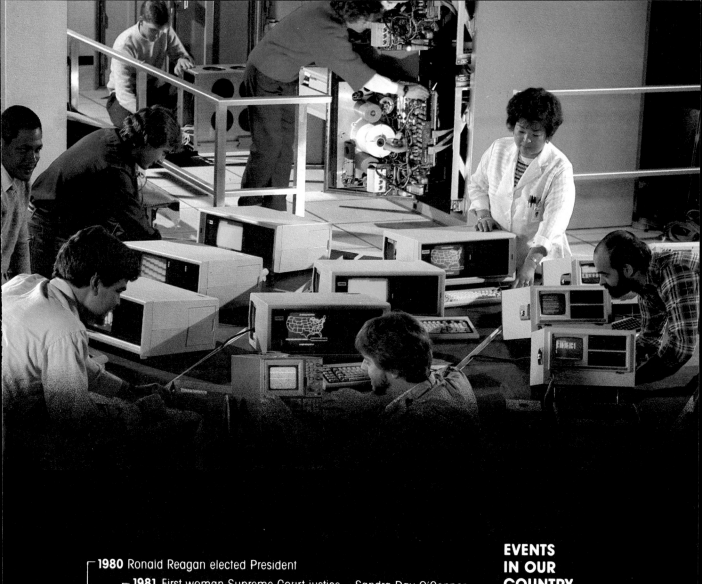

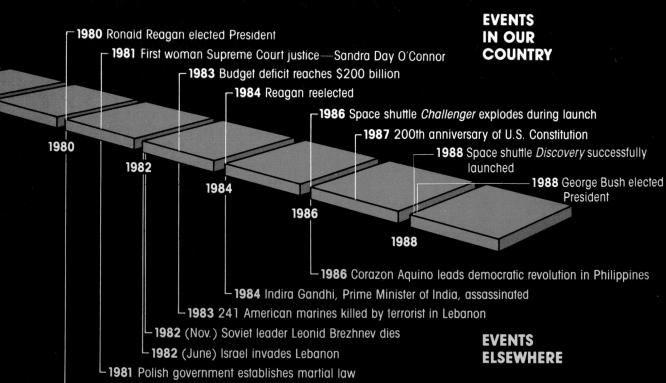

1980 Ronald Reagan elected President

1981 First woman Supreme Court justice—Sandra Day O'Connor

1983 Budget deficit reaches $200 billion

1984 Reagan reelected

1986 Space shuttle *Challenger* explodes during launch

1987 200th anniversary of U.S. Constitution

1988 Space shuttle *Discovery* successfully launched

1988 George Bush elected President

1980

1982

1984

1986

1988

1986 Corazon Aquino leads democratic revolution in Philippines

1984 Indira Gandhi, Prime Minister of India, assassinated

1983 241 American marines killed by terrorist in Lebanon

1982 (Nov.) Soviet leader Leonid Brezhnev dies

1982 (June) Israel invades Lebanon

1981 Polish government establishes martial law

1980 Polish workers start Solidarity union

Barry Goldwater, the Republican candidate for President in 1964. Two years later, Reagan, who had never held a political office, ran for governor of California and won. His speeches on radio and television had a lot to do with his victory.

After two successful terms as governor of the nation's largest state, he sought the Republican nomination for President in 1976. He was narrowly defeated by President Gerald Ford. Still, Reagan was not to be denied. In 1980 the Republicans chose him to run against incumbent Democratic President Jimmy Carter.

Winning the Presidency   During the 1980 campaign, Reagan spoke of the need to restore respect for the United States thoughout the world. He said that American military power had been allowed to

Ronald Reagan stressed patriotism in his campaign for the presidency.
■ What is Reagan appealing to in this poster?

AMERICA
REAGAN COUNTRY

slip and must be rebuilt. He also favored cutting taxes and reducing government regulation of business. Reagan won in a landslide, receiving 483 electoral votes to Carter's 49. The Republicans also gained 12 seats in the Senate to take control of that body for the first time since 1954.

At the age of 69, Ronald Reagan was the oldest person ever to be elected President. Two months into his first term, his life was almost cut short when a disturbed young man named John Hinckley, Jr., tried to assassinate him. As Reagan left a Washington hotel, the young man fired several shots from a small handgun, hitting the President and three other people. Reagan was rushed to a nearby hospital, where doctors removed a bullet that had stopped near one of his lungs. The President made a rapid recovery and was soon back at his desk in the White House.

Reagan's Economic Program   In that first term, Reagan proved to be one of the most successful Presidents in winning the support of Congress for his programs. Following his recommendations, Congress cut $35 billion out of the **federal budget** that President Carter had proposed for 1981. The budget is the official estimate of the amount of money the government will take in and the amount it will spend over a 12-month period. The cuts made by Congress included funds for aid to cities, public housing, public health, education, and welfare. Critics said these cuts would take too much away from the poor. The President's reply to the critics was that the truly needy would be protected.

The President also got Congress to pass an income tax cut for individuals, totaling 25 percent over 3 years. This was the largest tax cut in American history. There were also tax cuts for businesses. Reagan said that these cuts would leave

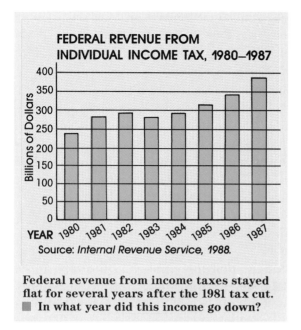

FEDERAL REVENUE FROM INDIVIDUAL INCOME TAX, 1980–1987

Billions of Dollars

Source: *Internal Revenue Service, 1988.*

Federal revenue from income taxes stayed flat for several years after the 1981 tax cut. ■ In what year did this income go down?

more money for people to invest in factories and equipment. American industry could then become more productive and compete more successfully with other countries. Tax cuts would also leave Americans with more money to spend on goods and services. This would help the economy grow and provide more jobs.

Relaxing Regulations President Ford had taken a few steps toward reducing federal regulation of businesses in 1975. President Carter had gone still further in this direction. During Carter's administration, air travel, rail freight, trucking, long-distance telephone service, natural gas, and cable television were all fully or partially deregulated.

President Reagan was committed to reducing federal regulation even more. After a week in office, he ended all remaining controls on the price of oil and gas, saying that this would encourage Americans to produce more of these fuels. Reagan also relaxed some regulations designed to encourage conservation and prevent pollution.

The New Federalism To reduce the size of the federal government, President Reagan wanted to shift certain programs from the federal government to the states. These would include some welfare and health-care programs. Some tax revenues would go to the states to help them pay the costs. The President called this plan the **New Federalism**.

Most governors were cautious about the plan. They feared that it would cost more than their states could afford. Some also felt that the programs were really the responsibility of the federal government.

A few programs were shifted to the states during Reagan's presidency but not as many as Reagan had originally intended. In fact, despite the President's pledge to cut the size of the federal government, there were over 170,000 more federal employees near the end of 1988 than there had been when Reagan took office.

A Military Buildup Reagan believed that the United States had fallen behind the Soviet Union in the production of arms. He won congressional approval for huge increases in defense spending. This included funds for a new missile. A **missile** is a weapon that can be launched from the ground, sea, or air against a target many miles away.

For several years the Soviet Union had been placing medium-range nuclear missiles near its European border. These Soviet missiles could reach targets in the European NATO countries in 10 minutes. The NATO countries warned that if the Soviet missiles were not removed, they would install their own. When talks with the Soviets produced no agreement, American missiles were put in place in Great Britain and West Germany.

Reagan also persuaded Congress to approve the beginning of research on a new defense program called the **Strategic Defense Initiative**, or **SDI**. Because this was a plan for an antimissile system in space, it came to be known popularly as "Star Wars." Such a system would be incredibly complex and would require huge expenditures for research, but President Reagan believed it could be put into place by the year 2000.

If the SDI system worked, it would act as a shield against missiles fired at the United States. Many scientists doubted, though, that it was possible to create a foolproof antimissile system. Others feared that proceeding with SDI would make it impossible to reach an agreement on arms control with the Soviets. (See page 758.) Despite these doubts, Congress approved funds for SDI research.

Economic Losses and Gains President Reagan promised that his programs would bring down inflation and also balance the federal budget by the end of his first term in office. The budget is balanced when the amount that the government takes in in taxes and other revenue is equal to the amount that it spends. For 12 years in a row before Reagan became President, there had been federal **budget deficits**—that is, the government had spent more than it had taken in.

When a budget deficit occurs, the federal government must borrow to cover it. This new debt is added to the amount the government already owes from past deficits. The total amount the government owes is called the **national debt**.

Despite Reagan's predictions, during the first 2 years of his presidency the economy got worse instead of better. Annual budget deficits climbed. Interest rates soared to all-time highs. Many businesses shut down or cut back their operations. Unemployment rose to 11 percent, the highest rate since the Great Depression.

On the other hand, with less demand for goods and services, the inflation rate did fall. By the end of 1982, it was down to 5 percent per year.

Then came a turnaround. Interest rates dropped sharply, and the economy picked up some steam. Automobile factories, retail stores, and other businesses

One component of SDI is a neutral particle beam accelerator. These scientists are working on one at Los Alamos National Laboratory in New Mexico.
■ **What does SDI stand for?**

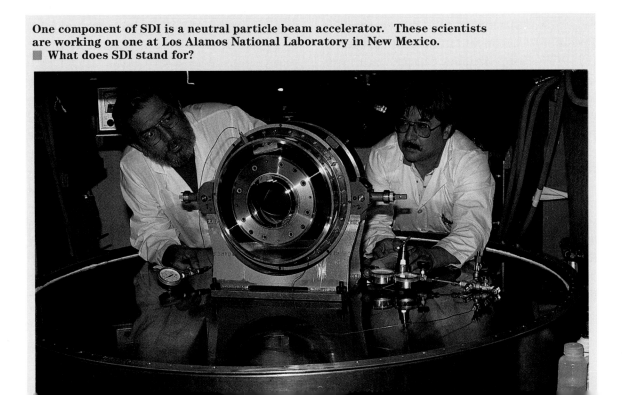

reported rising sales. Whole new industries, such as the personal computer industry, were started by American technological know-how. New jobs were created, and unemployment declined.

Inflation also remained low. It fell to less than 4 percent in 1984 and remained low throughout the 1980s with the help of lower oil prices. After selling at a high of $40 a barrel in 1980, oil prices leveled off to $12 to $14 by the end of the decade. This in turn kept interest rates relatively low.

The Election of 1984   At the end of his first term, Ronald Reagan was one of the most popular Presidents of the twentieth century. When he decided to run for another term in 1984, the Republican party renominated him without opposition.

In the Democratic party there was a spirited contest for the presidential nomination. The leading candidates were Walter Mondale, who had been Carter's Vice President; Gary Hart, a senator from Colorado; and the Reverend Jesse Jackson, a longtime civil rights leader. Jackson broke new ground as the first black to mount a serious campaign for the presidency. He gathered more than 20 percent of the vote in the Democratic primaries.

In the end the Democrats nominated Mondale. He then made history by choosing as his vice presidential candidate Representative Geraldine Ferraro of New York. Ferraro became the first woman nominated to run for national office by one of the major political parties.

In his campaign, President Reagan was able to point to continuing good news on the economy. Reagan asked Americans if they were better off than they had been when he came into office. Most felt that they were. Reagan also said that he had strengthened the United States militarily

Geraldine Ferraro was the first woman nominated for Vice President by one of the nation's major political parties.
■ Who ran for President with her?

and that the country had regained respect around the world. He declared that there was a growing spirit of pride in America.

Mondale, on the other hand, pointed with alarm to Reagan's huge budget deficits and the soaring national debt. He also charged that the policies of the Reagan administration ignored the needs of the poor. Mondale said he would raise taxes to cut the deficit and put money into needed programs.

None of the Democrat's arguments made a dent in the popularity of President Reagan. On election day, voters gave Reagan a sweeping victory. He received 59 percent of the popular vote and carried 49 states, winning 525 electoral votes to just 13 for Mondale.

The Budget Deficit Grows   One of the most difficult problems Ronald Reagan and Congress wrestled with in Reagan's second term was the huge budget deficit, then more than $200 billion a year. As each year's deficit was piled onto what the government already owed, the national debt grew and grew. By 1986 it stood at 2 *trillion* dollars — $2,000,000,000,000. The debt had doubled in 6 years, and it was headed nowhere but up.

To get the deficit under control, Congress in 1985 enacted the Gramm-Rudman-Hollings Act. This law set deficit targets for the next 5 years, with each year's target lower than the previous year's. If Congress and the President failed to lower spending or raise revenue enough to meet those targets, across-the-board spending cuts would be made auto-matically, to be divided equally between defense spending and domestic spending. The law called for the deficit to disappear altogether by 1991.

Tax Reform   Over the years, Congress had created many **tax loopholes**. These special rules allowed some businesses and individuals to avoid paying some of their taxes. Supporters of such loopholes usually claimed that it was in the nation's best interest to grant tax breaks to certain kinds of businesses and business practices. But by the middle of the 1980s, both parties and the American public expressed a growing demand to Congress to make the income tax laws simpler.

President Reagan strongly agreed. His efforts helped win the support that was needed in Congress to pass the Tax Reform Act of 1986. This law lowered the tax rates of people with high incomes, but it also closed many of the loopholes that had allowed them to avoid paying taxes. It also freed some 6 million working families with low incomes from paying any income tax. The law was not supposed to change the amount of taxes the government would collect. It did, however, shift much of the tax burden away from individuals and families and onto large corporations.

Most people agreed that the new law was fairer than the one it replaced. It was the most important reform of the tax system in 40 years.

Prosperity for All?   The overall American economy continued to thrive in President Reagan's second term. Still, not all the economic news was good.

Farmers in the 1980s experienced their worst time since the Great Depression. They saw their cost of doing business rise while the prices of farm goods fell. Many were unable to repay their

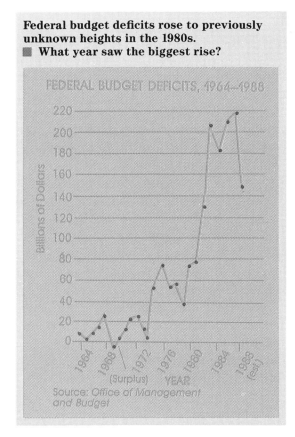

Federal budget deficits rose to previously unknown heights in the 1980s.
■ **What year saw the biggest rise?**

FEDERAL BUDGET DEFICITS, 1964–1988

Billions of Dollars

220, 200, 180, 160, 140, 120, 100, 80, 60, 40, 20, 0

1964, 1968, 1972, 1976, 1980, 1984, 1988 (est.)

(Surplus)   YEAR

Source: Office of Management and Budget

During the early 1980s, many farmers lost their land, machinery, and farm animals in auctions.
■ What type of farm is this?

loans. A devastating drought in 1988 further strained the farming community.

The states that produce oil were hit especially hard during the Reagan years. The demand for oil decreased due to an emphasis on fuel conservation. Auto and home owners welcomed lower fuel prices, but falling prices brought distress to oil states such as Colorado, Louisiana, Oklahoma, and Texas.

While unemployment was highest in the farm and oil states, the unemployment rate throughout the country remained over 6 percent. The rate was higher among blacks and young people. The number of American families living in poverty was about the same when Reagan left office as when he began his presidency.

Immigration Reform   Among those struggling to get by were untold millions of immigrants who had entered the United States illegally. Most of these were from countries in the Americas, especially from neighboring Mexico. They came to be called undocumented aliens — that is, foreign visitors who lacked the papers, or documents, to show that they had entered the country legally. Many of these people lived in fear that they might be forced to leave the United States.

In 1986, Congress passed the Immigration Reform Act. This new law enabled undocumented aliens who had lived in the United States continuously since 1981 to become legal residents. To discourage the illegal entry of more aliens in the future, the law made it a crime for employers to hire immigrants who did not have documents to prove that they had entered the United States legally.

The Trade Deficit   One of the greatest economic problems was the nation's worsening trade deficit. A **trade deficit** occurs when we as a nation import, or buy, from other countries more goods than we export, or sell, to other countries.

753

When President Reagan took office in 1981, the trade deficit was already $40 billion a year. Six years later it had climbed to $170 billion. Most of this total was the result of importing cars, oil, clothing, stereos, televisions, and electrical and electronic products.

An event in October 1987 dramatically revealed the weakness of the American economy. The stock market index, which measures the number of stocks bought and sold each day, dropped 95 points—the largest one-day fall ever. Many more people were selling stocks than were buying them. In one day, stocks on the American stock market dropped in value by $500 billion! Stock markets around the world panicked in response to "Black Monday." Some people compared what had happened to the "Crash of '29."

The severe stock market drop in 1987 did not result in a disastrous business depression. Laws passed after the stock market crash of 1929 and the depression of the 1930s created reforms to prevent this. The stock market rebounded slowly as investors acted with caution.

While experts differed over the causes of the "Crash of '87," nearly all agreed that the expanding trade deficit was at the heart of the problem. The trade deficit continued to be a problem throughout the 1980s.

Space Shuttles: Triumph and Disaster

In the early months of the Reagan administration, NASA sent into space its first manned mission in 6 years. The *Columbia* was different from all the vehicles that had made the trip before. It was a **space shuttle**. The shuttle, shaped like an airplane, was designed to be landed under its own power by its pilot and then reused in other space missions.

Over the next few years, NASA added two more shuttles, *Challenger* and *Discovery*, to its fleet. They flew more and more frequent missions, with heavier cargoes, larger crews, and more experiments to perform. Some shuttle missions took permanent satellites into space and launched them. One crew in 1984 repaired a satellite that had been launched 4 years earlier. NASA began to view its shuttles as "space trucks," making frequent round-trips for pickups and deliveries.

Then, on the unusually cold morning of January 28, 1986, disaster struck. The shuttle *Challenger* exploded in midair, just 73 seconds after being launched on its latest mission. All seven brave members of its crew were killed.

One of those seven was Christa McAuliffe, a high school social studies teacher from Concord, New Hampshire. McAuliffe had been chosen from among thousands of competitors to be the first ordinary citizen

Trade deficits grew rapidly in the 1980s.
▪ **In what year did the trade deficit almost double in size?**

SELECTED UNITED STATES INTERNATIONAL TRADE DEFICITS, 1965–1988

Sources: Through 1985, Economic Report of the President; 1986–1988, Department of Commerce.

The *Discovery* shuttle was successfully launched on September 29, 1988.
■ What is attached to the rocket booster?

NASA sent into space. She had planned to teach lessons on the mission and the shuttle program that would be televised to classes across the country. Instead, those classes saw a fiery explosion, followed by trails of smoke against an empty sky.

A presidential commission investigated the disaster. It found the cause to be a faulty O-ring on one of the booster rockets that lifted the shuttle into the sky. This rubbery ring, not much thicker than a big rubber band, was intended to seal the sections of the booster together, but freezing temperatures caused it to fail. The commission also made the disturbing discovery that some engineers who had helped to build the rocket had warned that this might happen in cold weather. They had even tried to stop this *Challenger* mission, but they were overruled.

Following these revelations, NASA found new ways to replace the flawed booster and repair its own tarnished image. Space flights did not resume until September 1988 with the successful launch of the *Discovery* shuttle.

CHECKUP

1. What were President Reagan's views on (a) taxation, (b) military spending, (c) the regulation of business, (d) the role of the states?
2. What was the Reagan administration's record on (a) inflation, (b) budget deficits, (c) unemployment?
3. What is the connection between a yearly federal budget deficit and the national debt?
4. **Thinking Critically** Why did many Americans favor tax reform in 1986?

Foreign Affairs Under Reagan

What were the major problems the Reagan administration had to confront in its foreign policy?

VOCABULARY

Contras	terrorism
martial law	

Trouble in Central America While President Reagan could point to many successes in winning support for his domestic programs, his record in foreign policy was more mixed. During his administration much attention was focused on Central America, especially on the countries of El Salvador and Nicaragua.

In El Salvador, rebel groups that included Communists threatened to overthrow the government. The United States had reason to believe that the Soviet Union and Cuba were sending arms to these rebels by way of Nicaragua. The United States increased its economic aid to El Salvador and sent 50 military advisers to help train its army.

Many Americans were uncomfortable with this policy. They said that the government of El Salvador violated human rights and killed thousands of its own people each year. President Reagan, however, believed that stopping the spread of communism in the region had to come before any human rights policy.

By the end of 1986, the United States had poured $1.5 billion in economic aid and $500 million in military aid into El Salvador. The war had already taken 60,000 lives. Still, no end was in sight.

Aiding the Contras In El Salvador the Reagan administration backed the government against the rebels. In neighboring Nicaragua it backed rebels fighting the government. The Nicaraguan government was controlled by the Sandinistas. (See page 742.) They jailed political opponents and closed down newspapers that criticized their rule. They also established close ties with the Soviet Union and Cuba. In fact, the Reagan administration feared that the Sandinistas would turn their country into another Cuba. Through the Central Intelligence Agency (CIA), the administration secretly provided equipment, training, and money to the **Contras**, rebel groups seeking to overthrow the Sandinista government. These groups took their name from the Spanish word meaning "against."

Public opinion polls showed that while Americans disliked the Sandinistas, they were overwhelmingly opposed to United States involvement in Nicaragua. Some members of Congress, much of the press, and many other nations also criticized Reagan's policy. Despite this opposition, the President succeeded in getting Congress to go along with his request for funds for the Contras. Still, few people believed that the small, disorganized Contra movement would ever be able to overthrow the Sandinista government.

Grenada and Haiti Important developments occurred in two Caribbean island nations. In 1983, Communist forces took over the government of tiny Grenada and had the prime minister and other officials killed. With the approval and cooperation of a number of Grenada's worried island neighbors, the United States sent in troops and restored a moderate government.

In Haiti a popular uprising in 1986 forced dictator Jean-Claude "Baby Doc" Duvalier to flee the country. Duvalier and his father, "Papa Doc," had ruled the country for 3 decades through torture and fear, and had amassed a fortune at the expense of the Haitian people. Duvalier took much of this fortune with him when he fled. A military group replaced Duvalier and promised democratic elections within a year, but the year came and went with no elections.

People Power in the Philippines
Meanwhile, on the other side of the world the cause of democratic government took a large step forward. In 1986, voters in the Philippine Islands threw out the increasingly corrupt government of President Ferdinand Marcos.

In his place they elected Corazon Aquino (kôr ä zōn′ ä kē′ nō), the widow of Benigno Aquino, a leading opponent of Ferdinand Marcos. Her husband had been assassinated in 1983. Aquino had not been involved in politics before her husband was killed, but she joined the struggle to overthrow Marcos. When the United States government pressured Marcos to hold an election, his opponents united behind Aquino.

At first Marcos claimed victory. Then groups of nonpartisan observers and a delegation from the United States Congress reported massive fraud in both the voting and the counting. Next, some members of the armed forces took over their camps to protest Marcos's attempt to steal the election. When soldiers loyal to Marcos were sent to crush the rebellion, millions of Filipinos filled the streets of the capital, Manila, and blocked their way.

Within days, Marcos, at the urging of President Reagan, fled to exile in Hawaii. Aquino was sworn in as president of the Philippines. The United States promptly recognized the new government, and Congress voted to increase foreign aid to the Philippines.

Corazon Aquino (left) campaigns in the streets of Cebu City. Aquino became president of the Philippines in 1986.
■ What type of vehicle is Aquino riding in?

Twice during the next year, dissatisfied elements in the Philippines armed forces tried but failed to overthrow Aquino's government. In 1987 the Filipino people voted their approval of a new constitution drawn up by the new government.

Relations with the Soviet Union
President Reagan believed that the Soviet Union was behind much of the world's trouble. During his presidency the United States and the Soviet Union moved farther apart than they had been for years. Reagan did end Carter's ban on grain sales to the Soviet Union, enabling American farmers to sell some of their surplus grain to that country. But he strongly discouraged the sale of high-technology products by both the United States and its European allies. Reagan claimed that these goods strengthened the Soviet military.

Events in Poland contributed to the worsening relations with the Soviet Union. In 1980, Polish workers started a

In late 1986, President Reagan and Soviet leader Gorbachev held a summit meeting in Reykjavik, the capital of Iceland.
■ Why, do you think, are meetings between world leaders important?

labor union called Solidarity. This union won great popular support as it fought for increased freedom for the Polish people. In December 1981, under strong pressure from Moscow, the Polish government imposed **martial law**, or rule by the military, and crushed Solidarity.

The United States led the Western nations in denouncing this action. It showed, they said, the real attitude of the Soviet bloc toward freedom.

Relations Worsen   Relations reached a new low in September 1983 when a Soviet pilot shot down a South Korean passenger airliner, killing 269 people including 60 Americans. The airliner had strayed into Soviet airspace, and the Soviets claimed it was on a spy mission. Many nations condemned the Soviets for this action.

The U.S.S.R. was also condemned for its continuing war in Afghanistan. When Soviet troops had entered that country in 1979, they had expected to crush any resistance, install a friendly government, and return home quickly. Afghan rebels based in the mountains fought back, however, and would not be defeated. By the middle of the 1980s, the Soviet Union was eager to find a way out of Afghanistan.

Arms Control   In such an atmosphere, a new agreement to limit arms seemed all but impossible. The issue of arms control was too important to ignore. Meetings between representatives of the United States and the Soviet Union resumed in 1985. President Reagan agreed to a "get acquainted" meeting with the new Soviet leader, Mikhail Gorbachev (gôr′ bə chôf), in late 1985. At that meeting the two leaders agreed to meet again in 1986.

This second meeting took place in Reykjavik (rāk′ yə vik), Iceland, in October 1986. Reagan and Gorbachev negotiated seriously about large reductions in the number of nuclear weapons held by each side. However, no agreement was reached. Finally, in 1987, the Intermediate Nuclear Forces (INF) Treaty was signed in Washington. This treaty outlawed all intermediate-range missiles.

A Nuclear Accident   Due to these talks, it was clear that both sides would continue to seek a way to control nuclear arms.   If any reminder of the nuclear threat to human existence was needed, it came in April 1986.   In that month the worst accident in the history of nuclear power occurred at a nuclear power plant at Chernobyl (chèr nō′ bəl) in the Soviet Union.   Radiation took the lives of at least 30 people and will shorten the lives of countless others.   More than 135,000 people had to be evacuated from their homes, many permanently.   Winds carried the deadly radiation hundreds of miles across the Soviet Union and into neighboring countries in Europe.

Involvement in Lebanon   In the mid-1970s a civil war in Lebanon between Christian and Moslem groups threatened to tear that country apart.   Syrian troops,

NASA's Landsat (Land satellite) took this picture of Chernobyl in the Soviet Union.   Red indicates vegetation; blue shows built-up areas.
 When was this satellite photograph taken?

entering Lebanon supposedly to restore peace, remained to occupy a large part of the country. Meanwhile the Palestine Liberation Organization (PLO) used southern Lebanon as a base for attacks on Israeli settlements.

Determined to drive the PLO from its borders, Israel invaded Lebanon in June 1982. Israeli forces drove all the way to Beirut, Lebanon's capital and the headquarters of the PLO. Western countries finally arranged a cease-fire, but the PLO had to agree to leave Lebanon.

A new Lebanese government then requested the United States, France, and Italy to send small peacekeeping forces to Beirut. The hope was to give the new government time to get established, end the fighting between Moslems and Christians, and get all the Syrian and Israeli forces out of the country.

In October 1983 a radical Moslem group blew up a United States marine barracks in Beirut, killing 241 Americans.

President and Mrs. Reagan attend a memorial service for the marines killed in Beirut.
■ **Who are the seated men being greeted by the Reagans?**

Several months later the United States and the other nations with peacekeeping forces in Lebanon withdrew their troops.

Israeli forces pulled back from Lebanon the following year. Still, peace did not return to war-torn Lebanon. Christians and Moslems continued to fight, and various Moslem groups fought among themselves. The United States was learning how limited was its power to influence governments and events thousands of miles away.

Terrorism Increases   The 1980s saw a rise in international **terrorism**. Terrorism is the organized use of violence against innocent civilians in an attempt to advance one's political goals. Terrorists championing a number of causes planted bombs in buildings, seized airliners, gunned people down on streets and in airports, and seized hostages. In Lebanon, various groups seized citizens of the United States and of several European countries, killing some and holding others as hostages.

Support for these terrorists came from the Middle Eastern countries of Libya, Syria, and Iran. Colonel Muammar Qaddafi (mü′ ə mär kə dä′ fē), the Libyan leader, often spoke out in praise of terrorist actions and provided places for terrorists to train. An official of the United States government called Libya "the nerve center of terrorist training."

The United States took the lead in opposing international terrorism. President Reagan urged other nations to stand firm against terrorists' demands and not to make deals for the return of hostages. To do so, he said, would only reward the terrorists and encourage them to take still more hostages. Reagan also urged allies not to deal with governments that supported terrorism. When a terrorist's bomb killed an American soldier and

Born: 1911, Tampico, Illinois.
Education: Eureka College.
Training: Radio announcer, actor, public official.
To presidency from: California.
Position when elected: Private citizen.
Political party: Republican.
Married: (1) Jane Wyman, (2) Nancy Davis.
Children: Two daughters, two sons.
Other facts: A play-by-play sports announcer for radio stations in Iowa. Became an actor in motion pictures and played in more than 50 films, many of them westerns. Made training films for United States Army Forces in World War II. Served for 6 years as president of film actors' union. Twice elected governor of California. Likes to spend weekends at California ranch.
During his presidency: The birthday of Martin Luther King, Jr., was made a national holiday.

RONALD REAGAN
40th President
1981 • 1989

wounded 50 others in West Berlin in 1986, the United States struck back. Acting on evidence that Libya was directly involved in the bombing, President Reagan sent American war planes to bomb a number of targets in Libya.

A Confused Policy In 1980, Iraqi forces had invaded Iran in a border dispute. Since that time, Iraq and Iran had been involved in a costly, bloody war. Because of Iran's hostile attitude toward the United States, President Reagan prohibited the sale of arms to Iran. He also urged all other countries, especially our allies, not to sell military equipment to Iran. In late 1986 the United States citizens learned that the Reagan administration was secretly dealing with Iran.

In 1986 a pro-Iranian group in Lebanon held six Americans hostage. Hoping to gain their return, and also to improve relations with Iran in the future, the Reagan administration secretly agreed to sell arms to a group in Iran. Thus, while urging our allies not to sell arms to that country and not to make deals for the return of

hostages, the United States was secretly doing both.

Some of the money received for the weapons had then been sent secretly to the Contras in Nicaragua so that they could buy arms. Many Americans believed that members of the administration had clearly violated United States law. They had withheld information from the President and the American people. The Iran-Contra hearings in 1987 uncovered these findings.

CHECKUP

1. What events in Central American countries occupied the attention of the Reagan administration?
2. What contributed to the worsening of American relations with the U.S.S.R. during Reagan's presidency?
3. How did the Reagan administration respond to terrorism in the Middle East?
4. What did some Americans mean when they said that Nicaragua might become another Cuba?

5. **Thinking Critically** Why was the war in Afghanistan called the Soviets' Vietnam?

The Struggle for Equality Broadens

How was the idea of equality broadened in the years leading up to the two hundredth anniversary of the Constitution?

An Important Anniversary   In 1987, Americans celebrated the anniversary of one of the most important events in our history. That year the Constitution was 200 years old. Under this great document our country has grown from a young republic of barely 4 million people to a mighty nation of over 240 million.

Students examine a copy of the Constitution, the original of which was signed in 1787. ■ What are its first three words?

During these 2 centuries, the government set up by the Constitution has been tested again and again, and it has been found strong and flexible enough to preserve and extend our democratic way of life. The Constitution and its amendments have guaranteed our most basic freedoms: free speech, a free press, the right to assemble, the right to worship as we please. They have assured people accused of crimes that they would have fair trials. All Americans, regardless of race, color, or sex, have the right to vote. We are protected in the enjoyment of our civil rights, and we are guaranteed the equal protection of the laws. Under this great charter of liberties, we have moved ever closer to reaching the promise of America — equal rights and opportunity for all, and the chance for every person to be all that he or she can be.

We know that before these goals are achieved, some barriers must be overcome. Inequality, injustice, discrimination, and crippling poverty remain. But as the noted historian Richard Hofstadter has written:

> Americans do not abide [i.e., accept] very quietly the evils of life. We are forever restlessly pitting ourselves against them, demanding changes, improvements, remedies.

Among these "changes, improvements, remedies" is the struggle by many Americans to end discrimination and gain equal rights for themselves and others.

A Great Mexican American Migration In the United States today, there are some 20 million Hispanic Americans. These people or their ancestors came from lands that were long ago colonized by Spain — Mexico, Puerto Rico, Cuba, and countries

Migrant workers move from one farming region to another to help harvest crops. These workers are picking spinach on a Michigan farm.
■ **Why, do you think, is the spinach packed in wooden crates?**

in Central and South America and in the Caribbean Sea. Hispanics are the second-largest and fastest-growing minority group in the United States.

The largest group of Hispanics is the Mexican Americans. They number some 11 million or 12 million. Most live in the Southwest, but there are large communities in other parts of the country as well.

Some Mexican Americans are descended from families that lived in the American Southwest before that land became part of the United States. Most,

however, are part of the migration from Mexico that began after 1900. This migration became especially large after 1940.

Many of the newcomers became migrant workers on large farms in California and Texas. **Migrant workers** traveled from one farm and one part of the country to another to find work planting, cultivating, and harvesting crops. They received low pay and worked in poor conditions.

In 1962 Cesar Chavez (cha′ vās) decided to organize these farm workers. Chavez, who with his wife had eight children to raise, gave up a well-paid job to spend all his time working for the migrants. He formed a union later known as the United Farm Workers (UFW). Chavez, like Martin Luther King, Jr., believed in nonviolence and insisted that his followers accept this principle.

In 1965 the farm workers went on strike against the grape growers in California. The strike lasted 5 years, but in the end the UFW won improved wages and working conditions.

Mexican Americans Today Today many Mexican Americans still work on farms, but more than four out of five live in cities. Many of these live in separate neighborhoods, which they call barrios. Many people in the barrios continue to speak Spanish as their first language and to hold on to their familiar culture—just as many other immigrant groups have done. The Spanish language and culture have been a major source of strength and pride.

Mexican Americans have begun to organize to improve their position. By the 1980s they were taking a larger part in government. Several served in Congress. Henry Cisneros (siz när′ ōs) of San Antonio, Texas, became the first Mexican American mayor of any of our largest cities. As more Mexican Americans voted, they could expect to elect more candidates who would pay attention to their needs and wishes.

Puerto Ricans to the Mainland The second-largest Hispanic group is the Puerto Ricans. Puerto Ricans are United States citizens, whether they live on their home island or on the United States mainland. Puerto Rico has its own constitution, and its people govern themselves. It is not, however, a state. It is governed as a

In a bilingual classroom students speak both English and Spanish. These students are learning their basic subjects partly in Spanish and in English.
■ What language is on the chalkboard?

commonwealth under a one-of-a-kind arrangement with the United States government.

Since the 1940s, Puerto Rico has made great strides in improving its economy. Even so, poverty and unemployment remain. Beginning after World War II, many Puerto Ricans decided to leave *la isla verde*—"the green island"—to look for work on the mainland. Today about 2 million people of Puerto Rican descent live on the mainland.

Puerto Ricans have gradually improved their position despite some barriers they had to break down. Each year larger numbers of Puerto Ricans in the United States than before are going to college and getting good jobs. They are also gaining political power as men and women of Puerto Rican descent serve in Congress, in state legislatures, and in many offices in their own communities.

Women Seek Equality   There are more women than men in the United States. Women are a majority group, not a minority group. Yet women have suffered from some of the same kinds of discrimination that minorities have known.

Many women entered the work force in the 1950s and 1960s, but they continued to find barriers in many fields. Few were promoted to high-level jobs — the jobs that carried not only higher pay but also the power to make important decisions. Women were often paid less than men for the same work. Rarely did a woman hold an important job in federal, state, or local government.

In 1966 some 300 women and men formed the National Organization for Women, or NOW. NOW's first goal was to help both women and men become aware of the unequal treatment of women and to change their thinking about it.

Soon other groups organized to promote equality for women. Some concentrated on the issue of jobs and pay. Others aimed at getting more women elected and appointed to public office. Together these efforts came to be called the **women's liberation** movement.

Led by NOW and other such groups, women made important gains between the 1960s and the 1980s. They were aided by several actions of the federal government. The Civil Rights Act of 1964 forbade discrimination on the grounds of sex as well as race. By the early 1970s the government was actively enforcing this position. It also required schools and colleges receiving federal money, and companies doing business with the government, to set goals for hiring qualified women and minorities. Another law of this period, the Equal Employment Opportunity Act of 1972, required employers to give equal pay to men and women for equal work.

Women's Political Goals   During the 1970s and 1980s, women were elected and appointed to public office at all levels of government. Women served as governors and mayors, and in the House and the Senate. A growing number were appointed as judges. In 1981, Sandra Day O'Connor became the first woman justice of the United States Supreme Court. In 1986 the governor's race in Nebraska and the Senate race in Maryland provided voters with evidence of how much had changed. In those elections, both major parties nominated women as their candidates.

The women's movement failed, though, to gain its major political goal. This goal was a proposed amendment to the United States Constitution that would

Chief Justice Burger greets Justice Sandra Day O'Connor.
■ Why was O'Conner's appointment important?

ban all discrimination based on sex. In 1972, Congress passed this **Equal Rights Amendment**, which the movement came to refer to as **ERA**. It read:

> Equality of rights under the law shall not be denied or abridged by the United States or by any state on account of sex.

Many states approved the amendment.

Still, there was opposition to ERA. Some of the opposition came from women. One group, called Stop ERA, was headed by an Illinois woman named Phyllis Schlafly. Schlafly and others argued that ERA was not needed because women already had equal rights under the law. They predicted that the amendment would damage family life and wipe out other legal protections women had won over the years. Some feared it would lead to women being drafted into the armed forces. President Reagan also expressed opposition to ERA. When the deadline for ratifying the amendment came on June 30, 1982, only 35 states — 3 short of the needed 38 — had approved it.

The Struggle of Native Americans   In the early 1950s the government had changed its policy of encouraging tribal land-owning and tribal life for American Indians. The new plan was called **termination**. Under this plan the federal government would terminate, or end, the reservation system. Lands would be divided among members of the tribes, who would be encouraged to sell them off, move to the cities, and enter the mainstream of American life.

For most Native Americans, termination made things worse, not better. Many who moved to the cities could not get jobs. They found it hard to adjust to the "cement prairies." President Eisenhower ended the new policy soon after it started.

Many American Indian leaders wanted the government to restore the reservation system and to provide more assistance. They believed that tribal life should be strengthened and that American Indians should be able to choose their own leaders to run their reservations.

To work for these goals, a number of Native Americans in 1968 organized the **American Indian Movement**, or **AIM**. Some AIM members believed that only dramatic action could call attention to the plight of their people. In 1969, a group of Indians took over the abandoned prison on Alcatraz Island in San Francisco Bay. The Indians held it for months before being forced off. For several days the following year, another group occupied the building that housed the Bureau of Indian Affairs in Washington, D.C. In 1973, armed AIM members took over the village of Wounded Knee, South Dakota, for more than 2 months. They demanded the return of lands taken from Indians over the centuries. The AIM members chose this spot for their action because Wounded Knee was the site of a massacre in 1890 in which almost 200 Indians were killed by federal troops.

By the 1980s, Native Americans could point to a few gains. An act of Congress in 1975 gave them a greater voice in running their own reservations. In several states they won court cases in which they had sued to have land returned to them. But for most Indians, life remained a struggle. The average Indian family continued to live in poverty and poor health.

Black Americans   The year 1978 was the tenth anniversary of the death of Martin Luther King, Jr. It was also the tenth anniversary of the Kerner Commission's report on ghetto riots. (See page 724.) A new study was made to see whether the

The Statue of Liberty

Its official name is *Liberty Enlightening the World*. That is what the French sculptor Frédéric Auguste Bartholdi called his gigantic statue. To millions of immigrants seeing it for the first time on entering New York Harbor, it was the Lady of the Harbor or Lady Liberty. To most Americans and to millions the world over it is better known as the Statue of Liberty.

Bartholdi created his statue in France in the 1870s, and in 1884 the people of that country presented it as a gift to the United States. The statue was mounted on a pedestal on a tiny island in New York Harbor, and on July 4, 1886, it was officially opened to the public.

For the next century the Statue of Liberty stood in the harbor as both a symbol of American liberty and a welcome to newcomers to these shores. But the years took their toll on the great statue. Rust weakened its iron framework. Air pollution wore thin the copper covering on the statue's uplifted hand and torch.

For the needed repairs to be made, the statue had to be closed to the public in 1984. Finally on the weekend of July 4, 1986, with fireworks lighting the evening sky and thousands of boats jamming the harbor to witness the event, the Statue of Liberty was opened again—as good as new, and ready to begin its second century as a symbol of freedom in the United States of America.

---

situation of black Americans had changed much. The study reported important and dramatic changes.

As a whole the nation's 25 million blacks have gained enormously in the last decade. . . . Many urban blacks, perhaps 30 percent, have worked their way into the middle class and have moved to the suburbs or to better housing within the cities.

Still, for millions left in the ghettos the situation had not improved. It may even have become worse. People lived in poverty, with little hope for the future.

These trends continued into the 1980s. By the middle of that decade, the percentage of all blacks who went to college had caught up with the percentage of whites. Black men and women were entering fields that had long been closed to them. But unemployment among black teenagers, mainly those who were not finishing school and not getting job training, was running between 40 and 50 percent. And it remained true that blacks' average income was only a little more than half the average income of whites.

On the twentieth anniversaries of King's death and the Kerner Commission, the struggle to win equal rights for all Americans had not yet ended. But great gains had been made. The America of the 1980s was far different from the America of the 1950s.

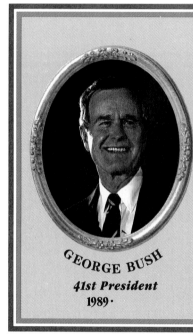

Born: 1924, Milton, Massachusetts.
Education: Yale University.
Training: Ambassador to the United Nations, Director of the CIA, Vice President.
To presidency from: Texas.
Position when elected: Vice President of the United States.
Political party: Republican.
Married: Barbara Pierce.
Children: Four sons, one daughter.
Other facts: Served on active duty as a pilot in the Pacific and received Distinguished Flying Cross and three Air medals. Co-founder of firm pioneering offshore oil-drilling equipment. Served on many national committees and was chairman of the Task Force on Terrorism. Served two terms as Vice President under Ronald Reagan. Active in the Episcopal church and in other civic and philanthropic concerns.

GEORGE BUSH
41st President
1989·

Entering the 1990s   George Bush was elected President of our country on November 8, 1988. Mr. Bush, who had served as Vice President under Ronald Reagan, became our nation's 41st President. The Republican ticket of George Bush and Dan Quayle defeated Democrats Michael Dukakis and Lloyd Bentsen. The Republicans won 54 percent of the popular vote. George Bush soundly defeated Michael Dukakis in the Electoral College by winning 426 votes to the Democrat's 112. Mr. Bush was the first person since 1836 to be elected President while serving as Vice President.

As our nation enters the 1990s under a new President, we can find a great deal to be deeply satisfied about. The nation's economy produces more goods and services than any other nation. Our 243 million people are among the freest and most prosperous in the world. The United States remains the land of opportunity.

However, there is more to be done. Although most Americans enjoy a high standard of living, 13 percent of the people in the country — one of every seven — still live in poverty. Even with major advances toward equality for all, the goal remains a distant dream for many. Other challenges lie ahead: protecting the environment, developing new sources of energy, rebuilding the cities, reviving America's industrial might, and maintaining a high standard of living for a rising population. Lying ahead, too, is the greatest challenge of all — that of finding the way to peace in the dangerous nuclear age.

Americans can find strength in the knowledge that we have met other challenges in our past. This gives reason for great confidence as the United States enters its third century as a nation.

CHECKUP

1. What are the two largest Hispanic groups among the people of the United States?
2. What political gains have women made in the 1980s?
3. How has the position of black people in American society changed since the time of Martin Luther King, Jr.?

4. **Thinking Critically** Which two challenges facing Americans do you think are most important? Why?

Understanding Prefixes

GREEK AND LATIN PREFIXES

You have probably heard the expression "It's Greek to me!" about something you did not understand. Actually, you know more Greek than you think — and Latin, too. Many of the words in the English language come from these two ancient languages. Many of the prefixes do too. A prefix is a unit of speech that is attached to the beginning of a word and modifies, or changes, the word's meaning. For example, the prefix *auto* comes from the Greek word meaning "self." An autobiography is a biography by oneself. An autograph is a signature by one's own hand. An automobile is a vehicle that moves under its own power.

A common prefix from Latin is *bi*, meaning "two." Someone who is bilingual speaks two languages. A bicycle is a two-wheeler. If you know what a three-wheeler is called, you know another prefix that comes from Latin.

Prefixes modify words in many ways. Some change words into negatives. *Disapprove* means "to not approve." Something that is *mislabeled* is wrongly labeled. If something is *unpleasant*, it is not pleasant.

Some prefixes describe when something happened. *Prewar* means "before the war."

Postwar means "after the war." Other prefixes have to do with size and amount. America is a *multicultural* society — it is made up of many cultures.

Following are some commonly used prefixes and their meanings. Some are negative prefixes. Others tell where, when, how many, or how much.

Prefix	Meaning
bi	two
dis	away, apart, opposite
inter	between
mis	wrongly
multi	many
non	not
pre	before
sub	under
tri	three
un	not

SKILLS PRACTICE

Skim back through Chapter 31 and look for words that have these or other frequently used prefixes. Write as many of them as you can find on a grid.

MAIN IDEAS

1. Ronald Reagan took over the presidency in 1981, planning to cut taxes, reduce the budget deficit, and increase defense spending.
2. Reagan presided over a time of prosperity, but federal budget deficits increased.
3. The 1980s saw an increase in turmoil in Central America and in tension between the United States and the Soviet Union.
4. Hispanic Americans, women, Native Americans, and black Americans made important gains in the years leading up to the two hundredth anniversary of the United States Constitution.

VOCABULARY REVIEW

On a separate sheet of paper, write **True** if the statement is true and **False** if it is false. If the statement is false, replace the underlined terms to make the statement true.

1. If the federal budget has a deficit, the government has taken in <u>more</u> money than it has spent.
2. Under Reagan's New Federalism, welfare and health programs were to shift <u>from the federal government to the states.</u>
3. The tax loopholes ended by the Tax Reform Act of 1986 were special rules <u>requiring some people to pay more taxes.</u>
4. Our nation's trade deficit grew larger because the value of our imports was <u>greater</u> than the value of our exports.
5. Unlike earlier spacecraft, the space shuttle could be flown like an airplane and then <u>used again.</u>
6. Under martial law the <u>news media</u> took over the government of Poland and arrested many Solidarity leaders.
7. In the 1980s, terrorist attacks on <u>civilians</u> increased in the countries of the Middle East and elsewhere.
8. In the years after World War II, many Mexican American migrants found work in the <u>computer factories</u> of California and Texas.
9. The Equal Rights Amendment to the Constitution would have outlawed <u>all discrimination based on sex.</u>
10. The government's termination policy <u>started a system of reservations for Native Americans.</u>

CHAPTER CHECKUP

1. What were some of the economic gains and losses during Ronald Reagan's two terms as President?
2. Why were Americans and many of our allies shocked to learn about the sale of arms to Iran?
3. What arguments were given for and against the Equal Rights Amendment?
4. In what ways have conditions changed for some Hispanic Americans since the early 1960s?
5. **Thinking Critically** How might the United States reduce its international trade deficit?
6. **Thinking Critically** What do you think history classes will be learning about the 1980s during the tricentennial of the United States Constitution in 2087?

APPLYING KNOWLEDGE

1. In a small group, investigate the causes of the 1986 space shuttle disaster. You will want to use library copies of newspapers and magazines from the weeks and months just after the explosion, and possibly the report of the government's investigating panel (the Rogers Commission). Present your group report orally to the class. You may want to make models or prepare diagrams to illustrate the important points of your presentation.
2. Why would 38 states have had to approve ERA for the amendment to become part of the Constitution? Write your answer in paragraph form. (*Hint:* You will be able to find the reason in the Constitution itself. See pages 194–219 of your book for the text of the Constitution.)

REVIEWING VOCABULARY

1. inflation   After World War II the United States experienced a period of high inflation. Inflation was also a problem in the 1970s and the early 1980s. What happens to prices in a time of inflation? Does a dollar buy more or less? Why will workers seek larger pay raises during a period of inflation than at other times?

2. nonviolent resistance   Martin Luther King, Jr., believed that nonviolent resistance was the best way to end segregation and racial discrimination. What are the advantages of seeking to change unjust laws through nonviolent means? Are there any disadvantages?

3. exile   Many exiles live in the United States today. Can you think of any particular country or countries from which these exiles have come? What is the difference between an exile and any other kind of immigrant?

4. trade deficit   In 1986 the international trade deficit of the United States almost reached $170 billion. What causes a trade deficit? What are some of the things a country can do to reduce its international trade deficit?

5. terrorism   The 1970s and 1980s saw a rise in terrorism around the world. Much of this terrorism was aimed at Americans. What are some of the tactics that terrorists use? Why is it often difficult for governments to deal with the problem of international terrorism?

EXPRESSING YOURSELF

1. Thinking like a planner   Suburbs have been booming since the 1950s. Today they are developing many of the same problems as cities. You are a city planner and have been asked to recommend ways to help a suburban community avoid some of these problems. What are the problems, and what can be done to avoid or eliminate them?

2. Compare and contrast   The Marshall Plan was an attempt to help rebuild the economies of European countries in the late 1940s. The Alliance for Progress was an attempt to help countries in the western hemisphere in the 1960s. How were these plans similar? How did they differ?

3. What if . . . ?   The United States fought a long and costly war in Vietnam. This war had many consequences in the United States. What if the United States had not entered that war? Discuss four ways in which the recent history of the United States might have been different.

4. What would you do?   Your family has lived in the same community for four generations. You have a good job with the biggest company in town. One day the company announces that it is moving to another part of the country. You can move with the company, or you can stay in town and look for a job. What would you do? Why?

5. In your opinion   Congress has been asked to spend several billion dollars to explore space. Some people say that all this money should be spent instead on dealing with the needs and problems of people here on earth, in our own country. What do you think?

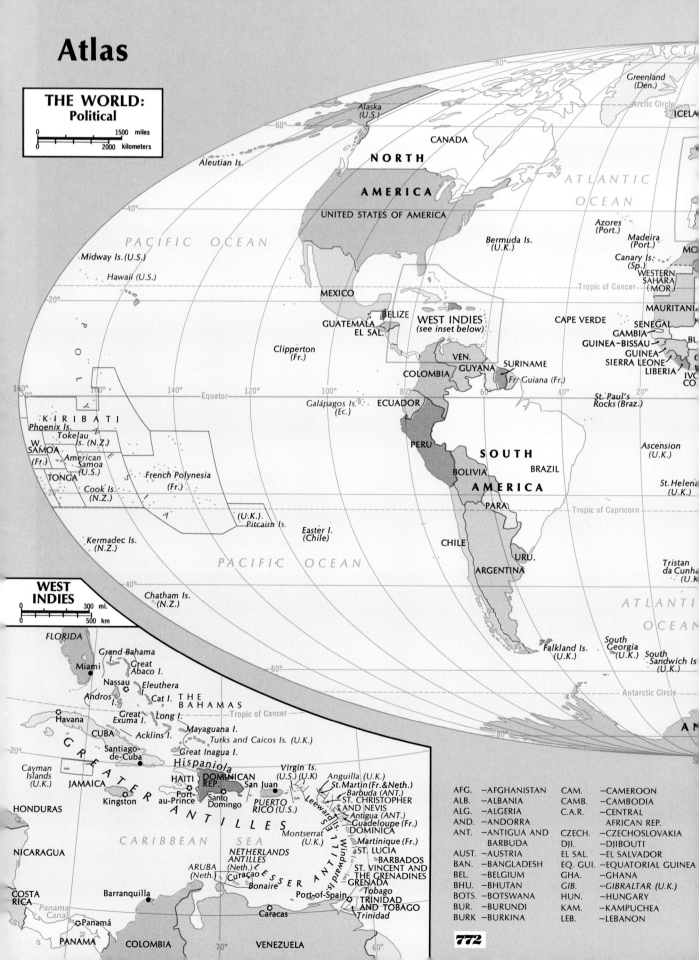

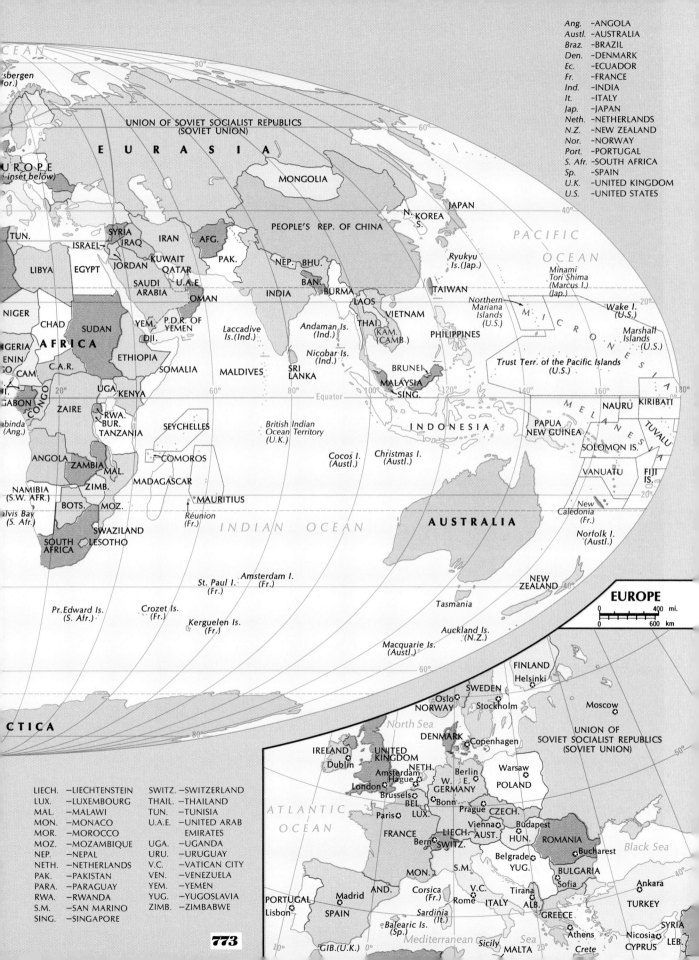

Ang. –ANGOLA
Austl. –AUSTRALIA
Braz. –BRAZIL
Den. –DENMARK
Ec. –ECUADOR
Fr. –FRANCE
Ind. –INDIA
It. –ITALY
Jap. –JAPAN
Neth. –NETHERLANDS
N.Z. –NEW ZEALAND
Nor. –NORWAY
Port. –PORTUGAL
S. Afr. –SOUTH AFRICA
Sp. –SPAIN
U.K. –UNITED KINGDOM
U.S. –UNITED STATES

OCEAN
sbergen
(or.)

EURASIA

UNION OF SOVIET SOCIALIST REPUBLICS
(SOVIET UNION)

MONGOLIA

UROPE
(-inset below)

N. KOREA
S.

JAPAN

PACIFIC

TUN.
SYRIA   IRAN
ISRAEL   IRAQ
JORDAN   KUWAIT
         QATAR
LIBYA   EGYPT   SAUDI   U.A.E.
                 ARABIA OMAN

AFG.

PEOPLE'S REP. OF CHINA

OCEAN

Ryukyu
Is.(Jap.)

Minami
Tori Shima
(Marcus I.)
(Jap.)

PAK.

NEP. BHU.

TAIWAN

NIGER
CHAD   SUDAN
GERIA
ENIN
GO CAM. C.A.R.
GABON ZAIRE
abinda   UGA. KENYA
(Ang.)

AFRICA   ETHIOPIA
YEM. P.D.R. OF
DJI. YEMEN

SOMALIA

BAN.
INDIA   BURMA

LAOS
THAI.   VIETNAM
KAM.
(CAMB.)

PHILIPPINES

Northern
Mariana
Islands
(U.S.)

Wake I.
(U.S.)

Marshall
Islands
(U.S.)

Laccadive
Is.(Ind.)

Andaman Is.
(Ind.)

Nicobar Is.
(Ind.)

MALDIVES

SRI
LANKA

BRUNEI

MALAYSIA
SING.

Trust Terr. of the Pacific Islands
(U.S.)

NAURU   KIRIBATI

RWA.
BUR.
TANZANIA

SEYCHELLES

British Indian
Ocean Territory
(U.K.)

Cocos I.
(Austl.)

Christmas I.
(Austl.)

INDONESIA

PAPUA
NEW GUINEA

SOLOMON IS.

TUVALU

ANGOLA
ZAMBIA
MAL.
ZIMB.

COMOROS

MADAGASCAR

NAMIBIA
(S.W. AFR.)

BOTS. MOZ.

MAURITIUS

Réunion
(Fr.)

INDIAN OCEAN

AUSTRALIA

VANUATU

FIJI
IS.

New
Caledonia
(Fr.)

alvis Bay
(S. Afr.)

SWAZILAND

SOUTH   LESOTHO
AFRICA

St. Paul I.
(Fr.)

Amsterdam I.
(Fr.)

NEW
ZEALAND

Norfolk I.
(Austl.)

CTICA

Pr.Edward Is.
(S. Afr.)

Crozet Is.
(Fr.)

Kerguelen Is.
(Fr.)

Tasmania

Auckland Is.
(N.Z.)

Macquarie Is.
(Austl.)

EUROPE

400 mi.

0   600 km

FINLAND
Helsinki

SWEDEN

Oslo   Stockholm
NORWAY

Moscow

North Sea

DENMARK
Copenhagen

UNION OF
SOVIET SOCIALIST REPUBLICS
(SOVIET UNION)

IRELAND
Dublin

UNITED
KINGDOM
London

NETH.

Amsterdam
Hague

Berlin
W. E.
GERMANY

Warsaw

POLAND

Brussels
BEL.

Bonn

Prague CZECH.

ATLANTIC

OCEAN

Paris

LUX.

FRANCE

Bern
SWITZ.

LIECH.
Vienna
AUST.

S.M.

MON.

Budapest
HUN.

ROMANIA

Bucharest

Black Sea

Belgrade
YUG.

BULGARIA

PORTUGAL
Lisbon

Madrid

SPAIN

AND.

Corsica
(Fr.)

Sardinia
(It.)

Balearic Is.
(Sp.)

V.C.
Rome ITALY

Tirana
ALB.

GREECE

Sofia

Ankara

TURKEY

SYRIA
LEB.

Athens

Nicosia CYPRUS

GIB.(U.K.)

Mediterranean

Sea

Sicily

MALTA

Crete

LIECH. –LIECHTENSTEIN
LUX. –LUXEMBOURG
MAL. –MALAWI
MON. –MONACO
MOR. –MOROCCO
MOZ. –MOZAMBIQUE
NEP. –NEPAL
NETH. –NETHERLANDS
PAK. –PAKISTAN
PARA. –PARAGUAY
RWA. –RWANDA
S.M. –SAN MARINO
SING. –SINGAPORE

SWITZ. –SWITZERLAND
THAIL. –THAILAND
TUN. –TUNISIA
U.A.E. –UNITED ARAB
          EMIRATES
UGA. –UGANDA
URU. –URUGUAY
V.C. –VATICAN CITY
VEN. –VENEZUELA
YEM. –YEMEN
YUG. –YUGOSLAVIA
ZIMB. –ZIMBABWE

773

BRITISH COLUMBIA
Vancouver Pacific Time Zone
ALBERTA
SASKATCHEWAN
CANADA
MANITOBA
WASHINGTON
Olympia ★ Seattle
Spokane
Mountain Time Zone
Central Time Zone
Portland
Salem ★
Eugene
OREGON
Great Falls
Helena ★
MONTANA
Missouri R.
Grand Forks
NORTH DAKOTA
Bismarck ★
Fargo
MIN
IDAHO
Boise
Billings
Idaho Falls
Snake R.
Pocatello
WYOMING
Rapid City
Pierre ★
SOUTH DAKOTA
Sioux Falls
Salt Lake City ★
West Valley
Provo
Casper
L. Platte R.
NEBRASKA
Omaha
Reno
Sacramento ★
Carson City ★
NEVADA
San Francisco
UTAH
Laramie
Cheyenne ★
Grand Island
Lincoln ★
S. Platte R.
Platte R.
Denver ★ Aurora
COLORADO
Colorado Springs
KANSAS
Topeka
CALIFORNIA
Las Vegas
Wichita
Tulsa
Los Angeles
ARIZONA
Santa Fe ★
Albuquerque
NEW MEXICO
OKLAHOMA
Oklahoma City ★
San Diego
PACIFIC OCEAN
Phoenix ★ Mesa
Lawton
Tucson
Las Cruces
Dallas
TEXAS
Austin ★
Houston
ASIA
SOVIET UNION
ELEVENTH TIME ZONE IN U.S.S.R.
TENTH TIME ZONE IN U.S.S.R.
Arctic Circle
ALASKA
Alaska Time Zone
Yukon R.
Fairbanks
Pacific Time Zone
CANADA
MEXICO
Rio Grande
Monday
International Date Line
Sunday
BERING SEA
Willow ★ Anchorage
Juneau ★
Gulf of Alaska
Hawaii-Aleutian Time Zone
ALEUTIAN ISLANDS
West longitude

0   200 miles
0   300 kilometers

774

UNITED STATES OF AMERICA: Political

CANADA

Central Time Zone

Eastern Time Zone

Atlantic Time Zone

ONTARIO

QUEBEC

NEW BRUNSWICK

PRINCE EDWARD ISLAND

NOVA SCOTIA

Duluth

Lake Superior

MICHIGAN

Quebec

MAINE

Bangor

OTA

St. Paul

Minnea-
polis

WISCONSIN

Green
Bay

Lake Michigan

Madison   Milwaukee

Grand
Rapids

Lansing   Detroit

Lake Huron

Montreal

Ottawa

Burlington

Montpelier   VT.

Rutland

N.H.

Concord

Augusta

Portland

Manchester

Nashua   Boston

MASS.   Worcester

Springfield   Pawtucket
Providence

Hartford   R.I.   Warwick

CONN.

Albany

Toronto

L. Ontario

Buffalo   **NEW YORK**

Cleveland

Lake Erie

Rockford

IOWA

Cedar
Rapids

Davenport

Chicago   Gary

Des
Moines

Fort
Wayne

OHIO

Columbus

INDIANA

Indianapolis

ILLINOIS

Springfield

PENNSYLVANIA

Pittsburgh

Wheeling

W.VA.

Harrisburg

Philadelphia

Bridgeport   New
Haven

Newark   New York

Jersey
City

Trenton

NEW JERSEY

Newark

Wilmington

Baltimore

MD.   Dover

Rockville

Washington   Annapolis

D.C.   **DELAWARE**

Kansas
City

Kansas
City

Missouri R.

St. Louis

Jefferson
City

MISSOURI

Louisville

Frankfort

Lexington

Hunting-
ton

Charleston

KENTUCKY

VIRGINIA

Richmond

Norfolk   Virginia Beach

CONN. — CONNECTICUT
D.C. — DISTRICT
OF COLUMBIA
MASS. — MASSACHUSETTS
MD. — MARYLAND
N.H. — NEW HAMPSHIRE
R.I. — RHODE ISLAND
VT. — VERMONT
W.VA. — WEST VIRGINIA

Fort
Smith

North
Little Rock

Little
Rock

ARKANSAS

Memphis

Nashville

TENNESSEE

Knoxville

Greensboro   Raleigh

**NORTH
CAROLINA**

Charlotte

Columbia

**SOUTH
CAROLINA**

North Charleston

Charleston

Shreveport

MISSISSIPPI

Meridian

Jackson

Birmingham

ALABAMA

Montgomery

Columbus

GEORGIA

Atlanta

Savannah

**UNITED STATES
OF AMERICA:
Political**

○ National capitals

★ State capitals

● Other cities

| 0 | 100 | 200 miles |
| 0 | 100 | 200 | 300 kilometers |

LOUISIANA

Baton Rouge

New Orleans

Biloxi

Mobile

Tallahassee

Jacksonville

FLORIDA

**ATLANTIC
OCEAN**

GULF   OF   MEXICO

Miami

Nassau

BAHAMAS

HAWAII

Niihau   Kauai

Pearl City   Oahu

Honolulu   Molokai

Lanai   Maui

Same scale
as main map

Hawaii-Aleutian
Time Zone

Hawaii
Kailua   Hilo

Tropic of Cancer

Havana

CUBA

ASIA

ARCTIC OCEAN

GREENLAND (Den.)

ICELAND

Bering Sea

Beaufort Sea

• Barrow

Yukon R.
Alaska (U.S.)

• Fairbanks
Gulf of Alaska
• Anchorage
• Dawson

Arctic Circle

Thule •

Baffin Bay

Pond Inlet •

• Godthaab

Labrador Sea

• Juneau

Great Bear Lake

Port Radium •

Great Slave Lake

C A N A D A

Goose Bay •

Seven Islands •

Gander •
St. John's •

PACIFIC OCEAN

• Edmonton

Churchill •

Hudson Bay

• Victoria
• Vancouver
• Calgary

Lake Winnipeg

Quebec •
Montreal •
Ottawa ✪
Halifax •

• Seattle
• Portland
• Spokane
• Regina

• Winnipeg

Great Lakes

Columbia R.

Missouri R.

Toronto •
Buffalo •
Boston •

San Francisco •

Great Salt L.

Salt Lake City •

Minneapolis •
St. Paul •
Milwaukee •
Chicago •

Detroit •
Cleveland •
New York •

U N I T E D   S T A T E S   O F   A M E R I C A

Omaha •

Pittsburgh •
Philadelphia •
Washington ✪
Baltimore •

Los Angeles •

Colorado R.

• Denver

Kansas City •

Cincinnati •

San Diego •

Phoenix •

St. Louis •

Arkansas R.

Ohio R.

Norfolk •

Guadalupe I. (Mex.)

Tropic of Cancer

El Paso •

Dallas •

Memphis •

Atlanta •

Bermuda Is. (U.K.)

G. of California

Rio Grande

San Antonio •

Houston •
New Orleans •

ATLANTIC OCEAN

Monterrey •

GULF OF MEXICO

• Miami

Grand Bahama I.
Great Abaco I.
Eleuthera I.
Nassau ✪
Cat I.
Andros I.
Gr. Exuma I.
Long I.
Acklins I.

THE BAHAMAS

M E X I C O

Guadalajara •

Havana ✪

CUBA

Mayaguana I.

PUERTO RICO (U.S.)
Virgin Is. (U.S.&U.K.)

Mexico City ✪

Cayman Islands (U.K.)

Santiago-de-Cuba •

Gr. Inagua I.

DOMINICAN REPUBLIC

Orizaba •

JAMAICA

Kingston ✪

HAITI
Port-au-Prince ✪
Santo Domingo ✪

ANTIGUA AND BARBUDA
ST. CHRISTOPHER-NEVIS
Guadeloupe (Fr.)
DOMINICA
Martinique (Fr.)
ST. LUCIA

Belmopan ✪
BELIZE

GUATEMALA
Guatemala ✪
HONDURAS
San Salvador ✪
Tegucigalpa ✪
EL SALVADOR
NICARAGUA
Managua ✪

CARIBBEAN SEA

Neth. Antilles (Neth.)
Aruba (Neth.)

ST. VINCENT AND THE GRENADINES
GRENADA

San José ✪
COSTA RICA

Panama Canal

Panamá ✪
PANAMA

SOUTH AMERICA

TRINIDAD AND TOBAGO

Den. –DENMARK
Fr. –FRANCE
Neth. –NETHERLANDS
Mex. –MEXICO
U.K. –UNITED KINGDOM
U.S. –UNITED STATES

NORTH AMERICA:
Political

✪ National capitals

• Other cities

0   500 miles
0   800 kilometers

776

100°   90°   80°   70°

West longitude

Barranquilla
Cartagena
Maracaibo
Valencia
Caracas
Port-of-Spain
TRINIDAD AND TOBAGO
Barquisimeto
Cúcuta
San Cristóbal
VENEZUELA
Orinoco R.
Medellín
Bucaramanga
Bogotá
Georgetown
Paramaribo
Cayenne
GUYANA
SURINAM
Fr.
Guiana
(Fr.)
Malpelo I.
(Col.)
COLOMBIA
Cali

Col. —COLOMBIA
Fr. —FRANCE
U.K. —UNITED KINGDOM

Quito
ECUADOR
Guayaquil
Iquitos
Manaus
Amazon R.
Belém
São Luis
Equator
Fortaleza
Trujillo
PERU
Recife
Maceió
B R A Z I L
Callao
Lima
Cuzco
Salvador
Arequipa
Lake
Titicaca
La Paz
BOLIVIA
Brasília
(Federal
District)
Sucre
PACIFIC
OCEAN
Belo
Horizonte
Chuquicamata
Rio de Janeiro
Antofagasta
PARAGUAY
São Paulo
Niterói
Santos
Asunción
Curitiba
San Felix I.
(Chile)
San Ambrosio I.
(Chile)
Tucumán
Tropic of Capricorn
Juan Fernández Is.
(Chile)
Córdoba
Santa
Fe
Paraná
Paraná
Pôrto Alegre
CHILE
Rosario
URUGUAY
ATLANTIC
OCEAN
Valparaiso
Santiago
Buenos Aires
Montevideo
La Plata
Rio de la Plata
Concepción
ARGENTINA
Mar del Plata
Bahía Blanca

Falkland Is. (U.K.)
(Malvinas Is.)
Punta Arenas
Strait of
Magellan
West longitude
777

SOUTH AMERICA:
Political

✵ National capitals

● Other cities

0   500 miles
0   800 kilometers

ATLANTIC OCEAN

Madeira Is. (Port.)

PORTUGAL
Lisbon

SPAIN
Madrid
Valencia
Barcelona
Balearic Is. (Sp.)

Bordeaux
FRANCE
Paris
Brussels 5 12
London
Dublin
IRE.
UNITED KINGDOM
Glasgow
Amsterdam 14
Hague 14
Hannover
Hamburg
Bonn
GER.
Berlin
Munich
Prague 7
Vienna 3
Wrocław
POLAND
Warsaw
Budapest 8
ROM.
Bucharest
BUL.
Sofia
Belgrade
YUG.
Tirana 1
GREECE
Athens
Crete (Gr.)

North Sea
DEN.
Copenhagen
Göteborg
Stockholm
Oslo
Bergen
NORWAY
SWEDEN
FINLAND
Helsinki
Tallinn
Riga
Leningrad
Kaliningrad
Murmansk
Narvik
Archangel
Novaya Zemlya
Barents Sea
Spitsbergen (Nor.)
North Land
ARCTIC OCEAN

Marseilles
Nice 13
Corsica
ITALY
Rome 16
Naples
Palermo
Sardinia
Sicily
Valletta
MALTA
Mediterranean Sea

Bern 11
Milan
2
18
E U R O P E

Moscow
Kiev
Kharkov
Saratov
Krasnodar
Volgograd
Odessa
UKRAINE
Black Sea
Istanbul (Constantinople)
Izmir
Ankara
TURKEY
Kazan
Perm
Ufa
Sverdlovsk
Chelyabinsk
Magnitogorsk
Orenburg
Kuibyshev
Volga R.
UNION OF SOVIET (SOVIET UNION)
Omsk
Novosibirsk
Tomsk
Ob R.
Yenisei R.
A S I A

NICOSIA
CYPRUS
Beirut
10
SYRIA
Damascus
ISRAEL
Jerusalem
Amman
JOR.
Sinai Pen.
IRAQ
Baghdad
Basra
Abadan
9 Kuwait
Caspian Sea
Aral Sea
TURKESTAN
Baku
Tashkent
SINKIANG
Urumchi
Tehran
IRAN (PERSIA)
Kabul
AFGHANISTAN
Islamabad
Jammu and Kashmir
TIBET
Lahore
Delhi
New Delhi
NEP.
Katmandu
PAKISTAN
Karachi
Hyderabad
Ahmadabad
INDIA
Bombay
Hyderabad
Ganges R.
Indus R.

AFRICA
Red Sea
Mecca
SAUDI ARABIA
Riyadh
Manama 4
Doha 15
Abu Dhabi
UNITED ARAB EMIRATES
Empty Quarter
YEMEN ARAB REPUBLIC
San'a
PEOPLE'S DEM. REP. OF YEMEN
Aden
Madinat ash Sha'b
OMAN
Masqat
Arabian Sea
Socotra (P.D.R. Yemen)
Laccadive Is. (Ind.)
MALDIVES
Male
Colombo
SRI LANKA
Madras
INDIAN OCEAN

BAN. —BANGLADESH
BHU. —BHUTAN
BUL. —BULGARIA
DEN. —DENMARK
GER. —GERMANY
IRE. —IRELAND
JOR. —JORDAN
KAM. —KAMPUCHEA
NEP. —NEPAL
ROM. —ROMANIA
YUG. —YUGOSLAVIA
1—ALBANIA
2—ANDORRA
3—AUSTRIA
4—BAHREIN
5—BELGIUM
6—BRUNEI
7—CZECHOSLOVAKIA
8—HUNGARY
9—KUWAIT
10—LEBANON
11—LIECHTENSTEIN
12—LUXEMBOURG
13—MONACO
14—NETHERLANDS
15—QATAR
16—SAN MARINO
17—SINGAPORE
18—SWITZERLAND

East longitude

EURASIA: Political

Gr. —GREECE
Ind. —INDIA
Jap. —JAPAN
Nor. —NORWAY
Port. —PORTUGAL
Sp. —SPAIN
U.K. —UNITED KINGDOM
U.S. —UNITED STATES
U.S.S.R.—SOVIET UNION

✪ National capitals
● Other cities

0   800 mi.
0   1200 km

779

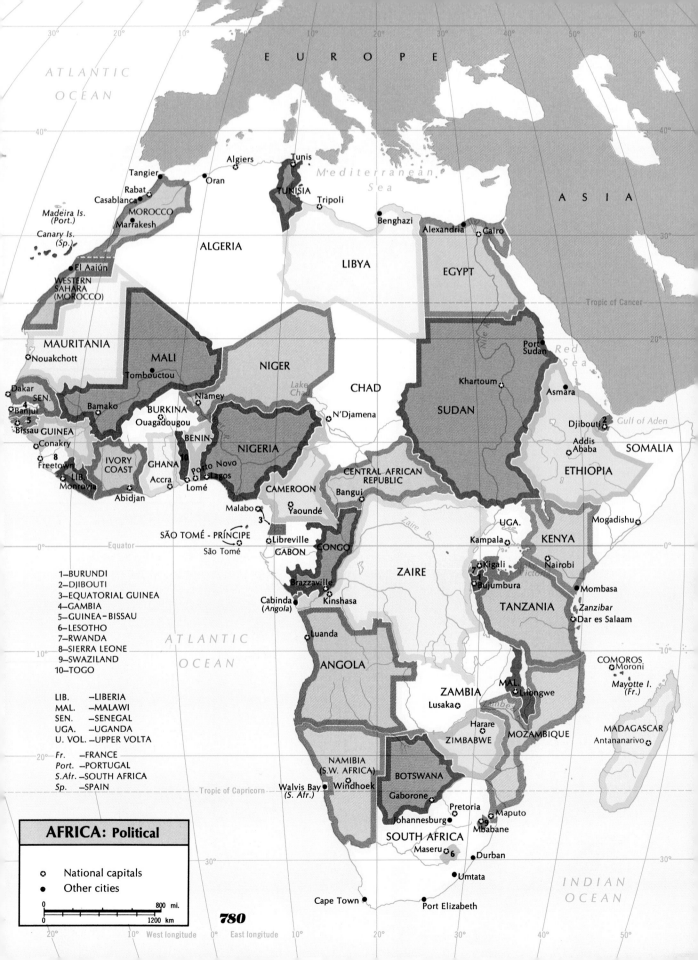

AFRICA: Political

✣ National capitals

● Other cities

0   800 mi.

0   1200 km

1—BURUNDI
2—DJIBOUTI
3—EQUATORIAL GUINEA
4—GAMBIA
5—GUINEA-BISSAU
6—LESOTHO
7—RWANDA
8—SIERRA LEONE
9—SWAZILAND
10—TOGO

LIB. —LIBERIA
MAL. —MALAWI
SEN. —SENEGAL
UGA. —UGANDA
U. VOL. —UPPER VOLTA

Fr. —FRANCE
Port. —PORTUGAL
S.Afr.—SOUTH AFRICA
Sp. —SPAIN

EUROPE

ATLANTIC OCEAN

ASIA

Mediterranean Sea

Algiers
Tunis
Oran
TUNISIA
Tripoli
Tangier
Rabat
Casablanca
MOROCCO
Marrakesh
Benghazi
Alexandria
Cairo

Madeira Is. (Port.)
Canary Is. (Sp.)

El Aaiún
WESTERN SAHARA (MOROCCO)

ALGERIA
LIBYA
EGYPT

Tropic of Cancer

MAURITANIA
Nouakchott
MALI
Tombouctou
NIGER
CHAD
SUDAN
Khartoum
Port Sudan
Red Sea
Asmara
Djibouti
Gulf of Aden

Dakar
SEN.
Banjul
Bissau GUINEA
Conakry
Freetown
LIB.
Monrovia
Bamako
BURKINA
Ouagadougou
Niamey
N'Djamena
Lake Chad
Addis Ababa
SOMALIA

Mogadishu

IVORY COAST
GHANA
Accra
BENIN
Porto Novo
Lagos
Lomé
NIGERIA
CAMEROON
Yaoundé
Bangui
CENTRAL AFRICAN REPUBLIC
ETHIOPIA

Abidjan
Malabo
SÃO TOMÉ - PRÍNCIPE
São Tomé
Libreville
GABON
CONGO
Brazzaville
Kinshasa
ZAIRE
Zaire R.
UGA.
Kampala
KENYA
Nairobi
Mombasa

Equator

ATLANTIC OCEAN

Cabinda (Angola)
Luanda
ANGOLA
Kigali
Bujumbura
TANZANIA
Zanzibar
Dar es Salaam

COMOROS
Moroni
Mayotte I. (Fr.)

ZAMBIA
Lusaka
MAL.
Lilongwe
MADAGASCAR
Antananarivo

Harare
ZIMBABWE
MOZAMBIQUE

NAMIBIA (S.W. AFRICA)
BOTSWANA
Gaborone
Pretoria
Maputo
Mbabane

Tropic of Capricorn
Walvis Bay (S. Afr.)
Windhoek
Johannesburg
Maseru
SOUTH AFRICA
Durban

Umtata

Cape Town
Port Elizabeth

INDIAN OCEAN

780

West longitude   East longitude

PRESIDENTS AND VICE-PRESIDENTS OF THE UNITED STATES

President	Birth-death	State*	Term	Party	Vice-President
George Washington	1732–1799	Va.	1789–1797	None	John Adams
John Adams	1735–1826	Mass.	1797–1801	Federalist	Thomas Jefferson
Thomas Jefferson	1743–1826	Va.	1801–1805	Democratic-	Aaron Burr
			1805–1809	Republican	George Clinton
James Madison	1751–1836	Va.	1809–1813	Democratic-	George Clinton
			1813–1817	Republican	Elbridge Gerry
James Monroe	1758–1831	Va.	1817–1825	Democratic-	Daniel D. Tompkins
				Republican	
John Quincy Adams	1767–1848	Mass.	1825–1829	National	John C. Calhoun
				Republican	
Andrew Jackson	1767–1845	Tenn.	1829–1833	Democratic	John C. Calhoun
			1833–1837		Martin Van Buren
Martin Van Buren	1782–1862	N.Y.	1837–1841	Democratic	Richard M. Johnson
William H. Harrison	1773–1841	Ohio	1841	Whig	John Tyler
John Tyler	1790–1862	Va.	1841–1845	Whig	....
James K. Polk	1795–1849	Tenn.	1845–1849	Democratic	George M. Dallas
Zachary Taylor	1784–1850	La.	1849–1850	Whig	Millard Fillmore
Millard Fillmore	1800–1874	N.Y.	1850–1853	Whig	....
Franklin Pierce	1804–1869	N.H.	1853–1857	Democratic	William R. King
James Buchanan	1791–1868	Pa.	1857–1861	Democratic	John C. Breckinridge
Abraham Lincoln	1809–1865	Ill.	1861–1865	Republican	Hannibal Hamlin
			1865		Andrew Johnson
Andrew Johnson	1808–1875	Tenn.	1865–1869	Democratic	....
Ulysses S. Grant	1822–1885	Ill.	1869–1873	Republican	Schuyler Colfax
			1873–1877		Henry Wilson
Rutherford B. Hayes	1822–1893	Ohio	1877–1881	Republican	William A. Wheeler
James A. Garfield	1831–1881	Ohio	1881	Republican	Chester A. Arthur
Chester A. Arthur	1830–1886	N.Y.	1881–1885	Republican	....
Grover Cleveland	1837–1908	N.Y.	1885–1889	Democratic	Thomas A. Hendricks
Benjamin Harrison	1833–1901	Ind.	1889–1893	Republican	Levi P. Morton
Grover Cleveland	1837–1908	N.Y.	1893–1897	Democratic	Adlai E. Stevenson
William McKinley	1843–1901	Ohio	1897–1901	Republican	Garret A. Hobart
			1901		Theodore Roosevelt
Theodore Roosevelt	1858–1919	N.Y.	1901–1905	Republican	
			1905–1909		Charles W. Fairbanks
William H. Taft	1857–1930	Ohio	1909–1913	Republican	James S. Sherman
Woodrow Wilson	1856–1924	N.J.	1913–1917	Democratic	Thomas R. Marshall
			1917–1921		Thomas R. Marshall
Warren G. Harding	1865–1923	Ohio	1921–1923	Republican	Calvin Coolidge
Calvin Coolidge	1872–1933	Mass.	1923–1925	Republican	....
			1925–1929		Charles G. Dawes
Herbert C. Hoover	1874–1964	Calif.	1929–1933	Republican	Charles Curtis
Franklin D. Roosevelt	1882–1945	N.Y.	1933–1937	Democratic	John N. Garner
			1937–1941		John N. Garner
			1941–1945		Henry A. Wallace
			1945		Harry S. Truman
Harry S. Truman	1884–1972	Mo.	1945–1949	Democratic	....
			1949–1953		Alben W. Barkley
Dwight D. Eisenhower	1890–1969	N.Y.	1953–1957	Republican	Richard M. Nixon
			1957–1961		Richard M. Nixon
John F. Kennedy	1917–1963	Mass.	1961–1963	Democratic	Lyndon B. Johnson
Lyndon B. Johnson	1908–1973	Texas	1963–1965	Democratic	....
			1965–1969		Hubert H. Humphrey
Richard M. Nixon	1913–	N.Y.	1969–1973	Republican	Spiro T. Agnew
			1973–1974		Agnew/Ford
Gerald R. Ford	1913–	Mich.	1974–1977	Republican	Nelson R. Rockefeller
James Earl Carter	1924–	Ga.	1977–1981	Democratic	Walter Mondale
Ronald Reagan	1911–	Calif.	1981–1985	Republican	George Bush
			1985–1989		George Bush

*State of residence at election

GLOSSARY

The page references tell where each entry first appears in the text.

┌─ KEY TO PRONUNCIATION ───┐

a	hat, cap					zh	measure, seizure
ā	age, face	i	it, pin	ou	house, out	ə	represents:
ã	care, air	ī	ice, five	sh	she, rush		a in about
ä	father, far	ng	long, bring	th	thin, both		e in taken
ch	child, much	o	hot, rock	ŦH	then, smooth		i in pencil
e	let, best	ō	open, go	u	cup, butter		o in lemon
ē	equal, see	ô	order, all	ů	full, put		u in circus
ėr	term, learn	oi	oil, voice	ü	rule, move		

This Key to Pronunciation is from *Scott, Foresman Intermediate Dictionary,* by E.L. Thorndike and Clarence L. Barnhart. Copyright © 1983, by Scott, Foresman and Company. Reprinted by permission.

└──┘

A

abolitionist (ab ə lish′ ə nist). Person opposed to slavery and in favor of ending it. p. 290.

acquit (ə kwit′). To set free; to declare not guilty. p. 134.

Adams-Onis Treaty (ad′ əmz ō nis′ trē′ tē). Treaty signed in 1819 between the United States and Spain that gave Florida to the United States and decided the boundary between the United States and Spanish territory in the Southwest. p. 268.

agriculture (ag′ rə kul chər). Raising crops and livestock; farming. p. 27.

AIM. See *American Indian Movement.*

Albany Plan of Union (ôl′ bə nē plan ov yün′ yən). A plan proposed by Benjamin Franklin in 1754 for a Grand Council with representatives from each American colony and a president general to be appointed by the British king. p. 122.

Alien and Sedition Acts (ā′ lē ən and si dish′ ən akts). Four laws enacted by the Federalists in 1798 in response to French actions and with the hope of destroying the Republican party. p. 234.

Alliance for Progress (ə lī′ əns fôr prog′ res). United States program started under President Kennedy to help countries in the Western Hemisphere. p. 690.

allies (al′ īz). Groups or nations that unite for a special purpose. p. 108.

amendment (ə mend′ mənt). Formal change or addition. p. 183.

American enterprise (ə mer′ ə ken en′ tər prīz). Energy and will of Americans to undertake big new projects to benefit themselves and their country. p. 310.

American Federation of Labor (ə mer′ ə ken fed ə rā′ shən ov lā′ bər). Organization of trade unions that was established in the 1880s. Its goal was to organize workers by crafts and skills. p. 502.

American Indian Movement (ə mer′ ə ken in′ dē ən müv′ ment), or *AIM.* Movement organized in 1968 by a number of American Indians to restore and strengthen the reservation system and tribal life. p. 766.

Amnesty Act (am′ nə stē akt). Bill passed after the Civil War that allowed most Confederate officials to take part in state and national government. p. 402.

Anaconda Plan (an ə kon′ də plan). Strategic plan devised by the Union to defeat the South in the Civil War. It was named after the snake that wraps itself around its victims and crushes them. p. 370.

anarchist (an′ ər kist). Person who wants to do away with all government and laws. p. 500.

annexation (an ək sā′ shən). Taking a country or other territory and making it part of one's own country. p. 323.

annotation (an ə tā′ shən). Note added to point out or explain something in a text. p. 14.

Anti-Federalist (an tē fed′ ər ə list). Opponent of a federal government. p. 187.

apprentice (ə pren′ tis). Person bound by contract to a skilled worker for the purpose of learning a trade or craft. p. 92.

arbitration (är bə trā′ shən). Settlement of a dispute by an impartial person or group. p. 534.

archaeologist (är kē ol′ ə jist). Scientist who studies objects, ruins, and other evidence of human life from the past. p. 20.

architect (är′ kə tekt). Person who designs and draws plans for buildings. p. 474.

aristocrat (ə ris′ tə krat). Person of high social standing. p. 57.

armada. See *Invincible Armada.*

armistice (är′ mə stis). Cease-fire, or halt to fighting, by agreement between warring nations. p. 585.

Articles of Confederation (är′ tə kəlz ov kən fed ə rā′ shən). Document that listed the powers of the central government and the powers of the states in the period immediately following the Revolutionary War. p. 174.

artifact (är′ tə fakt). Any object made by a person. p. 30.

assassination (ə sas ə nā′ shən). Murder of a political figure for a political purpose. p. 710.

assembly (ə sem′ blē). Legislative branch of a government, usually the lower house of two lawmaking bodies in the legislature. p. 87.

assembly line (ə sem′ blē līn). Process by which several workers construct a product by each adding different parts as it moves past them. p. 596.

astronaut (as' trə nôt). Pilot or crew member who travels in a spacecraft into space. p. 2.

Atlanta Compromise (at lan' tə kom' prə mīz). Strategy suggested by Booker T. Washington in a speech in 1895. He advised blacks to give up attempts to achieve social equality and instead strive for opportunities to develop skills. p. 420.

Atlantic Charter (at lan' tik chär' tər). Statement signed by the United States and Great Britain in 1941 expressing their aims for an end to World War II. p. 648.

atlas (at' ləs). Collection of maps. p. 9.

Axis powers (ak' sis pou' ərz). Name given to Italy, Germany, and Japan, the countries that fought against the Allies in World War II. p. 644.

B

Bacon's Rebellion (bā' kənz ri bel' yən). A clash between Virginia's frontier people and the royal government of the colony in 1676. p. 98.

Bank Charter Bill (bangk chär' tər bil). Bill proposed by Henry Clay in 1832 to issue a new charter for the Second Bank of the United States. p. 280.

bank holiday (bangk hol' ə dā). Four-day period in 1933 when President Franklin Roosevelt closed all banks in the country. p. 624.

Bank of the United States (bangk ov thə yü nī' tid stāts). National bank chartered in 1791 to issue bank notes, lend money to the government, and serve as a place for deposit of the government's money. p. 225.

Barbary States (bär' bər ē stāts). Countries along the northern coast of Africa. p. 257.

battle of Fallen Timbers (bat' əl ov fô' lən tim' bərz). 1794 battle in which General Anthony Wayne defeated the 12 Indian tribes of the Northwest Territory. p. 251.

Bessemer process (bes' ə mėr prô' ses). Process discovered by Henry Bessemer in the 1800s to make steel quickly and cheaply. p. 458.

bilingual (bī ling' gwəl). Knowing and using two languages. p. 57.

bill of rights (bil ov rīts). Statement of the basic rights of the people of a state or nation; first ten amendments to the Constitution of the United States, which state the basic rights held by citizens of the United States. p. 189.

Black Codes (blak kōds). Acts passed in the legislatures of Southern states after the Civil War to place restrictions on freed blacks. p. 401.

Black Hawk's War (blak hôks wär). War in 1832 between the United States and the Sauk and Fox Indians led by Chief Black Hawk. p. 290.

blacklist (blak' list). List of people who are disapproved of or are to be punished. p. 494.

"bleeding Kansas" (blē' ding kan' səs). Nickname given to the Kansas Territory in the 1850s because of the fighting over the slavery issue. p. 353.

blitzkrieg (blits' krēg). German word meaning "lightning war," used to describe a type of warfare that is rapid and very violent. p. 647.

board of directors (bôrd ov də rek' tərs). A group of people, elected by stockholders, who make major decisions about how a corporation will be run. p. 465.

border states (bôr' dər stāts). States between the North and the South that stayed in the Union during the Civil War. p. 369.

Boston Massacre (bôs' tən mas' ə kər). Skirmish in 1770 between a mob of colonists and 10 British soldiers in Boston in which 5 colonists were killed. p. 134.

Boston Tea Party (bôs' tən tē pär' tē). Event on the night of December 16, 1773, during which chests of tea belonging to the British East India Company were thrown into Boston Harbor by patriotic colonists disguised as Indians. p. 137.

Boxer Rebellion (bok' sər ri bel' yən). Uprising against foreigners in China in 1900. p. 556.

boycott (boi' kot). Organized campaign in which people refuse to have any dealings with a particular group or business in order to force a change. p. 500.

bread colonies (bred kol' ə nēz). Name given to the middle colonies in the 1700s because of the amount of grain raised there. p. 102.

Brown v. Board of Education of Topeka (broun v. bôrd ov ej ù kā' shən ov tō pē' kə). Supreme Court case that decided the "separate but equal" doctrine should not apply to schools and that led to the order for the desegregation of public schools. p. 713.

budget deficit (buj' ət def' ə sit). Shortfall when the government spends more in a year than it takes in in that year. p. 750.

Bull Moose party (bùl müs pär' tē). Another name for the Progressive party led by Theodore Roosevelt in the presidential election of 1912. p. 537.

burial mound (ber' ē al mound). Round mound or pile of earth used as a burial place by Native Americans. p. 30.

C

Cabinet (kab' ə nit). Group of advisers to the President of the United States. p. 222.

California gold rush (kal' ə fôrn' yə gōld rush). Period of time when many people hurried to California to search for gold. p. 332.

Camp David accords (kamp dā' vid ə kôrds'). Treaty signed in March 1979 in the United States by Israel and Egypt, aimed at establishing peace in the Middle East. p. 741.

capital (kap' ə təl). Money that people or companies invest in factories, machines, or other businesses. p. 465.

caption (kap' shən). Description or explanation accompanying an illustration. p. 13.

carbon 14 (kär' bən 14). Substance found in all living things, used by archaeologists and geologists in dating materials. p. 24.

carpetbagger (kär' pit bag' ər). Name given to Northern whites who moved to the South after the Civil War. p. 402.

cartographer (kär tog' rə fər). Person who makes maps. p. 9.

cash crop (kash krop). Crop grown for sale rather than for use by the farmer. p. 73.

caucus (kô' kəs). Meeting of party leaders to choose candidates for public office. p. 228.

cede (sēd). To give up or surrender something. p. 253.

censure (sen′ shər). To find fault with; to condemn. p. 705.

census (sen′ səs). Government count of the number of people in a country. p. 234.

Centennial State (sen ten′ ē əl stāt). Nickname given to Colorado, which became a state in 1876, the one-hundredth anniversary of the United States. p. 442.

charter (chär′ tər). Written permission from a government giving a group of people the right to settle or trade in a certain area. p. 72.

Cíbola (sib′ ō lə). Region north of Mexico, believed by the early Spanish explorers to contain vast treasures. p. 64.

city manager (sit′ ē man′ i jər). A person appointed by a city's commissioners to run the city government. p. 529.

civil rights (siv′ əl rīts). Basic rights to which all American citizens are entitled. p. 417.

Civil Rights Act of 1964 (siv′ əl rīts akt ov 1964). Law that prohibited discrimination because of a person's color, race, national origin, religion, or sex. p. 720.

civil service (siv′ əl sėr′ vis). System under which people are appointed to jobs in the offices of government. p. 414.

clapboard (klap′ bôrd). Thin, narrow board, thicker at one edge than the other. p. 114.

Clayton Antitrust Act (klā′ tun an′ tē trust akt). Law passed to prohibit companies from engaging in practices that reduce competition. p. 540.

closed shop (klōzd shop). Place of work that hires only union members. p. 702.

coexistence (kō ig zis′ tans). Living together in peace. p. 686.

cold war (kōld wôr). Prolonged struggle for power between nations. It is diplomatic and economic rather than military. p. 677.

collective bargaining (kə lek′ tiv bär′ gə ning). Process during which a union represents the workers and bargains for them with the employer. p. 631.

colony (kol′ ə nē). Place that is ruled by another country. p. 47.

commission (kə mish′ ən). Part of the sale or business done that is paid to the person who did it. p. 105.

commission government (kə mish′ ən guv′ ərn mənt). Form of city government in which an expert is appointed to run each department. p. 529.

Committee of Correspondence (kə mit′ ē ov kôr ə spon′ dəns). Colonial group whose members maintained contact with and sent news through letters to other such groups prior to the War for Independence. p. 135.

Common Sense (kom′ ən sens). Pamphlet published by Thomas Paine in January 1776 in which he urged the colonies to declare their independence from Great Britain. p. 149.

commonwealth (kom′ ən welth). Nation, state, or other political unit that has its own authority but is voluntarily united with another; officially used to describe Puerto Rico. p. 764.

Compromise of 1850 (kom′ prə mīz ov 1850). Plan proposed in 1850 by Senator Henry Clay to end the North-South controversy. p. 347.

Compromise of 1877 (kom′ prə mīz ov 1877). Agreement that settled the disputed presidential election of 1876 and ended the period of Reconstruction. p. 409.

Comstock Lode (kum′ stok lōd). Richest vein of silver in the West, discovered in 1859 in what is today Nevada. p. 443.

concentration camp (kon sən trā′ shən kamp). Camp where political prisoners, prisoners of war, refugees, or members of an ethnic group are held by order of the government. p. 655.

Concord group (kon′ kôrd grüp). Group of American writers who lived near Concord, Massachusetts, in the 1800s. p. 304.

Confederate States of America (kən fed′ ər it stāts ov ə mer′ ə kə). Name taken by the southern states that withdrew from the United States in 1860 and 1861 and organized their own government. p. 358.

confederation (kən fed ə rā′ shən). Loose grouping of states, with some powers held by a central government, but most retained by the states. p. 174.

Congress of Industrial Organizations (kong′ gris ov in dus′ trē al ôr gə nə zā′ shənz). Group of labor unions formed in 1938 and organized according to industries. It merged with the AFL in 1955. p. 637.

conquistador (kon kē′ stä dôr). One of the men who led the Spanish expeditions to the New World in the 1500s; the Spanish word for conqueror. p. 49.

conservation (kon sər vā′ shən). Managing natural resources in such a way as to prevent their waste or complete destruction. p. 535.

constitution (kon stə tü′ shən). Set of basic laws by which a nation, state, or group of people is governed. p. 78.

consumer credit (kən sü′ mər kred′ it). Device by which one can buy goods with a small payment at the time of purchase and pay the rest in monthly installments. p. 598.

consumer goods (kən sü′ mər gùdz). Things that are made or grown by producers and used by people. p. 598.

containment (kən tān′ mənt). Act of confining a political or military force within its current geographical boundaries. p. 678.

Continental army (kon tə nen′ təl är′ mē). Military force established by Continental Congress in the War for Independence. It was commanded by George Washington. p. 146.

Continental Association (kon tə nen′ təl ə sō sē ā′ shən). A group of delegates from each colony formed to unite the colonies against the British. p. 138.

contour line (kon′ tùr līn). Line on a map that is the same distance above or below sea level. p. 4.

Contras (kon′ trəz). Rebel groups seeking to overthrow the left-wing Sandinista government of Nicaragua in the 1980s. p. 756.

convoy (kon′ voi). To travel together for protection. p. 582.

cooperative (kō op′ ə rā tiv). Organization owned and operated for the benefit of those who use its goods and services. p. 508.

Copperheads (kop′ ər heds). Democrats opposed to the policy of Abraham Lincoln in the Civil War. p. 387.

corporation (kôr pə rā′ shən). Group of people who pool their capital to set up a business and who own shares of stock in it. p. 465.

cotton gin (kot′ ən jin). Machine used to separate the cotton fiber from its seeds. p. 244.

cow town (kou toun). Town on a railroad line that grew because cattle were driven there for shipment. p. 448.

creole (krē′ ōl). A person born in Spain's American colonies of Spanish parents. p. 53.

crop lien system (krop lēn sis′ təm). System in which landowners could buy supplies on credit by giving shopkeepers a lien on their crops. This was a pledge to repay the shopkeeper when the crops were sold. p. 404.

culture (kul′ chər). Way of life of a group of people, including their customs, traditions, and values. p. 34.

customs duties (kus′ təms dü′ tēs). Taxes paid on imported goods. p. 562.

D

dame school (dām skül). Small private elementary school run by a woman in her home. p. 112.

Dawes Act (dôz akt). Law passed in 1887 that permitted Indians to own land on reservations for farming. p. 441.

D-day (d-dā). June 6, 1944, the day the Allies began the invasion of France in World War II. p. 653.

debtor (det′ ər). Person who owes something, usually money, to another person. p. 89.

Declaration of Independence (dek lə rā′ shən ov in di pen′ dəns). Document that stated the reasons why the American colonies desired to be independent of British control. p. 150.

Declaration of Sentiments (dek lə rā′ shən ov sen′ tə mənts). Document that declared women's equality with men. It listed ways in which society discriminated against women. p. 296.

Declaratory Act (di klar′ ə tor ē akt). Act by which Parliament declared that it had the authority to tax and pass laws in the colonies. p. 130.

demilitarize (dē mil′ ə tə rīz). To remove armed troops from an area. p. 643.

Democrat (dem′ ə krat). Member of one of the two main political parties in the United States. The party was derived from the Democratic-Republican party. p. 276.

Democratic-Republican party (dem ə krat′ ik ri pub′ lə kən pär′ tē). Political party of the early 1800s, which was made up of Anti-Federalists. It was the forerunner of today's Democratic party. p. 226.

demographer (di mog′ rə fər). One who studies the characteristics of human populations. p. 10.

depression (di presh′ ən). Economic condition in which business is very bad and large numbers of people are unemployed. p. 281.

détente (dā tänt′). Relaxing of tensions, especially between nations or political groups. p. 731.

dictator (dik′ tā tər). Ruler having complete and uncontrolled authority over a nation. p. 642.

diplomacy (də plō′ mə sē). Handling of important dealings between nations. p. 551.

direct primary (də rekt′ prī′ mer ē). System by which members of a party vote to select their party's candidates. p. 524.

dividend (div′ ə dend). Money that stockholders receive as their share of the company's profits. p. 465.

domestic (də mes′ tik). A household servant. p. 482.

domino theory (dom′ ə nō thir′ ē). Idea that if one country falls to the Communists, the next or neighboring country will inevitably fall in turn. p. 726.

draft (draft). Process by which men are selected for military service without their expressed consent. p. 377.

Dred Scott case (dred skot cās). United States Supreme Court case that upheld the right of the master to his slave as property and declared the Missouri Compromise of 1820 unconstitutional. p. 354.

drought (drout). Long period of dry weather with no rain. p. 29.

dry farming (drī fär′ ming). Techniques used in farming areas that have little water. p. 452.

Dust Bowl (dust bōl). Area in the Great Plains in which soil erosion, caused by a long period of drought and poor farming methods, resulted in severe dust storms. p. 634.

E

effigy mound (ef′ ə jē mound). Mound or pile of earth built in the shape of an animal or human being. p. 31.

egalitarian (i gal ə tār′ ē ən). Person who believes all people are equal and have the same social, political, and economic rights. p. 302.

Eisenhower Doctrine (ī′ zən hou ər dok′ trən). Statement issued by President Eisenhower declaring that the United States would offer economic aid to the countries of the Middle East and defend them from attack by Communist countries. p. 688.

elector (i lek′ tər). One of the people chosen by the state legislature to elect the President. p. 190.

electricity (i lek tris′ ə tē). Form of energy. It can produce light, heat, motion, and magnetic force. p. 467.

elevation (el ə vā′ shən). Height of the earth's surface, usually expressed in feet or meters above or below sea level. p. 4.

Emancipation Proclamation (i man sə pā′ shən prok lə mā′ shən). Proclamation issued by President Lincoln on January 1, 1863, that declared all slaves in the rebelling states to be free. p. 375.

Embargo Act (em bär′ gō akt). Law passed in 1807 that forbade American ships and foreign ships from carrying American goods to other countries. p. 259.

empire (em′ pīr). Territories and peoples under the control of a powerful nation. p. 49.

encomienda (en kō myen′ dä). A large estate where a group of Indians lived under a Spanish colonist's care and supervision. p. 52.

enumerated articles (i nü′ mə rāt əd ar′ tə kəlz). List of colonial products that could be shipped only to England or to other English colonies. p. 126.

GLOSSARY

GLOSSARY

GLOSSARY

785

environment (en vī′ rən mənt). Everything in an area that affects the growth and development of living things, including land, water, plants, animals, and climate. p. 34.

Equal Rights Amendment (ē′ kwəl rīts ə mend′ mənt) or *ERA.* Proposed (1972) amendment to the United States Constitution that would ban all discrimination based on sex; defeated in 1982. p. 766.

Era of Good Feeling (ir′ ə ov gùd fē′ ling). Period following the War of 1812 (during the presidency of James Monroe) when the United States experienced peace and unity. p. 267.

executive branch (eg zek′ yə tiv branch). Part of the government that is headed by the President and is responsible for carrying out laws passed by Congress. p. 184.

exile (eg′ zīl). Person forced to leave his or her country. p. 691.

exodus of 1879 (ek′ sə dəs ov 1879). Emigration of black people from the South to the West. p. 421.

extinct (ek stingkt′). No longer existing. p. 22.

F

factor (fak′ tər). Person who does business for another; a trading agent. p. 105.

famine (fam′ ən). A very great shortage of food. p. 480.

Far East (fär ēst). Countries of eastern Asia and Southeast Asia. p. 42.

Farmers' Alliance (fär′ mərz ə lī′ əns). Regional organizations of farmers formed in the 1880s to help solve their problems. p. 509.

favorite son (fā′ vər it sun). Candidate favored by the delegates or people from one state or section. p. 274.

federal budget (fed′ ər əl buj′ it). Estimate of the amount of money that the United States government will take in and spend over a 12-month period. p. 748.

federal government (fed′ ər əl guv′ ərn mənt). Form of government in which power is divided between the national government and the governments of the states. p. 187.

Federalist (fed′ ər ə list). Person who supported the principle of federal government. p. 187.

Federalist papers (fed′ ər ə list pā′ pərz). Series of articles written in support of the Constitution. p. 188.

Federalist party (fed′ ər ə list pär′ tē). Political party in the United States that believed in a strong central government and favored the ratification of the Constitution. p. 226.

federal republic (fed′ ər əl ri pub′ lik). Government of the United States, in which powers are shared by the states and central government. It is based on the consent of the people through elected representatives. p. 190.

Federal Reserve System (fed′ ər əl ri zerv′ sis′ təm). Federal system of banks consisting of 12 Federal Reserve banks, which provide services for the private banks in their district. p. 539.

"Fifty-four forty or fight" (fif′ tē fôr fôr′ tē ôr fīt). A campaign slogan used in the presidential election of 1844 by Americans who were for the expansion of America as far north as 54°40′. p. 321.

fireside chat (fīr′ sīd chat). Name given to the reports President Roosevelt gave over the radio to the American people. p. 626.

First Continental Congress (ferst kon tə nen′ təl kong′ gris). Meeting in September 1774 of delegates from the American colonies assembled in Philadelphia to discuss colonial grievances against Great Britain. p. 138.

Folsom man (fōl′ səm man). Person of a prehistoric culture thought to have lived in North America at the end of the most recent Ice Age. p. 24.

Force Bill (fôrs bil). Law passed in 1833 giving the President authorization to use the army and navy to collect tariff duties. p. 279.

forty-niners (fôr tē nī′ nərz). Name given to gold seekers who came to California in the gold rush of 1849. p. 332.

49th parallel (49th par′ ə lel). Parallel established as the boundary between the Oregon country and British-controlled Canada. p. 321.

Fourteen Points (fôr′ tēn points). American terms of peace outlined by President Wilson to end World War I. p. 586.

Freedmen's Bureau (frēd′ mənz byùr′ ō). Governmental agency set up in 1865 to help freed slaves. p. 400.

free state (frē stāt). State in which slavery was illegal. p. 269.

frontier (frun tir′). Farthest unsettled edge of a country. p. 251.

Fugitive Slave Law (fyü′ jə tiv slāv lô). Law requiring that runaway slaves be picked up and returned to their masters. p. 348.

Fundamental Orders (fun də men′ təl ôr′ dərz). Constitution drawn up by the Connecticut Colony in 1639. It has been called the world's first written constitution. p. 81.

G

Gadsden Purchase (gadz′ den pėr chəs). Strip of land purchased by the United States from Mexico in 1853 for $10 million. Today it is the southern parts of New Mexico and Arizona. p. 328.

genocide (jen′ ə sīd). The killing of an entire ethnic, national, or religious group. p. 654.

Gentlemen's Agreement (jen′ təl mənz ə grē′ mənt). Agreement between the United States and Japan that would allow Japanese children to attend public schools if the Japanese would not let more workers come to the United States. p. 558.

geologist (jē ol′ ə jist). Scientist who learns about the earth by studying rocks and rock formations. p. 24.

geometric mound (jē ə met′ rik mound). Mound or pile of earth built in the form of a circle, a square, or parallel lines. p. 31.

Gettysburg Address (get′ ēz bərg ə dres′). Speech given by President Lincoln on November 19, 1863, at the site of the battle of Gettysburg. The occasion was the ceremony dedicating a part of the battlefield as a cemetery for those who had died in the battle. p. 383.

ghetto (get′ ō). Section of a city where members of a minority group live. It is usually crowded and run-down. p. 724.

GI Bill of Rights (jē ī bil ov rīts). Bill that provided government aid to the veterans of World War II. p. 696.

Gilded Age (gil′ did āj). Name given to the years following the Civil War, describing a flashy, get-rich-quick society. p. 412.

glacier (glā′ shər). Large body of ice formed from snow that moves slowly down a mountain or valley and spreads outward over a large area of land. p. 20.

gold standard (gold stan′ dərd). Belief that the money supply of a country should be based on gold only. p. 511.

governor's council (guv′ ər nərz koun′ səl). Upper house in the legislature of most colonies. Members of the council were appointed by the governor. p. 132.

grammar school (gram′ ər skül). Public elementary school, usually attended by boys, to prepare children for college. p. 112.

Grange (grānj). Organization of farmers who sought to improve their situation. p. 508.

Great American Desert (grāt ə mer′ ə ken dez′ ərt). Name given by an exploration expedition in the 1820s to the lands between the Missouri River and the Rocky Mountains. p. 316.

Great Compromise (grāt kom′ prə mīz). Connecticut Compromise; a proposal that created two houses of Congress, one in which states would be represented by population, and one in which states would be represented equally. p. 183.

Great Society (grāt sə sī′ ə tē). Program favored by President Lyndon B. Johnson for improving the domestic welfare of all people in the United States. p. 722.

greenback (grēn′ bak). Paper money printed on green paper that was issued by the Union to help pay war expenses. p. 379.

Green Revolution (grēn rev ə lü′ shən). Advances in agriculture that led to an increase in production. p. 698.

guerrilla (gə ril′ ə). Member of an armed band that carries on hit-and-run warfare apart from a country's uniformed forces. p. 165.

Gulf of Tonkin Resolution (gulf ov tän′ kin rez ə lü′ shən). Act that allowed the United States government to take military action in Vietnam. p. 727.

H

hacienda (hä syen′ dä). A plantation or ranch where a Spanish colonist ran an encomienda. p. 52.

Harlem Renaissance (här′ ləm ren ə säns′). Revival of arts and culture in the black community in New York City in the 1920s. p. 607.

Hartford Convention (härt′ fərd kən ven′ shən). Meeting in 1814 of New England's Federalist leaders in Hartford, Connecticut, at which they discussed their discontent with the War of 1812. p. 264.

Hessian (hesh′ ən). German soldier hired to fight for the British in the American War for Independence. p. 157.

Holocaust (hol′ ə kôst). Great or complete destruction; the mass extermination of European Jews by the Nazis during World War II. p. 655.

Homestead Act (hōm′ sted akt). Law passed in 1862 that offered citizens the opportunity to acquire 160 acres of government land for a small fee provided they lived on it and farmed it for 5 years. p. 406.

hostage (hôs′ tij). Person who is seized by another person or group and is held captive in order for the captors to obtain a demand. p. 743.

hot line (hot līn). Direct telephone line between the United States and the Soviet Union, offering immediate communication in an emergency. p. 693.

House of Burgesses (hous ov bèr′ jis əs). Representative assembly in colonial Virginia. A step toward self-government. p. 74.

Hudson River School (hud′ sən riv′ ər skül). Group of American artists of the 1800s who painted scenes of areas along the Hudson River. p. 305.

Huguenot (hyü′ gə not). French Protestant of the sixteenth or seventeenth century. p. 97.

human rights (hyü′ mən rīts). Basic rights to which all humans are entitled. p. 741.

I

Ice Age (īs āj). Most recent time that the Northern Hemisphere was covered by glaciers. p. 20.

impeach (im pēch′). To charge a public official with doing something illegal while in office. p. 398.

imperialist (im pir′ ē ə list). Person who favors the policy of extending the rule of one country over other countries or lands. p. 546.

impress (im pres′). To seize by authority for public use. p. 230.

inauguration (in ô gyə rā′ shən). Ceremony to put someone in office. p. 220.

indenture (in den′ chər). Contract by which a person agrees to work for a certain period of time in exchange for free passage to a foreign land. p. 96.

Indies (in′ dēz). Name used in the fifteenth and sixteenth centuries to refer to India and nearby lands. Europeans also used the name to refer to newly discovered lands in the Western Hemisphere. p. 42.

indigo (in′ də gō). Plant from which blue dye is made. p. 88.

Industrial Revolution (in dus′ trē əl rev ə lü′ shən). Period of great change in the way people worked and lived. It was brought about by the development of power-driven machines. p. 243.

industrial union (in dus′ trē əl yün′ yən). Union made up of all the workers in one industry. p. 637.

inflation (in flā′ shən). Economic condition in which the value of money decreases and the price of goods increases. p. 702.

initiative (i nish′ ē ə tiv). Right of citizens outside the legislature to introduce new laws. p. 510.

injunction (in junk′ shən). A court order that enjoins people, or tells them that they must or must not do something. p. 503.

interchangeable parts (in tər chānj′ jə bəl partz). Parts that are made exactly alike and are capable of being used in place of each other in manufactured products. p. 245.

GLOSSARY

international law (in tər nash' ə nəl lô). Body of rules that countries agree to follow in controlling their relations with each other. p. 574.

Interstate Commerce Act (in' tər stāt kom' ərs akt). Law passed in 1886 that determined the rates railroads could charge shippers. It also set up the Interstate Commerce Commission (ICC) to see that the law was carried out. p. 508.

intervene (in tər vēn'). To come between two people or groups to help settle a disagreement. p. 561.

Intolerable Acts (in tol' ər ə bəl akts). Four laws passed by Parliament to punish the people of Massachusetts for the Boston Tea Party. p. 137.

inventory (in' vən tôr ē). Stock of unsold goods. p. 619.

Invincible Armada (in vin' sə bəl är mäd' ə). Large fleet of ships sent by King Philip of Spain in 1587 to invade England. p. 71.

ironclad (ī' ərn klad). Ship protected by iron plates. p. 371.

iron curtain (ī' ərn kėr' tən). Imaginary wall or line separating the countries of Eastern Europe from the other nations. p. 677.

irrigate (ir' ə gāt). To bring water to crops, usually through canals, ditches, or pipes. p. 28.

island-hopping (ī' lənd hop' ing). Allied plan for fighting the Japanese in the Pacific during World War II. The Allies seized key islands and bypassed others. p. 656.

isolationist (ī sə lā' shə nist). Person who favors the policy of his or her nation keeping to itself and not having political or economic relations with other nations. p. 648.

J

Jay's Treaty (jāz trē' tē). Treaty signed in 1794 that resolved several problems that existed between the United States and Great Britain. p. 230.

Jim Crow (jim krō). Phrase used to describe the system of separate but equal facilities for black people. p. 418.

joint-stock company (joint stok kum' pə nē). Company organized so that many people own stock in the company. The stockholders share the profits and lose only what they invested, should the company fail. p. 72.

judicial branch (jü dish' əl branch). Part of government that decides the meaning of laws and sets up courts to try those who disobey laws. p. 184.

Judiciary Act of 1789 (jü dish' ē er ē akt ov 1789). Act passed by Congress in 1789 that set up the basic framework of the federal court system, including the Supreme Court, 3 circuit courts, and 13 district courts. p. 222.

K

Kansas-Nebraska bill (kan' zəs nə bras' kə bil). Bill creating the territories of Kansas and Nebraska from the land of the Louisiana Purchase. p. 351.

Kellogg-Briand Pact (kel' ôg brē än' pakt). Treaty signed in 1928 in which many countries agreed to settle disputes by peaceful means. p. 612.

Kitchen Cabinet (kich' ən kab' ə nit). Group of advisers to the President, including several politicians and newspaper people who President Jackson considered to be closer to the ordinary people than his Cabinet members were. p. 287.

Knights of Labor (nīts ov lā' bər). Organization started in 1869 to unite all skilled and unskilled workers into one union. p. 499.

Ku Klux Klan (kü kluks klan). Secret society formed by Southern whites after the Civil War to maintain white supremacy. p. 404.

L

labor union (lā' bər yün' yən). Group of workers joined together for the purpose of protecting the interests of its members. p. 494.

latitude (lat' ə tüd). Imaginary lines that circle the earth in an east-west direction, parallel to the Equator and indicating angle north or south of the equator; used with *longitude* to give numerical coordinates to every place on earth. p. 6.

League of Nations (lēg ov nā' shənz). Organization formed in 1920 to promote cooperation among nations and maintain peace following World War I. p. 586.

Leatherstocking Tales (leŦH' ər stok ing tālz). Series of novels written by James Fenimore Cooper about an American frontiersman. p. 304.

legend (lej' ənd). Story passed down over many years that may or may not be true. p. 68.

legislative branch (lej' is lā tiv branch). Part of government responsible for making laws. p. 184.

legislature (lej' is lā chər). Body of government responsible for making laws. p. 84.

lend-lease (lend lēs). Policy of making a loan of goods or services to an ally and receiving goods or services in return. p. 648.

Lewis and Clark expedition (lü' is and klärk eks pə dish' ən). Expedition running from 1804 to 1806 that explored the western lands. p. 254.

life expectancy (līf ek spek' tən sē). Average age to which a person usually lives. p. 521.

Lincoln-Johnson plan (ling' kən jon' sən plan). Plan by which Confederate states were readmitted into the Union. p. 394.

llama (lä' mə). South American animal that is related to the camel but is smaller and has no hump. p. 38.

local colorist (lō' kəl kul' ər ist). Author who writes a tale set in a specific region of the United States and makes the scenery, characters, and dialogue typical of that region. p. 429.

long drive (lông drīv). Herding large numbers of cattle from ranches over the plains to a rail line for shipment east. p. 447.

longitude (lôn' jə tüd). Imaginary lines that circle the earth in a north-south direction, intersecting at the north and south poles and indicating angle east or west of the prime meridian; used with *latitude* to give numerical coordinates to every place on earth. p. 6.

loose interpretation (lüs in tėr prə tā′ shən). Belief that Congress has certain implied powers that are not exactly stated in the Constitution. p. 224.

Lost Colony (lôst kol′ ə nē). English colony founded on Roanoke Island off the coast of North Carolina in 1587. The settlers of this colony later disappeared without a trace. p. 72.

Louisiana Purchase (lü ē zē an′ ə pėr′ chəs). Region of land the United States bought from France in 1803. It extended from the Mississippi River west to the Rocky Mountains and from Canada south to the Gulf of Mexico. p. 253.

Loyalist (loi′ ə list). Colonist who was a supporter of Great Britain and King George III. p. 148.

Lusitania (lü si tā′ nē ə). British passenger ship sunk without warning in May 1915 by a German submarine. p. 576.

lynching (linch′ ing). A murder committed by a mob. p. 419.

M

manifest destiny (man′ ə fest des′ tə nē). Belief held in the 1840s that the territorial expansion of the United States to its natural limits was right and inevitable. p. 328.

Marshall Plan (mär′ shəl plan). United States program for aiding the economic recovery of Europe after World War II. p. 679.

martial law (mär′ shəl lô). Rule by the military, often imposed in a time of real or imagined crisis. p. 758.

mass transit (mas tran′ sit). Way of moving a great number of people from one place to another at the same time. Trains, subways, buses, and airplanes are types of *mass transit*. p. 8.

Mayflower Compact (mā flou′ ər kom′ pakt). Document drawn up and signed by the Pilgrims aboard ship by which they agreed to make laws as needed for the colony's good and to obey these laws. p. 75.

mechanical reaper (mə kan′ ə kəl rē′ pər). Machine that cuts grain or harvests a crop. p. 313.

mercantilism (mėr′ kən ti liz əm). Economic system by which a government controls agriculture, industry, and commerce so that the country sells more goods than it buys and thereby increases the money wealth of the nation. p. 105.

mercenary (mėr′ sə ner ē). Soldier serving in the army of a foreign country for wages. p. 157.

merger (mėr′ jer). Process by which two or more companies combine to make a single company. p. 610.

mestizo (me stē′ zō). A person born in Spain's American colonies of mixed European and Indian ancestry. p. 53.

Mexican Cession (mek′ sə kən sesh′ ən). Land given to the United States by Mexico as part of the Treaty of Guadalupe Hidalgo. p. 328.

Middle Passage (mid′ əl pas′ əj). The long voyage from Africa to the Americas of slaves held in slave ships. p. 99.

migrant worker (mī′ grənt wər′ kər). Person who travels from one place to another to find work. p. 763.

militarism (mil′ ə tə riz əm). Policy of placing emphasis on the military power of a country. p. 571.

militia (mə lish′ ə). Organized military force made up of able-bodied citizens, not regular soldiers, that is usually called upon in emergencies. p. 120.

mint (mint). Place where coins are made by government authority. p. 234.

Minuteman (min′ it man). Member of an army of citizens ready to fight the British at "a minute's notice" during the War for Independence. p. 139.

missile (mis′ əl). Self-propelled rocket that can be launched from the ground, sea, or air to hit a target many miles away. p. 749.

mission (mish′ ən). Settlement consisting of a church, other buildings, and land for the purpose of teaching Christianity to nonbelievers. p. 52.

Missouri Compromise (mə zùr′ ē kom′ prə mīz). Compromise by which Missouri was admitted to the Union as a slave state and Maine was admitted as a free state. p. 269.

mobilize (mō′ bə līz). To assemble the armed forces and prepare for war. p. 571.

Mongoloid (mong′ gə loid). Person belonging to the race characterized by yellow skin, slanting eyes, prominent cheekbones, and straight dark hair. p. 22.

monopoly (mə nop′ ə lē). Sole control of an entire industry. p. 136.

Monroe Doctrine (mən rō′ dok′ trən). Statement issued by President Monroe in 1823 declaring that European nations should not interfere with American nations or try to claim additional territory in the Western Hemisphere. p. 268.

Mormon (môr′ mən). Member of the Church of Jesus Christ of Latter-day Saints, whose beliefs are based on the teachings of Joseph Smith. p. 329.

Mound Builders (mound bil′ dərz). Group of prehistoric Indians who lived in central and eastern North America, especially in the Ohio River and Mississippi River valleys. They built mounds of earth as burial places or as the foundation for a wooden building. p. 30.

Mountain Men (moun′ tən men). Fur trappers who lived in the mountains, were wise in the ways of the wilderness, and played an important part in the expansion of the United States in the 1800s. p. 316.

muckraker (muk′ rāk ər). Person who writes about wrongdoing in business and politics. p. 528.

mulatto (mü lät′ ō). A person born in Spain's American colonies of mixed European and black ancestry. p. 53.

mutiny (myü′ tə nē). Open rebellion against the person or people in authority, such as soldiers rebelling against their officers. p. 167.

N

national anthem (nash′ ə nəl an′ thəm). A country's official patriotic song. p. 263.

national debt (nash′ ə nəl det). The total amount the federal government owes. p. 750.

GLOSSARY

nationalism (nash′ ə nə liz əm). Feeling of loyalty to one's country. p. 266.

nativist (nā′ tə vist). Person who wanted to reduce or end immigration. p. 486.

NATO. See *North Atlantic Treaty Organization.*

Navigation Acts (nav ə gā′ shən akts). Acts passed by the English parliament in the 1600s for the purpose of regulating colonial trade. p. 126.

Neutrality Acts (nü tral′ ə tē akts). Several laws passed by Congress between 1935 and 1937 to keep America out of war. p. 644.

Neutrality Proclamation (nü tral′ ə tē prôk lə mā′ shən). President George Washington's declaration that the United States would not take sides in the 1793 war between France and Great Britain. p. 229.

neutral rights (nü′ trəl rīts). Rights associated with being neutral, or not taking sides in a quarrel or war. p. 258.

New Deal (nü dēl). Policies introduced by President Franklin D. Roosevelt in the 1930s to fight the Great Depression and improve the economic and social welfare of the United States. p. 624.

New Federalism (nü fed′ ər ə liz əm). Name given to President Reagan's domestic program, which reduced and eliminated certain federal programs and shifted other programs from the federal government to the states. p. 749.

New Frontier (nü frən tēr′). The slogan of John F. Kennedy's presidency, referring to the challenges and opportunities the nation faced at the beginning of the 1960s. p. 710.

New Immigration (nü im ə grā′ shən). People coming to the United States from eastern and southern Europe, beginning in the 1800s. p. 481.

New Jersey Plan (nü jėr′ zē plan). Small States plan; the proposal that all states should be represented equally in Congress. p. 183.

New South (nü south). A South in which manufacturing and commercial interests would play a more important role. p. 405.

New World (nü wėrld). Western Hemisphere. p. 47.

nomadic (nō mad′ ik). Moving from place to place. p. 439.

nominate (nom′ ə nāt). To choose a person as candidate for office. p. 228.

nominating convention (nom′ ə nāt ing kən ven′ shən). Meeting of party members from all states to nominate the presidential candidates. p. 284.

nonimportation agreements (non im pôr tā′ shən ə grē′ mənts). Agreements signed by colonial merchants, who pledged not to import any British goods until Parliament repealed the Stamp Act. p. 130.

nonviolent resistance (non vī′ ə lənt rē zis′ təns). Refusal to obey laws that one believes to be unjust, but without resorting to violence. p. 714.

North Atlantic Treaty Organization (nôrth at lan′ tik trē′ tē ôr gə nə zā′ shən), *or NATO* (nā′ tō). Alliance of 14 non-Communist countries formed for joint military defense. p. 680.

Northwest Ordinance (nôrth west′ ôr′ də nəns). Law passed in 1787 that set up a system for governing the Northwest Territory. p. 180.

Northwest Passage (nôrth west′ pas′ ij). Nonexistent water route sought by early explorers to provide a short-cut from Europe to Asia and the East Indies through North America. p. 54.

Northwest Territory (nôrth west′ ter′ ə tôr ē). Territory north of the Ohio River from the Appalachian Mountains to the Mississippi River. It now forms Ohio, Indiana, Illinois, Michigan, Wisconsin, and part of Minnesota. p. 164.

nullification (nul ə fə kā′ shən). Belief that a state could nullify, or declare void, a national law within its own boundaries. p. 277.

nullify (nul′ ə fī). To cancel or veto. p. 277.

O

oil refinery (oil ri fī′ nər ē). Industrial plant where gasoline and other products are separated from the crude oil that is taken out of the ground. p. 469.

Old Immigration (ōld im ə grā′ shən). People coming to the United States from the countries in northern and western Europe starting in the 1700s. p. 481.

Old Northwest (ōld nôrth west′). Name given to Northwest Territory after the purchase of Louisiana from France. p. 256.

Old Southwest (ōld south west′). Name given to the area south of the Ohio River between the Appalachians and the Mississippi River after the Louisiana Purchase. p. 256.

omnivorous (om niv′ ər əs). Eating both plants and animals. p. 26.

Open Door policy (ō′ pən dôr pol′ ə sē). All nations having the same opportunities and privileges, even within another country's sphere of influence. p. 556.

open range (ō′ pən rānj). Government-owned lands in the northern plains on which cattle ranchers grazed their herds for free. p. 450.

orbit (or′ bit). To travel a circle around the earth. p. 2.

Oregon Trail (ôr′ ə gən trāl). Route from Missouri to Oregon used by settlers moving to the Northwest in the 1800s. p. 319.

oronoco (ôr ə nō′ kō). Mild tobacco from an area in South America near the Orinoco River. p. 73.

overseas empire (ō vər sēz′ em′ pīr). Lands controlled by distant countries. p. 546.

overseer (ō′ vər sē ər). Person hired to supervise others or their work. p. 337.

P

pacifist (pas′ ə fist). Person opposed to war who favors settling all disputes between nations by peaceful means. p. 651.

pamphlet (pam′ flit). Paper-covered booklet. p. 84.

Parliament (pär′ lə mənt). Lawmaking body in Great Britain. p. 127.

party. See *political party.*

patent (pat′ ənt). Document giving an inventor the right to be the only person to make or sell his or her invention for a certain period of time. p. 234.

Patriot (pā′ trē ət). Person who loves and loyally supports his or her country. In the struggle against the British, a person who fought for the independence of the American colonies. p. 148.

patroon (pə trün′). Owners of large grants of land received from the Dutch government in colonial times. p. 60.

patroon system (pə trün′ sis′ təm). System by which Dutch government gave away large grants of land in North America to promote settlement. p. 61.

Peace Corps (pēs kôr). Agency of the United States government that sends volunteers with various skills to other countries to help improve conditions. p. 690.

Peace Democrat (pēs dem′ ə krat). Northern Democrat opposed to the Civil War. p. 387.

peninsulares (pen in sü lär′ ās). Major officeholders of the Spanish empire in America, so called because they were born in Spain, which is on the Iberian Peninsula, and usually returned there after their term of service. p. 53.

perjury (pėr′ jər ē). Act of lying while under oath. p. 737.

petition (pə tish′ ən). Formal request to someone in authority for a privilege or a right; often a written document containing the signatures of the people making the request. p. 65.

Pickett's charge (pik′ its chärj). Famous charge led by the Confederate general Pickett during the battle of Gettysburg. p. 382.

"Pikes Peak or Bust!" (pīks pēk ôr bust). Cry used by the thousands of people rushing to Colorado Territory after gold was discovered there in 1858. p. 442.

Pilgrim (pil′ grəm). Person who travels on a religious journey. Specifically, one who settled in Plymouth colony in 1620. p. 75.

Pinckney's Treaty (pingk′ nēz trē′ tē). Treaty signed in 1795 that settled the dispute between the United States and Spain over the western and southern boundaries of the United States and the issue of navigation on the Mississippi River. p. 231.

plantation (plan tā′ shən). Large farm on which one main crop is grown. p. 73.

platform (plat′ fôrm). Statement of goals or plan of action of a group. p. 509.

Plessy v. Ferguson (ples′ ē vėr′ səz fėr′ gə sən). Case in which the Supreme Court ruled that the "separate but equal" policy did not violate the Fourteenth Amendment. p. 419.

pogrom (pō′ grəm). Organized massacre of a group of people, especially of Jews. p. 482.

political democracy (pə lit′ ə kəl di mok′ rə sē). People taking part in the process of choosing leaders and influencing their government. p. 284.

political machine (pə lit′ ə kəl mə shēn′). Smoothly run political organization. p. 491.

political map (pə lit′ ə kəl map). Map that shows national and state boundaries and the names and locations of towns and cities. p. 4.

political party (pə lit′ ə kəl pär′ tē). Organization of people who hold similar views on policies a government should follow and who choose candidates for public office and work to get them elected. p. 226.

politics (pol′ ə tiks). Art or science concerned with guiding or influencing government. p. 243.

popular sovereignty (pop′ yə lər sov′ rən tē). Doctrine existing before the Civil War that gave people living in a new territory the right to decide by vote whether they wanted slavery in their territory. p. 351.

population explosion (pop yə lā′ shən ek splō′ zhən). Rapid increase in the number of people in an area. p. 100.

Populist (pop′ yə list). Member of the People's party, a national political party formed in the 1880s. p. 509.

portage (pôr′ tij). Carrying boats or provisions for short distances on land, from one body of water to another, or around a falls or rapids. p. 55.

precipitation (pri sip ə tā′ shən). Moisture that falls to the earth's surface in the form of rain, snow, sleet, hail, fog, or mist. p. 8.

prehistoric (prē his tôr′ ik). Time before there were written records. p. 20.

presidio (pri sid′ ē ō). Military post or fort in an area under Spanish or Mexican control. p. 53.

prime minister (prīm min′ ə stər). Chief minister in certain governments. p. 123.

privateer (prī və tir′). Privately owned armed ship built to attack and capture enemy merchant ships. In the War for Independence, privateers joined the United States in fighting the British. p. 163.

Proclamation of 1763 (prok lə mā′ shən ov 1763). Royal order issued by the king of Great Britain that prohibited colonists from settling on land west of the Appalachians. p. 125.

Progressive movement (prə gres′ iv müv′ mənt). Period of reform in the United States in the early 1900s. p. 527.

prohibition (prō ə bi′ shən). The legal effort to forbid the sale and drinking of alcoholic beverages, begun nationally in 1919 after the Eighteenth Amendment was ratified, and repealed in 1933 by the Twenty-first Amendment. p. 605.

promotional literature (prə mō′ shə nəl lit′ ər ə chər). Literature in the form of a pamphlet, advertisement, book, or letter used to develop interest in a person, product, or plan. p. 94.

propaganda (prop ə gan′ də). Plan or method for spreading ideas to further a cause. p. 134.

proprietary colony (prə prī′ ə ter ē kol′ ə nē). Colony granted by the British government to a person or persons who then had full power of ownership and could appoint the governor and other officials. p. 86.

proprietor (prə prī′ ə tər). Person who received a large grant of land from the king. p. 86.

protective tariff (prə tek′ tiv tar′ if). Tax on imports so that imported goods cannot be sold at lower prices than domestic goods. p. 266.

protectorate (prə tek′ tər it). Place or country under the protection of another country. p. 561.

provisional government (prə vizh′ ə nəl guv′ ərn mənt). Temporary government. p. 320.

public utility (pub′ lik yü til′ ə tē). Company that offers a service to the public, such as selling water, gas, and electricity. p. 524.

pueblo (pweb′ lō). Spanish word for "town." p. 28.

puncheon (pun′ chən). A split log. p. 114.

Puritan (pyür′ ə tən). Member of a group who wanted a more simple church organization in the Church of England in the 1600s. p. 78.

Q

Quaker (kwā′ kər). Member of a Christian group called the Society of Friends. Quakers favor simple religious services and are opposed to war. p. 84.

Quartering Act (kwôr′ tər ing akt). Act issued by the British in 1765 that ordered the colonial governments to furnish quarters and provisions for British troops in the colonies. p. 127.

Quebec Act (ki bek′ akt). A 1774 act that extended the boundaries of the Canadian province of Quebec to include all territory north of the Ohio River and east of the Mississippi River. p. 138.

quota (kwō′ tə). Fixed or limited number. p. 602.

R

radical (rad′ ə kəl). Person who favors extreme changes or reforms, especially in politics. p. 601.

Radical Republican (rad′ ə kəl ri pub′ lə kən). Member of Lincoln's party who believed he was too sympathetic toward the South. p. 387.

radioactivity (rā dē ō ak tiv′ ə tē). Property of some elements by which they give off energy as a result of the spontaneous decay of the nuclei of their atoms. p. 24.

ratify (rat′ ə fī). To approve. p. 187.

ration (rash′ ən). To limit the amount of something that someone can buy or use. p. 582.

rebate (rē′ bāt). To pay back part of the money paid. p. 470.

recall (re′ kôl). Procedure by which the people can vote to remove an elected official from office before his or her term has ended. p. 526.

Reconstruction (rē kən struk′ shən). Name given to the period following the Civil War (1865–1877). p. 392.

Reconstruction Act of 1867 (rē kən struk′ shən akt ov 1867). Bill placing Southern states under military rule until Reconstruction was complete. p. 398.

Red Scare (red skãr). Fear of Communist plots in America after the Russian Revolution in 1917. p. 601.

referendum (ref ə ren′ dəm). Process by which citizens vote directly to pass or reject a proposed law. p. 510.

reform (ri fôrm′). To change conditions with the hope of making them better. p. 294.

relief map (ri lēf′ map). Map that shows the elevation, or height, of the earth's surface. p. 4.

relocation center (rē lō kā′ shən sen′ tər). Camp where groups of people are sent to live on government orders. p. 665.

"Remember the Alamo!" (ri mem′ bər ŦHə al′ ə mō). Battle cry used to raise an army to fight for the independence of Texas. p. 324.

"Remember the Maine!" (ri mem′ bər ŦHə mān). Popular slogan in the United States in 1898, after the battleship *Maine* was blown up at Havana. p. 552.

reparations (rep ə rā′ shənz). Payment or other compensation for wrong or injury; payments made by a defeated country for damages inflicted during war. p. 586.

repeal (ri pēl). To cancel or do away with. p. 130.

Republic of Texas (ri pub′ lik ov tek′ səs). Independent nation formed in 1836 after the Texas victory over Mexico. p. 324.

Republican party (ri pub′ lik ən pär′ tē). One of the two major political parties in the United States. Formed in the mid-nineteenth century by opponents of slavery. p. 353.

reservation (rez ər vā′ shən). Public land set aside, or reserved, by the government for the use of Native Americans. p. 436.

revenue (rev′ ə nü). Money coming in. p. 266.

revolution (rev ə lü shən). A sudden, complete change. p. 189.

Roosevelt Corollary (rō′ zə velt kôr′ ə ler ē). Policy announced in 1904 that stated the United States would intervene in the Latin American republics to see that their debts were paid. p. 561.

Rough Riders (ruf rī′ dərz). Cavalry regiment, led by Theodore Roosevelt, that was recruited for the war with Spain in 1898. p. 553.

royal colony (roi′ əl kol′ ə nē). Colony directly under the control of the king. p. 74.

S

SALT II (sôlt tü). Treaty between the United States and the Soviet Union to limit weapons. p. 742.

sanitation (san ə tā′ shən). Making clean and healthful conditions, especially in terms of water supply, garbage, and sewage. p. 488.

scalawag (skal′ ə wag). Term used in the South after the Civil War to describe a white Southerner who sided with the new state governments. p. 403.

SDI. See *Strategic Defense Initiative.*

sea dog (sē dôg). English sea captain who was secretly encouraged by Queen Elizabeth to raid Spanish settlements and ships. p. 70.

secession (si sesh′ ən). Formal withdrawal from an organization. p. 278.

Second Continental Congress (sek′ ənd kon tə nen′ təl kong′ gris). Body of delegates from the 13 colonies that acted as a central government during the Revolutionary War. p. 146.

sectionalism (sek′ shə nə liz əm). Policy of placing great importance on a single section or region of a country. p. 275.

segregated (seg′ rə gā ted). Set apart. p. 418.

Selective Service Act (si lek′ tiv sėr′ vis akt). Law passed by Congress in 1917 that required all men of a certain age to register for the draft. p. 580.

self-determination (self di tèr mə nā′ shən). People choosing their form of government. p. 586.

self-government (self guv′ ərn mənt). Belief that people can and should rule themselves. p. 74.

"separate but equal" (sep′ ər it but ē′ kwəl). Policy of separating blacks from whites in public facilities, such as schools and waiting rooms, while maintaining equal facilities for each. p. 419.

Separatist (sep′ ə rə tist). Person wishing to separate from the Church of England; a Pilgrim. p. 75.

settlement house (set′ əl mənt hous). City building where various kinds of services are provided for the poor people of a neighborhood. p. 490.

Seven Cities of Gold (sev′ ən sit′ ēz ov gōld). Cities north of Mexico that were believed by early Spanish explorers to contain vast treasures. p. 64.

Seventh of March speech (sev′ enth ov märch spēch). Speech given by Daniel Webster in which he expressed approval for Clay's compromise. p. 346.

sharecropping (shār′ krop ing). Farming land for the landowner in return for a share of the crop produced. p. 404.

Shays's Rebellion (shāz′ ez ri bel′ yən). Uprising of farmers in Massachusetts after their lands were seized for overdue taxes. Viewed by many as proof of the need for a stronger central government. p. 177.

Sherman Antitrust Act (shėr′ mən an tē trust′ akt). Law passed in 1890 that declared trusts and any other ways of restricting trade to be illegal. p. 508.

sit-in (sit′ in). Form of protest in which a group of people remains seated for a long period of time in a public place. p. 715.

skyscraper (skī′ skrā pər). Very tall building. p. 474.

slave state (slāv stāt). State in which slavery was legal. p. 269.

Social Security Act (sō′ shəl si kyür′ ə tē akt). United States Government program started in 1935 to provide pensions to retired persons and their dependents. p. 630.

sod (sod). The top layer of soil covered with grass. p. 451.

solar energy (sō′ lər en′ ər gē). Power from the sun. p. 739.

space satellite (spās sat′ ə līt). Object made by people that is launched by rocket into space and circles the earth. p. 709.

space shuttle (spās shut′ əl). A space vehicle designed to be landed under its own power by its pilot and then reused in other space missions. p. 754.

speculation (spek yə lā′ shən). Buying or selling when there is a large risk, in hope of making a profit. p. 616.

sphere of influence (sfir ov in′ flü ens). Area or country where another nation has gained special privileges and rights for itself. p. 556.

Spice Islands (spīs ī′ ləndz). Islands off the coast of Southeast Asia, important in the fifteenth and sixteenth centuries for spices such as cloves, nutmeg, and pepper. p. 59.

spoils system (spoilz sis′ təm). Practice of rewarding party members with government jobs. p. 285.

square deal (skwâr dēl). Phrase used by Theodore Roosevelt to describe his idea of government, in which everyone was treated fairly. p. 534.

squatter (skwot′ ər). Person who settles on land without owning it or paying any rent. p. 88.

stalemate (stāl′ māt). Situation in which neither side can win. p. 685.

Stamp Act (stamp akt). Act passed in 1765 that required the use of stamps in the American colonies on all legal documents and other papers, including almanacs, newspapers, pamphlets, and wills. p. 128.

Stamp Act Congress (stamp akt kong′ gris). Meeting in 1765 of delegates from nine colonies to discuss colonial problems. p. 130.

stereotype (ster′ ēə tīp). Mental picture of a whole group that is exaggerated or oversimplified and often based on emotion. p. 362.

stock (stok). Share in the ownership of a company. p. 72.

stock market (stok mär′ kit). Place where shares of stock in corporations are bought and sold. p. 616.

Strategic Defense Initiative (strə tē′ jik di fens′ in ish′ ə tiv), or *SDI*. A new defense program calling for an antimissile system in space, for which research was begun during the Reagan administration. p. 750.

strict interpretation (strikt in tėr prə tā′ shən). Belief that the federal government could do only what the Constitution specifically gave it the power to do. p. 225.

strike (strīk). Job stoppage by workers to get an employer to agree to their demands. p. 494.

submarine (sub′ mə rēn). Ship that can operate under water. p. 575.

subsidy (sub′ sə dē). Gift of land or money from the government. p. 461.

suffrage (suf′ rij). Right to vote. p. 296.

Sugar Act (shủg′ ər akt). A 1764 act that raised duties on sugar, wine, cloth, and coffee imported into the American colonies from areas not belonging to Great Britain. p. 127.

summit conference (sum′ it kon′ fər əns). Meeting of the top leaders of the major powers to consider common problems. p. 686.

Sunbelt (sun′ belt). Southern and western parts of the United States. p. 699.

Sussex Pledge (sus′ iks plej). Agreement by the German government stating that German submarines would no longer torpedo passenger ships or merchant ships without warning. p. 577.

sweatshop (swet′ shop). Business in which workers were employed under unhealthy conditions for long hours with poor wages. p. 426.

T

table furniture (tā′ bəl fėr′ nə chər). Wooden dishes used for meals. p. 115.

tariff (tar′ if). Tax on imports or exports. p. 220.

"taxation without representation" (tak sā′ shən wiŦH′ out rep ri zen tā′ shən). Issue in the American colonies when Parliament levied taxes in the colonies without the approval of the colonial legislature. p. 130.

tax loophole (taks lüp′ hōl). A special rule that allows some businesses and individuals to avoid paying some of their taxes. p. 752.

Tea Act (tē akt). A 1773 act that granted the British East India Company a monopoly on the sale of tea to the American colonies. p. 136.

Teapot Dome (tē′ pot dōm). Name of a hill in Wyoming that lay over an oil deposit reserved for the navy; leasing of the oil field became the subject of a scandal during the 1920s. p. 609.

technology (tek nol′ ə jē). Amount of scientific knowledge and kinds of tools a people have. p. 39.

Teller Amendment (tel′ ər ə mend′ mənt). Part of the resolution passed by Congress that recognized Cuban independence. It said America would not take over Cuba. p. 553.

temple mound (tem′ pəl mound). Mound or pile of earth that is flat on top and was used as a foundation for a wooden building or temple. p. 31.

tenement (ten′ ə mənt). Apartment building in a city, usually with poor safety and sanitary conditions. p. 488.

tepee (tē′ pē). Tentlike shelter used by certain tribes of Native Americans. The tepee was made of buffalo skins stitched together, draped over poles, and secured to the ground. p. 36.

termination (tėr mə nā′ shən). Ending of something. p. 766.

terrace (ter′ əs). Flat surface on the side of a steep hill or mountain, constructed to make crop-growing possible. p. 28.

terrorism (ter′ ər iz əm). The organized use of violence against innocent civilians in an attempt to advance one's political goals. p. 760.

Three-fifths Compromise (thrē fifths kom′ prə mīz). Agreement reached at the Constitutional Convention that said for every five slaves owned, three would be counted for the purposes of taxation and representation in Congress. p. 185.

"Tippecanoe and Tyler, too" (tip ē kə nü′ and tī′ lər tü). Campaign slogan used by the Whig party in the presidential election of 1840 to get their candidates, William Henry Harrison and John Tyler, elected. p. 283.

Toleration Act (tol ə rā′ shən akt). Law passed in 1649 guaranteeing freedom of worship to all Christians in Maryland. p. 87.

Tory (tôr′ ē). Name sometimes given to colonists who supported Great Britain and King George III; named after the political party in Great Britain that supported the king. p. 148.

totalitarian (tō tal ə tār′ ē ən). Government that has total power over its people. p. 642.

total war (tō′ təl wär). War in which all of a nation's resources are used to further the national goals. p. 661.

Townshend Acts (toun′ zend akts). British law that placed taxes on glass, lead, paper, paint, and tea imported from England by colonial merchants. p. 131.

township (toun′ ship). Surveyors' division of land in the Northwest Territory; a square measuring 6 miles (10 km) along each side and subdivided into 36 square sections measuring 1 mile (1.6 km) along each side. p. 250.

trade deficit (trād def′ ə sit). The amount by which a nation's imports, or goods bought from other countries, exceed its exports, or goods sold to other countries. p. 753.

trade union (trād yün′ yən). Group whose members work at a single skilled trade. p. 499.

Trail of Tears (trāl ov tērz). Name given by the Cherokee to their journey from Georgia to Oklahoma after they had been forced off their land by the United States government. p. 290.

traitor (trā′ tər). Person who aids the enemies of his or her country. p. 167.

treason (trē′ zən). Act of aiding the enemies of one's country. p. 167.

treaty of alliance (trē′ tē ov ə lī′ əns). Treaty signed by France and the United States in 1778 in which France pledged its support to the Americans in their struggle for independence from Great Britain. p. 161.

Treaty of Ghent (trē′ tē ov gent). Treaty signed in 1814 between the United States and Great Britain, ending the War of 1812. p. 263.

Treaty of Greenville (trē′ tē ov grēn′ vil). Treaty signed in 1795 after the Indians' defeat at Fallen Timbers. It set up a boundary between Indian lands and land open to American settlers. p. 251.

Treaty of Guadalupe Hidalgo (trē′ tē ov gwä də lüp′ ā hē däl′ gō). Treaty signed in 1848 between Mexico and the United States that ended the Mexican War. p. 327.

Treaty of Paris (1763) (trē′ tē ov par′ is). Peace treaty that ended the French and Indian War. p. 124.

triangular trade route (trī ang′ gyə lər trād rüt). The course of trading ships between three points—for example, the West Indies, Africa, and the United States. p. 104.

tribe (trīb). Group of people held together by family and social ties, geography, or custom. p. 23.

tributary (trib′ yə ter ē). Stream that flows into a larger stream or body of water. p. 7.

Truman Doctrine (trü′ mən dok′ trən). Declaration in 1947 that the United States would help free peoples resist communism. p. 678.

trust (trust). Organization that controls several different companies or corporations. p. 470.

tsar (zär). Title of the rulers of the Russian empire. p. 61.

Tweed Ring (twēd ring). Corrupt group led by New York political boss, William Tweed; the ring robbed the New York City treasury of millions of dollars. p. 407.

tycoon (tī kün′). A business leader who achieves exceptional wealth and power. p. 469.

tyranny (tir′ ə nē). Harsh and unfair government. p. 129.

U

Uncle Tom's Cabin (ung′ kəl tomz kab′ ən). Famous antislavery novel written by the American writer Harriet Beecher Stowe. p. 362.

Underground Railroad (un dər ground′ rāl′ rōd). System by which people opposed to slavery secretly guided fugitive slaves to safety in free states or Canada. p. 348.

Union party (yün′ yən pär′ tē). Name used for the Republican party during the presidential election of 1864. p. 388.

unit (yü′ nit). Special part or section, as in a book. p. 13.

United Nations (yü nī′ tid nā′ shənz). Worldwide organization formed after World War II to promote peace and social and economic welfare. p. 674.

urban renewal (ėr′ bən ri nü′ əl). Programs to restore the run-down areas in American cities. p. 710.

V

vaquero (vä kär′ ō). Spanish word for "cowboy." p. 53.

vaudeville (vô′ də vil). Type of show that featured a variety of acts. p. 518.

veto (vē′ tō). Right of a person such as a President or governor to refuse to approve bills passed by the legislature. p. 132.

viceroy (vīs′ roi). The vice-king who stood in the place of the Spanish king and governed a viceroyalty in America. p. 53.

viceroyalty (vīs roi′ əl tē). One of the regions of the Spanish empire in America. p. 53.

Vietnamization (vē et nə mi zā′ shən). United States plan to train and equip South Vietnamese troops to take over the fighting in their country. p. 729.

vigilante (vij ə lan′ tē). Member of a group that captures and punishes criminals without the sanction of the law. p. 444.

Vikings (vī′ kingz). Bold seafaring people from the Scandinavian countries who raided European coastal towns and explored distant lands. p. 45.

Vinland (vin′ lənd). Place along the coast of North America visited by the Vikings, and named after the many wild grapes they found there. p. 45.

Virginia Dynasty (vər jin′ yə dī′ nəs tē). Virginians who headed the United States government during the first quarter of the nineteenth century. p. 265.

Virginia Plan (vər jin′ yə plan). Large State plan, or the proposal that states should be represented in Congress according to population. p. 183.

W

War Democrat (wôr dem′ ə krat). Northern Democrat who supported the war effort. p. 387.

War Hawk (wôr hôk). Person, especially a member of Congress, who supported the War of 1812. p. 260.

warrant (wôr′ ənt). Written order issued by a judge or other authorized person that gives an official the right to make a search or an arrest or to carry out other acts. p. 127.

Western civilization (wes′ tərn siv ə lə zā′ shən). High-level culture beginning in Europe in the fifteenth century and characterized by a strong emphasis on technology. p. 39.

Western Front (wes′ tərn frunt). Line of the battlefront across Belgium and France during World War I. p. 573.

Whig (hwig). Member of a political party that was formed in the United States in the early 1830s in opposition to President Andrew Jackson and the Democratic party. p. 281.

Whiskey Rebellion (hwis′ kē ri bel′ yən). Rebellion in 1794 of Pennsylvania farmers against paying taxes on whiskey. It was put down by federal troops. p. 227.

White House (hwīt hous). Official residence of the President of the United States, in Washington, D.C. p. 233.

Wilderness Trail (wil′ dər nis trāl). Path cleared and marked by Daniel Boone that ran from eastern Virginia through the Cumberland Gap into Kentucky. p. 248.

women's liberation (wi′ mənz lib ə rā′ shən). Group organized to promote equality for women. p. 765.

women's rights (wi′ mənz rīts). Movement for equality between men and women. p. 291.

workweek (wėrk wēk). Part of the week during which work is done. p. 668.

writ of assistance (rit ov ə sis′ təns). Document that gave a British official looking for smuggled goods the right to enter and search a ship or building. p. 133.

X

XYZ affair (eks wī zē ə fär′). Incident that occurred during negotiations to end a dispute between France and the United States during the Adams administration. p. 232.

Y

yellow journalism (yel′ ō jėr′ nə liz əm). Writing that makes use of sensational headlines and exaggerated news stories. p. 550.

BIOGRAPHICAL DICTIONARY

A

Adams, Abigail (ad' əmz, ab' ə gāl) (1744–1818). Wife of President John Adams. Her letters show her keen interest in public affairs. p. 114.

Adams, John (ad' əmz, jon) (1735–1826). Second President. p. 237.

Adams, John Quincy (ad' əmz, jon kwin' zē) (1767–1848). Sixth President. p. 275.

Adams, Samuel (ad' əmz, sam' yə wəl) (1722–1803). A Revolutionary War Patriot. Leader of Sons of Liberty. p. 129.

Addams, Jane (ad' əmz, jān) (1860–1935). Organized Hull House, a settlement house for helping the poor, in Chicago in 1889. p. 490.

Alcott, Louisa May (ôl' kot, lü ē' zə mā) (1832–1888). An author of books for children and young people. p. 425.

Anderson, Marian (an' dər sən, mar' ē ən) (1902–   ). A concert singer who helped lessen discrimination against black people in the field of music. p. 635.

Anthony, Susan B. (an' thə nē, sü' zən) (1820–1906). A leader in the movement for women's rights. p. 296.

Armstrong, Neil A. (ärm' strong, nēl) (1930–   ). Astronaut, and first person to land on the moon. p. 732.

Arthur, Chester A. (är' thər, ches' tər) (1829–1886). Twenty-first President. p. 416.

Attucks, Crispus (at' əks, kris' pəs) (1723?–1770). A black sailor killed in 1770 in the Boston Massacre. p. 134.

Audubon, John James (ôd' ə bən, jon jāmz) (1785–1851). American naturalist and painter famous for his paintings of birds and animals. p. 307.

Austin, Stephen F. (ô' stən, stē' vən) (1793–1836). Leader of Americans who settled in Texas when the region was a part of Mexico. p. 322.

B

Barton, Clara (bär' tən, kla' rə) (1821–1912). A nurse in Union hospitals during the Civil War. Later founded the American Red Cross. p. 379.

Beckwourth, James (bek' wərth, jāmz) (1798–1867?). A free black from St. Louis. Became a mountain man and guide in the West. p. 318.

Bell, Alexander Graham (bel, al ig zan' dər grā' əm) (1847–1922). Inventor of the telephone (1876). p. 466.

Bethune, Mary McLeod (bə thyün', mā rē mə kloud') (1875–1955). A black educator. Was an adviser on minority affairs in Franklin Roosevelt's administration. p. 635.

Black Hawk (blak hôk) (1767–1838). Chief of the Sac Indians of Illinois. Led his people in fighting the whites in Black Hawk's War. p. 290.

Boone, Daniel (bün, dan' yəl) (1734–1820). Frontiersman who blazed the Wilderness Trail for early settlers traveling to Kentucky. p. 114.

Bradford, William (brad' fərd, wil' yəm) (1590–1657). Governor of the English colony at Plymouth, in New England. He wrote a history of the Pilgrim settlement. p. 76.

Bridger, Jim (brid' jər, jim) (1804–1881). Mountain man and guide in the western mountains. p. 318.

Brown, John (broun, jon) (1800–1859). Fanatical abolitionist. Attacked proslavery settlers in Kansas. Led raid at Harpers Ferry, Virginia. p. 353.

Bruce, Blanche K. (brüs, blanch) (1841–1897). United States senator from Mississippi, 1875–1881. The first black to serve in the Senate. p. 403.

Bryan, William Jennings (brī' ən, wil' yəm jen' ingz) (1860–1925). Unsuccessful Democratic candidate in presidential elections of 1896, 1900, and 1904. p. 512.

Buchanan, James (byü kan' ən, jāmz) (1791–1868). Fifteenth President. p. 356.

Bunche, Ralph (bunch, ralf) (1904–1971). Diplomat. Head of United Nations group that arranged a truce between Israel and the Arabs in 1949. p. 687.

Burr, Aaron (bėr, a' rən) (1756–1836). Anti-Federalist follower of Jefferson. Vice President, 1801–1805. Killed Alexander Hamilton in a duel. p. 233.

Bush, George (bush, jôrj) (1924–   ). Forty-first President. p. 768.

C

Cabot, John (kab' ət, jon) (1450–1498). Italian sea captain who explored for England. He made a voyage to Newfoundland and another voyage along the North American coast. p. 70.

Calhoun, John C. (kal hün', jon) (1782–1850). Senator from South Carolina. Champion of the South and of states' rights. p. 241.

Carnegie, Andrew (kär' nə gē, an' drü) (1835–1919). Built iron and steel industry in late 1800s. Bought up steel companies and combined them. Profited from growth of railroads and growth of cities. p. 456.

Carter, James Earl "Jimmy" (kär' tər, jāmz ėrl "jim' ē") (1924–   ). Thirty-ninth President. p. 741.

Cartier, Jacques (kär tyā', zhäk) (1491–1557). French explorer. Made three voyages to North America. Explored the St. Lawrence River region. p. 54.

Catlin, George (kat′ lən, jôrj) (1796–1872). American artist famous for his realistic scenes of American Indian life. p. 307.

Champlain, Samuel de (sham plān′, sam′ yə wəl də) (1567?–1635). French explorer and colonizer. Founded Quebec in 1608. Called the Father of New France. p. 54.

Chavez, Cesar (chä′ vās, sā′ sär) (1927–   ). A leader for equal rights for Mexican Americans. Organized union for migrant workers. p. 763.

Churchill, Winston (chèr′ chil, win′ stən) (1874–1965). Prime Minister of Great Britain during World War II (1940–1945) and again later (1951–1955). p. 648.

Clark, George Rogers (klärk, jôrj rö′ jərz) (1752–1818). Revolutionary War colonel. Captured British forts north of the Ohio River. p. 164.

Clark, William (klärk, wil′ yəm) (1770–1838). One of leaders of the Lewis and Clark expedition, which explored the land gained by the Louisiana Purchase. p. 254.

Clay, Henry (klā, hen′ rē) (1777–1852). Representative and senator from Kentucky. He proposed the Missouri Compromise and the Compromise of 1850. p. 241.

Clemens, Samuel L. (kle′ mənz, sam′ yə wəl) (1835–1910). A writer of books, using the name Mark Twain. Grew up in Hannibal, Missouri. Was a Mississippi steamboat pilot. p. 339.

Cleveland, Grover (klēv′ lənd, grō′ vər) (1837–1908). Twenty-second and twenty-fourth President. p. 510.

Clinton, George (klin′ tən, jôrj) (1739–1812). Anti-Federalist governor of New York in the late 1700s. Vice President from 1809–1812. p. 188.

Cody, William F. "Buffalo Bill" (kō′ dē, wil′ yəm "buf′ ə lō bil") (1846–1917). A scout, cowboy, and buffalo hunter. Later made tours with his Wild West show. p. 449.

Columbus, Christopher (kə lum′ bəs, kris′ tə fər) (1451–1506). Native of Genoa, Italy. Sailing in the service of Spain, reached the West Indies in 1492. His voyages led to the exploration and colonization of the Americas. p. 42.

Coolidge, Calvin (kü′ lij, kal′ vən) (1872–1933). Thirtieth President. p. 610.

Cooper, James Fenimore (kü′ pər, jāmz fen′ ə môr) (1789–1851). An author who wrote novels about frontier people and American Indians. p. 304.

Cortes, Hernando (kôr tez′, âr nän′ dō) (1485–1547). Spanish conqueror of the Aztec Indians. Established the Spanish empire in Mexico. p. 49.

Cullen, Countee (kul′ ən, kount′ ē) (1903–1946). Black American poet who participated in the Harlem Renaissance of the 1920s. p. 607.

D

Davis, Jefferson (dā′ vəs, jef′ ər sən) (1808–1889). Mississippi plantation owner and senator who became President of the Confederate States of America. p. 366.

Debs, Eugene V. (debz, yü jēn′) (1855–1926). Labor leader. Head of the American Railway Union. p. 503.

Dewey, George (dü′ ē, jôrj) (1837–1917). Commander of the United States Pacific fleet in 1898. Captured Manila in the Spanish-American War. p. 544.

Dickinson, Emily (dik′ ən sən, em′ ə lē) (1830–1886). Great American poet of the late 1800s. Only a few of her 1,700 poems were published in her lifetime. p. 427.

Dix, Dorothea (diks, dôr ə thē′ ə) (1802–1887). A reformer who worked for better care and treatment of the mentally ill. p. 298.

Douglas, Stephen A. (dug′ ləs, stē′ vən) (1813–1861). Senator from Illinois. Proposed the Kansas-Nebraska bill. Defeated in the presidential election of 1860. p. 346.

Douglass, Frederick (dug′ ləs, fred′ rik) (1818–1895). Former slave who became a leading abolitionist. Publisher of an abolitionist newspaper, *The North Star.* p. 291.

Drew, Charles (drü, chärlz) (1904–1950). Black doctor who, during World War II, developed the first blood bank. p. 664.

Du Bois, William Edward Burghardt (dü boiz′, wil′ yəm ed′ wərd bèrg′ hart) (1868–1963). Black leader and co-founder of the NAACP. He differed with Booker T. Washington on tactics for black advancement in the Gilded Age. p. 420.

Dulles, John Foster (dul′ əs, jon fôs′ tər) (1888–1959). Secretary of state in Eisenhower's Cabinet. p. 686.

Du Sable, Jean Baptiste Pointe (dü sä′ bəl, zhôn bäp tēst′ pwänt) (1745–1818). Black fur trader in New France. Ran a trading post near the place where Chicago was later built. p. 64.

E

Edison, Thomas Alva (ed′ ə sən, tom′ əs al′ və) (1847–1931). Inventor of the electric light bulb, phonograph, motion-picture machine, and other devices. p. 466.

Eisenhower, Dwight D. (īz′ ən hou ər, dwīt) (1890–1969). Thirty-fourth President. p. 707.

Emerson, Ralph Waldo (em′ ər sən, ralf wôl′ dō) (1803–1882). Writer and philosopher who lived in Concord, Massachusetts. p. 304.

Estevanico (əs tā bä nē′ kō) (?–1539). Black African member of the party of Spanish conquistadores that first explored the lands of the southwest. p. 63.

F

Farragut, David (far′ ə gət, dā′ vəd) (1801–1870). Union naval officer during the Civil War. The first person to hold the rank of the admiral in the United States Navy. p. 383.

Fillmore, Millard (fil' môr, mil' ərd) (1800–1874). Thirteenth President. p. 351.

Fitzgerald, F. Scott (fits jer' əld, skät) (1896–1940). American novelist and short-story writer of the 1920s and 1930s. p. 606.

Ford, Gerald (fôrd, je' rəld) (1913–   ). Thirty-eighth President. p. 738.

Ford, Henry (fôrd, hen' rē) (1863–1947). Manufacturer of the Model T and other Ford cars. Introduced the assembly-line method of making cars. p. 594.

Foster, Stephen (fôs' tər, stē' vən) (1826–1864). Composer of popular American songs. p. 308.

Franklin, Benjamin (frang' klən, benj' ə mən) (1706–1790). Publisher, statesman, and scientist. Signer of Declaration of Independence. p. 92.

Fremont, John C. (frē' mont, jon) (1813–1890). Explorer and army officer in the Far West. p. 316.

Fulton, Robert (fûl' tən, räb' ərt) (1765–1815). Invented the first practical steamboat in 1807. p. 311.

G

Garfield, James A. (gär fēld, jāmz) (1831–1881). Twentieth President. p. 416.

Garrison, William Lloyd. (gar' ə sən, wil' yəm loid) (1805–1879). Publisher of an abolitionist paper, *The Liberator.* p. 291.

Garvey, Marcus ((gär' vē, mar' kəs) (1887–1940). Black leader who started a "back to Africa" movement. p. 600.

Gates, Horatio (gātz, hə rā' shō) (1728?–1806). Revolutionary War general. Fought at battle of Saratoga. p. 160.

Glenn, John (glen, jon) (1921–   ). First American to orbit the earth in space (1962). p. 2.

Glidden, Joseph (glid' dən, jō' zəf) (1813–1906). Invented barbed wire for fences used on the Great Plains. p. 452.

Goethals, George (gō' thəlz, jôrj) (1858–1928). Army engineer in charge of building the Panama Canal. p. 565.

Gompers, Samuel (gom' pərz, sam' yə wəl) (1850–1924). Longtime head of American Federation of Labor. p. 494.

Gorgas, William C. (gôr gəs, wil' yəm) (1854–1920). Army medical officer who put an end to yellow fever in Panama. p. 564.

Grant, Ulysses S. (grant, yü lis' ēs) (1822–1885). Eighteenth President. p. 407.

Greeley, Horace (grē' lē, hôr' əs) (1811–1872). Influential editor of the New York *Tribune.* p. 302.

Greene, Nathanael (grēn, nə than' yəl) (1742–1786). Revolutionary War general. Fought in North Carolina. p. 166.

Grimké, Angelina (grim' kē, an jə lē' nə) (1805–1879) and **Sarah** (sar' ə) (1792–1873). South Carolina–born Quaker sisters who worked for women's rights and an end to slavery. p. 290.

H

Hamilton, Alexander (ham' əl tən, al ig zan' dər) (1755–1804). Secretary of the treasury in Washington's Cabinet. A leader in forming the policies of the Federalists. p. 174.

Harding, Warren G. (här ding, wôr' ən) (1865–1923). Twenty-ninth President. p. 609.

Harrison, Benjamin (har' ə sən, benj' ə mən) (1833–1901). Twenty-third President. p. 512.

Harrison, William Henry (har' ə sən, wil' yəm hen' rē) (1773–1841). Ninth President. p. 283.

Hay, John (hā, jon) (1835–1905). Secretary of state in McKinley's Cabinet. p. 556.

Hayes, Rutherford B. (hāz, ruTH' ər fərd) (1822–1893). Nineteenth President. p. 415.

Hearst, William Randolph (hèrst, wil' yəm ran' dôlf) (1863–1951). Publisher of the New York *Journal.* p. 550.

Hemingway, Ernest (hem' ing wā, èr' nəst) (1899–1961). American novelist and short-story writer. p. 606.

Henry, Patrick (hen' rē, pa' trik) (1736–1799). A Virginia Patriot in the Revolutionary War period. Noted for his fiery speeches. p. 129.

Hobby, Oveta Culp (hôb' ē, ō vē' tə kulp) (1905–   ). Secretary of health, education, and welfare in Eisenhower's Cabinet. p. 707.

Homer, Winslow (hō' mər, winz' lō) (1836–1910). An artist who painted landscapes and other subjects. p. 428.

Hoover, Herbert (hü' vər, hèr' bərt) (1874–1964). Thirty-first President. p. 621.

Houston, Sam (hyü' stən, sam) (1793–1863). Leader of the Texas army that defeated Mexican troops. Elected first president of the Republic of Texas. p. 324.

Howard, Oliver O. (hou' ərd, äl' ə vər) (1830–1909). Head of the Freedmen's Bureau, which helped freed slaves. Founded Howard University. p. 400.

Hudson, Henry (hud' sən, hen' rē) (?–1611). English sea captain who explored for the Netherlands. Claimed lands in eastern America for the Dutch. p. 59.

Hughes, Charles Evans (hyüz, chärlz ev' ənz) (1862–1948). Republican candidate in presidential election of 1916. Later was secretary of state and Chief Justice of the Supreme Court. p. 577.

Hughes, Langston (hyüz, lang' stən) (1902–1967). A poet who was part of the Harlem Renaissance. p. 607.

Humphrey, Hubert H. (hum' frē, hyü' bərt) (1911–1978). Vice President under Lyndon Johnson. p. 728.

Hutchinson, Anne (huch′ ən sən,   an) (1591–1643). A leader for freedom of religion. Put out of Massachusetts, she moved to Rhode Island. p. 80.

I

Irving, Washington (ėr′ ving,   wôsh′ ing tən) (1783–1859). An author who wrote history and stories of the Dutch people in New York. p. 304.

J

Jackson, Andrew (jak′ sən,   an′ drü) (1767–1845). Seventh President. p. 279.

Jackson, Helen Hunt (jak′ sən,   hel′ ən hunt) (1830–1885). An author who wrote about the government's treatment of Indians. p. 424.

Jackson, Thomas J. "Stonewall" (jak′ sən, tom′ əs "stōn′ wôl") (1824–1863). Confederate general in the Civil War. p. 371.

Jay, John (jā, jon) (1745–1829). First Chief Justice of the Supreme Court. Arranged Jay's Treaty with Great Britain. p. 230.

Jefferson, Thomas (jef′ ər sən, tom′ əs) (1743– 1826). Third President. p. 259.

Jenney, William Le Baron (jen′ ē, wil′ yəm lə bar′ ən) (1832–1907). An architect whose design led to skyscrapers. p. 474.

Johnson, Andrew (jon′ sən,   an′ drü) (1808– 1875). Seventeenth President. p. 396.

Johnson, Lyndon Baines (jon′ sən, lin′ dən bānz) (1908–1973). Thirty-sixth President. p. 729.

Johnson, Tom (jon′ sən,   tom) (1854–1911). Reform mayor of Cleveland in the early 1900s. p. 528.

Johnston, Joseph E. (jon′ stən, jō′ zəf) (1807– 1891). Confederate general in the Civil War. p. 373.

Jones, John Paul (jōnz,   jon   pôl) (1747–1792). Revolutionary War naval officer. Sank or seized British merchant ships. p. 163.

Joseph (jō′ zəf) (1840?–1904). Nez Percé Indian chief who surrendered to U.S. Army in 1877. p. 436.

K

Kelley, Florence (kel′ ē,   flôr′ əns) (1859–1932). Reformer who worked for laws regulating child labor. p. 526.

Kelley, Oliver H. (kel′ ē,   äl′ ə vər) (1826–1913). Founded the Grange, a farm organization, in 1867. p. 507.

Kellogg, Frank (kel′ ôg,   frangk) (1856–1937). Secretary of state in Coolidge's Cabinet. p. 612.

Kennedy, John F. (ken′ ə dē,   jon) (1917–1963). Thirty-fifth President. p. 710.

Key, Francis Scott (kē,   fran′ səs   skät) (1779– 1843). Author of the words of "The Star-Spangled Banner." p. 263.

King, Martin Luther, Jr. (king,   mär′ tən   lü′ thər) (1929–1968). A leader in civil rights movement, using nonviolent methods. Awarded Nobel Peace Prize. p. 714.

Kissinger, Henry (kis′ ən jər,   hen′ rē) (1923–). National security adviser in the Nixon administration. Later the secretary of state in Nixon's Cabinet. p. 731.

Knox, Henry (noks, hen′ rē) (1750–1806). Revolutionary War general and first secretary of war. p. 144.

L

La Follette, Robert (lə   fôl′ ət,   räb′ ərt) (1855– 1925). Governor of Wisconsin and senator from Wisconsin. Accomplished many reforms in government. p. 524.

Lease, Mary Elizabeth (lēs, mā′ rē   ə liz′ ə bəth) (1850–1933). An effective spokeswoman for farmers in 1890s. p. 504.

Lee, Robert E. (lē, räb′ ərt) (1807–1870). Leading Confederate general in the Civil War. p. 373.

Levitt, William (lev′ ət,   wil′ yəm) (1907–   ). New York builder and developer who mass-produced suburban houses in the years after World War II. p. 696.

Lewis, John L. (lü′ əs, jon) (1880–1969). Head of United Mine Workers. Helped to form CIO. p. 637.

Lewis, Meriwether (lü′ əs,   mer′ ə weᴛʜ ər) (1774– 1809). One of leaders of Lewis and Clark expedition, which explored the land gained by the Louisiana Purchase. p. 253.

Lewis, Sinclair (lü′ əs,   sin′ klãr) (1885–1951). Author of novels and plays dealing with life in the early 1900s. p. 516.

Liliuokalani (li lē ə wō kə län′ ē) (1838–1917). Last queen of Hawaii. p. 548.

Lincoln, Abraham (ling′ kən,   ā′ brə ham) (1809– 1865). Sixteenth President. p. 388.

Lindbergh, Charles A. (lind′ bərg,   chärlz) (1902– 1974). The first aviator to fly alone across the Atlantic. p. 602.

Lockwood, Belva (lok′ wůd,   bel′ və) (1830–1917). A New York lawyer and a candidate for President in 1884. p. 422.

Lodge, Henry Cabot (lôj,   hen′ rē   kab′ ət) (1850– 1924). United States senator from Massachusetts. Opposed American membership in League of Nations. p. 589.

Long, Stephen (long,   stē′ vən) (1784–1864). Explored the northern Great Plains in the 1820s. Called this region the Great American Desert. p. 316.

Ludington, Sybil (lud′ ing tən, sib′ əl) (1761–1839). Daughter of a New York colonel, she made a moonlit ride to collect his troops for battle with the British in 1777. p. 159.

M

MacArthur, Douglas (mə kär′ thər, dug′ ləs) (1880–1964). General in United States Army. In World War II, commanded forces in the Philippines and the southwest Pacific. Commanded United Nations forces in Korean War. p. 657.

McCarthy, Joseph R. (mə kär′ thē, jō′ zəf) (1908–1957). Senator from Wisconsin who accused many in the government of being Communists in 1950s. Censured by the Senate for his methods. p. 704.

McClellan, George B. (mə klel′ ən, jôrj) (1826–1885). Union general in the Civil War. At one time headed the Army of the Potomac. p. 370.

McCormick, Cyrus Hall (mə kôr′ mək, sī′ rəs hôl) (1809–1884). Inventor of a mechanical reaper, the first of many machines that changed farming. p. 313.

McGovern, George (mə guv′ ərn, jôrj) (1922–   ). Democratic candidate in presidential election of 1972. p. 735.

McKinley, William (mə kin′ lē, wil′ yəm) (1843–1901). Twenty-fifth President. p. 532.

Madison, James (mad′ ə sən, jāmz) (1751–1836). Fourth President. p. 264.

Magellan, Ferdinand (mə jel′ ən, fèrd′ ən and) (1480?–1521). Explorer for Spain. Sailed around South America and across the Pacific. Killed in the Philippine Islands, but one of his ships returned to Spain in 1522, the first ship to sail around the world. p. 47.

Mann, Horace (man, hôr′ əs) (1796–1859). A leader in getting Massachusetts to provide the first free public elementary schools. p. 300.

Marion, Francis (ma′ rē ən, fran′ səs) (1732?–1795). A guerrilla fighter in South Carolina in the Revolutionary War. Known as the Swamp Fox. p. 165.

Marshall, George C. (mär′ shəl, jôrj) (1880–1959). Chief of staff of the army in World War II. Secretary of state in Truman's Cabinet. Proposed Marshall Plan of economic aid for Europe. p. 678.

Marshall, John (mär′ shəl, jon) (1755–1835). Federalist leader in Virginia. Chief Justice of the Supreme Court from 1801 to 1835. p. 229.

Marshall, Thurgood (mär′ shal, thèr′ gùd) (1908–   ). Lawyer who won case against segregation in public schools. Later was first black to be appointed a justice of the Supreme Court. p. 712.

Mason, George (mā′ sən, jôrj) (1725–1792). Prominent Virginian. A leader in government. p. 115.

Meade, George G. (mēd, jôrj) (1815–1872). Union general in command at battle of Gettysburg. p. 382.

Millay, Edna St. Vincent (mil ā′, ed′ nə sänt vin′ sənt) (1892–1950). A poet who wrote in the first half of 1900s. p. 607.

Mitchell, William "Billy" (mich′ əl, wil′ yəm "bil′ ē") (1879–1936). General in Air Service of U.S. Army. Called for greater use of military airplanes. p. 640.

Monroe, James (mən rō′, jāmz) (1758–1831). Fifth President. p. 266.

Montezuma (mônt ə zü′ mə) (1466–1520). Last ruler of the Aztecs, he was conquered and killed by Hernando Cortes. p. 50.

Morris, Gouverneur (mor′ əs, gəv ər nùr′) (1752–1816). Delegate from Pennsylvania to Constitutional Convention. p. 186.

Morse, Samuel F. B. (môrs, sam′ yə wəl) (1791–1872). An artist and inventor of the telegraph. p. 306.

Mott, Lucretia (mot, lü krē′ shə) (1793–1880). Leader in women's rights movement. p. 294.

N

Nast, Thomas (nast, tom′ əs) (1840–1902). German immigrant who became the leading political cartoonist of the late 1800s. p. 408.

Nimitz, Chester W. (nim′ əts, ches′ tər) (1885–1966). Admiral in World War II. Commanded naval forces in the central Pacific. p. 656.

Nixon, Richard M. (nik′ sən, rich′ ərd) (1913–   ) Thirty-seventh President. p. 737.

O

O'Connor, Sandra Day (ō kôn′ ər, san′ drə dā) (1930–   ). First woman justice of the Supreme Court. p. 765.

Oglethorpe, James (ō′ gəl thôrp, jāmz) (1696–1785). English nobleman who founded the Georgia colony as a refuge for debtors. p. 89.

Oliver, James (äl′ ə vər, jamz) (1823–1908). Invented the chilled-iron plow for use on the Great Plains. p. 452.

P

Paine, Thomas (pān, tom′ əs) (1737–1809). Author of *Common Sense*, the 1776 pamphlet that urged the colonists to declare their independence. p. 149.

Parker, Cynthia Ann (pär′ kər, sin′ thē ə an) (1827?–1864). A white woman captured by Comanche Indians when she was a child. Married a Commanche and remained with the Indians in Oklahoma. p. 341.

Paterson, William (pat′ ər sən, wil′ yəm) (1745–1806). Delegate from New Jersey to Constitutional Convention. p. 183.

Penn, William (pen, wil′ yəm) (1644–1718). Quaker who established the colony of Pennsylvania and the city of Philadelphia. Called the colony a "holy experiment." p. 84.

Perkins, Frances (pėr′ kənz, fran′ səs) (1882–1965).Secretary of labor in Franklin Roosevelt's Cabinet. The first woman to hold a Cabinet post. p. 636.

Pershing, John J. (pėr′ zhing, jon) (1860–1948). Army general who commanded the American Expeditionary Force in World War I. p. 582.

Pickett, George E. (pik′ ət, jôrj) (1825–1875). Confederate general in the Civil War. Led an attack at battle of Gettysburg. p. 382.

Pierce, Franklin (pėrs, frang klən) (1804–1869). Fourteenth President. p. 353.

Pinckney, Eliza Lucas (pingk′ nē, ə lī′ zə lü′ kəs) (1722–1793). Managed a plantation in South Carolina. Experimented in growing indigo. p. 116.

Pinckney, Thomas (pingk′ nē, tom′ əs) (1750–1828). Statesman who arranged Pinckney Treaty, a pact with Spain. Son of Eliza Lucas Pinckney. p. 228.

Pitcher, Molly (pich′ ər, mäl′ ē) (1754?–1832). Wife of a Revolutionary War soldier. Took part in battle of Monmouth. Real name Mary Ludwig Hays. p. 164.

Pizarro, Francisco (pə zär′ ō, frän sēs′ kō) (1470?–1541). Spanish explorer. Conquered the Incas in Peru. p. 51.

Poe, Elizabeth Arnold (pō, ə liz′ ə bəth är′ nəld) (1787?–1811). Actress and singer. Mother of Edgar Allan Poe. p. 240.

Polk, James K. (pōk, jāmz) (1795–1849). Eleventh President. p. 324.

Ponce de León, Juan (pôn′ sə dā lā ōn′, hwän) (1460–1521). Spanish explorer who discovered Florida in 1513. p. 47.

Powderly, Terence V. (pou′ dər lē, ter′ əns) (1849–1924). Labor leader. Head of Knights of Labor. p. 500.

Pulitzer, Joseph (pyü′ lət sər, jō′ zəf) (1847–1911). Publisher of the New York newspaper *The World.* p. 550.

R

Rainey, Joseph Hayne (rā′ nē, jō′ zəf hān) (1832–1887). First black member of House of Representatives. Was a member of Congress from South Carolina. p. 403.

Randolph, A. Philip (ran′ dôlf, fil′ əp) (1889–1979). Civil rights leader during and after World War II. p. 664.

Randolph, Edmund (ran′ dôlf, ed′ mənd) (1753–1813). Attorney general in Washington's Cabinet. p. 222.

Reagan, Ronald (rā′ gən, rän′ əld) (1911–   ). Fortieth President. p. 761.

Revere, Paul (rə vēr′, pôl) (1735–1818). Silversmith in Boston. An active Patriot before and during the Revolutionary War. p. 120.

Riis, Jacob (rēs, jā′ kəb) (1849–1914). Newspaper reporter in New York City. He wrote about the terrible living conditions in tenements. p. 488.

Rockefeller, John D. (rok′ ə fel ər, jon) (1839–1937). Formed Standard Oil Company in 1870. Gained control of the oil refining industry. p. 469.

Roosevelt, Eleanor (rō′ zə velt, el′ ə nôr) (1884–1962). Worked for the benefit of blacks and other minorities. Head of United Nations Commission on Human Rights. Wife of Franklin Roosevelt. p. 623.

Roosevelt, Franklin D. (rō′ zə velt, frang′ klən) (1882–1945). Thirty-second President. p. 650.

Roosevelt, Theodore (rō′ zə velt, thē′ ə dôr) (1858–1919). Twenty-sixth President. p. 535.

S

Sacajawea (sak ə jə wē′ ə) (1787?–1812). Shoshone Indian woman. A valuable member of the Lewis and Clark expedition. p. 254.

Sampson, Deborah (sam′ sən, deb′ rə) (1760–1827). Woman who disguised herself as a man to enlist as a soldier in the American Revolution. p. 170.

Scott, Dred (skät, dred) (1795?–1858). Missouri slave whose lawsuit demanding freedom gave rise to a landmark Supreme Court decision. p. 354.

Scott, Winfield (skät, win′ fēld) (1786–1866). Army general who took Mexico City in the Mexican War. p. 326.

Sequoya (sə kwoi′ ə) (1770?–1843). A leader of the Cherokee Indians. Devised an alphabet for writing their language. p. 290.

Serra, Junipero (ser′ ə, hü nē′ pāe rō) (1713–1784). Spanish explorer and Roman Catholic priest who started nine missions in California. p. 330.

Seward, William (sü′ ərd, wil′ yəm) (1801–1872). Secretary of state in Lincoln's Cabinet. Purchased Alaska from Russia. p. 374.

Shays, Daniel (shāz, dan′ yəl) (1747?–1825). Former officer who led a farmers' rebellion against high taxes and crushing debt in Massachusetts in 1786. p. 177.

Shepard, Alan (shep′ ard, al′ ən) (1923–   ). First American to ride a rocket into space (1961). p. 2.

Sherman, Roger (sher′ mən, räj′ ər) (1721–1793). Delegate from Connecticut to Constitutional Convention. Proposed the Great Compromise. p. 150.

Sherman, William T. (sher′ mən, wil′ yəm) (1820–1891). Union general in the Civil War. Led march through Georgia. p. 385.

Sholes, Christopher L. (shōlz, kris′ tə fər) (1819–1890). Inventor of the first practical typewriter (1867). p. 426.

Sims, William (simz, wil′ yəm) (1858–1936). Admiral in the United States Navy in World War I. p. 582.

Sinclair, Upton (sin klär′, up′ tən) (1878–1968). A writer who exposed conditions in the meat-packing business. p. 535.

Sirica, John (sə rē′ kə, jon) (1904–   ). Judge for the trial in the Watergate scandal in the Nixon administration. p. 736.

Slater, Samuel (slā′ tər, sam′ yə wəl) (1768–1835). Brought knowledge of machines for spinning and weaving cotton from England to Rhode Island. Started textile factory system. p. 243.

Smith, Alfred (smith, al′ frəd) (1873–1944). Democratic candidate for President in 1928. First Roman Catholic nominated for that job. p. 613.

Smith, John (smith, jon) (1580–1631). Leader of the English colony at Jamestown, Virginia. Explored the coast of New England. p. 68.

Sousa, John Philip (sü′ zə, jon fil′ əp) (1854–1932). Composer of popular marches in the late 1800s. p. 431.

Stanton, Elizabeth Cady (stan′ tən, ə liz′ ə bəth kā′ dē) (1815–1902). Organized first women's rights convention at Seneca Falls, N.Y., in 1848. p. 294.

Steffens, Lincoln (stef′ ənz, ling′ kən) (1866–1936). Journalist who exposed corruption in city governments. One of the muckrakers. p. 528.

Stevens, Thaddeus (stē′ vənz, thad′ ē əs) (1792–1868). Congressman from Pennsylvania. A leader of Radical Republicans in Reconstruction years. p. 404.

Stowe, Harriet Beecher (stō, har′ ē at bē′ chər) (1811–1896). Author of the antislavery book *Uncle Tom's Cabin.* p. 362.

Strauss, Levi (strous, lē′ vī) (1829–1902). German immigrant who made a fortune selling denim pants known as Levi's and founded what is today the world's largest clothing company. p. 444.

Stuyvesant, Peter (stī′ və sənt, pēt′ ər) (1610?–1672). Dutch governor of New Netherland from 1647 until the English took it over in 1664. p. 82.

Sullivan, Louis (sul′ ə vən, lü′ əs) (1856–1924). An architect. Designed tall city buildings. p. 476.

Sylvis, William (sil′ vəs, wil′ yəm) (1828–1868). Labor leader. Head of National Labor Union. p. 499.

T

Taft, William Howard (taft, wil′ yəm hou′ ərd) (1857–1930). Twenty-seventh President. p. 536.

Tarbell, Ida (tär′ bəl, ī′ də) (1857–1944). One of the muckrakers. Exposed the methods used by John D. Rockefeller. p. 528.

Taylor, Zachary (tā′ lər, zak′ ə rē) (1784–1850). Twelfth President. p. 331.

Tecumseh (tə kum′ sə) (1768?–1813). Chief of the Shawnee Indian tribe. Organized Indians west of the Appalachians against white settlers. p. 248.

Tilden, Samuel J. (til′ dən, sam′ yə wəl) (1814–1886). Governor of New York. Democratic candidate in disputed presidential election of 1876. p. 408.

Truman, Harry S. (trü′ mən, har′ ē) (1884–1972). Thirty-third President. p. 704.

Truth, Sojourner (trüth, sō′ jərn ər) (1797?–1883). A black reformer who worked for abolitionism and women's rights. p. 296.

Tubman, Harriet (tub′ mən, har′ ē ət) (1820?–1913). A slave on Maryland plantation who escaped to Philadelphia. She returned south many times to lead other slaves to freedom. p. 336.

Twain, Mark (twān, mark) (1835–1910). See Samuel L. Clemens.

Tweed, William M. "Boss" (twēd, wil′ yəm "bôs") (1823–1878). Head of a corrupt ring in New York City. p. 407.

Tyler, John (tī lər, jon) (1790–1862). Tenth President. p. 321.

V

Van Buren, Martin (van byü′ rən, mär′ tən) (1782–1862). Eighth President. p. 281.

W

Wagner, Robert (wag′ nər, räb′ ərt) (1877–1953). Senator from New York. Author of Wagner Act, which dealt with labor relations. p. 631.

Wallace, George (wäl′ əs, jôrj) (1919–   ). Alabaman who was third-party candidate in the presidential election of 1968. p. 729.

Warren, Earl (wôr′ ən, ėrl) (1891–1971). Chief Justice of the Supreme Court from 1953 to 1969. Head of commission to investigate assassination of President Kennedy. p. 711.

Washington, Booker T. (wôsh′ ing tən, bùk′ ər) (1856–1915). A black educator and a spokesman for black Americans. p. 420.

Washington, George (wôsh′ ing tən, jôrj) (1732–1799). First President. p. 228.

Weaver, James (wē′ vər, jāmz) (1833–1912). Populist candidate in presidential election of 1892. p. 509.

Weaver, Robert (wē′ vər, räb′ ərt) (1907–   ). Secretary of housing and urban development in Lyndon Johnson's Cabinet. First black Cabinet member. p. 724.

Webster, Daniel (web′ stər, dan′ yəl) (1782–1852). Senator from Massachusetts. A noted orator who supported a strong national government. p. 241.

Wheatley, Phillis (hwēt′ lē, fil′ əs) (1753?–1784). Black poet who was brought to Boston as a slave in 1761. p. 169.

Whitman, Walt (wit′ mən, wôlt) (1819–1892). A poet who wrote during the last half of the 1800s. p. 427.

Whitney, Eli (wit′ nē, ē′ lī) (1765–1825). Inventor of the cotton gin. He also helped develop the system of interchangeable parts. p. 244.

Williams, Roger (wil′ yəmz, räj′ ər) (1603?–1683). Puritan minister. An advocate of religious freedom, he started the first settlement in Rhode Island. p. 79.

Wilson, Woodrow (wil′ sən, wŏod′ rō) (1856–1924). Twenty-eighth President. p. 589.

Winnemucca, Sarah (win ə muk′ ə, sar′ ə) (1844–1891). Daughter of a Paiute chief, she wrote and lectured about the mistreatment of her people. p. 424.

Woodhull, Victoria (wŏod′ həl, vik tôr′ ē ə) (1838–1927). Social reformer and Equal Rights party candidate for President in 1872. p. 422.

Wright, Orville (rīt, ôr′ vəl) (1871–1948) and **Wilbur** (wil′ bər) (1867–1912). Ohio brothers who invented the airplane. p. 534.

Y

Young, Brigham (yung, brig′ əm) (1801–1877). Mormon leader who started a settlement near the Great Salt Lake in 1847. p. 329.

INDEX

Q

Pure Food and Drug Act, 535
Puritans, 78–79, 97

Qaddafi, Muammar, 760
Quakers, 84
Quartering Act, 127, 131, 138
Quayle, Dan, 768
Quebec, 54, 55, 57, 124, 138, 147
Quebec Act, 138
Queen Anne's War, 108
Quincy, Josiah, 134
Quinton, Amelia, 423

R

Radical Republicans, 387, 395–399
Railroads, 310, 524
    and economic growth, 463
    and growth of cities, 477
    and rebates, 470, 508
    in West, 447, 461–463
Rainey, Joseph, 403
Raleigh, Walter, 71, 72
Randolph, Edmund, 223
Reagan, Ronald, 743, 746–748
    and arms issue, 749–750, 758
    economic program of, 748–749, 750
    and federal regulations, 749
    and foreign affairs, 756–761
    and Soviet Union, 757–759
Reaper, mechanical, 313
Recall, 526
Reconstruction, 392, 394, 406–407
    carpetbaggers and scalawags during, 402–403
    and Congress, 394–399
    Freedmen's Bureau, 400
    Lincoln-Johnson plan for, 394

military occupation of South, 398. *See also* Civil War
Reconstruction Act of 1867, 398, 402
Reconstruction Finance Corporation (RFC), 621
Red Scare, 600–601, 704
Referendum, 510, 526
Reform movements in 1800s, 284–288, 298–303, 534–535. *See also* Progressive movement
Religion
    in English colonies, 75, 78, 84
    freedom of, 87
    reform of in 1800s, 302
    separation of church and state, 81
Relocation centers, 665
"Remember the Alamo!" 324
"Remember the Maine!" 552
Renault, Phillipe, 64
Reparations payments, 587
Republican party
    and Abraham Lincoln, 357–358
    and blacks, 419
    emerges as dominant party, 407
    naming of, 276, 353
Revere, Paul, 120, 134–135, 139, 142
Revolutionary War. *See* American Revolution
    allies in, 150
Rhode Island, 79–81, 84, 85, 243–244
Rice, 88, 102
Richmond, Virginia, 10
Ricketts, M.O., 421
Riis, Jacob, 488–489
Roanoke, settlement of, 71–72
Roaring Twenties, 606
Rochambeau, Jean Baptiste, 167, 169
Rockefeller, John D., 469–470, 528

Rocky Mountains, 4, 55
Rolfe, John, 68, 70, 73
Rolfe, Thomas, 68
Roman Catholic Church, 87, 322
Rommel, Erwin, 651
Roosevelt Corollary, 561–562, 612
Roosevelt, Eleanor, 623, 635, 636
Roosevelt, Franklin D., 61, 622, 623, 650
    death of, 659
    early programs of, 626–631
    elected President, 624
    First Inaugural Address, 625
    and programs after reelection, 631–632
    and World War II, 644. *See also* New Deal
Roosevelt, Theodore, 61, 528, 531–532, 535, 551
    and coal-mining strike, 533–534
    foreign policy of, 557–562
    and Panama Canal, 564
    reforms of, 534–535
    and Roosevelt Corollary, 561–562
    and Spanish-American War, 553–554
Ross, Betsy, 179
Rough Riders, 553–554
Royal colony, 74
Russia, 61–62, 557. *See also* Soviet Union
Russian Revolution, 583–584
Russwurm, John B., 302

S

Sacajawea, 254–256
Sacco, Nicola, 601–602
Sadat, Anwar El, 740–741
St. Augustine, Florida, 53, 109
St. Clair, Arthur, 250
St. Lawrence, Gulf of, 54, 108

St. Lawrence River, 54, 56, 57
St. Leger, Barry, 158, 160
Salem, Peter, 170
Salmon, 34–35
Salomon, Haym, 161
SALT (Strategic Arms Limitation Talks), 731
SALT II, 742
Samoa, 547
Samoset, 76
Sampson, Deborah, 170
San Jacinto, battle of, 324
San Juan Hill, battle of, 553–554
San Salvador, 44–45
Sandia Cave, New Mexico, 25
Sanitation, in cities, 488
Santa Anna, Antonio, 323, 324
Santa Maria, 44
Santa Rosa Island, 25
Saratoga, battle of, 160
Sawyer, Philetus, 524
Scalawags, 403
Scandinavians, 480
School Law of 1647, 79
Schools
    public, 79, 287–288
    in South, 403. *See also* Education
Schuyler, Philip, 147, 160
Scots-Irish, 97–98, 359
Scott, Dred, 354–356
Scott, Winfield, 326, 350, 370
Search warrant, 127
Secession, 278, 358
Secondary sources, 172
Sectionalism, 275, 277–278
Sedition Act, 236–237
Segregation, 418, 712–713. *See also* Discrimination
Selective Service Act, 580
Self-government, 74
Senate, 183, 190
Seneca Chief, 309
Seneca Falls convention, 296, 302

INDEX

INDEX

INDEX

CREDITS